INTEGRATED MARKETING COMMUNICATIONS

Strategic Planning Perspectives

KEITH J. TUCKWELL
ST. LAWRENCE COLLEGE

PEARSON

Prentice Hall

Toronto

To Esther...and our children, Marnie, Graham, and Gordon

National Library of Canada Cataloguing in Publication

Tuckwell, Keith J. (Keith John), 1950–
    Integrated marketing communications : strategic planning perspectives / Keith J. Tuckwell.

Includes bibliographical references and index.
ISBN 0-13-140538-1

    1. Communication in marketing. 2. Sales promotion. 3. Advertising. I. Title.

HF5415.123.T82 2004   658.8'02   C2004-901412-9

0-13-140538-1

Vice President, Editorial Director: Michael J. Young
Acquisitions Editor: Laura Paterson Forbes
Marketing Manager: Steve McGill
Senior Developmental Editor: Paul Donnelly
Supervising Editor: Avivah Wargon
Copy Editor: Madeline Koch
Proofreader: Gilda Mekler
Production Coordinator: Deborah Starks
Page Layout: Anne MacInnis
Art Director: Mary Opper
Cover and Interior Design: Lisa LaPointe
Cover Image: Ray Boudreau

Statistics Canada information is used with the permission of the Minister of Industry, as Minister responsible for Statistics Canada. Information on the availability of the wide range of data from Statistics Canada can be obtained from Statistics Canada's Regional Offices, its World Wide Web site at **http://www.statcan.ca**, and its toll-free access number 1-800-263-1136. The Statistics Canada CANSIM II database can be accessed at **http://cansim2.statcan.ca/**.

1 2 3 4 5   09 08 07 06 05

Printed and bound in the United States of America.

Brief Contents

Contents

Dear IMC Professor:

Please read the following questions and answer them with a simple yes or no.

1. Are you tired of seeing the same core content in the first four or five chapters of a specialized marketing textbook that is included in an introductory-level marketing textbook?

2. Do you find it difficult to deliver a solid IMC course in a 14-week or 15-week cycle with the textbook you are currently using?

3. Do your students feel intimidated by voluminous hardcover textbooks that emphasize theory at the expense of practical applications?

4. Do you find it challenging getting your students to read lengthy, heavy, hardcover textbooks?

5. Are you sensitive to the price that students must pay for 4-colour textbooks?

If you answered yes to two or more of these questions you will be very interested in knowing more about *Integrated Marketing Communications: Strategic Planning Perspectives*.

This new Canadian textbook, the first of its kind on the subject of integrated marketing communications, is built on one fundamental premise: "The goal of most IMC courses is to provide students with the vital information they need to create, implement, and evaluate an integrated marketing communications plan. To accomplish this goal, the student must appreciate what the various components of IMC are and how they interact with one another to solve marketing problems."

Most IMC textbooks inundate students with information they have already learned in other courses. To dwell on core information over and over again wastes valuable time, time that could be devoted to learning new material and time that could be better spent applying concepts. Time is a precious commodity in a one-semester course!

Students frequently question the price they pay for textbooks. If they buy a marketing communications textbook and the first four chapters are not covered in the classroom because it was part of another course, are they getting fair value for the price they are paying? When they become disgruntled, they question the value of the rest of the book.

Other textbooks on IMC are Canadian editions of American books. They are theory-intensive and do not spend much time on strategic planning principles. None of them includes an actual IMC plan. In contrast, this textbook is truly Canadian and includes all kinds of examples and illustrations that students can quickly relate to, plus planning models they can quickly refer to. If you accept the notion that being familiar with something makes it easier to understand and apply, your students will be better equipped to develop a marketing communications plan after they have read this book.

This textbook is written in a friendly, open manner. It carefully balances the presentation of relevant theories and concepts with applied situations. Your students will even find the book enjoyable to read. The sleek presentation of material in a two-colour, softcover format guarantees the book will be purchased, opened, and read. The price is attractive to student budgets!

All of the key topics associated with integrated marketing communications are covered in 12 chapters. The amount and depth of the content is ideally suited for 14- or 15-week courses of 45 to 60 hours. Rejoice! You can cover all of the material and not be pressed for time!

If the intention of your course is to introduce students to integrated marketing communications, or if the intention is to integrate all components of the mix into a marketing communications plan, for certain this is the book for you. Check out the planning models in any of the chapters and the actual plan that is included in Appendix 2.

Integrated Marketing Communications: Strategic Planning Perspectives offers essential perspectives on planning marketing communications in a concise, tidy, and affordable format. If this is the type of book you and your students require, I would encourage you to give it careful consideration when you make your next adoption decision.

Sincerely,

Keith Tuckwell

Preface

The very nature of marketing communications is changing rapidly. Companies that specialize in various aspects of communications such as advertising, sales promotion, direct-response, or any other area find their clients are making new demands upon them. Clients are looking for integrated marketing and communications solutions for their business problems from one central source. Consequently, specialized communications agencies are evolving into marketing communications agencies. The concept of integrated marketing communications is taking hold in the marketplace!

This textbook meets the needs of this changing marketplace. The content of the book pays equal attention to the various components of the marketing communications mix while stressing the need to coordinate appropriate components into an integrated plan. There are individual chapters devoted to advertising (creative and media issues are treated separately), direct response communications, online and interactive communications, sales promotion, public relations, event marketing and sponsorships, and personal selling. The objective is to show students how the various components might interact with each other in order to create and implement a marketing communications plan that will resolve a business problem.

The book is divided into four essential parts.

Part 1: Understanding Integrated Marketing Communications

This section presents an overview of essential inputs that a manager would consider when developing a marketing communications plan. The content included in Chapter 1, Integrated Marketing Communications: An Overview, introduces the various components of the marketing communications mix and summarizes the essential concepts dealing with consumer behaviour, organizational behaviour, and target marketing. This material typically occupies four or five chapters in competing textbooks.

Chapter 2 shifts the focus to strategic planning. Relationships are drawn between plans and planning at various levels of an organization and how they are integrated. The structure and content of a marketing plan and a marketing communications plan are examined in order to show how plans work together to resolve marketing problems. Chapter 3 introduces the concept of branding and branding strategy. Discussion about branding is strategically located in the textbook to precede detailed coverage of the components of the marketing communications mix. Branding strategies and brand positioning strategies are often the focal points of marketing communications strategies.

Part 2: Planning for Integrated Media

This section examines planning considerations for traditional media choices. Chapter 4, Advertising—Creative Planning, introduces the communications process and the various planning concepts that are considered when briefing an agency about message requirements. The role of strategies and tactics—and the distinctions between them and creative objectives—are considered. Chapter 5 presents the media planning process and stresses the importance of planning an effective yet efficient media plan. The various strategic decisions that are made about media usage are discussed in detail.

Chapter 6 introduces the rapidly expanding field of direct-response communications. Since direct response relies on database management techniques, there is considerable emphasis on customer relationship management practices and the key role played by individualized marketing communications strategies in fostering solid customer relationships. Chapter 7 examines the emerging role of the Internet and other interactive media and how online media strategies can be effectively merged with offline media strategies.

Part 3: Planning for Integrated Marketing

Because organizations look for synergy, the objective is to integrate related marketing practices with the media strategies already presented in the book. Chapter 8 introduces the various sales promotion alternatives that are frequently employed in integrated marketing communications plans. The roles of consumer promotions and trade promotions are examined in detail. Chapter 9 examines the role of public relations in communications. The content focuses on the various techniques that are available, planning procedures, and measurement techniques.

Chapter 10 examines the emerging role of event marketing and sponsorships in contemporary marketing. It introduces the criteria for participating in event marketing and the steps and procedures for planning an event. Chapter 11 covers the role of personal selling in a variety of business settings. Personal selling adds a human component to the integrated marketing communications mix, and for this reason plays a very important role in establishing and building solid customer relationships.

Part 4: Measuring Plan Performance

This section examines the role of various research procedures for evaluating the effectiveness of marketing communications programs. Chapter 12 introduces some fundamental methodologies for collecting and analyzing primary research data and distinguishes between qualitative and quantitative data. The role and influence of collecting and interpreting information on the development of marketing communications strategies are considered.

UNIQUE FEATURES

- This text is presented in a practical, friendly, student-oriented style and provides a good balance between theory and practice. The emphasis on planning makes it an excellent resource for courses that involve developing marketing communications plans or for courses that want to introduce students to the various components of the marketing communications mix.
- This book is written from a Canadian perspective. Careful consideration was given to all of the input that was gathered from Canadian instructors during the review process. For this reason, the book and much of its illustrative content will be very familiar to your students. Such familiarity will make it easier for students to apply the planning concepts that are presented.
- The key topics that comprise a complete IMC course are presented in 12 chapters. The amount and depth of content is ideally suited for courses of 14 or 15 weeks' duration. You, the instructor, will have time to cover all of the material.
- Essential topics that are important for the development of integrated marketing communications strategies are reviewed in only one chapter. Chapter 1—Integrated Marketing Communications: An Overview—introduces the concept of integrated

marketing communications, reviews various consumer behaviour and organizational behaviour concepts that are considered when an organization identifies targets and develops communications strategies, and evaluates several ethical issues related to marketing communications messages.

- Each chapter includes at least two IMC Highlight vignettes. These short inserts reflect important aspects of marketing communications planning or provide actual illustrations of how organizations apply marketing communications concepts. Among the featured organizations and brands are familiar names such as Cirque du Soleil, Canadian Tire, Mazda, Viagra, SOS, Moore's, Moosehead, Frito-Lay, Country Style, and Saturn.

- There is a unique emphasis on planning throughout the book. Chapter 2 provides an overall model for organizing and structuring a marketing communications plan. Each of the individual chapters on the various components of the marketing communications mix includes a model for developing that component of the plan, while showing how it is integrated with other components to form an integrated marketing communications plan. The concept of integration is reinforced throughout the book.

- Chapter 3 presents a thorough discussion of branding and the important role that branding and branding strategies play in the development of marketing communications strategies. This chapter describes the importance of brand positioning strategies and the relationships between brand positioning and marketing communications strategies.

- Appendix 1—Media Buying Principles and Media Information Resources is a supplement that provides additional media details and shows students some fundamental procedures for estimating costs and buying media time and space in a variety of media and other components or the marketing communications mix. Students can quickly refer to media buying information in this specific section of the book.

- An integrated marketing communications plan is included in Appendix 2. The plan for Mobicox, a relatively new pharmaceutical product that is prescribed to arthritis patients, is the topic of the plan. This plan shows how Boehringer Ingelheim employed advertising, public relations, and Web-based communications to launch the drug. Various creative illustrations are included with the plan.

- The book includes countless visual illustrations that specifically demonstrate an important application of marketing communications. Most will be well-known names to your students and include companies and brands such as BMW, Kellogg's, Kraft Foods, Harley-Davidson, Fairmont Hotels, Harvey's, Dell, BMO Bank of Montreal, Pepsi-Cola, Sears, Honda, Colgate-Palmolive, Gillette, and many more. Since each of these companies faces unique situations, the way in which they use integrated marketing communications is also unique.

PEDAGOGY

Learning Objectives Each chapter starts with a list of learning objectives directly related to the key concepts contained in the chapter

Advertisements, Figures and Charts Throughout each chapter, key concepts and applications are illustrated with strong visual material. Sample advertisements and other forms of marketing communications augment the Canadian perspective and demonstrate key aspects of marketing communications strategy and execution.

Key Terms Key terms are highlighted in boldface in the text and in colour on page margins, where they are accompanied by definitions. Students also have quick access to key terms and definitions in the glossary at the end of the book.

Weblinks Helpful internet sites are identified throughout the book and are easily identifiable by the Weblinks icon shown here in the margin.

Chapter Summaries The summary at the end of each chapter reinforces major points and concepts.

Review Questions, Discussion and Application Questions Both sets of questions allow students to review material and apply concepts learned in the chapter.

Appendix 1: Media Buying Principles and Media Information Resources The essentials of buying media time and space in various media outlets are covered in this section.

Appendix 2: Mobicox—An Integrated Marketing Communications Plan This plan shows how various elements of marketing communications combine to form an integrated marketing communications plan. Creative visuals actually used to implement the message strategy are included.

Glossary A glossary of all key terms and definitions appears at the end of the textbook.

Supplements

INSTRUCTOR'S RESOURCE CD-ROM (ISBN 0-13-127045-1)

This valuable tool is an all-in-one resource package that provides quick and easy access to the following supplements.

INSTRUCTOR'S RESOURCE MANUAL

Prepared by the author, the Manual includes learning objectives, chapter highlights that can act as lecture outlines, additional illustrations of key concepts that can be built into lectures, and answers to review and discussion questions. A selection of Canadian case studies that can be used for developing marketing communications strategies and plans is also included. The Manual also provides summary commentaries on each of the video segments in the video library that accompanies the textbook.

TESTGEN

A series of questions for each chapter has been prepared to test students on the material they have studied. The mix of questions will challenge the student's ability to understand concepts and apply concepts. The TestGen software enables instructors to view and edit questions, generate tests, and print the tests in a variety of formats. It also allows instructors to administer tests on a local area network, have tests graded electronically, and have their results prepared in electronic or printed reports.

POWERPOINT SLIDES

A complete set of slides that are specifically designed or culled from the textbook is available electronically. The accompanying Digital Image Gallery provides full-colour versions of ads from the textbook that you can incorporate into your own presentations.

CBC/PEARSON EDUCATION CANADA VIDEO LIBRARY (ISBN 0-13-127039-7)

The videos that accompany the first edition of the textbook cover a broad range of marketing communications topics. Appropriate video segments have been secured from two CBC shows: *Undercurrents* and *Venture*. These are available as a separate supplement in VHS format, or you can link to the videos online at the Companion Website.

COMPANION WEBSITE

The companion website at <**www.pearsoned.ca/tuckwell**> is a handy reference for students. The site includes practice questions, experiential exercises, case studies, web links to related sites, CBC videos, and more. Visit the site for a learning experience.

Acknowledgements

Many organizations and individuals have contributed to the development of this book. I would like to sincerely thank the following organizations for their cooperation and contribution:

3M Canada

Apple Canada

Ashton Green

BMO Bank of Montreal

BMW Canada

Boehringer Ingelheim

Campbell's Soup Company Limited

Canada.com

Canadian Advertising Rates and Data

Canadian Business Magazine

Canadian Geographic Magazine

Canadian Tire

Cara Operations

CIBC Canadian Imperial Bank of Commerce

CKCO Television

The Clorox Company of Canada

Colgate-Palmolive Canada

Cottage Life Magazine

Dell Canada

Fairmont Hotels

Fred Deeley Imports Ltd.

Gallup & Robinson

Garnier Canada

General Mills Canada

The Gillette Company

Givenchy

The Globe and Mail

Honda Canada

Internet Advertising Bureau

Kellogg Canada Inc.

Kimberley-Clark

Kraft Canada

Labatt Breweries of Canada

Maple Leaf Foods

Marriott Hotels

McDonald's Restaurants

McNeil Consumer Healthcare

Millward Brown

Molson Canada

Moosehead Breweries

NCH Promotional Services

Nestlé Canada

Neutrogena

Outside Magazine

Parmalat Canada

Pattison Outdoor Advertising

Pepsi-Cola Canada

Porsche

Procter & Gamble

RBC Financial

Remtulla Euro RSCG

Rolex Canada Limited

Saturn Canada

Save.ca

Sears Canada

Sharp Electronics

Shell Oil

Shoppers Drug Mart

St. Lawrence Broadcasting Company

TaylorMade Golf

Tim Hortons

TIM-BR Mart

Transcontinental Publications

TSN

UPS

Viceroy Homes

Visa Canada

Weyerhaeuser Canada

For undertaking the tedious task of reviewing this book at various stages of development, and for the time and energy they devoted to the review process, I would like to thank the following people profusely:

Cathy Ace, University of British Columbia

Mary Blais, Fanshawe College

Brad Davis, Wilfrid Laurier University

Steve Janisse, St. Clair College

Marianne Marando, Seneca College

Albert Mastromartino, Sir Sandford Fleming College

Peter Mitchell, British Columbia Institute of Technology

Judy Nash, Southern Alberta Institute of Technology

Elizabeth O'Neil, University of Guelph

Beth Pett, Niagara College

Deb Reyner, Conestoga College

Harold Simpkins, Concordia University

Heather Stevens, George Brown College

Jayne Van Dusen, Algonquin College

From Pearson Education Canada I would like to thank Kelly Torrance for seeing the wisdom of pursuing this project initially. I would also like to thank Laura Forbes, Acquisitions Editor; Paul Donnelly, Senior Developmental Editor; Avivah Wargon, Supervising Editor; Deborah Starks, Production Manager; my copy editor, Madeline Koch; and Lisa Brant, for her help with photo research.

I would sincerely like to thank David Sharpe, vice-president and creative director at Remtulla Euro RSCG, and two of his colleagues, David Rutherford and Chris Lemme, for providing the marketing communications plan and supporting creative figures for Mobicox that appear in Appendix 2. I would also like to thank their client, Boehringer Ingelheim, for allowing the Mobicox launch campaign to be used in such an important way in the book.

As always I would also like to thank my family for their support and cooperation. Finding the time to write a third book was challenging and required a lot of creative timetabling. To Marnie, Graham, and Gord—thanks so much! A very special thank you goes to my wife, Esther, for her patience, support, and guidance in the past year!

Keith J. Tuckwell
2004

A Great Way to Learn and Instruct Online

The Pearson Education Canada Companion Website is easy to navigate and is organized to correspond to the chapters in this textbook. Whether you are a student in the classroom or a distance learner you will discover helpful resources for in-depth study and research that empower you in your quest for greater knowledge and maximize your potential for success in the course.

Companion Website

[www.pearsoned.ca/tuckwell]

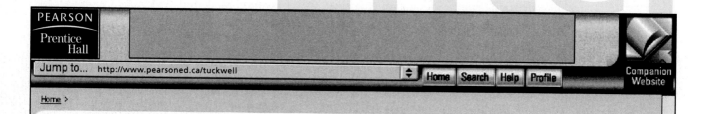

PEARSON Prentice Hall

Jump to... http://www.pearsoned.ca/tuckwell ⬍ Home | Search | Help | Profile

Companion Website

Home >

PH Companion Website

Integrated Marketing Communications: Strategic Planning Perspectives, by Keith J. Tuckwell

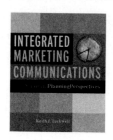

Student Resources

The modules in this section provide students with tools for learning course material. These modules include:
- Learning Objectives
- Destinations
- Quizzes
- Internet Exercises
- PowerPoint Presentations
- Glossary
- CBC Videos

In the quiz modules students can send answers to the grader and receive instant feedback on their progress through the Results Reporter. Coaching comments and references to the textbook may be available to ensure that students take advantage of all available resources to enhance their learning experience.

Instructor Resources

The modules in this section provide instructors with additional teaching tools. Downloadable PowerPoint Presentations and an Instructor's Manual are just some of the materials that may be available in this section. Where appropriate, this section will be password protected. To get a password, simply contact your Pearson Education Canada Representative or call Faculty Sales and Services at 1-800-850-5813.

PART

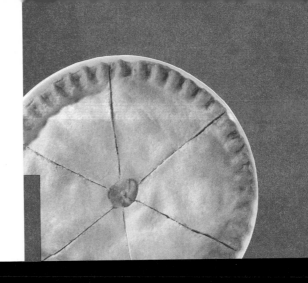

Understanding Integrated Marketing Communications

Part 1 focuses on several introductory issues that are associated with the development of integrated marketing communications programs. Chapter 1 introduces the components of the integrated marketing communications mix and then discusses some essential consumer behaviour concepts and business-to-business buying characteristics that organizations consider when developing communications strategies.

Chapter 2 introduces the student to essential strategic planning principles while drawing relationships between planning at various levels of an organization. The structure and content of a marketing plan and marketing communications plan are presented in detail. The intent is to show how integrated planning provides solutions to marketing problems.

Chapter 3 concentrates on issues related to branding strategy. Essentially, marketing communications strategies are the primary vehicle for building the image of a brand or company. Since brand positioning is the focal point of most marketing communications strategies, the role that positioning strategy statements play in the development of communications campaigns is examined in detail. The role and influence of packaging and product design strategies and their effect on brand image are also examined.

INTEGRATED MARKETING COMMUNICATIONS: AN OVERVIEW

After studying this chapter you will be able to:

LEARNING OBJECTIVES

appreciate the role of integrated marketing communications planning in business today,

identify the components of the integrated marketing communications mix,

identify the conditions that have led to the emergence of integrated marketing communications,

explain how consumer behaviour concepts influence marketing communications strategies,

assess the information needed to identify and select target markets,

explain how unique characteristics of organizational buying behaviour influence marketing communications, and

evaluate the ethical issues that surround marketing communications messages.

Organizations today are searching for complete solutions for their communications needs. In the past it was quite common for separate departments within an organization to prepare communications plans independently. If communications plans were prepared externally, various tasks would be assigned to distinct and separate organizations that were specialists in certain areas. Typically, an advertising agency would handle creative and media assignments, a company with expertise in sales promotion would develop consumer promotion programs, while a public relations firm would develop programs to build an organization's image. In such a system, each firm operated independently, not knowing what the others were doing. When communications plans were implemented, they often headed in different directions or delivered a different message about the company.

The business environment has changed dramatically in the past ten years. The influence of technology alone has forced business organizations to examine how they deliver messages to their target markets. Generally speaking, there has been a movement toward targeted media and away from mass media. As well, companies are experimenting with new communications concepts such as *product placement* and *product seeding* in order to create a "buzz" for new products. Customer behaviour has changed. The average consumer relies less on newspapers and television and more on computers and telephones for receiving news and commercial messages. And the nature of competition has moved from being just competitive to being hypercompetitive. Companies are going to market with new products much more quickly than they used to.

Changes like these have influenced how an organization communicates with its customers, whether they are individual consumers or businesses. No longer do companies rely on disjointed strategies from a variety of sources, even though those sources are experts at what they do. The goal of communications now is to deliver the same message through a variety of media in order to have a synergistic impact on the target. Furthermore, the development of message strategy is now in the hands of fewer external suppliers. Many traditional advertising agencies have evolved into marketing communications agencies. They have either hired expertise or acquired companies that specialize in different aspects of communications, for example, public relations, sales promotion, direct response communications, and so on. The range of services and the level of specialization that agencies provide are much greater than before. In effect, these agencies are changing with their client's needs and are providing integrated marketing communications solutions.

The Integrated Marketing Communications Mix

Integrated Marketing Communications

The coordination of all marketing communications in a unified program that maximizes the impact on the intended target audience.

Integrated marketing communications involves the coordination of all forms of marketing communications in a unified program that maximizes the impact on consumers and other types of customers. It embraces many unique yet complementary forms of communication: media advertising (a focus on message strategies and media strategies in a traditional media environment), direct response communications (communications that encourage immediate action), interactive communications (internet, CD-ROM, and instant messaging text), sales promotions (both consumer and trade promotions), public relations, event marketing and sponsorships, and personal selling (see Figure 1.1). Effective communications integration also considers the role of packaging and its impact on consumers at point-of-purchase and the role that all employees of an organization play in communicating a positive attitude about a company to its various publics. Any customer touch-point is part of integrated marketing communications.

How an organization plans and manages the various components of the mix is important. Rarely does an organization employ all components at one time on a particular project, but rather it selects and uses those components that are deemed appropriate for resolving the situation at hand. For the components used, the message delivered by each must be complementary. Integration of message strategy, regardless of the medium, is key to generating maximum impact on the target audience.

FIGURE **1.1** The Integrated Marketing Communications Mix

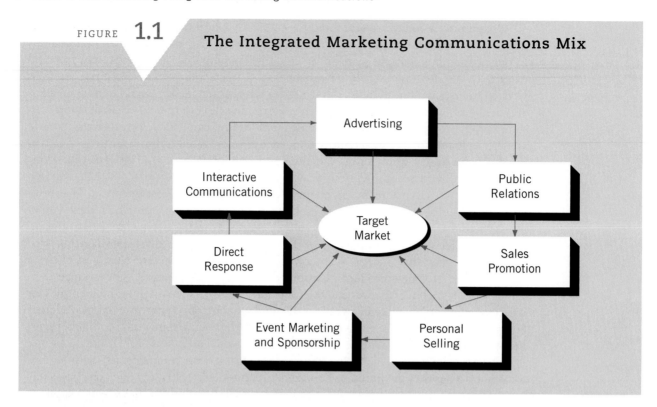

Clients look for a "total solutions" communications approach to resolve their business problems. There is a demand for comprehensively planned, seamless campaigns. However, since the communications industry is structured in a rather fragmented manner with specialized agencies competing for a client's attention, a total solutions approach is not always feasible. The industry is not yet structured in a manner that allows for a holistic approach to communication delivered by people with broad experience and training across many communications disciplines. Though acquisitions and expansion have occurred among the largest agencies, they are only slowly evolving into marketing communications agencies. Even under such an umbrella, various operating divisions often create plans for the same client independently rather than collectively. There is much work to be done!

Managing branded communications through today's ever-evolving matrix of potential consumer/customer touch-points is becoming increasingly complex. Both marketing organizations and their agencies need to stop for a moment and re-evaluate their long-term goals. Key issues remain the level and intensity of the planned service, organizational structures and execution processes, and the overall approach to compensation, performance, and accountability.[1]

Let's start the discussion about integrated marketing communications by clearly explaining the fundamental nature of each form of marketing communication.

ADVERTISING

Advertising

A form of marketing communications designed to stimulate a positive response from a defined target market.

Advertising is a persuasive form of marketing communication designed to stimulate a positive response from a defined target market. In the context of the integrated marketing communications mix, good advertising (advertising that has an impact on the audience) will influence the behaviour of that audience—that is its primary function. Assuming that the advertising helps create a positive attitude toward a specific product or company in the customer's mind, that customer may be motivated to purchase the product or look favourably upon it.

Product Advertising
Advertising that provides information about a branded product to help build its image in the minds of customers.

Advertising can be either product-oriented or promotion-oriented. **Product advertising** provides information and helps build an image for the product, whether it's a brand or a company. In doing so, the features, attributes, and benefits of the product are presented in a persuasive manner. With reference to Figure 1.2, the ad for Tylenol 8 Hour stresses one key benefit to potential users: the product provides long-lasting relief. That is a compelling argument for buying this product.

FIGURE **1.2**   **A Benefit-Oriented Advertisement Used to Launch Tylenol 8 Hour**

Need pain relief that works as long as you do?
New TYLENOL® 8 HOUR relieves tough muscle pain for up to 8 hours.

For a Trial Offer visit www.TYLENOL8HOUR.ca

Source: Provided by McNeil Consumer Healthcare.

General Motors Canada
www.gm.ca

Promotional Advertising
Advertising that communicates a specific offer to encourage an immediate response from the target audience.

Several large companies are among the leading product advertisers in Canada: General Motors, Procter & Gamble, Ford Motor Company, Sears, and HBC (Hudson's Bay Company). These companies are also among the leaders in integrated marketing communications. General Motors, for example, also communicates online through its company website, is active in direct response communications with prospective customers, uses sales promotions extensively to offer more attractive prices to customers, and is constantly in the news thanks to the success of its public relations program.

Promotional advertising is designed to accomplish a specific task—usually to communicate a specific offer to elicit some kind of immediate response from the customer. Including some kind of coupon or contest promotion with a print advertisement, for example, is a form of promotional advertising. In this case, the content of the ad presents the features and primary benefit to help build the image and also provides an incentive for customers to buy. Automobile manufacturers, for example, are well known for their rebate programs and low-cost financing programs, both of which are advertised heavily in order to attract customers. Packaged goods manufacturers use coupons and other incentives to encourage more immediate action by consumers. These form an integrated marketing communications strategy even though they involve only two components of the marketing communications mix.

DIRECT RESPONSE COMMUNICATIONS

Direct Response Communications
The delivery of a message to a target audience of one; message can be distributed by direct mail, direct response television, and telemarketing.

Direct response communications involves the delivery of a message to a target audience of one. As the term implies, "direct" means direct from the marketing company to a specific user or prospective user of a company's product. Direct mail is the most common form of direct response communications. Other forms of direct response include direct response television (DRTV), telemarketing, and catalogues. This segment of the communications industry is growing at a much faster pace than traditional forms of advertising. Time-pressed consumers, for example, find the convenience of direct response appealing. They can learn of a product's benefit and actually buy it if they so desire all in one stage.

Figure 1.3 includes the content of a direct mail package that was used as part of the launch strategy for Tylenol 8 Hour tablets. The mailing includes product information, sample tablets, and a $2.00 coupon on the first purchase of the product. The direct mail execution was a key element of the launch campaign since it was designed to encourage trial purchase. A television and print advertising campaign was implemented to generate awareness and interest for the brand, another example of successful integration.

Direct response communications was once the domain of direct marketing organizations such as magazine publishers and record companies. Consumers had a less-than-favourable image of direct response companies. Now, however, all kinds of blue chip companies are involved in direct response communications and consumers are much more receptive to receiving and reacting to messages received through the direct response techniques.

INTERACTIVE COMMUNICATIONS

Technology is changing so rapidly that there is little doubt that communications by way of electronic devices will be the future of marketing communications. Thus far, however, consumers have been reluctant to accept marketing communications distributed on the internet. The behaviour of internet users is such that they avoid or barely tolerate the intrusion of commercial messages. That said, advertisers are finding more effective ways of delivering messages online and it is expected that consumers will come to perceive the internet as a medium much like television. Consumers must realize that the online services they take for granted have to be paid for by someone. Advertising revenue is vital for the survival of internet service providers.

FIGURE **1.3** **A Direct Mail Package Containing Product Information and Trial Purchase Incentives**

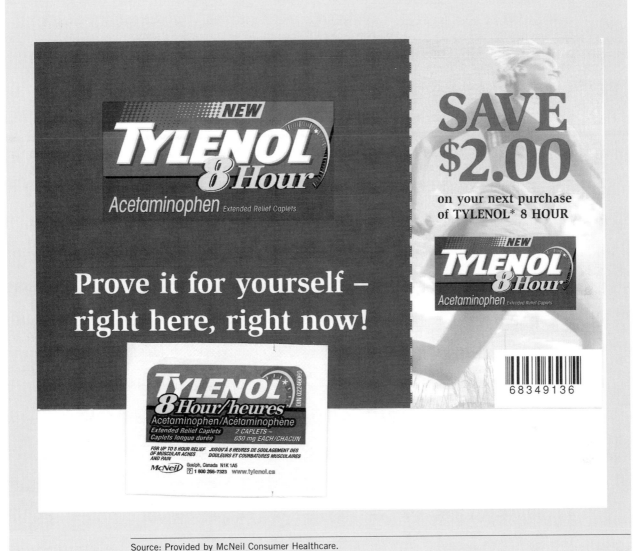

Source: Provided by McNeil Consumer Healthcare.

The new emphasis that business organizations place on *customer relationship management (CRM)*, combined with their ability to manage internal databases, is forcing them to move toward direct and interactive communications. At present, organizations communicate through their own websites and through various forms of online advertising such as banner ads, pop-ups, and sponsorships. These and other new forms of communications will play an increasing role in the communications mix in the future. CRM is discussed in more detail later in this chapter.

SALES PROMOTION

Sales Promotion
An activity that provides incentives to bring about immediate response from customers, distributors, and an organization's sales force.

Sales promotion involves special incentives to stimulate an immediate reaction from consumers and distributors. An organization's promotion expenditures tend to be divided between consumers and distributors. Strategies that include coupons, free samples, contests, and cash refunds or rebates are classified as consumer promotions. The direct mail campaign included in Figure 1.3 is a good example of how sales promotions are integrated with media advertising. Offering price discounts to distributors for purchasing goods in large quantities or for performing some kind of marketing or merchandising task on behalf of a marketing organization is classified as a trade promotion.

The marketing organization is constantly challenged on how to divide the sales promotion budget between consumers and trade customers. Regardless of how the budget is allocated, it is imperative that consumer promotion strategies be aligned effectively with consumer advertising programs (to pull the product through the channel of distribution) and that trade promotions be aligned effectively with personal selling programs (to push the product through the channel of distribution). In a business organization, the sales force is responsible for implementing the trade promotion plans. Again, the integration of various marketing communications programs pays off for the organization.

PERSONAL SELLING

Personal Selling
Face-to-face communication involving the presentation of features and benefits of a product or service to a buyer; the objective is to make a sale.

As the term implies, **personal selling** involves the delivery of a personalized message from a seller to a buyer. That message presents the features, attributes, and benefits of a product or service. Personal selling is important in so many situations, whether the seller is a car salesperson in a DaimlerChrysler showroom, a store clerk in Best Buy, or the Kraft sales representative presenting a new product to a buyer at the head office of Loblaws.

All kinds of compelling advertising for new automobiles encourage consumers to visit dealer showrooms. That money can go to waste if a salesperson at a dealership is unprepared to handle customer inquiries effectively. And what about that new line of Post cereal that Kraft is trying to sell to Loblaws? If the buyer doesn't accept the offer put forth by the Kraft sales representative, Kraft faces a significant setback. For example, if the listing discounts or quantity discounts are not sufficient, no amount of advertising will help sell the product—it simply will not be available at Loblaws. The job of the sales representative is to secure widespread distribution of the product, one customer at a time, and in a timely manner. The availability of the product in stores must coincide with the scheduling of media advertising. If that is not the case, a lot of advertising money could be wasted.

PUBLIC RELATIONS

Public Relations
A form of communications designed to gain public understanding and acceptance.

Public relations are a form of communications that is primarily directed toward gaining public understanding and acceptance. Public relations messages influence the attitudes and opinions of interest groups to an organization. Traditionally, public relations messages have focused on issues rather than on products or services, but marketing organizations now appreciate the role that public relations and publicity campaigns can play in generating positive attitudes toward products.

Public relations rely placing messages in the media that require no payment. In effect, they can generate "free" exposure. For example, a company issues a press release announcing a new product. The release includes all the virtues of the product, where it will be available, and how it will be advertised. Stories about the new product will appear on television newscasts and in newspaper and magazine articles. Such exposure offers a legitimacy that advertising does not have. To demonstrate, public relations played a key role in Vancouver's bid to host the 2010 Winter Olympic Games. Hollywood movie producers rely heavily on public relations to generate publicity for new movie releases—it creates the necessary hype they so desire!

Vancouver Olympic and Paralympic Winter Games (2010)
www.city.vancouver.bc.ca/olympics/

Public relations also play a major role when a company finds itself in a crisis. Senior managers of an organization must be prepared to deal with the media and issue effective communications when unpleasant circumstances arise, for instance, a product recall or a matter of public safety involving the company. Such was the case when the City of Toronto found itself in the midst of the SARS disaster. In such cases, good public relations help to reassure the public that the situation is being dealt with quickly and effectively.

EVENT MARKETING AND SPONSORSHIPS

Event marketing

The process, planned by a sponsoring organization, of integrating a variety of communications elements with a single event theme.

Sponsorship

The act of financially supporting an event in return for certain advertising rights and privileges.

Molson Canada
www.molson.com

Event marketing and sponsorships are related yet different activities. **Event marketing** involves planning, organizing, and marketing an event, whether it is an event for a company or a brand of a company, that integrates a variety of communications elements. **Sponsorship** simply means that a company provides money to an event in order to enjoy specified marketing privileges for being associated with the event. Molson, for example, is involved in event marketing through CART Racing (the Molson Indy races that run in Toronto, Montreal, and Vancouver each summer). Molson defrays the cost of holding such events by selling sponsorships to other companies. Those companies have advertising and signage privileges at the event and can use the event logo to help market their product to the public.

In the past decade, event marketing and sponsorships have become more prominent in the marketing communications mix. Although the benefits of event marketing are difficult to measure, an organization does know that it can reach its target market directly when it associates with the right event. In the example cited here, Molson knows that beer drinkers find auto racing a very popular sport. Molson invests its event marketing and sponsorship budget wisely by selecting those sports that its best customers prefer. As well, Molson effectively combines its racing association with other elements of marketing communications. In the months leading up to the various Canadian races, Molson is active with media advertising, public relations, and sales promotions. All activities are designed to create awareness and interest—and sell tickets to the races.

In summary, contemporary organizations realize there are significant benefits to be achieved if all forms of marketing communications are integrated successfully. For certain, integration fosters a cooperative approach to communications planning, presents a unified message, and creates a higher level of impact on the target audience. The Cirque du Soleil implemented an integrated communications campaign to launch a three-city Canadian tour in 2002. For insight into the campaign and the results it achieved, refer to the IMC Highlight **A Sellout for Cirque du Soleil**.

Factors Encouraging Integrated Marketing Communications

Several key issues and trends will continue to affect marketing and marketing communications practice. Among these issues and trends are the strategic focus on relationship marketing commonly referred to as customer relationship management (CRM), the expanding role of database marketing, the sudden and dramatic impact of the internet and other communications technologies, and greater demand for efficiency and accountability in organizations.

CUSTOMER RELATIONSHIP MANAGEMENT

Business today is all about relationships: the relationships that an organization has with its customers, distributors, and suppliers. A relationship may involve numerous companies working together to achieve common goals, or it may only involve one company trying to

IMC Highlight

A SELLOUT FOR CIRQUE DU SOLEIL

Cirque du Soleil is a well-known Canadian entertainment troupe that has received accolades from all over the world, and it was thought that those accolades would be a double-edged sword when it came time to market Varekai in 2002. More than 33 million people worldwide have experienced the magical animal-free spectacle.

In Canada in 2002, three tour stops were planned: Quebec City, Montreal, and Toronto. Cirque hadn't performed in Canada for three years, so there was some fear that the Canadian pubic might have abandoned the troupe. It was decided to create a campaign that would be as untraditional as the product itself. The marketing objective was to sell 70 percent of the tickets prior to the premiere in each city. Another objective was to increase the database of "Cirque Club" members by 50 percent. The media budget was $900 000.

The anchor of the marketing communications plan was a redesigned website (cirquedusoleil.com). The site would offer an intimate place to experience the Cirque phenomenon. The campaign started with a teaser postcard that was sent to all members in the existing database, inviting them and their friends to join the online Cirque du Soleil for free.

They would be the first to receive news, have first rights to tickets, and have access to exclusive content such as a webcast of the troupe's performance at the Academy Awards.

The campaign relied on low-level buzz-generating tactics rather than a full-blown media blitz. Print and outdoor ads appeared in Toronto, Montreal, and Quebec City with the tagline "The sun will shine in Toronto" (or Montreal or Quebec City). Additional support came in the form of radio announcements, celebrity-studded premiere parties, and press events. "It was all about creating the buzz of a circus caravan rolling into town," according to Mario D'Amico, the troupe's Vice-President of Marketing.

The campaign was a success. The tickets were so hot that 90 percent were sold in each city by premiere day, and all tickets were sold by the end of each city's run. The website was so captivating that it was awarded the Best of Show prize at *Marketing*'s Digital Marketing Awards in 2003. Membership in the Cirque club climbed from 68 000 to 350 000 people—significant ammunition for the next marketing communications campaign.

Adapted from Andrea Zoe Aster, "Cirque's Sun Shines Brightly," *Marketing*, December 16, 2002.

Customer Relationship Management (CRM)

A process that enables an organization to develop an ongoing relationship with valued customers.

Corporate Culture

The values, beliefs, norms, and practices shared by all employees of an organization.

build a meaningful relationship with its consumers. **Customer relationship management** programs are concerned with establishing, maintaining, and enhancing long-term relationships; they involve collecting information about customers that can be used to develop and sustain those relationships. These programs call for internal marketing, that is, they involve all employees in the role of marketing ambassadors. External marketing and marketing communications programs are designed to approach customer groups (targets) collectively and each customer individually, when applicable.

For relationship management programs to be successful, an organization gives the customer the first and final say. Such an attitude by all employees is referred to as corporate culture. **Corporate culture** refers to the values, beliefs, norms, and practices shared by all employees of an organization. A successful organization thinks "customer" all the time. At 3M, for example, all employees consider themselves to be in the customer care business, and in all forms of communications the company uses the phrase "3M Innovation" to present unified messages to customers. 3M has an identity strategy in place with the goal of making 3M Innovation a recognizable and trustworthy element in all relationships the company has with channel partners, investors, employees, customers, the media, and so on. As part of 3M's vision, the company abides by the 3M brand promise: "Practical and ingenious solutions that help customers succeed."[2]

Caring for customers in today's business environment calls for equal consideration to attracting new customers and to retaining existing customers. Typically, the more traditional means of communication are used to pursue new customers, and nontraditional media such as telemarketing, online communications (email), and loyalty programs are used to retain and enhance the customer relationship. Specific loyalty programs such as Air Miles and Canadian Tire money keep customers coming back. In the case of Air Miles, consumers show loyalty to all the companies that participate in the program in order to derive maximum benefit from the points collected. Further discussion of a CRM programs appears later in this chapter.

EXPANDING ROLE OF DATABASE MANAGEMENT TECHNIQUES

Database Management System
A system that collects information about customers for analysis by managers in order to facilitate sound business decisions.

Database management systems involve the continuous collection of information about customers, and have been developing and growing rapidly. Consequently, companies can contact consumers directly more easily than they were previously able to do. Companies analyze the information to predict how likely the customer is to buy, and then develops a message precisely designed to meet that customer's unique needs. Technological advances allow a company to zero in on extremely small segments of the population, often referred to as niches. The ultimate goal is to aim directly at the smallest segment—the individual.

There was a time when direct marketing practices were frowned upon by leading companies. It was something that only desperate companies practised. How the times have changed! Today database marketing has emerged as a major thrust, to which more traditional forms of communications are added. Bell Canada, for example, is one of Canada's largest advertisers in the traditional mass media. Bell is also one of Canada's largest database and direct response marketing organizations. Bell keeps in close contact with its customers in order to serve them better and generate incremental business from them.

Database marketing and relationship marketing are closely related. The database is the internal vehicle that facilitates implementation of customer relationship management programs. For additional information about database marketing and CRM, see the section on "Direct (Customized) Segmentation" later in this chapter.

THE INTERNET AND OTHER COMMUNICATIONS TECHNOLOGIES

The internet and the World Wide Web are now vital means of communicating information about goods and services and conducting business transactions with customers. Companies are exploring new forms of advertising made available by the internet, and in many cases are adding an online component to their traditional media advertising. The internet is a new and exciting medium and is becoming a primary medium to reach customers on an individual basis. It truly is a vehicle that facilitates relationship marketing because it involves continuous interaction in the pre-transaction, transaction, and post-transaction stages of a purchase.

Due to its newness, organizations are struggling in terms of how to integrate internet communications effectively. Many organizations jumped in very quickly, and, as the old saying goes, they learned from their mistakes. What is perplexing about online communications is how it differs from traditional forms of communications. "It's a bit of direct response, it's a bit of broadcast, it's a bit of print, and it's a bit of technology," comments one observer.[3] Finding external communications expertise that is knowledgeable in all these areas has also been a challenge. Nonetheless, the web is a medium that seems to offer unlimited potential.

Internet communications are growing more slowly than expected but current evidence suggests a bright future. In the United States, expenditures on internet communications now exceed radio advertising. Online communications in the U.S. amounted to US$5.7 billion (2.4 percent of total advertising expenditures) in 2002.[4] Furthermore, consumers are spending less time watching television and more time online. That shift has consequences for how media budgets are allocated. Colgate-Palmolive Company announced recently that online communication is the most cost-efficient way to promote toothpaste to 18- to 49-year-olds, and the company has adjusted its marketing communications budget accordingly.[5]

The penetration of satellite communication is increasing in Canada. Satellite dishes combined with a myriad of cable channels have fragmented the television-viewing audience to the point where mass-market television campaigns make little sense. As indicated above, the internet has changed consumers' behaviour—they refer to the traditional media less than they used to for news and information. As a consequence, smart managers are adding more electronic communications strategies. Beyond the internet, CD-ROMs and text messaging through mobile telephones is growing in popularity. It is estimated that by the time this book is published there will be 150 million cellphone subscribers in North America, a marketing communications explosion just waiting to happen.[6]

THE DEMAND FOR EFFICIENCY AND ACCOUNTABILITY

Organizations now understand that scarce resources can be put to better use if the efforts of individual activities are coordinated. A coordinated effort encourages synergy, which in turn should encourage a stronger impact on the target audience. There is intense pressure on managers today to be more accountable for producing tangible results for their marketing communications investment. Therefore, communications strategies that are efficient are popular, as are strategies that can be measured easily in terms of return on investment. Senior management likes the idea of tangible results. Such a demand is fuelling interest in electronic communications because consumer responses to the communications can be tracked electronically and without cost. Similar measurements are not possible when traditional forms of communications are employed.

The campaign for the 2004 Toyota Echo saw public relations, cinema advertising, conventional advertising, and direct marketing work together effectively, and is the result of Toyota's management decision to combine all communications departments into one integrated group. According to Peter Renz, Toyota Canada's national manager of public relations and advertising, "We combined all departments in order to ensure that we were speaking with a consistent voice and were sending out a consistent message all the time. It's given us an opportunity to think more 'out of the box' in terms of ideas. With all disciplines working together there are tremendous efficiencies."[7]

Consumer Behaviour Essentials

A basic understanding of some important behavioural concepts is essential, because such knowledge is applied directly in the development of marketing communications strategies. Knowledge in the areas of needs and motives, personality and self-concept, attitudes and perceptions, reference groups, and families is considered when an organization plans its marketing communications strategies.

Consumer Behaviour
The combined acts carried out by individuals choosing and using goods and services, including the decision-making processes that determine these acts.

Consumer behaviour is defined as the acts that individuals perform in obtaining and using goods and services, including the decision-making processes that precede and determine these acts.[8] In the context of marketing and marketing communications, it is imperative that organizations understand what influences consumers' behaviour. Consequently, organizations invest considerable sums of money on marketing research in order to understand consumers better. Information is power, as they say.

NEEDS AND MOTIVES

Need
The perception of the absence of something useful.

Motive
A condition that prompts an individual to take action to satisfy a need.

There is a direct link between needs and motives. Individuals have a **need** when they perceive the absence of something that is useful to them. A **motive** is a condition that prompts the individual to take action to satisfy the need. Consumers are motivated by friends and family members or they can be influenced by what they see and read in the media, or by broadcast messages on radio and television. An appealing presentation of a product's features and benefits as they relate to a target's needs is often good enough to stimulate action—a purchase decision. "I need (want) whiter clothes, so I buy Tide." That's the power of advertising!

Maslow's *hierarchy of needs* and *theory of motivation* have had a significant impact on marketing and marketing communications strategies. Maslow classified needs from lower level to higher level. His theory is based on two assumptions:

1. When lower-level needs are satisfied, a person moves up to higher-level needs.
2. Satisfied needs do not motivate. Instead, behaviour is influenced by needs yet to be satisfied.

Maslow states that individuals move through five levels of needs as shown in Figure 1.4. Numerous advertising examples can be cited to show how needs theory is applied. For example, safety needs are used to motivate people to buy life insurance and retirement plans. A tagline such as "Like a good neighbour, State Farm is there," exudes the message of protection and security.

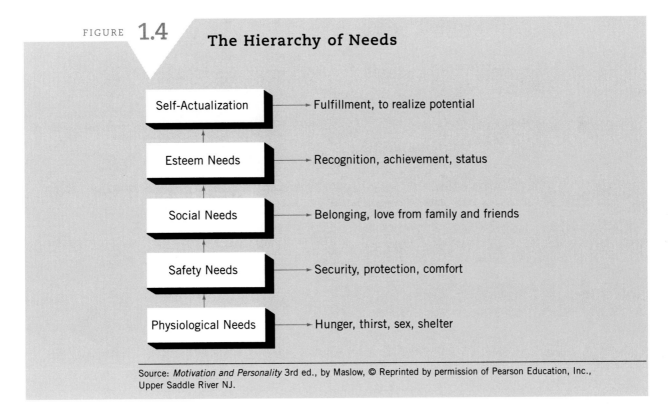

FIGURE 1.4 **The Hierarchy of Needs**

Source: *Motivation and Personality* 3rd ed., by Maslow, © Reprinted by permission of Pearson Education, Inc., Upper Saddle River NJ.

Social needs are extremely important to style-conscious youth who want to fit in with their peers. Take, for example, recent clothing fashions worn by girls 12 to 15 years old. More and more of them are wearing cleavage-baring crop tops and ultra-low-rise pants that expose their pelvic bones, emulating their favourite pop stars. Clothes for girls have never been so skimpy. These girls are trying to convince their moms and dads that it is all about girl power, but they are often unaware of how their dress is being interpreted.[9] Fashion designers and retailers such as Abercrombie & Fitch and La Senza Girl are reaping the benefits. Children today are more affluent than previous generations. As an economic power, they are being bombarded with messages on how to look and how to dress.

The advertisement for the BMW X5 that appears in Figure 1.5 appeals to potential buyers on two levels of needs: safety and esteem. For consumers who want to enjoy the rugged outdoors, both levels of need come into play. The ad appeals to both the rational side and emotional side of consumer buying behaviour.

FIGURE **1.5** | The BMW X5 Appeals to Safety Needs and Esteem Needs

PERSONALITY AND SELF-CONCEPT

Personality

A person's distinguishing psychological characteristics that lead to relatively consistent and enduring responses to the environment in which that person lives.

Personality refers to the individual's distinguishing psychological characteristics that lead to relatively consistent and enduring responses to the environment in which that person lives. Personality is influenced by self-perceptions, which in turn are influenced by family, reference groups, and culture. An understanding of that self-concept provides clues to how to communicate with consumers. According to Maslow, we have certain needs that must be satisfied. The self-concept, however, goes a step further and focuses on our desires.

According to self-concept theory, the self has four components: real self, self-image, looking-glass-self, and ideal self.[10]

1. *Real Self:* An objective evaluation of one's self. You as you really are.
2. *Self-Image*: How you see yourself. It may not be the real self but a role you play with yourself.
3. *Looking-Glass Self:* How you think others see you. Your view of how others see you can be quite different from how they actually see you.
4. *Ideal Self*: How you would like to be. It is what you aspire to.

Based on these descriptions, the real self and self-image are less significant. In contrast, the looking-glass self and ideal self seem dynamic—they focus more on desires, the way we would like to be perceived. Consequently, many communications campaigns revolve around the looking-glass self and the ideal self. Marketing communicators know that consumers buy on emotion. They present messages for goods and services that make them feel better and look better, for they know the next level of fulfillment is attractive. To demonstrate, why is it that a man will spend $1500 or more on a suit at Harry Rosen when a less expensive suit will offer similar benefits? The answer lies somewhere in the looking-glass self or the ideal self. The image created by high prices and effective communications attracts an upscale clientele to Harry Rosen's stores. Harry Rosen has cultivated its image using a combination of media advertising, public relations, personalized service, and customer relationship management programs. Their job is to make the customers feel good about every purchase they make. Those customers are on the move and want to make a statement about themselves.

How men react to the aging process provides another good illustration of the self-concept theory. Today's men are falling prey (as women have in the past) to feeling insecure about aging. They are now getting manicures and skin treatments and many are pursuing cosmetic surgery—those love handles are the first things to go. It seems that white teeth, nice skin, and a red-hot wardrobe are now requirements of the ultimate male package. Magazines such as *Men's Health* and *Maxim* are effective delivery vehicles for the message that physical imperfection, age, and an underdeveloped fashion sense are potentially crippling disabilities. As a result, new products such as face scrubs, moisturizers, and cleansing products, long regarded as female beauty aids, are springing up for males. Nivea for Men and Neutrogena Men are examples of such product lines (see Figure 1.6). As one industry critic observes, "Males are evolving from being a John Wayne to being more like Niles Crane."[11]

ATTITUDES AND PERCEPTIONS

Attitude

An individual's feelings, favourable or unfavourable, toward an idea or object.

Attitudes are an individual's feelings, favourable or unfavourable, toward an idea or object. People form attitudes based on what they hear, read, and see about a product as well as from the opinions of others they have faith in. Friends, for example, certainly have a dramatic impact on the attitudes held by youth. Trendsetters and opinion leaders who embrace new products quickly also influence how consumer attitudes are shaped.

As a rule, organizations present their product in accordance to attitudes held strongly by their target audience. It makes little sense to go against the grain—many an organization has discovered it is very expensive to try to change an attitude. The "force fit" strategy does not work! To demonstrate, only a few years ago it would be an exception to the rule if a brand were to target the gay community. Such a move presented real risk—the core consumers might desert the brand in favour of a brand that is more mainstream. Today, society is more tolerant of gay relationships, as such a lifestyle is now out in the open. Beer and alcohol companies have been quick off the mark in taking advantage of such an attitude shift. A print ad for Miller Lite shows two twenty-something males sharing an intimate moment. The headline reads, "Twist one off" followed by a subhead that reads, "It's your Miller Time—35 years proud." Captain Morgan's rum has targeted gays by sponsoring Pride Week celebrations in Toronto. Captain Morgan, in the flesh, hits Pride party venues dressed in his pirate suit to promote the brand's variety of rum drinks.[12]

FIGURE 1.6 Perceptions of One's Image Plays a Role in Advertising

Give him the gift of healthy-looking skin.

RAZOR DEFENSE™
Gentle Face Scrub
Neutrogena® MEN
Minimizes Razor Irritation

RAZOR DEFENSE™
Shave Gel
Neutrogena® MEN
Minimizes Razor Irritation

RAZOR DEFENSE™
Face Lotion
Neutrogena® MEN
Minimizes Razor Irritation

Introducing
Neutrogena®
M E N

Source: Courtesy of Neutrogena.

Perception

The manner in which individuals receive and interpret messages.

Perception refers to the manner in which individuals receive and interpret messages. Given the prevailing model of human behaviour, it is safe to say that consumers accept messages that are in line with their needs, personality, self-concept, and attitudes, and ignore or reject messages that are not. Theory states that we are selective about the messages we receive and that there are three levels of selectivity:

1. *Selective Exposure:* Our eyes and minds notice only information that interests us.
2. *Selective Perception:* We screen out messages that conflict with our attitudes.
3. *Selective Retention:* We remember only what we want to remember.

To demonstrate, time-pressed consumers, particularly women who balance a working career with household responsibilities, have adjusted their attitude toward the foods their children eat. It would be nice to pack milk, a sandwich, and a piece of fruit for the children's lunch each day, but preparation takes time. The mother now looks for prepackaged snacks that can be easily thrown in a knapsack and can be eaten on the go. Such a fundamental shift in attitude has led to a booming packaged snack food market. These mothers are now very receptive to messages for anything from Quaker Chewy Granola Dipps to Oreo cookie bars to Squeez 'n Go portable puddings. Hostess Frito-Lay is making life simpler by packing chips in portable canisters. The cans fit neatly into backpacks or a car-cup holder—a product concept well suited for dashboard dining, which is another trend among today's busy households.[13]

Busy mothers also search for nutritional and convenient snacks to fit their own lifestyle. Kellogg's responds with products such as Special K bars (see Figure 1.7). The Special K brand has already been positioned to appeal specifically to women. The former advertising slogan for the brand "Look good on your own terms" recently gave way to a new slogan "Keep it simple."

REFERENCE GROUPS

Reference Group or Peer Group

A group of people who share common interests that influence the attitudes and behaviour of its members.

A **reference group**, or **peer group**, is a group of people with a common interest that influences the attitudes and behaviour of its members. Reference groups include schoolmates, sports teams, fraternities and sororities, and hobby clubs. There is considerable pressure on members to conform to the standards of the group—a desire to "fit in." Take, for example, the mild hazing that occurs among rookies of a college or university sports team or the rituals associated with joining a fraternity.

In terms of marketing and marketing communications, it is common for brands to associate with a particular situation or lifestyle the target consumer could become interested in. Skateboarders and snowboarders, for example, have their own style of clothing and display a distinct behaviour when they congregate. Mountain Dew transformed itself from a brand with virtually no image to a "hip" brand when it launched the "Do the Dew" advertising campaign. The ads were edgy and contained lots of action and loud music to grab the attention of teens. Ads like those for Mountain Dew suggest to teens they can join such a group or be part of a subculture by purchasing a particular product. To enhance its connection with teens, Mountain Dew also sponsors numerous skateboard competitions across North America each year. Event marketing is now an integral aspect of Mountain Dew's marketing communications strategy.

FAMILY INFLUENCES

Each member of a family has some influence on the behaviour of other family members and thus an influence on buying decisions. Perhaps the biggest influence on behaviour within families today relates to the *changing roles* and *responsibilities* of family members. Traditional attitudes, roles, and responsibilities are out—nothing is what it seems anymore.

Households are different. There are same-sex households, lone-parent households, and dual-income (two-worker) households. In the dual-income household, much of the decision-making is shared between partners. No longer can the maker of a household product assume the woman is the primary buyer and a financial advisor cannot assume that the man makes all of the investment decisions. To do so would be foolish. Companies that are in

FIGURE **1.7** **Manufacturers are Developing Nutritional Food Products to Match the Needs of Busy Lifestyles**

NUTRITIONAL INFORMATION (per bar)

Energy..95 cal

Carbohydrates..18 g

Fat..1.8 g

Times you'll think about pastry...................................0

Keep it simple.

tune with these types of changes are double targeting—they are devising marketing strategies that reach both genders effectively. Financial companies and automobile manufacturers recognize the role and influence of women in matters of financial planning and major buying decisions, and are devising new campaigns that take advantage of such knowledge.

Identifying and Selecting Consumer Target Markets

Knowledge and understanding of consumer behaviour provide the foundation on which potential target markets are identified and pursued. At one time, companies made products and hoped that the public would buy them. They followed a "marketing to the masses"

Market Segmentation
The division of a large market into smaller homogeneous markets based on common needs and characteristics.

approach to business. In today's business environment, businesses devise their marketing and marketing communications strategies based on the concept of **market segmentation**. When a market is segmented, it is divided into smaller homogeneous markets or segments based on common needs or characteristics. Typically, it is a three-step process: identifying market segments by profiling the primary user, selecting the segments that offer the greatest profit potential, and positioning the product so it appeals to the target market. Volvo, the Swedish car company, develops and markets cars to a target market interested in safety. Through effective marketing communications, Volvo cars are positioned in the customer's mind as the safest car to drive.

Micro-segmentation or Micro-marketing
The identification of very small yet profitable market segments.

Continual changes in technology are dramatically affecting how companies identify and pursue target markets. For example, with the capability to reach individual consumers directly with unique marketing strategies, segments (targets) are now potentially so small that new terms such as **micro-segmentation** and **micro-marketing** have emerged. Now a company can make sufficient profit in a very small segment through efficient production and marketing. At one time, for example, automobile makers needed to sell a volume of 250 000 for a new car to be a success. Today, the figure is as low as 50 000. Unique cars are being marketed to unique customer groups. The MINI, once a working class car for the masses in Britain, is now targeted directly at twenty-something urban professionals in North America.

When a target market is identified, the result is a profile of the primary customer and perhaps secondary customer based on demographic, psychographic, and geographic variables.

DEMOGRAPHIC SEGMENTATION

Demographic Segmentation
The identification of target markets based on characteristics such as age, income, education, occupation, marital status, and household formation.

With **demographic segmentation**, target markets are identified and pursued on the basis of variables such as age, gender, income, occupation, marital status, household formation, and cultural mix. For planning purposes, an organization must keep track of trends in each of these areas in order to adjust their strategies when necessary. Let's examine some essential demographic trends that will influence the direction of future marketing and marketing communications planning.

THE POPULATION IS GETTING OLDER

Older age groups are growing the fastest in Canada. The population aged 45 to 64 increased 35.8 percent from 1991 to 2001, as a result of the entry of baby boomers into this age group. It is projected to grow another 30 percent by 2011, when nearly one third of the population will be between 45 and 64. The seniors segment aged 65 and over currently accounts for 13 percent of the population (15 percent by 2011). At the other end of the age spectrum, 26 percent of the population was aged 19 or younger, down from 28 percent in 1991. If fertility remains low, this could fall to less than 23 percent by 2011.[14] Figure 1.8 shows population trend information by age.

By 2020 it is projected that one half of the population will be older than 45. These segments tend to be wealthy as they are free of financial obligations associated with raising a family. The combination of age and wealth make the over-45 segment an attractive market. Traditionally, marketing organizations have given priority to attracting new, younger customers. Prudent marketers will be shifting their focus to attracting and retaining older customers in the future.

To illustrate the effect of age change, consider the condition of companies such as Levi-Strauss and McDonald's. Both are suffering today in terms of sales and profit. Baby boomers grew up with Levi's and are the customer who built the brand. Today's youth won't go near the brand—they won't wear their parents' jeans. Unfortunately, parents' demand for jeans isn't what it used to be, so Levi's is suffering. McDonald's recently announced its first quarterly loss in the history of the company. The influence of

FIGURE **1.8**

Canada's Population and Growth Rates by Age Segments

(All population figures in millions)

Age Segment	1991	2001	2011	%Growth 2001 - 2011
0–4	1.91	1.70	1.64	–3.1
5–12	3.04	3.23	2.77	–14.1
13–24	4.57	4.81	4.98	3.6
25–34	4.87	3.99	4.17	4.4
35–44	4.37	5.10	4.51	–11.5
45–64	5.37	7.29	9.47	29.9
65–69	1.07	1.13	1.49	31.3
70–79	1.44	1.82	1.99	8.9
80+	0.66	0.93	1.33	42.7
Total	**27.30**	**30.01**	**32.36**	**7.8**

Source: Adapted from the Statistics Canada publication "Profile of the Canadian population by age and sex: Canada ages, 2001 Census (Analysis series)," Catalogue 96F0030, July 2002.

boomers is being felt here as well. Boomers have moved on to more upscale restaurants (roadhouse and other sit-down style restaurants) and there are fewer young people coming up to replace them at McDonald's.

URBAN GROWTH

The trend to urbanization continues in Canada. In 2001, 79.4 percent of Canadians lived in an urban area with a population of 10 000 or more, compared to 78.5 percent in 1996. From 1996 to 2001, the nation's population continued to concentrate in four broad urban regions: the extended Golden Horseshoe in southern Ontario, Montreal and its adjacent region, the Lower Mainland of British Columbia and southern Vancouver Island, and the Calgary-Edmonton corridor. By 2001, 51 percent of Canada's population lived in these regions, compared to 49% in 1996. Halifax continues to strengthen its position as the major urban centre of Atlantic Canada, accounting for 39.6 percent of Nova Scotia's population. The census metropolitan area with the strongest rate of growth by far is Calgary. The population of Calgary (951 400) increased 15.8 percent between 1996 and 2001, about twice the rate of Edmonton.[15]

The nature of Canada's urban population has a direct effect on marketing and marketing communications planning. Gone are the days of a national strategy. With the population so clustered, companies now devise plans that are regional in nature or dwell specifically on key urban areas. A brand may be available nationally in terms of geography, but the way it is positioned and the nature of the message could be very different from one area to another. Such a trend also helps explain the popularity of regional brands. In Atlantic Canada, for example, Keith's is a leading brand of beer. A national brand such as Molson Canadian has to adapt its national strategy to suit the needs of Atlantic beer drinkers if it is to make any headway in that region.

HOUSEHOLD FORMATIONS ARE DIFFERENT

Trends such as the postponement of marriage, the pursuit of careers by women, increases in divorce rates, and same-sex partnerships are producing new households in Canada. The mythical "Ozzie and Harriet" family is long gone. As of 2001, only one in four families consisted of a married mother and father with two or more children. That cozy imagery of Janet and Wayne Gretzky with two of their children in a Gap ad, likewise, is a mythical one, in that only 44 percent of families are composed of two parents who are married or living common law with children.[16] Contemporary households are described by expressions such as lone-parent families (the result of divorce), blended families (the result of remarriage or common-law arrangements), and same-sex families (the result of more openness and acceptance of gay lifestyles).

With families evolving so dramatically, other changes are also occurring. Between 1981 and 2001, smaller households represented the fastest growth in Canada. There are now as many one-person households as there are those with four or more people. The average household size decreased in the same period from 2.9 to 2.6 persons.[17]

No longer can marketing and marketing communications strategies be tailored to the traditional family. Products and services must be fashioned to fit all kinds of family situations, and again this calls for more micro-marketing strategies. Companies in the household and packaged-goods business, for example, have to offer a variety of sizes to meet the needs of such household variation. They must also be cognizant of who is making the buying decisions. To present a product improperly or in an old-fashioned way—that is, according to traditional roles and responsibilities—could be harmful to a brand's development.

ETHNIC DIVERSITY CONTINUES

Canada's ethnic diversity continues to present new challenges for marketing organizations. Canadian culture is represented by many diverse subcultures (subgroups of a larger population). These subcultures have distinct lifestyles based on religious, racial, and geographic differences. As of 2001, Canada's visible minorities totalled 5.7 million or about 18 percent of the population. The largest minority groups are Chinese (23 percent of ethnic population), South Asian (21 percent), black (19 percent), and West Asian/Arabs (13 percent). Canada's subcultures tend to be in three key regions: Ontario, Quebec, and British Columbia. Furthermore, 75 percent of visible minorities live in four cities: Toronto (37 percent), Vancouver (15 percent), Montreal (14 percent), and Calgary/Edmonton (9 percent).[18]

Since ethnic communities are concentrated geographically, they are accessible market niches that organizations can pursue with targeted marketing communications programs. Burger King chanced onto ethnic marketing communications following its introduction of the BK Veggie burger (a beef-free soy burger). Veggie burgers were a hit among Toronto's East Indian population, whose religious beliefs forbid consumption of beef. Burger King launched an ad campaign that promoted the BK Veggie burger on a grander scale to East Indians. The ads aired on East Indian television programs appearing on local stations in Toronto and Vancouver.[19]

Burger King
www.burgerking.com

GENDER ECONOMICS

Gender has always been a primary means of distinguishing product categories. Personal care products, magazines, and fashion goods are typically categorized to the gender of the buyer. As discussed earlier, more and more women are pursuing careers, so their changing roles and responsibilities in a household have influenced the buying decision process. Today, it is quite common for women to be the primary decision maker, or at the very least key decisions are shared by the partners living together. Why so? A marketing research study conducted by

Thompson Lightstone about marketing efforts of companies revealed that women control 80 percent of the consumer dollar spent, yet the majority of women consumers surveyed felt they weren't taken nearly as seriously as men. A majority of men and women said understanding and reaching women should be a company's top priorities.[20]

How organizations perceive gender roles has to be reflected in their marketing communications campaigns. The self-concept theory plays a key role in how females are portrayed in advertising—it is essential to communicate to a woman based on how she sees herself or wants to see herself. It should speak to her as an individual, one who defines her individuality today differently from how she will define it tomorrow. It understands that women are different from men. Aero (a chocolate bar) experienced a 42 percent increase in sales, moving from number 8 to number 2 in a very competitive market, when it targeted women specifically. Lean Cuisine's "Real Women" TV campaign, with women describing what they had for dinner the night before, resulted in a 10 percent sales increase in a product category experiencing flat growth. Lean Cuisine's website (see Figure 1.9) is also very popular with women. The site provides information specifically tailored to women's needs and lifestyles and the company now considers it a primary vehicle for keeping in touch with regular customers. For more insight into the importance of reaching women see the IMC Highlight **Take Me Seriously**.

PSYCHOGRAPHIC SEGMENTATION

Psychographic Segmentation

The identification of a target market according to lifestyle characteristics such as activities, interests, and opinions.

Psychographic segmentation examines individual lifestyles in terms of activities, interests, and opinions (commonly referred to as AIOs). Psychographics supplements demographics and serves a very useful purpose. An examination of lifestyle trends helps marketing organizations understand why two people who are demographically identical behave in different ways and purchase different types of goods and services.

Messages about products are delivered to targets in such a manner that they are associated with the targets' lifestyle. The personality of the product matches the personality of the target. Canada's beer industry uses psychographic information to devise one campaign after another for a variety of beer brands. The two leading national brands, Labatt Blue and Molson Canadian, continually present images and lifestyles that are attractive to male beer drinkers aged 19 to 29. Such campaigns tend to dwell on the concept that guys need to get together to do their thing—anything from enjoying the rugged outdoors to frequenting bars to watching sports on television.

Numerous research studies have been conducted in an effort to classify consumers into psychographic cells. One such company, Millward Brown of Toronto, has classified Canadians into six psychographic cells within two broad segments: traditionalists or non-traditionalists. For a summary of the cells, see Figure 1.10.

Another system of classifying consumers is VALS. VALS is an acronym for values and lifestyles. Developed and refined by SRI Consulting Business Intelligence, this system reflects a real-world pattern that explains relationships between personality traits and consumer behaviour. VALS uses psychology to analyze dynamics underlying consumer preferences and choices. It asserts that people express their personalities through their behaviour. For a summary description of the various VALS classifications, see Figure 1.11.

When devising a communications strategy for a new motorcycle, the F650CS, BMW focused on the target's lifestyle. The bike was designed specifically to attract a new, younger demographic of riders. According to Hendrik von Kuenheim, president and CEO of BMW Group in Canada, "These riders want a bike that expresses their individuality and expands their already exciting lifestyle." Since bike owners tend to be very brand loyal, this is BMW's way of attracting young first-time buyers. One of the ads in the campaign is called "Grand Canyon." The picture is a breathtaking photograph of the famous canyon. The copy line reads: "You feel the urge to hang-glide across the Grand Canyon." Below the picture of the bike it adds: "But what you really need is a ride on the new F650CS."

BMW Canada
www.bmw.ca

FIGURE **1.9**   **Offering Information Online Is a Key Aspect of Lean Cuisine's Communications Strategy**

Source: Reprinted by permission of Nestle Canada.

The BMW campaign placed heavy emphasis on lifestyle imagery. As well, it tore a page out of Apple Computer's strategy book and offered the bike in three youth-oriented colour schemes: azure blue metallic, golden orange metallic, and beluga blue. The objective of the campaign is to appeal to a younger, hip group always on the lookout for a new adventure.[21] The print ads ran in *Toronto Life* and *Outdoor Canada* magazines (see Figure 1.12).

Psychographics allow a company to position its products better in the marketplace. Purchase decisions based on needs not yet satisfied, or based on a self-concept yet to be realized, furnish ammunition for compelling campaigns that focus on lifestyle

TAKE ME SERIOUSLY

First, some facts about women:

- Women constitute 46.4 percent of Canada's labour force.
- Women make up 52.7 percent of professionals.
- Employed women and women entrepreneurs are the primary decision-makers in households, influencing 95 percent of purchasing decisions.

Beyond these statistics, it is widely accepted that women influence at least 80 percent of all car purchases. There are approximately 1.1 million cars sold annually in Canada, so that means women have a say in 800 000 car-buying decisions a year. Such data should make any company take notice. And the smart companies do!

Volvo of Canada may pull away from its competitors with the launch of its first SUV, the XC90. It has been designed specifically for the needs and tastes of the primary family caregiver—the mother. Female focus groups contributed input from the drawing-board stage onward throughout the development of the XC90. The car is advertised on television programs and networks that attract the greatest number of female viewers.

Chrysler's commitment to impressing female consumers is signalled by their recently formed partnership with Céline Dion and Sony Music Entertainment. The three-year deal includes advertising, cross-promotions, and the creation of a "Chrysler song." In Canada, Chrysler's official spokesperson is Diana Krall. Both Krall and Dion are meant to "epitomize the drop-dead gorgeous personality of our brand" and prompt customers to "have love affairs with our cars." Ads for Chrysler products appear frequently in magazines targeted at women. In fact, the interest expressed in women by car companies has produced new advertising revenue for magazines such as *Chatelaine, Canadian Living, Elm Street,* and *Family.*

Women are also the hottest target market among general merchandise retailers. Zellers recently launched several initiatives that target mothers directly. "She spends twice as much as others in our stores," said David Strickland, senior vice-president of marketing. Retailers that understand the multi-task nature of a mother's daily routine are trying to make the shopping experience less stressful, a little more relaxed, a little more fun. If they can do so, shoppers will spend more money.

Zellers has set up a panel of 140 mothers who are questioned five times a year about their roles and needs. The panels have influenced numerous marketing and merchandising practices. For example, mothers find everyday low pricing more convenient than the practice of bouncing prices up and down. Zellers shifted to everyday low pricing, which is the cornerstone of rival Wal-Mart. Research also indicated a need for in-store double strollers with one of the seats designed for a toddler. These are now available in all stores. Zellers is now installing play areas with televisions and VCRs in its in-store diners. While shopping, moms do need a break!

Adapted from Terry Poulton, "The 80% Factor," *Strategy*, November 18, 2002, pp. M11–12, and Marina Strauss, "Merchants Making Moms Their Mark," *Globe and Mail*, March 25, 2002, p. B1.

associations. Such campaigns tap into the emotional side of the brain. For consumers who take the plunge and buy, the decision often has to be justified to others. Have you ever had to present rational arguments for an emotional purchase decision?

GEOGRAPHIC SEGMENTATION

Geographic Segmentation
The identification of target markets based on the regional, urban, or rural location of the customers.

Geographic segmentation refers to the division of a geographically expansive market into smaller geographic units. In Canada and the United States, for example, many companies manage their companies regionally with specific marketing plans for certain areas. A plan in Atlantic Canada would be different from a plan in Ontario. A plan for the Northeastern United States would be different from a plan for the South (Georgia, Florida, and Louisiana), and so on.

In Canada, Quebec presents the biggest challenge in terms of marketing and marketing communications. Many companies assume that translating a message from English to French is sufficient to attract the French-speaking population. Such a flawed premise only

FIGURE **1.10**   **Lifestyle Segments in Canada**

Segment	% of Population	Characteristics
Traditionalists		
Day-to-Day Watchers	24	The status quo; don't like change; motivated by familiarity and security; influenced by quality, brand name, and authority figures.
Old-Fashioned Puritans	18	Prefer simpler times, conservative values; motivated by price and quality; influenced by value messages and sales discounts.
Responsible Survivors	12	Frugal shoppers; have money but don't like parting with it; shop at low-end stores; heavy television viewers.
Non-traditionalists		
Joiner Activists	16	Idealists, liberal minded; willing to spend; motivated by information; influenced by rational messages (quality, service, and price).
Bold Achievers	15	Aggressive and confident; success oriented; innovators in terms of buying new items; influenced by messages stressing gratification.
Self-Indulgents	14	Resent authority; want easy road to success; motivated by self-gratification; buy impulsively; price not a factor; influenced by messages stressing gratification.

Adapted from studies conducted by Millward Brown.

leads to alienation and rejection of the brand in question. Figure 1.13 highlights the main differences between English Canada and French Quebec. McDonald's, for example, is well known for its advertising slogans. Some recent ones include "We love to see you smile" and "There's a little McDonald's in everyone." McDonald's never considers a direct translation of its English taglines in Quebec. For instance, it uses "J'M" pronounced as "J'aime," meaning "I like." Advertising spots for the French Quebec market are produced by Cossette Communication Marketing Group, a Montreal-based advertising agency.

Toyota Canada
www.toyota.ca

Toyota Canada is another company that pays specific attention to Quebec. According to Chris Pappas, manager of vehicle marketing, "We try to make sure backdrops could be Montreal or Quebec City as Quebecers are more sensitive to the appearance of their geographical landmarks. We think the awareness and perception of Toyota is better in the Quebec market because of it."[22]

Given the migration of the population to urban markets (discussed earlier in this chapter), it is possible to devise marketing and marketing communications strategies that are tailored specifically to regions or individual urban centres. Where possible, however, many companies will develop universal strategies that are appropriate for all of North America, or even for the global marketplace. The phrase "Thinking globally and acting locally" is also a common theme among marketing organizations today. Either approach can work if the strategy is the right one. The key to success seems to be flexibility and a willingness to make changes when and where necessary.

FIGURE **1.11** The VALS™ Segments

VALS places American adult consumers into one of eight segments based on their responses to the VALS questionnaire. The main dimensions of the segmentation framework are primary motivation and resources.

Primary Motivation An individual's primary motivation determines what in particular about the self or the world is the meaningful core that governs his or her activities. Consumers are inspired by one of three primary motivations: ideals, achievement, and self-expression

Resources A person's tendency to consume goods goes beyond age, income, and education. Energy, self-confidence, intellectualism, novelty seeking, innovativeness, leadership, and vanity play a key role. These personality traits in conjunction with demographics determine an individual's resources

Summary Description of Each VALS™ Segment

Innovators
- Exhibit all three primary motivations (see above).
- Successful, sophisticated, take charge people; high self-esteem.
- Receptive to new ideas and technologies.
- Cultivated tastes for upscale, niche products.
- Established and emerging leaders in business.
- Possessions reflect cultivated tastes.

Thinkers
- Motivated by ideals.
- Mature, satisfied, and comfortable people.
- Value order, knowledge, and responsibility.
- Seek information in the decision-making process.
- Moderate respect for status quo but open to new ideas.
- Conservative, practical consumers who seek value.

Achievers
- Motivated by desire for achievement.
- Goal-oriented lifestyles.
- Deep commitment to career and family.
- Politically conservative and respect authority.
- Value consensus, predictability, and stability.
- Buy established, prestige products that demonstrate success.

Experiencers
- Motivated by self-expression.
- Young, enthusiastic, and impulsive.
- Like new, offbeat, and risky things.
- Spend heavily on fashion, recreation, and socializing.
- Purchases reflect desire to look good and to be "cool."

Believers
- Motivated by ideals.
- Conservative people with traditional values and beliefs.
- Moral codes deeply rooted in family and community.
- Follow established routines.
- Choose familiar products (exhibit loyalty).

Strivers
- Motivated by achievement.
- Trendy; concerned about the approval of others.
- Money defines success.
- Active consumers demonstrate an ability to buy.
- Impulsive within financial constraints.

Makers
- Motivated by self-expression.
- Practical people; value self-sufficiency.
- Experience the world by doing (e.g., fixing. building, etc.).
- Live within traditional context of family.
- Respect government and authority.
- Unimpressed with material possessions.

Survivors
- No strong primary motivation.
- Live focused lives and have few resources.
- Comfortable with the familiar; concerned with safety.
- Meet needs rather than fulfilling desires.
- Cautious consumers; loyal to favourite brands; price oriented.

Adapted from SRI Consulting Business Intelligence, "Welcome to VALS," <**www.sric-bi.com/VALS**> (November 2003).

FIGURE **1.12** **An Understanding of a Target's Psychographic Profile Often Leads to Lifestyle Imagery in Advertising**

You feel the urge to windsurf across the Pacific Ocean,

but what you really need is a ride on the new F650CS.

With its spirited, go anywhere, do anything sense of independence, together with your need to get away from it all, the F650CS is your best chance to ride off into the sunset.
© BMW Canada Inc. "BMW" and the BMW logo are trademarks of BMW AG, used under licence by BMW Canada Inc.

F650CS

www.bmw.ca
1-800-667-6679

Motorcycles

DIRECT (CUSTOMIZED) SEGMENTATION

Direct or Customized Segmentation

The identification of a target audience at the level of the individual; marketing programs designed for and communicated to individual customers.

Mass Customization

The development, manufacture, and marketing of unique products to unique customers.

Direct or customized segmentation means that a company provides differentiated products and services, prices, and delivery strategies for each customer. By marketing online, companies are also capable of interacting with individual customers by personalizing messages, products, and services. The combination of operational customization—that is, the development and manufacture of unique products for unique customers—and marketing customization is often referred to as **mass customization**.

As discussed earlier in the chapter, contemporary organizations focus much of their efforts on customer relationship management (CRM). CRM enables a company to provide real-time service by developing an ongoing relationship with a valued customer by effectively using information the company has about that individual. CRM is designed to

FIGURE 1.13

The Uniqueness of the French Quebec Market

Many marketing executives must decide whether to develop unique marketing strategies for the Quebec market. Are the language and cultural differences significant enough to justify such an investment? Here are just a few of the unique characteristics of the French Quebec market.

Attitudes and Opinions	French Quebecers %	Rest of Canada %
I enjoy keeping fit.	59	48
I prefer low-fat or light foods.	43	33
I consider myself to be a risk-adverse investor.	42	18
I like to dine at fine restaurants as often as possible.	41	26
I seldom make a financial move without expert advice.	31	22
I am more of a spender than a saver.	22	32
A career should be an individual's first priority.	20	34
Health-related issues are given too much attention these days.	39	27

Personal Consumption	French Quebecers %	Rest of Canada %
Buy lottery tickets	68	56
Drink wine	60	47
Own personal life insurance	49	27
Shop at specialty stores for fruit and vegetables	45	23
Ride a bike	44	28
Use a cell phone	11	23
Own a swimming pool	13	4
Eat snack cakes	55	20

You be the judge. Should unique marketing strategies be devised for this market?

Adapted from Andrea Haman, "Quebecers Snub Diets and Compacts for Port and Luxury cars," *Strategy*, April 9, 2001, p. 14. Figures cited from PMB 2000 (two-year database).

attract, cultivate, and maximize the return from each customer the company does business with. By effectively using information that is stored in a database, a company can increase the life of a customer relationship, enhance customer sales and profits, and convert low-profit customers to more profitable customers.

An organization may compile information about customers: past volumes, prices and profits generated, buying practices, frequency of purchase, buying practices, and so on. This information is used in **database marketing**, and can be combined with demographic, psychographic, media-related, and consumption information on customers in order to target them more effectively. Information is available from a variety of external sources including Statistics Canada, Canada Post, and marketing intelligence companies such as Nielsen Marketing Research and Millward Brown.

The electronic era has resulted in an information explosion that allows for the storage and transfer of great amounts of customer data in a short time. What has emerged is a concept called data mining. **Data mining** is the analysis of information to establish relationships among pieces of information so that more effective marketing strategies can be identified and implemented. Data mining techniques look for informational patterns and nuggets within the database.[23] The goal is to identify prospects most likely to buy or buy in large volume, and to provide input on how best to communicate with the customer.

Database Marketing
The use and analysis of accumulated information on customer buying behaviour in order to develop more effective marketing strategies.

Data Mining
The analysis of information to determine relationships among the data and enable more effective marketing strategies to be identified and implemented.

IBM has an interesting perspective on data mining and customer relationship management. IBM believes that companies must evaluate a variety of information sources in order to create dossiers on individuals. By doing so the company can figure out better ways to encourage patronage and ultimately achieve the goal of mass customization—designing unique products and delivery strategies for unique customers. IBM has established a division to develop and market products that will help clients manage their customer relationships.[24]

To demonstrate how new forms of segmentation are changing the ways companies do business, consider the following example. In the past, neighbourhoods were classified and described on the basis of the profile of the typical resident. It was believed that all households had similar characteristics—demographics, attitudes, and lifestyles. This was called **cluster profiling** or **geodemographic segmentation**. When information was analyzed, clusters emerged, and they were given descriptions such as "Mortgaged in Suburbia," "Canadian Establishment," and "Suburban Nesters." The descriptions alluded to the neighbourhood's profile.

Geodemographic Segmentation or Cluster Profiling
The identification of target markets according to dwelling areas defined by geographic and demographic variables, based on the assumption that like people seek out residential neighbourhoods in which to cluster with their lifestyle peers.

It is now possible to pinpoint individual houses by satellite and then obtain the name of the owner through local property assessment rolls. The name is combined with data available from Statistics Canada and other sources described above. The marketing organization now has sufficient information to develop a customized offer that is sent to someone personally. Neighbours may not receive the same offer. That's direct (customized) marketing! This technology will result in greater usage of direct response and internet communications between organizations and their customers in the future. Furthermore, through websites, organizations are collecting all kinds of valuable information about their customers. It seems that many visitors to a site willingly give up personal information in order to access the information they want at the website. For more information about how segmentation and targeting concepts are applied, see the IMC Highlight **You Are What You Drive**.

Business Markets and Buyer Behaviour

The buying process of organizations is very different from consumer buying. In a nutshell, organizations exhibit more rational behaviour than consumers—consumers do a lot of buying based on emotion. The **business-to-business (B2B) market** is managed by individuals in an organization responsible for purchasing goods and services needed to produce a product or service, or promote an idea. This market includes business and industry, governments, institutions, wholesalers and retailers, and professions.

Business-to-Business (B2B) Market
A market of goods and services needed to produce a product or service, promote an idea, or operate a business.

The business market has several characteristics that distinguish it from consumer markets. Business markets have fewer buyers and those buyers tend to be concentrated in industrial areas in and near large cities; the buying criteria are very practical, with decisions based on the best buy according to predetermined requirements, and there is a usually formal buying process for evaluating product and service alternatives. Business buying processes have changed dramatically because of advancing technology and the benefits derived from buying goods online.

Regardless of location or the numbers of buyers, the key issues that a business organization must address when marketing to other businesses are the criteria established by the buying organization. In most situations, those requirements are established in advance and companies can compete with each other by submitting bids. The buyer customarily chooses the bid with the lowest price, assuming the criteria have been met. So, what are those requirements?

- **Quality:** Buyers want consistent quality on every order. What they buy could have a direct impact on the quality of goods they in turn produce and market.
- **Service:** Buyers want reputable suppliers who provide prompt service and believe that the initial order is simply the start of a business relationship.

YOU ARE WHAT YOU DRIVE

The automobile industry relies heavily on market segmentation. In fact, the industry that invented the mass-marketing assembly line is emphasizing its capacity for customization. The general story line is micro-segmentation. Take the MINI for example. Once a cheap mass market car made in Great Britain and once known as the Cooper Mini, BMW's retooled version is now going after the narrowest of demographic slivers: twenty-something urban professionals who don't mind driving at eye level with a Chevy Suburban's wheels.

Maritz Automotive Research recently released a psychographic cluster analysis that sorted Canadian drivers into ten segments. At one extreme is the "Car Lover," a young male driver who devours car magazines for all the technical information. His dream is to own a Porsche Cayenne, a German sports utility vehicle. At the other end, is the "No Frills" buyer, a female looking for low-priced transportation. She opts for a Chevy Cavalier.

With all the special incentives and other discounts offered these days, carmakers have to differentiate cars through the look of the product. In the quest for niches, they will go as far as spinning off new companies. That's what Toyota did when it launched Lexus (a luxury car) and will be doing for Scion, a military-looking SUV targeted at young buyers. The Scion will be a customized vehicle created by the customer at an online dealer showroom.

Car tastes in Canada vary considerably from one region to another. The luxury market is restricted to four cities: Toronto, Vancouver, Montreal, and Calgary. In Vancouver, the Asian influence makes Japanese luxury cars (Lexus and Acura) popular. In Toronto, European luxury cars (BMW and Mercedes) are more popular. Vancouverites are outdoors people, so it's no coincidence the city is Canada's top SUV market.

What about the other regions? Alberta is the largest market for pickup trucks—the bigger the better! Saskatchewan and Manitoba follow the Prairie preference for SUVs and pickups, though not to the same degree as Alberta. Ontario is a melting pot—anything goes there. Quebec has its own character and car-buying trends could reflect an anti-English sentiment. Quebecers have a pragmatic outlook toward cars and opt for reasonably priced cars that can navigate their complicated expressways. Suzuki, Mazda, and Hyundai are popular there.

When you consider the differences in buying preferences in Canada, based largely on the unique needs, attitudes, perceptions, and lifestyles exhibited by customers from one region to another, you clearly see why companies must develop and implement unique marketing and marketing communication strategies for regions or key urban markets. The plans carefully consider trends in demographics, psychographics, and geographics that vary from one area to another.

Adapted from Christopher Shulgan, "Auto Biography," *Report on Business Magazine*, January 2003, pp. 46–50.

- *Continuity of Supply:* Buyers want suppliers that can provide goods over the long term. A steady source of supply ensures consistent production scheduling.
- *Price:* Buyers evaluate price in conjunction with the other criteria. The lowest price is not always accepted. Potential long-term savings could outweigh an initial low price.

In order to ensure that the right buying decision is made, organizations employ a formal or informal approach. A formal approach involves a **buying committee**. The committee is made up of key representatives from various functional areas of the company such as Finance, Marketing, Manufacturing, Purchasing, and so on). A committee takes a very rational approach when evaluating alternatives and participants need to know that costly decisions are shared decisions.

A **buying centre** is an informal purchasing process, with individuals in an organization involved in the purchasing process but not necessarily having direct responsibility for the actual decision. These roles are summarized in Figure 1.14.

In terms of marketing or marketing communications, the seller must know who on the committee or within the buying centre has the most influence. Once that is known, the best means of communicating can be determined. Based on the nature of business buying, it becomes clear that personal selling and direct forms of communications are vital components when trying to influence the decisions of business buyers.

Buying Committee

A formal buying structure in an organization that brings together expertise from the various functional areas to share in the buying decision process.

Buying Centre

An informal purchasing process in which individuals in an organization perform particular roles but may not have direct responsibility for the actual decision.

FIGURE **1.14**

The Buying Centre

Role	Description	Example
Users	Those in the organization who use the product directly.	If the product is a personal computer, any end-user in the organization.
Influencers	Those who define the product specifications.	An engineer.
Buyers	Those with the authority to buy.	A purchasing manager.
Deciders	Those with the power to finalize the purchase.	Where high-cost decisions are involved, the CEO may be the decider.
Gatekeepers	Those who control the flow of information to the members of the buying centre.	A purchasing manager may also fulfill the role of gatekeeper.

INTEGRATION AND PARTNERING INFLUENCES B2B COMMUNICATIONS STRATEGIES

Business markets have embraced customer relationship management in an attempt to establish efficient business systems. CRM promotes the seamless transfer of information throughout the channels to ensure the efficient and continuous flow of goods. Forming partnerships with suppliers implies a long-term relationship. Therefore, to be part of a CRM system the marketer must be more familiar than ever with the role the product plays in the customer's operation. Collecting information about the customer and operations is crucial.

Eprocurement

An online, business-to-business marketplace through which participants can purchase goods and services from one another.

The internet has created buying opportunities through **eprocurement**. This is an internet-based, business-to-business buying marketplace through which participants can purchase supplies and services from one other. It is an all-inclusive system that allows buyers to solicit multiple bids, issue purchase orders, and make payments. The combining of CRM practices with eprocurement systems fosters long-term relationships between buyers and sellers and presents a situation where participants are directly influenced by the decisions of other participants. This clearly is the future of business-to-business buying and marketing. Companies will either be part of the system or they will watch it unfold from the sidelines.

The strategies employed to reach business customers are also evolving. Yet, in spite of all the technological advances and the direct nature of the buying and selling process, customers must still be made aware of the product alternatives that are available. Creating awareness is always the first step. Therefore, the need for print advertising directed at business customers will continue, along with the need for strong personal sales contact. Event marketing in the form of trade show participation will help keep marketing organizations on a buyer's radar screen, and direct marketing techniques such as direct mail and internet-based communications will become more of a priority. A website containing essential product information is indispensable to B2B marketing situations. The same tools are employed in consumer marketing; they are just given different priority.

A recent survey published by the Centre for Media Research provides interesting insight into business buying behaviour and the media that influence buyers. It suggests that simultaneous media usage presents a challenge for business-to-business marketers. Nearly half the respondents said traditional communications methods such as print, direct mail, and outdoor advertising are "not important" to them. In contrast, 44 percent said the internet was "somewhat important," 81 percent said word of mouth was "very important" or "important," and 88 percent said they "sought the advice of others" before making a decision.[25] This clearly indicates that products must live up to the promise made by any form of marketing communications.

Ethical Issues Confronting Marketing Communicators

The communications strategies employed by organizations often come under attack from consumers and other interest groups. Some of the concerns that are commonly raised are the use of violent or dangerous imagery, the use of sexual imagery, gender stereotyping, and misleading advertising. This section will highlight each issue briefly so that readers can formulate their own opinions in ethical issues.

VIOLENT OR DANGEROUS IMAGERY

Labatt Breweries was forced to pull a television commercial for Blue a few years ago because it showed a group of twenty-something males and females racing downhill in supermarket carts on very busy city streets. There were all kinds of near accidents along the way. It was an action-packed commercial that captured the essence of the brand's "Out of the Blue" advertising theme. Similarly, an ad for Imperial Margarine showed an animated suicidal potato, upset by an empty tub of margarine, jumping off a microwave and impaling itself on a fork as Air Supply's "All Out of Love" plays in the background. According to Mike Welling, vice-president of brand development at Unilever, "We were trying to highlight the rich, creamy taste of Imperial by demonstrating, in a *Romeo and Juliet* fashion, how sad the food felt because the Imperial was all gone."[26] Welling elaborated by stating, "we spent time researching the idea to make sure it's seen in much the same way as cartoons today." Perhaps the research should have included a broader cross-section of the population.

In both cases, enough people took exception to the ads that Advertising Standards Canada, the industry body committed to creating and maintaining community confidence in advertising, requested both companies stop showing the ads. ASC administers the Canadian Code of Advertising Standards, a code that promotes the professional practice of advertising and forms the basis upon which advertising is evaluated in response to consumer complaints. In response, creative directors say, "It's no wonder Canada has a reputation for timid and boring advertising when agencies and clients are conditioned to stay away from the creative edge."[27] You be the judge.

SEXUAL IMAGERY

A very common complaint about advertising involves the use of sex to sell something. There's an old saying: "Sex sells!" So what's the beef with Canadian consumers? Critics charge that advertisers use more and more sex each passing year. Using sex appeals in an appropriate manner and for appropriate products seems natural, but gratuitous sex is something consumers shouldn't have to tolerate.

One Carlsberg beer ad featured a woman boasting about the bedroom skills of her male companion. The woman's gestures suggested the oral sex was something else. An earlier Carlsberg commercial showed a man and a woman lustily groping each other in a motel doorway (the room number: 69). The punch line to the ad was that the couple was actually married. Usually, it is the people beyond the target market that complain about such ads. The people whom Carlsberg was targeting (thirty-something males and females)—people entering their "Carlsberg years"—were not objecting. Perhaps the sexual portrayals did go a bit too far, but they did break through the clutter of television advertising. You be the judge.

GENDER STEREOTYPING

Advertising is constantly under attack for portraying women as objects, not necessarily sex objects, but as objects men desire. Considering the changing composition of Canadian households and the changing roles and responsibilities of males and females, advertisers are reducing gender stereotyping. In fact, the Advertising Standards Council reports there is a growing concern about the exploitation of men in advertising.[28]

Reverse stereotyping is demonstrated in a commercial for Finesse shampoo. The commercial titled "Poem" shows a male reciting a poem about his wife to an audience of men, a group of confused husbands pathetically trying to learn how to communicate with their wives. The men were portrayed as bumbling and ineffective, but give credit to Finesse. The ad was targeted at married women over the age of 30; they know what men are really like and perhaps saw the humour in the portrayal. Stereotyping may be an issue, but in the whole scheme of things, if it helps build the brand isn't a little bit okay? You be the judge.

MISLEADING ADVERTISING

Sometimes an advertiser does make wild and unsubstantiated claims about a product. The Ford Motor Company, for example shows its trucks pulling objects it couldn't possible pull—a ship out of the water, for example. It's an exaggerated demonstration that simply portrays the strength and durability of the vehicle. It is questionable whether an ad like this would cause concern among consumers.

Pantene Pro-V conditioner found itself in some hot water with some of its claims. The ads claim that Pantene Pro-V "improves the condition of damaged hair. The pro vitamin complex penetrates while the conditioning formula helps strengthen your hair." A leading dermatologist refutes this claim by saying, "It is physically impossible to effect permanent change. It's just a temporary coating on the surface of the hair." On one hand, ads with claims such as these routinely blur the line between what's right and what's wrong. On the other hand, the same consumer may just enjoy buying the hope and not need to have it pan out. Many personal care products tend to stretch the truth somewhat. Does it hurt anyone?

The examples above suggest that advertisers do create messages that stretch the limits of the law and the imagination of consumers. Perhaps that is what makes advertising interesting. In later chapters you will learn much more about the strategies and execution techniques that are routinely employed by marketing organizations. As business students, you should review these techniques from two perspectives: the business that is sending the message and the customer that is receiving the message.

Summary

The rapid pace of change in business today has forced organizations to re-examine and change the way they communicate with customers. More than ever before, organizations are demanding integrated marketing strategies to help resolve marketing problems and to take advantage of new opportunities.

The integrated marketing communications mix is composed of seven unique yet complementary components: advertising, direct response communications, interactive communications, sales promotion, personal selling, public relations, and event marketing and sponsorships. The organization evaluates marketing situations and employs the components of the mix that will effectively and efficiently reach its target market.

Several key issues and trends have led to the emergence of integrated marketing communications. Among the key issues are the strategic focus on customer relationship management (CRM), the expanding role of database marketing, the dramatic impact of the internet, and greater demand by senior managers for efficiency and accountability for the resources that are invested in marketing communications.

In the process of developing marketing communications strategies, an organization must understand and apply various consumer behaviour concepts. Among these concepts are needs and motives, personality and self-concept, attitudes and perceptions, reference groups, and family. Research into these factors provides clues on how to reach customers with a more effective message.

Marketing communications programs consider the unique needs and desires of a specific target market. Target markets are identified on the basis of common characteristics that are classified according to demographic, psychographic, and geographic variables. Trends in each of these areas are analyzed and a consumer profile of a designated target market emerges. Organizations then determine which targets are worth pursuing. Contemporary technology now allows for direct communications with individual customers. These new techniques are part of CRM programs. CRM is a practice that is designed to attract, cultivate, and maximize the return from individual customers.

Business buying behaviour is different from consumer buying behaviour. While consumers tend to be swayed by emotion, business buyers maintain a rational approach when making buying decisions. Business buying is based on predetermined criteria according to quality, service, continuity of supply, and price. Decisions are made formally by a buying committee or informally by a buying centre. Technology and relationship marketing practices have taken hold in business-to-business (B2B) marketing. Companies must adapt to this way of doing business or perish. Tools such as personal selling, event marketing, direct response, and interactive communications will play a prominent role in the future.

When devising marketing communications strategies, an organization often confronts some ethical issues. Typically, it does not wish to do harm or misrepresent its products based on inappropriate claims or images. Some of the key ethical issues involve the use of violent or dangerous images, the use of sexual images, inappropriate gender portrayals, and misleading advertising claims. If an ad is found to be objectionable, it is common for the advertiser to alter or remove that ad from distribution.

Key Terms

Review Questions

1. Identify and briefly explain the components of the integrated marketing communications mix.

2. Briefly describe the key issues and trends that have led to the emergence of integrated marketing communications.

3. "An understanding of Maslow's hierarchy of needs and theory of motivation has a direct influence on advertising strategy." Explain.

4. According to the self-concept theory, the self has four components. Identify and briefly describe each component.

5. How important is assessing customer attitudes when developing an advertising campaign? Explain.

6. What role and influence do reference groups play when a consumer is deciding what products to buy?

7. What are the key elements of demographic segmentation, psychographic segmentation, and geographic segmentation?

8. Identify the basic trends in Canada that must be considered when identifying and selecting demographic targets.

9. What is meant by the term direct or customized segmentation?

10. What essential criteria do organizational buyers consider when making buying decisions?

11. What is the difference between a buying committee and a buying centre?

Discussion and Application Questions

1. How have integration and partnerships influenced marketing communications strategies in business-to-business markets? Explain.

2. "Relationship marketing practices will dramatically alter marketing communications strategies in the future." Is this statement true or false? Conduct some online secondary research and form an opinion on this statement.

3. "Due to the geographic and cultural diversity of Canada, regional marketing communications strategies should be commonplace; instead, organizations rely upon national strategies." What direction should companies be taking and why? Consider both sides of the situation before making a decision.

4. From the following list of goods and services identify what you think is the most important marketing communications tool for building and sustaining the brand. Provide some justification for your choice.

   a) Labatt Blue
   b) BMW Automobiles
   c) Michelin (tires)
   d) RBC Financial Group

5. Cite some examples and provide actual illustrations of companies or brands that use the following consumer behaviour theories when developing communications strategies. Provide a description that relates the theory to the practice.

   a) Hierarchy of needs and theory of motivation
   b) Personality and self-concept
   c) Reference groups
   d) Family influences

6. Visit the Statistics Canada website and gather the most up-to-date statistics on Canadian household formations. Consider two or three prominent brands of Canadian household goods or retail organizations: do they reflect contemporary households? If not, what are the potential consequences?

7. The chapter discussed various methods (demographic segmentation, psychographic segmentation, and geographic segmentation) for identifying target markets. Provide some new examples of companies or brands that employ each of these methods when attempting to motivate their target customer to buy.

Endnotes

1 Kevin Astle, "Mending Broken Eggs," *Marketing*, July 14–21, 2003, p. 9.

2 3M, <**www.3m.com**> (November 2003).

3 Bernadette Johnson, "Advertisers Revisiting the Web: Study," *Strategy*, February 12, 2001, pp. 1, 14.

4 Based on data compiled for "Ad Age Special Report: 100 Leading National Advertisers," *Advertising Age*, June 23, 2003, pp. 2–14.

5 David Ticoll, "Ads on the Web? It's Time to Get Serious," *Globe and Mail*, April 25, 2003, p. C1.

6 "Unplugging Data," *Advertising Age*, March 6, 2000, p. S50.

7 Richard Rotman, "When Worlds Combine," *Marketing*, September 29, 2003, p. 8.

8 James F. Engel, David T. Kollatt, and Roger D. Blackwell, *Consumer Behaviour*, 2nd edition (New York: Holt Rinehart Winston, 1973), p. 5.

9 Deborah Fulsang, "Mom, I'm Ready for School," *Globe and Mail*, September 28, 2002, p. L1.

10 John Douglas, George Field, and Lawrence Tarpay, *Human Behaviour in Marketing* (Columbus, OH: Charles E. Merrill Publishing, 1987), p. 5.

11 Jack Neff, "Marketer's Rush into Men's Care Category," *Advertising Age*, July 29, 2002, p. 6.

12 "Ahoy Ye Pride Partiers," *Marketing*, July 8, 2002, p. 15.

13 Lisa D'Innocenzo, "On-the-Go Snacks Are Where It's At," *Strategy*, September 9, 2002, pp. 1, 17.

14 Statistics Canada, "Profile of the Canadian Population by Age and Sex: Canada Ages," press release, July 16, 2002.

15 "Demographic Statistics," *The Daily*, Statistics Canada, March 28, 2002.

16 Anne Kingston, "Nuclear Family Atomized," *National Post*, October 23, 2002, pp. A1, A14.

17 Barbara Wickens, "How We Live," *Maclean's*, November 4, 2002, p. 46.

18 Jo Marney, "Counting Ethnic Canadians In," *Marketing*, June 4, 2001, p. 24.

19 Patrick Lejtenyi, "Call in the Specialists," *Marketing*, June 4, 2001, pp. 19, 22.

20 Joanne Thomas Yaccato, "What Women Really Want," *Strategy*, November 18, 2002, p. M19.

21 Patrick Allossery, "The Element of Risk," *Financial Post*, April 15, 2002, p. FP12.

22 Nancy Carr, "Does a Distinct Society Need Distinct Creative?" *Strategy*, April 9, 2001, p. 13.

23 Ross Waring, "The Promise and Reality of Data Mining," *Strategy*, June 7, 1999, p. D9.

24 David Eggleston, "We've Come a Long Way Baby," *Strategy Direct Response*, November 8, 1999, p. D13.

25 Media Post, **www.mediapost.com**, June 19, 2003.

26 "Unilever Drops Suicidal Potato," *Marketing*, March 26, 2001, p. 1.

27 Angela Kryhul, "Stifling Nuisance or Helpful Guide?" *Marketing*, March 11, 2002, p. 6.

28 John Heinzl, "Labatt Forced to Yield to ASC Again," *Globe and Mail*," April 10, 1999, p. B3.

2

STRATEGIC PLANNING PRINCIPLES

After studying this chapter you will be able to:

identify essential external trends
and conditions that influence
organizational planning,

describe the steps in the strategic
planning process,

identify the distinctions and
relationships among the various
types of plans,

characterize the essential elements
of a corporate plan,

outline the structure and content of
a marketing plan,

outline the structure and content of
a marketing communications plan,
and

show how integrated marketing
planning provides solutions to
marketing problems.

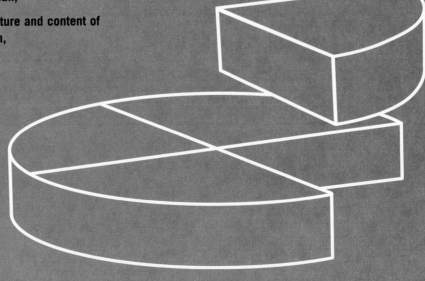

All business planning is an integrated process that involves planning at three levels of an organization: corporate planning (planning conducted by senior executives), marketing planning (planning conducted by brand and marketing managers), and marketing communications planning (plans designed by communications specialists based on guidelines provided by brand and marketing managers). When a planning system works properly, each level of planning is linked to the other levels. Corporate plans provide guidance and direction for marketing plans and marketing plans provide direction for marketing communications plans.

How plans are struck varies considerably from company to company. There is no perfect model to follow. Some organizations produce very detailed plans, while others take a more action-oriented approach. The common factor among all companies should be integration, meaning integrating one plan with another and integrating all the pieces of a plan together so that a consistent strategic direction is followed when the plans are implemented. What this chapter presents is a potential model for preparing strategic plans. Students should recognize that it can be altered in order to fit specific needs of an organization.

Strategic Planning and Factors Influencing Planning

Strategic Planning

The process of determining objectives and identifying strategies and tactics to help achieve objectives.

Strategic planning is the process of determining objectives (setting goals) and identifying strategies (ways to achieve the goals) and tactics (specific action plans) to help achieve objectives. Based on this definition, a strategic plan includes three common variables:

- **Objectives:** Statements of what is to be accomplished in terms of sales, profit, market share, or other measures.
- **Strategies:** Statements that outline how the objectives will be achieved, such as the direction to be taken and the allocation of resources needed to proceed.
- **Tactics:** Action-oriented details, including precise details about the cost and timing of specific activities.

Strategic planning is a cyclical process in most organizations. It is an annual occurrence that calls for plans to be updated constantly based on the latest conditions that prevail in the marketplace. Therefore, the essential ingredient in any plan is a firm understanding of the external factors that will influence the potential direction a company will proceed in. Furthermore, in the business marketplace today, change is occurring so fast that it is absolutely essential that a company keep abreast of change. A company's strategic plan is influenced by changes in the economy, among consumers, technology, laws and regulations governing business practices, and competitor activities. Occurrences and trends in each of these areas have an impact on the nature and direction of corporate plans, marketing plans and marketing communications plans. This section discusses briefly the nature and implications of these influences (see Figure 2.1).

ECONOMIC INFLUENCES

The general state of the economy has a direct impact on how aggressive or conservative a company is with its business plans. Should it be investing in marketing and marketing communications to expand its business or should it conserve funds to protect profit margins? The general state of the economy is determined by growth rates in the gross domestic product, inflation rates, levels of employment, the value of the Canadian dollar in relation to foreign currencies, and income distribution among consumers. The relationship among these variables is dynamic. For example, if the value of the gross domestic product has dropped for a few consecutive years, if levels of employment have been dropping, and if real income has been dropping marginally from year to year, the economy could be in recession. If consumers aren't spending, marketing organizations might adopt a conservative approach and control investment in marketing and marketing communications.

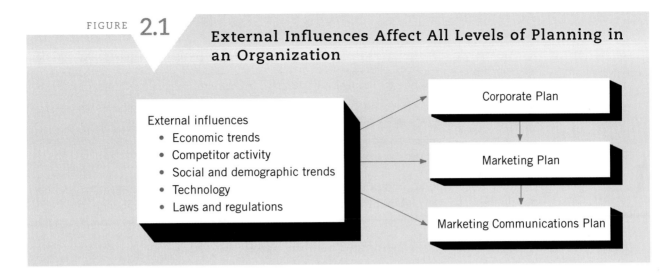

FIGURE **2.1**

External Influences Affect All Levels of Planning in an Organization

External influences
- Economic trends
- Competitor activity
- Social and demographic trends
- Technology
- Laws and regulations

Corporate Plan

Marketing Plan

Marketing Communications Plan

Based on all kinds of factors, a country's economy goes through cycles. Those cycles are recession, depression, recovery, and prosperity. In contrast to the scenario described above, an economy where gross domestic product is expanding, where real incomes are expanding and employment is plentiful, would indicate recovery or prosperity. Such an economy would call for aggressive investment in marketing and marketing communications to take advantage of the increases in consumer spending.

The North American economy was directly influenced by the terrorist attacks of September 11, 2001. Consumers and business travellers stayed home and the travel and hotel industries suffered considerably. Many hotel and airline companies had no alternative but to lay off employees, reduce marketing expenditures, and curb expansion plans. While consumer confidence is slowly rebounding, companies have had to adjust their strategic planning accordingly.

COMPETITOR INFLUENCE

Assessing the activities of competitors is probably the most thoroughly analyzed aspect of marketing planning. Such analysis provides input into how one brand can differentiate itself from the others and perhaps stand out more in the eyes of consumers. Most Canadian markets are very competitive and described as being an **oligopoly** (a market with a few major brands) or as being **monopolistically competitive** (a market with all kinds of brands). In either case, the consumer has a choice of what brand to buy, and the effectiveness of the marketing and marketing communications strategies will influence the decision.

Competition comes in two forms: direct competition and indirect competition. **Direct competition** is competition from alternative products and services that satisfy the needs of a target market. **Indirect competition** is competition from substitute products that offer customers the same benefit. In today's hypercompetitive marketplace, the lines between direct and indirect competition are becoming blurred. McDonald's true competitors at one time were other hamburger restaurants such as Burger King and Wendy's, but now, based on expanding menus (due to competitive influences), McDonald's competes with KFC, Swiss Chalet, and Pizza Hut, and with even more upscale roadhouse-type establishments such as Kelsey's. McDonald's is in the restaurant business today, so it has to be conscious of what all other restaurants are doing in order to develop new strategies to grow its business.

The brand Coca-Cola Classic is very aware of the activities of the brand Pepsi-Cola. Pepsi continues to invest heavily in distribution and marketing communications programs to edge closer to the leading brand. While defending its position, Coca-Cola must

Oligopoly
A market situation in which only a few brands control the market.

Monopolistic Competition
A market in which there are many competitors, each offering a unique marketing mix; consumers can assess these choices prior to making a buying decision.

Direct Competition
Competition from alternative products and services that satisfy the needs of a common market.

Indirect Competition
Competition from substitute products that offer the same benefit as another type of product.

The Coca-Cola Company
www.cocacola.com

also be aware of what other beverage companies are doing and what consumers are demanding. Colas are direct competitors; packaged juice drinks and water are indirect competitors. With consumers trending toward healthier alternatives, juices and waters are becoming the preferred choices. They are the growth segments of the beverage market. Therefore, Coca-Cola must look beyond traditional soft drinks. Coca-Cola is in the beverage business, not the soft drink business. Its marketing and marketing communications strategies must change based on such broader-based competition.

SOCIAL AND DEMOGRAPHIC INFLUENCES

Chapter 1 presented in detail several demographic tends that must be considered when developing a strategic plan. Here is a quick recap of the key trends in Canada:

- The rate of population growth is slowing down and the population is getting older.
- The population is concentrated in urban markets.
- Households are getting smaller and the structure is changing (there are fewer traditional households and more non-traditional households).
- The population is becoming more ethnically diverse.
- Gender equality is altering decision-making processes.

In addition to these trends, the lifestyles of Canadians are changing. As a population, Canadians are generally more health conscious than ever before. They are concerned about social issues such as education, health and welfare, and the natural environment in which they live. People have awakened to how fragile nature is and they no longer take for granted natural resources such as water. Furthermore, consumers are demanding better corporate citizenship and many companies are responding (see Figure 2.2). Consumers like to buy products from companies they perceive to behave in a socially responsible manner. To this end, companies are marketing goods and services that respond to consumers' interest in outdoor and recreational activities and foods that are either natural or better for the diet. Consumers can now choose among low-fat products, low-sodium products, healthier menus at fast food restaurants, automobiles that get better fuel mileage, and so on. Companies are also responding by implementing micro-market communications strategies to be as efficient as possible with relatively scarce marketing budgets.

In addition to recognizing fundamental changes in social trends, an organization must also respond to change within segments of the population. As discussed in Chapter 1, strategies are now devised to meet the unique needs of very small target markets. For the purposes of targeting and defining common characteristics in population subgroups, Canada's population is divided into categories: traditionalists, baby boomers, Generation X, and millennials. For a description of each segment, see Figure 2.3. Automobile companies must create models and marketing communications plans that attract young car buyers. Lately, most manufacturers have focused on the 18- to 25-year-old segment, commonly referred to as Generation Y. Gen-Yers, it seems, want it all: price, a nice buying experience, and a vehicle they won't be embarrassed to be seen in. Models such as the Honda Civic, Saturn Vue, and Toyota Matrix have pursued this segment aggressively through various forms of marketing communications.

TECHNOLOGY INFLUENCE

New products are coming to market so fast that consumers simply cannot grasp them all. Can anyone possibly keep up with the changes occurring in the telecommunications industry? How many electronic gadgets do we need simply to stay in touch? The technological environment consists of the discoveries, inventions, and innovations that provide for marketing opportunities. New products, new packaging, and new forms of communications are the direct result of technological advancement.

FIGURE **2.2** **An Advertisement Communicating Social Responsibility**

After the fruit is harvested, we make sure it gets picked.

If you're like most people, the last thing you think about when you pick up a few oranges at the supermarket is how they got from the grove into your hand. Well, chances are good it was in special corrugated packaging made by Weyerhaeuser. In fact, nearly everything you buy is shipped in corrugated boxes, so using forest resources wisely when we make them is our top priority. Today, we average nearly 60 percent recycled content in our containers. And 5 of our 8 mills use nothing but recycled fiber. We want to make sure there are always plenty of trees—the ones that provide food and the ones that deliver it.

▲ Weyerhaeuser
The future is growing
www.weyerhaeuser.com

Source: Weyerhaeuser Company

In terms of product development, companies are harnessing the power of virtual reality, the combination of technologies that allows users to experience three-dimensional, computer-generated environments through light, sound, and touch. Virtual reality has helped firms to gather reactions to new car designs and other potential products.[1] How people communicate and conduct buying transactions is also affected by technology. The Internet has had an overwhelming impact on commerce and communications as websites

FIGURE **2.3** **Canada's Population Segments**

Traditionalists

Born before 1946, they came of age in the shadow of two world wars and the Depression. They are disciplined, patriotic, and loyal, with a strong appreciation for hierarchy and tradition.

Baby Boomers

Born between 1946 and 1964, they grew up during the turbulent 1960s and '70s. They are idealistic and optimistic and driven by a desire to make a difference. Because of large numbers, they must compete to get ahead. They are ambitious.

Generation Xers

Born between 1965 and 1980, they entered the job market in the wake of a worldwide recession. They are skeptical and independent, and reluctant to rely on jobs and institutions for security. They are techno-literate and entrepreneurial, and challenge traditional ways of doing business.

Millennials

Born between 1981 and 1999, they inherited some of the idealism of their baby boomer parents, but with a strong dose of pragmatism. They are comfortable with technology and have grown up multi-tasking. They expect to hold more than one job at a time.

Source: Adapted from Ellen Schwartz, "Talkin' 'Bout My Generation(s)," *Costco Connection*, September/October 2002, p. 21.

and web-based communications seem imperative for reaching a tech-savvy public. Canadians have embraced ATMs and debit cards at an unprecedented rate, and 65 percent of customers already use banking e-services. In fact, five national banks introduced electronic person-to-person payment systems (P2P) in 2002. The service allows money to be transferred instantly by e-mail.[2]

The latest statistics available suggest the Internet will become a preferred channel for communicating with customers and for conducting transactions. A survey conducted by Statistics Canada revealed that the Internet is an ideal medium for reaching a desirable target market described as male and female between the ages of 15 and 44, college or university educated, household incomes of $40 000 plus, with an urban skew.[3] In conjunction with customer relationship management (CRM) programs, the Internet offers direct and interactive contact with customers.

LEGAL AND REGULATORY INFLUENCE

Strategic plans are affected by new developments in the political and legal arenas. Most laws and regulations governing business practice are created by federal and provincial legislation. As well, many industries establish and abide by their own self-regulation policies and practices. In some cases, the self-regulation guidelines are more stringent. Industry Canada regulates Canadian businesses through the *Competition Act*. The Act has three purposes: to maintain and encourage competition, to ensure small businesses have equal opportunity to participate in trade, and to provide consumers with product choice and competitive prices.

It cannot be assumed that all businesses follow the letter of the law and, in all honesty, many companies conduct their business and marketing practices unscrupulously.

The scandals associated with companies such as Enron and Worldcom certainly opened our eyes to unethical practices. In another instance, how telemarketing techniques are implemented often creates negative perceptions among consumers. For example, telemarketing, if used properly, is an effective technique for generating sales. However, the constant and persistent barrage of calls at inappropriate times only serves to turn the customer off. At present, the federal government and several provincial governments are revising consumer protection laws to reflect the explosive growth in e-commerce and the surge of complaints by people and small businesses doing business on the Internet. According to Bob Runciman, former Consumer Affairs Minister in Ontario, "the times have left the law behind the marketplace."[4]

In terms of marketing communications, companies have to be careful about what they say to consumers. Exaggerated product claims to promote an important benefit that lack proper substantiation, claims that improperly quote sale prices to make a sale look better than it really is, and any other form of misleading advertising will cause problems for a company. Advertisers should follow the Canadian Code of Advertising Standards. The Code contains regulations about gender portrayal, product claims, price claims, advertising involving product comparisons, and advertising to children. The Code is administered by Advertising Standards Canada, a group representing advertisers and advertising agencies.

STRATEGIC PLANNING PROCESS

Corporate Plan

A strategic plan formulated at the executive level of an organization to guide the development of functional plans in the organization.

Marketing Plan

A short-term, specific plan of action that combines strategy and tactics.

This section will draw the relationships between the plans at various levels of the organization. The corporate plan originates at the top of the organization and is largely based on input from senior executives. Most objectives are financial in nature and become the goals that must be shared by all of the company's divisions or products. Typically, the **corporate plan** is not an exhaustive document. Once the corporate plan has been struck, the various functional areas, including marketing, start their planning process. Refer to Figure 2.4 for a visual illustration.

A **marketing plan** is developed for each one of a company's products, which sets out the objectives for all brands. The plan determines how the various elements of the marketing mix will be employed so that they have the desired impact on the target market.

FIGURE **2.4** **Strategic Planning: Links between Various Organizational Plans**

The corporate plan provides guidance to the marketing plan and the marketing plan provides guidance for the marketing communications plan. All plans are based on the same background information and any analysis stemming from that information. Corporate plans are strategic in nature. Marketing plans and marketing communications plans are both strategic and tactical in nature.

The target market is identified through some combination of demographic, psychographic, and geographic variables, and a positioning strategy statement guides the development of the plan.

Once the role of marketing communications has been determined, specific plans are then developed for the various components of the marketing communications mix. At this stage, the goal is to develop a synergistic communications plan that will have all components delivering the same basic message about the product. As discussed in Chapter 1, advertising will achieve awareness and interest objectives and help build brand image over an extended period. Other variables, such as sales promotion, event marketing, public relations, and personal selling, perform more immediate tasks and are designed to achieve desire and action—a purchase. The integration of all components in a strategic plan will help achieve short-term and long-term objectives. The saying that "A chain is only as strong as its weakest link" appropriately describes the relationships among various components of the marketing communications mix and the relationship between marketing and marketing communications. As in war, a unified attack has a better chance of success!

For additional insight into the importance of strategic planning read the IMC Highlight **The "Attitude" Counts**.

J. Walter Thompson
www.jwt.com

IMC Highlight

THE "ATTITUDE" COUNTS

According to Tony Pigott, CEO of J. Walter Thompson in Toronto, marketing is in real trouble and there is no shortage of evidence. He cites some of the world's leading consumer products companies—Procter & Gamble, Kraft, Nestle, and Unilever, among others—that have in recent years made it known that they are seeking ways to revamp their marketing approaches.

These companies are eliminating marginal brands, shifting to customer relationship models, moving to performance-based compensation models for their partner agencies, and creating their own internal marketing communication processes. It seems the inventors of modern marketing feel there is a better way! But is that all that has to change?

In Pigott's view, it is attitude, especially the attitude among senior executives, that has to change. They need to "elevate the importance of marketing and communications to the highest rank," he says. "They need to look for key indicators of potential success the same way analysts assess EBITDA [earnings before income tax, depreciation, and amortization], cost of goods, or supply-chain efficiencies." What does marketing look to?

Pigott points to three key indicators:

Involvement of the CEO: The CEO must be actively involved in marketing decisions and directions. As they say, "What interests my boss fascinates me."

A Cohesive End-to-End System: Silos rule the day. Specialists and suppliers operate separately. Different tools (communications alternatives) and turf wars among partners conspire to create disintegration and inconsistency. What's needed is a fully engaged total communications planning system that embraces all disciplines and activities at all points of customer contact.

Ideas: There has to be a branding idea at the heart of the business. To dramatize the importance of a brand idea, consider the problem a copywriter by the name of Frances Garrity faced in the 1960s. Frances pulled an all-nighter on a new assignment and presented her ideas to the boss in the morning. The boss rejected everything and asked if she had anything else. She pulled a single sheet of paper out of the garbage can. On it was written, "A Diamond is Forever." That phrase became the inspirational core for De Beers marketing for more than 40 years. It has guided several billion dollars in marketing worldwide.

In the context of integrated marketing and integrated marketing communications, simple phrases like "A Diamond is Forever" express the fundamental promise and distinctiveness of the brand. Good planning produces good ideas. Good ideas make an organization successful. Commitment at the top, commitment throughout an organization, and commitment among external partners to work together are the keys to success.

Adapted from Tony Pigott, "Marketing in Crisis," *Marketing*, November 11, 2002, pp. 12–14.

The Corporate Plan

The mission statement is the guiding light for all forms of strategic planning. A **mission statement** is a statement of an organization's purpose and an indicator of the operating philosophy the organization follows. A good mission statement is customer oriented and marketing oriented, considers the competition, and looks to the long term. In other words, once a company establishes its mission, it must provide adequate time and resources to carry through with it. Here is an example of a mission statement:

> Our mission is to be the leader in all markets we participate in. In order to fulfill this mission, the Corporation must strive for profitable growth, surpass customer expectations with innovative products and services, foster an entrepreneurial spirit and provide employees with the opportunity to achieve their professional goals. —Bombardier Inc.

For the record, Bombardier Inc. manufacturers and markets aircraft, commuter and regional rail transportation vehicles, locomotives, and freight cars. Bombardier is a company that earns $21 billion a year and generously contributes to the economic and social well-being of the communities in which it operates.[5]

With the mission confirmed, executive attention turns to setting corporate objectives, determining strategic direction, and allocating resources. **Corporate objectives** are statements of a company's overall goals. These objectives are usually financial in nature and are used to evaluate the effectiveness or ineffectiveness of a company's strategic plan and the people who manage the organization. At the end of the year, actual financial results are compared to the objectives. The degree of success is there for all concerned to see. Here are a few examples of corporate objectives:

- To increase company sales revenue from $50 000 000 to $60 000 000 in 20XX.
- To increase category market share (share in a market for all company brands) from 25 percent to 30 percent in 20XX.
- To increase return on investment from 10 percent to 15 percent in 20XX.
- To exhibit constructive social responsibility by investing in research and development to discover environmentally friendly new products.

Objectives statements like these have direct impact on the development of marketing objectives and strategies. All company brands must contribute to achieving the company's goals. It is the total of sales revenues for various brands, for example, that comprises overall company sales revenue. The market share of several company brands, say Maxwell House, Chase & Sanborn, Nabob, and General Foods International Coffees, make up Kraft Canada's total market share in coffee.

When an organization determines its corporate strategy, it considers several factors: marketing strength, degree of competition in current or new markets under consideration, financial resources, research and development capabilities, and management commitment to particular goals. It is common for a company to follow numerous strategic directions at the same time, largely due to the dynamic nature of the marketplace. To follow one direction and fail could have a negative long-term effect on the company.

A variety of strategic options are given due consideration. Among the options are a penetration strategy, an acquisition strategy, a new product development strategy, and a strategic alliance strategy. All these strategies imply a desire for growth. In some cases, a company may decide to get smaller. While that may seem odd, many companies find that too much expansion can have disastrous results on profits. Growing sales at the expense of profit doesn't make sense! In such cases, a company may decide to consolidate operations by selling off various divisions or products. The goal is to return to the business it knows best. Molson Inc. did just that in the early and mid-1990s. The company's profits were declining sharply so the decision was made to exit the retailing market (Beaver Lumber), the chemical market (Diversey Chemical), and the sports and entertainment market (Montreal Canadiens and the Molson Centre in Montreal). Molson returned to its roots—beer!

A **penetration strategy** involves aggressive marketing of a company's existing products. The goal is to build the business by taking customers from the competition or by expanding the entire market. McDonald's, for example, is constantly juggling its menu, altering its prices, and revamping restaurants to differentiate itself from other restaurants. Coca-Cola does the same thing in order to fend off Pepsi and retain its leadership position in the soft drink market. Brands like these aggressively protect their position.

New products, the result of **new product development strategy**, offer another option for growth-minded companies. New products create new revenue streams at a much greater rate than simply trying to expand existing products. Back to McDonald's for an example: In trying to meet the demands of healthier lifestyles and healthier eating, McDonald's launched a Lighter Choices Menu, which includes a veggie burger, low-fat yogurt parfait and a selection of salads (see Figure 2.5). Already the light-meal business has exceeded expectations. It accounts for 6 percent of the company's $2.2 billion sales in 2002.[6]

Rather than invest in something new, some companies prefer to buy their way into a market by following an **acquisition strategy**. Why did PepsiCo buy the Quaker Oats Company at a cost of $13.4 billion? To get its hands on Gatorade, the dominant brand in the growing sports drink beverage category.[7] With such a purchase, PepsiCo is more of a competitive threat to Coca-Cola. Both companies are in the beverage business, not just the soft drink business.

Strategic alliances, when separate companies with complementary strengths join resources to satisfy their shared customers, are now very popular among companies searching for ways to reduce costs or improve operating efficiency. Canadian National (CN) has formed several alliances with customers and distributors to achieve such goals. CN and Schneider Logistics, General Motors' logistics partner in the highly competitive aftermarket parts business, joined forces to produce a distribution chain that would provide optimal performance. Rail traffic flows from GM's central parts distribution centre in Flint, Michigan, to 12 distribution centres across the United States. Dedicated CN logistics professionals work on site in Flint to manage day-to-day rail activity, coordinating Schneider Logistics and interfacing with a number of other rail carriers to maximize performance. For the service, CN receives base compensation and can receive incentives that are tied to continuous improvement in asset utilization and car supply.[8]

Senior executives also make decisions about the financial resources that are allocated to marketing and other functional divisions of the company. Prior to embarking on marketing plans for individual products, the vice-president of marketing usually knows how much money is available for marketing purposes. That person distributes the money among each of the company's brands. Competition among brand managers for such a scarce resource creates some very interesting marketing plans and presentations. Most companies have brands that are stars, and they are given budget priority. What's left is divided among the remaining brands.

Marketing Planning

With the details of the corporate plan determined, the marketing department starts the process of marketing planning. **Marketing planning** involves analyzing, planning, implementing, and controlling marketing initiatives to satisfy target market needs and achieve organizational objectives. In contrast to corporate plans, marketing plans are short term in nature (one year), specific in scope (they involve precise actions for one product), and combine both strategy and tactics (they are action oriented). The marketing plan should also include a **contingency plan** to provide alternative courses of action in the event that new circumstances arise.

FIGURE **2.5**   **McDonald's Launches New Products to Satisfy Changing Taste Preferences**

Source: Dick Locek/CP Photo Archive (upper left); courtesy of McDonald's restaurants of Canada Limited (right).

The process involves four basic steps:

1. *Analyzing Market Opportunities:* The market conditions are evaluated to identify the best opportunities for the company, considering its expertise and resources.
2. *Developing Marketing Strategies:* A positioning strategy is designed in the context of satisfying target market needs and managing a product though its life cycle. During the life of a product, positioning strategies can change.
3. *Planning and Implementing Marketing Programs:* Basic decisions are made about how the marketing mix will be used. A budget is drawn up to allocate resources to the various activities recommended.
4. *Managing Marketing Programs:* Programs are put in place to evaluate and control the effectiveness of the marketing effort.

There is no perfect format for a marketing plan, although Figure 2.6 offers an illustration. Marketing plans vary considerably from one organization to another in length, detail, and content. This section will examine the content of a marketing plan, but readers must realize that the content of a plan is modified to suit the needs of each specific organization. Essentially, a marketing plan is divided into two major sections. The first section is a compilation of background information about the market, target market, competition, and product. The second section is the plan itself; it contains the objectives, strategies, and tactics for the product for the year ahead, and provides specific details about how the budget is allocated and the timing of all activities.

MARKET BACKGROUND

SWOT Analysis

An analysis procedure that involves an assessment of an organization's strengths, weaknesses, opportunities, and threats.

The direction a marketing plan takes is directly influenced by internal conditions (strengths and weaknesses) and external conditions (opportunities and threats). As indicated earlier, the first step in planning is analysis. In marketing terms, such an analysis is referred to as a SWOT analysis. The acronym **SWOT** stands for strengths, weaknesses, opportunities and threats.

Strengths and Weaknesses The internal capabilities and resources are reviewed to determine the relative condition of a brand and determine its capability to pursue new directions. The review considers a variety of controllable marketing factors, and may extend to the areas of manufacturing, finance, human resources, and technology. Any limits on current strengths may justify developing new strengths.

Opportunities and Threats The manager reviews the data and information external to the organization, focusing on the economy, social and demographic trends, technology, and social responsibility issues. Trends in each of these areas influence the direction marketing strategies will take. Opportunities are prioritized, and threats are classified according to seriousness and probability of occurrence. The absence of marketing action in either area could hinder the development of a brand.

A variety of information is collected and analyzed. The goals of a SWOT analysis are to capitalize on strengths while minimizing weaknesses and to take advantage of opportunities while fending off threats. In addition to reviewing the contingency plan to deal with "what if" scenarios that could pop up, the SWOT analysis should review the following information. Refer to Figure 2.7 for an illustration of a marketing plan model.

External Influences

- *Economic Trends:* The current and predicted states of the economy are considered. Is the economy growing (recovery or prosperity) or is it sputtering (recession)? Appropriate statistical information is evaluated in this section of the plan.
- *Social and Demographic Trends:* Basic trends in age, income, immigration, migration, and lifestyles are evaluated to identify potential target markets. For example,

FIGURE 2.6 **The Marketing Planning and Control Process**

Once plans are developed and implemented, evaluation and control procedures are implemented during the plan period (e.g., quarterly reviews). At that stage there is an opportunity to revise marketing objectives and strategies according to current market conditions.

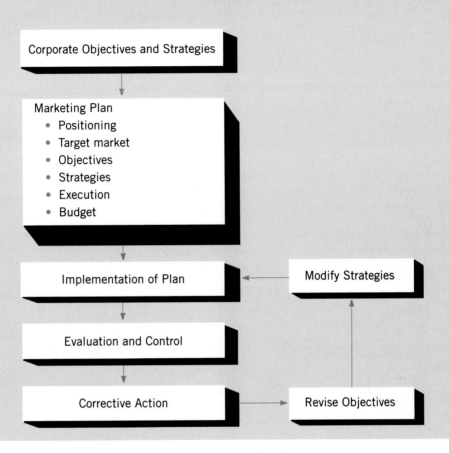

the aging of Canada's population will be a factor influencing positioning strategies in the future. There will be a new emphasis on older age groups.

- *Technology Trends:* Technological trends that affect buyer behaviour have to be determined. Technology quickens the speed with which new products come to market and the way companies deliver messages about products to customers.
- *Regulatory Trends:* A company should always stay abreast of changes to any laws and regulations affecting the marketing of its products. For example, new nutritional labelling laws came into play in 2003. Food companies had to revise all of their packages to meet the new standards.

Market Analysis

- *Market Size and Growth:* A review of trends over several years is considered for the purposes of making sales projections for the year ahead. Is the market growing or declining, and how fast?
- *Regional Markets:* Sales trends by region are analyzed in order to determine what areas need more or less attention in the year ahead. Some markets may be growing while others are not. A regional analysis helps determine priorities.

FIGURE **2.7**   **An Illustration of a Marketing Plan Model**

MARKETING BACKGROUND	MARKETING PLAN

MARKETING BACKGROUND

External Influences
- Economic trends
- Social and demographic trends
- Technology trends
- Regulatory trends

Market Analysis
- Market size and growth
- Regional market size and growth
- Market segment analysis
- Seasonal analysis

Competitor Analysis
- Market share trends
- Marketing strategy assessment

Target Market Analysis
- Consumer data
- Consumer behaviour

Product (Brand) Analysis
- Sales volume trends
- Market share trends
- Distribution
- Marketing communications
- New product activity

MARKETING PLAN

Positioning Strategy
- Positioning strategy statement

Target Market Profile
- Demographic
- Psychographic
- Geographic

Marketing Objectives
- Sales volume
- Market share
- Profit
- Other

Marketing Strategies
- Product
- Price
- Marketing communications
- Distribution

Marketing Execution (Tactics)
- Product
- Price
- Marketing communications
- Distribution
- New products
- Marketing research
- Service
- Partnerships and alliances

Budget and Financial Summary
- Budget allocations (by activity, by time of year)
- Brand financial statement

Timeline or Calendar
- Activity schedule

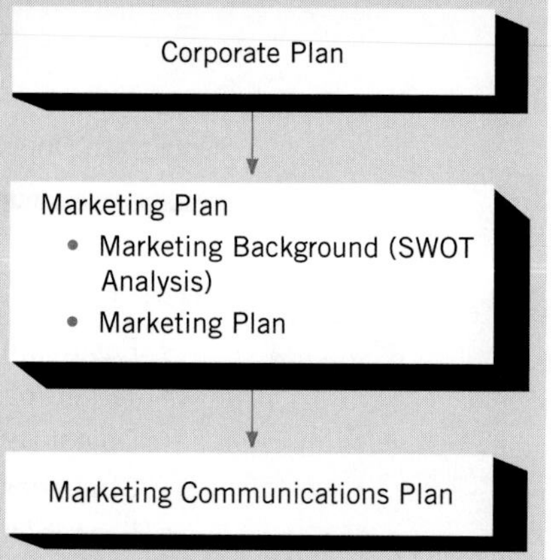

Corporate Plan

↓

Marketing Plan
- Marketing Background (SWOT Analysis)
- Marketing Plan

↓

Marketing Communications Plan

- **Market Segment Analysis:** There could be numerous product segments in market. For example, in the hotel industry there are budget hotels, mid-priced hotels, and luxury hotels. Are all segments growing at the same rate, or are some segments doing better than others? Interpretive comments about the various segments should be included.

- **Seasonal Analysis:** Seasonal or cyclical trends over the course of a year are examined. For example, volume trends for beer and barbecue-related items would be much higher in the spring and summer seasons. The timing of proposed marketing activities would consider such trends.

Target Market Analysis

- *Consumer Data:* The profile of primary users (and secondary users if necessary) is reviewed for any changes during the past few years. The aging population and lifestyle changes could be affecting the profile of product users.

- *Consumer Behaviour:* The degree of customer loyalty to the market and products within a market is assessed. To what degree are customers brand loyal? Do they switch brands and how frequently do they do so? Knowledge of such behaviour has a direct influence on advertising and promotion strategies. Should the plan attract new customers, prevent existing customers from departing, or do both?

Product (Brand) Analysis

An assessment of a brand's past performance is included in this section of the plan. An attempt is made to link past marketing activities to the performance of the brand. Have previous strategies been successful and will changes be needed in the year ahead?

- *Sales Volume Trends:* Historical volume trends are plotted in order to forecast sales for the year ahead.

- *Market Share Trends:* Market share is a clear indicator of brand performance. Market share trends are examined nationally, regionally, and by key market in order to determine areas of strength and weakness. Is the brand's market share growing faster or slower than competitors' shares. Where are the priorities for improving market share?

- *Distribution:* The availability of the product nationally and regionally is reviewed. Regional availability will affect how much marketing support a brand will receive. Should the new plan focus on areas where distribution is high or low?

- *Marketing Communications:* Current activities are assessed to determine if strategies need to be retained or changed. A review of expenditures by medium, sales promotions, and events and sponsorships is necessary in order to assess the impact of such spending on brand performance.

- *New Product Activity:* Sales performance of recently implemented initiatives is evaluated. For example, the performance of new product formats, sizes, flavours, and so on is scrutinized to determine the impact of those factors on sales and market share.

Competitor Analysis

In order to plan effectively, a manager should know competitors' products as well as his or her own product. A review of marketing mix activities for key competitors provides essential input on how to revise marketing strategies. A brand must react to the actions of another brand or suffer the consequences of lack of action.

- *Market Share Trends:* It is common to plot and review the market share trends of all brands from year to year. Such analysis provides insight into what brands are moving forward and what brands are moving backward.

- *Marketing Strategy Assessment:* An attempt is made to link known marketing strategies to competitor brand performance. What is the nature of the competition's advertising, sales promotions, events and sponsorships, and interactive programs? How much are the competitors investing in these areas? Have they launched any new products or implemented any new distribution, pricing, or communications strategies? What changes are anticipated in the year ahead?

MARKETING PLAN

The SWOT analysis leads directly into the development of the action plan. The plan section clarifies the positioning strategy of the company's brands, establishes objectives for the year, determines how the various elements of the marketing mix will be employed, and outlines the investment and timing of all activities that are recommended.

Positioning Strategy

Positioning
The selling concept that motivates purchase, or the image that marketers desire a brand to have in the minds of consumers.

Positioning Strategy Statement
A summary of the character and personality of a brand and the benefits it offers customers.

Positioning refers to the selling concept that motivates purchase, or the image that marketers desire a brand to have in the minds of customers. The **positioning strategy statement** has a direct impact on the nature of the message that must be communicated to consumers. Visa's positioning strategy statement is as follows:

> To reinforce our leadership position in the credit card market, and to establish it as the preferred provider for all future purchases.

The positioning statement clearly identifies where the company wants the product to be in the market and what message must be communicated to customers. The strategy statement provides guidance and direction for marketing strategies. Furthermore, it serves as the standard for considering what strategies to use and not use. For example, if a marketing communications agency presents a new creative strategy for the brand, the client will evaluate it against the positioning strategy statement to see whether the new creative plan fits with the strategy.

Target Market Profile

At this stage, the manager identifies or targets a group of customers that represents the greatest profit potential. As discussed earlier, a target market is defined in terms of similar needs and common characteristics based on:

- *Demographic Profile:* Characteristics such as age, gender, income, education, and ethnic background are considered. Depending on the nature of the product, some characteristics are more important than others. Some may not be important at all. For example, is the brand for males, females, or is it gender neutral? If the product is expensive, income will be an important factor.

- *Psychographic Profile:* The lifestyle profile includes three essential characteristics: the target's activities, interests, and opinions. Knowledge about customer behaviour provides clues on how to best reach the customer with a compelling message. As discussed in Chapter 1, many advertising campaigns are designed in such a way that a brand associates itself with a lifestyle or desired lifestyle of the target market. Research about consumers compiled by research organizations such as Millward Brown and SRI Consulting Business Intelligence (refer to the discussion of VALS in Chapter 1 for details) is useful when describing target markets based on psychographic information. Information about media consumption is relevant to the customer profile; knowledge of what media customers refer to most frequently affects how funds are allocated across different media and other forms of marketing communications. For example, if the target market spends a lot of time online and less time watching television than it used to, such knowledge could influence media strategy.

- *Geographic Profile:* The urban nature of Canada's population means geography has a significant influence on marketing strategy. Therefore, the profile considers the location of the target market in terms of region or key market. Geography is typically a key influence on how a budget is allocated across the country. Does a brand invest in regions of strength or regions that need shoring up?

Target Profile
A description of a customer group based on demographic, psychographic, and geographic variables.

Harley-Davidson
www.harleycanada.com

Marketing Objective
A statement that identifies what a product will accomplish in a one-year period, usually expressed in terms of sales, market share, and profit.

To demonstrate **target profiling**, consider the description of the primary customer for a Harley-Davidson motorcycle. Biker gangs do not keep Harley-Davidson in business! Their customer is described as:

Males, 40 to 55 years of age, earning $75 000 plus annually, living in major cities. They are "weekend warriors" who want to get away from the office. They are lawyers, doctors, or corporate executives looking for a way to alleviate stress. About 25 percent are new to biking and 45 percent have previously owned a Harley; 30 percent have come from a competing brand. Women account for 15 percent of purchasers.

This illustration aptly portrays a combination of demographic, psychographic, and geographic characteristics, at least the ones that are important to Harley-Davidson.[9] Figure 2.8 shows a sample of Harley-Davidson communications.

Marketing Objectives

Marketing objectives are statements that identify what a product will accomplish in a one-year period. Similar to corporate objectives, they tend to focus on financial measures such as sales and profits or other quantitative yardsticks. Objectives may also be qualitative in nature and include new product introductions, product line extensions, the launch of new packaging, and so on.

To illustrate how marketing objectives are written, let's assume you are the brand manger for Crest toothpaste. At present, Crest is the challenger in the market with a market share of 26.4 percent. The market leader is Colgate with a 40.8 percent market share. The toothpaste market has been experiencing annual rates of growth of between 4 percent and 6 percent in recent years and is currently estimated to be worth $134 million.[10] You might set out the marketing objectives for Crest for the year ahead like this:

- To increase market share from 26.4 percent to 28.5 percent in 2005.
- To increase dollar sales from $35,376,000 to $39,958,800 in 2005 (assumes a market growth of 5 percent and achievement of market share objective).
- To successfully introduce three new line extensions in 2005 to extend Crest's presence further in the oral care market.
- To improve distribution levels in Quebec from 75 percent to 85 percent (in stores carrying toothpaste) in 2005.

Objectives are written so they can be measured in order to facilitate evaluation at the end of the plan period. Were the objectives achieved or not? Was the plan too aggressive or not aggressive enough? It will depend on the dynamics of the marketplace over the next 12 months.

Marketing Strategies

Marketing Strategy
A plan of action that shows how the various elements of the marketing mix will be used to satisfy a target market's needs.

Marketing strategies are the master plans for achieving the objectives. The importance of having a good strategy must be emphasized. There is a saying that "Good strategy with weak execution can produce reasonable results." There is another saying: "Poor strategy with good execution produces terrible results." The reason these have become such common sayings is that they are true. The goal should be to have the right strategy and then simply to work on better execution as time goes on. Most professional hockey or football coaches would agree with this principle.

In the development of the marketing strategy, the role and contribution of each component of the marketing mix are identified. Priority may be given to certain components depending on the nature of the market. For example, the success of a brand of beer depends largely on the impact of advertising on the target market. The nature of the message and the amount of money invested in advertising are critical decision areas for achieving differentiation. In the hotel market, price (low price or high price, depending

FIGURE **2.8** **Harley-Davidson Motorcycles Targets Middle-Aged Males by Placing Ads in Magazines that Segment Reads**

Source: Courtesy of Larter Advertising

on market segment) and services offered (product) receive more emphasis, because they are critical factors that determine competitive advantage (see Figure 2.9).

The total amount of money that will be invested in the product will be identified in the strategy section of the plan. There are various methods for arriving at a budget. Some methods estimate sales first and then base the marketing or marketing communications budget on sales. Other methods develop the budget first, a method based on the premise

FIGURE **2.9** **Fairmont's Differential Advantage is a Promise of Sophisticated Elegance in a Relaxing Environment**

Source: Courtesy of Fairmont Vancouver Airport

that investing in marketing communications creates sales, so that the budget is not the outcome of sales. Regardless of the method used, the budget must be carefully calculated and defended when the plan is presented to the marketing managers. Figure 2.10 shows further details about budget methodologies.

Marketing Execution (Tactics)

Tactics (execution)
Action-oriented details that outline how a strategic plan will be implemented.

The **tactics (execution)** outlined in the plan are program details drawn directly from the strategy section of the plan. Such details will identify what programs are to be implemented, how much they will cost, what the timing will be, and who will be responsible for

FIGURE 2.10

Methods for Determining a Marketing Budget

Method	Procedure
Percentage of Sales	A predetermined percentage of forecasted sales is allocated to marketing or marketing communications.
Fixed Sum / Unit	A predetermined dollar amount per unit sold is allocated to marketing or marketing communications.
Industry Average	The average amount (current or forecasted) spent on marketing or marketing communications by all brands in a market is allocated to marketing.
Advertising Share/Market Share	Invest at a level to retain share (ad share equals market share); invest at a level to build market share (ad share is greater than market share).
Task (Objective)	Define the task, determine the activities to achieve the task, and associate a cost to the activities.

implementation. The unique action plans provide specific details for the four primary decision areas—product, price, distribution, and marketing communications—as well as secondary areas such as marketing research, service, and potential partnerships and alliances.

Typically, only the key elements of various marketing communications plans (advertising, sales promotion, Internet communications, public relations, direct response, and so on) are included in the marketing plan. The assumption is that specific communications plans are based on the same marketing objectives and marketing strategies described in the marketing plan. Specific and lengthier information about marketing communications strategies and tactics is presented in their respective plans or a marketing communications plan.

Budget and Financial Summary

In order for a marketing plan to be improved, it is crucial to show the financial implications of the activities to be undertaken. Senior executives like to know how the company's money will be spent and how profitable the investment will be. Therefore, the budget section will itemize all activities and indicate the associated cost. Major areas such as media, consumer promotion, trade promotion, and marketing research are often subdivided into more specific activities.

In many companies, the brand managers and marketing managers are responsible for bottom-line profitability for their brands. If so, a financial statement for the brand is included. Such a statement should provide some financial history for the previous year, current year, and a forecast for the plan year. Senior executives are interested in seeing progress in marketing terms and financial terms. The financial statement will include such measures as sales, market share, cost of goods sold, gross profit, marketing expenses, and net profit before taxes.

Evaluation and Control

Marketing Control

The process of measuring and evaluating the results of marketing strategies and plans and of taking corrective action to ensure marketing objectives are achieved.

It is quite common for an organization to plan for semi-annual or quarterly reviews to assess its financial position. Marketing and marketing communications managers often fear such reviews because it is a time when budgets are frequently given the axe. Nonetheless, evaluation of activities is essential, because changes will likely be necessary while a plan is in mid-stream. **Marketing control** is the process of measuring and evaluating the results of marketing strategies and plans and then taking corrective action to ensure the marketing objectives are attained. Refer back to Figure 2.6 for a visual illustration of evaluation and control.

The evaluation process also provides an opportunity to change marketing strategies if necessary. If financial obligations are not being achieved, then new strategies must be explored. Furthermore, it is an opportunity to review key financials such as sales, costs, and profits and reforecast the figures for the balance of the year. If the original objectives are not achievable, they should be modified, as should the marketing activities and expenditures that support the product.

Marketing Communications Planning

Since plans have to be struck well in advance of their implementation date, the marketing communications plan is developed simultaneously with the marketing plan so that its key components can be integrated into the marketing plan. The various components of marketing communications rely on the same input (background information, target market profiles, and positioning strategy statements), as do other components of the marketing mix. A marketing communications plan model is included in Figure 2.11. To demonstrate how a marketing and marketing communications plan are integrated, read the IMC Highlight **Continuous Improvement at Canadian Tire**.

A **marketing communications plan** is usually prepared by an outside organization. Depending on the nature of the plan, it could be an advertising agency, public relations company, or sales promotion company, or any combination. At some point, all the agencies working on the same plan must compare notes to ensure that their strategies are synchronized. Each aspect of the marketing communications plan has its own objectives, strategies, and tactical plans. In fact, it is crucial that the role and contribution of each component—advertising, sales promotion, public relations, direct response, interactive communications, event marketing and sponsorships, and personal selling—be identified. Similar to the components of the marketing plan, the role of the communications components will vary depending on the nature of the product and the market. As well, some components are suited for achieving long-term objectives while others are suited for short-term objectives. The key to success is the integration of the various components to produce a unified approach to building the brand (or company).

Marketing Communications Plan

A plan that identifies how the various elements of marketing communications will be integrated into a cohesive and coordinated plan.

MARKETING COMMUNICATIONS OBJECTIVES

In general terms, marketing communications objectives are very diverse and tend to involve

- building awareness and interest in the product,
- altering perceptions held by consumers about the product,
- differentiating the product from others by presenting unique features and benefits,
- attracting new target markets to the product,
- encouraging greater usage of the product,
- offering incentives to get people to buy the product,
- creating goodwill and fostering a positive public image (usually for a company),
- creating leads for follow-up at a later date, and
- motivating distributors to carry the product.

To continue with the Crest toothpaste example in the marketing objectives section, Crest is a firmly established and well-known brand, so awareness objectives are not relevant. However, here are some examples of other marketing communications objectives Crest might identify:

Crest
www.crest.com

FIGURE 2.11 **A Marketing Communications Plan Model**

MARKETING COMMUNICATIONS OBJECTIVES

- Identify what is to be accomplished

MARKETING COMMUNICATIONS STRATEGIES

- Identify the role/importance of mix components
- Budget Available

CREATIVE PLAN

- Objectives (what to say)
- Strategies (how to say it)
- Execution (specific details)

MEDIA PLAN

- Objectives
- Strategies
- Criteria for reaching target
- Rationale for media selection
- Execution (cost, coverage, and timing details)

DIRECT RESPONSE PLAN

- Objectives
- Strategies
- Tactics
- Budget

INTERACTIVE COMMUNICATIONS PLAN

- Objectives
- Strategies
- Tactics
- Budget

SALES PROMOTION PLAN

- Objectives
- Strategies
- Tactics
- Budget

PUBLIC RELATIONS PLAN

- Objectives
- Strategies
- Tactics
- Budget

EVENTS AND SPONSORSHIP PLAN

- Objectives
- Strategies
- Tactics
- Budget

PERSONAL SELLING PLAN

- Objectives
- Strategies
- Tactics
- Budget

CALENDAR OF EVENTS

- Week
- Month

BUDGET SUMMARY

- Total and allocation by various plans

Note: These plans assume adequate input is provided from the background section of the marketing plan. See Figure 2.7 for details.

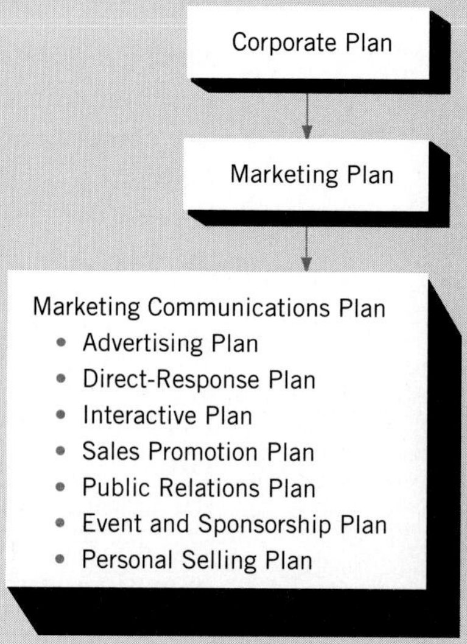

Corporate Plan

↓

Marketing Plan

↓

Marketing Communications Plan
- Advertising Plan
- Direct-Response Plan
- Interactive Plan
- Sales Promotion Plan
- Public Relations Plan
- Event and Sponsorship Plan
- Personal Selling Plan

- To achieve a brand preference score of 40 percent among primary buyers of toothpaste products.
- To achieve a trial purchase rate of 25 percent among competitive brand users by offering incentives that encourage brand switching.
- To alter consumers', perceptions about brand image so that potential users perceive Crest to be an innovative product and market leader.

These objectives imply that marketing communications will be an integrated effort including activities beyond advertising. For certain, sales promotions (both consumer and

CONTINUOUS IMPROVEMENT AT CANADIAN TIRE

Canadian Tire is a very successful organization but in recent years has been under intense pressure from American retailers such as Home Depot and Wal-Mart, as well as various Canadian hardware companies that have merged together. So, to be ready for the future, Canadian Tire implemented a new positioning strategy in 2002 that called for ambitious growth and an improved shopping experience for its customers.

The strategy is a five-year plan that involves new advertising, new in-store designs and layouts, new products, and new merchandising strategies. It is an integrated approach based on a new positioning strategy that uses the phrase "Let's get started." Marketing and marketing communications will play a pivotal role. The primary objective is to differentiate Canadian Tire further from the competition by offering better product quality.

The "Let's get started" campaign reinforces the message that Canadian Tire is the perfect place to start something new—whether it's a hobby, a project, or a sports season. The television ads are upbeat, with a country-rock type song and images of people enjoying life with products purchased at Canadian Tire. Elements of the campaign have been integrated into the company's corporate communications strategy, in-store signage, catalogues, the company's website, and radio and television ads.

Canadian Tire sees the new positioning strategy as the foundation for a long-term brand-building and image-building program. At the core of the message are the products sold at Canadian Tire. The company wants to be known as a place where you can get new and innovative items. In 2002 alone the company created 16 commercials that featured different products. Canadian Tire also continues to expand its popular private label products, Mastercraft (tools) and Motomaster (auto parts). A new line called Yardworks has been added in the lawn and garden tools and outdoor power equipment categories.

The financial goal for Canadian Tire is to grow by $1.4 billion by 2007. If it achieves its goal, company sales revenue will reach $6.7 billion. The five-year strategic plan is the path Canadian Tire will follow to get there. "Let's get started." Competitors beware!

Adapted from Chris Powell, "Starting from Its Strengths," *Marketing,* December 16, 2002.

Canadian Tire
www.canadiantire.ca

trade), public relations, and internet communications will be employed. Advertising and sales promotions will satisfy the first two objectives, and public relations and internet communications will satisfy the third objective. A brand such as Crest uses all components of the marketing communications mix in order to retain its position in the marketplace relative to Colgate (another leading brand). The ad for Crest that appears in Figure 2.12 creates awareness for a new line extension. Crest has incorporated Scope mouthwash (another Procter & Gamble brand) into the Crest formula to offer a dual benefit to consumers.

MARKETING COMMUNICATIONS STRATEGIES

The marketing communications strategy provides a basic outline of how the various components of the mix will be used. As indicated by the Crest toothpaste example, all components may not be used, and those that are used are often ranked in terms of priority and what they are able to achieve.

This section of the strategy also identifies the budget allocated to marketing communications and how funds will be allocated to the various activities. What percentage of the budget will be allocated to advertising, to sales promotions, to event marketing, and so on?

Creative Plan

A plan that outlines the nature of the message to be communicated to the target audience; involves the development of creative objectives, creative strategies, and creative execution.

Advertising Plan

The advertising plan is divided into two primary areas: creative (message) and media. The **creative plan** is concerned with what message will be communicated and how it will be communicated to the target market. The message usually stresses the most important attribute of the product, that which is most important to the customer. Where claims of

FIGURE **2.12** **An Ad Creates Awareness for a New Line Extension**

performance are made, proper substantiation is provided. That hints at the "how" aspect of creative planning. Agencies draw on such techniques as humour, sex, emotions, and even facts to tempt us to buy something. To illustrate, consider what Energizer does when it advertises batteries. The ads say that Energizer batteries last longer. In the demonstration, the now-famous bunny keeps going, and going, and going! Complete details about creative planning are presented in Chapter 4.

Media Plan

A strategy that outlines the relevant details about how a client's budget will be spent; involves decisions about what media to use and how much money to invest in the media chosen in order to reach the target audience effectively and efficiently.

The **media plan** involves strategic decisions about what media to use and how much money to invest in the media that are chosen. The overall goal of any media plan is efficiency: the plan must effectively reach the target audience at the lowest possible cost. Since a company invests considerable sums in media advertising, wise decisions about usage are critical. Other media decisions involve timing, what markets to advertise in, how much money to allocate to regional markets and to key markets (cities), how long the campaign should last, and so on. Developing a media plan is complicated and best left to media specialists. More details about media planning for traditional mass media options are presented in Chapter 5.

Direct Response Plan

Direct response communications has a significant advantage over traditional mass media advertising; the direct results of the investment can be determined. The fact that direct response techniques can be accurately measured for success or failure makes it attractive to companies that stress accountability in their operations. It has taken considerable time for large companies to adopt direct response techniques (see Figure 2.13). The negative image of direct mail advertising, for example, formerly made such a technique unattractive. Advancing technology, database marketing practices, and customer relationship management programs have fostered interest in marketing and communicating directly to individuals. Now all forms of direct response are popular. More details about direct response communications are included in Chapter 6.

Interactive Communications Plan

Earlier discussion about internet communications stated that acceptance of advertising messages online was growing very slowly. Online consumers perceive internet ads to be an intrusion, forgetting that the internet is a medium much like television or newspapers. However, with each passing year, as consumers spend more time online, the commercial aspects of the internet are becoming more acceptable. Certainly among youth, the internet is becoming the medium of choice for personal communications. Widespread acceptance of commercial communications is just around the corner.

Among the communications alternatives available to companies wanting to advertise online are banner ads, sponsorships at websites where a target market congregates, and email. Other interactive options include CD-ROMs and instant text messaging through mobile telephones. The advertisement for BMW motorcycles in Figure 2.13 on the next page includes a CD that shows the exhilaration of driving such a vehicle. Interactive communications strategies are discussed in more detail in Chapter 7.

Sales Promotion Plan

Sales promotions concentrate on reaching and influencing consumers, trade customers (distributors), and a company's sales force. Funds allocated to promotion strategies are traditionally divided between consumer promotions and trade promotions. Consumer promotions focus on objectives such as encouraging trial purchase, repeat purchase, or simply getting customers to buy a product in greater quantity. Refer to Figure 2.14 on page 63 for an illustration of a promotion incentive designed to achieve trial and multiple purchases.

Trade promotions are designed to encourage merchandising and marketing support among distributors. Getting a product listed and on the store shelves of major supermarkets,

FIGURE **2.13** **A BMW Motorcycle Advertisement Includes a CD to Enhance the Connection with the Customer**

85mb worth of information...
unlimited worth of riding experiences.

for example, requires offering financial incentives to retailers such as Safeway, Sobeys, Loblaws, and others. In Canada, prominent retailers have significant clout with manufacturers and as a result considerable sums are spent on trade promotions each year. Sales promotion planning is discussed in detail in Chapter 8.

Public Relations Plan

Public relations involve communicating with various groups beyond customers. For example, companies communicate with governments, prospective shareholders, the financial community, the media, and community groups. Typically, the goal of such communications is to enhance the company's public image. Public relations can be either corporate oriented or product oriented. At the corporate level, public relations are an important communications tool in times of crisis, to show the public what the company is doing to resolve the crisis. PR can also be used to tell the public about the positive things a company is doing, say for example, creating awareness of its environmental programs.

FIGURE **2.14** **Manufacturers Offer Incentives to Encourage Trial and Repeat Purchases**

Source: Kraft Canada

In a product sense, public relations play a role in generating interest in new products or spreading "news" about an existing product. Such communications are the result of a public relations plan that is designed to secure media support for newsworthy information. The nature of public relations is such that written or broadcast news about a company or its products can be of more value. A third-party endorsement through public relations can have greater impact on consumers than does advertising. Furthermore, companies spend considerable sums on advertising, whereas public relations is an "unpaid" form of communications for the most part. For that reason alone, its usefulness must be exploited. Public relations planning is presented in more detail in Chapter 9.

Event Marketing and Sponsorships

Events and sponsorships now play a more prominent role in the marketing communications mix. Organizations are attracted to events because they present opportunities to reach a target market as a group in one location. The audience can be quite large in the case of a major-league sports event or comparatively small, such as a local theatre production. Decisions about what events to support are important and careful planning is needed if the organization is to achieve maximum value from participation. A variety of communications elements must be built into the plan to show how the event will be supported. All of this information is documented in the communications plan. Event marketing and sponsorship planning are presented in Chapter 10.

Personal Selling Plan

Personal selling plays a key role, especially in business-to-business market situations. As indicated earlier, personal selling techniques create desire and action. The role of a sales representative is to present the benefits of products and show how they resolve a customer's problem. The sales representative is also responsible for presenting the marketing and merchandising support plans to distributors who resell the company's products. In this regard, there is a direct link to the media advertising, trade promotion, consumer promotion, and event marketing and sponsorship components of the marketing communications plan. Customers must be made aware of all activities that will potentially influence sales.

A sales manager directs the activities of the sales department and is responsible for setting sales objectives that are part of the marketing communications plan. Arriving at realistically achievable sales objectives calls for much discussion and negotiation with marketing executives. The manager is also responsible for developing the sales strategies and tactics that will be employed by the sales representatives. Personal selling is discussed in more detail in Chapter 11.

MEASURING AND EVALUATING MARKETING COMMUNICATIONS

The final step in the marketing and marketing communications planning process involves measurement and evaluation. It is essential that an organization monitor all programs in order to distinguish effective activities from ineffective activities. There's a famous expression about marketing planning and budgeting: "50 percent of my budget works and 50 percent doesn't work. But I don't know which is which." Yes, a lot of marketing decisions are made on instinct, but many more are based on hard and fast measurements.

In marketing communications, some activities are difficult to measure and very often too much burden is placed on communications. It is such a visible aspect of marketing that it convenient for senior managers to be critical of it. Each element of marketing communications should be accountable for what it can accomplish. If it is advertising, awareness scores can be measured; if it's public relations, brand mentions in the press may be a means of measuring success; if it's event marketing, the number of new clients that come on stream may be a useful measure. Each component can be measured and evaluated in unique and different ways. This topic is discussed in detail in Chapter 12.

Summary

Strategic planning is an integrated process that involves developing plans at three different levels of an organization. The planning process is cyclical and is subject to constant change based on conditions in the marketplace. To stay on top of things, an organization monitors changes in the economy, competitive activity, consumers, technology, and laws and regulations.

A marketing communication plan (its direction and content) is influenced by a marketing plan and a corporate plan. When one plan is complete, it provides direction to the next plan. Planning usually starts with the corporate plan, a document prepared by senior executives. Corporate planning starts with the development of a mission statement followed by corporate objectives and strategies. When deciding upon a strategy, the organization evaluates its marketing strength, degree of competition, financial resources, research and development capabilities, and management expertise.

Marketing planning involves four steps: analyzing market opportunities, developing marketing strategies, planning and implementing marketing programs, and managing marketing programs. In performing these steps, target markets are identified, positioning strategies are developed, and marketing strategies and tactics for all components of the marketing mix and marketing communications mix are documented in a marketing plan.

The marketing communications plan identifies the various communications objectives for the year and the strategies that will be employed to achieve them. The plan is subdivided into specific areas, depending on which components of the mix will be employed. The advertising plan focuses on creative and media decisions. In the creative plan, objectives and strategies (what to say and how to say it) are identified. The media plan states the media objectives by identifying the target market, how often its members should be reached, and when they should be reached. The media strategies rationalize the use of media alternatives and provide detailed information about how the budget is allocated.

If the plan is an integrated plan, other components of the mix are included. Depending on the situation a brand or company faces, the plan could include sales promotions, public relations, events and sponsorships, direct response communications, interactive communications, and personal selling. Objectives, strategies, and tactics for each are included in the plan. The goal is to have a unified plan—all forms of marketing communications delivering a single message to a target market in a convincing manner.

Key Terms

acquisition strategy	46	media plan	61
contingency plan	46	mission statement	45
corporate objective	45	monopolistic competition	39
corporate plan	43	new product development strategy	46
creative plan	59	oligopoly	39
direct competition	39	penetration strategy	46
indirect competition	39	positioning	52
marketing communications plan	57	positioning strategy statement	52
marketing control	56	strategic alliance	46
marketing objective	53	strategic planning	38
marketing plan	43	SWOT analysis	48
marketing planning	46	tactics (execution)	55
marketing strategy	53	target profile	53

Review Questions

1. What are the external trends and conditions that should be considered when commencing a new planning cycle?

2. What are the key components of a corporate plan? What guidelines does the corporate plan provide to operational plans such as marketing and marketing communications?

3. What is a mission statement and what role does it play in planning?

4. Marketing planning involves four essential steps. Identify and briefly describe each step.

5. What role does a positioning strategy statement play in developing a marketing strategy?

6. Marketing strategies are the master plans for achieving objectives. What does this statement mean?

7. What is the difference between marketing strategy and marketing execution?

8. What is meant by marketing control and how does it influence marketing planning?

9. What are the essential decision areas for a creative plan and a media plan?

10. What is the relationship between the various components of an integrated marketing communications plan?

Discussion and Application Questions

1. "Marketing communications objectives are diverse by nature but a good campaign must have a specific focus." What does this mean?

2. Some of the world's leading marketing organizations are in financial and marketing trouble—McDonalds, the GAP, and Levi Strauss, to name a few. Has their position been affected by poor planning? Conduct some online research on one of these companies and try to formulate a position on the matter. Can you offer any recommendations to improve the situation?

3. Review the IMC Highlight **Continuous Improvement at Canadian Tire**. Despite intense competition from American retailers, Canadian Tire continues to roll on. What are the key factors contributing to its success?

4. Evaluate the marketing situation for the following companies. What makes them unique and what is their differential advantage(s) compared to their primary competitors? Develop a positioning strategy statement for each company based on your assessment of the situation.

   Canadian Tire

   Tim Hortons

   Roots

5. Using a variety of online sources, conduct a market analysis for a branded product of your choosing. The market analysis should include the following information:

   a) Market size and growth

   b) Importance of regional markets

   c) Market segment analysis (which segments are growing, declining, etc.)

   d) Seasonal analysis

   What conclusions can you draw from your analysis?

6. Compare and contrast the marketing communications strategies of two competing brands (a brand leader and a brand challenger). Do these brands use all elements of the marketing communications mix or do they selectively use only certain elements? What conclusions can you draw based on your analysis of each brand? Some brands to consider might be:

   a) Coca-Cola and Pepsi-Cola

   b) Colgate toothpaste and Crest toothpaste

   c) Dove soap and Oil of Olay soap

7. Analyze the marketing communications strategies for an automobile (car or truck) of your choosing. Based on the images portrayed in any and all forms of marketing communications, describe in detail the target market that automobile is pursuing. Provide a profile based on demographic, psychographic, and geographic characteristics.

Endnotes

1 Philip Kotler, *A Framework for Marketing Management*, 2nd edition (Upper Saddle River, NJ: Prentice-Hall, 2003), p. 104.

2 Tyler Hamilton, "Cash Is in the E-mail," *Toronto Star*, February 11, 2002, pp. E1, E2.

3 Patrick Brethour, "Women Narrow Internet Gender Gap," *Globe and Mail*, March 27, 2001, pp. B1, B2.

4 Colin Perkel, "Consumer Laws to Be Revamped," *Toronto Star*, August 11, 2001, p. E5.

5 Bombardier Annual Report, 2002.

6 Marina Strauss, "Healthy Foods Taking Bite out of Market," *Globe and Mail*, September 28, 2002, p. B1, B5.

7 Brad Foss, "Pepsi Seals Quaker Deal," *Globe and Mail*, December 5, 2000, p. B4.

8 Canadian National Railway Company, Annual Report, 2001.

9 "Money Hog," an advertorial appearing in the *National Post*, Driver's Edge Section, January 3, 2002, p. DO11.

10 Lesley Young, "Shampoo Shakeup," *Marketing*, May 27, 2002, p. 9.

BRANDING STRATEGY

After studying this chapter you will be able to:

describe the concept of branding and the role it plays in marketing communications and other business-building programs,

identify the various components of a brand,

describe the benefits of branding for organizations and consumers,

characterize the various stages of brand loyalty,

describe the role and importance of brand positioning and its relationship to marketing communications plans,

explain various brand positioning strategies commonly used in marketing communications, and

describe the role and influence of packaging and product design in the brand-building process.

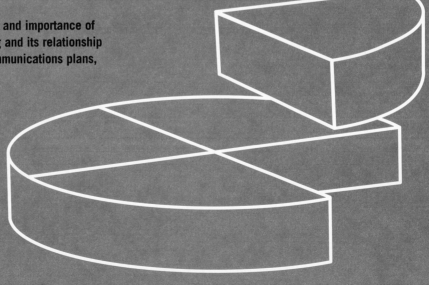

Think of marketing and marketing communications as a loop. The loop starts somewhere and ends somewhere, but exactly where? Well, it starts with the brand and ends with the brand. Marketing and marketing communications programs create awareness for the brand (the start of the loop). All kinds of messages are sent to consumers through a variety of touch-points such as packaging, personal selling, events, promotions, news articles, and advertising. Collectively, these messages heighten the interest and desire for the brand. While all this is happening, competing brands are doing the same thing. The goal for all brands: to get the consumer into the store to buy their brand. The consumer is now standing in front of a store shelf looking at all the different brands. Which one does he or she buy? The customer takes action and places one brand in the shopping cart. Which one? The loop just closed.

What this loop principle suggests is that every form of communication is going to have some kind of impact. The impact of the message and its ability to stimulate action are determined by what a brand has to offer (e.g., a compelling reason why someone should buy it) and the convincing way in which the message is delivered to potential customers. Essentially, the brand offering and the message communicated to consumers form the backbone of brand strategy and positioning strategy. This chapter provides insights into how brand strategy and positioning strategy are developed and show the influence of marketing communications in developing a relationship between the customer and the brand. Communications is the glue that holds or binds the customer to the brand.[1]

Defining the Brand

Just what is a brand? Ask the question and you will get hundreds of different answers. Every "expert" has a different take on what a brand is. The *Dictionary of Marketing Terms* defines a **brand** as an identifying mark, symbol, word(s), or combination of same, that separates one company's product from another company's product. Brand is a comprehensive term that includes all brand names and trademarks.[2]

Brand

An identifying mark, symbol, word or words, or combination of mark and words that separates one product from another product.

In today's hypercompetitive marketing environment, branding is a hot button. Marketing executives are busy trying to find or build their brand essence, brand architecture, or brand DNA. Maybe it's a little overdone! That said, brands and branding have been around for centuries; only recently has the concept worked its way into everyday conversation. Not surprisingly, even the experts have different interpretations about what a brand is. Here's how some experts define a brand[3]:

> A promise that is publicly conveyed to customers by everything they can observe: the brand name and logo, advertising, the way they are treated by representatives of the brand, signage, storefront, billing statements, displays, shopping environment... *Rodney Underhill, Richards Group, Dallas*

> A name, logo and/or symbol that evokes, in existing and potential customers, a perception of "added value" for which they will pay a premium price. *John Torella, J.C. Williams Group, Toronto*

> A product with a personality. *Chris Staples, Rethink, Vancouver*

While these people disagree on what a brand is, there is a common thread, and that is that marketing communications in any form has an impact on how customers perceive a brand. It seems that a brand is more than just a tangible product. It can embrace intangible characteristics as well. Customer perceptions of brands are largely based on the brand name and what it stands for. It is an image they hold of a brand over an extended period and that image is based on what they have learned about the brand. For example, such brand names as Porsche or Jaguar suggest a certain quality or status. Nike sells shoes, but the brand represents a kind of rebellious spirit. Apple is a user-friendly, different kind of computer, and Volvo is well known for being a safe automobile. These images are the result of good marketing and marketing communications programs. Perhaps Landor Inc., a branding consulting firm, offers the best and simplest definition of a brand: a brand is "the sum of all characteristics, tangible and intangible, that make the offer unique."[4]

Based on the definition of a brand and the thoughts on what a brand is, as provided above, it can be seen that different components of a brand work together to distinguish one product from another. The key components of a brand are:

Brand Name
That part of a brand that can be spoken.

Wordmark
The stylized treatment of the brand name.

Brandmark or Logo
A unique design, symbol, or other special representation of a brand name or company name.

Brand Name The **brand name** is the part of the brand that can be spoken. It may consist of a word, letter, or group of words and letters. Nike, Starbucks, Gatorade, WD40, eBay, Tide, and Wal-Mart are brand names. Brand names are usually presented with their own unique font style. The stylized treatment of the brand name serves the same function as a symbol and is referred to as a **wordmark**.

Brandmark or Logo The unique design, symbol, or other special representation of a brand name or company name is referred to as the **brandmark** or **logo**. Some interesting brandmarks include Apple computer's famous apple with a bite taken out of it, Coca-Cola Ltd.'s unique bottle design and red cap, and Nike's famous swoosh (see Figure 3.1). As of 2000, 97 percent of American citizens recognized Nike's swoosh logo. From a marketing perspective, you couldn't ask for anything more. However, so ubiquitous is the logo that it represents negative images to many consumers—for many it represents two social ills: the commercialization of sports and the globalization of capitalism.[5] That's not good for business!

FIGURE **3.1** **A Selection of Famous Logos**

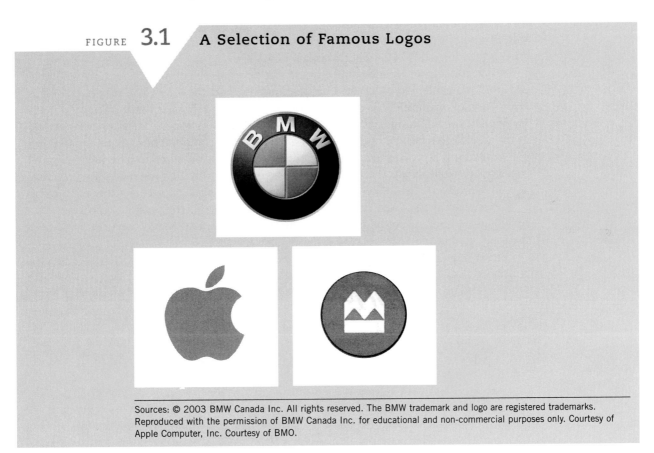

Sources: © 2003 BMW Canada Inc. All rights reserved. The BMW trademark and logo are registered trademarks. Reproduced with the permission of BMW Canada Inc. for educational and non-commercial purposes only. Courtesy of Apple Computer, Inc. Courtesy of BMO.

Trademark That part of a brand that is granted legal protection so that only the owner can use it. The symbol ™ is the designation of a registered trademark. Trademarks can include the brand names and symbols described above. "Coke"® and "Coca-Cola"® and the unique style in which these names are printed are registered trademarks of Coca-Cola Ltd.

What to name a brand is a critical decision. Consequently, companies spend considerable time and money developing and testing brand names. When you think of it, virtually every marketing activity undertaken revolves around the brand name. It has to be distinctive and meaningful. It has to be the right name. Considering the proliferation of brands in the marketplace, there are a lot of brand names out there that aren't right.

Brand names come in many different forms. They can be based on people (Calvin Klein and Elizabeth Arden), places (Air France, Air Canada, and Monte Carlo), animals (Mustang and Dove), inherent product meaning (Ticketmaster and Lean Cuisine), product attributes (Bounty towels and DieHard batteries), or they can be completely made up to simply sound scientific or attractive (e.g., Intel, Murano, and Miata).

Brands are more than just a tangible product. A company adds other dimensions that differentiate it in some way from other products designed to meet the same need. These differences may be rational and tangible, or they may be emotional or intangible entities related to what the brand represents. Through marketing communications, the "personality" of a brand evolves, and the combination of brand attributes (tangibles) and brand personality (intangibles) are what influence brand choices by consumers. The key for any brand is to be perceived as offering something unique. You could probably name at least ten different brands of deodorant. Why does one person buy Gillette, another Mennen, another Right Guard, another Axe, and so on?

Brand management has played a key role in the growth and development of Mazda automobiles. "Zoom-Zoom," a phrase that has been popularized based on the success of an integrated marketing communications campaign, expresses Mazda's unique combination of brand attributes and brand personality. For more insight into Mazda's branding strategy, read the IMC Highlight **Mazda's DNA**.

Sony
www.sony.ca

When something unique about a brand stands out in the customer's mind, favourable decisions are made. Consider the brand name Sony and the image you may have of this brand in your own mind. No doubt you recognize Sony as a brand that makes good quality products and a brand with a good reputation. *Forbes* magazine describes Sony as one of the world's five best companies. Such a position is a compliment to Sony's marketing vision. Among Sony's innovations are the VCR and the Walkman. The key to Sony's success is twofold: it was the first electronics company to build products of high quality as well as products that looked attractive—style is part of the brand equation. According to *Forbes*, "Sony consistently introduces products that delight people, capturing their imaginations. Sony's products stop you in your tracks. The brand acquires an almost mythical quality."[6]

Brands may be more that physical products and services. Whenever and wherever a consumer is choosing between alternatives, brands play a role in the decision-making process. Today, marketers are even branding products that were once described as commodities. Commodities such as milk (Neilsen and Beatrice), bananas (Chiquita), water (Perrier and Evian), pineapples (Dole), and microprocessors (Intel) are all branded. An extensive advertising campaign using a now famous phrase "Intel Inside" convinced the public that Intel's computer chips offered a higher level of performance than other chips. Consumers seek out computers that have the Intel chip.

Sears
www.sears.com

Endorsement
A situation where a celebrity speaks highly of an advertised product.

Branding also applies to retail organizations. Sears, for example, spends a considerable sum each year reminding customers what Sears stands for. It also advertises many of its private label brands, such as Kenmore, Craftsman, and Die Hard. These sub-brands have their own image and reputation and are perceived to be as good as manufacturer's branded goods. People (famous people) are branded. Consider how far the name Martha Stewart extends into the marketplace. Her name appears on magazines, books, catalogues, television, and radio shows, in merchandise available at Sears and Canadian Tire, and online. Diana Krall and Tiger Woods are people whose services (**endorsements**) are requested by various organizations. For endorsing products, they earn a considerable amount of money. The entertainment world thrives on branding. In fact, movies are the launching pad for the merchandise that is sold around the movie theme. Recent examples include *Star Wars*, *Lord of the Rings*, and *Hulk*.

MAZDA'S DNA

"Zoom-Zoom." It's a memorable slogan for a very effective advertising campaign. For the past four years, Mazda has been airing television commercials that are very different from anything it had done before. Gone is the previous message "The Practical Car, The Enjoyable Car. That's Mazda." The initial campaign that started in 1999 was based on the creative concept of "New Ideas That Stir Emotions." In 2002, that concept evolved into "Zoom-Zoom."

Let's trace the steps and see why Mazda altered its communications strategy. The "New Ideas That Stir Emotions" concept was to be a key aspect of Mazda's re-branding strategy. According to Mazda, the globalization of free markets, the emergence of "borderless" economies, and the subsequent intensification of competition mean the strength of a company's brand is more important than ever before. In fact, the development of a strong, consistent brand that consumers identify with is a necessary condition for survival in the marketplace.

Brand management is now the centre of Mazda's business strategy. One of the company's overall goals is to develop a keen understanding of Mazda target customers and to delight them through concentrated efforts in the areas of product, service, and communication. Mazda has become a customer-driven company that wants to attract customers to its brand and foster the development of a long-lasting, emotional connection with them.

The new communications campaign was part of a worldwide brand positioning strategy. Mazda describes its brand in terms of product attributes and personality. Like human DNA, the unique attributes of the product are distinctive design, exceptional functionality, and superbly responsive handling and performance. On the personality side, Mazda defines itself as stylish, insightful, and spirited. When these brand attributes and personality are combined you have "New Ideas That Stir Your Emotions." Now an integral aspect of Mazda's corporate culture, this strategic direction provides a foundation for developing new products, services, and communications at every level of the company.

In 2002, the campaign evolved into "Zoom-Zoom." Zoom-Zoom aims to recreate the fun-to-drive feeling of Mazda vehicles. Zoom-Zoom is a phrase children use when they imitate the sound of a car engine. It expresses fascination with motion experienced by a child playing with a toy car or riding a bike. The Mazda brand conveys this feeling in its products and Zoom-Zoom captures this feeling perfectly. Mazda offers driving experiences for customers who still have that childlike fascination with motion. This is the emotional connection that Mazda seeks with its customers. The Zoom-Zoom theme and the boy who appears in the commercials are easy to remember. It is a very likeable advertising campaign that has made an impact all over the world.

Adapted from <www.mazda.com> and <www.mazda.com.hk>.

The Benefits of Branding

Both consumers and the organization benefit from branding. Some of the benefits for consumers are as follows:

- Over time, the brand name suggests a certain level of quality. Consumers know what to expect; they trust and have confidence in the brand.
- There can be psychological rewards for possessing certain brands. For example, buying a brand new BMW automobile might suggest achievement to the owner. The automobile says something about the drivers; it expresses their self-image.
- Brands distinguish competitive offerings, allowing consumers to make informed decisions. Such brand names as Cup-A-Soup (Lipton), Mr. Clean (Procter & Gamble), and Frosted Flakes (Kellogg's) suggest clear messages or benefits about the product.

Over time, a relationship develops between a consumer and the brand; it's like a bond. Consumers offer their trust and loyalty in return for consistent product quality from the brand. A brand is a promise delivered. A brand protects its place in the consumer's mind by keeping its promise.[7] Good brands are personal. They become an integral part of people's lives by forging emotional connections.[8]

Brands play a key role and offer numerous benefits to an organization as well. At the operational level, they help to plan production runs, maintain inventory counts, and facilitate order processing and delivery. In a marketing context, the key benefits are:

Unique Selling Point (USP)

The primary benefit of a product or service that distinguishes it from its competitors.

- A good brand name communicates the point of difference, or **unique selling point (USP)**, and highlights the distinctive value added. A name such as Lean Cuisine, for example, addresses two benefits: "lean" communicates low calories and "cuisine" implies it tastes good. The brand name is meaningful and pleasant sounding.

- Branding allows for the creation and development of an image. For example, Volvo is recognized as being a "safe" automobile. Nike suggests an independent spirit. Maytag stands for dependability. For these brands, extensive advertising campaigns have instilled such images in the customer's mind.

- Satisfied customers will make repeat purchases and hopefully remain loyal to the brand. Such loyalty stabilizes market share and provides for certain efficiencies in production and marketing. Reliable estimates of future sales facilitate internal brand planning.

Creating and using brand names are crucial aspects of product management, since the attributes of the brand, the package, the logo, and brand image collectively influence other marketing and marketing communications activities. A brand name stands for much more than simply differentiating one brand from another. For more information about the importance of a brand name see the IMC Highlight **A Good Name Means Everything**.

BRAND LOYALTY

Brand Loyalty

The degree of attachment to a particular brand expressed by a consumer.

Brand loyalty is defined as the degree of consumer attachment to a particular brand. Loyalty is influenced by such factors as marketing communications (what is said about a brand), family or peer pressure, and friendship with a salesperson. For example, someone intending to buy a new car might return to the same dealer and person he or she has bought from before. Satisfaction based on experience with a product or an individual breeds loyalty.

Brand loyalty is measured in three distinct stages: brand recognition, brand preference, and brand insistence (see Figure 3.2).[9]

FIGURE **3.2**   **The Stages of Brand Loyalty**

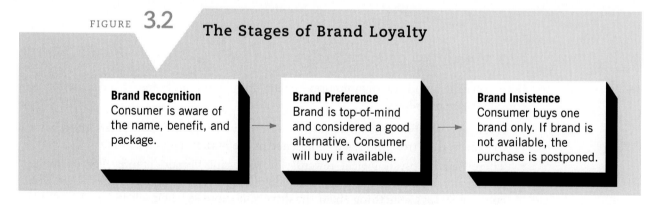

Brand Recognition
Consumer is aware of the name, benefit, and package.

Brand Preference
Brand is top-of-mind and considered a good alternative. Consumer will buy if available.

Brand Insistence
Consumer buys one brand only. If brand is not available, the purchase is postponed.

Brand Recognition

Customer awareness of the brand name and package.

Brand Preference

The situation where a brand is perceived as an acceptable alternative by a customer and will be purchased if it is available.

In the early stage of a brand's life, the marketing objective is to create **brand recognition**. It is imperative to communicate the brand name, the unique selling point, and what the product looks like (e.g., the package if it is a consumer good, or the look and style if it is a shopping good such as an automobile or appliance). Incentives such as coupons and low-cost financing may be offered to encourage an initial purchase.

When a brand achieves the status of **brand preference**, it is on a short list of brand alternatives that the consumer will consider buying. Such a position is good because consumers only retain a select group of brand names in their minds for any product category.

A GOOD NAME MEANS EVERYTHING

If it's true that "you are what you drive," then branding in the automobile industry involves crucial decisions about brand names. Car companies spend millions each year developing, testing, marketing, researching, and registering new names.

According to Frank Delano, president of a New York–based brand specialist company, "A good name is everything. The name is king for any product. It's the most important thing in the marketing picture." A name says as much about the car as it does about the consumer. Are you a Taurus or an Aries? Are you a Cougar or a Mustang?

Historically speaking, car names have run the gamut. They have been inspired by distinctive, affluent places: Park Avenue, Fifth Avenue, and Capri. They have stressed social rank: Marquis, Diplomat, and Ambassador. They have been exotic animals: Viper, Mustang, and Cobra. They have been rugged geographic terrains: Dakota, Montana, and Yukon.

Cars have become the mechanical extension of the driver's personality. Your car tells others about your status, your preferences, and the socioeconomic group you belong to—or wish to belong to. Executives on the rise love those luxury European sports cars!

According to Ian Forsyth, president of Nissan Canada, "A name that can be used globally, or at least in large geographic areas of the world, is a true asset." Such a strategy reduces the investment in advertising necessary to build and sustain a brand. For this reason, Nissan invents its names. Among them are Sentra, Altima, Maxima, and Murano.

Most manufacturers hope they never have to change a name, but car brands do come and go. Perhaps the real test of a good brand name is how memorable it is and how quickly a consumers can link it to a manufacturer. Good names have longevity—Honda still markets the Civic (launched in 1973), Accord (1976), and Prelude (1978). It's not a coincidence that Honda and many of its sub-brands are consistently given high ranks for product and service quality. A classic example of good brand strategy and good marketing (in addition to a good product!).

Despite the time and energy that car companies invest in brand names, there have been all kinds of failures. The classic is the Edsel, a 1950s car named for one of Henry Ford's sons. So unsuccessful was the car, the name became synonymous with automotive futility. Just recently, General Motors dropped the Pontiac Aztek from its lineup. Rudely nicknamed "Ass Crack" among competitors, the radically styled not-quite-a-car, not-quite-a-truck "crossover utility vehicle" featured a built-in cooler and foldout tent but never captured the public's imagination. No amount of marketing communications could convince enough buyers to take a chance, and endure the stares and taunts of fellow drivers.

Adapted from Vinay Menon, "Wheels of Fortune in a Car's Name," *Toronto Star*, January 24, 2002, pp. A1, A22, and Paul Brent, "Farewell, Old Dog," *National Post*, June 7, 2003, p. FP6.

Furthermore, it is an indication that the message strategies and other marketing strategies are working; the customer knows something about the brand, has evaluated it in relation to his or her needs, and will purchase it if available when it is needed.

Brand Insistence

A situation where the consumer searches the market for the specific brand.

At the **brand insistence** stage, a consumer will search the market extensively for a particular brand. No alternatives are acceptable, and if the brand is not available the consumer will likely postpone the purchase until it is. Such an enviable position shows the type of bond that can develop between a brand and a consumer. As suggested earlier, consumers want consistent quality from their brands. The famous Coca-Cola marketing debacle of 1985 confirms how brand insistence works. Coca-Cola made the decision to replace Coca-Cola with a new formula. When the change was implemented the backlash from customers was so swift and strong that the company had to bring back the original formula under the name Coca-Cola Classic. Some critics insist that Coca-Cola is a brand that has gone beyond brand insistence. So strong is the bond with consumers, the product cannot be changed, ever.

A Hundred Monkeys
(naming and branding
consultants)
www.ahundredmonkeys
.com

Since one of the tasks of marketing is to keep customers loyal, smart companies plan and implement loyalty programs. Starbucks encourages loyalty through a coffee card program and Canadian Tire offers Canadian Tire "money" that is redeemable on future purchases. Loyalty-oriented marketing programs are presented in Chapter 8.

Consumers in the brand insistence stage often become advocates for the brand. So convinced are they that their brand is the best, they will openly recommend it to others. As discussed in Chapter 1, a word-of-mouth network is a powerful communications tool that influences buying decisions. To illustrate, many users of Apple computers are advocates. They often belong to Mac user groups (MUGs) and frequently end up in "religious wars" with PC users. The same can be said of owners of Harley-Davidson motorcycles, commonly know as HOGs. To Harley owners, there is no other kind of motorcycle.

BRAND EQUITY

Brand Equity
The value of a brand to its owners.

Brand equity is a confusing term that has been historically defined different ways for different purposes. For our purposes, **brand equity** is defined as the value of a brand in its holistic sense to its owners as a corporate asset.[10] The value of the asset is the result of effective marketing strategies over an extended period, and reflects the brand's position and status in the marketplace, and in the hearts and minds of the customers who purchase it regularly. In the Coca-Cola example cited earlier, the attitudes and feelings that consumers showed for Coca-Cola suggests it has extremely high brand equity. Brand equity is influenced by several variables: brand name awareness, the degree of loyalty expressed by customers, perceived quality, and the brand's association with a certain attribute. The quality and effectiveness of marketing and marketing communications play a key role in linking brands and consumers together. Coca-Cola is consistently ranked as the leading global brand in terms of value, at US$69.64 billion.[11] Eight of the world's top 10 brands are American (see Figure 3.3).

Starbucks
www.starbucks.ca

To illustrate the concept of brand equity and how it develops, consider the Starbucks brand. In less than a decade, Starbucks transformed itself from a fledgling whole-bean coffee retail chain into a globally recognized coffee emporium for gourmet enthusiasts. At Starbucks, the consumer sips gourmet coffee in a warm and friendly environment. Each store is carefully designed to enhance everything the customers see, hear, smell, or taste. Company management envisioned Starbucks to become a "personal treat" for its customers, whether it was a convenient stop to and from work, a refreshing break in the day or a place to relax at night. It would be a comfortable gathering spot between the workplace and the home.[12] The environment of the store (the added value) complemented the pleasurable coffee-tasting experience (the physical product). With annual sales of close to US$3 billion and a core group of very loyal customers, Starbucks is a brand with high brand equity. Starbucks presently ranks 93rd on the global brand value list and is on the rise.

Building the Brand

Building a brand (building brand equity) is the responsibility of the brand manager (or category manager or marketing manager depending on a company's organizational structure). A **brand manager** is responsible for developing and implementing the marketing plans for the brands he or she is responsible for. The process of building a brand involves four essential steps (see Figure 3.4 for a visual illustration)[13]:

Brand Manager
An individual assigned responsibility for the development and implementation of marketing programs for a specific product or group of products.

1. Identify and establish brand values and positioning strategy.
2. Plan and implement brand marketing programs.
3. Measure and interpret brand performance.
4. Grow and sustain brand equity (managing a brand through its life cycle).

Since the concept of brand equity has already been discussed, the remaining discussion in this chapter will focus on brand values and positioning, and the development of marketing programs.

FIGURE **3.3**

Brand Equity: The World's Top 10 Brands

Rank	Brand	Brand Value (US$ billion)	Country of Ownership
1	Coca-Cola	70.45	U.S.
2	Microsoft	65.17	U.S.
3	IBM	51.77	U.S.
4	GE	42.34	U.S.
5	Intel	31.1	U.S.
6	Nokia	29.44	Finland
7	Disney	28.04	U.S.
8	McDonald's	24.70	U.S.
9	Marlboro	22.18	U.S.
10	Mercedes	21.37	Germany

Some other popular brands are ranked as follows: Ford (14th), Sony (20th), Budweiser (22nd), Pepsi-Cola (23rd), Dell (29th), and Nike (33rd). No Canadian brand was ranked in the top 100 brands.

The criteria considered for ranking brands include:

- the percentage of revenues generated by the brand,
- projected net earnings for that segment of the business,
- a charge for the cost of owning the assets is deducted from the brand value,
- strength of potential earnings based on the brand's market leadership, its stability, and its ability to cross geographical and cultural borders.

Brand rankings were calculated by Interbrand Corp.

Adapted from "The 100 Top Brands," *Business Week*, August 4, 2003, p. 72. Reprinted by special permission of The McGraw-Hill Companies, Inc.

ESTABLISHING CORE VALUES AND BRAND POSITIONING

Core Values
The primary attributes and benefits a brand delivers to the customer.

Attribute
A descriptive feature of a product.

Benefit
The value a customer attaches to a brand attribute.

What does a brand stand for? The answer to that question will relate to the core values of a brand. **Core values** are the primary attributes and benefits a brand delivers to the customer. An **attribute** is a descriptive feature. A **benefit** is the value consumers attach to a brand attribute. Very often the core values can be expressed in a very short statement about the brand. Here are a few examples:

- Sunlight laundry detergent: No matter how dirty your clothes get, Sunlight gets them clean.
- Tide laundry detergent: Removes the really tough stains from any type of material.
- Cheer laundry detergent: Gets clothes clean in any water temperature.

The laundry detergent category is a large and very competitive product category. These examples demonstrate the primary attribute and benefit of three leading brands. True to form, they all have the same proprietary benefit but each brand takes a different angle on how to communicate the benefit. That's brand differentiation. Sunlight uses the tagline "Go ahead. Get dirty" in its advertising and shows people participating in outdoor activities where clothes really do get dirty, and then Sunlight comes to the rescue. Tide advertises that it gets the "tough stains" out. The other brands have their own unique approaches to advertising as well. For an illustration, see Figure 3.5.

FIGURE **3.4**

The Brand-Building Process

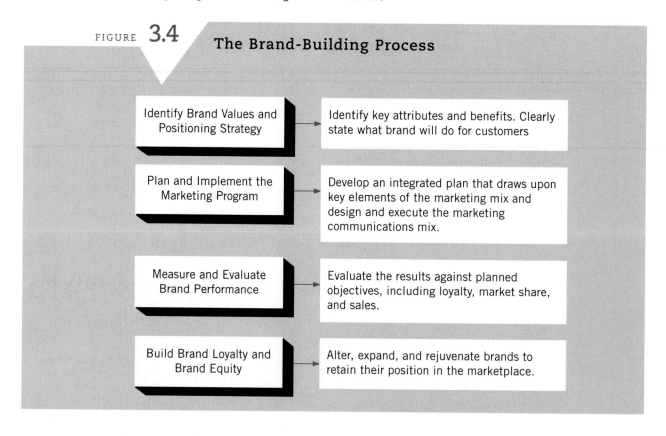

Identify Brand Values and Positioning Strategy	Identify key attributes and benefits. Clearly state what brand will do for customers
Plan and Implement the Marketing Program	Develop an integrated plan that draws upon key elements of the marketing mix and design and execute the marketing communications mix.
Measure and Evaluate Brand Performance	Evaluate the results against planned objectives, including loyalty, market share, and sales.
Build Brand Loyalty and Brand Equity	Alter, expand, and rejuvenate brands to retain their position in the marketplace.

Brand Positioning Concepts

Positioning

The selling concept that motivates purchase, or the image that marketers desire a brand to have in the minds of consumers.

As discussed in Chapter 2, **positioning** is the selling concept that motivates purchase, or the image that marketers desire a brand to have in the minds of customers. It is a strategy influenced by core brand values and the values offered by competing brands. Simply stated, each brand wants to differentiate itself from competitive offerings. Therefore, positioning involves designing and marketing a product to meet the needs of a target market and creating the appropriate appeals to make the product stand out from the competition in the minds of the target market. The result is a clearly defined positioning strategy statement that provides guidance for all marketing and marketing communications strategies. The strategy statement provides a compelling reason why potential customers should buy the brand. Figure 3.6 illustrates the importance of positioning.

Typically, a brand sticks to a single-benefit positioning strategy, but for many brands and companies the competition is so intense that additional benefits become the focus of marketing communications. For example, Wal-Mart focuses on its low prices, a value-oriented positioning strategy, but given the degree of competition and the expectations of retail shoppers, Wal-Mart also promotes friendly service and product selection. Subway focuses on the health benefits from eating fresh food, but promotes all of the different breads that the sandwiches are served on. There are products that are specifically designed to offer multiple benefits and by doing so may have an edge on the competition. The introduction of Colgate 2in1 toothpaste in a small plastic container is such an example: the product combines the primary benefit of cavity prevention with an additional benefit such as fresher breath or whiter teeth—an attractive selling point. To remain competitive, Crest launched a similar line that combines two of their leading brands in toothpaste. Crest toothpaste now includes Scope mouthwash in its formula.

FIGURE **3.5**   **Brands Differentiate by Focusing on a Unique Attribute**

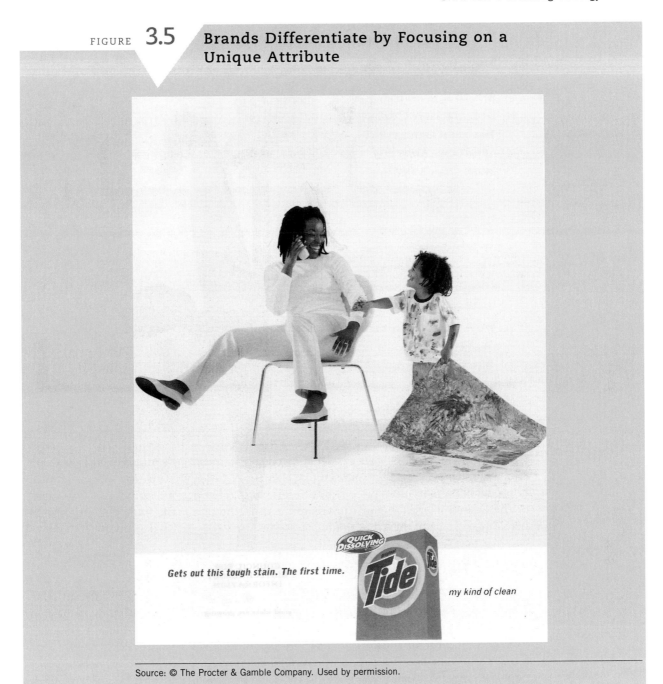

Source: © The Procter & Gamble Company. Used by permission.

The positioning strategy statement should be clear, concise, and uncomplicated while addressing the target market's need and the primary benefit to be offered. Here is an actual positioning strategy statement for the Visa credit card:

> To reinforce our leadership position in the credit card market, and to establish it as the preferred provider for all future products.

One can start to see how such a statement is used as input for developing a communications strategy. All consumer-directed communications for Visa use the tagline "All you need" as a means of summarizing their primary benefit. When you look back at the positioning statement, the relationship between the positioning strategy and the communications strategy starts to crystallize. For an illustration of Visa advertising, see Figure 3.7.

FIGURE **3.6** **The Importance of Positioning**

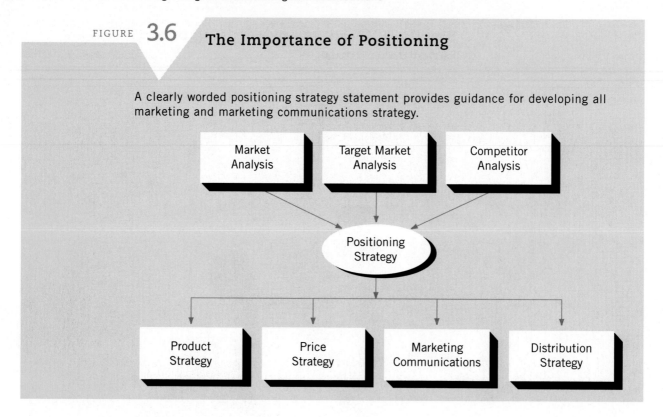

A clearly worded positioning strategy statement provides guidance for developing all marketing and marketing communications strategy.

There are all kinds of ways a product can be positioned in the minds of customers but typically they relate back to some crucial element of the marketing mix such as product or product differentiation, price (low or high price), channel of distribution advantages, or the desired image a brand can create for itself through marketing communications. Let's discuss some of these positioning strategies.

PRODUCT DIFFERENTIATION

Product Differentiation Strategy

A plan of action for communicating meaningful attributes and benefits of a product to a target market.

Here's what the product is! Here's what the product does! That's product differentiation —nothing could be more straightforward. When a **product differentiation strategy** is employed, the product will communicate meaningful and valued differences in order to distinguish itself from competitive offerings. Such differences focus specifically on what the product may offer, and refer to the form of the product (size, shape, or physical structure), performance quality (it lasts longer!), durability (ability to withstand stress), reliability (it won't break down), or style (the look and appearance of the product or package).

To illustrate product differentiation positioning, consider the launch of Oscar Meyer's Leaner Lunchables (a Kraft product). Regular Lunchables were experiencing flat sales largely due to negative publicity generated by the media attention given to the childhood obesity epidemic. Lunchables' high fat and sodium content was mentioned in the media as an example of the growing problem.[14] The new leaner line is designed to satisfy nutritional requirements and still offer the convenience parents look for when putting lunches together. Lunchables offer solid nutritional content in a fun product that kids enjoy—a great combination for parents who are confused over what to buy their children for lunch.

In the fast-food restaurant category, Harvey's has taken a bold step to differentiate itself from other chains. While a perception exists that fast food is fattening, and competitors such as McDonald's and Wendy's are promoting healthier menus, Harvey's is returning to its roots and promoting great-tasting grilled hamburgers and serving them

FIGURE **3.7** The Phrase "All You Need" Summarizes Visa's Positioning Strategy

IF LIFE WERE LIKE THAT, YOU WOULDN'T NEED A *VISA* CARD.

Source: Visa Canada Association. Photography by Shin Sagino.

with the toppings that their customers want. They also launched the Big Harv, a 6-ounce burger (see Figure 3.8). Harvey's does offer healthier choices. They just don't tout the fact. Harvey's identifies itself with the guy who likes to barbecue beef.[15] Harvey's new advertising slogan aptly portrays their positioning strategy: "Long live the grill."

FIGURE **3.8** Harvey's Differentiates from Other Fast Food Restaurants by Promoting Grilled Hamburgers

Source: Harvey's Restaurants.

BRAND LEADERSHIP POSITIONING

Leadership Positioning
A marketing strategy in which a product presents itself as a preferred choice among customers.

As the name suggests, **leadership positioning** is a strategy often employed by brand leaders. Good marketing and marketing strategies from the past have helped such a product achieve an enviable position in the marketplace and in the minds of customers. These brands have high brand equity. Therefore, the message such a brand delivers is designed to reinforce its lofty position. Probably the classic example (pardon the pun) of leadership positioning is Coca-Cola Classic. In most North American markets, Coca-Cola Classic is the number-one brand, and in terms of brand equity it is recognized as the most valuable brand name globally. In advertising, Coca-Cola Classic struts its stuff. The brand has used phrases such as "Coke is It," "Can't beat the real thing," "Always Coca-Cola," and "Real" to reinforce its position.

A few years ago, Hall's cough drops launched an advertising campaign featuring a hoarse-throated, very bad golfer unable to yell "fore" to warn other golfers of his stray shots. The ad campaign repositioned the brand somewhat in the consumer's mind by moving it beyond the winter cold season. The campaign helped grow the category of which Hall's held 70 percent market share, and the brand had a significant boost in sales in the off-season.[16] Hall's is the undisputed market leader and continues to grow the category. Other brands are so far behind they have a difficult time competing with Hall's. Quick! Name one competitor.

HEAD-ON POSITIONING (COMPARATIVE POSITIONING)

Head-on Positioning
A marketing strategy in which one product is presented as an equal or better alternative to a competing product.

Head-on positioning involves a comparison of one brand with another. Typically, the brand doing the advertising presents itself as being better than another brand. The message focuses on an attribute that is important to the target market. To dramatize the claim of superiority or whatever the claim may be, it is common to demonstrate how both brands perform. For example, we often see popular brands of household products use head-on positioning strategies, such as Tide laundry detergent's television advertising campaign that compared Tide to five other popular brands. The ad's tagline was "Tide is my kind of clean!"

Perhaps the most famous illustration of this strategy is the "Pepsi Challenge." In television commercials, non-believers were challenged in a taste test. Once they experienced the taste of Pepsi-Cola, their conclusion was rather obvious. Another execution actually shows a Coca-Cola deliverymen enjoying the taste of an ice-cold Pepsi.

INNOVATION POSITIONING

Innovation Positioning
A marketing strategy that stresses newness (based on a commitment to research and development) as a means of differentiating a company or a brand from competing companies and brands.

An innovation is a product, service, or idea that is perceived by consumers as new. **Innovation positioning** is a marketing strategy that stresses that newness as a way to differentiate its brand from the competition. Adding oat bran to a breakfast cereal is considered a *continuous innovation* since it only constitutes a small change in the nature of the product. A *discontinuous innovation* is something like a personal computer or a digital camera, something that has an impact on society and the way we do things. A company that employs innovative strategy uses continuous innovation to stay one step ahead of the competition. Periodically, it will also discover and launch that breakthrough product that will separate it from competitors. Innovation is a mindset of the company!

3M is a company that invests heavily in research and development to improve products constantly and bring new products to market. Its range of products is diverse, including anything from unique consumer products such as Post-It Notes and Scotch tape to highly technical electronic equipment used in hospitals and industry. From a branding perspective, the 3M brand stands for trust, leadership, and quality. To the customer, it is a guarantee of quality and reliability. When the company uses the 3M brand, it is leveraging its reputation and creating distinctive, relevant differentiation through the unique features and benefits of its products and services. It is proud of its innovations and promotes that message loud and clear to all of its publics, and phrases such as "Innovative and Practical Solutions" and "Leading through Innovation" tie all its communications together into an integrated package.[17]

PRICE (VALUE) POSITIONING

Price Positioning
A marketing strategy based on the premise that consumers search for the best possible value given their economic circumstances.

A **price positioning** strategy is based on the premise that consumers search for the best possible value given their economic circumstances. Some consumers search for low prices, others are willing to pay more for something perceived as offering good value, and still others don't even look at price. Some people shop for high-end goods and services and expect to pay a lot for the products they buy.

Wal-Mart seems to have a lock on low price positioning strategy in the North American retail marketplace. So firmly entrenched is its image in the minds of consumers, based on persistent messages that show prices being slashed on store signs, that consumers automatically think Wal-Mart offers the best value. Their slogan "We sell for less. Everyday." reinforces the message.

Another retailing example shows how high price positioning is an effective strategy. In terms of men's fashion, Harry Rosen comes to mind. In spite of a weak economy over the past few years and a trend toward more casual fashions, Harry Rosen has survived at the high end of the market. The Harry Rosen image has been carefully cultivated over time so that customers know exactly what to expect when they shop there.

At Harry Rosen's a suit can cost anywhere from $1500 to $10 500. Harry Rosen keeps its edge on the competition by carrying many exclusive products, and by moving to customer relationship marketing, pitching wares directly to individual customers in mailings and through special events. According to retail consultant John Williams, Harry Rosen is "unique in North America and maybe the world. There's no other chain of high-quality menswear of any significance." Put a bit differently, Larry Rosen (president and son of the founder) states, "A man looks powerful, authoritative, confident and professional in a suit. To get the right suit that man knows where to shop—Harry Rosen."[18]

CHANNEL POSITIONING

Channel Positioning
A marketing strategy based on an organization's position in its distribution channel and its market coverage.

Dell Canada
www.dell.ca

Some companies gain competitive advantage based on their **channel positioning** and their degree of market coverage. To demonstrate, consider the enviable position Dell Computer finds itself in. From nowhere, Dell conquered such corporations as IBM, Compaq, and Apple based solely on its methods of selling and delivering computers to customers. Dell was the first (an innovator) to sell computers directly to customers—by telephone initially, and then by the internet with no retail outlets. The entire business was built on a non-conventional strategy for the industry (see Figure 3.9).

Awareness of such a selling strategy was the responsibility of an extensive marketing communications program that embraced all of the mass media. A mass media communications strategy complemented Dell's direct marketing strategy. Consumers were convinced that buying computers directly would save them money. Dell made the promise and then delivered the goods. The rest is history. Dell is now the leading personal computer company in North America.

In the soft drink business, consumers can purchase Coca-Cola and Pepsi-Cola in virtually any supermarket in North America. These brand leaders have significant leverage among distributors based largely on their brand equity. Being readily available certainly enhances the prospects of purchase. Distribution is an important factor, because it must be tied closely to the timing of marketing communications execution. The challenge of matching distribution with marketing communications is less for Coke and Pepsi. The same can't be said for most other brands.

LIFESTYLE (IMAGE) POSITIONING

Lifestyle or Image Positioning
A marketing strategy based on intangible characteristics associated with a lifestyle instead of tangible characteristics.

In very competitive markets where product attributes of so many brands are perceived to be equal by consumers, it is difficult to follow the positioning strategies outlined above. **Lifestyle or image positioning** involves moving away from the tangible characteristics of the product toward the intangible characteristics (things that aren't there, for example). Marketing communications play a key role in establishing an image for a brand. The "Do the Dew" campaign that was mentioned earlier in the chapter is a good example of how action-oriented images can dramatically alter how a target perceives a brand. Mountain Dew became a popular product among the skateboarder set or youth who perceived themselves to be living on the edge. Mountain Dew is now an avid sponsor of skateboard competitions throughout North America. Event marketing is perceived to be a unique way of reaching the elusive teen market, a market that tends to shun traditional forms of marketing communications.

FIGURE **3.9** **A Channel-Oriented Positioning Strategy (Buy Direct from Dell) Separates Dell from Competitors**

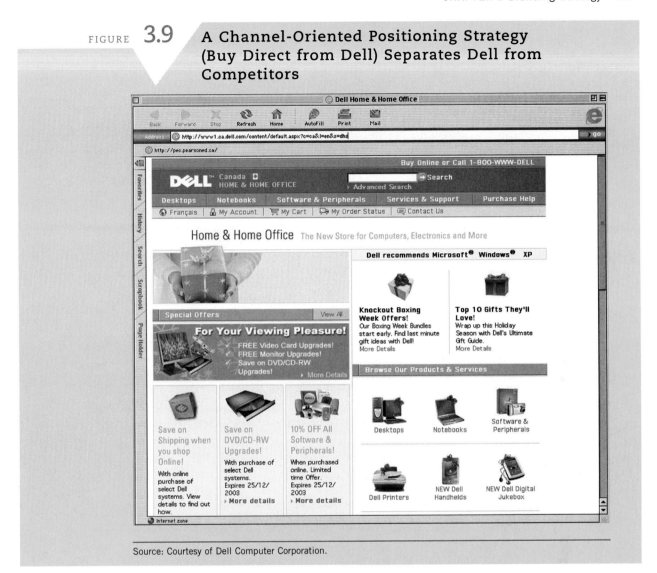

Source: Courtesy of Dell Computer Corporation.

The use of psychographic information allows companies to develop campaigns that are based on the lifestyle or desired lifestyle of the target market. A product like Mountain Dew is positioned to fit in or match the lifestyle of the customer. Generally speaking, lifestyle positioning involves using emotional appeal techniques such as love, fear, adventure, sex, and humour to influence the target. Furthermore, the image, if it is to work, must be communicated through every media vehicle and brand contact, including logos and special events. Other industries that employ lifestyle positioning extensively include automobiles and beer. For example, it is common to see the rugged outdoors associated with SUVs and young urban professionals driving a luxury car. And don't forget all those young men bonding together over a few brews. An illustration of lifestyle imagery appears in Figure 3.10.

PLANNING AND IMPLEMENTING MARKETING AND MARKETING COMMUNICATIONS PROGRAMS

To build brand loyalty and brand equity requires effective marketing programs: activities that produce a strong and favourable association to a brand in a consumer's memory. It is an information transfer process that considers two essential factors. First, decisions must

FIGURE **3.10** **Lifestyle Imagery Positions Competing Brands in the Customer's Mind**

©2003 Porsche Cars North America, Inc. Porsche recommends seat belt usage and observance of all traffic laws at all times. Specifications for comparison only.

Art not imitating anything.

Consider this bold collaboration. You and the incomparable 911 Carrera. Wrap yourself in the driver's seat, feel the surge of the hand-assembled, rear-mounted 320-hp engine, and every twist and bend of the road becomes pure artistry. Contact us at 1-800-PORSCHE or porsche.com.

The 911 Carrera

Source: Courtesy of Porsche. Photo by Georg Fischer.

be made about how to employ various brand elements. These decisions involve brand names, trademarks, and characters. Second, appropriate marketing strategies must be developed to communicate the brand values and brand positioning strategy.

The most common brand elements are brand names, logos, symbols, characters, packaging, and slogans. The content of most advertising in any medium, from television to print to websites, usually includes these elements. Characters sometimes become more famous than the brand itself. Some very popular brand characters include the A&W Root Bear, the Pillsbury Doughboy, Tony the Tiger, and the Energizer Bunny, to name only a few. As discussed in the positioning strategy section of this chapter, slogans are commonly used in advertising to summarize the core value of the brand. Phrases such as "There's a little McDonald's in everyone" do have an impact on people. Interestingly enough, McDonald's recently announced that it was implementing its first global communications campaign and the new slogan will be "I'm lovin' it." In terms of planning, McDonald's challenged all of its agency partners worldwide to brainstorm for new ideas. Though it was not a competition among agencies, many strategic concepts were brought forward. The winning strategy was created by Heye & Partner, an advertising agency in Munich, Germany. Other agencies around the world will now develop executions based on the "I'm lovin' it" strategy.[19] For more insight into the role that characters in advertising perform refer to Figure 3.11.

FIGURE **3.11** **Advertising Icons of the 20th Century**

Some people might consider character icons to be hopelessly old-fashioned nowadays. But their warmth, personality, and humour may be just what a brand needs in a forever changing marketplace. Here are the top 10 advertising icons of the 20th century.

1. **The Marlboro Man**
2. **Ronald McDonald**
3. **The Green Giant**
4. **Betty Crocker**
5. **The Energizer Bunny**
6. **The Pillsbury Doughboy**
7. **Aunt Jemima**
8. **The Michelin Man**
9. **Tony the Tiger**
10. **Elsie the Cow**

Rankings are based on a survey conducted by *Advertising Age* magazine.

Adapted from Angela Kryhu, "The Great Canadian Icon," *Marketing*, June 26, 2000, p. 11.

Advertising characters like these play a key role in developing consumer perceptions about a brand. They contribute to building brand equity over time. Here's another list of characters. Will they become as popular?

- **Ray and Carl**—the lovable and funny Blockbuster animals
- **Colonel Sanders**—the animated version used by KFC
- **The Maytag Repairman**—several different actors have performed in this role
- **A&W Root Bear**—that lovable bear that never speaks
- **The Man from Glad**—he disappeared for a while but has returned looking slightly younger.

Based on the numerous examples already cited in this chapter, it should be abundantly clear that marketing communications is the "voice" of a brand's (or company's) positioning strategy. Regardless of the medium selected, that voice must deliver a message with clarity and continuity. If the communications strategies are executed effectively, and with sufficient financial support, the desired message and image should be planted in the customer's mind.

To illustrate, consider the stark contrast with which Apple computers and accessories are presented to potential customers. Personal computers are technical in nature and while competitors dwell on all kinds of technical jargon in their communications, Apple talks about why its computers are fun to use. Apple doesn't want to be seen as just another computer company. It wants to be perceived as a different computer company. The products are available in a rainbow of colours and their whimsical style of advertising is unique. Apple's slogan "Think different" is an appropriate tagline to summarize the company's positioning strategy.

In terms of how the various elements of the marketing communications mix are employed, advertising should be viewed as an aerial attack on the audience it reaches. It is the most visible form of communications, a form of communications that creates awareness and interest in a brand. Advertising gets people talking about a brand. It creates hype. The other forms of marketing communications play more specific roles and should be viewed as the ground attack. Communications in the form of sales promotions, personal selling, and event marketing, for example, help create desire and action. They provide the stimulus that gets the wallet out of the pocket or purse. The internet has become a useful vehicle for providing detailed information. Therefore, with all points of contact delivering the same message, a brand begins to build momentum. The brand-building process has begun.

For more insight into brand building strategies read the IMC Highlight **Fame and Fortune Do Not Come by Chance**.

Packaging and Brand Building

The package is what consumers look for when they are contemplating a purchase. For new products especially, the look of the package must be instilled in the customer's mind. For that reason, it is very common for the package to play a key role in introductory marketing communications programs. Over time, consumers start associating specific colours with a brand and they know exactly what they are looking for when trying to spot a brand on a cluttered store shelf. Tide, for example, is strongly associated with the colour orange; Tetley tea is associated with the colour blue.

In today's competitive environment, packaging is playing a more significant role in differentiating one brand from another. The type and style of container may change during the product life cycle to spruce up the image of a brand, even though the product itself may not change. On the other hand, a new form of a product usually means a new package or a redesigned package. It is important, however, to maintain brand identity. Deodorant brands, for example, are available in spray (aerosol cans or rigid plastic spray containers), powder (soft plastic containers), and lotion formats (rigid plastic containers with roll-on applicators). From one container to another, the design of the package has a common look and colour scheme (see Figure 3.12).

A revolution is occurring in packaged-goods marketing, as marketers see packages having a growing influence on purchase decisions amid ongoing media fragmentation. Changes in media and consumer lifestyles are now forcing a dramatic shift, making the package itself an increasingly important selling medium. Examples such as H.J. Heinz Co.'s ketchups in colours ranging from green to blue in uniquely designed packages to tempt kids have scored millions of dollars worth of free publicity by being first of a kind. Marketers are also investing significant sums of money into research and development to win consumer loyalty with package designs that make life easier. It seems that packaging is being recognized as a key element in integrated marketing practice.[20]

IMC Highlight

FAME AND FORTUNE DO NOT COME BY CHANCE

Every day people are bombarded with brands pursuing their cash. Only a select few brands rise above the rest, their names instantly recognizable, desirable, and durable. They are the super brands. Some of the names in this category include Ferrari, Gucci, Nike, and Coca-Cola.

Brands like these teach marketers valuable lessons. Fame and, especially, fortune do not come by chance. Brand experts from the advertising, manufacturing, and retail communities point to a complex strategy of identity, creativity, quality, investment, and, above all, a magical relationship with the customer as the keys to success.

The first thing a brand needs is desirability. People have to really want to associate themselves with it. The emotional appeal might be the exclusivity of a Rolex watch or the sense of belonging that comes with owning a Harley-Davidson motorcycle. In a retailing environment, great brands go well beyond the concept of brand identity, with advertising, shop layouts, and products blending together into a personality.

Nike, one of the world's most readily identifiable brands, has a mission: "to bring inspiration and innovation to every athlete in the world." So successful is Nike, that the "swoosh" logo has become a synonym for sporting success rather than just a shoe label.

Once a brand has captured the imagination of the public, its identity needs to be nurtured, protected, and targeted at specific customers frequently. Automobile brands such as BMW and Volkswagen have attracted car buyers with new versions of the famous Mini and the Beetle, very popular brands in their own right that sell because of their name and funky modern-looking designs.

But for all of the hefty investment in marketing, a brand's eventual success relies on the most fickle and least controllable element—the customer. "The strength of your brand comes from the customer. You have to respect and feed what the customer expects from you, maintain your identity and authenticity," says Franco Cologni, head of the watch division at Swiss luxury group Richemont.

Earning customer loyalty and proving a brand's real worth is going to be more important than ever before. Trademarks and brands if they are authentic and truly connect the buyer to the brand will be perceived as more of a "trustmark" than a trademark. Successful brands consistently prove their value and authenticity to consumers.

Adapted from Jane Barrett, "Careful Nurturing Drives Superbrands," *Financial Post*, November 15, 2002, p. DO 13.

While package decisions fall under the category of brand management, the package is a very important touch-point with consumers. Familiarity with a package helps build trust between the consumer and the brand, so, ultimately, the package is a factor that can influence consumer loyalty. A good package serves three functions: it protects the product, it markets the product, and it offers convenience to consumers.

PROTECTING THE PRODUCT

How much protection a product needs depends on how often it changes hands in the distribution process. For example, how long does it sit in a warehouse, how will it be transported, what kind of handling will it experience, and how much protection from exposure to heat, cold, light, and moisture will it need? Milk, for example, is traditionally packaged in bags and cartons, but the recent introduction of plastic containers in single serving sizes (yes, milk is being positioned as a "refreshing" beverage) has increased the shelf life of milk. Potato chips are packed in oversized bags to protect the chips while being transported or handled.

MARKETING THE PRODUCT

In its marketing role, the package does the same thing an advertisement in any medium would do. The design and colour scheme should be coordinated so that the overall

FIGURE **3.12** A Consistent Brand Identification Across All Product Formats Is Important

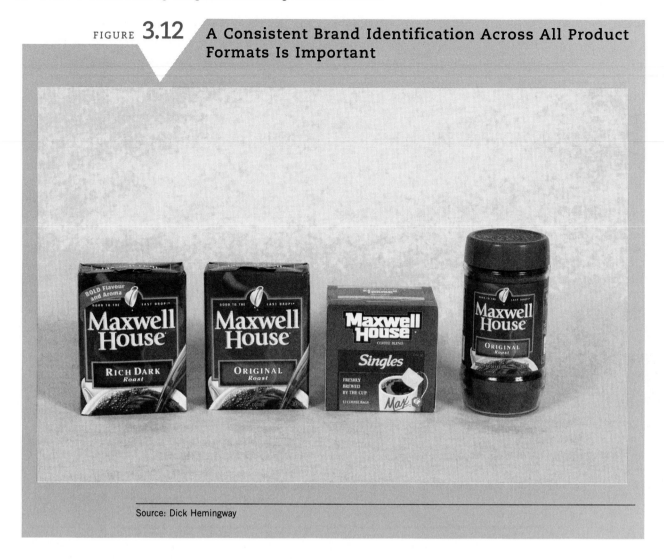

Source: Dick Hemingway

look of the package creates a good impression. The package should be attractive and eye catching in order to grab the attention of consumers. It should contain useful information and the benefits that will give consumers a reason to buy it. Becel margarine, for example, is positioned as a healthy eating alternative and the phrase "Takes your health to heart" appears in all forms of marketing communications for the brand, including the package.

Studies have shown that changes in colours, graphics, or configuration can dramatically alter a consumer's perception of the same product. To illustrate, consider the case of Nabisco Bits & Bites. The product was packaged in a cracker-style box, and sales had stagnated. Insight obtained through marketing research revealed that the package undermined the social image of a snack. Nabisco needed a package that would be as convenient as a potato chip bag. The solution was a standup foil pouch with a resealable opening. Between 1996 and 2000, sales of Bits & Bites tripled, all due to the package change. Nabisco then extended the pouch pack to other product lines.[21]

The Bits & Bites example shows that packaging can have psychological implications, so it is important to keep in touch with consumers. The package helps consumers form opinions about quality, value, and performance.

Packages can be used to communicate information about promotional offers such as coupons, contests, and giveaways. Since promotions of this nature are temporary, a package "flash" is usually added to the front panel of the package to draw attention to the offer. Details of the offer would appear on the side, back, or inside the package (see Figure 3.13).

Beyond transferring essential information about a brand, marketers must be aware of legal and regulatory requirements associated with packaging. The universal product code (UPC) symbol (a series of black lines that identify each item of a product line) is mandatory on all packaged goods. Other mandatory information includes the volume or weight designation and the company name and address. On prepackaged food products, nutritional information is now mandatory. Where appropriate and with substantiation from marketing research and approval from the appropriate government authority, a company can now make specific health claims about brands on the packages.

PROVIDING CONVENIENCE

A package should be easy to carry, open, handle, and reseal (if appropriate). Liquid detergents, for example, should be easy to pour without spills (on some brands the plastic lid is the measuring device for dispensing the product). No-drip spouts on products such as mustard and ketchup also offer convenience. If a product is heavy or bulky, handles should be built into the package design. Other examples of convenience include resealable plastic lids on margarine containers, twist-off caps on beer, wine, and soft drinks, straws on fruit juice containers, and canned goods with moulded metal bottoms that allow for stacking on store shelves.

Branding by Design

Not all kinds of product are sold in a package. What attributes sell an appliance, an automobile, a computer, the services offered by a bank, and so on? For durable goods like cars and computers, the key influencer in the buying decision could be the design—the look and style of the product and the image it projects about itself. Consumers want products that fit in with their lifestyle or the decor of their home furnishings. For products like mutual funds, trusts, and other financial offerings—products that are truly intangible—consumers are primarily influenced by the brand image as perpetuated by effective marketing communications programs.

Let's examine durable goods first. At one time, designers followed one basic premise: form follows function. This is a good premise because consumers want durable goods to perform specific functions dependably and reliably. Shopping for a stove or a dishwasher involved comparing the interior and exterior features of the brands carried by a store. Since all brands offered the same benefits, the decision was based largely on the brand name and the perceptions the consumer held about the brand name. At some point, manufacturers started offering kitchen appliances in a variety of colours; design elements became very important in the buying decision. Today, kitchen appliances are electronic in nature and have a modern appearance.

Today, the onslaught of new technologies with all their mysterious, invisible digital powers has created a kind of technophobia that threatens to alienate society from the benefits technology brings. Automobiles and computers are two categories that demonstrate this new way of thinking. The goal for design is to make technology less hostile, less intrusive, and friendly.[22]

Ten years ago, personal computers were ugly beige and black boxes (many brands still are!). They had sharp, uninviting edges and less-than-user-friendly operating systems. When Apple introduced the iMac, things started to change. Suddenly beige and black were out and colours such as orange, aqua, grey, and green were in. The boxy shape gave way to a more human, rounded egg shape. The iMac was a hit! Apple has

FIGURE **3.13** **A Package Face Communicates Details of a Promotional Offer**

Source:Dick Hemingway

redesigned the iMac with a 15-inch flat-screen monitor attached to a dome base with an adjustable, stainless steel arm. No longer does a person move in order to suit the computer screen. The iMac screen moves with the touch of a finger, and the dome contains the technology that makes the iMac one of the fastest personal computers ever (see Figure 3.14).

The Cadillac is another product where product design has had a dramatic influence on brand image. Traditionally a luxury car for men 55 years of age and older, Cadillac sales were dropping. Customers were looking more favourably at Japanese and European brands such as BMW, Mercedes, Lexus, and Infiniti. The imported brands offered better technology and more contemporary design characteristics. To rejuvenate interest in the Cadillac, General Motors completely redesigned the Cadillac and launched a series of new models over the past five years.

Cadillac's design goal was to simplify functions, alter perceptions about the car, and provide pure pleasure for the owner. Cadillac now sports a solid contemporary look with all kinds of new electronic gadgetry built into the engine and cabin. The 2004 Cadillac XLR, a two-seater roadster, is a bold example of the design goals. Ten years ago Cadillac would not market such an automobile. The XLR was a direct response to public demand. The exterior features a bold, chiselled form, seven-spoke wheels, and a unique egg-crate grill. The luxurious interior cabin features eucalyptus wood, brushed aluminum accents, and form-fitting leather bucket seats. The Cadillac XLR is being positioned as a car for drivers to drive and enjoy.

On the services side of things, consider the problem that the Bank of Montreal was facing. The bank had dropped significantly in consumers' minds in terms of ranking despite major expansion into wealth-management products. People were not aware that they could get anything from mutual funds to complex financial planning assistance from the bank. It embarked upon a rebranding program that had to communicate the perception that what they were offering was above banking and better than banking.

Archrival RBC Royal Bank had already undertaken an extensive rebranding program. To remain competitive, the Bank of Montreal had to follow. FutureBrand, a company specializing in developing brand strategies, worked on its branding program. "The critical element of any rebranding is understanding what the current narrative about the brand is, as well as the business strategy to date. Then you clarify what's going to change and distill it into a narrative explaining why the changes are a good thing."[23]

BMO
www.bmo.com

Distilling a complex rebranding into an instantly recognizable message is crucial. The result was a new persona for the bank, which is now known as BMO. BMO positioned all of the bank's product lines under one consistent brand. The new identity system introduced the name "BMO Financial Group" but linked it back to the Bank of Montreal. For an illustration of the rebranding program, see figures 3.15 and 3.16. An extensive marketing communications program was implemented to communicate

FIGURE **3.14** **Apple Computer Offers Consumers Distinctive Designs**

Source: Courtesy of Apple Computer, Inc.

the new name to the Canadian public. All touch-points with consumers—from stationery to ATMs to websites to bank signage—carry the BMO name. Such a change is a huge internal and external undertaking.

There are perils associated with identity changes. The transformation of Standard Oil into Exxon Corp. is an example. Exxon was merely a casual suggestion of an employee and was among 10 000 potential names that were considered. The firm spent US$100 million on new stationery and signage for the new name and logo. It was left with a sign that said nothing to anybody. And chronic name changes at the world's largest media firm have coincided with poor financial results. Time Inc., Warner Bros., and America Online Inc., thrived as independent entities. The combined Time Warner Inc., created in 2001 as AOL Time Warner and changed again in 2003, is a debt-laden behemoth that has destroyed billions of dollars in shareholder wealth.[24]

FIGURE **3.15** **An Illustration of BMO Bank of Montreal's New Corporate Identity System**

Source: Courtesy of BMO.

FIGURE **3.16** **BMO Bank of Montreal Logo**

Source: Courtesy of BMO.

Summary

Developing a sound brand strategy and positioning strategy is the first step in the brand building process. Having the right strategy is important since consumers form their impressions about a brand based on what they hear and see about it. Therefore, marketing organizations use branding as a means of identifying products and building an image.

Branding offers several benefits for consumers. It suggests a consistent degree of quality, provides psychological rewards (e.g., a better self-image) for possessing certain brands, and it distinguishes competing brands from one another. Good brands are personal and they often become integral parts of people's lives. For manufacturers, the brand name communicates a point of difference, allows for the creation of an image, and helps build brand loyalty. Over time consumers come to trust what a brand stands for and express their satisfaction in varying degrees of brand loyalty. Loyalty is expressed in terms of brand recognition, brand preference, and brand insistence.

The brand-building process involves four essential steps: identifying brand values and positioning strategy, planning and implementing a marketing program, measuring and interpreting brand performance, and growing and sustaining brand equity. Brand values are the primary attributes (descriptive features) and benefits (the values consumers attach to a brand). Positioning refers to the image a marketer wants the brand to have in the customers' mind. A positioning strategy is based on an important element of the marketing mix. Some of the common positioning strategies include product differentiation, brand leadership, head-on (comparative), innovation, price and value, channel efficiency, and lifestyle.

When implementing a brand strategy, all elements of the marketing mix and the marketing communications mix come into play. The marketing communications mix is the voice of a brand's positioning strategy. A good strategy that is executed efficiently should instill the desired image about a brand in the customer's mind. In this regard, all elements of the communications mix work together to deliver a consistent message.

Packaging and product design play key roles in differentiating brands and help determine consumer perceptions. A good package design will protect the product, market the product, and provide consumers convenience in handling and using the product. Package designs should be unique and attractive in order to grab the attention of consumers as they pass by. Expensive durable goods rely on the design of the product to create images in the consumer's mind. The design must be functional yet attractive to the eye. Style and appearance are important influences on buying decisions for cars, appliances, computers, and other consumer electronic goods. Goods such as these are often an expression of one's self-image.

Key Terms

attribute   75

benefit   75

brand   68

brand equity   74

brand insistence   73

brand loyalty   72

brand manager   74

brand name   69

brand preference   72

brand recognition   72

brandmark   69

channel positioning   82

core values   75

endorsement   70

head-on positioning   81

image positioning   82

innovation positioning   81

leadership positioning   80

lifestyle positioning   82

logo   69

positioning   76

price positioning   81

product differentiation strategy   78

unique selling point (USP)   72

wordmark   69

Review Questions

1. Identify and briefly explain the key components of a brand.
2. Identify two benefits of branding for consumers and two benefits of branding for organizations.
3. Identify and briefly explain the three stages of brand loyalty.
4. What is brand equity and how does a brand build it?
5. "A brand is a set of core values." What does this statement mean?
6. Define what positioning is and state the importance of having a clearly worded positioning strategy statement.
7. What is the difference between head-on positioning and brand leadership positioning? Provide an example of

each not mentioned in the chapter.
8. If a brand is using a product differentiation positioning strategy, what will the advertising message focus on? Provide an example of this strategy not mentioned in the chapter.
9. If a brand is using a lifestyle positioning strategy, what will the advertising message focus on? Provide two examples of this strategy not mentioned in the chapter.
10. What essential roles does a package perform in the marketing of a brand? Briefly explain.
11. Explain the role and influence that the design of a product can have on prospective buyers.

Discussion and Application Questions

1. "A brand is more than the physical product." Explain.
2. "Selecting the name for a new product is a critical decision." What are the essential issues in naming a

brand? Conduct some online secondary research to get to the bottom of this issue.
3. Select a lifestyle advertising campaign that you think is particularly effective.

Write a brief report or make a brief presentation on why you think it is effective.

4. Explain the relationship between brand positioning and the development of an effective marketing communications strategy.

5. Evaluate the marketing situation for one of the following companies or brands. What makes this company (brand) unique and what is its differential advantage(s) compared to the primary competitors? Based on what you know of this company (brand) and what you see or hear in terms of marketing communications, develop a positioning strategy statement for the company (brand).

   a) Apple
   b) Wal-Mart
   c) La Senza
   d) Listerine
   e) Gatorade

6. Using a company or brand of your choosing, examine the relationship between its name, logo, and advertising slogan (e.g., "GE brings good things to life"). Are these brand and communications elements permanently entwined or can any of the elements be changed in order to build the brand's image? What are the benefits and risks associated with any kind of change?

7. Assess the role that package design plays in building a brand's image. To justify your position provide an example of a package design that you perceive to be good and a design that you perceive to be less than good. What is the relationship between the package design and other forms of marketing communications?

Endnotes

1 Jo Marney, "Bringing Consumers Back for More," *Marketing*, September 10, 2001, p. 33.

2 *Dictionary of Marketing Terms*, Barron's Educational Series, Inc., 1994.

3 John Heinzl, "The Attack of the Brand Flakes," *Globe and Mail*, November 24, 2000, p. E1.

4 "A Dictionary of Branding Terms," <**www.landor.com/index.cfm?fuseaction=cBranding .getLexicon**> (November 2003).

5 Kevin Keller, *Strategic Brand Management* (Upper Saddle River, NY: Pearson Education, 2003), p. 106.

6 Bill Robinson, "Five Best Companies," *Forbes*, <**www.forbes.com/2002/08/01/ 0801marketers.htm**> (November 2003).

7 Allan P. Adamson, "What's Your Brand's Job?" *Advertising Age*, September 16, 2002, p. 18.

8 Jill Rosenfeld, "Experience the Real Thing," *Fast Company*, January 2000, Issue 31, p. 184.

9 Dale Beckman, David Kurtz, and Louis Boone, *Foundations of Marketing* (Toronto, ON: Holt Rinehart and Winston, 1988), pp. 316–317.

10 "A Dictionary of Branding Terms," <**www.landor.com/index.cfm?fuseaction=cBranding .getLexicon**> (November 2003).

11 "The 100 Top Brands," *Business Week*, August 5, 2002, pp. 95–99.

12 Howard Shultz, *Pour Your Heart Into it* (New York: Hyperion), 1997

13 Kevin Keller, *Strategic Brand Management* (Upper Saddle River, NY: Pearson Education, 2003), p. 44.

14 Stephanie Thompson, "Kraft to Introduce Leaner Lunchables," *Advertising Age*, November 11, 2002, pp. 3, 41.

15 Dana Flavelle, "Harvey's Bucks Lean Trend with Big Harv," *Toronto Star*, September 18, 2003, p. C2.

16 Lesley Young, "In-house Inspiration," *Marketing*, April 1, 2002, p. 14.

17 3M Worldwide, <www.3m.com> (November 2003).

18 Virginia Galt, "Return of the Suit Seen in 'Dress to Impress' Times," *Globe and Mail*, September 6, 2002, p. B5.

19 "McDonald's Unveils "I'm lovin' it" Worldwide Brand Campaign," Press Release, September 2, 2003, <**www.mcdonalds.com/corporate/press/ corporate/2003/09022003**> (November 2003).

20 Kate Fitzgerald, "Packaging Is the Capper," *Advertising Age*, May 5, 2003, p. 22.

21 Carey Toane, "Success Is in the Bag," *Marketing*, October 9, 2000, p. 25.

22 "Connecting with Design," *Globe and Mail*, October 18, 2002, p. B13.

23 Terry Poulton, "Communicating the New You," *Strategy*, October 7, 2002, p. 23.

24 David Olive, "Name Game Woes," *Toronto Star*, January 20, 2002, pp. C1, C3.

PART II

Planning for Integrated Media

Part 2 examines the steps, considerations, and procedures for developing message strategies and media strategies in the traditional media: television, radio, newspaper, magazines, various forms of out-of-home advertising, and direct response media. Message and media strategies for the interactive media are also presented.

In Chapter 4, the basic elements of the communications process are introduced along with the various stages of creative planning. Because creative plans are based on clearly defined objectives, strategies, and executions, the chapter draws clear distinctions among these three planning concepts. It finishes with a discussion of various creative appeal techniques and execution techniques that are employed by advertisers to present compelling messages to customers.

Chapter 5 describes the media planning process. Media planning involves identifying media objectives, strategies, and execution. The development of a sound media strategy is crucial, so considerable time is devoted to discussing primary issues that influence media strategy. Strategic decisions are largely influenced by the budget available and the strengths and weaknesses of each medium in the context of the problem the advertiser is attempting to resolve.

Chapter 6 examines the growing field of direct response communications. Direct response plans rely on database management techniques, and the chapter devotes considerable time to how organizations use information sources. Various direct response media options are introduced and the strengths and weaknesses of each option are examined.

In Chapter 7, the emerging role of the internet is examined. The various strategies for delivering effective online messages are discussed and perspectives are offered regarding how to effectively integrate online messages with offline messages and related communications strategies.

CHAPTER 4

ADVERTISING: CREATIVE PLANNING

After studying this chapter you will be able to:

identify the basic elements of the communications process,

explain the various stages of creative planning,

explain the role of a creative brief and describe the content of such a document,

distinguish between creative objectives, creative strategies, and creative execution,

describe the role of creative objective statements,

appreciate the variety of appeal techniques for developing creative strategies, and

assess the various execution techniques for best presenting creative strategies.

From the previous chapter you have learned about the strategic planning process and seen how various elements of the marketing and marketing communications mix converge in a master plan of some kind. The role and nature of the individual plans—the plans for advertising, direct response, internet, sales promotion, public relations, events and sponsorships, and personal selling—are the focus of the remainder of the book. Separate external organizations may be responsible for developing these plans. Therefore, in the planning and development stages there is much communication between a company and its external suppliers.

This chapter will focus specifically on one aspect of advertising, that being the development and implementation of the message. The initial section introduces some fundamental communications concepts that are common to all of the components of the marketing communications mix. It is followed by a discussion of the creative planning process. Creative planning relies upon essential input from the marketing plan and involves the development of a separate plan that outlines the creative objectives, creative strategies, and creative execution (tactics).

Communications Essentials

The marketplace is dynamic and consumers are exposed to hundreds of messages each day from all kinds of sources. What do consumers recognize and recall at the end of the day? Can they say with certainty they saw a television commercial for Diet Pepsi and recall someone singing Rod Stewart's "Forever Young." Do they remember that Chevy trucks are "Like a Rock"? Do they recall a woman having an "organic" experience while using Herbal Essences shampoo? The answer is not likely. In very simple terms, there is so much commercial clutter out there that consumers remember very little. The challenge, therefore, is to develop a message in any form (broadcast or print) that will break through the clutter and leave a lasting impression on the audience. Easier said than done!

An understanding of the communications process and how consumers receive and interpret messages is essential. In Chapter 1 various consumer behaviour concepts were introduced—concepts such as needs and motives, attitudes and perceptions, reference groups and family influences. Knowledge and application of these concepts influence the nature and content of a commercial message and the degree to which it is accepted and retained by consumers.

Communication is defined as transmitting, receiving, and processing information. Communication occurs when the message that was sent reaches its destination in a form that is understood by the intended audience. Commercial communications does not have to be a complex science. Simply stated, an organization develops a message, selects the right media to deliver it, and, if all things are planned effectively, it will reach the consumers and have an impact on them. Developing the message is referred to as **encoding**; that is, the message is transformed into some attention-getting form such as a print advertisement, a direct response mailing piece, an article about the product in a newspaper, and so on. The message is then **transmitted**, usually by the media (television, radio, newspapers, magazines, outdoor advertising, internet, and so on) or through personal selling.

In the delivery of the message, however, certain complications arise along the way. For example,

- the message was not in line with customer attitudes,
- the message did not reach the intended target with the desired frequency,
- the message delivered by the competition was more convincing,
- the competition spent more on advertising and had higher share of mind, or
- new competitors entered the market and invested heavily in advertising.

Circumstances such as these are referred to as **noise**, and dilute the impact of an advertiser's message. Whether or not a message breaks through the clutter is usually determined

---

Communication

The transmission, receipt, and processing of information between a sender and a receiver.

Encoding

The transformation of a message into a meaningful format such as an advertisement, a mailing piece, or an article in a newspaper.

Transmission

The sending of a message through a medium such as television, radio, newspapers, magazines, outdoor advertising, internet, and so on, or through personal selling.

Noise

Any potential form of disruption in the transmission of a message that could distort the impact of the message.

by the relationships between three separate factors: the quality of planning when developing message strategy, the execution of the plan being on target with the right timing and frequency, and the impact of competitive messages. The advertiser has control over the first two factors but no control over the third.

Competing products are sending very similar messages to the same target market, creating noise. The objective, therefore, is to break through the noise. To do so, the message must be relevant to the consumer. For instance, the product's benefits must satisfy a need or suit the lifestyle of the target, and be presented in such a manner that the brand becomes a preferred alternative. If this occurs, positive feedback in the form of consumer action will occur. However, if the message does not break through (if it is perceived as dull, uses the wrong types of appeals, or is simply confusing to the target), then no action will occur. Negative action indicates a need to revisit the creative strategy and execution and make changes where necessary. Refer to Figure 4.1 for an illustration.

FIGURE **4.1**   **The Communications Process**

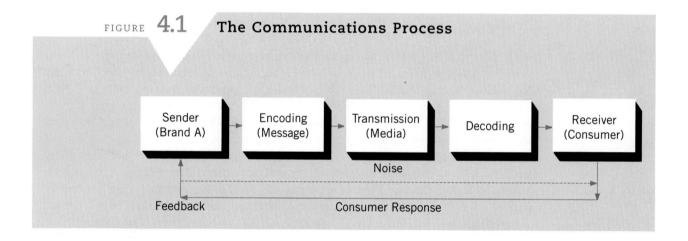

Understanding the processing that goes on in the consumer's mind also helps with the development of advertising messages. A consumer passes through a series of stages on the way to taking action. Advertising can influence the consumer at each stage. One such model is referred to as ACCA—awareness, comprehension, conviction, and action. This model is part of a theory called DAGMAR, which stands for Defining Advertising Goals for Measured Advertising Response. An advertising goal is a specific communication task to be accomplished among a defined audience in a given period. The task should be measurable, with benchmarks in existence in order to assess achievements.

The effectiveness of an advertising campaign is usually linked back to this model. For example, an advertiser wants to know (in percentage terms) the level of awareness of its product among the target market, whether or not it is perceived as being a preferred brand. Furthermore, the advertiser may want to know what percentage of the target market has tried the product (in the case of a new product campaign). Post-campaign marketing research studies measure the achievement of the objectives.

An advertisement (or campaign) that achieves good scores with respect to awareness, comprehension, and conviction is likely to succeed. The desired action in the form of someone buying the product will likely occur. To protect its investment in advertising, an organization may also conduct marketing research while message strategy is in the development stage. The message is tested for likeability, persuasiveness, and likelihood of purchase. Research measures that exceed the norms of other products in the category would suggest the advertiser is on to something. The various marketing research techniques used to evaluate advertising effectiveness are discussed in Chapter 12. The following is a description of each behaviour stage:

- *Awareness:* In this stage, the customer learns something for the first time. In an advertising context, a message tries to plant the brand name and the primary benefit offered in the customer's mind. Awareness can be measured by aided and unaided recall tests.
- *Comprehension:* At this stage, the consumer is expressing interest. The message is perceived as relevant. The brand is evaluated on the basis of need satisfaction. It is in the consumer's cognitive realm, and becomes a candidate for potential purchase. A like or dislike for a brand can be measured using attitude scales.
- *Conviction:* At this stage, the consumer expresses stronger feelings toward the brand based on the perceived benefits it offers. The brand has moved higher in the consumer's frame of reference and become a preferred brand in his or her mind. In other words, a new attitude or a change in attitude about something has occurred. There may be sufficient motivation to take action and buy the product.
- *Action:* At this stage, the desired action occurs. The consumer buys the brand for the first time, visits the dealer showroom, or calls that 1-800 number!

This is the beginning of a customer relationship. An organization will invest a considerable amount of money in advertising and other forms of marketing communications to achieve one basic goal: to get the target customers to buy the product. The message delivered by marketing communications is nothing more than a promise, a promise that motivates someone to buy. The product must then live up to the expectations created by the marketing communications. As we say, no amount of advertising can make up for a lousy product.

A second theory of communications revolves around the degree of involvement the consumer has with a product in the purchase decision-making process. The extent of involvement, described as either high involvement or low involvement, has implications for the development of marketing communications strategy. Referred to as the FCB Grid, the grid was developed by Richard Vaughan, a senior vice-president of Foote, Cone, and Belding Advertising (see Figure 4.2).[1]

Foote Cone & Belding
www.fcb.com

Products that are included in Quadrant One are expensive and require a rational decision-making process during which alternatives are evaluated. Since the consumer

FIGURE **4.2** **An Illustration of the FCB Grid**

HIGH INVOLVEMENT

Quadrant 1	**Quadrant 2**
High Importance (expensive)	High Importance (expensive)
Rational Decision	Emotional Decision
Example: Automobile or computer	**Example:** Designer Clothing
Quadrant 3	**Quadrant 4**
Low Importance (less expensive)	Low Importance (less expensive)
Rational Decision	Emotional Decision
Example: Detergent	**Example:** Soft drink, beer

LOW INVOLVEMENT

Source: Adapted from **www.public.iastate.edu/~geske/FCB.html**. Reproduced with permission.

will probably spend an extended period of time assessing alternatives, the message strategy would have an informative tone and style, and the media selected to deliver the message would be conducive to a long copy format (e.g., newspaper and magazines, websites, and CD-ROMs). Products in Quadrant Two are also high involvement but consumers evaluate alternatives more on emotion. For example, designer clothing is bought to make the consumer feel good, feel sexy, or show status. Marketing communications must generate emotional responses and create an image that people will buy. The message will appeal to higher level needs, the looking glass self, and the ideal self. Television ads, glossy and visual magazine ads, and special inserts are effective media for such products.

Products that are included in Quadrant Three are low-involvement products that require rational decisions. Products such as household cleaning products, paper products, and other everyday items are in this category. Marketing communications should give the consumer a compelling reason to buy (e.g., it lasts longer, as in a battery, or it is fast-acting, as in a headache remedy). Consumers are unlikely to read extensive copy for these types of products so the message must be short. A catchy slogan might act as a reminder (e.g., Maxwell House "Good to the last drop."). Television, magazine ads with strong visuals, and point-of-purchase material are effective media choices.

Products that are included in Quadrant Four are low-involvement, emotional decisions. The products are not expensive but they make the consumer feel good. Examples of such products include snack foods, beer and alcohol, and soft drinks. There are not many rational reasons for buying these types of products, so it is common for messages to adopt a "feel good" strategy. For example, there is an abundance of lifestyle-oriented messages among popular Canadian beer brands. It is the image or lifestyle association that the consumer buys into. Television, outdoor, and point-of-purchase play a role in delivering messages for these products.

MARKETING COMMUNICATIONS PLANNING PROCESS

The various elements of the strategic planning process were presented in Chapter 3. This chapter concentrates on the advertising planning process, but will recognize the relationships between advertising and the other forms of communication. Once the relationships are established, the chapter will then focus on creative planning. Media planning concepts are presented in Chapter 5.

All aspects of a marketing communications plan are based on the same set of information. The current situation a brand or company faces is analyzed, a problem or opportunity is identified, and a plan of action is developed and implemented. As part of the planning process, the role and contribution of each element in the marketing communications mix are also identified. Separate plans, designed to achieve specific objectives, are developed for each element of the mix. Once completed, the key elements of these plans are integrated into the master plan—the marketing plan (see Figure 4.3).

ADVERTISING PLANNING—CREATIVE

Advertising

A form of marketing communications designed to stimulate a positive response from a defined target market.

Advertising is defined as a paid form of a non-personal message communicated through the various media by industry, business firms, not-for-profit organizations, and individuals. Advertising is persuasive and informational and is designed to influence the behaviour or thought patterns of the audience.[2] The advertising plan is usually developed by an advertising agency, an external partner that works closely with the client. The agency is responsible for developing and managing the client's advertising. Historically, agencies focused their energy on creative and media planning but in today's environment, they have expanded into other areas, such as direct response, marketing research, internet communications, and public relations.

FIGURE 4.3   **Creative Planning**

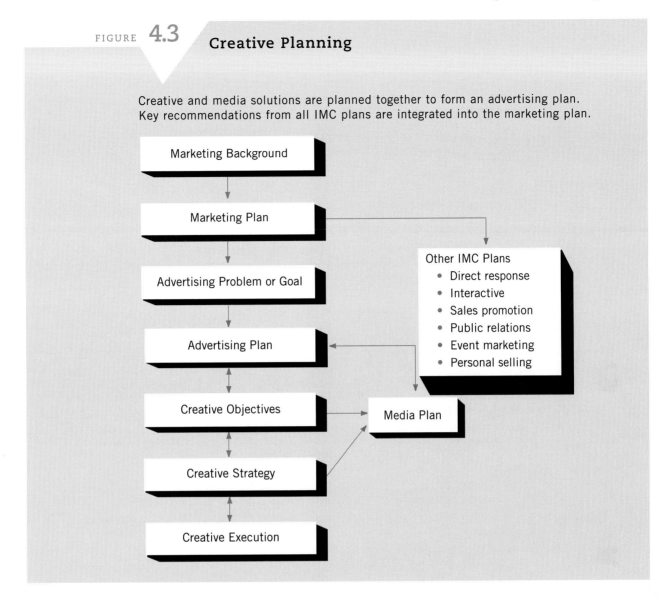

Creative and media solutions are planned together to form an advertising plan.
Key recommendations from all IMC plans are integrated into the marketing plan.

Marketing Background

Marketing Plan

Advertising Problem or Goal

Other IMC Plans
- Direct response
- Interactive
- Sales promotion
- Public relations
- Event marketing
- Personal selling

Advertising Plan

Creative Objectives

Media Plan

Creative Strategy

Creative Execution

Creative Brief

A document developed by a client organization that contains vital information about the advertising task at hand; it is a useful tool for discussions between the client and its advertising agency.

The starting point for any new advertising project is the creative brief. A **creative brief** is a business document developed by the company that contains vital information about the advertising task at hand. The information is discussed with advertising agency personnel so that copywriters, art directors, and creative directors fully understand the nature of the assignment. The brief is a discussion document and the content can change based on the nature of discussion between the client and agency. In some cases, certain sections are actually left blank, awaiting discussion between the two parties. For example, when it comes to developing creative strategy, that's the responsibility of the agency. Clients that provide too much direction are "stepping on toes." The content of a creative brief is contained in Figure 4.4.

Information that is provided by the client includes market background information, a statement that identifies the problem to be resolved or the overall goal to be achieved, and a list of communications objectives that relate to the behaviour process a consumer goes through when determining what brands to buy. As discussed earlier in the chapter, these objectives deal with issues such as awareness, preference, and action. The client also provides a positioning strategy statement to guide the development of the creative plan. The positioning strategy statement directly influences the creative objectives. For

FIGURE **4.4**   **Content of a Creative Brief**

Market Information (information from marketing plan)

- Market profile
- Brand profile
- Competitor profile
- Target market profile
- Budget

Problem and Overall Objective

- Identification of the problem that advertising will resolve
- Statement of the overall goal for advertising to achieve

Advertising Objectives (based on problem or goal)

- Awareness
- Interest
- Preference
- Action
- New image
- New targets

Positioning Strategy Statement

- A statement of brand benefits, brand personality, or desired image

Creative Objectives

- Key benefit statement
- Support claims statement

Creative Strategy

- Tone and style
- Central theme ("big idea")
- Appeal techniques

Creative Execution

- Tactical considerations
- Production decisions

Note: The nature and content of a creative brief varies from company to company. A working model is presented here to show the typical content of a creative brief. Some companies include a problem statement or an overall goal, while others include both. Advertising objectives usually concentrate on one or two issues so the campaign remains focused on the problem at hand.

our discussions here, creative objectives deal with the content of the message to be delivered (e.g., what is the primary attribute and benefit to be communicated to the target market?). The remaining elements of the creative brief—the creative strategy and creative execution—are the responsibility of the agency. That's what they get paid to do!

Once the creative brief is finalized, the spotlight shines upon the copywriter and art director, a team charged with developing the creative concept or the "big idea," as it is often referred to, that will be the cornerstone of the campaign. At this point, the agency's creative team immerses itself in details about the brand, target market, and competition so that it can fully appreciate the current situation.

Let's examine the content of the creative brief in more detail. Since the market background information is drawn from the marketing plan, that section will not be discussed in this chapter. Simply refer back to Chapter 3 if you need more details. The market background section includes information about the market, brand, key competitors, a profile of the primary target market, and budget. Knowing a brand's market position and how consumers perceive it is important to developing message strategies. Knowing how competitors advertise their products is also important. The agency wants to ensure it recommends new and innovative ideas to its clients. An example of a creative brief is contained in Figure 4.5.

Problem Identification

Advertising plans are usually designed to resolve a particular problem or pursue an opportunity. For example, an established brand will review its marketing strategy each year and make changes in strategic direction when necessary. Factors such as the stage at which a brand finds itself in the product life cycle, the intensity of competition, and changing preferences among target consumers are evaluated in the review process. Any change in direction has an impact on marketing communications strategies.

Problem Statement
A brief statement that summarizes a particular problem to resolve or an opportunity to pursue and serves as the focus of an advertising strategy.

Overall Goal
The objective of an advertising campaign.

Based on this creative brief model, the situation is encapsulated in a **problem statement**. Other models may require a statement that describes the **overall goal** of the campaign. Regardless of which option is used, advertising can only accomplish one thing at a time. A campaign must have a central focus. Simply stated, it's "Here's what we want to achieve!" To illustrate, consider the following examples:

- To create or increase brand awareness.
- To alter perceptions currently held by consumers about a brand.
- To present a completely new image for a brand.
- To launch a new product into the marketplace.
- To attract a new target market to a brand.
- To create awareness and trial purchase for a brand line extension.

These examples suggest focus. Any brand would have a difficult time if it were to reposition itself in the market while trying to attract a new target market. Consumers currently using the brand would be utterly confused by the messages they see and hear.

Advertising Objectives

Once the overall goal is determined, specific advertising objectives are identified. Typically, these objectives are quantitative in nature so that the plan can be evaluated for success or failure at a later date. Furthermore, advertising objectives may be behavioural in nature or they may focus on the content of the message (e.g., what to say about the product).

Advertising objectives should only deal with issues that advertising (the creative plan and media plan) can resolve. For example, a new product campaign will focus on awareness and preference objectives. The objective is to build awareness gradually by presenting a message that informs consumers about what the product is and what it will do for them. Refer to the advertisement in Figure 4.6 for an example. If the market is very competitive and several brands are strong, the advertising objectives will focus on building preference. The message will focus squarely on unique attributes that show how the advertised brand performs better than other brands. When a product reaches maturity, the focus will shift again. Advertising objectives will focus on ways to encourage frequency of use by current customers or ways to attract new customers. To demonstrate how advertising objectives are written, consider the following examples:

- To achieve an awareness level of 60 percent for Brand X in the defined target market within 12 months of product launch.

FIGURE **4.5**

An Example of a Creative Brief

This is an example of a creative brief for a public service campaign designed to increase awareness for the Centre for Addiction and Mental Health and its efforts to make the public more understanding of depression and what can be done for those who suffer from it.

BACKGROUND INFORMATION

- 3 million Canadians suffer from clinical depression.
- Only one third of sufferers seek help because they are afraid of being "labelled."
- 80 percent of suicides are by people suffering from a depressive illness.
- 40 percent of cases are diagnosed in people under the age of 20.
- Depression accounts for 30 percent of all disability claims in Canada.

PROBLEM

- The public knows little about depression. It is a silent disease with a prevailing stigma surrounding it. Many perceive it to be a simple coping deficiency that "weak" people have and that those people will, and can, snap out of it. Or they are just feeling "blue." Depression is a misunderstood illness.

OVERALL GOALS

- To create awareness about depression as a disease and to influence the public's attitudes about how to deal with people suffering from it.
- To make the public aware of the Centre for Addiction and Mental Health and the services it provides.

COMMUNICATIONS OBJECTIVES

- To remove the social stigma that surrounds depression and sell understanding of the disease.
- To encourage those who may have the disease to seek help.
- To raise awareness of the Centre for Addiction and Mental Health.

CREATIVE OBJECTIVES

- To communicate that depression is an illness and is the result of a chemical imbalance in the brain of sufferers, and that it can be controlled with modern medication and professional counselling.
- To communicate that people with depression can't help themselves. Those who have it or think they have it need to know they are not to blame, and that there is compassionate help available to deal with it.

CREATIVE STRATEGY

- Dramatically portray the real suffering situations (at work, at home, etc.) that people with depression go through each day by using compelling, human, and empathetic headlines and images.

CREATIVE EXECUTION

- Black and white ads of various sizes will be placed in the print media.
- Similar images will be depicted on Centre's website.
- Images will portray empathy and compassion.

Compiled with the assistance of David Sharpe, Vice-President and Creative Director, Remtulla Euro RSCG Advertising.

FIGURE **4.6**   **An Advertisement Designed to Raise Awareness of a New Product**

Source: Courtesy of Gillette.

- To achieve a trial purchase rate of 25 percent for Brand Y in the defined target market within 12 months of product launch.
- To reposition (or re-image) Brand Z in the customer's mind by presenting messages depicting a completely new and contemporary image.

The first two examples are quantitative in nature and can be easily measured for achievement at the end of the plan period. If the objectives are achieved, it indicates that current advertising strategies are working. If they are not achieved, the client and agency can re-evaluate the situation and make appropriate changes. The third example is not quantitative in nature but it can be measured. Assuming the current image of the brand is known, a marketing research study near the end of the plan period can be conducted to determine if current customers have a different view of the brand. If they do, it would indicate the current creative strategies are working.

Let's examine a few of these challenges in more detail and determine how they influence the direction of creative planning.

Creating or Increasing Brand Awareness

Creating awareness is always the first challenge for advertising. The higher the level of awareness, the stronger the likelihood that consumers will buy the product. Achieving high levels of awareness depends on how memorable the message is and perhaps how frequently the message is delivered. The medium used to deliver the message will also influence awareness levels. The right plan will use the right medium, but the size of the budget often dictates media selection. Nonetheless, the use of a medium such as television may create higher levels of awareness than magazines or outdoor advertising, and so on.

Encouraging Trial Purchase

Creating awareness and interest in a brand is one thing, but getting the wallets out is another. Sometimes incentives have to be offered to give consumers an extra nudge. If the timing of the incentive is right, positive action will be taken. Therefore, many advertisements are designed specifically to include special offers, anything from cents-off coupons to manufacturers' rebates to low-cost financing. These incentives serve a specific purpose. They help reduce the risk associated with purchasing something for the first time (see Figure 4.7). For expensive goods such as cars and computers, where the risk is very high, they can help encourage consumers to buy in a time frame that is desirable for the manufacturer.

Considering how the consumer's mind works, people want to know they are making the right decision. If the product lives up to the promise, as presented in advertising, subsequent purchases will be made without incentives. Consumers today are looking for better value in the products and services they buy and, as a result, incentive-oriented advertising is now more prominent than in the past.

Attracting New Target Markets

In order to attract a new target market, say a younger age group than the audience the brand currently appeals to, a new message strategy is needed. The tone and style of advertising may have to change. To illustrate, consider what Tetley tea has been doing in its recent global adverting campaign. For 30 years, messages about the brand have been based on those loveable animated characters known as the "tea folk." Tetley is the leading brand in Canada, and the world's second best-selling tea brand.

The Tetley Group
www.tetley.com

Why mess with success? Two years ago the Tetley Group (a British-based company) was acquired by Tata Tea Limited (a large Indian tea company). In the process of defining new marketing objectives and strategies, there has been a clash of corporate cultures. Tata's primary goal is to pass Lipton and become the leading brand of tea. To do so, it decided to shed the working-class image of the brand in favour of a slick, modern campaign that would attract the next generation of tea drinkers. The tea folk were old-fashioned. If tea was to be positioned as a modern lifestyle choice to a new generation of tea drinkers, a new strategy was needed. The brand's new spokesperson is Ewan McGregor (*Trainspotting* and *Moulin Rouge*), quite a difference from the figures he replaced.[3] You be the judge. Was this a wise decision to make?

FIGURE **4.7** **An Offer That Combines Advertising and Sales Promotion (Free Sample) to Encourage Trial Purchase. Sample was glued to a magazine advertisement**

New Crystal Light Singles go wherever you go.

Crystal Light transforms water.

Crystal Light is an "Extras" Food Choice Value: 250 mL = 1 ⊞.

TANGERINE·GRAPEFRUIT

Crystal Light Singles

LOW CALORIE DRINK MIX

Artwork and design by Head Gear Animation

Source: Kraft Canada.

Encouraging Preference

For an established brand in growth or mature markets, the objective is to stand out from competing brands. Therefore, the thrust of marketing activities is on product differentiation. Advertising messages focus on existing or new attributes the brand offers. Where continuous improvement programs are in place, it is possible for a brand to become better with age. Regardless of the situation, preference is only achieved if a brand is perceived to be superior to the other alternatives available. Automobiles are redesigned periodically to bring a new look to the market, food products are reformulated to improve the taste, cleaning products are reformulated with newer, fresher scents, and deodorants are changed so that they last longer. Refer to Figure 4.8 for an illustration.

Changes such as these must be communicated to consumers. Having advertising messages focus on something new about the brand may be just enough to position the brand in a better light with consumers. Sporting goods products like golf clubs and skis are good examples of this. Modest changes in product attributes for existing brands such as Calloway and Nike (golf) and Rossignol and Solomon (skis) become the focus of new ad campaigns from year to year. The convincing nature in which the message is presented helps stimulate greater interest and desire among customers. Golfers and skiers tend to be very receptive to messages that promise enhanced performance.

Altering Perceptions Held by Consumers

To build a brand sometimes requires consumers to adopt a different view of the brand. The quickest way to alter an image is to launch a completely new advertising campaign with an entirely different message. The style and personality of the message will be different in order to create a new image in the customer's mind. The Hudson's Bay Company has been struggling with perception issues for years, all the time watching its market share of the department store market drop at the hands of Wal-Mart and Sears.

Hudson's Bay Company
www.hbc.com

A recent campaign for the Bay that used the tagline "Shopping is good" seemed to fall on deaf ears. Consumers didn't understand what it meant. Consumer perceived the Bay to be leaders in fashion style but thought the fashions were too expensive for the average budget. The Bay's primary target is working mothers 35 to 54 years old, with two kids and a $50 000 income. In this family, the budget is tight. What consumers didn't know was that the Bay has been adding lower-priced merchandise for several years. In fact, the fashion lines range from everyday value to high-end fashion. To address the perception issue, the Bay launched a new campaign using the tagline "More than you came for." The message stresses affordability, something previous campaigns didn't do. The ads prominently feature the Bay's house brands and trumpet the "everyday low price" strategy that was recently adopted. Through marketing research, the Bay learned that consumers were looking for better value and they preferred everyday low prices to sale prices.[4] Advertising's role is to make the customers aware of the changes.

For more insight into setting advertising objectives and how a campaign is designed to achieve the objective, see the IMC Highlight **Out of the Closet: The Viagra Launch**.

Positioning Strategy Statement

Positioning strategy has been discussed in the previous two chapters. Therefore, comments here will simply reinforce the necessity of having a clearly worded positioning strategy statement and how it is applied in developing an ad campaign. The positioning strategy statement indicates the benefits a brand offers, states what the brand stands for, and is a reflection of a brand's personality. These are the essential inputs assessed by the creative team when it develops the message strategy. It can be the trigger that leads to discovery of the "big idea."

Moosehead Beer
www.moosehead.ca

To illustrate how positioning strategy influences creative planning, consider a recent Moosehead beer campaign. Over time, a clear definition of Moosehead's brand character has emerged. In a nutshell, Moosehead's positioning strategy statement is as follows:

Enjoyment of the great outdoors.

You might ask what that has to do with the consumption and sale of beer. Well, previous campaigns strongly associated the brand and moose graphic with lots of Canadian wilderness imagery. Advertising helped build the brand's image. Focus groups revealed

FIGURE **4.8**   **Products are Redesigned to Rekindle Consumer Interest in Them**

Perhaps you don't recognize the all-new Accord. Completely understandable, considering it's been redesigned in nearly every respect. It now boasts distinctive European styling, the increased horsepower of an i-VTEC™ engine or an available 240-horsepower V6, and amenities usually reserved for luxury automobiles. Are you ready for it?

Accord, is that you?

The all-new Accord.   **HONDA**
www.honda.ca

Source: Honda Canada Inc.

that consumers actually reject seeing the brand in any other setting. Moosehead is anything but a mainstream beer. It's about tranquility, the sense of individual power, and freedom to choose. It's an independent beer much like a moose standing tall, it's the alpha male. You see, a brand's positioning is actually determined by the consumer!

OUT OF THE CLOSET: THE VIAGRA LAUNCH

Pharmaceutical marketing in Canada is governed by a tight set of laws and regulations, the most critical of which is not being able to identify brand names for prescription drugs. So what does an agency do to spark interest in a product when it is in a virtual straitjacket? Taxi, a Toronto-based ad agency, met the challenge by developing an innovative campaign that a very conservative company, Pfizer, had the guts to run with.

The overall goal of the campaign was: "to destigmatize E.D. (erectile dysfunction), to bring it out of the closet." The quickest way to generate buzz for such a delicate issue was to use television. The initial two spots did not identify the brand, but managed to break through the clutter and get people talking. The first spot featured a man in a doctor's office completing a checkup. He wants to broach the subject with the doctor but chickens out. Consumers are then urged to call their doctor if they suffer from E.D. The second spot was similar to U.S. advertising in that a former professional hockey player (Guy Lafleur) was a spokesperson. Sitting in a locker room, he urges men to come forward and ask for help.

Then came the now famous branded spot. The spot is called "Good Morning" and it shows a man leaving the house hopping and bouncing along to a song "Good Morning, Good Morning." The song was a 1950s type of tune. The guy is full of energy and is having a very good morning indeed. On the way to work he cartwheels, leapfrogs, and, laughing, enters an elevator full of people. And why was the man so happy? Well, he got lucky the night before! The closing super on the screen read: "Viagra. Talk to your doctor."

According to Pfizer, the third commercial helped change perceptions. It showed that overcoming the problem had an emotional benefit as well as a physical benefit. "It led to one of those creative leaps where we realized that showing a man feeling much happier would be the best approach to deliver the message."

Has the campaign worked? While Pfizer won't reveal specific results, over one million prescriptions have been written for Viagra in Canada. The advertising generated all kinds of media publicity that provided all kinds of buzz for the problem (E.D.) and the solution (Viagra). Viagra has been prescribed for 16 million men in 70 different countries. *Fortune* magazine estimates sales to be US$2 billion.

Adapted from Terry Poulton, "Good Morning Runaway Sales," *Strategy*, July 29, 2002, p. 23.

The Moosehead positioning is reflected in new creative that shows classic outdoorsy scenes such as sunset and a peaceful lake and a deck chair at the end of a dock. The new slogan, "Refreshingly Independent," acknowledges the presence of the consumer and the connection between the consumer's mindset and the brand's personality (see Figure 4.9).[5] The outdoor theme is a territory that is unique in beer campaigns and is potentially a domain solely owned by Moosehead. For a niche beer, that's good strategy.

CREATIVE OBJECTIVES

Creative Objective

A statement that clearly indicates the information to be communicated to the target audience.

Creative objectives are statements that clearly indicate the information to be communicated to the target audience. What to say about a brand in general terms is usually included in the creative brief. While formats may vary, objective statements tend to involve a key benefit statement and a support claims statement, because the content of an ad or an ad campaign needs focus.

When determining what to say about a brand, and how to say it, the copywriter and art director refer to the advertising objective for context. As discussed earlier in the chapter, the advertising objective may be *to achieve brand awareness, encourage trial purchase, attract a new target, encourage preference*, or *alter a perception*. Somehow, the objective and the primary reason for buying the brand must be related together so that a cohesive message is presented to the consumer.

FIGURE **4.9** **An Ad That Reflects Moosehead's Positioning Strategy: "Enjoyment of the Great Outdoors"**

Source: Courtesy of Moosewood Breweries Limited.

Key Benefit Statement

A statement of the basic selling idea, service, or benefit promised the consumer by the advertiser.

- *Key Benefit Statement:* The **key benefit statement** expresses the basic selling idea, service, or benefit that the advertiser promises the consumer. This benefit should be the primary reason for buying a particular brand instead of competitive brands. The benefit can be something tangible, such as better performance, better quality, lower price, longer lasting, and so on, or it can be something intangible or psychological, such as the status and prestige that come with ownership. With reference to the positioning strategy described above, the key benefit for Moosehead is intangible. The brand appeals to beer drinkers in pursuit of independence and freedom, a desire to be different than mainstream brand drinkers.

Support Claims Statement
A substantiation of the promise made in the key benefit statement.

- ***Support Claims Statement:*** **A support claims statement** describes the characteristics that will substantiate the promise. It provides proof of the promise based on criteria such as technical performance data, comparative product testing, and any other data generated from marketing research. Good support claims give customers a real reason why they should buy the product. Support claims statements are less important for brands touting intangible benefits. Lifestyle imagery, for example, relies on the image presented and the connection between the image and the consumer who sees it to substantiate the promise.

Pine-Sol
www.pinesol.com

To demonstrate the application of and relationships between advertising objectives, key benefits, and support claims statements, consider the situation that Pine-Sol was facing. Pine-Sol ranks second in market share behind Mr. Clean and ahead of Lysol. Research showed Pine-Sol as old fashioned, too strong for everyday use, with an overpowering smell. It suffered from back-of-the-cupboard syndrome. The advertising objective was to alter these perceptions. The solution was found in consumer research. Younger women wanted strength, but not the strength Pine-Sol stood for. In exploratory research, the women talked about different types of clean: the clean for when friends dropped by and the clean for when the mother-in-law dropped by. Out of this came the idea for a new level of clean: the thorough clean. Therefore, the *key benefit statement* for Pine-Sol might read as follows:

> For mothers in search of a cleaner that will *thoroughly* clean their floors and counters, Pine-Sol works best (the promise).

The *support claims statement* might read like this:

> While other leading brands get your floors and counters clean, Pine-Sol cleans and disinfects more thoroughly. It even cleans the dirt you don't even know about such as accidents and spills that go undetected (the proof).

Pine-Sol's message was communicated in a unique manner. The ads charmingly dramatize real life and included situations mothers could readily identify with (see Figure 4.10). One commercial showed a small boy whose "aim" is off in the bathroom. Another showed a dog resting on the kitchen table instead of his basket. In research women said "that's my life." The ads make them think of Pine-Sol differently than before.[6]

A new ad for Mott's Fruitsations offers another illustration. The objective of the ad is to create brand awareness and trial purchase of Mott's new unsweetened applesauce blends. The product is positioned to fit with the healthier eating preferences of today's consumers. The key benefit is that the product is all natural. There are no refined or processed sugars added. The visual image of the sliced apple and the headline "No sugar added," along with the product visual and the sub-headline "Ditto," supports the promise. The ad clearly and convincingly presents a case for trying the product (see Figure 4.11).

Ads for Colgate Total toothpaste offer another illustration. The promise made is clear: Colgate helps fight tooth decay and helps prevent gingivitis. Consumers are attracted to brands that offer dual benefits (a form of product differentiation). The proof is even clearer: Colgate is the only toothpaste to earn the Canadian Dental Association seal of approval for gingivitis reduction and for the prevention of tooth decay. The endorsement by a third party enhances the credibility of the message. The CDA seal and an explanation appear in all forms of advertising.

CREATIVE STRATEGY

With the decisions about what to say in advertising determined, the creative team turns its attention to creative strategy. This is where the advertising agency starts to earn its keep. What the team searches for is the "big idea," or the central concept or theme that an entire campaign can be built around. All kinds of discussion and experimentation take place. It is an exercise in brainstorming. The guiding light is the positioning strategy. When the ad

FIGURE **4.10** An Ad Focusing on a Key Benefit: "A Thorough Clean"

"BAD AIM"

VIDEO: Open on a shot of an empty bathroom.
Now a little boy runs into the bathroom.
The little boy begins to pee in the toilet.
SFX: Tinkling in toilet.
SUPER: Pine-Sol cleans the dirt you know about.
VIDEO: Suddenly, his mom calls from downstairs. The boy turns to respond to her call, and in doing so pees on the floor.
MOM: Max! We're going!
SFX: Tinkling on floor.
VIDEO: He turns back and casually finishes up.
SUPER: And the dirt you don't.
VIDEO: Cut to a mid-shot of Pine-Sol Original bottle.
SUPER: The thorough clean.

Source: The Clorox Company of Canada.

agency pitches its ideas to the client, the client evaluates the idea based on how it fits with the positioning strategy. Simply put: Is the big idea on strategy or off strategy?

The **creative strategy** is a statement of how the message will be communicated to the target audience. It deals with issues such as the tone and style of message, the central theme that will be adopted, and the appeal techniques that will be employed. It is a statement about the personality a brand will project to consumers.

- *Tone and Style:* In an attempt to break through the clutter of competitive advertising, copywriters and art directors agonize over decisions about tone and style. Such a fundamental decision has direct impact on how a campaign evolves over time and how the brand's personality gets ingrained in the customer's mind. Single words often describe the tone and style that is recommended. For example, the message will be presented in a persuasive manner, an informative manner, a conservative manner, a friendly manner, a contemporary manner, a straightforward manner, an upbeat manner, and so on and so on. What approach will have the most impact on the target audience? Obviously, knowledge about the target audience that is gleaned from the demographic and psychographic profiles plays a key role in this decision.

Creative Strategy

A plan of action for how the message will be communicated to the target audience, covering the tone and style of message, the central theme, and the appeal techniques.

FIGURE **4.11** **An Ad to Create Awareness and Trial for an All-Natural Fruit Product**

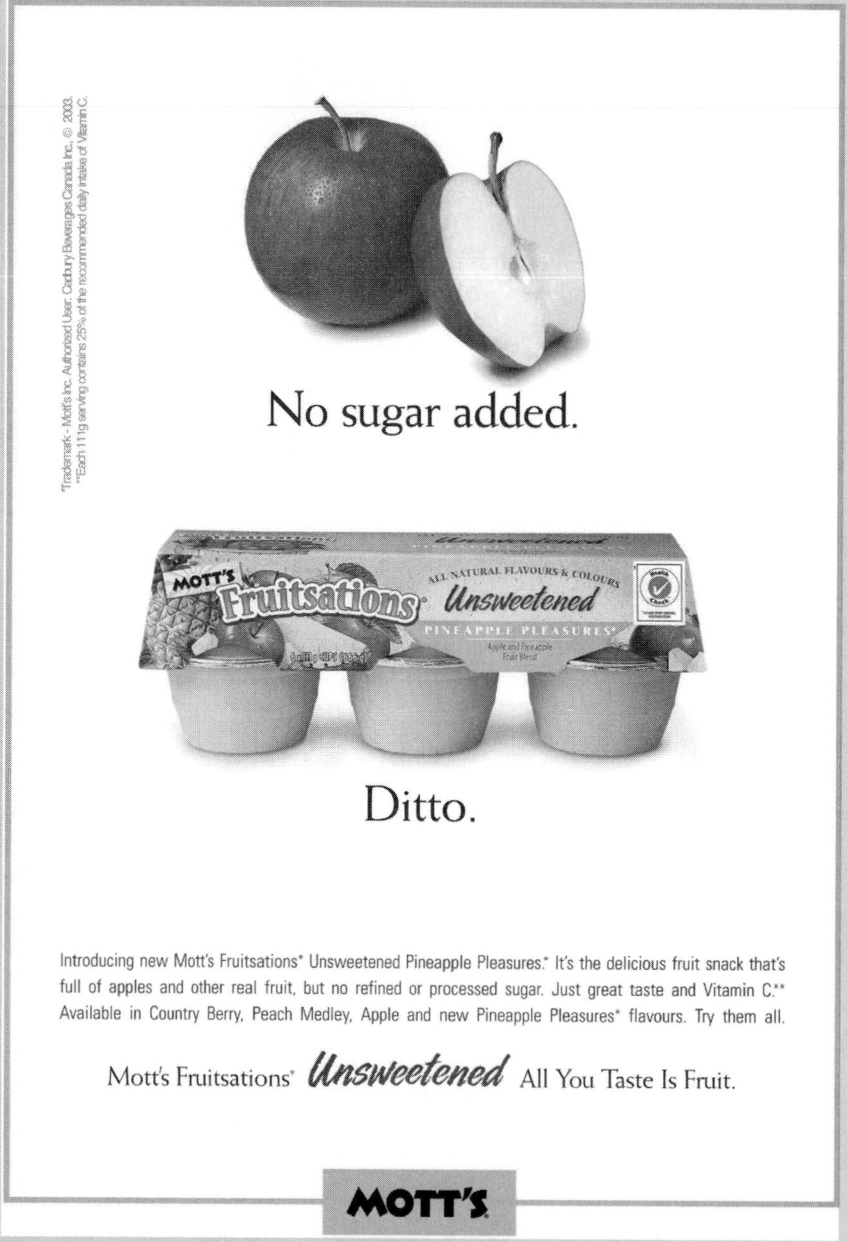
*Trademark - Mott's Inc. Authorized User: Cadbury Beverages Canada Inc. © 2003.
**Each 111g serving contains 25% of the recommended daily intake of Vitamin C.
No sugar added.
MOTT'S
Fruitsations
ALL NATURAL FLAVOURS & COLOURS
Unsweetened
PINEAPPLE PLEASURES
Ditto.
Introducing new Mott's Fruitsations* Unsweetened Pineapple Pleasures.* It's the delicious fruit snack that's full of apples and other real fruit, but no refined or processed sugar. Just great taste and Vitamin C.** Available in Country Berry, Peach Medley, Apple and new Pineapple Pleasures* flavours. Try them all.
Mott's Fruitsations* Unsweetened All You Taste Is Fruit.
MOTT'S

Source: Cadbury Beverages Canada Inc.

Central Theme or "Big Idea"
The glue that binds various creative elements of a campaign together; transferable from one medium to another.

- ***Central Theme:*** The **central theme** or **"big idea"** is the glue that binds the various creative elements of the campaign together. As such, the theme must be transferable from one medium to another. For example, when someone sees an ad in print form (newspaper, magazine, or outdoor), it should conjure up images and meaning from something they have seen on television (a 30-second commercial). What the theme will be is truly the key decision the creative team makes. For the theme to see the light of day, it must be presented to the client in a very convincing manner. For a brand such as Maytag (appliances), the central theme is dependability. That is also the key benefit the brand offers. The idle Maytag repairman, a character strongly associated with the brand name, is the means by which dependability is communicated.

A recent advertising campaign for Diet Pepsi aptly demonstrates how good decisions about tone, style, and theme have a positive impact on consumers. Diet Pepsi was losing ground to Diet Coke and Diet Pepsi was being ruled by the image of regular Pepsi. Diet Pepsi's primary target market is young adults (the twenty-something crowd). They are making their first big, important decisions such as where to live, their career choice, and who to have relationships with. Marketing research revealed they didn't want to lose their spontaneity and spirit even though they were getting older. Therefore, the big idea had to consider the youthful feelings of a maturing audience. Too much youth and Diet Pepsi would wind up back in regular Pepsi territory. Too little, and the brand would be just plain dull.

The creative team recommended a "Forever Young" theme (see Figure 4.12 on p. 118). The tone and style of ads, particularly on television, were "kind of wacky." They portrayed a temporary break from maturity, not a breakdown in their entire way of life. Apparently, mature diet cola drinkers still long for some crazy moments of their past. In one ad a young man working in a men's shop spots a customer's underwear peeking out of his pants and gives him a wedgie. He then asked, "How's that fit?" The ad ends with the tagline "Taste the one that's forever young."[7] In the race for market share, Diet Pepsi and Diet Coke are now in a dead heat, proof that the right kind of advertising works.

APPEAL TECHNIQUES

How to make an advertisement appealing to the customer is another key decision. What techniques will be employed to bring the product benefit claims and theme to life? What can we do creatively to break through the perceptual barriers in the consumer's mind? There isn't a single, definitive formula for success, but there is a tendency to classify appeal techniques into certain areas. For example, when you see an ad, does it make you snicker? Does it draw a tear? Does it make you think? How consumers respond to an ad is usually related to the effectiveness of the appeal. The following is a discussion of some of the more common appeal techniques.

Positive Appeals

Presenting the message in a positive manner is always a safe approach, but it is also a very common approach. If combined effectively with the right theme, positive appeals will work. However, if the creative execution lacks impact, it will wind up being just another ad. McDonald's is one of the country's biggest advertisers and dominates its market. The company is proud of its accomplishments so its ads reflect its position. The theme of McDonald's advertising does change from time to time but the ads remain consistent in how they appeal to their target. Television ads usually include music and positive interactions among family members and between family members and employees. The message is delivered in an upbeat manner. Taglines such as "There's a little McDonald's in everyone" aptly reflect the positive style of advertising. Admit it, the McDonald's tagline is a phrase you do sing along to!

Negative Appeals

Unless you are Buckley's cough mixture, you don't say bad things about your product. "Tastes awful, but it works," is now a famous slogan coined by Buckley's. Following a philosophy of "do what your momma says and you will get better," Buckley's has experienced new popularity and a positive increase in market share based solely on its negative style

FIGURE **4.12** **An Illustration of Diet Pepsi's Central Theme or "Big Idea"**

Agency:	BBDO Canada	Title:	"Comb-Over"
Client:	Pepsi-Cola Canada Ltd.	Length:	30-second English Television
Product:	Diet Pepsi	Date:	01.02

We open on a balding man standing on a sidewalk somewhere. He is looking away, but turns towards camera as the camera approaches him
ANNOR VO: I see you're drinking Diet Pepsi. Is there anything else youthful you'd like to experience?

MAN: (thinking for a moment and then pointing at his bald head) Yeah...I'd like to have back all the hair I had in high school.

MUSIC: (The song "I Ran" from the Flock of Seagulls starts to play.)
Panning up we follow our hero walking towards camera - indeed he has his high school hair back – it's unfortunately the same 1980s Flock of Seagulls hairstyle he wore as teenager.

We see our hero in the middle of a serious business meeting.

His hair is casting an unusual shadow on the projection screen – disrupting the meeting.

Then we see our hero waiting for a serve.

His new hair is blocking 90% of his vision. His opponent winds up and serves. Just as our hero takes the ball in the head.

We match-dissolve back to our original scene – our hero looks back towards camera.
MAN: (thinking) Oh second thought, I'll stick to the Diet Pepsi.

ANNOR VO: Taste the one that's forever young. Diet Pepsi.

Source: Pepsi-Cola Canada Ltd.

of advertising. For other products, though, negative appeals usually present a situation the consumer would like to avoid, such as stolen traveller's cheques (American Express), the theft of an automobile (CIBC auto insurance), and kids making a mess in the kitchen (any brand of paper towel). These situations are quickly resolved when the product appears to save the day—a convincing demonstration that usually seals the deal. A leading brand such as American Express eliminates potential fear and anxiety by saying "American Express. Don't leave home without it."

Humorous Appeals

Taking a light-hearted approach to communicating benefits can work effectively. In fact, many critics believe that for advertising to be successful it must entertain the audience. If true, then an advertisement that causes the audience to break into a smile or giggle should break through the clutter. Dairy Queen used humour in a campaign for its Blizzard product. Two goofballs who appear to have indulged in more than just dessert are sitting around a table. One holds a Blizzard upside-down in each hand and chants "bawk, bawk, bawk—dude, dude" while the other does an air drumming routine. The voiceover deadpans, "Yeah, they're thick." Is it the two guys or the Blizzard that's thick? The irreverent humour is bang on for the youth market with the dudes and the product sharing the same attributes. The commercial cleverly includes a product demonstration and there is wall-to-wall branding throughout.

One of the major weaknesses of using humour is that it can wear out prematurely. After a few exposures, the audience may not find the message funny. The commercial described above for Dairy Queen could get annoying after you've seen it a dozen times. Advertisers must also be wary of sarcastic humour that could insult cultural groups. Humour can backfire and bring on unwanted negative publicity. Furthermore, the use of humour allows for considerable creative latitude. The creative team must ensure that the humour does not get more attention than the product. To keep the message fresh, a pool of commercials is needed so that individual spots can be rotated in and out of a media schedule.

Sexual Appeals

Sex in advertising! It will spark some controversy, some good, some not so good. When sexual appeals are used in advertising, certain values and attitudes toward sex are being sold to consumers along with the products. Consider, for example, a recent commercial for Elastoplast bandages. Who would think that a sexual connotation would suit such a product? The commercial, titled "Hide the Evidence," for its Fast Healing bandage is all about covering up wounds inflicted in close encounters with the other sex. To hide some scratches, the man puts a bandage on his shoulder. When he returns home, and casually embraces his wife, he notices she is wearing one, too. The erotica in the ad doesn't steal the show but rather reinforces the primary message. The result is an ad that not only catches the eye; it leaves a very clear impression of Elastoplast's benefits.

Elastoplast
www.elastoplast.ca

Some sexual advertisements are subtle, while others are blatant. Doug Robinson, Chair and Creative Director at Ammirati Puris, says, "It's simply a reflection of general trends in the entertainment world. People are using more provocative imagery and language. Whether you like it or not videos and movies are opening doors."[8] Robinson's ad agency developed a controversial television ad for Carlsberg beer in which a woman alludes to her friend's prowess at giving oral pleasure. The ad raised a few eyebrows!

Sex is a strong physiological need, just behind self-preservation, and sexual desire is an instinctive reaction, so why not use it in advertising? The only real issue is the way in which it is used. Clearly, explicit sex increases the risks for the advertiser, since it may alienate consumers at large. But, if core customers do not find it offensive, the advertiser may truly be on to something. Beiresdorf Canada Inc., the marketer of Elastoplast bandages, did take a risk when it aired the commercial described above. To eliminate some of that risk, the commercial was scheduled for airing late in the evening and the company sponsored the hit show *Sex and the City*. The image in Figure 4.13 is a form of sexual appeal.

Emotional Appeals

Emotional appeals presented effectively will arouse the feelings of an audience. To demonstrate, consider the style of advertising used to promote social causes: anything

FIGURE **4.13**   **An Advertiser Using a Sexual Appeal Technique**

Source: Parfums Givenchy Canada, Ltd.

from drinking and driving to spousal abuse to quitting smoking. In one TV ad that encourages people to stop smoking, a mature woman talks of the perils of second-hand smoke. Her husband, a smoker, is dead and she suffers from emphysema. Such a message leaves the viewer with a disturbing feeling.

Tapping into people's emotions also works in a positive setting. There is no disputing the popularity and dominance of Tim Hortons in Canada. In terms of annual dollar sales, the company is as big as McDonald's. Good marketing and good advertising has helped build the business. Hortons' image advertising campaign titled "True Stories" effectively uses emotional appeals by showing real emotional connections between customers and the company. A recent television spot shows a Canadian student away from home attending the University of Glasgow. Through visual imagery and words, the ad says you don't know what you miss until you are away from it—an important lesson in life. To make his place feel more like home all kinds of Canadian paraphernalia adorned the student's residence but it wasn't until the Tim Hortons coffee maker and coffee arrived that it really felt like home. Yes, it's another feel-good story from a Canadian icon.

Lifestyle Appeals

Advertisers using lifestyle appeal techniques try to associate their brand with the lifestyle or desired lifestyle of the audience they are trying to reach. Some of the appeals already discussed, such as sexual appeals and emotional appeals, are frequently included as elements of a lifestyle campaign. Other elements may include action, adventure, and excitement to stimulate desire. Lifestyle appeals are popular among advertisers owing to the greater availability of psychographic information about Canadian consumers.

Many beer brands use lifestyle appeals in order to establish an image firmly in the minds of drinkers 19 to 29 years of age. If you are what you drink, then there is a brand of beer for you. A relatively new category of drinks called "alcopops" has adopted a similar strategy. Also referred to as coolers, this is the fastest growing category in the food and beverage industry worldwide. Unlike wine coolers, alcohol-based coolers appeal to both genders. Smirnoff Ice is one of the leading brands and success is attributed to the style of advertising. One ad called "Train" depicts partygoers transforming a subway car into a rolling nightclub. Another spot called "Hairnet" shows a group of twenty-something guys sneaking into a dance bar by telling the bouncer they work in the kitchen. The similarity to beer ads is no accident. Says brand manager Steve Doyle, "There's no doubt about it. We're targeting beer drinkers and trying to provide them with an alternative to beer."[9] To be a product like a beer, you must portray the product like a beer. Smirnoff Ice and other competitors have to fit the lifestyle of the target market.

Even durable goods such as electronics components, televisions, and major kitchen appliances use lifestyle appeal techniques. Ads typically show situations that families can readily identify with, such as a home environment that has a very contemporary look. Figure 4.14 on page 122 shows how Sharp appeals to a modern lifestyle.

Comparative Appeals

In comparative advertisements, the promise and proof are shown by comparing the attributes of a given product with those of competing products—attributes that are important to the target market. The comparison should focus on the primary reason for buying the product. Comparisons can be direct, such as when the other brand is mentioned and shown. Or they can be indirect, with only a reference to another leading brand or brands. The Pepsi-Cola taste test challenge led to an all-out assault on Coca-Cola when Pepsi advertising made claims of taste preference for Pepsi by Coca-Cola drinkers. It is quite common for a brand of paper towels such as Bounty to show the ease with which it cleans up a mess while the competitors are shown disintegrating on contact with moisture.

Comparative campaigns are usually undertaken by a "challenger" brand, a brand that ranks behind the category leader in terms of market share. Showing comparisons where the challenger performs better than the market leader is a convincing presentation. It will make consumers think more about the brand they currently use. Such a strategy presents several risks. The brand leader could fight back. If so, the brand that made the comparison may need adequate financial resources to fight an advertising war. As well, any claims must not mislead the public. If they do, the market leader could instigate legal proceedings to get the offending brand to offer proof of its claims. Critics of comparative appeals firmly believe a brand should stand on its own merits. Why cloud the issue by bringing in competing brands?

FIGURE **4.14** GE Appeals to the Lifestyle of a Young Contemporary Family

Appliances That Make Your Kitchens Stand Out

GE Appliances
www.geappliances.ca
1-800-361-1100

Source: Courtesy of Camco.

Factual Appeals

Certain product categories lend themselves to a straightforward style of advertising. The ads simply state what the product will do and back it up with information that is plain for the customer to understand. Over-the-counter pharmaceuticals use this technique frequently. Brands in this category rely on technical information or scientific data to validate claims. Advil says it's for "today's kind of pain." Advil offers fast relief for the things that slow you down. Phrases such as "safe, reliable, and doctor recommended" verify the claim.

And what do the competitors say? Motrin ads say, "It's for people who don't fool around with pain." Unlike acetaminophen pain relievers, which alter perceptions of pain, Motrin works at the source of the pain (that makes it sound better!). Category leader Tylenol says, "Doctors recommend Tylenol more than all other brands combined to reduce fever and temporary relief of minor aches and pains." The third-party endorsement by doctors has a definite impact. These competitive examples aptly depict the intent of factual appeals.

Factual appeals are very appropriate for products that are expensive or complex. In these cases, there is usually a high degree of involvement by consumers in the decision-making process. Information (detailed information) provided by advertising is helpful. Furthermore, the rational buying behaviour in the business-to-business marketplace is conducive to factual appeals.

For a good illustration of how S.O.S. Soap Pads broke through the clutter of cleaning products advertising, read the IMC Highlight **Saving Our Saucepans**.

CREATIVE EXECUTION

In the creative execution stage of creative planning, specific decisions are made regarding how to best present the message. If product comparisons are used, what kind of demonstration technique will be employed? Will sexual appeals be subtle or blatant? If lifestyle appeals are used, what kind of backdrops and settings will be needed? If music is called for, what kind of music will it be? If it is a print campaign, will the ads be copy dominated or image dominated? Will artwork or photography be the key visual element? How big will the ads be? There is a host of decisions to be made.

IMC Highlight

SAVING OUR SAUCEPANS

S.O.S. is a long-established brand name, but since it had not been advertised in some time it was not top of mind with consumers. It is a product designed for heavy-duty cleaning jobs. Sales were declining because of changes in consumers' eating habits (less fatty oil) and cooking habits (less frying).

However, S.O.S. remains the best thing for stuck-on, burnt-on, really bad stains on pots, pans, and bakeware. The advertising challenge for Clorox (the manufacturer) and Palmer Jarvis DDB (the ad agency) was "how to get S.O.S. back into people's top of mind, and remind them to think of S.O.S. first when they are thinking of dirty dishes."

The target was described as women 35 to 54 years, who work, have children, and have busy, active households. Palmer decided to use magazines as the primary medium. These women read publications such as *Chatelaine, Canadian Living,* and *Canadian House & Home.* The creative challenge was to develop an ad that would stand out from the clutter of household product advertising that appeared in these magazines. All ads look similar and all brands make similar kinds of product claims.

Few people today are aware that when the product was initially launched the acronym S.O.S. stood for "Save Our Saucepans." However, there is a high level of awareness for the nautical term S.O.S. standing for "Save Our Ship." Voilà! The big idea emerged!

The combination of the brand name and what the product does best—save people from unimaginable messes—led to the concept of a Titanic-style ad. Strategically, it is a negative appeal technique—a situation people would like to avoid. In terms of execution, dishes were strategically placed in a sink to resemble a sinking ship. The breakthrough visual is a great link to the brand name and the single copy line "S.O.S. First for every disaster" was a great reminder of the primary benefit of using S.O.S.

So impressed with the creativity of the ads was the Titanic International Society that it requested copies for its 2003 national meeting in Ottawa. S.O.S. sponsored of the event.

Adapted from Melanie Johnston, "That Little Blue Pad," *Marketing*, April 8, 2002, p. 10.

The agency creative team evaluates specific ideas that it thinks have the potential to convert its vision of an ad into reality. In doing so, the team must answer two basic questions:

1. What is the best or most convincing way to present the brand's benefits to motivate the consumer to take action?
2. Is there a specific technique that will effectively convince consumers that this is the right brand for them?

For example, if a decision is made to use a celebrity as a spokesperson, who will the celebrity be? Will it be a famous rock star, movie star, or sports personality? A lot of behind-the-scenes discussion goes on for decisions of this magnitude. The following are some of the more commonly used presentation tactics.

Product Demonstrations

Product as Hero
A creative execution technique in which the advertised product is shown coming to the rescue.

Torture Test
A creative execution technique in which the product is subjected to extreme conditions to demonstrate its durability.

For products that want to make claims regarding performance (e.g., dependability, reliability, speed), demonstrations work well. As mentioned above, the simplest appeal is to say or show the product and what it will do. In print advertising, "a picture says a thousand words." On television, showing the product in use is often the simplest and most direct way to make a claim. The intensity of competition among brands sometimes calls for more dramatic demonstrations. A technique referred to as **product as hero** (the product comes to the rescue when the consumer is facing a really tough situation) is often the answer. Categories such as household cleaning products are famous for such a technique (see Figure 4.15). If a product really wants to drive home an important claim, there's the **torture test**. This technique was made famous by Timex watches with its "It takes a licking and keeps on ticking" campaign. The exaggerated demonstrations for the watch certainly verified the primary claim of durability, and at a reasonable price.

Testimonials

Advertisers that follow a traditional approach to advertising frequently use testimonials. In a testimonial, a typical user of the product presents the message. Real people in ads are often perceived to be more credible than models and celebrities who are paid handsomely to sell a certain brand. The "True Stories" Tim Hortons campaign referred to earlier involves a series of testimonials by everyday customers who tell a story about why Tim Hortons plays such an important and enjoyable role in their lives. The commercials present kind of a "folksy" image that regular customers can identify with. When you think about it, after all, Tim Hortons is part of the daily grind of a lot of people.

The popularity of reality-based television has spawned *reality-based advertising*. Labatt Breweries and Tim Hortons are two advertisers that launched national campaigns featuring real people in roles that are usually left to actors. "There's more room for magic and spontaneity because the people are not so rehearsed," says executive creative director Paul Wales of Creative Enterprise Selling. The new Labatt Blue campaign features the slogan "Cheers. To Friends," and realistically depicts what guys do when they are hanging out with their friends. The first ad is a montage of scenes that looked like they were shot by a hand-held video camera. The guys knock over an outhouse with a friend inside, show another guy being launched head first into a paper towel display in a supermarket, and show two guys fishing off a dock sitting in La-Z-Boy armchairs. Anything goes![10] These kinds of commercials are produced for a fraction of the fees of regular commercials, a real bonus for advertisers—assuming they work.

Endorsements

Star power is the heart of a celebrity endorsement execution. Stars from stage, screen, music, and sports form the nucleus of celebrity endorsers. Among the biggest and most expensive celebrities are Tiger Woods (Nike, American Express, and Buick, among other brands and companies) and Britney Spears (Pepsi-Cola).

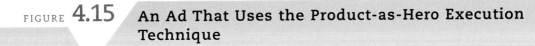

FIGURE **4.15** **An Ad That Uses the Product-as-Hero Execution Technique**

Source: Scott Paper Limited.

TD Waterhouse decided to use celebrities for the first time. Going all out, stars such as Jerry Orbach (*Law & Order*), Jackie Chan (movies and martial arts expert), Geena Davis (movie star), and Phil Jackson (Los Angeles Lakers basketball coach) appear individually in television and print ads. According to a TD Waterhouse executive, "The campaign captures the personal dimension of investing. The personalities were selected to bring life to the differences in how people choose to invest." In one commercial, Jackie Chan fights off the bad guys while reading a research report. In another spot, Phil Jackson is asked about a recent trade he made. Turns out it was a trade in his TD Waterhouse account. TD Waterhouse is spending US$100 million on the campaign in the U.S. It is their largest investment ever in advertising.[11]

Ford of Canada and its dealer associations have built a campaign in Canada on retired hockey star Wayne Gretzky. Says Dean Tesser, Director of Marketing, "The new campaign aims to provide a unified message from all Canadian Ford dealers by using a 'Canadian icon' who appeals to all demographics." The campaign uses the theme and tagline "Built for life in Canada." Gretzky appears in television and print ads, dealer advertising, and promotional materials and on Ford's website.[12]

Do celebrities work? That's a tough question to answer but one asked frequently by clients. There isn't a definitive answer but let's look at a situation and try to pass judgment. Where would Nike be in the golf business without Tiger Woods? Nike has invested millions in Tiger Woods. In return, he alone has put Nike on the golf map. Star power like that does attract advertisers, and an audience.

Taglines and Slogans

Tagline
A short phrase that captures the essence of an advertised message.

Slogan
A short phrase that captures the essence of an entire advertising campaign.

Despite all of the time, energy, and money that go into developing an ad campaign, consumers only remember bits and pieces of the message. The most important thing for them to remember is the brand name and the primary benefit. To reinforce the primary benefit and the central theme of a campaign, and to reflect the positioning strategy of the brand, the creative team develops a **tagline** for individual ads, or a **slogan** that will appear in all forms of advertising. The slogan provides continuity within an advertising campaign. Several ads that appear in figures in this chapter include a slogan. Pine Sol, for example, says it is "The thorough clean" and Diet Pepsi is "Forever Young."

Of the things that consumers remember about a brand, the slogan is something they have a tendency to recall. The repetition of messages consumers receive over an extended period helps ingrain the slogan in the customer's mind. From time to time the slogan will change, especially when a brand or company wants to change its image. However, it is more common for the slogan to remain in place even if the creative strategy and creative execution are completely new. The brand name and the slogan are important variables that help build a brand's equity. Figure 4.16 lists some popular and longstanding brands and slogans.

FIGURE **4.16**

Some Popular Brands and Slogans

Visa	"It's everywhere you want to be."
Volkswagen	"Drivers wanted."
Burger King	"Have it your way."
Bounty	"The quicker picker-upper."
KFC	"Finger lickin' good."
Avis	"We try harder."
Nike	"Just do it."
Lays	"Betcha can't eat just one."
Infiniti	"Accelerating the future."
Nissan	"Shift"
L'Oreal	"Because you're worth it."

A slogan is a key element of brand identification. Many of these slogans have stood the test of time. They are strongly associated with the brand name and appear in all forms of advertising.

Summary

The marketing communications process begins with a sender (the advertiser) developing a message to be sent by the media to the receiver (the consumer or business customer). The goal of marketing communications is to break through consumers' perceptual barriers while recognizing that competitors' messages are trying to do the same. When messages are developed, consideration is given to how consumers receive and interpret messages. The consumer's mind goes through a series of stages: awareness, comprehension, conviction, and action.

Creative planning is a sequential process that involves analyzing market and customer information, identifying problems and opportunities, setting goals and objectives, and developing creative strategies and tactics. The planning cycle starts with a creative brief, a document prepared by the client for discussion with the advertising agency. The brief includes relevant background information, identifies problems, goals, and advertising objectives. The document acts as a guideline for the creative team when it is brainstorming for new ideas.

Once the advertising objectives are identified, the creative team begins work on creative objectives, strategies, and execution. Advertising objectives provide focus to the creative challenge (e.g., the objective is to create awareness, build preference, alter perceptions, encourage trial purchase, and so on). Creative objectives are statements that clearly identify the information to be communicated to the target market. They include a key benefit statement (a promise) and a support claims statement (proof of promise). Usually the client and agency collaborate when finalizing these statements.

Creative strategy is concerned with the tone, style, theme, and appeal techniques that are used to influence consumers to take action. Among the more commonly used strategies are positive and negative approaches, using humour, sexual, emotional and lifestyle appeals, offering factual information, and comparisons with other products.

At the creative execution stage, specific decisions are made on how to implement the strategy. Some of the specific techniques that are commonly used include product demonstrations, testimonials from everyday users of the product, and celebrity endorsements. A good campaign will include a slogan. The slogan serves two essential roles. First, it communicates the essential idea the advertiser wants associated with the product and, second, it maintains continuity within an advertising campaign. In combination with the brand name, a good slogan helps build brand equity.

Key Terms

advertising	102	noise	99
"big idea"	116	overall goal	105
central theme	116	problem statement	105
communication	99	product as hero	124
creative brief	103	slogan	126
creative objective	112	support claims statement	114
creative strategy	115	tagline	126
encoding	99	torture test	124
key benefit statement	113	transmission	99

Review Questions

1. Briefly explain the behavioural stages a consumer passes through prior to making the decision to buy a particular product.
2. What is a creative brief and what role does it play in the development of an advertising campaign?
3. In the context of creative planning, what is meant by the "big idea"?
4. Ad campaigns should have focus and aim toward an overall goal. Identify and briefly explain three specific goals a campaign may try to achieve.
5. How important is a positioning strategy statement and what role does it play in creative planning?

6. What is the difference between a key benefits statement and a support claims statement?

7. Briefly describe the various appeal techniques commonly used in advertising.

8. Briefly explain the following creative execution terms:
   a) product as hero and torture test
   b) testimonial and endorsement
   c) tagline and slogan

Discussion and Application Questions

1. Are humorous advertising campaigns effective? Conduct some online secondary research on humour in advertising and present a case for or against the use of humour.

2. "Lifestyle advertising strategies are ineffective because they communicate little about the product." Is this statement true or false? Conduct some online secondary research about lifestyle advertising and present a position on this issue.

3. "Good execution of a poor creative strategy will create positive results for the brand (company)." Is this statement true or false? Assemble some data that either support or negate this statement.

4. Clip an ad that catches your imagination from a magazine in your household. After assessing the ad, try to determine the advertising objective, the creative objective (key benefit statement), and the creative strategy (appeal technique). Can you figure out what the advertiser intended when the ad was in the development stages?

5. Assess a series of advertisements for one brand. Pick a popular brand that uses several different media. Based on everything you know about that brand based on the marketing communications you

are exposed to, write a positioning strategy statement that reflects the intentions of the brand. What message or image does the company want to instill in the customer's mind?

6. Select two brands that compete directly against one another. Assess the creative strategies and creative executions used by each brand. Since both brands are trying to reach and influence the same target market using advertising, which brand has more impact on consumers? Which style of advertising is more effective? Justify your position.

7. Find separate products or services that use the following creative appeal techniques.
   a) Negative appeals
   b) Humorous appeals
   c) Comparative appeals
   d) Emotional appeals
   e) Lifestyle appeals

8. What is your assessment of that strategy in terms of potential impact on the target market? Justify your position.

9. Assess a brand advertising campaign that features a celebrity spokesperson. Will that spokesperson have an influence on the intended target? What are the benefits and drawbacks of using a celebrity spokesperson?

End Notes

1 "Ad Education," Iowa State University <www.public.iastate.edu/~geske/FCB.html> (November 2003).

2 *Dictionary of Marketing Terms*, Baron's Educational Series, Inc., 1994, p. 13.

3 Edna Fernandes, "Tetley Tea Folk Just Too Common for the Brand's New Owners," *Financial Post*, December 9, 2002, p. FP6.

4 Hollie Shaw, "Bay Ads Trade Flash for Practical," *Financial Post*, August 23, 2002, p. FP3.

5 Patrick Allossery, "Best Place for a Moose Is Outdoors," *Financial Post*, May 6, 2002, p. FP6.

6 "Packaged Goods Other," Cassies insert in *Marketing*, November 18, 2002, p. 5.

7 Susan Heinrich, "Forever Young: Pepsi Campaign

Wins Top Cassie," *Financial Post*, November 16, 2002, p. FP7.

8 Wendy Cuthbert, "Racy Ads Pushing the Boundaries," *Strategy*, September 25, 2000, p. 20.

9 John Heinzl, "Spirit Coolers Proving Hot," *Globe and Mail*, June 28, 2002, p. B9.

10 Susan Heinrich, "Advertisers Say It's Time to Get Real," *Financial Post*, March 3, 2003, p. FP4.

11 "TD Waterhouse Launches $100 Million Ad Campaign," Press Release, TD Waterhouse, September 21, 1999 <www.tdwaterhouse.com/home/press/releases/092199.html> (November 2003).

12 "Gretzky Driving Ford Campaign," *Marketing*, November 25, 2002, p. 1.

CHAPTER 5

ADVERTISING: MEDIA PLANNING

After studying this chapter you will be able to:

describe the steps involved in media planning,

distinguish among media objectives, media strategies, and media execution,

describe the various factors that influence media strategy decisions, and

outline the characteristics, strengths, and weaknesses of mass media advertising alternatives.

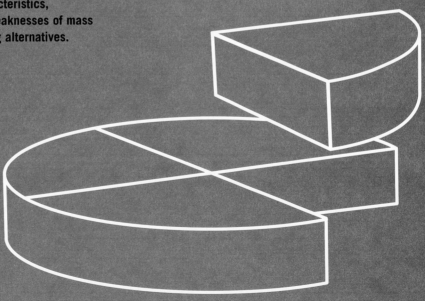

As mentioned in Chapter 4, the creative plan and media plan are developed at the same time and depend on the same information from the marketing plan. This chapter will focus specifically on the development and implementation of the media plan. Developing a media plan is a complex process. The primary goal of the agency media planners is to reach a target market efficiently. In doing so, they consider all kinds of strategic issues, along with conditions in the marketplace and what competitors are doing.

Efficiency in media planning can be loosely defined as gaining maximum exposure at minimum cost. In following this mantra, the agency planners must develop and execute a plan that achieves the client's objectives within certain financial constraints. As in the case of the creative plan, the media plan is part of a broader marketing communications plan and marketing plan. Therefore, the direction a media plan takes must fit in with and be coordinated (timed) with activities recommended in other marketing communications areas. Coordinating various communications activities creates synergy and maximizes the impact of the plan on competitors in the channel of distribution and on consumers.

Media Planning

Media planning involves developing a plan of action for communicating messages to the right people (the target market), at the right time, and with the right frequency. Both the client and the agency play a role in media planning (see Figure 5.1). The client's role focuses on providing necessary background information and then evaluating the recommendations that the agency makes. The agency assesses the information provided by the client and then prepares a strategic plan that will meet the client's objectives. Because there is a considerable amount of money involved, clients scrutinize media plans carefully.

Media Brief

A document that contains essential information for developing a media plan; used to stimulate discussion between a client and agency.

Information provided by the client is contained in a **media brief** (much like the creative brief discussed in Chapter 4). The media brief is a document that contains essential information for developing the media plan and is used as a starting point in the discussion between a client and the agency. It includes some or all of the following information.

MARKET PROFILE

Any relevant information about the current state of affairs in the market is useful to media planners. Such information includes historical sales data of leading brands, market share trends of leading brands, and rates of growth in the market. Is the market growing, flat, or declining?

COMPETITOR MEDIA STRATEGY

In general terms, what media do major competitors use, and how much money do they invest in media advertising? What the competitors are doing has some influence on the strategic directions that will be recommended. For example, if key competitors dominate a particular medium, it may be prudent to select another medium to reach the same target. Whatever competitive information is available should be in the hands of the media planners.

TARGET MARKET PROFILE

Perhaps the most important ingredient for a media plan is a thorough understanding of the target market. As discussed earlier, targets are described on the basis of demographic, psychographic, and geographic variables. The target profile must be clearly defined and key variables must be expanded upon. For example, knowing the activities and interests of the target (psychographic considerations) enables a media planner to select the best times and best places to advertise. As well, information about how the

FIGURE **5.1** Media Planning

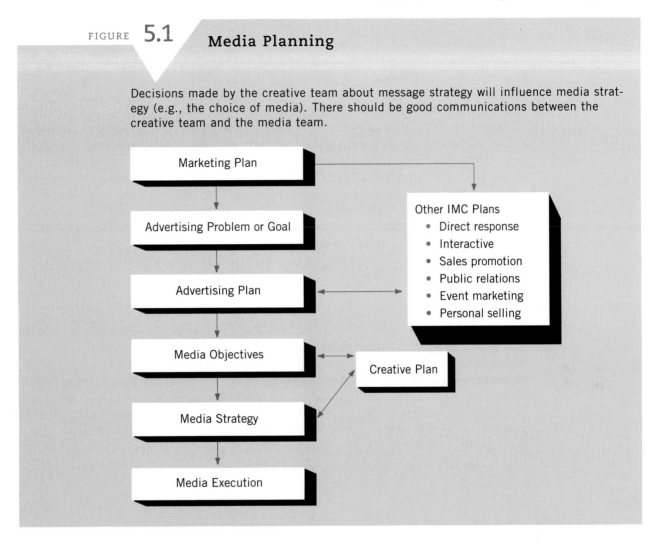

Decisions made by the creative team about message strategy will influence media strategy (e.g., the choice of media). There should be good communications between the creative team and the media team.

- Marketing Plan
- Advertising Problem or Goal
- Advertising Plan
- Media Objectives
- Media Strategy
- Media Execution

Other IMC Plans
- Direct response
- Interactive
- Sales promotion
- Public relations
- Event marketing
- Personal selling

Creative Plan

target refers to the media (e.g., what media the target refers to most frequently) helps the planner to allocate funds across the recommended media.

MEDIA OBJECTIVES

Based on marketing priorities, the client usually identifies key objectives. Objectives tend to focus on target market priorities by identifying primary targets and secondary targets, the nature of the message and its influence on media selection, the best time to advertise, and the geographic market priorities. Depending on the problem at hand or the overall goal of the campaign, the client may also identify priorities for reach, frequency, and continuity of message.

MEDIA BUDGET

Since media advertising is but one media expenditure, the funds available come from the marketing plan budget. In most cases, the client has already identified the amount that will be allocated to media advertising. Knowing the size of the budget is essential, because it provides the framework for the media planner's strategic thinking. Is there enough for television? Will this be strictly a print campaign? Is this a national campaign or will it be restricted to regional markets? Will this campaign rely on a few media or will it be a multimedia effort? The budget points the planners in a certain direction.

Once the media planners have been briefed on the assignment, they begin discussing potential alternatives. Their goal is to devise a media strategy and tactical plan (execution) that will achieve the stated objectives. Once the media plan has been presented to the client and approved, agency media buyers negotiate with the media to buy the time and space. The media buyer's task is to deliver the maximum impact (on a target audience) at a minimum cost (client's budget).

Media planning is quantitative by nature. Agency personnel are experts in media trends and have all kinds of statistical information available to figure out what media are best suited to the client's needs. Furthermore, the sophistication of computers and media software has enhanced the ability of media planners and media buyers to generate more efficient media plans. Once a plan has been implemented, the agency evaluates the plan in a post-buy analysis. A **post-buy analysis** is an evaluation of actual audience deliveries calculated after a specific spot or schedule of advertising has been run. The actual audience may be different from the estimated audience that was identified in the plan. The question to be answered is whether the plan delivered the audience it was supposed to.

Post-Buy Analysis
An evaluation of actual audience deliveries calculated after a specific spot or schedule of advertising has run.

The Media Plan

Media Plan
A strategy that outlines the relevant details about how a client's budget will be spent.

The **media plan** is a document that outlines the relevant details about how a client's budget will be spent. Objectives are clearly identified, strategies are carefully rationalized, and execution details are precisely documented. The costs associated with every recommendation are put under the microscope when the agency presents the plan to the client. Because of the money involved, media plans often go through numerous revisions before being approved by the client. The structure and content of a media plan are the focus of this section of the chapter. Figure 5.2 summarizes the content of a media plan, although the content of a media plan varies from one agency to another. This model is strictly a guideline.

MEDIA OBJECTIVES

Media Objective
A statement that outlines what a media plan is to accomplish (who, what, when, where, or how).

Media objectives are clearly worded statements that outline what the plan is to accomplish. They provide guidance and direction for developing media strategies. If worded correctly, priorities will emerge. For example, there could be customer priorities, regional market priorities, and timing priorities. These priorities are based on historical information, the current situation a brand finds itself in, and the problem that the advertising plan must resolve. Such issues are part of the background information included in the media brief. For example, a plan may have a national focus, regional focus, or it may simply run in a few urban markets that are given priority.

Media objectives typically deal with the following issues:

- **Who:** Who is the target market? The target market profile is defined in terms of demographic, psychographic, and geographic characteristics. Media planners use this profile to match the target with a compatible media profile. For example, magazines know their readership profile, radio stations know their listener profile, and television networks know who watches specific shows. Refer to the media strategy section of this chapter for detailed discussion about target market matching strategies.

- **What:** What is the nature of the message to be communicated? Media planners must be informed about the message strategy. For example, is the message strategy information intensive (lots of copy) or image intensive (lots of visuals)? Does the budget permit television and, if so, is the creative team giving television due consideration? Issues such as these strongly suggest that basic creative and media decisions be made at the same time. Clients should provide guidance in this area. If certain media are mandatory, the client should say so.

FIGURE **5.2** **The Structure and Content of a Media Plan**

Media Budget

- Total budget available (from client's marketing plan)

Media Objectives

- Who (is the target market)
- What (is the message)
- When (is the best time to advertise)
- Where (are the priority markets)
- How (important is reach, frequency, and continuity)

    Note: Media objectives are usually clear, concise statements.

Media Strategy

- Target market matching strategy (shotgun, profile match, rifle)
- Market coverage
- Timing
- Reach considerations
- Frequency considerations
- Continuity considerations
- Media selection rationale
- Media rejection rationale

    Note: Media strategies expand upon the objectives and provide details about how the objectives will be achieved.

Media Execution

- Blocking chart (calendar showing timing, weight, and market coverage)
- Budget summary (allocations by media, time, and region)

- ***Where:*** Where are the market priorities geographically? The budget plays a key role in this decision. Typically, a brand has regions of strength and weakness. A media plan could be devised to correct a situation in a problem region. In such cases, these could cutting back media spending in a strong region in order to allocate more to a weaker region. In other situations, regions may be treated equally with media funds allocated based on population patterns. If this is to be a key market plan only, what key markets are given priority? The number of markets that must be reached and the level of intensity (media investment) are factors largely based on the budget.

- ***When:*** When is the best time to reach the target market? For example, is the product a seasonal product such as a sun lotion or ski boot? If so, the media strategy will consider a heavier schedule of advertising in the pre-season, a time when consumers are starting to think about summer or winter activities. Knowledge of the target's daily schedule also plays a role in timing decisions. For instance, a busy executive who rises early and arrives home late may not have much time to spend with the media. How and when is the best time to reach this person? When is the best time to reach a student? Knowledge of media consumption patterns by the primary target is essential.

- ***How:*** The question of how conjures up all kinds of media issues. How many people to reach, how often to reach them and for what length of time? These are strategic issues that are best left to the media planners at the ad agency. However, some basic guidance from the client is provided. For example, if the plan is for a new product, the absolute number of people reached and how often they are reached may be given priority. If a product is firmly established and the goal of the plan is to simply remind the target, then length of time may be given priority. Refer to discussion about reach, frequency and continuity in the next section for more details.

MEDIA STRATEGY

Media Strategy
A plan for achieving the media objectives stated in the media plan; typically justifies the use of certain media.

Media strategy focuses on how media objectives will be achieved while outlining how to reach the target market as effectively and efficiently as possible. Given the scarcity of clients' financial resources and their demands for accountability, having the right media strategy is crucial. Clients want to see a reasonable return for their investment. A media strategy addresses how often to advertise, how long to advertise, where to advertise, and what media to use, and will rationalize why only certain media are recommended. Strategic decisions are linked directly to the media objectives. The various factors that influence media strategy are discussed below.

Target Market Profile

For some products and companies, the target description may be broad in scope. For example, a newspaper's primary readers include adults of all ages and income groups. In contrast, the primary buyer for a Lexus automobile may be described as a male business executive, 35 to 49 years old, earning $75 000 annually, living in an urban market of 1 million plus. The extent of the target's description directly influences media strategy decisions.

Lexus
www.lexus.com

The task of the media planner is to match the profile of the target market as closely as possible with the profile of the medium (e.g., the readership profile of a magazine or the listener profile of a radio station). The more compatible the match, the more efficient the strategy will be. For example, to reach that Lexus buyer, executive-oriented business magazines such as *National Post Business*, *Canadian Business*, and *Report on Business* are good matches. Figure 5.3 illustrates a readership profile. The same executive may watch television but to place an ad in primetime hours would reach people well beyond the target description. This would not be efficient. There are three basic target market matching strategies: shotgun, profile matching, and rifle.

Shotgun Strategy
A tactic involving the use of mass media to reach a loosely defined target audience.

- If a **shotgun strategy** is used, the target market's profile has a broad scope. The message is placed in media that reach a broad cross-section of the population. For example, television reaches all ages, although viewing by certain age groups varies by time of day. To reach teenagers and adults, primetime television does the job. In the United States, the cost of placing one 30-second spot on "Friends," NBC's popular comedy show, is US$455 700.[1] The same spot on Global Television in Canada would cost approximately CA$40 000. Television is an expensive medium.

Radio TV Ad Spot.com
www.radiotvadspot.com

For advertisers on a tighter budget but with a diverse target market, options such as daily newspapers and out-of-home advertising are attractive. Out-of-home options include billboards, transit shelters, and subway stations. They reach a diverse population but generally cost less than television.

Profile-Matching Strategy
A media tactic that involves matching the demographic profile of a product's target market with a specific medium that has a similar target profile.

- If a **profile-matching strategy** is used, the target market profile is carefully defined by demographic, psychographic, and geographic variables. For example, assume a target profile described as follows: female head of household, working or stay-at-home mother, college or higher education, $50 000 household income, suburban lifestyle, with interests that include home decorating, entertaining, and travel. Several magazines are good possibilities for reaching such a woman: *Chatelaine*, *Canadian Living*,

FIGURE **5.3**

Readership Profile of *Canadian Business* Magazine

Characteristic	Canadian Adults % Composition	Readers per copy	Canadian Business Readers % Composition	Index
Age				
18–24	12	120 000	12	100
25–34	18	227 000	22	120
35–49	32	430 000	41	129
50–64	21	207 000	20	95
65+	16	59 000	6	34
Occupation				
Senior Managers	2	48 000	5	208
Other Managers	10	197 000	19	180
Professionals	5	102 000	10	200
Sales/Tech/Teaching	9	167 000	16	172
MOPEs	18	348 000	33	190
SOHO	13	290 000	28	213
Household Income				
$75 000+	22	398 000	38	173
$100 000	10	226 000	22	219
$125 000	5	140 000	13	255
Personal Income				
$50 000	13	288 000	28	210
$75 000	4	123 000	12	300
$100 000	2	67 000	6	300
Education				
College Grad+	49	683 000	66	133
University Degree	37	573 000	55	148

Notes

1. MOPES are Managers, Owners, Professionals, and Executives.

2. SOHO means Small Office/Home Office.

3. The index is calculated by dividing the % of *Canadian Business* readers by the % of Canadian adults in the various categories. The index shows where *Canadian Business* readers are in relation to the Canadian average.

INTERPRETATION
Based on the above readership statistics, *Canadian Business* magazine is a good profile match for advertisers wanting to reach highly educated adults 25 to 49 years old with above-average personal income and household incomes, including senior managers, professionals, and business owners.

Adapted from the Canadian Business Media Kit, 2003.

Canadian Home & Country, and *Homemaker's*. The primary reader of each magazine is reasonably close to the description of the target. In contrast, *Canadian Business* magazine appeals to upper-income males and females commonly referred to as MOPES (managers, owners, professionals, and entrepreneurs).

Profile matching can extend to television as well. Conventional networks such as CTV and Global have been losing viewers to specialty networks such as TSN (sports), YTV (youth), and the Outdoor Life Network (OLN), among others. Specialty networks offer programming that is tailored to specific demographics. OLN caters to twenty-something males and females with programs that are action- and adventure-oriented. YTV reaches children and tweens (kids 11 to 14 years old) with appropriate program content.

Rifle Strategy

A strategy that involves using a specific medium that effectively reaches a target market defined by a common characteristic.

- In the **rifle strategy**, a common characteristic such as an activity or interest binds a target market together. For example, golfers are golfers, whether they play at a public club, an exclusive private club, or anywhere in between. All golfers look for similar equipment. They cross both genders and most income groups. Therefore, a publication such as *Score Golf* or *Golf Canada* offers a means of reaching the target directly. Enthusiasts look to these kinds of publications for information about the products that are advertised there. Business publications target specific industries; therefore, to target decision makers within a particular industry, its trade publications are attractive. To reach people employed in the hospitality industry, for instance, a publication such as *Hotel & Restaurant* is an option.

In Chapter 1, the concepts of database marketing and customer relationship management were discussed. A rifle strategy is ideally suited for organizations that practise these concepts. Non-traditional media such as the internet, CD-ROMs, direct mail, and telemarketing can reach customers on an individual basis. These media are discussed in more detail in appropriate chapters of this textbook.

Nature of the Message

Creative strategy and media strategy should be developed simultaneously in order to generate a synergistic effect in the marketplace. Planners should cooperate to ensure that the right message is delivered by the right medium. If a rational appeal technique is used with factual information to be communicated, then print media options take precedence. If emotional appeals are used and if action and adventure are prominent in the message, television is good. If sales promotion incentives are part of the message, a combination of media may be called for. Television may be used to generate awareness of a contest, for example, while print media and in-store communications provide more details.

The media campaign that launched the Infiniti G35 luxury car shows how target market characteristics and consumer behaviour influenced the direction of creative strategy and media strategy. For insight into this campaign, read the IMC Highlight **Power That Couldn't Be Ignored**.

Geographic Market Priorities

With regard to where to advertise, strategic decisions must be made on how to divide a budget among the areas where advertising will be scheduled. A company or brand rarely advertises nationally on a continuous basis. It is common for some national advertising to occur during the course of a plan, but it is supplemented by additional advertising in markets where specific problems need to be resolved. In other instances, a brand might decide just to advertise in key urban markets. The top five Canadian markets reach about 40 percent of the total population—and much of the success (or failure) in Canada is governed by how successful the brand is in those four markets. Usually, the budget determines the extent of market coverage. Some of the coverage options include the following.

POWER THAT COULDN'T BE IGNORED

A research study conducted by Leger Marketing among consumers about what media influences awareness of new cars revealed that television was most popular by far (56 percent of respondents). That was followed with newspaper and magazine ads (14 percent), word of mouth (8 percent), car reviews and news stories (7 percent), and direct marketing (5 percent). Of course, these data apply to any kind of car. But perhaps the luxury car buyer views the media differently.

The advertising challenge facing the Infiniti G35 launch involved what to stand for (the message strategy) and how to stand out (the media strategy). Infiniti's media research indicated that the luxury car buyer is a heavy newspaper reader. Despite the findings mentioned above, automotive marketers believe newspapers are the most vital component of the media mix. All manufacturers combined allocate about 70 percent of their media budgets to newspapers.

Infiniti was trying to attract luxury buyers who normally look at European makes—BMW, Audi, and Mercedes-Benz. European car enthusiasts usually value performance as a key motivator. Since the 260-horsepower G35 can outperform its European rivals, the car was positioned as an awe-inspiring performance vehicle. Creative strategy focused on presenting power in an elegant, witty, and smart way. It would be power that couldn't be ignored. Multiple creative executions with tremendous stopping power communicated exactly what the G35 and Infiniti stood for. The ads had a sophisticated look that matched well with the Infiniti brand image. The tagline for the campaign was "Accelerating the future."

Because the luxury segment is extremely competitive, media strategy and execution were aggressive. A multimedia campaign that included newspapers, selective magazines, outdoor, and unprecedented online advertising launched the G35. A superboard (extra big billboard) in Toronto rounded out the campaign. All print ads were full colour and full page. Black-and-white ads appeared in automotive supplements of major daily newspapers.

Initial results were extremely positive. First-month sales targets were exceeded by 57 percent, Infiniti had its best sales month ever, and showroom traffic was much higher than usual.

Adapted from John Roumelis, "How to Get Noticed...Fast," *Marketing*, May 6, 2002, p. 26.

Infiniti
www.infiniti.com

Category Development Index (CDI) or Market Development Index

The percentage of category sales in a geographic area in relation to the total population of that area.

National Coverage Such a strategy assumes widespread availability of the product with all geographic areas figuring equitably in the success of the product. For example, if product sales as expressed as a percentage of total sales by region are close to population splits by region, a national strategy is an option. Funds can be allocated across media that reach the national market. Network television shows in prime time (*Friends, CSI, Everybody Loves Raymond*, etc.) and national magazines such as *Maclean's* are good alternatives. Of course, the precise description of the target audience and the budget also influence this kind of strategy. Primetime television and general-interest magazines reach a broad cross-section of the population and the cost in absolute terms (the actual cost per ad) is high.

Regional Coverage A regional strategy involves an evaluation of each region's contribution to a brand's (or company's) success. Funds are allocated so that no particular region has an advantage or disadvantage—at least, that's the theory. The reality is different. Some regions will over-contribute to sales while others will under-contribute. An organization might assess the value of a region by analyzing two different indexes. The first index is called a market development index or **category development index (CDI)** and is a percentage of category sales (e.g., a category like instant coffee) in an area in relation to the population in that area compared to the sales throughout the entire country in relation to the total population. For example, if the sale of instant coffee in British Columbia represents 10 percent of total sales and BC represents 12 percent of the population, the CDI is 83.3 (10 divided by 12). BC would be considered an underdeveloped region. Conversely, if Ontario represents 42 percent of instant coffee sales and Ontario represents 38 percent of the population, the CDI would be 110.5 (42 divided by 38). Ontario would be described as an overdeveloped instant coffee market.

A **brand development index (BDI)** works the same way. It is a percentage of a brand's sales in an area in relation to the population in that area compared to the sales throughout the entire country in relation to the total population. For example, if Maxwell House instant coffee has 15 percent of its Canadian sales in BC and only 12 percent of the population lives there, the BDI for BC would be 125. This would indicate that BC is an important area for the brand; the brand is very popular there. Refer to Figure 5.4 for some additional calculations of the brand development index, which help explain why certain regions get disproportionate funds. There is only so much money to be allocated. For example, in a market where a brand is underdeveloped but potential for growth is present, that brand may temporarily receive additional funds that will be taken away from a region where the brand is doing well. The BDI is commonly used when determining regional media budgets.

In terms of media selection, a planner will focus on regional media opportunities to reach the target market. Television networks offer regional packages (e.g., all stations within a region) and national magazines such as *Chatelaine*, *Canadian Living*, and *Reader's Digest* offer numerous regional editions.

Key Market Coverage A third alternative is to give priority to those members of the target market residing in key urban markets. Usually there are predetermined criteria to determine what markets will receive media support. If population is the criterion, a planner will consider other strategic factors first and then go down the market list until the media budget is exhausted. Canada's top five cities (Toronto, Montreal, Vancouver, Ottawa-Hull, and Calgary) account for 40.6 percent of the population, while the top ten cities account for 51.7 percent.[2] Given that the population is migrating steadily toward cities in Canada, a key market plan is a good option.

While this strategic approach seems equitable, smaller cities may never receive media support. For example, no city in the Atlantic region is among the top ten. If the Atlantic region doesn't receive media support, expectations for the brand should be lowered appropriately. In terms of media selection, key market plans offer the most flexibility and choice. Local market television stations, daily newspapers, outdoor and transit advertising, and radio are attractive alternatives. Which ones to choose depends on the media preferences of the target market and the budget.

Timing of Advertising

Information about the target market and cyclical patterns in sales influence decisions about when to schedule advertising. The best time could refer to the time of day, day of week, or time of year. For products with a cyclical sales pattern, the media schedule may follow the ebb and flow of sales. If the media plan is for a new product, the planners may decide to hit the market heavy and frequently in a short period. Lower levels of advertising are scheduled later in the plan cycle. Typically, a media schedule is planned in flights. A **flight** is a period of time in which advertising is scheduled. Rarely is advertising scheduled continuously—tough creative scheduling just makes it seem like it is. There are many options available for planning the timing of a media schedule, all based on unique situations a brand (company) faces. Refer to Figure 5.5 for an illustration of the media schedules discussed below.

- A **skip schedule** calls for scheduling on an alternating basis. For example, ads are scheduled one week and not the next, or one month and not the next. This cyclical pattern follows for the duration of the campaign. A skip schedule strategically stretches a budget over an extended period while maintaining the effect of the advertising in the marketplace.

- A **pulse schedule** involves scheduling advertising in flights but with different weights (the amount invested in media) and durations (the length of time). Such a schedule

Brand Development Index (BDI)

The percentage of a brand's sales in an area in relation to the population in that area.

Flight

A period of time in which advertising is scheduled.

Skip Schedule

The scheduling of media advertising on an alternating basis.

Pulse Schedule

A scheduling of media advertising in flights of different weight and duration.

FIGURE **5.4**

Considerations for Allocating Budgets by Region

One method of determining the importance of a region for a brand (company) is to compare actual sales volume (as a percentage of total sales) to the region's population (as a percentage of Canada's population). Such an analysis is called a **brand development index (BDI)**. The BDI is determined by dividing the sales volume percentage by the regional population percentage.

Region	Sales Volume %	Population %	BDI
Atlantic Region	7.6	7.6	100.0
Quebec	21.5	23.9	89.9
Ontario	42.5	38.5	110.4
Prairie Region	13.4	16.8	79.8
British Columbia	15.0	13.2	113.6
Total	**100.0**	**100.0**	—

Example: The BDI in Ontario is 110.4. The BDI was determined by dividing 42.5 by 38.5

Analysis: Based on the BDI in each region, Ontario and BC over-contribute to sales while Quebec and the Prairies under-contribute. The media planner can concentrate advertising dollars in areas where the brand enjoys most usage. Another option is to transfer some funds from Ontario and BC to Quebec and the Prairies to help improve sales in those regions. Other factors can influence such a decision.

looks random but the weight and frequency of the spending patterns are carefully rationalized. To demonstrate, assume a schedule has three flights. The first is four weeks long and heavy, the second is six weeks long at a low level, and the third flight is four weeks long and heavy. There is a period of four weeks with no advertising between each flight. The variation in flights creates a "pulsing" effect.

Seasonal Schedule

Scheduling media advertising according to seasonal sales trends.

- Many products are seasonal in nature so media advertising follows a **seasonal schedule**, with most of the advertising in the pre-season to create awareness and interest prior to the beginning of the seasonal purchase cycle. Banks and financial institutions have a heavy schedule of RRSP advertising in January and February, for example, as the tax-deduction deadline for contributions is the end of February.

Blitz Schedule

The scheduling of media advertising so most spending is front-loaded in the schedule.

- A **blitz schedule** is best suited for new products that want to hit the market with a bang—a multimedia strategy at a heavyweight level. Lots of money is spent in a very short period. Once the blitz is over, media spending tapers off considerably and some media are dropped from the schedule.

Build-up Schedule

The scheduling of media advertising so that the weight of advertising starts out light and gradually builds over a period of time.

- Frequently referred to as a teaser strategy, in a **build-up schedule** media advertising is scheduled at low levels initially and gradually builds (as more weight is added) as time passes. Often a teaser campaign is launched well before the product is available on the market (hence the name). The advertising creates a pent-up demand for the product when it becomes available. Hollywood movie releases use this strategy frequently.

FIGURE **5.5**

Media Scheduling Alternatives

Effective scheduling patterns improve the efficiency of the media plan. Each of these media schedules serves a unique purpose and meets specific media objectives.

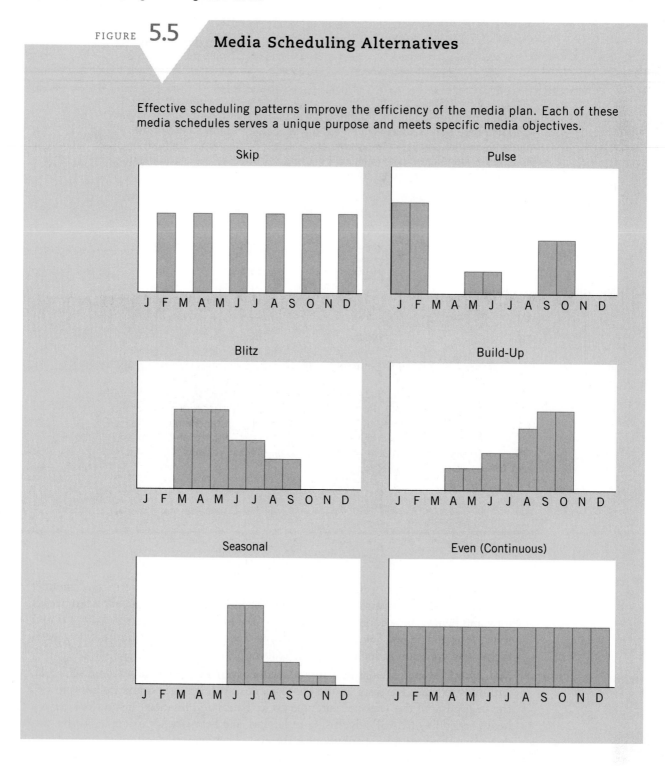

Even Schedule

The uniform schedule of media advertising over an extended period.

- Often referred to as a continuous schedule, the **even schedule** involves the purchase of advertising time and space in a uniform manner over a designated period. This schedule is best suited for large advertisers that need to sustain a certain level of advertising spending due to competitive pressures. Such a spending pattern is not very common.

Canmedia Planning
www.canmedia.com

Reach
The total unduplicated audience exposed one or more times to a commercial message during a specific period.

Frequency
The average number of times a message has been exposed to an audience over a period of time, usually a week.

Gross Rating Points (GRPs)
An expression of the weight of advertising in a media schedule; calculated by multiplying reach by frequency.

Continuity
The length of time required in an advertising medium to generate the desired impact on the target audience.

Media Execution
The translation of media strategies into specific media action plans; involves recommending specific media to be used in the plan and negotiating the media buys.

Reach/Frequency/Continuity

Media planners must decide on the reach, frequency, and continuity needed to achieve advertising objectives. Much like a riddle, these three factors interact and, if planned effectively, will have a synergistic effect on the target market. It is unrealistic to have maximum reach, frequency, and continuity at the same time. Priorities are based on the situation and the budget.

- **Reach** is the total unduplicated audience (individuals or households) exposed one or more times to an advertiser's schedule of messages during a specific period (usually a week). It is expressed as a percentage of the target population in a geographically defined area. For example, a television ad on Ottawa's CJOH-TV may reach 40 percent of the households in the Ottawa region.

- **Frequency** is the average number of times a target audience has been exposed to an advertising message over a period of time, usually a week. It is calculated by dividing the total possible audience by the audience that has been exposed at least once to the message. Frequency may also refer to the number of times a publication is issued or the number of times a commercial is aired. The media planner must decide what combination of reach and frequency is appropriate for achieving the advertising objectives. In the case of a new product where awareness objectives prevail, the emphasis is on reach (and frequency if there is enough budget). A mature product that is trying to defend its position may opt for more frequency and aim the message at a precisely defined target market.

- Media planners use gross rating points as a method of designing a media schedule. **Gross rating points (GRPs)** are calculated by multiplying the total reach (the unduplicated audience) of the proposed schedule by the frequency (the average amount of exposures) in the proposed schedule. It is an expression of the weight of advertising in a market. To illustrate, assume the weekly reach is 50 percent of targeted households in a particular city and the average number of exposures is 3.5. The GRP level would be 175 (50 x 3.5). Depending on how important particular markets are, an advertiser usually varies the weight level (the GRP level) from one market to another. For more detailed illustrations of GRPs, refer to Appendix 1, "Media Buying Principles and Media Information Resources," at the end of the book.

- **Continuity** refers to the length of time required to ensure impact on a target market through a particular medium. During that period, a consistent theme is communicated (e.g., "Well Made. Well Priced. Well Dressed," the theme for Moores, a men's clothing chain). Since advertising is scheduled in flights, continuity decisions deal with how long a flight will be. Will the schedule be four weeks, six weeks, or eight weeks?

Media planners must juggle reach, frequency, and continuity throughout the entire campaign. An increase in any of these variables will increase the cost of advertising, so there would have to be a corresponding decrease somewhere else.

In combination with the strategic variables described above, the media planners must recommend what media to use. Their media plan will include reasons why certain media were accepted and certain media were rejected. Knowledge of the target market's media preferences and the budget available has a direct and powerful influence on media selection. The section of this chapter titled "Assessing Media Alternatives" discusses the various media in more detail. Figure 5.6 offers additional information about the relationships between reach, frequency, and continuity.

MEDIA EXECUTION

The final stage of the media planning is media execution. **Media execution** is a process of fine tuning the media strategy and translating it into specific action plans. This

FIGURE 5.6

The Relationship among Reach, Frequency, and Continuity

Reach is the number of people potentially exposed to a message in one week.
Frequency is the average number of times a person is exposed to a message in a week.
Continuity is the length of time required to generate impact on a target market.

The relationship among these three variables is dynamic. Since the media budget is usually a fixed amount of money, if one variable is given more priority, then another variable will be given less priority. Otherwise, you will spend beyond the budget. Examine the numbers in the chart. Each plan is different but they achieve the same number of gross impressions.

Gross impressions are calculated by multiplying reach x frequency x continuity.

Variable	Reach	Frequency	Continuity	Impressions
Plan 1	500 000	4	6 weeks	12 000 000
Plan 2	250 000	8	6 weeks	12 000 000
Plan 3	125 000	8	12 weeks	12 000 000

INTERPRETATION
Each plan is different. The first plan stresses reach, the second stresses frequency, and the third stresses continuity. The costs of each plan would be about the same. It's all in the numbers!

involves comparing various options within a class of media for cost efficiencies, finalizing a schedule in the form of a calendar or blocking chart, and allocating the budget in detail by specific activity. Then the agency buys the media time and space.

Media Selection

Selecting the right media to resolve the problem at hand is a three-step decision process: selecting the general type of media, selecting the class of media within type, and selecting the particular medium. Of the media discussed in this chapter, the first decision involves what mix of media to use. Among television, radio, newspapers, magazines, and out-of-home, any combination is possible (direct response and interactive media are discussed in separate chapters). For the second decision, let's assume that magazines and television are the media chosen and that the campaign is national in scope. Will general-interest magazines, men's or women's magazines, or special-interest magazines be chosen? What television networks will be chosen? The characteristics of the target market will influence these decisions.

For the third decision, let's also assume the target market is men and women between 35 and 49, living in major cities across Canada. Magazines that reach both males and females would be selected: *Maclean's, Time,* and *Reader's Digest* are candidates. Conventional television networks such as CTV, CBC, and Global are also candidates.

Cost per Thousand (CPM)
The cost of delivering an advertising message to 1000 people.

When selecting specific media, the cost efficiencies of each alternative are analyzed. To demonstrate, magazines are compared on the basis of **CPM (cost per thousand)**. CPM is the cost incurred in delivering a message to 1000 readers. It is calculated by dividing the cost of the ad by the circulation of the publication in thousands. Therefore, if an ad cost $20 000 and the circulation was 500 000, the CPM would be $40.00 ($20 000 divided by 500 000). When comparing publications that reach the same target market, the ones with the lowest cost per thousand are the most efficient at reaching the target.

Media planners also assess media alternatives qualitatively. In other words, do numbers tell the complete story? Factors such as editorial content, quality of reproduction, and demographic selectivity can lead the media planner to prefer one magazine over another, even if the preferred magazine has a higher CPM. Perhaps there are more pass-along readers of one publication than another. If more people are exposed to the ad then the real costs of reaching the target are lower than the CPM. Daily newspapers, television networks, and radio stations can be compared on a similar basis. The actual cost of advertising varies from one medium to another (see Figure 5.7). Appendix 1, "Media Buying Principles and Media Information Resources," also has additional information about media selection and how various alternatives are compared when making decisions about what media to use.

Media Calendar or Blocking Chart
A document that shows allocation of a brand's media budget according to time of year and type of medium.

Media Schedule and Budget Allocations

The final stage for the media planners is developing the media calendar and assigning estimated costs to all activities. A **media calendar** or **blocking chart**, as it is also referred to, summarizes in a few pages all the details of the media execution (e.g., media usage, market coverage, weight levels, reach and frequency, and the timing of the campaign).

FIGURE **5.7** **Comparing Media Alternatives for Efficiency**

Magazine	Cost (1P, 4-color)	Circulation (000)	CPM
Report on Business	18 800	363.7	$51.69
National Post Business	15 910	311.3	$51.10
Canadian Business	14 000	80.5	$173.91

Newspaper	Cost (1000 lines)	Circulation (000)	CPM
Globe and Mail	27 400	363.7	$75.33
National Post	15 280	311.3	$49.08
Toronto Star	15 900	454.8	$34.96

Rates from *CARD*, April 2002. Magazines ads are full colour; newspaper ads are black and white.

Analysis: Based on CPM, the cost of reaching 1000 readers, *Report on Business* and *National Post Business* are comparable. *Canadian Business* is significantly higher, so advertisers may select *Report on Business* and *National Post Business* first. The cost of reaching a *Globe and Mail* newspaper reader is much higher than the *National Post* reader. The *National Post* is a comparatively new newspaper and to attract advertisers it offers advertising rates much lower than the *Globe and Mail*. The *Globe and Mail* is an established, trusted newspaper; that will be factored into the media decision. The *Toronto Star* reaches a broader cross-section of the population in a cost-efficient manner, but does not have much national reach.

Accompanying the calendar is a detailed budget. Typically, the media budget classifies spending by medium, region, and time of year. Because plans change during the course of the planning cycle, clients and agencies must know how much money is committed at any point in time, in case there is a need to cancel activities. Taking the axe to the budget while the plan is in midstream is both common and frustrating for managers.

Media Buying

Metromark Media Buying Services
www.metromarkcorp.com

Once the client approves the media plan, media buyers execute the plan. Buyers work with media representatives to negotiate final prices for the various activities. If the required elements of the plan are unavailable, buyers are responsible for making replacement buys that will achieve the same objectives. The demand for key time periods in television and preferred spaces in magazines and newspapers means that good timing and effective negotiations skills on the part of the buyer are critical elements of the media buy. In the role of negotiator, the media buyer seeks favourable positions and rates to maximize efficiency and achieve the objectives set out in the plan.

Appendix 2, "Mobicox—An Integrated Marketing Communications Plan," is an example of an actual media plan, and includes applications of the various media strategy and execution principles discussed in this chapter.

Assessing Media Alternatives

Primary Medium
A medium that receives the largest allocation of an advertiser's budget.

Secondary Media
Media alternatives used to complement the primary medium in an advertising campaign.

Media planners choose between traditional media alternatives and non-traditional alternatives. The former category include television, radio, newspapers, magazines, and out-of-home advertising. The latter includes media such as the internet, CD-ROMs, video games, and telephones, all of which are interactive forms of media. Typically, a planner will include several media in the plan, as people refer to more than one medium for information. In the hectic world of today's consumers, the simultaneous use of media is popular. Teens, for example, are online while watching television. Adults frequently read the newspaper or a magazine while watching television. Knowing the right combinations for various age groups will influence media decisions.

Because consumers refer to so many different media, media planners usually recommend a **primary medium**, which will be allocated most of the budget, and support it with **secondary media**, which complement the primary medium and receive less of the budget. As mentioned earlier, a medium such as television is ideal for creating awareness quickly, whereas print media are good for communicating detailed information over a longer period. The combination of the two media is usually effective. This section will analyze the major mass media alternatives and highlight the pros and cons of each. Chapters 6 and 7 will focus on direct response and interactive forms of advertising.

TELEVISION

The Canadian television industry is divided among three types of networks: conventional national networks of the CBC, CTV, and Global; conventional regional networks such as Radio-Canada and TVA in Quebec (both are French-language networks); and specialty channels such as TSN, MuchMusic, YTV, and others offered by the various cable companies. Cable companies also offer a pay-per-view service but consumers must rent a special decoder to access the channels. These channels offer first-run movies and sports and entertainment specials.

Digital cable channels (the latest in television technology) were recently launched in Canada. Appealing to niche markets, some of the new channels include Leafs TV (news about the Toronto Maple Leafs and their games), Lone Star TV (old westerns), Men TV (television with a shot of testosterone), and PrideVision TV (the world's first gay, lesbian, bisexual, and transgendered television network). So far, their penetration in the market and impact on conventional broadcasters have been minimal. There are also two direct-to-home options available: Bell ExpressVu and Star Choice. Both carry an extensive list of national and international channels that reach consumers by satellite.

Budget permitting, advertisers are magically drawn to television. It is a multi-sense medium that is ideal for product demonstrations and appeals to consumers on an emotional level. As well, the reach potential is incredibly high. On an average day, 76 percent of Canadians view television at least once, and 39 percent of adults watch television at least once in prime time.[3] With television, media planners have four options: network advertising, selective-spot advertising, local spot advertising, and sponsorships.

Network Advertising
Advertising from one central source broadcast across an entire network of stations.

- **Network advertising** on networks such as CTV and Global is suitable for products and services that are widely distributed and have large media budgets. When a spot is placed on the network, the message is received in all network markets. The CTV Network, for example, comprises 21 stations and reaches 99 percent of English-speaking Canadians. Popular primetime shows such as *Survivor*, *ER*, *CSI*, and *Friends* attract big-budget advertisers.

Selective Spot
Commercial time during a network show that is allocated back to regional and local stations to sell.

- At the regional or local level, stations fill the balance of their schedules with non-network programs and sell **selective spots** directly to interested advertisers. Local stations are also allocated a certain portion of a network program to sell directly. That's why you may see an ad for a local restaurant on "Hockey Night in Canada."

  Strategically, selective spots benefit advertisers using a key market media strategy. For a large-budget advertiser, there is an opportunity to increase the level of advertising in local markets judged as priorities. Small-budget advertisers can simply choose the markets they wish to advertise in. Ads for national spots and selective spots are negotiated and scheduled by an advertising agency as part of the overall media buy.

Local Spot
Advertising bought from a local station by a local advertiser.

- With **local spots**, local advertisers such as independent retailers and restaurants buy time from local stations. Since local market advertisers don't usually work with an advertising agency, the stations usually provide assistance in the development and production of commercials for local clients.

Sponsorship
The act of financially supporting a show in return for certain advertising rights and privileges.

- **Sponsorship** allows an advertiser to take "ownership" of a property that is targeted at its consumer audience. If the fit is right, the advertiser can leverage the sponsorship by extending the relationship to include consumer and trade promotions, and alternate media exposure. To illustrate, the Labatt Brewing Company holds the sponsorship rights to *Hockey Night in Canada*, a Saturday-night institution that draws a large audience. In addition to placing ads on the hockey broadcast, Labatt benefits from the prestige associated with such a high-profile show. Other sponsorship opportunities include other sports specials, miniseries, and docudramas. Good programming attracts good advertisers.

TV Trends: Challenges and Opportunities

Television advertising, as we know it, could change considerably in the coming years. The causes are rooted in the continuation of long-established trends: the proliferation of media outlets, audience fragmentation, unprecedented advertising clutter, and improved technology giving the viewer more control.

Generally, the number of hours a person spends viewing television each week has been drifting downward. The public's preoccupation with the internet is one reason for this decline. As well, there is so much choice available that even the most popular shows deliver an audience that is only a portion of what it used to be. Twenty years ago, prime-time viewing was spread across three major networks (NBC, CBS, and ABC) in the United States; collectively they controlled 88 percent of viewing, and a top-ten show would reach 25 percent of all households. Today, the same three networks account for only 38 percent of viewing and a top-ten show reaches only 13 percent of households.[4]

Technological advancements, particularly the introduction of the PVR (personal video recorder), could have a dramatic impact on conventional broadcasting and advertising. Much like a VCR, the PVR records programs in a digital format. When the consumer plays back the program, the commercials can be eliminated. The PVR is user-friendly. A viewer simply types in the shows to record and the machine does the rest. If consumers stop watching commercials, the networks lose advertising revenues and all of the wonderful shows the public take for granted won't get produced. Already, more that 80 percent of PVR users say they skip the commercials, so advertisers and broadcasters are understandably worried.[5] Fortunately, only 2 percent of American households and even fewer Canadian households have PVR technology thus far.

Given these trends, however, advertisers have two basic options: they can reduce investment in television advertising, making it less important in the mix than previously, or they can shift their investment entirely. While the latter option seems radical, many large advertisers are doing a lot of soul searching about their TV budgets. Other advertisers firmly believe that television will remain the dominant medium and that it's mandatory if the goal is to build brand image. For some additional insight into these and related issues, see the IMC Highlight **Well Made, Well Priced, Well Dressed**.

Some critics believe that the PVR will lead to the demise of the 30-second television commercial. However, a study conducted by the Yankee Group called "The Death of the 30-Second Commercial" maps out strategies for expanding on the traditional advertising

---

IMC Highlight

WELL MADE, WELL PRICED, WELL DRESSED

If the expression "Well Made, Well Priced, Well Dressed" rings a bell with you, it's because of a lot of good television advertising. Up until 1999, the only media used by Moores (men's clothing and shoes) were newspapers and flyers. Considering there are 114 stores across Canada, that meant 24 flyers a year and as many as 8 million inserts a year.

In 1999, Moores was acquired by California-based Men's Warehouse, a successful company that built its business through television advertising. Rather than just jump into TV, Moores tested a few alternatives in three test markets: Calgary, Edmonton, and Vancouver. One city got flyers only, a second got a combination of flyers and TV, and the third got TV only. In both the TV markets, a different type of customer started shopping at Moores. The new customer would spend more and wanted some of the more expensive product lines. Television advertising helped create a better brand image for Moores.

Based on the results, Moores went full steam into television. The impact of the switch in media strategy wasn't felt until about the six-month mark. By then, sales were up 12.6 percent compared to the previous year, a rate of growth surpassing average retail sales growth by far in Canada.

A few other prominent retailers are also reducing their dependence on flyers and switching to TV. Sears' media ratio is very print oriented: 85 percent print (all forms) and 15 percent broadcast. In 2003, the plan was to go to a 70 percent print, 30 percent broadcast split. That doesn't seem like much of a change, but consider that Sears spends $63 million annually in media advertising. The switch in ratio meant that $9.5 million more went into television.

Sears's rationale for the change is based on a desire to build its image. "Flyers work for sales and short-term events, whereas TV markets a brand," says Vincent Power, director of corporate communications at Sears. Sears plans on promoting many of its own brands on television: Kenmore appliances, DieHard batteries, and Nevada clothing will benefit. Canadian Tire has used a similar approach to advertising for years and has been very successful with it. The switch in media strategy fits well with Sears' overall marketing strategy. Sears is moving away from sales events and towards a regular price on a day-to-day basis.

Adapted from David Chilton, "Taking to Television," *Marketing*, December 9, 2002, p. 11.

approach; the trick, it seems, is to supplement the 30-second spot, not supplant it.[6] Can television advertising be delivered in a more compelling way? One alternative that seems to be working is product placement or branded content, as it is sometimes referred to.

Product placement or branded content refers to the visible placement of branded merchandise in television shows, films, or programming. Hollywood has been doing product placement in movies for years. In any given television show, numerous products are given exposure; such exposure has more credibility with the audience than regular advertising. The pilot to Fox's series *24* starring Kiefer Sutherland was commercial free but featured Ford automobiles throughout the show. A primetime reality show on Global called *No Boundaries* was the highest rated Canadian series in 2002. The show was created by the Ford Motor Company specifically to promote the Ford Explorer Sport Trac SUV to its target demographic: people interested in extreme sports. Since Ford owns the show, it can distribute it on any network around the world.[7] And for the winner of the challenge, guess what the grand prize was? Shows like this save the broadcasters money. Expect many more of them in the future. Preparation H might turn up on a sitcom someday!

Television provides advertisers a means of reaching huge numbers of people in a short space of time with a compelling message. Companies that can afford to advertise in prime time on shows like *Friends*, *Survivor*, *ER*, and *Law & Order* or on sports programming like *Hockey Night in Canada* or *NHL Playoffs* have high reach almost instantaneously. Television is an expensive medium, so to save money many advertisers are opting for 15-second commercials. If reaching a well-defined target is a priority, television is not a good option. The audience in prime time, for example, spans all ages. You will reach your target, but are paying for everyone else who is watching. Furthermore, clutter is a problem on television; there are simply too many ads. Given that ads are scheduled in a **cluster**, does an advertiser want to be the third or fourth commercial in a cluster of six? Consider that one ad on the 2003 Super Bowl cost US$2.1 million. The ad reached 85 million viewers.[8] Is it worth it? Refer to the discussion about CPM in the "Media Execution" section for more details, and consult Figure 5.8 for a summary of the advantages and disadvantages of television advertising.

Product Placement or Branded Content
The visible placement of brand name products in television shows, movies, radio, video games, and other programming.

Cluster
Commercials grouped in a block of time during a break in a program or between programs, or ads grouped in a section of a publication.

FIGURE **5.8** **Advantages and Disadvantages of Television Advertising**

ADVANTAGES

Impact—sight, sound, motion; demonstration; emotion
Reach—high reach in short space of time
Some targeting—sports and specialty cable channels reach niche targets
Coverage flexibility—local, regional, and national options

DISADVANTAGES

High cost—desired frequency (message repetition) increases absolute cost
Clutter—too many spots in a cluster negates potential impact
Audience fragmentation—abundance of channels lowers audience size (reach potential)
Technology—electronic equipment records programs and edits out commercials

RADIO

As of 2002, 909 radio stations operated in Canada: 290 AM stations and 619 FM stations. Collectively these stations reach 93 percent of the population, with FM stations being far more popular than AM stations. The average listener spends more than 21 hours a week with the radio when all locations for listening are included (home, work, vehicle, etc.). All radio stations are self-regulating, with no restrictions on the number of commercial minutes or on the placement of those minutes.[9]

Format
The type and nature of the programming offered by a radio station.

One of the major advantages of radio is its ability to reach selective target markets. The audience reached depends on the format of the station. **Format** refers to the type and nature of the programming offered by a station. Basically, the content is designed to appeal to a particular target group, usually defined by age and interests. In radio, everything is based on demographics.

The most popular radio station formats in Canada are adult contemporary, news/talk, and contemporary hits. In terms of market share, these three formats are significantly higher than the remaining formats. *Adult contemporary (AC)* stations play popular and easy-listening music, current and past, and generally appeal to an audience in the 25- to 49-year-old range. Adult contemporary is the top format, commanding a 27 percent market share. *News/talk* stations focus on frequent news reporting and caller phone-in shows that discuss newsworthy issues. Some stations focus on unique niches such as sports. In Toronto, for example, The FAN 590 is a niche station popular with sports-minded males. *Contemporary hit radio (CHR)* stations play the latest hits, mainly rock, and appeal to teens and 18- to 34-year-old adults. Top 40 stations are popular in major urban markets. Among the remaining radio formats are classical, album-oriented rock, country, classical rock, adult standards, modern rock, and gold.

Because of its ability to reach precisely defined demographic targets in local markets, radio can be an ideal component of a "key market" media plan. As well, it is a relatively inexpensive medium. An advertiser can achieve high frequency on a weekly basis. In fact, radio is often referred to as the "frequency medium." If frequency is the strategic priority, then radio is a good fit.

While reach potential is high, a radio audience is fragmented in major urban markets. If several stations compete for the loyalty of the same demographic, an advertiser would have to buy spots on all the stations in order to reach the target. That would drive the cost of advertising upward. Unlike TV, which is an evening medium, radio is a morning medium. In fact, breakfast time—between 8 am and 9 am—is the highest daily period for all demographics. Radio listening drifts downward as the day progresses, with a slight blip upward in the afternoon drive-home period (4 pm to 6 pm). Listening trends such as these can influence the placement (timing) of an advertiser's message.

For additional information about the advantages and disadvantages of radio advertising refer to Figure 5.9.

NEWSPAPERS

Circulation
The average number of copies per issue of a publication sold by subscription, distributed free to predetermined recipients, carried with other publications, or made available through retail distributors.

Canada has 105 daily newspapers, with a total average daily circulation of 5.2 million copies. **Circulation** is defined as the average number of copies per issue of a publication that are sold by subscription, distributed free to predetermined recipients, carried within other publications, or made available through retail distributors.

Industry research indicates that 56 percent of Canada's adult population read a daily newspaper on any given weekday. On the weekend, readership increases to 80 percent. Newspapers are a popular medium among advertisers. Net advertising revenues generated by newspapers rank second in Canada, behind only television.

Broadsheet
A large newspaper with a fold in its middle.

Newspapers are produced in two formats: broadsheets and tabloids. A **broadsheet** is a large newspaper with a fold in the middle. Most Canadian dailies are published as

FIGURE **5.9** **Advantages and Disadvantages of Radio Advertising**

ADVANTAGES

Target selectivity—station format attracts a defined audience (profile matching possible)
Frequency—reach plans rotate messages through entire audience weekly
Cost—very favourable compared to other media
Flexibility—stations and markets selected according to priority (key market strategy)

DISADVANTAGES

Audience fragmentation—multiple stations competing for the same demographic reduces station's audience potential
Message retention—sound-only medium; clever creative required

Tabloid

A smaller newspaper that is sold flat (not folded).

broadsheets, including circulation leaders such as *The Toronto Star*, *The Globe and Mail*, and *The National Post*. A **tabloid** is a smaller newspaper in terms of surface area. It is sold flat and resembles an unbound magazine. The Sun newspaper chain (*Toronto Sun, Ottawa Sun, Calgary Sun*, and so on) publishes all of its newspapers in tabloid format.

Community newspapers are small-circulation newspapers usually published weekly. The community paper is the voice of the community. As such, it is well read. Among English Canadians, community papers are read by 59.1 percent of the population. Among French Canadians, readership is 71.3 percent. The readership of community newspapers parallels the demographics of the community. For that reason, they are an excellent advertising medium for local businesses.

Newspapers generate revenues from different types of advertising:

- *National Advertising:* National ads are sold to advertisers and ad agencies by a national sales department. Advertisers in this category include products and services marketed nationally or regionally. Brand name food and beverages, automobiles, airlines, banks and financial institutions, computers, and telecommunications products and services fall into this category.

- *Retail Advertising:* Retail advertisers include department stores, supermarkets, drug stores, restaurants, and shopping malls. These retailers usually advertise sales or re-advertise the nationally branded merchandise they sell. Retail advertising generates a majority of revenue for a newspaper. It truly is a local market medium.

Classified Ads

Print advertising in which similar goods and services are grouped together in categories under appropriate headings.

Insert

A preprinted, free-standing advertisement specifically placed in a newspaper or magazine.

- *Classified Advertising:* **Classified ads** provide an opportunity for readers and local businesses to buy, sell, lease, or rent all kinds of goods and services. Typically, the classified section is well read and in many large dailies is a separate section of the newspaper, a testament to its significance.

- *Preprinted Inserts:* The preprinted **insert** (often referred to as a free-standing insert) is a dedicated piece of advertising inserted into the fold of a newspaper. Large users of inserts include supermarkets (Loblaws, Sobeys, and others), drugstore chains (Shoppers Drug Mart and others), large general merchandisers (Canadian Tire and Home Hardware), and automotive companies (GM, Ford, and others). Other national marketers, including the Liquor Control Board of Ontario, Dell Computer, and Bell Sympatico's high-speed internet service, have begun using inserts.

Preprinted inserts are catching on with marketing organizations, but they are not yet a staple item in a media planner's recommendations to clients. According to Wayne Clifton, vice-president of advertising at the *Toronto Star*, "It's a steadily growing business." He cites

Dell Computer and Sprint Canada as clients that frequently use inserts.[10] Perhaps it's the perception of inserts held by media planners that is holding them back.

For advertisers, newspapers offer geographic selectivity and high reach in local markets. Furthermore, newspapers and readers have a relationship with each other. Readers have a tendency to read the entire newspaper in their own unique and sequential manner. For this reason, they are likely at least to see an ad in the paper. Newspapers are an effective choice for reaching broadly defined adult target markets. Unfortunately, the papers' life span is very short (one day for dailies). As the old saying goes, "There's nothing as stale as yesterday's news." Newspapers also suffer from a clutter problem. **Clutter** refers to the amount of advertising in a medium. About 60 percent of newspaper space is devoted to advertising, so standing out in the crowd is a design challenge for the creative team.

See Figure 5.10 for a summary of the advantages and disadvantages of newspaper advertising.

MAGAZINES

Currently, more than 1600 magazines are published and distributed in Canada, 550 of which are classified as consumer magazines. Business magazines are another large category. The most popular consumer magazines include *Reader's Digest* (1 026 800 circulation), *Chatelaine* (717 200), and *Maclean's* (502 000).

Canadian consumer magazines are distributed on the basis of paid circulation or controlled circulation. **Paid circulation** refers to subscriptions and newsstand sales. Magazines such as *Maclean's*, *Chatelaine*, *Flare*, and *Canadian Business* are paid circulation magazines and rely on subscriptions, newsstand sales, and advertising space to generate revenues.

Some magazines are distributed free to a predetermined target audience based on demographic, geographic, job function, or some other characteristic. These are **controlled circulation** magazines. Typically, receivers of the magazines are in a unique position to influence sales, so they are attractive to advertisers wanting to reach them. City-oriented lifestyle magazines such as *Toronto Life*, *Ottawa Life*, and *Vancouver Magazine* are examples of controlled circulation magazines. Much of their circulation is

Clutter
The amount of advertising in a particular medium.

Canadian Magazine Publishers Association
www.cmpa.ca

Paid Circulation
The circulation of a newspaper or magazine that is generated by subscription sales and newsstand sales.

Controlled Circulation
The circulation of a publication that is distributed free to individuals in a specific demographic segment or geographic area.

FIGURE **5.10**

Advantages and Disadvantages of Newspaper Advertising

ADVANTAGES

Targeting capability—reaches a diverse adult audience in key geographic markets
Reach—ideal for reaching consumers in local markets frequently
Media environment—readers engage with paper based on editorial content; they are receptive to messages
Merchandising—national advertisers have cooperative advertising opportunities with local market retailers

DISADVANTAGES

Life span—daily; exposure to message reduced if paper not read on day of publication
Audience diversity—not suitable if target market profile is precisely defined (exception may be the *Globe and Mail*)
Clutter—lots of space devoted to advertising (many ads on one page)
Reproduction quality—primarily a black and white medium; speed of presses reduces colour quality

based on distribution to selected households, hotels, and motels in their respective markets. *Homemaker's/Madame au Foyer* are widely distributed magazines that combine paid circulation with controlled circulation. Combined, about 15 percent of their total audience receives the magazine free.

Business magazines are divided into various industry categories: food manufacturing and distribution, hardware trade, hotels and restaurants, telecommunications, engineering and construction, and so on. These magazines are very specialized, their content appealing to people employed in a certain industry or a particular job function. Some magazine titles include *Canadian Grocer, Hotel & Restaurant, Modern Purchasing,* and *Marketing Magazine.* The profile of readers is based on a common interest or function, so these magazines are an efficient means of reaching prospects with a business-to-business advertising message.

Magazines are ideal for advertising purposes. For advertisers using a profile-matching strategy or rifle strategy, they serve a useful role. Magazines are often referred to as a "class" medium rather than a "mass" medium. In other words, readership is well defined on the basis of demographic and psychographic variables (profile matching), and there are all kinds of magazines devoted to a particular interest or activity (rifle strategy). As well, many large-circulation consumer magazines offer regional editions, so if geography is a factor influencing the media strategy, magazines will be part of the solution. Magazines are read for their editorial content; therefore, advertisers' messages benefit from the prestige of being associated with the magazine and the quality it represents.

Clutter remains a problem in most consumer magazines. The clustering of ads at the beginning or end of a publication, for example, may mean that a reader skips over an entire section of ads on the way to reaching editorial content. Advertisers combat the problem by requesting specific locations in a magazine. Covers, for example, are preferred positions and command a higher price. If frequency is a key objective, magazines are not a viable option. Most are published monthly or every two months, so they are good for achieving reach among a defined target audience and delivering continuity of message from month to month. More information about the advantages and disadvantages magazine advertising appears in Figure 5.11.

FIGURE **5.11** **Advantages and Disadvantages of Magazine Advertising**

ADVANTAGES

Targeting capability—good reach based on readers' demographic (profile-matching strategy) and psychographic (rifle strategy) characteristics
Coverage flexibility—city, regional, and national magazines available
Life span—magazines tend not to be discarded right away; opportunity for multiple exposures to message
Quality—excellent colour reproduction
Environment—message benefits from the prestige of association with the magazine's quality and image
Pass-along readership—actual readership goes beyond the subscriber (added reach)

DISADVANTAGES

Clutter—abundance of ads appearing in the initial section (advertising domination in some magazines)
Cost—colour is an added cost in production of ad
Frequency—distribution is usually monthly or bi-monthly

OUT-OF-HOME ADVERTISING

Out-of-home advertising and the variety of alternatives included in its domain represent a highly visible and effective alternative for advertisers. Think about it. If you drive a car, travel by transit, or stroll through shopping malls, you are constantly exposed to out-of-home advertising messages.

If the goal of an advertising campaign is to reach as many people as possible, then out-of-home should be the medium of choice. Although considered by some to be "pollution on a stick," outdoor boards have become one of the hottest media. Advertisers are giving it more priority due to the specialization that has occurred in other media, especially television and magazines. Moreover, with an increasingly mobile population, out-of-home ads provide a convenient way to get a message to consumers.[11] The major classifications of out-of-home media include outdoor posters and transit advertising.

Outdoor Posters

Posters or Billboards

A common form of outdoor advertising; usually a picture-dominant advertisement with a minimum of copy.

Backlit Poster

A luminous outdoor sign printed on polyvinyl material.

Superboard or Spectacular

Outdoor advertising that is larger than a normal poster and much more expensive to produce; can include extensions beyond borders and electronic messaging.

Banner

In outdoor advertising, a large-size printed ad that is framed and mounted on the exterior of a building.

Mural Advertisement

A hand-painted outdoor ad painted on the side of a building.

Mall Poster

A form of advertising located inside shopping malls; relies only on pedestrian traffic.

Posters or **billboards**, as they are commonly referred to, are large sheets of poster paper mounted on a panel of some kind. To maximize reach potential, they are strategically located on major travel routes leading to or within a community's business and shopping districts. To maximize the frequency of message, and to extend daily viewing by consumers, posters are often illuminated. A powerful light beams upward from the bottom of the poster.

A step up in quality is the **backlit poster**. On a backlit the advertising message is printed on translucent polyvinyl material. When the posters are erected, lights shine through the material from behind the sign. The primary advantage is the image enhancement offered by this lighting; there is strong visual impact in the day and night. Backlits are strategically located at major intersections and on high-volume traffic routes. For the advertiser, they cost more.

A **superboard or spectacular** is an extremely large display unit positioned at the highest-volume traffic locations. It is created to the advertiser's specifications and can include space extensions, flashing lights, louvres, and electronic messaging. Since superboards are one-of-a-kind structures that are illuminated and frequently include moving objects, they require a long-term commitment from the advertiser due to the high expense of designing and constructing them. Spectaculars are beyond the budgets of most advertisers.

Banners are large vinyl banners framed and mounted on the outside of a building. They can be moved and re-used. **Mural advertisements** are hand-painted outdoor extravaganzas painted on the sides of buildings. They are very large—often the entire height of the building. If size really matters, these kinds of ads are real attention grabbers.

Mall posters differ from the posters described above because they rely only on pedestrian traffic and aren't exposed to vehicle traffic. Located in shopping malls, they are directed at consumers who are actually shopping; therefore, they are a useful medium for the mall's retailers. Mall posters are good for supplementing other media and for reinforcing a brand's primary selling message.

Outdoor posters are an ideal medium if an advertiser is using a shotgun strategy. Posters reach a large cross-section of a market's population in a short period. Frequently outdoor boards are included in a blitz or build-up schedule because they are good for launching new products where creating awareness for the brand name, brand logo, and package are important. Outdoor posters are also ideal for advertisers who want geographic flexibility. The advertiser selects only those urban areas that are given priority. There are a few drawbacks as well. The message must be brief, considering the circumstances in which people view outdoor boards. Since they reach a wide cross-section of the population, they are not a targeted medium. The message reaches people well beyond the target, so that will increase the cost of reaching an actual target customer.

Transit Advertising

People who use public transit are a captive audience for advertising messages. To relieve the boredom of travelling, ads offer a form of visual stimulation. I know from personal experience that passengers read the same ad over and over while riding a subway car or bus.

Interior cards are print advertisements contained in racks above the windows of transit vehicles (buses, street cars, subway cars, and rapid transit cars). The average time spent travelling is approximately 30 minutes, offering the advertiser the flexibility of including longer messages—not an option in other forms of outdoor advertising.

Two different posters are available on the outside of buses. The **king poster** is a very large poster that stretches along the side of a bus. A **seventy poster** is smaller and located on the tail end of the vehicle. The unique characteristic of bus posters is their mobility. They move through the city and are seen by motorists and pedestrians.

Superbus advertising involves painting the outside of a bus to carry one advertising message. Due to the costs, the advertiser must commit to a long-term contract with the transit company (usually one year). As part of the package, the advertiser gets all of the interior cards as well. Bus murals are also available, and appear on the driver's side or the tail of the bus, or both. These are applied using vinyl products and are sold for commitments of 12 weeks or more.

Transit shelter advertising involves two street-level backlit posters that are incorporated into the design of glass and steel shelters located at bus stops. These shelters offer high levels of exposure to motorists, pedestrian, and transit riders. Transit shelter advertising offers the advertiser strong visual impact, as the colour reproduction is of superior quality.

Station posters are advertisements located on platforms and at the entrances and exits of subway and light rail transit systems. They are available in a variety of sizes and are either paper posters or backlit posters. Passengers waiting on platforms are exposed to the advertising message. A variety of new and innovative concepts have recently been introduced. Among them are *stair risers* (ads that appear on the sides of steps that can be read from a distance), *ceiling decals* in vehicles, and *floor decals* on walkways and platforms. Another concept called *station domination* gives a single advertiser control of all advertising space in a subway station. These are good options for advertisers looking for new ways of standing out amid the clutter of out-of-home advertising.

From an advertising perspective, transit offers continuous exposure. That 30-minute ride provides ample opportunity to deliver an advertising message. In terms of advertising objectives, transit achieves both reach and frequency. Transit riders cut across all demographics, with the heaviest concentration being adults. Factors such as the increasing cost of operating a car and the increasing numbers of commuters traveling to and from a city each day have a positive effect on the reach potential of the medium. Like outdoor advertising, transit is suited for media strategies designed to reach a diverse audience in key markets. Refer to Figure 5.12 for additional details about the benefits and drawbacks of the various forms of out-of-home advertising.

Other Forms of Out-of-Home Advertising

It's everywhere! It's everywhere! There are all kinds of unique opportunities to reach consumers when they least expect it. Among the more popular options with advertisers are washroom advertising, elevator advertising, arena and stadium advertising, and cinema advertising.

Washroom advertising involves the placement of mini-posters in public washrooms, usually above urinals in men's washrooms and on the backs of stall doors. They are located in colleges and universities, sporting facilities, hospitals, restaurants, and bars. Levi's and Budweiser are two brands that use this form of advertising. According to Gino Cantalini, marketing manager for Budweiser, "They are innovative and offer

Interior Card
A transit ad in the rack above the window or near the door of a bus or subway car.

King Poster
An oversized poster attached to the sides of buses.

Seventy Poster
A small poster usually affixed to the back of a bus.

Superbus Advertising
An advertisement painted on the exterior of a bus.

Transit Shelter Advertising
Street-level advertisements incorporated into the design of the glass and steel shelters located at a bus stop.

Station Poster
An advertisement located on the platform or at the entrance or exit of subways and light rail transit systems.

Washroom Advertising
A mini-poster ad located in a public or institutional washroom; usually placed above the urinal and on the back of the stall door.

FIGURE **5.12**   **Advantages and Disadvantages of Out-of-Home Advertising**

OUTDOOR POSTERS

Advantages

Reach and frequency—reach a large general audience daily
Coverage flexibility—markets selected geographically (key market plan)
Compatibility—a good complementary medium to reinforce a message
(name, logo, slogan)
Awareness—often included in teaser and blitz campaigns for new products due to
reach potential

Disadvantages

Creative limitations—message must be concise; good visuals mandatory
Targeting—not suitable for reaching precisely defined targets
Cost—absolute costs high compared to other media (minimum four-week cycles)
Image—often referred to as "urban clutter"

TRANSIT

Advantages

Reach and frequency—riders receive same message daily, weekly, and monthly
Continuous exposure—trapped riders view same ad many times
Coverage flexibility—markets selected geographically, based on priority
(key market strategy)

Disadvantages

Targeting—a diverse cross-section of population, therefore some circulation wasted
Environment—cluttered and crowded environment in peak periods makes message
less visible

---

a certain degree of targeting."[12] Budweiser is reaching its audience in a location close to where purchase decisions are made.

Elevator Advertising
Advertising in display frames on elevator walls and on televisions mounted in the corner or above the door.

Elevator advertising is available in two forms: posters contained in display frames on the walls of elevators and slim-line televisions usually mounted in the top corner and tilted downward toward the passengers. The Elevator News Network (ENN) delivers up-to-date news and information along with ads on TV screens in office towers in major cities.

All arenas and stadiums in North America offer targeted reach to advertisers. In arenas that are home to professional hockey teams, advertising starts right above the front door, with companies paying megabucks to have an arena adorned with their name. GM Place in Vancouver, Air Canada Centre in Toronto, Corel Centre in Ottawa, and Bell Centre in Montreal are just some examples. In hockey arenas, there is also on-ice advertising, usually ads painted in the neutral zone between the blue lines. Signs can be installed behind the player's benches and in the penalty box. At ballparks, rotating signs behind home plate are popular, and there are courtside signs on basketball courts. These signs receive additional exposure when a game is broadcast on television.

Cinema Advertising
Print advertising inside film theatres and broadcast advertising on screens.

Cinema advertising offers a variety of options, everything from films and slides to posters, theatre promotions, ads printed on movie tickets, and more. Cinema advertising is growing in popularity with Canadian advertisers. Full-motion screen ads, most of which are 60 to 90 seconds long, versus the traditional 30-second TV spot, provide kinetic visuals with an audio accompaniment. Throw in a captive audience and engaging content, and you have a very powerful advertising medium.[13] To be effective, full-motion ads have to be energetic and take advantage of the huge screen and Dolby Digital sound. Lifestyle products such as automobiles and designer label fashions find cinema advertising attractive.

Summary

Media planning is a process of developing a plan of action for communicating messages to the right people at the right time. The end result is a media plan prepared by an advertising agency that covers all relevant media strategies and tactics. It is a document that is presented to the client for approval, and, once approved, is put into action.

The key elements of the plan are media objectives, media strategies, and media execution. Media objectives deal with five key issues: who to reach, what and how to present the message creatively, where to advertise, when to advertise, and how often to advertise. Media objectives establish priorities for the plan and provide guidance for developing media strategies.

Media strategy deals with the selection of appropriate media to accomplish the objectives. Strategies are influenced by variables such as the characteristics and behaviour of the target market; the nature of the message; the degree of market coverage desired; the best time to reach the target; competitive activity; reach, frequency, and continuity; an assessment of the benefits and drawbacks of the various media options; and the budget available.

The advertising agency makes specific recommendations regarding the media a client should use. Depending on the assessment of the situation, and assuming the client wants to use traditional mass media, there are numerous alternatives: television, radio, newspapers, magazines, outdoor posters in a variety of forms, and transit and transit shelter advertising. Some unique and newer options are also considered: washroom advertising, elevator advertising, advertising in arenas and stadiums, and advertising in cinemas. To meet the challenge, the advertising agency usually recommends a combination of media. Typically, there is one primary medium (a medium that receives a significant portion of the budget) supplemented with secondary media.

Media execution is the section of the media plan that outlines the specific tactics for achieving the media objectives. These include the specific media usage recommendations and summaries of how media funds will be allocated. Once the plan is approved, the agency media buyers negotiate the best possible prices with media representatives. The plan is then put into action.

Key Terms

Review Questions

1. What are the essential differences among media objectives, media strategies, and media execution?
2. Identify and briefly describe the key issues usually covered by media objective statements.
3. What is the difference between a profile-matching strategy, a shotgun strategy, and a rifle strategy? What media are best suited for each strategy?
4. What is the difference between the following market coverage strategies: national coverage, regional coverage, and key market coverage? What media are best suited for each strategy?
5. Briefly describe how the timing and amount of spending vary in the following media schedules: pulse, skip, blitz, and build-up.
6. Briefly describe the impact of reach, frequency, and continuity on strategic media planning.

7. What role does CPM play in media selection? How is it calculated?
8. Identify two key strengths and weaknesses for each of the following media: television, radio, magazines, newspapers, outdoor boards, and transit.
9. In television advertising, what is the difference between a network spot and a selective spot?
10. What is product placement?
11. Briefly describe the following media terms:
    a) Format (of a radio station)
    b) Broadsheet and tabloid
    c) Paid circulation and controlled circulation
    d) Clutter and cluster
    e) Posters and backlit posters (outdoor)
    f) Interior cards and exterior cards (transit)

Discussion and Application Questions

1. How will technological advances affect media strategy and media execution in the future?
2. Should the budget determine the media plan or should the media plan determine the budget? Briefly explain and establish an opinion on the issue.
3. Read the IMC Highlights **Power That Couldn't Be Ignored** and **Well Made, Well Priced, and Well Dressed**. Do you think television advertising will continue to play a key role in the future or will advertisers shift their preference to other media? Consider other external trends that may influence such a decision and provide sound arguments for your opinion.
4. Is it possible to implement a rifle media strategy by using television advertising? Justify your position by providing branded advertising campaigns that are scheduled effectively or

ineffectively on television networks and channels.

5. Assuming you can't have both high reach and high frequency, under what circumstances should reach take precedence? Under what circumstances should frequency take precedence? Be specific and provide examples.

6. Given the nature of Canada's population and where the bulk of the population is located, when is it practical to implement a national media campaign? When do regional media campaigns or key market media campaigns make economic sense?

7. Using resources that are available in your library or online, compare the CPMs for three different magazines that compete with each other. They must be magazines that reach a similar target audience and attract similar advertisers. Which magazine is the most efficient at reaching the target audience?

8. Assume you are about to devise a media plan to launch a new luxury automobile (such as a BMW, Audi, Lexus, or Infiniti). The new model is a very sleek-looking sporty car. The target market is males aged 35 to 49 living in urban markets. What magazines and newspapers would you use to reach this target and why would you recommend them? What target-market media-matching strategy would you use?

Endnotes

1 David Goetzl and Wayne Friedman, "Friends Tops Price List," *Advertising Age*, September 30, 2002, pp. 1, 58.

2 Canadian Media Directors' Council, *Media Digest*, 2002–2003, p. 7.

3 Canadian Media Directors' Council, *Media Digest*, 2002–2003, p. 13.

4 Andrew Green, "The Death of Prime Time," *Strategy*, November 18, 2002, p. 8 Media.

5 Matthew Fraser, "TiVo, PVRs Begin to Worry Advertisers, Broadcasters," *Financial Post*, January 20, 2003, p. FP3.

6 Anthony Crupi, "Will DVR Really Kill the 30-Second Ad?," CableWorld, September 29, 2003 <www.cableworld.com> (November 2003).

7 James Careless, "Stretching TV's Boundaries," *Marketing*, October 14, 2002, p. 19.

8 Wayne Friedman, "Super: Rates Up 10%; Six Slots Left," *Advertising Age*, January 13, 2003, p. 3.

9 Canadian Media Directors' Council, *Media Digest*, 2002–2003, p. 27.

10 Chris Powell, "Insert Your Ad Here," *Marketing*, November 11, 2002, pp. 32–34.

11 John Heinzl, "Billboards Enjoy Boom Times," *Globe and Mail*, June 16, 1999, p. M1.

12 David Carr, "Pinning Down the Young Folk," *Marketing*, November 27, 2000, p. 25.

13 Nate Hendley, "Cinema Advertising Comes of Age," *Marketing*, May 6, 2002, p. 16.

Direct Response Communications

After studying this chapter you will be able to:

LEARNING OBJECTIVES

describe the direct response marketing communications planning process,

describe the various forms of direct response communications,

assess the role of database management techniques in the design and implementation of direct response strategies,

evaluate various external sources of list information and evaluate the role of these lists in building an effective direct response campaign, and

explain the advantages and disadvantages of the various forms of direct response communications.

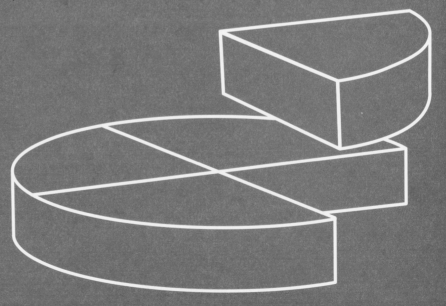

It was only a few decades ago that a mass marketing approach dominated the marketplace. Today, companies have the capability to deal with customers on an individual basis. In Chapter 1, the concepts of customer relationship management (CRM) and database marketing were introduced. Both concepts influence the development of programs that are designed to attract, cultivate, and maximize the return for each customer with whom the company does business. The end result is that companies are combining mass communications and marketing techniques with micro-marketing techniques. Database management and its influence on integrated marketing communications programs are discussed in more detail in this chapter. Information—that is, quality information—is the backbone of a direct response communications strategy.

Direct response communications involves direct mail, direct response communications in the mass media (mainly television, magazines, and newspapers), telemarketing, and catalogue marketing. Direct mail is the most common means of delivering messages directly to consumers, but advances in technology and database management techniques offer great potential for telemarketing and catalogues to become more important in the mix. Using database management techniques, a company can look at a customer over an entire lifetime and plan appropriate strategies to encourage good customers to buy more often or in larger quantities. Communicating directly with customers makes the entire process much more personal.

Direct Response Communications and Direct Marketing

Just how important are direct response communications and other direct marketing practices in Canada? Recent statistics suggest direct response communications and direct marketing have a significant impact on advertising expenditures and sales revenues for goods and services. Direct mail advertising alone accounts for $1.2 billion, or 13 percent, of net advertising revenues in Canada. As an advertising medium, it ranks third just behind television and daily newspapers and ahead of magazines, radio and outdoor advertising.[1] If investments in direct response television, telemarketing, and catalogue marketing were included, the percentage of total media expenditures would be much higher.

To understand the relationship between direct response communications and the sales it generates, let's review a few key figures from the United States. In 2001, the total investment in direct response television communications targeted at consumers was US$11.4 billion, resulting in sales of US$74.4 billion. In the business-to-business (B2B) sector, the investment was US$10.9 billion and sales were US$52.2 billion.[2] Such significant investments and sales revenues strongly suggest the increasing role that direct response communications play in the development of U.S. companies and their brands. Some of Canada's largest corporations have successfully integrated direct response communications with traditional forms of communications. These companies see the real value to be gained by managing customer relationships. Among these companies are Bell Canada, Rogers Communications, and Shaw Communications. The financial services market, which includes major banks and insurance companies, is also very active in direct response communications.

Direct marketing and direct response communications will continue to grow for several reasons. First, companies want managers to be more accountable for the expenditures they oversee. Executives are looking for more immediate sales returns for the dollars they invest. Direct response advertising can be measured for success quickly. Second, the trend toward niche marketing and micro-marketing suggests the importance of forming good relationships with customers. Because direct response communications can be personalized, they constitute an ideal medium for nurturing relationships. Third, the availability of database management techniques provides the fuel that direct response communications run on. Specific message strategies for individual customers are now a possibility, if the organization can effectively analyze the information in its database.

Advantages such as these clearly indicate why prudent marketing organizations include direct response as part of their communications mix.

It is important to remember that direct response communications is a subset of direct marketing. In other words, the communications program is a component of a much larger direct marketing program. What is the distinction between the two practices? In **direct marketing**, products are developed, messages about the products are sent directly to customers (consumers and B2B) through a variety of media, orders are accepted, and then distributed directly to customers. All wholesale and retail intermediaries are eliminated when direct marketing is practised.

In contrast, **direct response advertising** is advertising placed in any medium that generates an immediate and measurable response from the intended target. In a direct marketing campaign, direct response advertising plans involve the design and development of appropriate messages and the placement of messages in appropriate direct response media, in order to encourage immediate action by the intended target. Alternatively, direct response advertising may be designed to build brand image, alter a perception, or attract a new target, much like other forms of advertising. Therefore, direct response advertising can be part of a fully integrated marketing communications campaign. Figure 6.1 illustrates the direct response planning process and its relationship with other components of marketing communications.

If traditional mass media are used (newspaper, magazines, radio, and television), the message includes a return mail address, 1-800 telephone number, or a website address, where more information can be obtained or an order can be placed. Direct response advertising is capable of making a sale. Assuming adequate order taking and fulfillment strategies are in place, the entire transaction process from creating awareness to delivering the product is possible, and in a very short space of time.

Direct response communications can be divided between online communications and the more traditional forms. Online communications is presented in Chapter 7. The traditional forms of direct response communications are direct mail, direct response in the mass media (TV or print), telemarketing, and catalogue marketing:

- **Direct mail** is a printed form of communications distributed to prospective consumers by Canada Post or independent delivery agents (e.g., leaflets and flyers that may be dropped at a doorstep).

- **Direct response television (DRTV)** or **direct response print** refers to ads that appear in television commercials, extended commercials commonly referred to as infomercials, and print ads in newspapers and magazines. In each case, there is a direct call to action via a 1-800 number, return mail address, or website (see Figure 6.2).

- **Telemarketing** refers to outbound sales calls (a company calls the customer) or inbound sales calls (the customer contacts the company) to secure an order. All calls are usually handled through a central call centre.

- **Catalogues** are important communications vehicles among retail organizations. Typically, they are mailed or hand delivered by independent agents to existing customers. New customers may request catalogues through some form of direct response communications. Catalogues promote the sales of goods the retailer carries. They are also useful tools for communicating information about goods in B2B situations. In fact, many such catalogues are published on CD-ROMS and mailed directly to prospects.

It has taken considerable time for direct response communications to be accepted by blue chip marketing organizations. For years, traditional advertising agencies resisted using direct response; they were unfamiliar with this aspect of communications and saw it as a last-minute strategy when things weren't working well. It was for companies that didn't appreciate the impact of mass advertising. How the times have changed! Today, marketing organizations stress accountability and measurability. They want to know what they are getting for their investment. So pressure from clients instigated this change in the

Direct Marketing

A marketing system for developing products, sending messages directly to customers, and accepting orders through a variety of media, and then distributing the purchase directly to customers.

Direct Response Advertising

Advertising placed in a medium that generates an immediate and measurable response from the intended target.

Direct Mail

A printed form of direct response advertising distributed by Canada Post or independent delivery agents.

Direct Response Television (DRTV)

Advertising that appears on television and encourages viewers to respond by telephoning a toll-free number, by mail or online; often referred to as infomercials.

Direct Response Print

An ad in print media that issues a direct call to action via a toll-free number, return mail address, or online.

Telemarketing

The use of telecommunications to promote the products and services of a business.

Catalogue

A reference publication, usually annual or seasonal, distributed by large retail chains and direct marketing companies.

FIGURE **6.1** **Direct Response Planning Process**

Direct response campaigns are monitored continuously. If an offer isn't working (if results are lower than expected), it is common to alter the message during the campaign. Scripts for commercials and telemarketing campaigns can be changed quickly. In a direct response offer, the message, media, and fulfillment are equally important. Failure at the back end (fulfillment) undermines the impact of message and media strategies.

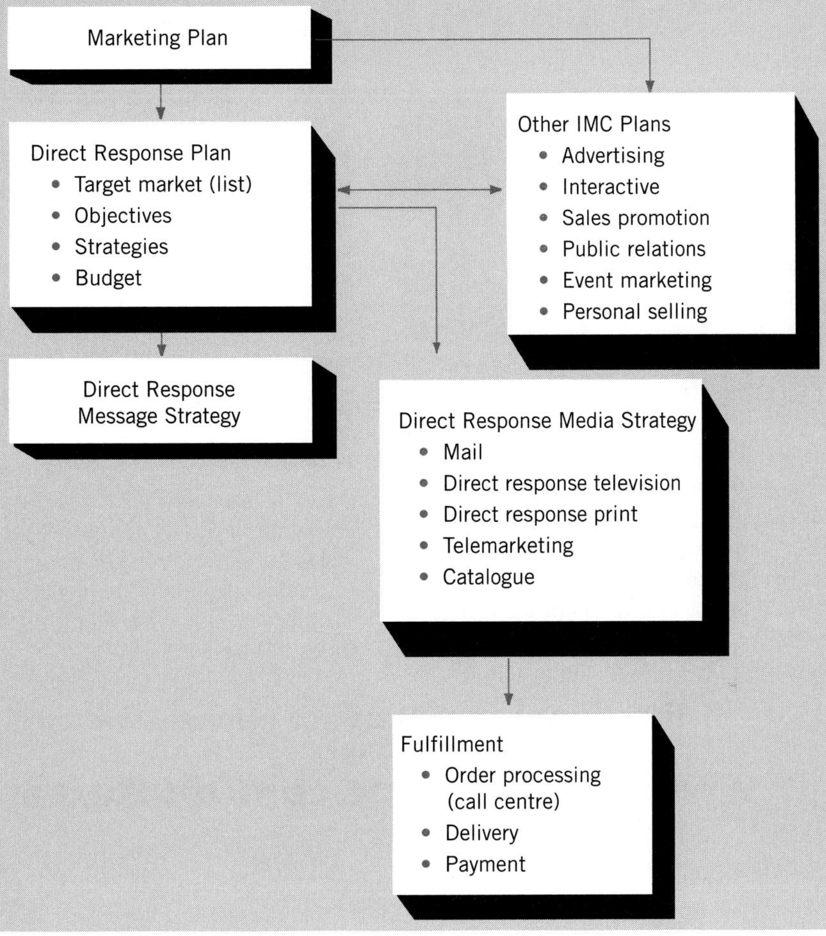

Marketing Plan

Direct Response Plan
- Target market (list)
- Objectives
- Strategies
- Budget

Other IMC Plans
- Advertising
- Interactive
- Sales promotion
- Public relations
- Event marketing
- Personal selling

Direct Response
Message Strategy

Direct Response Media Strategy
- Mail
- Direct response television
- Direct response print
- Telemarketing
- Catalogue

Fulfillment
- Order processing (call centre)
- Delivery
- Payment

advertising industry. Most large full-service agencies now offer direct response expertise or have access to it. Along the way, many traditional advertising agencies have acquired direct response agencies. There is an ongoing and general progression by agencies and marketers to treat direct response as a more important part of the communications mix.

The Roots of Direct Response Communications: Database Management

Whether it's mail or telephone communications, there needs to be a convenient and efficient means of contacting customers. As experts in direct response communications often state, it's the list that makes or breaks the campaign. By list, they mean the list that will be used to contact current customers or prospective customers directly. That list is the backbone of the entire campaign; the quality has a direct impact on the success or failure of the campaign.

FIGURE **6.2** **A Direct Mailing Promoting RBC Insurance**

CLICK NOW FOR A QUOTE
Value-priced insurance
from a company you can trust

Competitive quotes at a click

GUARANTEED FOR 60 DAYS

Now, getting a value-priced quote on home and auto insurance is quick, simple and confidential. Simply visit our secure website at www.rbcinsurance.com/quote/card today.

Affordable, convenient coverage

First, you'll receive a fair, competitive quote online within minutes. Then you can purchase your coverage with one toll-free call to RBC Insurance® by quoting your reference number. Our Licensed Insurance Advisors are available by phone to finalize your coverage and offer their best advice so you can be confident in choosing

RBC Insurance for your home and auto insurance needs. We'll guarantee your quoted rate for 60 days†. When your current insurance comes up for renewal, please contact us and we'll provide the coverage you need right away.

You can even enjoy the convenience of charging your payments to your RBC Royal Bank *Visa*.

Dependable service from quote to claim

Whether you need advice, a quote, coverage or our 24 hour emergency claims response service, you can count on our undivided attention. That's a promise from RBC Insurance – the insurance specialists of RBC Financial Group™.

If your insurance is up for renewal within the next 60 days, visit us at:

www.rbcinsurance.com/quote/card

You can get a quote online, 24 hours a day, seven days a week.
Or, call 1-877-230-7224 Monday to Friday, 8:00 a.m. to 8:00 p.m.

 **RBC Insurance**

Source: By permission, RBC Financial Group.

Companies recognize that it costs about six times as much to acquire a new customer as it does to keep an existing customer. Consequently, companies are compiling databases to keep track of existing customers and are forming relationships with them through the mail and electronic means. Obviously, the best list is a well-maintained and managed internal list of customers. Such a list is referred to as a **house list**. Since the best customers are current customers, it is much easier to get them to buy more of something than it is to attract a new customer. If the goal is to generate new business from new customers, then lists can be obtained from external sources.

House List
An internal customer list.

INTERNAL DATA SOURCES

A good database management system collects and maintains relevant information about customers. The information is stored in such a manner that managers have easy access to it when developing marketing strategies. For example, managers should be able to manipulate the data so that customer profiles will emerge, so that future purchase patterns can be forecast from those profiles. In other words, a thorough understanding of a customer's past purchasing behaviour should provide ammunition for predicting his or her future buying patterns.

COLLECTING DATA

The names and addresses of customers are the most common forms of internal data, but simply knowing who the customers are offers little perspective in developing a strategic plan. Factor in technology, and all kinds of information about customers can be combined. Keeping track of purchasing behaviour and then linking it to a name and address is very meaningful. Therefore, the database should identify what a customer purchases, how often the customer purchases, how much the customer spends on average, what brands of goods the customer prefers, and so on. Sophisticated retail organizations update this information automatically as goods are scanned through checkouts. From this information, buying behaviour profiles of a customer can be developed. Once the behaviour information is linked to the name and address, and perhaps also other demographic information, it is then possible to develop specific offers for specific types of customers. Plus the offer can be sent to each customer individually. Such profiles can also be used to search for new customers in external databases.

Adding external information to the database rounds out the profile of the customer. Information about customers using credit cards for purchases is readily available. Credit card companies such as Visa and MasterCard are sitting on nest eggs of information that marketing organizations can purchase. Statistics Canada makes available census data that are updated every five years. This information is available at reasonable cost to the marketing organization.

Statistics Canada
www.statcan.ca

And what about the demographic and psychographic information that was discussed earlier in the textbook? This information can be obtained from commercial research companies such as Millward Brown, among many others, or a company can hire an independent research company to conduct primary research to uncover such information. The combination of information dealing with age, gender, education, income, marital status, and household formation along with information about attitudes, lifestyles, interests, and hobbies form an arsenal of information ready for use in strategic planning. Procter & Gamble, for example, maintains a database of 50 000 studies and conducts 4000 to 5000 consumer studies a year in North America.[3]

ACCESSING DATA

The second step in database management is devising a storage system that allows managers to access information easily when it is needed. In the realm of marketing communications, sales representatives and sales managers need instant access to customer sales records as they prepare for sales calls. Customer service staff need access to historical information in order to handle complaints or simply serve customers better. Marketing managers and marketing communications managers need to clearly identify target customers and their behaviour in order to design special offers and communicate directly with them. To accomplish these kinds of tasks, relevant information must be convenient and accessible to all those who work with the database.

Data Mining

The analysis of information to determine relationships among the data and enable more effective marketing strategies to be identified and implemented.

The electronic era has resulted in an information explosion that now allows for the storage and transfer of a great amount of business data in a short time. What has emerged is a new concept called data mining. **Data mining** is the analysis of information that establishes relationships among pieces of information so that more effective marketing strategies are identified and implemented. Rather than looking at an entire data set, data mining techniques attempt to locate informational patterns and nuggets within the database.[4]

The goals of data mining are to produce lower marketing costs and to increase efficiency by identifying prospects most likely to buy in large volume. A firm's competitive advantage in the marketplace will depend increasingly on knowing the situation better than the competition and being able to take action rapidly, based on knowing what is going on.[5] Look no further than your local Wal-Mart to see data mining at work. Wal-Mart is the acknowledged leader in data mining with the capability of tracking sales on a minute-by-minute basis. It can also quickly detect regional and local market trends. Such knowledge allows Wal-Mart to customize each store's offerings while keeping suppliers abreast of how well their products are selling. Wal-Mart knows that rain gear is popular on the West Coast while wind gear is popular on the East Coast. Such information allows Wal-Mart to ship appropriate quantities to each region. It results in cost savings and an opportunity to group product lines together in its stores to drive sales.[6]

Data mining offers an organization two essential benefits. First, it provides a means of profiling the "best" customers and the "worst" customers. Clearly, in these times, greater emphasis must be placed on customers who produce sales and high profit margins for an organization. As well, consideration can be given to dumping customers who are costing more than they generate in profit. Why keep customers if they are not profitable? Second, data mining techniques allow an organization a means to predict future sales. Continuous compiling and analysis of data about current customers' sales histories should result in more accurate forecasts about what the future holds. As well, when a company wants to expand its business by attracting new customers, it can use the internal customer profile information as a guideline and then rent names from lists that have similar profiles.

For some insight into how Moosehead Breweries employs database marketing to manage customer relationships, read the IMC Highlight **Moosehead Builds Loyalty**.

EXTERNAL SOURCES

People who have a history of responding to mail offers tend to be attractive prospects for new offers. Buying by mail or from offers seen on television is part of their behaviour. Therefore, the challenge is to find prospects that have a similar demographic profile, and perhaps a psychographic profile that is close to the profile of current customers. A **list broker** can assist in finding these prospects. The buyer provides the broker with a profile of the target customer, and the broker supplies a list of potential prospects on a cost-per-name basis. Generally, a high-quality list is developed through a **merge/purge** process on a computer, whereby numerous lists are purchased, combined, and stripped of duplicate names. Names are purchased (actually rented) on a cost-per-thousand basis. The base rate for names is between $90 to $100 per thousand names. As the request for names becomes more sophisticated by adding more demographic and psychographic characteristics, the rate per thousand rises.[7]

One of the biggest suppliers of external data about households is Canada Post. Working from postal codes that isolate a neighbourhood or a city block, prospective households are identified when census data is added. For example, relevant statistics regarding the ages and incomes of homeowners in the area and the presence of children in those households could be attractive information for marketing organizations. There are three types of lists available:

Response Lists A **response list** is a list of proven direct-response buyers. It's a "hot" list so the price is high on a cost per thousand basis. Such lists include book-of-the-month buyers, CD music buyers, and people who routinely place orders with cooperative direct

List Broker

A company specializing in finding or developing lists for direct response purposes.

Merge/Purge

A process in which numerous lists are combined and then stripped of duplicate names.

Canada Post
www.canadapost.ca

Response List

A list of direct mail buyers who have previously bought based on direct response offers.

MOOSEHEAD BUILDS LOYALTY

How does a distant number-three company in the beer business compete with the likes of Labatt and Molson, the two market leaders that together control 90 percent of the Canadian market? They do it by staying small and focusing on their existing customers for growth. Moosehead is into customer relationship management.

CRM is often misunderstood and burdened with all kinds of technical jargon. Let's break it down. CRM simply involves collecting and analyzing customer information so that any activities the marketer implements will keep customers happy. It's a technique that will gradually grow a business.

When Moosehead evaluates what components of the marketing communications mix to use, it realizes that competing head-to-head in media advertising with giants like Molson and Labatt does not make much sense. Labatt spends $60 million a year in advertising and Molson close to $50 million. Moosehead can only afford $1.5 million. There has to be another way. Stephen Poirier, VP sales and marketing at Moosehead, believes that way is direct response marketing.

Moosehead focuses on its best customers by applying the old 20-80 rule: "20 percent of your customers drink 80 percent of your product." Starting from scratch, Moosehead built a database from personal contacts, contest entry forms, and an in-case survey. In the survey, respondents were asked a battery of questions about their consumption habits and brand preferences. Information about lifestyles, interests, hobbies, and activities was collected.

Moosehead's first effort at using the information was to pull all of the names that ranked fishing high on their list of favourite pastimes. Then the company sent a specially designed Moosehead fishing fly to each of them.

According to Poirier, this type of activity sets Moosehead apart. Instead of going after new customers, they reward existing customers in order to build brand loyalty. The occasional delivery of free goodies like the fishing fly adds value to the brand. Strategies like this will increase the number of touch-points Moosehead will have with the customer, and by managing the customer relationship they can maximize the lifetime value of individual customers.

Adapted from Kathleen Martin, "Hook, Line, and Sinker," *Marketing Direct*, August 21, 2000, p. 17.

---

marketing firms. For example, Time Life Products (an established direct mail marketing company) rents its list for $365/M ($365 for every one thousand names). A minimum purchase of 5000 names is required.[8]

Circulation Lists The word "circulation" indicates these lists are obtained from newspaper and magazine sources. **Circulation lists** can target consumers demographically, psychographically, and geographically. A publishing company, such as Rogers Communications, sells its list of subscribers to any other business that is interested in a similar target. A list management company is usually responsible for managing and renting all of the lists made available by the publisher.

For instance, *Canadian Living* magazine reaches women aged 25 to 49, with children, in households where incomes average $59 000 annually. Most recipients of the magazine are homeowners. The *Canadian Living* list has a base cost of $130/M, which rises as certain characteristics are added. There are also additional costs for requesting specific formats for the list (see Figure 6.3). Another example is *Cottage Life*, which reaches upper income households ($85 000 average), MOPEs (managers, owners, professionals, and executives), and multi-vehicle households. Its base rate is $160/M with added costs similar to *Canadian Living*.[9] Similar lists are available for trade and industrial publications.

Compiled Lists **Compiled lists** are assembled from government, census, telephone, warranty, and other publication information. Less expensive than circulation lists and response lists, these lists are very common in B2B marketing. Names of prospects can be assembled from various print sources such as *Fraser's Canadian Trade Index* and *Scott's Industrial Index*. Provincial and national associations such as the Canadian Medical Association provide lists of their physicians, as do other associations: accountants, engineers, purchasing managers, teachers, and so on.

Circulation List

A publication's subscription list that targets potential customers based on specified demographic characteristics, interests, or activities.

Compiled List

A direct mail list prepared from government, census, telephone, warranty, or other publication information.

FIGURE **6.3**

The Costs Involved in Renting a Direct Response List

Requirement	Canadian Living	Cottage Life
List Size	335 833	61 229
Minimum Order	5000	5000
Base Cost	$130/M	$160/M
Selects		
Male	$10/M	$10/M
Female	$10/M	$10/M
Key Records	$7/M	$7/M
Province	$10/M	$10/M
Other Selects		
Age	$20/M	N/A
Age/Income	$30/M	N/A
Direct Mail Sold	$10/M	$10/M
Rural	$10/M	N/A
Urban	$10/M	N/A
Cottage Location	N/A	$20/M

There are additional costs that depend on the format of the label required (e.g., peel-off, tape, e-mail, and disk).

CANADIAN LIVING READERSHIP PROFILE

- Household income $59 000
- 68% are 18 to 49 years old
- 64% are 25 to 54 years old
- 42% have children
- 77% are homeowners
- 233 157 identifiable females on list

COTTAGE LIFE READERSHIP PROFILE

- Household income $85 000
- 50% are MOPEs (managers, owners, professionals, and executives)
- Combined value of house and cottage is $670 000
- 70% have two vehicles

Adapted from Cornerstone List Management
<www.cornerstonewebmedia.com/CStoneWeb/Lists/CLMLists.aspx> (November 2003).

ONLINE DATABASES

Online Database
An information database accessible online to anyone with proper communications facilities.

Due to advancing technology there has been a surge in developing online databases. Information from commercial sources can now be transferred to an organization almost instantly. An **online database** is an information database accessible to anyone with proper communications facilities. For example, census data from Statistics Canada are readily available online. Most of Statistics Canada data are based on census data collected every five years. The nature of the information and reporting of the information is very detailed, covering dozens of demographic and socioeconomic topics such as family and household structures, income, occupation, education, ethnic background, and marital status. For a marketing organization, knowledge and understanding trend data are essential skills for planning effective marketing strategies.

From commercials sources, such as Dun & Bradstreet, marketing organizations can access information through directory databases. A **directory database** provides a quick picture of a company and its products (e.g., ownership, size in terms of sales revenue, company locations, numbers of employees, key management personnel and profitability). Examples of business directories that are available electronically include the *Canadian Key Business Directory* and the *Canadian Trade Index*. For businesses marketing goods and services to other businesses, the information contained in these directories helps identify real prospects.

Directory Database
A commercial database that provides information about a company.

The Tools of Direct Response Communications

Essentially, five primary media comprise the direct-response tool kit: direct mail, direct-response television, direct-response print media, telemarketing, and catalogues. At one time, direct mail marketing and direct marketing were often confused with one another, mainly due to the domination of mail in the direct response mix. Now that more organizations are implementing direct response programs more frequently, they are looking at the other alternatives as a means of solving marketing problems. Direct mail still dominates, but the other options are growing in importance. Let's examine each option in more detail.

DIRECT MAIL

The use of direct mail is widespread thanks to its ability to personalize the message by using names secured from internal databases or rented from external databases. As well, direct mail provides an opportunity to target customers demographically and geographically. For example, an organization might choose to do a mailing to a fairly general audience by distributing a magazine subscription leaflet to all households in Ontario, or by delivering a message to a very selective upper-income household in a concentrated area of a city. Moreover, direct mail provides an opportunity to "tell a story." Since the average mailing includes several pieces, an expanded story can be told about the product or service. Unlike the traditional mass media, the advertiser is not restricted by time (30 second commercials on TV or radio) or space (one page or less in a newspaper or magazine). Benefits such as these make direct mail an attractive option.

A typical direct mailing has several components, designed to serve a specific purpose:

Envelope The envelope is a critical component of the mailing. Since direct mail is usually unsolicited mail, the envelope has to suggest strongly why the recipient should read the contents. To demonstrate, Citi Financial did a direct mailing to solicit new members for its platinum MasterCard. In red ink on the envelope cover were the words, "The brilliance of platinum. The strength of Citibank. Plus, pay no interest and no annual fee. You're pre-approved." Persuasive copy like this might encourage someone to compare the costs of the Citibank card with the cards currently used. The envelope gets opened!

Letter The letter introduces the prospect to the product or service and encourages the receiver to read more about the offer in the other pieces included in the mailing. The letter may be unaddressed (delivered to the householder) or addressed (with the person's name and address). Addressed mail offers a certain degree of personalization and produces a higher response. Typically, the language used in the letter is persuasive, because the goal is to generate interest and desire and, ultimately, get the receiver to respond to the offer. In many mailings, the letter is not included. Instead, the leaflet or folder does all of the selling.

Leaflets and Folders These types of inserts can vary in size and structure. By definition, a **leaflet** is one page (though it may not be a full page), printed front and back, and

Leaflet
A one-page flyer that offers relevant information about a direct mail offer.

Folder

A direct response sales message printed on heavy stock that can be mailed with or without an envelope; may be several pages in length.

Incentive

A free gift or offer included in a direct mail package.

Statement Stuffer or Bounce Back

An ad or offer distributed in monthly statements or with the delivery of goods purchased by some form of direct response advertising.

containing vital information about the offer: here's what the product is and here's why you should buy it. Again the language is persuasive in nature. Visuals frequently support the copy. A **folder** can be larger in size and contain multiple pages. For example, a double page folded once results in a four-page layout. That amount of space gives the marketer ample room to sell. When an offer is put together, an **incentive** is often included to stimulate a more immediate response. Offering something for free catches the attention. An incentive might nudge a recipient interested in buying closer to taking action. The objective is to get that person to fill in the order form.

Order Form A well-designed order form is essential. It must be easy to read and communicate all details regarding price, additional costs such as shipping and handling charges, and means of payment (usually credit card information). The recipient must be able to place the order effortlessly.

Postage-Paid Return Envelope Eliminating the need for postage is another means of encouraging the recipient to take action. The combination of a clear and concise order form with a postage-paid return envelope makes it a no-hassle process from start to finish.

Figure 6.4 shows a direct mail offer, including several of the components described above.

Statement Stuffers A **statement stuffer,** or **bounce back,** is an additional offer that rides along with the delivery of another offer or with the delivery of a monthly statement. Capitalizing on the ease of purchasing by credit or on the knowledge that the customer uses related products or services, such mailings make it convenient for the customer to take action. Bounce backs commonly arrive with Sears, Visa, and MasterCard bills, or with utility statements like Enbridge Gas.

There are two basic options for delivering direct mail. The first is to deliver the mailing as a standalone piece. In this option, the organization bears all of the costs associated with developing the offer and distributing it to the target market. The second option

FIGURE **6.4** **The Various Components of a Typical Direct Mail Piece**

Source: Courtesy of *Outside* Magazine.

is to deliver the offer as part of a package that includes offers from other companies. In this option, the distribution costs are shared equally among all participants. That is the difference between solo direct mail and cooperative direct mail.

Solo or Selective Direct Mail
A unique advertising offer mailed directly to a target audience by a marketing organization.

Solo Direct Mail Also known as **selective direct mail**, with **solo direct mail** the organization prepares a unique offer and mails it directly to the target market. It is a standalone offer, much like the offer illustrated in Figure 6.4. As discussed earlier, today's technology makes it very convenient for organizations to assess buying information, devise unique offers for existing customers, and deliver offers directly to the customers. Such a plan of action sounds much more efficient than delivering a message blindly to all consumers on primetime television, daily newspapers, and national magazines. Furthermore, solo direct mail can play a key role in an organization's CRM program. It is an effective means of keeping the channel of communication open.

According to Nielsen Marketing Research, the median response rate for selective direct mailings is 12.5 percent.[10] If 100 000 letters were mailed to consumers 12 500 would be returned, either to request more information or to take advantage of the offer. Statistics such as these are one reason direct mail has become more popular. Marketers can predict the return on investment with reasonable accuracy. Selective direct mail is commonly used in B2B marketing situations as well.

Cooperative Direct Mail
A mailing containing specific offers from non-competing products.

Cooperative Direct Mail **Cooperative direct mail** refers to packages containing offers from non-competing products and services. Consumer goods companies commonly use this method; they are attracted to it because the costs are shared among all participants. A typical mailing might include coupons for packaged goods items, magazine subscription forms, preprinted envelopes offering discounts on film processing, order forms for direct mail offers, and so on. For packaged goods marketers in the food and drug industries, cooperative direct mail has proven to be an effective means of generating trial purchase. Response rates to coupon offers in direct mail are significantly higher (5 percent) than for similar offers in newspapers (1 percent) and magazines (1 percent).[11]

When deciding how and when to use direct mail advertising, a manager must evaluate the benefits and drawbacks of the medium. Figure 6.5 summarizes what direct mail has to offer.

DIRECT RESPONSE TELEVISION

Direct response television (DRTV) is gaining in popularity with advertisers. How so? If mass media advertisers such as Procter & Gamble and the RBC Financial Group are using the medium, then it clearly has something to offer other companies. Their leadership in DRTV will pave the way for others to follow. Essentially, there are three forms of direct response television: the 30- or 60-second commercial that typically runs on cable channels and sells gadgets and music products, the infomercial (a program-like commercial), and direct home shopping (as in The Shopping Channel).

The nature of direct response television advertising has changed over time. Once it was regarded as the "domain of schlock"; mainstream marketing organizations would not go near it. It was perceived as a last-resort tactic when all else failed. Perhaps what has changed the image the most, and in a very positive way, is both the gradual acceptance of infomercials and their improved level of quality. An **infomercial** is usually a 30-minute commercial that presents, in detail, the benefits of a product or service. Messages today are presented in a more acceptable manner; there is less "hard sell." Contemporary infomercials are positioned to inform consumers; in fact, many entertain consumers. The transfer of information is less intrusive. Consumers can simply evaluate the message and take action if they so desire.

Infomercial
A long commercial (e.g., 10 to 30 minutes) that presents in detail the benefits of a product or service.

Well-produced and highly informative infomercials are now being placed by serious mainstream marketing organizations. Included in the mix are pharmaceutical companies, banks and financial institutions, packaged goods companies, and automotive companies.

FIGURE **6.5** **Direct Mail as an Advertising Medium**

ADVANTAGES

Audience Selectivity—Targets can be precisely identified and reached based on demographic, psychographic, and geographic characteristics. It is possible to secure external lists that closely match internal lists.

Creative Flexibility—Unlike other media, the message can be copy oriented, visually oriented, or a combination of both. Because a mailing includes several components, there is ample time to expand on the benefits of the product.

Exclusivity—Mail does not compete with other media or other ads upon receipt. In contrast, magazines and newspapers include clusters of ads and create a cluttered environment to advertise in.

Measurability—Direct mail response is measured by the sales it generates. A sale can be directly linked to the mail offer (e.g., receipt of a phone call or order form in the mail). The success of a campaign is determined in a relatively short period.

DISADVANTAGES

Image—Direct mail is not a prestigious medium. Often perceived as junk mail, it can be easily discarded by the recipient.

Cost per Exposure—When all costs are included (e.g., printing, securing list, mail delivery, and fulfillment), total cost can be higher than an ad placed in another print medium, although selective targeting reduces waste circulation.

Lack of Editorial Support—As a standalone medium, compared to newspapers or magazines, it can't rely on editorial content to get people to read the message.

First movers into this arena include companies such as Ford, Bell, TD Canada Trust, and Procter & Gamble. These organizations evaluated the returns from their respective investments in mainstream advertising and decided that direct response communications would play a more vital role. The true benefits of database management are starting to pay off. As time goes on, direct response will play an even greater role in the communications mix.

According to a report from Nielsen Media Research, the greatest boost in U.S. advertising volume during 2001 came from the direct response sector, which was up 18 percent, a trend the firm believes was ignited by an increase in infomercials. In Canada, Scotiabank launched a 60-second direct response commercial that outlined the rewards of an RSP account. The ad portrayed the exchange between a husband and wife poring over their monthly budget, and explained how to make automatic contributions to an RSP, while offering a 1-800 number and a website address throughout. In a similar spot promoting mortgages for first-time homebuyers, Scotiabank received 5000 calls. The ad ran on Toronto Star TV, a station with 800 000 viewers weekly. Based on that level of response, Scotiabank has continued its direct response advertising.[12]

Direct-response commercials do not always have to sell something. In fact, a good infomercial can serve many different marketing communications objectives: it can establish leads, drive retail traffic, launch new products, create awareness, and protect and enhance brand image. Some companies are even referring to the medium as "BRTV" or "brand response television." What this means is that advertisers are pursuing a dual benefit—they are combining a branding message with a DRTV technique. The ad builds the brand attributes and generates an immediate response through a 1-800 number and the web. Its ability to do both is what excites the advertiser. Getting

into direct-response television is not cheap. According to Patty Booth, vice-president of Thane Direct, "It costs somewhere between US$150,000 and US$400,000 to produce a good 30-minute DRTV commercial."[13]

For additional insight into how Procter & Gamble uses DRTV, read the IMC Highlight **Old Dog, New Tricks**.

IMC Highlight

OLD DOG, NEW TRICKS

Who says packaged goods marketers aren't changing their ways? If traditional retailers are now carrying direct response products like OrangeGlo International's OxiClean, a brand built on direct response advertising, why shouldn't the reverse occur?

Even a packaged goods stalwart such as Procter & Gamble, a company built on brand management systems and mass advertising, is now giving direct response television a serious look. P&G started with a direct response ad for Swiffer WetJet, a motorized floor-cleaning machine. That was followed with a few infomercials. The impact was immediate. The direct response ads helped propel Swiffer WetJet past Clorox Co.'s rival Clorox ReadyMop. Such movement in market share gets the attention of top-level managers.

Recently, P&G tried a bare-bones direct response ad for Dryel, a home dry-cleaning kit, in addition to traditional

30-second ads. The pitch was to have consumers make the call to request coupons for the product. According to a P&G spokesperson, "Both brands are doing well. They are seeing increases in sales, shipments, and awareness. Success is attributed to the overall marketing communications effort of which DRTV is a piece."

P&G is starting to reap the rewards that direct response campaigns offer. Brands such as Swiffer and Dryel can enhance their databases based on the responses they receive, and then develop direct mail or e-mail offers aimed at building repeat sales of replacement supplies. In this case, P&G is attracting new customers and then continuing the relationship through additional sales.

Adapted from Jack Neff, "Direct Response Getting Respect," *Advertising Age*, January 20, 2003, pp. 4, 35.

Direct Home Shopping

A shopping service provided by cable television stations that offers products or services for sale by broadcast message.

Direct home shopping is a service provided by cable television, for example The Shopping Channel. Messages to prospects are presented in the form of close-up shots of the product or, in the case of clothing and accessories, by models wearing the goods. Items such as home gym equipment usually involve a full-scale demonstration. Details on how to place an order are broadcast frequently and a 1-800 number is usually shown continuously on the edge of the TV screen along with a description of the product.

Home shopping offers the shopper convenience. George Foreman, a former boxing champion, markets his cooking grill on The Shopping Channel. The Shopping Channel has annual sales in the $150 million range and sold 90 000 Foreman grills over a two-year period.[14] That's effective marketing communications!

Generally, the United States is well ahead of Canada in terms of direct response television and home shopping penetration. American companies embraced these techniques more quickly. The trend, however, suggests that the boom years for direct response television in Canada lie ahead.

DIRECT RESPONSE PRINT MEDIA

The print media—mainly newspapers and magazines—are good choices for communicating direct response offers or for fielding leads for future marketing programs. Given the local nature of daily newspapers, an organization can target prospects geographically. If the size of the budget restricts activity, then markets can be assigned priorities until the budget is exhausted. Local market retailers that want to take advantage of direct response techniques have a good option in newspapers.

A majority of magazines are targeted at specific audiences based on demographic and psychographic characteristics, so the direct response message can be sent to specific audiences based on criteria established by the advertiser. For example, a company marketing floating docks or cottage designs might want to reach cottage owners. A direct response ad placed in *Cottage Life* magazine will reach that target market. The basic point is that it is possible to identify magazines that closely match the profile of a company's best customers. If a direct response is the objective, the print ad should include a toll-free telephone number and a mailing address or website that facilitates the response (see Figure 6.6). Viceroy, a designer and builder of modular homes, for example, uses direct response print ads to get potential customers to order a catalogue or to visit a dealer. The catalogue contains colourful pictures and the floor plans for all of the models. A video about the company and how it constructs the cottages is also sent to the prospective customer. This is a good example of an effective, integrated direct response campaign.

Another option to consider is the insert. Inserts were briefly discussed in Chapter 5 in the discussion of newspapers. An **insert** can be a single-page or multiple-page

Insert

A preprinted, free-standing advertisement specifically placed in a newspaper or magazine.

FIGURE **6.6** **An Illustration of Direct Response Print Advertising**

Source: Courtesy of Viceroy.

Tip-in

An insert that is glued to a page in the publication using a removable adhesive.

document that is inserted into the publication. In some cases, the insert is actually glued onto a page (a gum-like glue that is easily removed when the insert is removed from the page). This type of insert is referred to as a **tip-in** (see Figure 6.7). Advertisers pay the publication insertion fees based on the cost per thousand. A single-page insert in the *Toronto Star*, for example, costs $37.00/M, and a 16-page insert costs $53.00/M.[15] Preprinted inserts can be used for other communications purposes—they are good hand-outs at trade shows and other promotional events and can be used to draw attention to products at the point-of-purchase. They can also be mailed directly to customers in the company's database.

FIGURE **6.7**   **Inserts Are Flexible and Can Be Used in Print Media, Direct Mail, and at Point-of-Purchase**

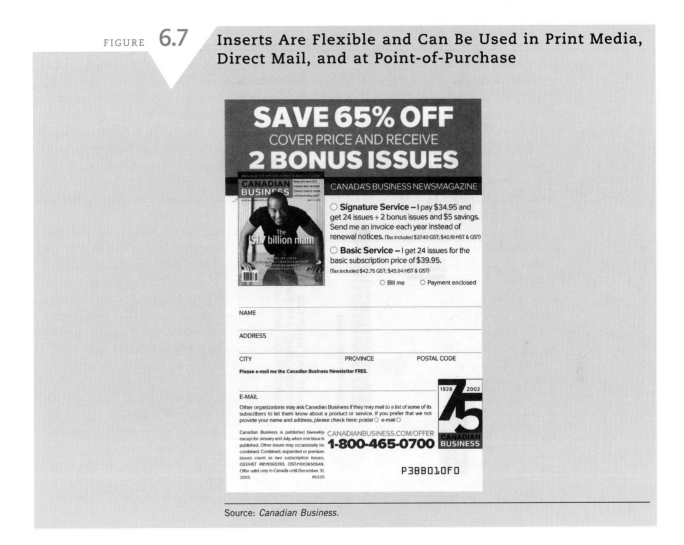

Source: *Canadian Business.*

TELEMARKETING

Why are people so rudely interrupted during their supper by a telemarketer—can't tele-marketers call at a more suitable time? Doesn't that sound like a common complaint? To a telemarketer, it's simply a fact of life. The best time to call is when the prospect is at home, and that's suppertime or shortly thereafter. Despite the negative feelings con-sumers have about telemarketing practices, it is a growing sector in marketing and mar-keting communications. Telemarketing communications are directly linked to direct response television campaigns. Working together, they are a potent combination for achieving all kinds of marketing objectives.

Most telemarketing activities are conducted by call centres. A **call centre** is a central operation from which a company operates its inbound and outbound telemarketing programs. In Canada, telemarketing generated $15 billion in sales revenues in 2001 alone.[16] As indicated above there are two forms of telemarketing: inbound and outbound. *Inbound telemarketing* refers to the calls received by an order desk, customer inquiry, and calls generated from toll-free telephone numbers promoted on direct response television commercials. *Outbound telemarketing* refers to calls made by company to customers to develop new accounts, generate sales leads, and even close a sale.

The call centre is a vital link in the database management system, because the telephone is a quick and convenient method of capturing information about customers. Any information that is obtained can be added instantly to the database. Cost-effective software is available to manage this task.

In direct response communications, much emphasis is placed on message and media decisions. For example, how will the offer be communicated to entice the target market and what media will it be placed in? Managing the inbound sales calls generated by commercials has traditionally been a weak link. Therefore, the better an organization plans its activities to meet call volume, capture data, present selling opportunities, and handle closing calls, the better the economics of the direct response campaign. To illustrate, consider that a national TV spot on a cable network for a direct response lead generation campaign can easily generate 500 or more inbound inquiries, 85 percent of which will occur within the first three minutes of airing.[17] The call centre has to be ready! If it has to dump the call, or if the consumer hears a busy signal and hangs up, the marketer's return on investment is undermined.

In the pursuit of direct response success, smart marketers understand there is more to it than simply extending the offer. The ability to manage the inbound call—a medium in its own right—demands planning and precision in order to maximize returns. It could be the start of a very fruitful customer relationship.

The primary advantage of telemarketing is cost. Compared to traditional forms of mass advertising and the cost of sending a salesperson into a business call, telemarketing offers considerable savings. To be effective, however, the telemarketing call must be carefully planned. There must be proper training and preparation of telemarketing representatives, just as there is for field sales representatives. Figure 6.8 summarizes the activities that can involve telemarketing.

Earlier in this section, the negative image of telemarketing was mentioned. Image is perhaps telemarketing's biggest drawback. A Canadian research study conducted by Ernst & Young found that 75 percent of Canadian consider marketing calls unwelcome and intrusive; they are ranked as one of the least-liked sales techniques.[18] People who react negatively to the calls simply hang up. Despite this behaviour, marketing organizations persist. To them, it's a game of averages. How many calls does it take to convert one customer? It's inexpensive to make those calls. Economies of scale rule the day!

CATALOGUES

Catalogues are reference publications, often annual, distributed by large retail chains and other direct marketing organizations. Catalogue marketing involves the merchandising of products through catalogue sales. When someone thinks of catalogues, the Sears catalogue comes to mind immediately, and for good reason. By the numbers, Sears is a $6.5 billion company in Canada. It has a network of 123 department stores, 42 furniture and appliance stores, more than 2200 catalogue merchandise pick-up locations, and the busiest commercial website in Canada. This combination of contact points means that Sears reaches 93 percent of Canadians.[19]

The Canadian catalogue market is underdeveloped, yet it offers great potential in the future. In the United States, catalogues generate $50 billion in consumer sales annually.

FIGURE **6.8**   **Telemarketing Performs Many Marketing Roles**

FUNDRAISING

- Inbound (donations)
- Outbound (solicitations)

SALES SUPPORT

- Generating leads
- Qualifying prospects
- Securing appointments
- Marketing research

PERSONAL SELLING

- Opening new accounts
- Selling existing accounts
- Selling marginal accounts

FULFILLMENT

- Accepting orders
- Maintaining customer records
- Invoicing and payment processing

CUSTOMER SERVICE

- Handling inquiries and complaints
- Help lines

L.L.Bean
www.llbean.com

A Canadian catalogue market would proportionately generate sales of more than US$5 billion. Currently, the Canadian catalogue market is only valued at US$2 billion.[20] Among the leading catalogue marketers in the Unites States are L.L. Bean and Lands' End. Given the technology of the day, many large U.S companies now put their catalogue on a CD-ROM.

As indicated above, the Sears catalogue is the largest in Canada and is distributed to more than 4 million households. Sears publishes two semi-annual catalogues (Fall & Winter and Spring & Summer) as well as numerous seasonal catalogues such as the Christmas Wish Book and sale catalogues. Sears is now a fully integrated marketing communications organization (see Figure 6.9). The company accepts orders by fax, e-mail, and online. Its 1-800 number is the most frequently called toll-free number in Canada.[21]

Canadian Tire is another leading catalogue marketing organization. Its catalogue is extremely popular and is referred to frequently. Eight out of ten Canadian households keep theirs until a new one arrives.[22] Both Sears and Canadian Tire see the value in catalogue and online marketing activities. Sales through catalogues definitely take away from store sales, but both companies are responding to their customers' demand for convenience. Customers today are into multi-channel shopping. Both companies effectively combine media advertising (television, print, and flyers) with non-traditional marketing communications (internet, direct mail, and catalogues). Canadian Tire also has one of the most popular loyalty programs in existence with its Canadian Tire money. The ongoing discounts that are based on dollars spent at Canadian Tire keep the customers coming back for more.

FIGURE **6.9** Sears Effectively Integrates Catalogue Marketing and Web Marketing

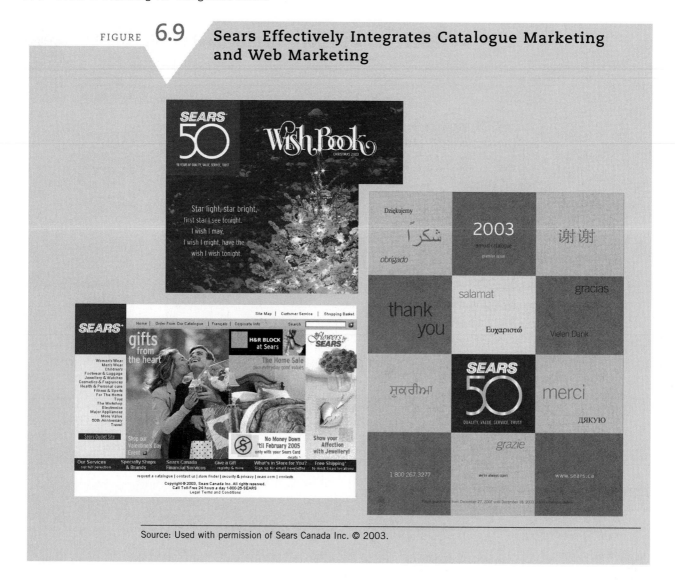

Source: Used with permission of Sears Canada Inc. © 2003.

Ashton Green
www.ashtongreen.com

There are many types of catalogues. In some industries, the catalogue is the dominant means of making sales. For example, more than 50 percent of gardening supply sales are made through catalogues. My household recently received a catalogue from Ashton Green, marketing "Cooking Tools that Work!" The 68-page catalogue includes almost every cooking utensil and accessory you could think of. Goods are shipped direct to consumers from the company's Ottawa location (see Figure 6.10). Catalogues are also widely used in business-to-business marketing. These catalogues are used by sales representatives and contain a complete listing and description of all products sold by the company. B2B marketers now put their catalogues on CD-ROMs so that customers can quickly access information about products they are interested in.

Rather than distribute catalogues, some companies have taken the concept a step further and are publishing their own magazines for distribution to current customers. The purpose is to stay in touch with customers after the sale. The Ford Motor Company launched *My Ford* magazine in 2001 and General Motors has a catalogue called *Vision* targeted directly at its Cadillac customers. These magazines are sent to customers at no cost to the customer and they are not profitable. However, both companies firmly believe the publications will influence buying decisions down the road. In the automotive industry, loyalty is increasingly crucial as competition swells and the quality gap among vehicle

FIGURE **6.10** **Catalogues Provide Consumers with Shopping Convenience**

Source: Courtesy of Ashton Green Limited.

brands closes. Therefore, any effort that builds rapport and keeps customers coming back is well worth the investment. A market research study shows that 38 percent of readers pass the magazine on to a friend. That's an added bonus for communicating product information.[23] The magazines include lifestyle articles appropriate for the target audience.

Summary

Direct response advertising is the third largest advertising medium in Canada and is growing at a pace faster than traditional mass media. Several factors are contributing to this growth: companies are looking for tangible returns for the money they invest in communications, direct response communications are a natural extension of database management programs, and direct response is a personalized medium that is ideal for enhancing customer relationships.

The foundation of direct response communications is the organization's database. An organization collects and analyzes data from internal and external sources. Customer or house lists record data about purchase transactions made by customers. This information is combined with demographic and psychographic information to form profiles of an organization's best customers. These customers are then targeted and reached through direct response communications. The analysis and manipulation of data constitute a process called data mining. The goal of data mining is to lower marketing costs and increase efficiency by identifying customers most likely to buy in large volume.

The success of a direct response campaign depends on the quality of the list used by the advertiser. Lists are available from list brokers and other secondary sources such as directories and trade indexes. Lists provided by brokers are rented on a cost-per-thousand basis. Advertisers can choose between response lists (the most expensive), circulations lists and compiled lists.

Direct mail is the most common form of direct response advertising. A direct mailing usually includes an envelope, letter, leaflet or folder, order form, and postage-paid return envelope. Each component performs a specific role in trying to get the recipient to take action. Advertisers choose between solo direct mail and cooperative direct mail. Solo distribution is more expensive but produces a higher response rate than cooperative distribution.

In recent years, direct response television has captured the attention of blue chip marketing organizations. An advertiser can choose between 30- and 60-second direct response commercials and infomercials, which are much longer and are more like a program than a commercial. Direct response commercials are effective if an organization wants to establish leads, build image, and launch new products. Infomercials are effective in situations where there are lots of details to communicate or for explaining complex products. By definition, direct response ads are capable of completing a transaction with the recipient.

Direct response ads in the print media are another option. Advertisers frequently use the print media to encourage prospective customers to call 1-800 numbers or to visit websites to get more information. As well, print is a good medium for distributing inserts. By selecting the right newspaper or magazine, the advertiser can target its primary customer.

There are two types of telemarketing. Inbound telemarketing refers to calls made by customers to an order desk. Outbound telemarketing refers to calls made by a company to prospective customers to generate leads and even close a sale. Telemarketing programs are usually outsourced to a call centre. Companies are attracted to telemarketing because of its low costs. It is much less expensive than face-to-face personal selling and mass advertising. Its major drawback is the negative perceptions people hold about this form of communication.

Catalogues are an underdeveloped alternative in direct response communications in Canada. However, companies such as Sears and Canadian Tire see the value of producing annual catalogues. As well, there are all kinds of specialty companies that produce catalogues that include descriptions, pictures, and prices of the products they market. Time-pressed consumers appreciate the convenience of catalogue shopping.

Key Terms

bounce back 168	house list 162
call centre 174	incentive 168
catalogue 160	infomercial 169
circulation list 165	insert 172
compiled list 165	leaflet 167
cooperative direct mail 169	list broker 164
data mining 164	merge/purge 164
direct home shopping 171	online database 166
direct mail 160	response list 164
direct marketing 160	selective direct mail 169
direct response advertising 160	solo direct mail 169
direct response television (DRTV) 160	statement stuffer 168
direct response print 160	telemarketing 160
directory database 167	tip-in 173
folder 168	

Review Questions

1. What is the difference between direct marketing and direct response advertising?

2. What are the major forms of direct response advertising?

3. Explain the concept of data mining. What impact does data mining have on marketing and marketing communications?

4. What is the role of the list broker in direct response advertising?

5. In the context of mailing lists, what does merge/purge refer to?

6. What are the differences among a response list, a circulation list, and a compiled list?

7. Briefly explain two advantages and two disadvantages of direct mail advertising.

8. Identify and briefly explain the components of a typical direct mail piece.

9. What is a statement stuffer?

10. What is the difference between a solo direct response campaign and a co-operative direct response campaign?

11. Identify and briefly explain the various direct response television alternatives.

12. What is the difference between an insert and a tip-in?

13. What is the difference between inbound telemarketing and outbound telemarketing?

Discussion and Application Questions

1. Will direct response communications play a more significant role in the marketing communications mix in the future? Through secondary research, identify those factors that will encourage or discourage the use of direct response communications, and formulate your position on the issue.

2. Direct mail advertising remains a popular medium for many profit-based and not-for-profit based organizations. Why? What are the benefits and drawbacks of using direct mail? Identify some organizations that successfully use direct mail advertising to help achieve their marketing goals.

3. Collect two or three direct mail pieces that have been delivered to your household address. Did the mailing reach the appropriate target market? What components did the mailing include, and how effective were they in communicating the message? Is the message convincing enough to act upon?

4. Assume you are about to develop a direct response advertising campaign

to launch a new and improved version of the George Foreman grill. The target market is male and female heads of households, with a family income of $50 000 or more, living in markets of over 100 000. The campaign will be national in scope. What direct response media would you use in the campaign? Assuming direct mail will be a component of the campaign, how would you find names for the mailing?

5. Conduct some research to find a company that has successfully used direct response advertising as part of an integrated marketing communications campaign (such as a major bank, financial services company, or not-for-profit fundraising campaign). What role did direct response communications play? Describe the successes that resulted from the direct response effort.

6. Is direct response advertising a viable option for Canadian packaged goods companies? Provide appropriate examples to illustrate your point of view.

Endnotes

1. Canadian Media Directors' Council, *Media Digest*, 2002–2003, p. 10.

2. Cara B. Dipasquale, "Accountable TV Ads: Direct Gets Respect," *Advertising Age*, June 24, 2002, p. 24.

3. Emily Nelson, "P&G Wants the Truth: Did You Really Brush Your Teeth?," *Globe and Mail*, June 1, 2002, p. M2.

4. Ross Waring, "The Promise and Reality of Data

Mining," *Strategy*, June 7, 1999, p. D9.

5 Kevin Marron, "Tools for Taming Data Chaos," *Globe and Mail*, September 6, 2002, p. T1.

6 Susan Pigg, "Diapers, Drinking, and Data," *Toronto Star*, August 16, 2002, pp. E1, E10.

7 Information obtained from a brochure published by *Target Source*, "Canada's Best Sources of New Consumer Responders," 1998.

8 Based on costs obtained from Accountable List Brokers, ListBroker <**www.listbroker.com**>, and direct responders Time Life.

9 Costs obtained from Cornerstone List Management <**www.cornerstonewebmedia.com/CStoneWeb/Lists/CLMLists.aspx**> (November 2003).

10 *A Special Presentation on Consumer Promotion Fundamentals*, NCH Promotional Services, 1998.

11 Ibid.

12 Lisa D'Innocenzo, "The Rise of the Infomercial," *Strategy*, July 15, 2002, pp. 1, 7.

13 Ibid.

14 Paul Brent, "Brawn + Brains = Bucks," *Financial Post*, March 29, 1999, pp. C1, C7.

15 *Canadian Advertising Rates and Data*, Rogers Media, September 2002.

16 Eve Lazarus, "The New Call Centre Mecca," *Marketing Direct*, February 12, 2001, p. 24.

17 Maria Eden, "One Call, Multiple Sales Opportunities," *Marketing Direct*, November 4, 2002, p. 16.

18 Mary Gooderham, "Level of Antipathy a Wake-Up Call for Telemarketers," *Globe and Mail*, May 7, 1997, p. c 11.

19 Dana Flavelle, "Sears Canada Turns 50 While Seeking to Rejuvenate Itself," *Toronto Star*, January 5, 2003, pp. E1, E11.

20 David Napier, "Northern Exposure," *Marketing*, April 27, 1997, p. 4.

21 "Sears Canada This Year's Directors' Choice," *Strategy Direct Response*, November 22, 1999, p. 10.

22 Stephen Theobald, "Canadian Tire's Flyer Grows Up," *Toronto Star*, March 15, 2001, p. E1.

23 "Automakers Hope Magazines Will Keep Buyers Loyal," *Toronto Sun Driver Source*, July 28, 2002, p. 12.

ONLINE INTERACTIVE COMMUNICATIONS

After studying this chapter you will be able to:

LEARNING OBJECTIVES

assess strategies for delivering effective messages using online advertising,

describe the various roles played by online communications in a marketing and marketing communications environment,

evaluate the various advertising alternatives that are available online, and

assess the potential of the internet as an advertising medium.

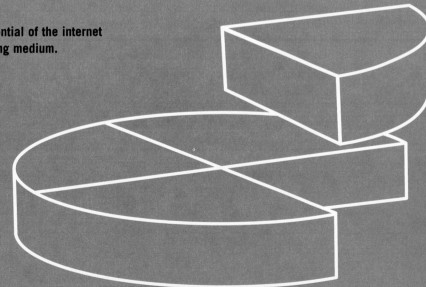

The decision to advertise online and how much to invest in such advertising is a difficult one. For some companies, when the internet became so popular, the decision was made quickly and the results were disastrous. It now seems that those companies that sat on the sidelines while they assessed what role the internet would play in their marketing communications mix are generating better results.

Online communications offer a high degree of personalization. Since personalization is one of the cornerstones of customer relationship management (CRM) programs, the internet should be attractive to marketers. The medium also offers the ability to listen to customers and learn from them, and to deliver content and services tailored to their responses and actions. Such an advantage must be made the most of. Since the medium is still new, however, companies are still trying to figure things out. Once they do, for certain it will play a more important role.

One company that has figured things out is General Motors. The leading advertiser in North America has repositioned its marketing budget to put more money into relationship marketing, including sponsorships and the internet. GM is looking for better ways to target customers, and it's a lot easier to identify prospects when they visit its GM websites than when they view its television commercials.[1] If GM is going in this direction, its competitors and large companies in other industries won't be far behind.

Interactive Marketing Communications

As with any new medium, it takes time to establish a presence in the marketplace. The internet has been an overwhelming success among consumers who search for information online, but the commercial side of the internet has met with consumer opposition. Advertising is perceived by many to be an intrusion; it is something that is there to stall them from doing what they want to do online. Slowly however, consumers are starting to realize that what they have begun to take for granted comes at a cost and that cost involves the placement and acceptance of advertising.

Unilever
www.unilever.com

Companies are exploring the internet; for most of them, it is still a new opportunity that will be added to the traditional marketing communications mix. The internet is a medium that allows a company to achieve what was once thought of as an unattainable goal: a personal, one-to-one relationship with consumers at all stages of a transaction—pre-transaction, transaction, and post-transaction. Unilever's Dove and many other brands have conducted research on the effectiveness of deploying online media in concert with offline media advertising. At the same time, Unilever is exploring an array of new rich-media formats and streaming technology as the internet continues to grow.[2] This chapter will explore the various opportunities available to companies and show how the internet can play a significant role in the integrated marketing communications mix.

Perhaps companies are confused about how to use the internet because of the various perceptions they hold about it. The reality is that the internet can do a host of things that other individual media can do. For example, it helps create brand awareness and build brand image. At the same time, it can go further than many other media because it can secure a purchase and make arrangements to have goods delivered. It is capable of closing the loop, from initial awareness to a buying decision in a very short period, assuming the website has ecommerce capabilities. Figure 7.1 illustrates how internet communications links with traditional advertising and ecommerce. The internet is a fast-paced medium unlike all others. "It's a bit of direct response, it's a bit of television, it's a bit of print, and it's a bit of technology," says one observer.[3] For these reasons, it is an exciting medium, and its potential must be exploited.

Beyond the internet is another interactive communications option: instant text messaging. The booming market for cellphones is fuelling interest in on-the-spot communications with people. CD-ROMS also offer a good opportunity to incorporate a

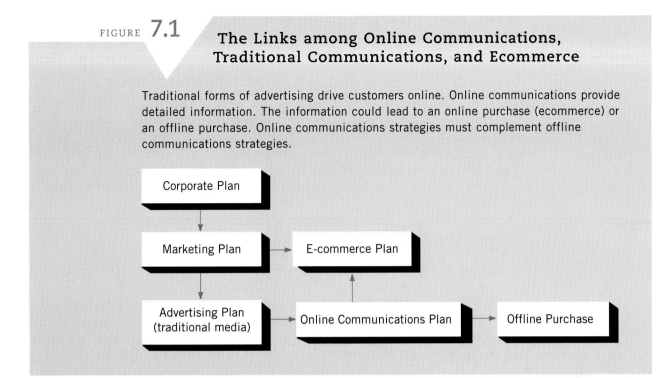

FIGURE **7.1**   **The Links among Online Communications, Traditional Communications, and Ecommerce**

Traditional forms of advertising drive customers online. Online communications provide detailed information. The information could lead to an online purchase (ecommerce) or an offline purchase. Online communications strategies must complement offline communications strategies.

message with bold and vivid graphics. They are proving useful in communicating complex messages and messages that require careful explanation and demonstration. These media are also discussed in this chapter.

THE INTERNET

Internet
A world-wide network of computer networks linked together to act as one in the communication of information.

World Wide Web
A system of internet servers that publish websites, which are specially formatted documents that contain graphics, audio, and video files and links to other websites.

The **internet** is a network of computer networks (independent, interconnected networks) linked together, like a global mail system in which independent entities collaborate in moving and delivering information. The **World Wide Web** is the collection of websites, which are documents that contain graphics, audio, and video files as well as links to other websites, on the internet. Users of the internet go to the websites that interest them and browse through the material for as long as they like. Along the way, they can be exposed to various forms of online advertising. In some cases, consumers must agree to view the ads before they are granted access to the material they are searching for. As indicated earlier, this creates some conflict but consumers are beginning to realize that commercial interests will ultimately rule the internet.

The reality of the internet is that consumers voluntarily visit specific websites. To get what they want, they also give up valuable information about themselves. Smart companies use the internet as a means of obtaining information for their database. It is a way to build a stockpile of information that can be mined at a later date. Once the information is analyzed, it can be translated into specific messages and marketing offers can be tailored to specific customer needs.

INTERNET USERS

All kinds of studies have been conducted to determine the profile of internet users. Since penetration of the internet is still growing rapidly, the profile of users is changing quickly. As potential customers, internet users are a moving target! At one time, the internet was the domain of upper-income, well-educated households, because access to computer technology was a prerequisite. As the price of technology has dropped, barriers to entry among lower-income households have been gradually eliminated. Marketers today can reach a more diverse audience.

The latest Canadian statistics available reveal that 48.7 percent of households have at least one regular internet user. The highest penetration remains in middle-income and upper-income households, though a full one third of lower-income households now have internet access. In terms of education, internet penetration in households with occupants who have high school or higher education is 64 percent, while penetration in households with children 18 years of age and under is 80 percent. On a regional basis, Ontario, British Columbia, and Alberta exceed the national average for penetration.[4] For additional details, refer to Figure 7.2.

INTERNET BEHAVIOUR

The internet is not yet the centre of the advertising or commercial universe. In fact, it is a long way off, considering the attitudes and behaviour of internet users. Trends definitely indicate that usage is increasing each year and that users are finding new and different reasons for using the internet. In December 2001, Canadians online at home spent 10 hours per week online compared to 8.5 hours a year earlier. Weekly users are also connecting more frequently: about 10.9 times per week compared to 8.5 times. Users with high-speed access spend up to 6 hours more a week online compared to users with regular dial-up service. The average online Canadian family spends more than 32 hours using the internet each week and 59 percent of families have actually bought something online.[5]

The primary activities of internet users are email and general browsing on the web. Although making actual purchases online with any consistency and frequency remains low, consumers use the web to research potential offline purchases. That's a step in the right direction! It also provides a good reason to communicate online. A user who sees something of interest (that is, an advertising message that creates awareness) can obtain information immediately by clicking the ad and visiting the website. Therefore, well-designed, well-placed, and well-targeted messages are useful tools for consumers who engage in online product research. Figure 7.3 provides some details on how people use the internet.

Online Marketing Communications

The internet provides access to customers all over the world and delivers information in ways that traditional broadcast media and print media cannot. Traditional media are passive by nature; the internet is interactive by nature. Traditional media target an audience; on the internet consumers target the content they are interested in and in the process are exposed to messages that should be of interest. The potential of the internet is huge—it will become the medium of choice for companies wanting to reach large numbers of people in a cost-efficient manner.

Thus far, however, the growth of internet advertising has been slow to take off. The most recent statistics show total internet advertising in Canada to be CA$118.4 million annually, or roughly 1 percent of all advertising revenues. In the United States, internet advertising amounts to CA$8.2 billion for a U.S./Canada ratio of 69:1.[6] This ratio confirms the extent to which the Canadian market is underdeveloped. At this level of spending, the internet is not yet a threat to traditional forms of advertising. It is still perceived by many organizations to be an additional medium that requires some experimentation in order to determine its true value.

The internet offers three significant marketing and marketing communications opportunities. First, from a communications perspective, it is an excellent medium for telling a story. The medium is ideally suited for extended copy and loads of visuals.

FIGURE **7.2**

A Profile of Canadian Internet Users
(Percentage of Households)

Demographic	1997	1999	2001
All Canada*	29.0	41.8	60.2
Home Access	16.0	28.7	48.7
Education			
Less than High School	8.9	16.1	29.9
High School/College	30.6	44.4	64.6
University Degree	59.2	70.1	85.8
Age			
Under 35	37.3	53.0	76.2
35–54	28.5	54.9	74.1
55–64	20.7	32.7	52.5
65 plus	9.3	10.1	19.3
Income			
Lowest Quartile $23 000 or less	12.2	18.8	31.6
Second Quartile ($23 000–40 000)	18.0	29.2	51.8
Third Quartile ($40 000–$70 000)	32.2	48.1	70.1
Highest Quartile ($70 000 plus)	53.5	71.2	87.3
Family Structure			
Single Family with Children	37.9	59.0	80.5
Single Family without Children	27.2	38.7	55.6
One-Person Family	16.4	22.1	36.2
Location			
Toronto	37.6	48.5	67.0
Montreal	24.0	39.1	60.1
Vancouver	35.5	49.7	69.1

* Internet access from home, work, school, public library, or some other location.

Adapted from the Statistics Canada publication "Connectedness series," Catalogue 56F0004, September 2003, and from the Statistics Canada CANSIM database <http://cansim2.statcan.ca>, Tables 358-0002, 358-0003, 358-0004 and 358-0005.

Mass Customization

The development, manufacture, and marketing of unique products to unique customers.

Second, from a marketing perspective, an organization can complete a sale online. In terms of securing action, the internet is very similar to direct response advertising (discussed in Chapter 6). Online storefronts such as those for Sears and Canadian Tire fall into this category. Third, the internet deals with the concept of mass customization. **Mass customization** refers to the capability of personalizing messages and ultimately products to a target audience of one. The marketer deals with each customer individually. Dell is already an expert at mass customization: traditional forms of advertising draw consumers

FIGURE **7.3**

Top Ten Uses of the Internet

Purpose of Use	1997	1999	2001
Email	13.3	26.3	46.1
General Browsing	13.6	24.3	44.3
Medical/Health Information	—	15.6	30.1
Travel Information/Arrangements	—	—	27.4
View the News	—	—	26.2
Government Information	—	12.7	25.6
Playing Games	—	12.3	24.4
Obtaining/Saving Music	—	7.8	23.3
Formal Education/Training	—	9.2	22.9
Financial Information	—	—	22.8

Greater penetration and acceptance of the internet have encouraged usage for a wide variety of activities. The internet is a valuable entertainment and research medium.

Adapted from the Statistics Canada publication "Connectedness series," Catalogue 56F0004, September 2003, and from the Statistics Canada CANSIM database <http://cansim2.statcan.ca>, Table 358-0006.

online to learn about Dell's computer products and, ultimately, to place an order. Dell operates one of the highest volume ecommerce sites in the world. The site receives 840 million page requests each quarter at 82 country sites in 21 languages. Dell understands how the internet works. Of the US$33 billion of revenue generated in the U.S., US$20 billion is transacted online (see Figure 7.4).[7]

Online Advertising

Advertising on a website or delivered electronically through email, cellphones or personal digital assistants.

Online advertising is defined as the placement of an advertising message on a website, usually in the form of a banner, pop-up ad, text ad, or animated ad that looks much like a television commercial, or delivered by email, or in the form of sponsorships. Online advertising can also be delivered to individuals through other electronic devices such as cellphones and personal digital assistants that are connected to the internet. Online advertising performs the same or similar roles as traditional media advertising. It can help create brand awareness, build or enhance brand image, provide a means to make a purchase, improve customer service and communications between customers and the company, and acquire meaningful data about potential customers (as in database management). With so many benefits to be gained, one can quickly see why online communications must be considered a vital component of the integrated marketing communications mix. This section will examine these roles in more detail.

Portal

A website that serves as a gateway to a variety of services such as searching, news, directories, email, online shopping, and links to other sites.

CREATING AWARENESS

Given the amount of time and the frequency with which consumers go online, there is ample opportunity for a company or brand to develop advertising that will generate awareness. The most obvious way to achieve awareness is to advertise on a web portal. A **portal** is a website featuring several commonly used services, such as news or searching, and serves

FIGURE **7.4**   **Dell Has One of the Highest-Value Ecommerce Sites in the World**

Source: Courtesy of Dell Computer Corporation.

Government of Canada
www.canada.gc.ca

Saturn Canada
www.saturncanada.com

as a starting point or gateway to other services, such as shopping, discussion groups, and links to other sites. Examples of such sites include Yahoo!, Canoe, Canada.com, Sympatico, AOL, and MSN; the Government of Canada's home page is also a portal to all the government services and directories. These are often sites that people are automatically routed to when they launch their browser. Banner ads (discussed later in the chapter) typically appear on these sites. While the standard banner cannot communicate much information, it can help create brand name awareness (see Figure 7.5). When the user clicks on the ad, he or she is routed to a website where more details can be communicated. This was precisely the strategy Saturn Canada used when it launched the Saturn Ion in 2003. Market research information revealed that 75 percent of Saturn's target market surfed the web, a compelling reason for using internet advertising.[8]

FIGURE **7.5** **Saturn Canada Uses Banner Advertising to Increase Awareness and Interest in the Saturn Ion**

Introducing the all-new Saturn ION
See where it takes you.

ION Click here

Introducing the all-new Saturn ION

Starring in
4 all-new animated featurettes

ION WIN free
MOVIE PASSES FOR LIFE† Click here

The online effort–which also encompasses banner (above) and big box (left) advertising, as well as a micro-site (top)–is the driving force behind a new integrated campaign for the Ion

Source: Courtesy of General Motors of Canada.

BRANDING AND IMAGE BUILDING

Brand building is the responsibility of marketing communications activities. The purpose is to have the public perceive the brand in a positive manner. Therefore, online communications must present a message and image consistent with and comparable to any traditional form of communication. Consumers actively seek out product information on company websites, so it is important that the site project an image in keeping with overall company image. Often consumers are routed to sub-pages on a website (e.g., a brand page). In this case, the brand page must comply with the brand's image and persona. The appearance, style, and tone of the messages communicated through online advertising or on a website should be consistent with traditional media advertising. It is now common for traditional forms of advertising to carry a website address to encourage people to visit the site. Such a practice fosters communications integration and helps produce a synergistic effect for the total communications effort.

Companies in the telecommunications, automotive, and financial services industries are masters at matching messages strategies among traditional and non-traditional forms of media. Automotive sites in particular do an excellent job of creating and building an image for a new car model. When an interested consumer or tempted car buyer first sees a new car in a print ad or on television, he or she almost automatically migrates to the internet for more information (see Figure 7.6).

FIGURE **7.6** **A Honda Print Ad Encourages People to Visit the Website for More Information**

Source: Honda Canada Inc.

OFFERING INCENTIVES

The internet is a good medium for implementing a variety of sales promotion activities. To encourage consumers to make their initial online purchase, price discounts are commonplace. Canadian Tire, for instance, offers unique and special deals online as a means of getting people comfortable with online buying. Once they realize it is a safe and convenient way to buy, they go back for more. Online coupon offers are available from companies that specialize in this business. One example is Save.ca, which identifies offers available from various manufacturers and services, takes requests for the coupons online, and then mails the coupons to consumers (see Figure 7.7).

Contests and sweepstakes are popular online promotions. Typically they encourage consumers to buy for the first time or they encourage brand loyalty (repeat purchases). Regardless, the true benefit to the company is the names and information that are collected through entry forms. For the chance of winning a prize, it is surprising how much personal information an individual will divulge to a marketing organization. This information can be used either to start or expand a database.

FIGURE **7.7** **The Internet Is a Useful Medium for Distributing Incentives to Prospective Customers**

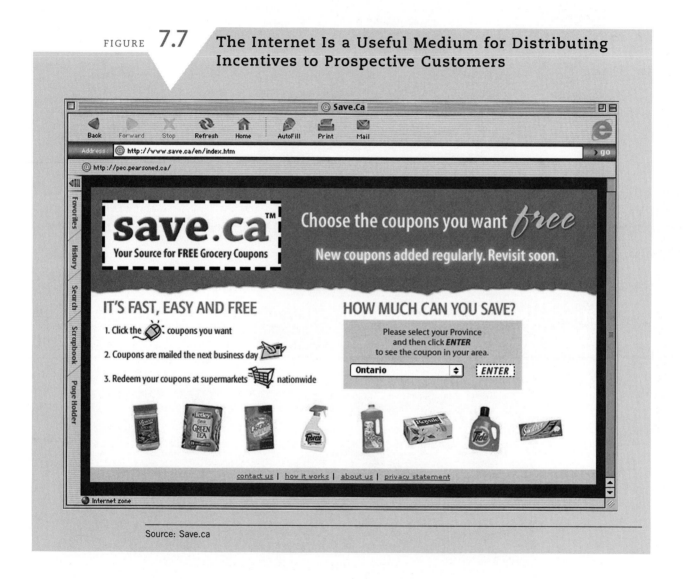

Source: Save.ca

GENERATING LEADS

In a business-to-consumer or business-to-business marketing situation, the internet is a useful medium for generating leads. As already indicated, consumers willingly disclose information when entering contests. Consumers and business people will also leave the same vital information when they are searching for information online. The stumbling block in retrieving the information they want is the transfer of personal or business information. However, online visitors are known to give out more details about themselves, or the business they are part of, so that they may retrieve the information they are searching for. Business sites often request information such as company size, number of employees, type of business, location, postal codes, email address, and so on. It's a fact of life in doing business online. This type of information, once analyzed and mined (data mining), can be used to identify potential targets (one-to-one marketing) and to customize messages and products that are suited that target. It's the start of CRM.

PROVIDING CUSTOMER SERVICE

In any form of marketing, offering good customer service is crucial. Satisfied customers hold positive attitudes about a company and are likely to return to buy more goods. Again, the internet plays a pivotal role. It can be an efficient and cost-effective way of providing service, assuming a company's website is well organized. Service demands by customers tend to be high. Therefore, any frustration a customer experiences when searching for service on a website will only compound the problem. Speed of service is a primary benefit offered by the internet. It goes without saying that customers should have quick and open access to service information. Carefully indexed FAQs (frequently asked questions) or key word searches are common ways to access online information quickly.

For specific questions and concerns, email is another good option. Of course, response time for handling email has unfortunately become a real issue. Making customers wait a few days for a response is not the type of service they expect. Successful online businesses don't forget that online activities must be backed up by a human component. They must pay close attention to inbound sales, order tracking, out-of-stock issues, deliveries and returns, and all the service issues associated with these tasks. All of these activities are part of a good CRM program.

USING EMAIL MARKETING

Working from a database, a company can email useful and relevant information to prospects and customers in order to build stronger relationships. Email offers a way to keep in touch with important customers. Unlike direct mail, which is perceived negatively, reaction to email marketing messages is generally more positive (the concept of opt-in email lists is discussed later in the chapter, as is unwanted email, or spam). Email is an efficient method of delivering new product information, information about promotional offers, customer newsletters, and viral marketing programs. Email campaigns cost $5 to $7 per thousand, compared with $500 to $700 per thousand for direct mail.[9] **Viral marketing** encourages the recipient of a message to send it on to a friend. Should one person send a marketing message to everyone in his or her address book, word would spread fast.

Viral Marketing
Online marketing that encourages the receiver of a message to pass it along to others in order to generate additional exposure.

CONDUCTING TRANSACTIONS

The business-to-business market is booming with online transactions, while the business-to-consumer market is showing promising signs of better things to come. Companies in a supply chain are linking together to form a B2B exchange. The goal of the exchange is to achieve efficiencies in the process of buying and selling. For example, many large retail chains such as Wal-Mart and The Bay allow suppliers access to sales information in their databases. They can see which colours, sizes, and styles are most popular. The manufacturer can schedule production runs and deliveries more effectively, knowing that such information is readily at hand. A steady supply of merchandise should be always available to the retailer.

Business-to-consumer transactions are starting to pick up speed as consumers become more comfortable with transferring sensitive information online. If consumers are not buying online, they are certainly doing a lot of research about products they buy offline. As an example, a website such as Autobytel.com bridges the gap between the

Frito-Lay
www.fritolay.com

internet and real-world buying by providing consumers information about various makes and models of cars. When the search is complete, Autobytel refers the consumer to the nearest dealer. Car manufacturers such as General Motors, Ford, and BMW also have elaborate websites that disseminate information but refer the user to dealers at the end of the search process.

For additional insight into the role the internet can play in a marketing communications program and the objectives it can help achieve, refer to the IMC Highlight **Web-Savvy Frito-Lay**.

IMC Highlight

WEB-SAVVY FRITO-LAY

Frito-Lay has been a perennial advertiser on mainstream television and has spent considerable sums over the years advertising at the Super Bowl. That way of thinking changed in 2002, when company marketers decided to pursue a different route to the hearts and minds of its market. Frito-Lay did not forego traditional media advertising. But to broaden its advertising reach, it decided that the internet would play a more important role.

Then marketing VP Cammie Dunaway said that the decision to go online stemmed from a study conducted by Teenage Research Unlimited. It showed that 92 percent of teens are online, 44 percent believe the internet has changed the way they get information about products, and significant numbers are watching less television. Such data suggest a much more aggressive online strategy.

Marketing objectives were established for the Frito-Lay brands. Online efforts had to

- be coordinated with television and in-store efforts for maximum integration,
- connect with teens in a way that appeals to the more typical gatekeeper (mothers),
- start building a one-to-one dialogue with Frito-Lay's consumers, and
- build sales.

Since other packaged goods marketers only spend 1 percent or 2 percent of their budget online, Doritos's 9 percent is very aggressive. One of the company's first moves was to take Frito-Lay advertising online to Doritos.com, offering teens the chance to view commercials that hadn't yet aired on TV. Frito-Lay streamed seven spots an average of 60 000 times each and garnered 57 000 votes on which ones were bold, daring, or neither.

One of the side benefits of the streaming was that Frito-Lay was able to gauge the popularity of one ad it was hesitant about. Positive and direct feedback made the decision to air the spot easier. Such quick feedback is not available by any other means. The internet also provided a great way to make consumer promotions relevant to teens. An online and offline promotion to win Microsoft Corp's Xbox game consoles required the entry of a special code from instant-win game pieces found on packages. The effort drove 700 000 registrations on Doritos.com, where consumers were offered the opportunity to exchange information about themselves for advance notice on new products and promotions; 43 percent opted into the database.

To build a better relationship with teens, Frito-Lay decided on quarterly promotions. One of the initial promotions was tied to MTV.com and offered a sweepstakes for a free spring break vacation. The promotion attracted 100 000 entries and 76 percent agreed to be on the database. This promotion and similar promotions that followed yielded a database of some 350 000 names over the course of 2002. To meet the objective of the one-to-one dialogue, the company established an email program that offers news of upcoming promotions and product information while speaking to teens on a personal level.

By the end of 2002, sales for Doritos were up 5 percent and although this growth can't be attributed just to online marketing efforts, Dunaway says, "It's something that makes me more confident that it's the right way to stay connected to this audience." Other packaged-goods marketers will soon realize that internet is where the eyeballs are for a very desirable target.

Adapted from Stephanie Thompson, "Virtual Path to Teen Tummies," *Advertising Age*, November 18, 2002, p. S-14.

Online Advertising

As indicated by the revenues generated by online advertising quoted above, it is apparent that advertisers at large are not embracing the medium. That said, some companies are using the internet successfully for advertising purposes and are enjoying tangible sales results. This section will examine the various opportunities for advertising online and provide some examples of success stories that other potential advertisers can learn from.

An advertiser has numerous opportunities available to advertise online. At present, banner advertising comprises most of the advertising, accounting for 58 percent of all ad revenue.[10] Banners have fallen short of expectations, however, and as a result advertisers are looking more seriously at sponsorships, rich media, interstitials, email advertising, and websites. Prior to examining the various alternatives, some basic online advertising terminology needs to be discussed. The internet is a unique, technological medium with a different terminology from traditional mass media.

- **Ad Views (Impressions):** The number of times a banner is downloaded onto a user's computer.
- **Ad Clicks:** The number of times users click on an ad banner (clicking transfers the user to another website).
- **Ad Click Rate (Clickthrough Rate):** The percentage of ad views that resulted in an ad click. This percentage determines the success of an advertiser in attracting visitors to click on its ad. For example, if during 500 000 ad views there are 10 000 ad clicks, the clickthrough rate is 2 percent. The formula is clicks divided by ad views.
- **Hit:** Each time a server sends a file to a browser, it is recorded in the server log file as a hit.
- **Page Views:** The number of times a user requests a page that may contain a particular ad. It indicates the number of times an ad was potentially seen or "gross impressions."
- **Visitor:** A unique user of a website.
- **Visit:** A sequence of page requests made by a visitor at a website. A visit is also known as a *session* or *browsing period*.

A site's activity is described in terms of visits and visitors. A site that reports it had 5 million page views, 50 000 visitors, and 500 000 visits last month would be doing very well. It means that the average visitor returns to the site 10 times each month and views 10 pages each visit. That's incredible "stickiness." **Sticky** sites are those where the visitors stay for an extended period of time. For instance, a financial site that offers the latest information in investment trading or a sports site that offers statistics, games, and fantasy pools tend to be sites that interested users view frequently.

Stickiness
A website's ability to keep people at the site for an extended period or to have them return to the site frequently.

WEB ADVERTISING FORMATS

A **banner** refers to advertising on a website, usually placed by a third party. Originally, banners were designed so they spread across a page in a narrow band, looking much like an outdoor banner or a banner that stretches across the bottom of a newspaper page. Not much copy can be included in a banner. The brand name, short selling point, and visual must convince the user to click on the ad, which links to another website. Smaller versions of the banner such as small squares, rectangles or circular ads are referred to as **buttons**.

Banner
In online advertising, an ad that stretches across a web page.

Button
A small online ad.

To simplify the buying and creative development process for agencies and their advertisers, the Internet Advertising Bureau (IAB) created a "universal ad package" that includes four sizes. The size of an ad is based on *Internet Measurement Units* (IMU), an expression of the width and depth of an ad. The ad formats are 300 x 250 IMU, 180 x 150 IMU, 160 x 600 IMU, and 728 x 90 IMU. The first two formats feature similar proportions to television, enabling easier creative development. The other two are

Skyscraper
A vertical box-shaped ad that appears on a web page.

Rectangle
A large ad, slightly wider than it is tall, on a web page.

designed to sit on the perimeter of the page, allowing the advertising message to be surrounded by other content.[11] Figure 7.8 shows various online ad sizes.

Advertising research conducted by the IAB has concluded that larger formats that are naturally more visible and provide more creative freedom are significantly more effective than smaller, standard-sized banners across all campaigns. In Figure 7.8, the oblong, vertical-shaped ads that appear to one side are called **skyscrapers**, whereas the large box-style ads are referred to as **rectangles**. With more size comes more creative opportunity. Ads have moved from being static messages and often include animation and movement to

FIGURE **7.8** **Universal Ad Package Sizes for Internet Advertising**

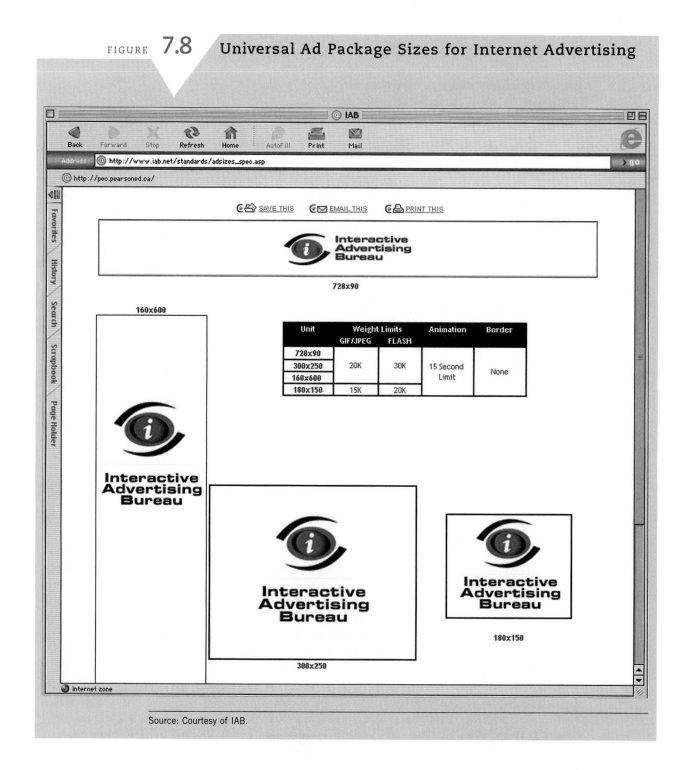

Source: Courtesy of IAB.

attract attention. Larger ads make it more difficult for users to avoid them and provide an opportunity to deliver a more complete message, even if the user doesn't click on the ad. Because of their size and better performance, they command a higher price. Cost must be factored into the equation when an advertiser decides to use online advertising. For insight into the effects of ad size on brand awareness and message association, refer to Figure 7.9.

FIGURE **7.9**

The Impact of Ad Size on Brand Awareness and Other Advertising Measures

Size of Ad	Brand Awareness	Message Association	Brand Favourability	Purchase Intent
Banner	1.8	2.4	0.3	0.2
Skyscraper	2.7	3.9	1.4	1.4
Large Rectangles	3.1	8.5	2.5	3.3

Large rectangles seem to offer the greatest benefit to advertisers. This information represents the point above the statistical baseline that helped increase the brand measure in absolute terms and is based on an aggregate of all online campaigns tested.

Reprinted with permission from the January 13, 2003 issue of *Advertising Age*. Copyright, Crain Communications Inc. 2003.

Animated Ad

A online ad that has a spinning motion or other form of action.

Animated ads are the type that spin or have some form of action. Clickthrough rates for animated ads are higher than static ads, suggesting that (good) creative influences user reactions to ads. Interactive ads, or rich media ads (see below), engage the viewer in some fashion. For instance, the viewer plays a game or responds to some questions. Clickthrough rates for these forms of ads are also higher.

INTERSTITIALS

Interstitial

An online ad that appears in a separate browser window while another web page is loading.

Meaning in between, an **interstitial** is an ad that appears in a separate browser window while another web page is loading. This type of ad is frequently referred to as a *pop-up* or a *pop-under*. The pop-up ad appears in a window that opens on top of the active window, and the pop-under appears behind it and is visible only after the active window is closed.

Because there is no warning when this type of ad will appear, it catches the user's attention by surprise. Such a tactic has positive and negative implications. The user will certainly catch the brand name but may view it negatively because many users object to receiving this kind of message—it's like that unsolicited telemarketing call. The intrusiveness of interstitials can be a drawback. Consumers who don't like them can use software that prevents them from appearing on screen. Since this style of online advertising annoys consumers the most, many portal sites—including AOL, iVillage, and Ask Jeeves—are reducing their number and frequency. In fact, proliferating new forms of rich media (see next section) are slowly replacing the garish, in-your-face, intrusive kinds of interstitials.[12]

In Canada, Bell Globemedia Interactive does not permit interstitials on any of its home pages, but does allow them on inside pages. A user will only see an ad twice during the duration of the campaign (the user's movement online is tracked!). According to Gary Fearnall, vice-president of sales for Bell Globemedia Interactive and president of the Internet Advertising Bureau of Canada, "Pop-ups in the right context can work."[13]

RICH MEDIA

Rich Media
Streaming video, audio, and special effects similar to television and used online.

Rich media are the graphical technologies such as animation and streaming video and audio that are used online to create special effects. Rich media allow for greater use and interaction. In their most sophisticated form, ads using rich media resemble television commercials.

The IAB has also established guidelines for rich media banners. Recommended formats include a wide banner that spans the top of a page, a skyscraper set off to the right or left, a large square box set in the middle of a page, and a smaller square unit. According to the guidelines, each can display 15-second animations.[14] Viewing these types of banners usually requires special software such as Flash, Shockwave, and Javascript.

Streaming Media
Audio or video delivered online in small, compressed packets of data that are interpreted by a software player as they are received.

Streaming media involve the continuous delivery of small, compressed packets of data that are interpreted by a software player and displayed as audio or full-motion video. The visitor views the content while the streaming is in progress; it does not have to be downloaded or saved on the viewer's computer. Streaming media is used extensively by radio station websites and sites such as cbc.ca. The similarity to television advertising makes it attractive to traditional advertisers. Consequently, this is a high-growth area of internet advertising. More to the point, rich media lends itself well to branding so it has quickly become the domain of the big consumer brands such as Coca-Cola, Nike, and Ford, among many others. Rich media are often sold as part of a package that includes other types of online advertising such as banners.

A recent option involves running commercials in a web video format and usually bundled with video content that users have requested. These ads are generally run exactly as they appear on TV. For instance, the popular sports site ESPN sells TV-style ads that are embedded in sports highlights. The highlights are only seen by people who have chosen to download the ESPN Motion software (about 1.8 million people). These people will see one highlight clip, followed by an ad, followed by another highlight clip, and so on. Advertisers that have been attracted to full-motion ads include Lexus, Warner Brothers (for the film *Matrix Reloaded*) and Universal (for the films *2Fast 2Furious* and *The Hulk*).[15]

The creativity aspect of rich media makes online advertising more sexy, fun, and something new to try. Delta Airlines has experienced real success with rich media in the form of increased brand awareness. Delta combines rich media and standard online ads on one page to maximize branding impact. According to Rob Sherrell, manager of interactive marketing at Delta, "Using rich media, you have an opportunity to tell people more about whatever the campaign objective is right there in the context of what they're doing," as opposed to sending them away to a different website.[16]

While use of rich media ads is growing right now, they will become increasingly common as users adopt high-speed internet access in greater numbers. These kinds of ads grab the viewer's attention more quickly and can deliver the message on a more emotional level. An organization's ability to adapt its messages to rich media technology could be the key to online advertising success. The advertiser will benefit because the viewer wants to receive the information. If viewers like what they see and read, in many cases they are able to click further and actually buy the product.

Advertising originally created for television and radio can be adapted for the purpose of advertising online. Clickthrough rates for rich media are significantly higher than for static ads. According to Real Networks, the rate for rich media averages 3.5 percent compared to static banners at 0.5 percent.[17]

SPONSORSHIPS

Sponsorship
A commitment online to advertise for an extended period or to sponsor a web page.

An online **sponsorship** is a commitment to advertise on a third-party website for an extended period. Sponsorships are the second most popular form of online advertising, accounting for 26 percent of advertising revenues. Advertisers are attracted to sponsorships on the basis of web content. If the content of a site is particularly interesting to an advertiser's target market, visitors are apt to visit the site frequently. For example, investors in the stock market frequently visit ROBtv.com, which broadcasts business news online. Business and recreational travelers visit weathernetwork.ca and sports junkies frequently visit tsn.ca and other sports sites. Brands that are closely linked to the content of these networks pursue sponsorships.

Perhaps some specific examples will clearly illustrate the benefit derived from sponsorships. On tsn.ca, Vector cereal (a brand positioned as an energy-boosting meal replacement) sponsors a hockey challenge, "Play the Vector Hockey Challenge." Nissan Canada sponsors the Ski Report on the Weather Network website. Two of Nissan's sports utility vehicles, the Pathfinder and Exterra, are positioned to suit outdoor lifestyles. The Pathfinder sponsors ski programs across Canada and refers to the skiing association in traditional media advertising. So the association with the Weather Network's Ski Report is a natural extension of that strategy. Quarto Communications Ltd., publisher of *Cottage Life* magazine and broadcaster of Cottage Life TV, offers sponsorships at its cotttagelife.com website. TIM-BR Mart advertises in the magazine and sponsors a web page titled "What's New." The page usually features projects involving lumber—docks, decks, and fences—a natural tie-in for a lumber retailer (see Figure 7.10).

With a sponsorship, the advertiser does not have to drive the viewer to a website. Instead visitors come to the site. The sponsor benefits from the status and prestige of the site it is associated with. Consumers trust the sites that they visit frequently on the web so a brand that is associated with the site could be perceived more positively through the sponsor association.

EMAIL ADVERTISING

Permission-based Email
Email sent to recipients who have agreed to accept email advertising messages.

Sponsored Email
Email that includes a short message from a sponsor along with a link to the sponsor's website.

One of the most promising applications in online advertising is email advertising, specifically permission-based email. **Permission-based email** is sent to recipients who agree to receive information in that form. In other words, people actively subscribe to the email service. This form of advertising is relatively inexpensive, response rates are high and easy to measure, and it is targeted at people who want information about certain goods and services. An offshoot of email advertising is sponsored email. With **sponsored email**, the email includes a short message from a sponsor along with a link to the sponsor's website.

Email advertising is similar to direct mail advertising, but at the same time it is very different. It does operate the same way insofar as it is based on a list contained in a database and it targets customers specifically interested in something. The difference, though, is that email advertising generates higher responses—and that is attracting advertisers' attention. Unlike any other form of online advertising, sending messages by email in this way seems quite acceptable to internet users. Users can subscribe and unsubscribe to email as they wish.

Opt-in Lists
A list of people who have agreed to receive messages via email.

Similar to direct mail, the success of an email campaign depends on the quality of the list. There are two kinds of lists. The lists are called **opt-in lists**, an appropriate name because consumers agree to have their names included. There are two kinds of opt-in lists. A *first-party list* comprises people who have specifically agreed to receive email from an organization. A *third-party list* is composed of names and addresses compiled by one company and sold to another. An example of email advertising generated from an opt-in list appears in Figure 7.11.

Spam
Unsolicited e-mail.

Although email advertising is attractive, that third-party list is what promotes spam. **Spam** is unsolicited email, even from reputable sources, and third-party lists can result in people receiving mail they do not expect. With a first-party list, subscribers agreed to receive messages; they might not have agreed to have their names are sold for marketing purposes. The use of the internet to send large volumes of email has infuriated many consumers, forced employees in organizations to waste precious time deleting junk email,

FIGURE **7.10** TIM-BR Mart Takes Advantage of a Sponsorship Opportunity at the *Cottage Life* Website

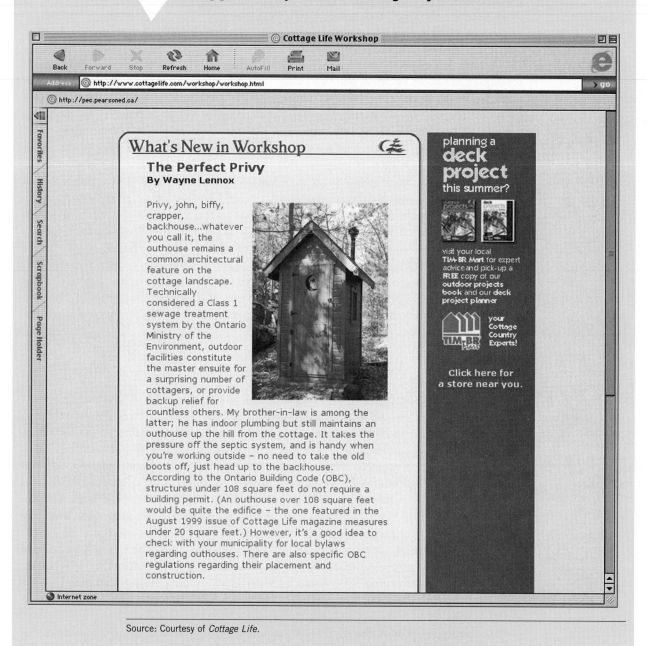

Source: Courtesy of *Cottage Life*.

overwhelmed the server capacities of many internet service providers, spread viruses as well as the fear of viruses, and hurt the business of legitimate internet marketers. This issue has to be addressed, for many of the efficiencies gained through the use of email are diminished as consumer suspicion rapidly grows with the flood of unsolicited commercial email.[18]

Database technology, being what it is today, makes it easy for marketers to obtain names and addresses. Typically, a site offers a subscription service and users who want periodic updates graciously divulge certain demographic information along with their email address. Online promotions and contests are another way of securing names and addresses.

FIGURE **7.11** **Marriott Uses Email Advertising with an Opt-in Mailing List**

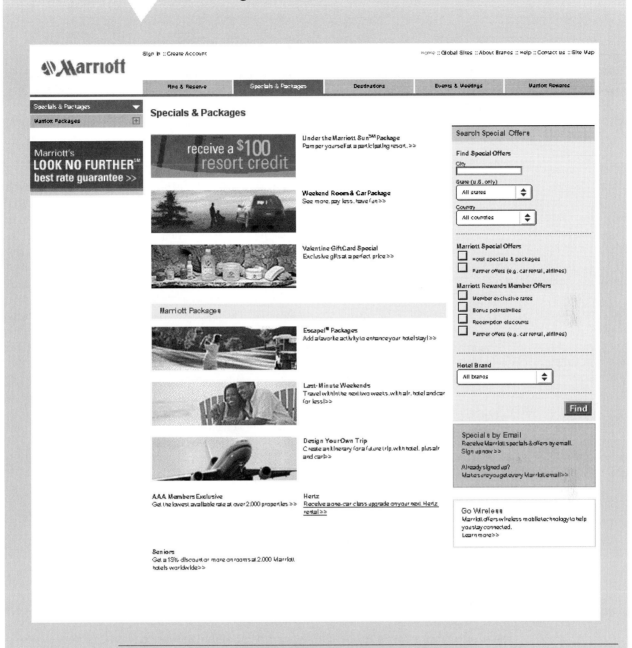

However, as indicated above, organizations should be careful how they distribute names to other organizations. There's a saying these days: "Permission rented is permission lost."

Despite such perils, advertisers see nothing but the upside of email advertising. For more insight into this area of online communications, see the IMC Highlight **Message Delivered**.

MESSAGE DELIVERED

Email marketing is finally poised to become a real threat to traditional direct mail marketing techniques. Until recently, email efforts were ranked low on the priority list, but now every major company has some kind of program in place.

Why is email marketing gathering momentum? A research study conducted by e-Dialog Inc. polled 300 marketing companies in the U.S. from a broad range of industries and found that one third of them named email as their most effective marketing tool—82 percent ranked it in the top three. The same survey indicated that the popularity of direct mail was declining. Clearly, marketers are transferring money from one form of direct marketing to another. The thinking is that direct mail has reached its peak—email will be the growth sector of the future.

The attraction to email marketing is for good reason. In fact, for several good reasons. First, email campaigns cost only $5 to $7 per thousand, compared to $500 to $700 per thousand for direct mail. Beyond cost, email programs are quicker to implement and they get results faster. Success or failure can be measured more easily. It's all the things that direct mail isn't.

Direct email marketing is quite different from spam or junk email in that it sends messages to people who have opted in to bulk mailing lists. People want to receive this information! Spam starts to enter the picture only when an organization sells its list to other organizations.

Email marketing serves a useful purpose in attracting customers and retaining them. Customer retention campaigns typically use mailing lists of people who have already agreed to receive information from a particular company, and customer acquisition campaigns must spread their net wider, targeting people who have agreed to receive ad messages about a particular category of product or service.

Email is a good vehicle for communicating complex messages that are often required to sell technology or a service designed for a niche audience. If the message is well designed, it can achieve immediate results by getting the recipient to click on a link to a website to fill in a form requesting more information.

While everything about email marketing seems positive, there is a downside. Clickthrough rates have declined recently according to surveys conducted by DoubleClick Inc., an internet measurement company. It reports a drop in opt-in list clickthroughs from 3.2 percent to 1.8 percent over a one-year period. Among first-party opt-in lists only, the clickthrough rate dropped from 9.7 percent to 8.3 percent. The drop may be the result of consumers' frustration with spam and the ever-increasing amount of marketing email. The challenge for marketers, therefore, is to make the message relevant to the person receiving it so that it is not considered spam, and to make the offer compelling enough that consumers want to act on it.

Adapted from Kevin Marron, "Email Gets the Message Across," *Globe and Mail*, September 27, 2002, p. B11.

Company Websites

Traditional media communications and online communications encourage users to visit a company or brand website. Clicking on an ad automatically takes you to the website. The purpose of the ad is to attract attention; once the person is at the website, the purpose is to deliver more meaningful and detailed information in an entertaining manner. The website provides an opportunity to tell a story. A company cannot tell or show as much through traditional media as inexpensively as it can on the internet. Advertising in the traditional media should always provide a website address and encourage potential customers to contact the site for additional information. This practice is becoming common, and marketing research studies indicate that 60 percent of website visitors are there because the site was mentioned in a print ad and 53 percent because of a television ad.[19]

Rolex, a very expensive and reputable brand of watches, advertises in upscale publications read by upper-income targets. Typically, the ads feature a closeup of the watch to highlight its elegance and beauty. Detailed information is available at the website (see Figure 7.12).

FIGURE 7.12 **The Combination of Elegant Print Advertising a a Website Enhances the Image of Rolex Watches**

The nature of information communicated on a website varies from one organization to another. For example, news and information organizations such as the *Globe and Mail* and *Maclean's* magazine provide copy-intensive information (they are online versions of their respective print editions). In contrast, automobile companies provide unique and vivid visual images of their latest makes and models along with technical specifications and related information. Many sites include contests and games to make the experience of visiting more entertaining. A fun experience leads to more frequent visits.

ebsites play a role in building brand awareness and brand preference, although mar- organizations are just now learning what that influence is. Marketing research con- l by the Internet Advertising Bureau reveals that media combinations that include ion, print, and websites generate higher awareness and preference levels than just ion and print (the traditional combination of most packaged-goods brands). e-Palmolive, for example, reveals that online was the most cost-efficient means of ig 18- to 49-year-olds for Colgate Total toothpaste. The brand altered its media mix easing the online component from 7 percent to 11 percent of the budget and reducing television from 78 percent to 74 percent. The result was incremental reach among light TV watchers and non-TV watchers, an audience it otherwise wouldn't have reached. Colgate generated higher preference ratings in a more economical manner.[20]

The internet, particularly websites, is the preferred and most effective form of media for advertisers trying to reach business decision-makers, according to a recent survey conducted by Nielsen//NetRatings. Of 1000 business decision-makers polled, 60 percent said the best way to reach them was through a website. Nearly 50 percent of the participants said the web has influenced them to make a purchase or obtain a service for their business. Related findings indicated that reference to television, newspaper, and magazines had declined. In B2B marketing, the web is the place to find out about new products and companies.[21]

Integrating Online Advertising into the Communications Mix

In light of the statistical evidence discussed earlier in this chapter, online advertising remains in its infancy stage. As organizations learn more about online technology and how advertising can be adapted to it, online advertising will grow. Lack of experience with the medium among advertisers and advertising agencies has contributed to the slow rate of adoption. Nonetheless, there are several advantages and disadvantages of online advertising that organizations must consider when deciding how and when to add it to the communications mix. Saturn Canada, a division of General Motors, has figured out how to use the internet. In fact, the internet was the cornerstone of the launch campaign for the Saturn Ion in 2003. For details of this integrated marketing communications campaign, read the IMC Highlight **Saturn's Virtual Launch**.

On the positive side of things, an advertiser can target an audience of one based on an individual's browsing behaviour and online preferences. A browser's cookies make such targeting possible. A **cookie** is an electronic identification tag sent from a web server to a browser to track a person's browsing patterns. The acceptance of cookies on a user's computer allows a website to be personalized to that individual's experience and allows for personalizing messages. Messages of interest to the user appear on the computer screen once his or her preferences have been determined.

As discussed earlier in the chapter, visitors tend to migrate frequently to websites that they trust and that contain information they value. For a profile of the users who visit some of Canada's more popular websites, see Figure 7.13.

Online advertising messages are delivered 24 hours a day, seven days a week. If the *timing* of a campaign is an issue, it's not a factor in the online advertising equation. As well, the message content can be altered at a moment's notice if need be. Because technology allows for constant monitoring of a campaign for success or failure, changes or cancellations can be made more quickly than in traditional media.

The *interactive nature* of the internet can be integrated into advertising campaigns. For example, the inclusion of a game or a contest provides an opportunity for interaction. Interaction combined with meaningful information leads to a higher degree of customer satisfaction. As indicated earlier, users tend to visit sites they enjoy frequently. Such

Cookie

An electronic identification tag sent from a web server to a user's browser to track the user's browsing patterns.

SATURN'S VIRTUAL LAUNCH

Picture this. A young guy is cruising down a deserted highway being followed by a UFO. As cool as 007, the driver steps on it and leaves the spacecraft far behind. It's not a movie, but a short television-style commercial called *Intergalactic Getaway* being shown on the Saturn Canada.com website. The commercial is one of four different commercials that were used to launch the new Ion, a car positioned for a younger, more aggressive-conscious audience.

The internet played a leading role in the launch of the Ion. Saturn's target market is among the largest users of the internet in the automotive industry. Up to 75 percent of Saturn drivers surf the web. The online effort (see Figure 7.5) combined forces with traditional media advertising to create a truly integrated marketing communications strategy. Online advertising included banners and an innovative email marketing campaign. Offline communications included television, direct mail, outdoor, cinema, and newspaper advertising.

The campaign was developed by three different divisions of Cossette Communication Marketing: Blitz, its data, direct response, and promotional arm; Nucleus, its planning division; and Cossette Interactive. Staff from each division brainstormed together as one marketing team. The goal was to target the new Ion at single urban dwellers between the ages of 18 and 40 who have a university education and an average household income of $35 000 or more.

Included in the launch was a promotion developed by Cossette. Titled "Movies for Life," it was a sweepstake that offered consumers a chance to win four movie passes a month for 25 years. Research showed that the target demographic went to the movies at least once or twice a month. The contest was promoted in theatres across Canada using a 60-second cinema spot, backlit posters, in-lobby banners, and ads in theatre magazines. Direct mail, including a stuffer in GM Visa card statements, was delivered to 40 000 drivers, including current Saturn owners. Television ads were picked up from Saturn's U.S.-based agency and included a tagline that directed viewers to the Saturn Canada website.

The website was the focus of the promotion. All forms of advertising encouraged consumers to visit saturncanada.com where they could register to win movies for life. The contest entries provided a database that Saturn could use immediately or in the future. Based on what they had learned from previous campaigns, Saturn knew that the internet was ideal for detecting "hot leads," people who are just about ready to buy a new car. To identify hot leads, Saturn asked entrants to answer questions about their car-buying plans, in addition to questions about personal information. Depending on their answers, a pop-up window or email then informed users that they qualified for a free test drive and two free movie passes, which could be redeemed at the dealership. This strategy encouraged qualified consumers to take a test drive.

The numbers of contest entries exceeded those of all previous contests. For Saturn, the strategy confirmed the value of incorporating the online medium into an integrated communications campaign. The website itself acted as a mini-destination site by showing the attractive features of the car in an interactive way. Other commercials in the campaign were called "The Cluster Conspiracy," "First Expressions," and "The Quad Coupe Equation." Each one intentionally had a B-movie quality and was created to show how the vehicle could be personalized to the driver. According to Eric LeBlanc, advertising and promotions manager at Saturn Canada, "The commercials were an exceptional idea from the agency. The little featurettes were a different way to deliver a message in an interactive manner."

Adapted from D.W. Dorken, "Saturn Sets a Virtual Scene," *Marketing*, April 21, 2003, pp. 8, 9.

satisfaction may be sufficient to motivate a purchase. The combination of entertainment (through interaction) and information provides a benefit no other medium can offer.

There are some obvious drawbacks to online advertising. While *penetration* of the internet is increasing each year, statistics reveal that just over half of Canadian households have access to the internet. People can access information from other locations, such as schools and the workplace, but leisurely access at home remains the domain of middle- and upper-income households and households composed of younger age groups. To be a truly effective medium, it must eventually offer reach comparable to the other mass media. In comparison, television reaches 99 percent of Canadian households.[22]

FIGURE **7.13** **A Target Market Profile of Some of Canada's Most Popular Websites**

Company	Traffic Monthly	Website Profile	User Profile
Chatelaine.com	Page Views: 6 000 000 Unique Visits: 500 000 Average Visit Length: 20+ min.	Canada's number-one site for women. Content consists of food, fashion, beauty, home and garden, family, work and money.	Women 25–49; 80% read Chatelaine; are time pressured; seeking time-saving solutions. Visually oriented; online ads considered useful.
Globeinvestor.com	Page Views: 60 000 000+ Unique visits: 240 000+	The leading investment information site, providing authoritative content and resources for investors.	Highly educated, affluent users. Reaches an at-work audience of engaged, internet-savvy investors.
Globeandmail.com	Page Views: 29 000 000 Unique Visits: 1,200,000+	A leading suite of online properties delivering the latest news from business and technology to national and international news.	Internet-savvy and affluent, household income of $107 000 or more; well educated; 88% MOPEs (managers, owners, professionals, and executives).
TSN.ca	Page Views: 26 000 000 Unique Visits: 1 000 000	Canada's sports leader for breaking news, streaming media, in-depth commentary, fantasy games, and pools	Coverage of all pro sports. Loyal sports fans; 58% male, 42% female; 67% of males are aged 18–34.

All of these sites have an advertising inventory that include banners, email marketing, sponsorships, pop-ups, pop-unders, and rich media. TSN also offers content integration, co-branding, and cross-marketing opportunities.

Adapted from *Webvertising 2002, An Offline Guide to Online Advertising Services*, published by *Marketing*, pp. 16–18.

Privacy, or, rather, the invasion of one's privacy by advertisers, is an important issue. Consumers tend to be wary of technology and its capabilities. The manner by which information is collected results in people being generally skeptical about how the information is used. They object to the sale of personal information for commercial purposes. Consumers needn't be concerned, but it is a situation where perceptions override reality. People transfer sensitive information all the time in other media (telephone, for example, and at point-of-purchase) and don't think twice about it. Consumers perceive the online environment differently, and some aspects of the internet have acquired a shady reputation. With registration, customers willingly give up information about themselves that is used for marketing purposes at a later date.

As time progresses, as advertisers and agencies become more familiar with online capabilities, and as consumers become more comfortable with the commercial aspects of the internet, the true benefits of the medium will be realized. What is known is that younger target audiences—a desirable audience for many advertisers—spend considerable time online. Since this is a hard-to-reach target through any medium, the internet represents an opportunity to reach them. The Frito-Lay example cited earlier in the chapter (see IMC Highlight **Web-Savvy Frito-Lay**) offers hope for other advertisers wanting to tap into the mindset of younger audiences. Frito-Lay Canada also sponsored a contest linked to Canadian professional football. Promoted as "CFL Fritos Fandemonium" on the TSN website, the contest prizes included trips to the 2003 Grey Cup Game (see Figure 7.14).

As already discussed, some advertisers are now showing their latest TV commercials on their websites in order to assess customer reaction to them. Levi-Strauss, for example, put three new ads on its site and asked people to vote for their favourite. The most popular spot, "Crazy Legs," then made its debut on the 2002 Super Bowl. According to Levi-Strauss, the media that influence youth are fragmented, so a multi-dimensional approach is essential. The website and online advertising extend the company's reach among youth.[23]

Text Messaging
The transmission of short text-only messages using wireless devices such as cell phones and personal digital assistants.

Text Messaging

It may be a generational thing but people under the age of 35 are into **text messaging**, the transmission of short text-only messages on wireless devices such as cellphones and personal digital assistants (PDAs), whereas people over 35 tend to shy away from it.

FIGURE **7.14**   **Frito-Lay Sponsors a Contest Promotion on the TSN Website**

Source: Courtesy of TSN.ca and Frito-Lay, Inc.

Owning a cellphone is one thing, but using one to take and send pictures, browse the internet, and play games is quite another thing. Does a person really need a gadget to do all of that? Apparently, some people do. At present, only 10 percent of North American adults have a PDA.[24] Marketing communications through cellphones and PDAs are growing, but at a slower pace than anticipated. The penetration is low because the baby boom generation has not embraced them. It will be younger consumers that make or break the PDA market.

Marketers interested in reaching the youth market are looking seriously at instant text messaging. It is one of the latest weapons in the arsenal of guerilla and field marketing tactics used to reach youth. Promotional tours and the distribution of free samples to selected youth markets are other strategies that have proven successful in recent years.

In Europe and Asia, the text messaging market is much more developed than in North America, so it's just a matter of time before things explode here. Since April 2002, the services offered by major wireless carriers in North America are compatible with one another. Consequently, text messaging is now perceived to be an ideal format to reach teens, and cellphone displays are fast becoming prime territory for advertisers with product information and special offers. They see it an opportunity to supplement traditional print and television advertising with interactive tie-ins. Teens tend to be a fickle audience and traditional approaches are not as effective as they once were.

A method called short message service (SMS) is a simplified text-messaging format that can electronically send out coupons for advertised products or special information on promotions. While these messages may not stimulate the audience to buy, they start them talking about the products that are advertised, such as the sneakers and CDs. How advertisers approach youth with cellphones must be carefully planned. If the messages are overly intrusive, their attempts could backfire. Too much commercialism is not a good thing among today's sceptical youth.

Teens and young adults have been attracted to text messaging because of its portability and low cost. In contrast, palm devices are too expensive and laptops are inconvenient. Email is too slow—kids are into instant messaging, whether on their cellphones or using online chat services such as ICQ. The sheer novelty of the cellphone is attractive to potential advertisers, but caution is required. It would be dangerous for carriers to open up their databases to commercial interests without having an opt-in from their customers.

AT&T
www.att.com

To demonstrate the applications of text messaging, consider what AT&T did with the *American Idol* series. Cellphone users (at their expense) could vote for or against the young would-be superstars on the show. A sense of intimacy and exclusivity made it a hit with teens. It was the right kind of content and value-added promotion for people who have a genuine interest. As with email, advertising through cellphones will work best if people have a choice to opt in. In Britain, about 1.5 billion personal and advertising-based text messages are sent each month. McDonald's was part of the British text message invasion, using it to distribute coupons that could be stored on cellphones for use at a later date.[25] In Canada, only 20 million messages were sent in all of 2002.

Labatt
www.labatt.com

In Canada, Labatt launched a first in the world of text messaging with a national, cross-carrier ad campaign and contest that featured prizes for the 2003 NHL Stanley Cup Playoffs (see Figure 7.15). The goal of the campaign was to connect Blue drinkers with their brand, as well as to introduce the brand's website, labattblue.ca. The online effort tied into a national in-case promotion called Labatt NHL Cup Crazy, featuring the six original NHL hockey teams on the beer bottles. To enter the contest, participants had to answer trivia questions successfully, using their cellphone and text messaging.[26]

FIGURE **7.15** Labatt Blue Experiments with Text Messaging to Connect with Its Target Market

Source: Courtesy of Labatt Canada.

Summary

Thus far, the internet has not lived up to commercial expectations, although the situation is gradually changing. As advertisers and agencies become more knowledgeable, the internet will become more acceptable. There will be a stronger understanding of how to integrate the medium into marketing communications strategies.

The behaviour of internet users is quite different from users of traditional media. Online users tend to be non-commercial in nature, but are slowly accepting the fact that commercial interests are essential if they are to continue accessing the information they have grown accustomed to. The challenge for advertisers is to create useful and entertaining messages while not alienating internet users.

Advertising online presents many opportunities for an organization. For certain, the internet can perform many of the functions that other media do. It plays a key role in achieving specific marketing objectives. Online advertising will help create brand awareness for the launch of new products and is an excellent medium for building brand image. The fact that so much information can be presented visually and in a tone and style comparable to television is a real asset. Companies also find the internet ideal for distributing buying incentives and for promoting contests. In both cases, information about consumers is collected to be added to a database for use at a later date. In a business-to-business context, online advertising is a means of generating leads. It is also a good medium for implementing customer service programs. Furthermore, unlike other media (except direct response advertising), online advertising can complete a transaction.

There is a variety of advertising alternatives to choose from. An organization can buy ads on various websites. Banners were the original form of online advertising and remain the dominant form. When a person clicks on an online ad, the viewer is transferred to the advertiser's website for more details. Ads have changed with the introduction of new technology. Gaining in popularity are rich media ads that include animation, audio, and video. These ads are streamed to a user's computer and appear much like television commercials when viewed.

Sponsorships are another advertising opportunity. A sponsorship involves a long-term commitment to advertise on third-party websites. Gaining in popularity is permission-based email advertising. Using lists generated from in-house databases or from other sources (rented lists), email represents a cost-efficient way to reach prospects and current customers.

As an advertising medium, the internet provides targeting capability at a very reasonable cost and also offers tracking capabilities that measure effectiveness in a variety of ways (e.g., clicks, clickthrough rates, leads, and purchases). Because it is available at all hours of the day, seven days a week, there is ample opportunity for brand and company exposure online. Some drawbacks of the internet include selective reach (higher educated and higher income households are the main users) and the perception among users that advertisers are invading their privacy. Security issues involving the transfer of sensitive information forestalls online purchases. Despite these drawbacks, online advertising will become more popular with advertisers and more acceptable to consumers, once they are more familiar with the medium.

A relatively new medium for advertisers is text messaging on cellphones and personal digital assistants (PDAs). Both electronic devices can offer internet access, making it very easy for advertisers to send messages to consumers. North American marketing organizations are well behind their overseas counterparts in using these devices for advertising. However, the tech-savvy youth generation, which relies heavily on cellphones, is the prime target for this new medium. Older generations are less likely to be part of this advertising revolution.

Key Terms

ad click rate (clickthrough rate) 193	portal 186
ad clicks 193	rectangle 194
ad views (impressions) 193	rich media 196
animated ad 195	skyscraper 194
banner 193	spam 197
button 193	sponsored email 197
cookie 202	sponsorship 196
hit 193	stickiness 193
internet 183	streaming media 196
interstitial (pop-up or pop-under) 195	text messaging 205
mass customization 185	viral marketing 191
online advertising 186	visit 193
opt-in lists (first-party or third-party) 197	visitor 193
page views 193	World Wide Web 183
permission-based email 197	

Review Questions

1. What is mass customization and how do internet-based communications facilitate its practice?

2. What are the primary marketing and marketing communications roles that the internet can provide marketing organizations? Identify and explain each role briefly.

3. In the context of online marketing communications, briefly explain what viral marketing is. Is it a worthwhile pursuit for marketing organizations?

4. Explain the following terms as they relate to online advertising:
   a) ad views (impressions)
   b) ad clicks
   c) ad click rate
   d) page views
   e) visits

5. What is banner advertising and how does it work?

6. Identify and briefly describe the various types of ads.

7. What is the difference between a pop-up ad and a pop-under ad?

8. What does rich media refer to and how does it work? What does streaming media refer to?

9. Briefly explain how an online advertising sponsorship works. What benefits does it provide? Illustrate the benefits with some examples.

10. Briefly explain the following email advertising terms:
    a) permission-based email
    b) sponsored email
    c) opt-in list
    d) spam

11. What is a cookie and what role does it perform in online communications and marketing?

Discussion and Application Questions

1. Identify and briefly explain two advantages and two disadvantages of internet-based advertising.

2. What future lies ahead for email advertising? Will it continue to grow or will consumers and businesses turn away from it? Conduct some online research on the issue and present a brief report of your findings.

3. "Persistent invasions of consumer privacy will be the undoing of online advertising." Is this statement true or false? Conduct some online secondary research to update the status of this issue. Report on your findings.

4. How important are websites to companies today? Examine their role in the marketing communications mix and present a position on what lies ahead for marketing organizations.

5. Can online advertising be successfully integrated into the marketing communications mix? Is integration universal or is it only appropriate for particular situations? Discuss.

6. Visit some commercial websites of your choosing. Evaluate these websites in terms of their ability to achieve certain marketing and marketing communications objectives such as building brand image, offering incentives, generating leads, and providing customer service. Are communications on the website coordinated with any other form of marketing communications?

7. Assess how consumer goods marketing organizations can use web-based communications to their advantage. Can it be an effective medium for building relationships with customers?

8. Assess the various online advertising alternatives such as banners, interstitials, and rich media. Which alternative is best at communicating with consumers?

9. Is it possible to launch a new product using online communications as the primary medium for creating awareness and interest? What strategies would be necessary to make such a plan work?

Endnotes

1 "GM Shows Way Toward the New Mix," *Advertising Age*, January 20, 2003, p. 20.

2 Tobi Elkin, "Up from the Bottom," *Advertising Age*, July 8, 2002, p. 36.

3 Bernadette Johnson, "Advertisers Revisiting the Web: Study," *Strategy*, February 12, 2001, pp. 1, 14.

4 Statistics Canada, "Household Internet Usage Survey," *The Daily*, September 18, 2003 <www.statcan.ca/Daily/English/030918/d030918b.htm> (November 2003).

5 Canadian Media Directors' Council, *Media Digest*, 2002–2003, p. 51.

6 Ibid., p. 53.

7 Michael Dell, "Leadership in the Internet Economy," address to the Canadian Club of Canada, April 7, 2000.

8 Chris Daniels, "Saturn Sets a Virtual Scene," *Marketing*, April 21, 2003, pp. 9, 9.

9 Kevin Marron, "E-mail Gets the Message Across," *Globe and Mail*, September 27, 2002, p. B11.

10 Canadian Media Directors' Media Council, *Media Digest*, 2002–2003, p. 53.

11 Dawn Anfuso, "IAB Introduces Universal Ad Package," *iMedia Connection*, December 12, 2002.

12 Tobi Elkin, "Intrusive Pop Ups Get Closer Scrutiny after iVillage Block," *Advertising Age*, August 5, 2002, p. 6.

13 John Heinzl, "Web Sites, ISPs Lopping Pop-up Ads," *Globe and Mail*, August 23, 2002, p. B10.

14 Stephanie Olsen, "Bigger Web Ads Endorsed by Industry," *CNET News.com*, December 11, 2002 <news.com.com/2100-1023-976933.html> (November 2003).

15 Carl Bialik, "TV Commercials Go Online, But Will Surfers Tune In?" *Wall Street Journal*, July 8, 2003.

16 Debra Aho Williamson, "Web Giants Cash In on Rich Media," *Advertising Age*, November 18, 2002, p. S-12.

17 Pamela Parker, "Branding Beyond Intuition," Streaming Media 101, Part V <**www.turboads.com/richmedia_news/2001rmn/ rmn20010822.shtml**> (November 2003).

18 Tyler Hamilton, "Ottawa Ponders Junk E-mail," *Toronto Star*, January 23, 2003, p. C5.

19 Kate Maddox, "Information Still Killer App on the Internet," *Advertising Age*, October 6, 1997, p. 48.

20 Tobi Elkin, "Net Advantages," *Advertising Age*, February 10, 2003, p. 29.

21 Tobi Elkin, "Study: Net Best to Get at Business," *Advertising Age*, September 9, 2002, p. 24.

22 Canadian Media Directors' Media Council, *Media Digest*, 2002–2003, p. 13.

23 Susan Heinrich, "Lipton Brisk Commercial Gets More Bang for Buck with Internet Site," *Financial Post*, April 8, 2002, p. FP6.

24 Jim Krane, "Boomers Cold on Palmtops," *National Post*, March 10, 2003, p. BE2.

25 Guy Dixon, "Companies Hope Teens Get Message—on a Cell Phone," *Globe and Mail*, February 21, 2003, p. B9.

26 "Labatt Text-Messages Hockey Trivia," *Marketing*, April 21, 2003, p. 10.

PART III

Planning for Integrated Marketing

Part 3 looks at non-traditional media choices and a variety of marketing and promotional choices that enhance the communications plan, because integrated marketing strategies combine these media with traditional media, producing a synergistic effect.

Chapter 8 introduces various sales promotion alternatives that are frequently used in integrated marketing communications plans. Discussion is divided between consumer promotions and trade promotions, with each area examined for its ability to achieve marketing and marketing communications objectives.

Chapter 9 describes the role of public relations communications in the integrated marketing communications mix. Various public relations techniques are introduced. The process of planning public relations activities is examined in detail, along with various measurement techniques used to determine the effectiveness of public relations messages.

Chapter 10 discusses the emerging role of event marketing and sponsorships in contemporary marketing. The criteria for participating in event marketing and the steps and procedures for planning an event are introduced, as are various evaluation techniques that determine the effectiveness of event marketing and sponsorship strategies.

In Chapter 11, the role of personal selling in a variety of business settings is examined. Personal selling adds a human component to the integrated marketing communications mix, and for this reason plays a very important role in an era where customer relationship management practices predominate. Key topics include the evolution of personal selling strategies, the fundamental roles and responsibilities of the sales representative, the steps in the selling process, and the need for proper planning and preparation.

SALES PROMOTION

After studying this chapter you will be able to:

distinguish between consumer promotions and trade promotions,

describe the steps in the sales promotion planning process,

assess the role of consumer promotions in achieving specific marketing communications and marketing objectives,

assess the role of trade promotions in achieving specific marketing communications and marketing objectives,

outline the nature of various consumer promotion and trade promotion activities, and

assess various criteria for integrating sales promotion strategies with other integrated marketing communications strategies.

This chapter examines the role of sales promotions in the marketing communications mix. Promotions are activities that focus on making a sale, usually in a short period of time. When planning and implementing promotions, the marketing organization provides an offer to customers in return for something they must do. Because the offer is valid only for a certain period, the impact of the offer, and its success or failure, can be measured quickly.

A wide variety of promotion offers are presented here, all of which are suited to achieving specific marketing and marketing communications objectives. The right promotion must be offered at the right time if the offer is to bring true benefit to the brand or company. In order to create awareness and interest in the promotion, there must also be media advertising to support it, and possibly some publicity generated by a public relations campaign. A coordinated effort is usually required to make a sales promotion a success. This chapter focuses on two distinct yet related areas of sales promotion: consumer promotion and trade promotion. An organization must consider strategies for both if it is to grow and prosper.

SALES PROMOTION

Sales promotion is defined as activity that provides special incentives to bring about immediate response from customers, distributors, and an organization's sales force. It is a strategy that encourages action by the recipient. According to the definition, three distinct groups are considered when planning sales promotion strategies. First, the consumer or final user must be motivated to take advantage of the offer and, second, the distributor (reseller of goods) must be motivated to support the offer by providing merchandising support. Third, the company's sales force must be motivated to sell the promotion to its trade customers. Because the intent of a promotion is to provide some added excitement to the product, an organization's sales representatives must present it enthusiastically to the trade distributors.

Consumer promotions are designed to stimulate purchases or to encourage loyalty. Among the options readily available are coupons, free samples, contests, rebates, price incentives, and rewards programs. These types of promotions are planned to help **pull** the product through the channel of distribution. An organization creates demand for the product by directing its promotional efforts directly at the consumer. The combination of advertising and promotions, for example, creates demand and causes consumers to look for the product in stores or request a service; by asking for it specifically, they put pressure on the retailer to provide it.

Trade promotions are less visible activities, given that they are offered to members of the channel of distribution. These promotions are price oriented and include options such as discounts and allowances, cooperative advertising funds, dealer premiums, and point-of-purchase materials. Offering financial incentives to distributors encourages them to support a manufacturer's promotion plans. Such promotions **push** the product through the channel of distribution. Refer to Figure 8.1 for a visual image of pull and push promotion strategies.

To be successful an organization must determine what type of promotion will contribute the most to achieving its objectives. In most cases, it is a combination of both. The real decision is to determine the extent to which each type of promotion is offered. Such a decision is based on the market analysis that precedes the development of any sales promotion plan. Sales promotion planning is discussed in the following section.

Sales Promotion Planning

Like any other component of the marketing communications mix, a sales promotion plan is but one component of a much larger plan. It must directly fit into the marketing communications plan and play a role in achieving the specific objectives that are identified

Sales Promotion

Sales promotion is divided into two primary areas: consumer promotion and trade promotion.

Consumer Promotion

Incentive(s) offered to consumers to stimulate purchases or encourage loyalty.

Pull

Demand created by directing promotional activities at consumers or final users, who in turn pressure retailers to supply the product or service.

Trade Promotion

An incentive offered to channel members to encourage them to provide marketing and merchandising support for a particular product.

Push

Demand created by directing promotional activities at intermediaries, who in turn promote the product or service among consumers.

FIGURE **8.1** **Pull and Push Promotion Strategies**

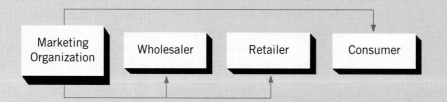

Pull—The promotion strategy is directed at consumers, who in turn request the product or service from distributors, and pull it through the channel.

Push—The promotion strategy is directed at distributors, who resell the product. Incentives help push the product from one distributor to another.

in that plan. Whereas advertising plans have a long-term perspective, and longer-term objectives, the sales promotion plan adopts a short-term view and achieves objectives of a more immediate nature. For example, while advertising is building a brand's image, sales promotions are implemented to encourage a spike in sales.

Sales promotions are activities that complement advertising. When you consider the primary goals of advertising—awareness, comprehension, conviction, and action—the primary goal of sales promotion is to focus on one specific area, and that's action. A well-timed promotional offer that coincides with an image-building advertising campaign could be just the incentive needed to get the customer's money out of that wallet or purse. Such a relationship suggests that integration of advertising strategies and promotional strategies is essential, and, on a larger scale, that their integration with online communications, events and sponsorships, and public relations is what promotes a brand or company with a sense of continuity.

Sales promotion planning involves developing a plan of action for communicating incentives to the appropriate target markets (consumers and trade customers) at the right time. Very often an external company (that specializes in sales promotion) will assume responsibility for developing and implementing the consumer promotion plan. As with developing an advertising plan, the specialist must be briefed. The client's role is to provide the necessary background information and then evaluate the promotion concepts put forth by the agency. The promotion agency must assess the information provided by the client and then prepare a strategic plan that will meet the client's objectives (see Figure 8.2). A sales promotion brief typically includes some or all of the following information.

MARKET PROFILE

An overview of sales and market share trends provides market perspective to the promotion planners. Knowing if the brand is a leader, challenger, or follower has an impact on the nature of the promotion they will ultimately recommend. It is important to know if the market is growing and what brands are growing in the market.

FIGURE 8.2 **The Sales Promotion Planning Process**

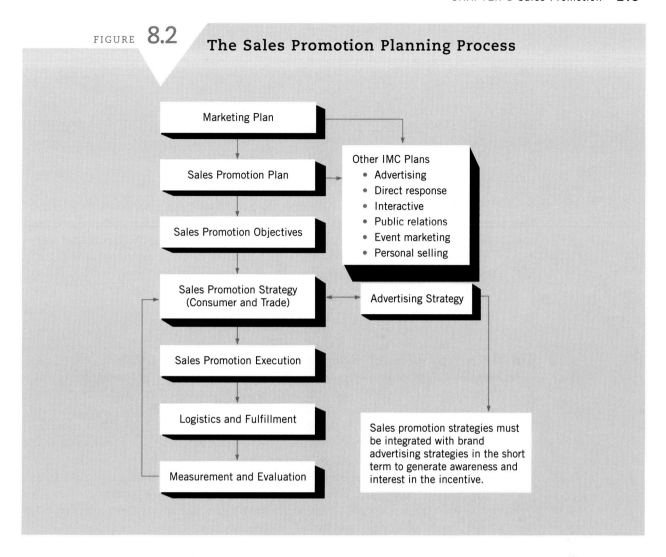

COMPETITOR ACTIVITY PROFILE

In general terms, what marketing communications strategies do key competitors rely upon? The role of the various elements of the mix will vary from one brand to another. What brands dominate the market and what are their mixes? An evaluation of this kind of information may suggest that various combinations of activities have more or less impact on customers. A review of competitors' recent sales promotions activities is essential.

TARGET MARKET PROFILE

Perhaps the most important aspect of planning a promotion is a good understanding of the target customer. As discussed earlier in the text, customers are described according to demographic, psychographic, and geographic characteristics. Additional information about shopping behaviour usually plays a role in developing a sales promotion plan. For example, are the customers price sensitive? Do they participate in contests? Where do they buy the product or service? As with any other form of planning, knowledge of consumer tendencies is power. In this case, it provides guidance for developing the incentive aspect of the promotional offer.

SALES PROMOTION OBJECTIVES

A variety of background factors will determine the objectives of the promotion campaign. Essentially, sales promotion plans focus on three distinct objectives: generating trial purchases, encouraging repeat or multiple purchases, and building long-term brand loyalty. Objectives for trade promotion plans concentrate on building sales and achieving merchandising support. These objectives are discussed in more detail in the consumer promotion and trade promotion sections of this chapter.

BUDGET

Funds for the sales promotion plan come from the overall marketing budget. In most cases, the client has already determined how much money is available for promotions. Knowing the size of the budget is crucial when the promotion agency is thinking about potential concepts. Will this be a large-scale national promotion or will it be restricted to specific regions? Will it involve an expensive grand prize or will there be a series of smaller prizes? How much media advertising support will be needed to create awareness for the promotion?

The Sales Promotion Plan

Sales Promotion Plan

An action plan for communicating incentives to appropriate target markets at the right time.

The **sales promotion plan** is a document that outlines the relevant details about how the client's budget will be spent. Objectives are clearly defined, strategies are justified, and tactical details are precisely documented. Similar to direct response communications plans, back-end considerations are very important. For example, if a fulfillment program is part of the package, details about how the offer will be handled from the time the consumer responds to the time the goods are delivered must be precisely planned. Promotions that include coupons, free samples, contests, rebates, and premiums might involve other companies that handle various aspects of the promotion. The inclusion of other companies adds to the cost of a promotion. The structure and content of a sales promotion plan are the focus of this section. Figure 8.3 summarizes the content of a sales promotion plan, but because the content of a plan varies from one company to another, it is only a guideline.

SALES PROMOTION OBJECTIVES

Sales promotion objectives are statements that clearly indicate what the promotion plan is to accomplish. As with other communications plans, objective statements should be realistically achievable, quantitative in nature in order to facilitate measurement, and directed at a carefully defined target market.

The nature of the promotion plan (that is, consumer promotion versus trade promotion) determines the objectives. Although objectives for both are quite different, they complement each other when implemented. Let's start with consumer promotion objectives.

The most common objective of consumer promotion is to encourage consumers to make a *trial purchase*. When a product is new, for example, an organization wants to establish acceptance as quickly as possible. Therefore, trial-oriented promotions are common (see Figure 8.4). Even when a product is in the growth stage of development, there is need to distinguish one brand from another. At that stage, incentives that encourage purchase of a specific brand remain essential. Media-delivered coupons are an excellent promotion tool for encouraging trial purchase.

The second objective is to *stimulate repeat purchases* by existing customers. An extension of this objective is to encourage consumers to make *multiple purchases* at one time. To illustrate, a well-conceived contest will encourage multiple entries by consumers. Persistent purchases of the brand in the contest ties the consumer to the brand for a period of time. Those consumers won't be buying a competitor's brand!

FIGURE **8.3**

The Content of a Sales Promotion Plan

Situation Analysis

- Market profile
- Competitor activity profile
- Target market profile

Budget

- Funds available

Sales Promotion Objectives

A. Consumer Promotion

- Trial purchase
- Repeat purchases
- Multiple purchases
- Brand loyalty

B. Trade Promotion

- New listings
- Sales volume
- Merchandising support

Sales Promotion Strategy

- Incentive or offer (save, win, or reward)
- Merchandise, cash, or combination
- Balance between consumer and trade

Advertising Strategy

- Broadcast
- Print
- In-store
- Web

Sales Promotion Execution

- Details of consumer offer (coupon, sample, contest, premium, rebate, loyalty promotion)
- Details of trade offer (trade allowance, performance allowance, cooperative advertising funds, dealer premiums, collateral materials, display materials, trade shows)

Logistics and Fulfillment

- Back-end plan to administer and implement the promotion

Budget and Timing

- Activity costs
- Calendar of events

The third objective deals with customer relationship management (CRM). Here, the objective is to *encourage brand loyalty* for an extended period. Traditionally, promotions encourage instant activity, but there are promotion alternatives that can meet both short-term and long-term brand objectives. Something as simple as the loyalty card offered by a local coffee shop helps keep a customer a customer. A coupon included in a box of Cheerios is a reward to the person for buying the brand. Rewards bring customers back.

The overall goal of trade promotions is to give sales a jolt in the short run. But such an accomplishment is usually the result of promotion strategies combined with other marketing strategies to influence trade customers and consumers. Therefore, trade promotion objectives must be confined to what they can realistically achieve. Generally speaking, trade promotion plans are designed to encourage distributors to carry a product and then sell it to retailers, and to increase the volume sold for products they already carry.

In the case of a new product, the first objective is to *secure a listing* with distributors. A **listing** is an agreement made by a wholesaler to distribute a manufacturer's product to the retailer it supplies. For example, when the head office of Canada Safeway or Sobeys agrees to list a product, it is then available to all of their retail outlets. Typically, trade promotions in the form of financial incentives are used to secure listings.

Listing

An agreement made by a wholesaler to distribute a manufacturer's product to the retailer it supplies.

FIGURE **8.4** **A Consumer Promotion Designed to Encourage Trial Purchase**

GET SOME NOW... ● AND SAVE!

50¢ OFF

With the purchase of any two (2) x 750g tubs **OR** any one 12-pack multi-pack of Astro™ Yogourt (any variety).

FREE CHATELAINE OFFER SEE DETAILS BELOW

WASABI-GINGER TUNA SALAD

RECEIVE 2 ISSUES OF CHATELAINE

FREE with 3 UPC's from any 750g tub or 12-pack multi-pack of ASTRO™ yogourt (any variety).

Source: Courtesy of Parmalat.

A second objective is to *build sales volume* on either a seasonal basis or a pre-determined cyclical basis throughout the year. For example, baking products are promoted in the pre-Christmas season and usually there are displays of such products in retail stores. In other cases, it is common for a company to offer temporary discounts for its key brands on a quarterly basis because they recognize that consistent activity keeps a popular brand in a preferred position with the trade and consumers. The nature of competition often dictates such a strategy.

A third trade objective is to *secure merchandising support* from distributors. Their support is crucial, because once the product leaves the manufacturer's warehouse the manufacturer is no longer in control of how it is sold. Consequently, funds are allocated to activities that get the product out of a distributor's warehouse and into displays on the retail sales floor. As well, the manufacturer will look for a sale price and perhaps a brand mention of the sale price in a retailer's advertising flyer. These activities constitute merchandising support.

Sales Promotion Strategy

Decisions about sales promotion strategy focus on the selection of the best promotion activity to meet the objectives. Decisions point the organization in a certain direction and, if agreed to, the tactical details are then developed. For example, on the consumer side of things, an organization can choose among coupons, free samples, contests, rebates, premiums, and loyalty programs. Other decisions may involve the selection of prizes. Should they be cash, merchandise, or a combination of both? The organization can use any one of these options or combine several to maximize the potential of the promotion.

Each of these options provides a different kind of incentive. For example, coupons and rebates save people money; contests give people a chance to win something; and samples, premiums, and loyalty programs offer something free with a purchase. As a result, the first decision relates directly to the incentive. Should the promotion program offer savings, a chance to win something, or a reward?

Key decisions about trade promotion strategy involve the allocation of funds among the different alternatives. Depending on the promotion objectives, preference may be given to listing allowances, trade and performance allowances, and cooperative advertising allowances. Alternatively, some combination of several of these allowances may be employed. The manager must also decide about the balance between consumer promotions (pull) and trade promotions (push). Successful promotions use both and are carefully integrated with other forms of marketing communications in order to maximize impact on the intended target audience.

The second component of the sales promotion strategy involves integration with the advertising strategy. You need to promote a promotion! In many cases, a brand will already be planning a brand-image campaign and several different media may be involved. Is special creative needed for the sales promotion? What media will be used to advertise the sales promotion?

With creative, the ideal situation is to have promotional creative blend effectively with existing brand creative. Therefore, separate but integrated messages must be prepared for the promotion. A promotion is an added incentive, so it temporarily becomes the brand's unique selling point. The combination of a strong ongoing sales message with the added bonus of a special offer will help achieve short-term and long-term objectives.

Gallup & Robinson
www.gallup-robinson.com

Marketing research by Gallup & Robinson recommended that marketers determine what they want to accomplish before embarking on a specific promotion plan. The marketer should evaluate any potential conflict between brand advertising and promotion advertising. Gallup & Robinson's research found that the ideal promotion offer draws attention to the ad and conveys a message about the product. Also, a strong association between the promotional offer and the advertised product tends to increase advertising recall and persuasiveness.[1] The lesson here is that the offer must be a good match for the product and the target market.

A sales promotion will only work if it receives the necessary media support, so another decision must be made about allocating funds specifically for promotion-related programs. Once that decision is taken, the media strategy will focus on two objectives: creating awareness for the promotion and providing details about how the consumer can take advantage of the promotion (e.g., how to send in order forms for premium offers or entry forms for contests).

Typically, a variety of broadcast and print media is selected. Television is an ideal medium for creating instant awareness of the promotion. High-impact television advertising in a short period (a blitz strategy) is common. In the case of a contest or sweepstakes promotion, television is ideal for creating excitement and for conveying a sense of urgency to consumers. It encourages them to take advantage of the offer right away. Television can also direct consumers to a website where all the details of the promotion are available.

FIGURE **8.5** A Contest Promotion Attracts New and Present Users and Helps Build Sales Volume in a Key Season

Print advertising and in-store advertising can assist in achieving awareness objectives while playing a key role in communicating details of the offer. Consumers are conditioned to look for details at point-of-purchase. In conjunction with trade promotion strategies, the ideal situation is to have brand displays in stores supported by posters and shelf-cards at the product's regular shelf location to draw attention to the promotion. Obviously, the nature and size of the promotion will dictate the degree of media support. A contest with a significant grand prize will garner abundant media support. For instance, brands such as Pepsi-Cola and Coca-Cola invest in media advertising to promote summer contests that offer huge grand prizes (see Figure 8.5). In contrast, a premium offer may simply be announced to the target market on the package itself and by shelf cards at point-of-purchase. The investment in media advertising would be low.

Furthermore, the trade customers must be made aware of consumer promotion offers. This task falls on the shoulders of the manufacturer's sales representatives. The manufacturer commonly prepares specific sales literature such as brochures, pamphlets, and display material for representatives to use to introduce the promotion. The sales representatives will integrate the consumer promotion offer with their trade promotion plans (a combination of pull and push) to maximize the impact of the dollars being invested in the promotion. A manufacturer will also consider direct mailings to trade customers and placing ads announcing the promotion in trade journals that their distributors refer to frequently. The sales representatives must sell the promotion to the distributors and show how it will affect their business positively. Their objective is to ensure the distributor orders sufficient inventory to cover the anticipated demand for the product and to encourage adequate merchandising support in their stores. If the trade customers are on board, the promotion will be successful. Their support is crucial.

LOGISTICS AND FULFILLMENT

The final phase of planning a promotion campaign involves working out all of the details of the offer. Depending on the nature of the promotion, there is a variety of dates and deadlines, there will be other companies involved in planning and implementing the offer, and a system will need to be put in place to deliver the goods to consumers, if the promotion so dictates. These are only a sampling of the potential decisions that are made.

To demonstrate the fulfillment process, let's assume that a major contest is the sales promotion offer. The grand prize is a trip to Disneyland, with a series of smaller prizes to be awarded to runners-up. Answers to the following questions start to create a plan of action for implementing the awareness and fulfillment sides of the promotion.

- When will the promotion be announced to the trade and to consumers?
- Who are the contest prize suppliers and what are the costs?
- How will consumers enter the contest? Who will design the entry form?
- Where will the entry forms be sent?
- What is the deadline for receiving entries?
- Who will draw the prizes?
- How will the prizes be delivered to the winners?
- What costs are associated with contest administration by a third-party organization?
- Who will the third-party organization be?
- Who will prepare in-store promotional materials?
- Who will print the promotional literature and what will it cost?
- How will media advertising be coordinated with the sales promotion offer?

Such a list of questions reveals the logistical implications for running a sales promotion offer. Needless to say, the entire promotion must operate seamlessly from the front end (announcing the promotion) to the back end (delivering prizes to winners). Organizations that try to implement a promotion of this nature on their own in order to save money do so at their own peril. It is much wiser to outsource the administration of the promotion to a specialist in this industry.

MEASUREMENT AND EVALUATION

Similar to any other marketing communications program, sales promotion activities must be evaluated for success or failure. As indicated earlier, a boost in sales is the immediate goal of most forms of promotion, but other factors beyond promotion also influence sales. Therefore, a promotion must be evaluated based on the objectives that were established for it. If the objective was to generate trial purchases, how many new users were attracted to the product? If the objective was loyalty, are current customers buying the product more frequently? To answer these questions, some pre- and post-promotion marketing research is necessary.

Specific promotions are also measured by response rates of consumers. For example, a coupon promotion could be assessed by the numbers of coupons returned. If the average return rate for coupons distributed by magazines is 1 percent and an offer draws a 2 percent response, the promotion could be judged a success. The incidence of trial purchase is higher than average sales. A contest is evaluated on the basis of the number of entries received. If the objective was 10 000 entries and only 7500 were received, the promotion could be judged a failure.

If there is a method of projecting revenues generated by a promotion, then it is possible to estimate some kind of financial payout from the promotion. The difference between revenues and costs would be the return on investment, because the costs of the promotion are known. Figure 8.6 illustrates how to evaluate the financial payout of a coupon offer.

FIGURE **8.6**

Evaluating the Financial Impact of a Sales Promotion Offer

This example shows the return on investment for a coupon offer distributed to households by cooperative direct mail. Costs and revenues are estimated to determine the return on investment.

Coupon Plan	
Face value of coupon	$1.00
Handling charge for retailer	$0.15
Handling charge for clearing house	$0.05
Distribution cost	$18.00/M
Distribution	2 million households
Printing cost (digest-sized ad with perforated coupon at bottom)	$12.00/M
Redemption rate (estimated)	5.0%
Retail price of product	$3.89

(Manufacturer receives about 65% of retail price when distributors' mark-ups are deducted)

Costs	Cost Calculation	Total	Grand Total
Distribution	2 000 000 x $18/M	$36 000	
Printing	2 000 000 x $12/M	$24 000	
Coupon redemption	2 000 000 x 0.05 x $1.20	$120 000	
Total cost		**180 000**	**$180 000**
Cost per coupon redeemed	180 000/100 000	$1.80	

Revenues			
Per unit of revenue	$3.89 x.65	$2.53	
Total revenue*	2 000 000 x 0.05 x 0.80 x $2.53	**202 400**	**$202 400**
Return on investment			**$22 400**

*With any coupon offer, there is a risk of coupons being returned without a purchase being made. This is referred to as misredemption. In this example, the misredemption rate is 20%, hence the .80 factor in the revenue calculation equation.

Boston Market
www.boston-market.com

A side benefit of consumer promotions is the collection of names. The names on entry forms from contests and order forms for premium offers and rebate offers can be added to the organization's database. Smart marketers seek additional information about consumers on promotion entry forms in order to develop more thorough customer profiles and to determine who their primary target market is.

When Boston Market restaurants entered Canada, consumer promotions played a key role in getting unfamiliar customers to visit. Figure 8.7 shows how Boston Market applied the sales promotion planning process. Their very unique offer generated extremely high response rates.

FIGURE **8.7**

Summary Example of a Sales Promotion Plan for Boston Market

SITUATION ANALYSIS

- Canadian consumers totally unaware of Boston Market
- Boston Market is a subsidiary of McDonald's Restaurants
- 650 locations in 28 U.S. states
- Food perceived as very good (home-cooked style); high incidence of repeat visits

SALES PROMOTION OBJECTIVES

- To show how Boston Market can benefit the everyday lives of consumers
- To generate traffic (trial usage)

TARGET MARKET

- Married households; two working adults; with or without children; suburban
- Time starved and searching for home replacement meals

SALES PROMOTION STRATEGY

- An incentive that ties into what the brand stands for: "Home-style meals made easy"
- Free sample offer to designated households in trading area

SALES PROMOTION EXECUTION

- Promotion theme: "Dinner on Us"
- Location: Mystery bag attached to front door knob of designated area households
- Message on bag: "Too much on your plate?" (a question to create curiosity)
- Incentive: Free meal for two (no strings attached)
- Action: Consumer must bring the dinner plate from the bag to the restaurant to get the free meals. Plate inferred a home-cooked meal away from home. The unique promotion would encourage positive word-of-mouth.
- Distribution: Different homes selected each Thursday

MEASUREMENT AND EVALUATION

- The Thursday rollouts created a high level of anticipation among households
- Very positive press coverage by local media (free advertising and endorsements)
- Redemption rate 70% (outstanding)

Adapted from Lisa McGillivray, "Bagging a Tasty Promo," *Marketing*, December 2, 2002, p. 15.

Country Style donuts is a distant second behind Tim Hortons in the coffee-and-donut market but has taken some bold marketing steps in the past few years to improve its situation. Sales promotion has played an integral role in its marketing communications strategies. For insight into their integrated marketing communications activities, read the IMC Highlight **Firing on All Cylinders**.

FIRING ON ALL CYLINDERS

It may seem hard to believe but Country Style was the originator of the coffee and donut concept in Canada and was the market leader long before anyone even heard of Tim Hortons. But that was long ago; the times are really different now. Country Style stood still and watched Tim Hortons sweep across the country, expanding like crazy.

Country Style had lost its way, but under the new leadership of recently appointed CEO Patrick Gibbons, repositioning for the future has been the company's mantra. One year into the job but with great retailing experience behind him, Gibbons implemented new menu additions, improved operational standards, closed inefficient locations, changed management, and implemented more promotional activities.

One of his first moves was to file for protection under the *Companies Creditor Arrangement Act*. He subsequently closed 120 stores, leaving about 150 in operation and another 150 smaller operations in gas station outlets (Sunoco and Shell).

Marketing communications would play a key role in Country Style's resurrection. The objectives of the campaign were to reacquaint customers with the new-look Country Style and to increase traffic counts. Sales promotions would play a key role. Looking to boost sales, the chain revamped its long-running "Turn Up a Winner" promotion in Ontario and offered bigger prizes, a new tag line "Love at first sip," a new jingle, more competitive prices, and partnerships with companies such as Hyundai, Air Transat, and Jumbo Video.

Gibbons changed the promotion from instant win, collect-and-win, and mail-in-and-win to instant gratification—everybody wins. Says Gibbons, "Such a tactic added value to our coffee product and it helped get people into the stores." To create awareness for the promotion, the investment in media advertising was significant. In Toronto, radio played at 350 GRPs a week for six weeks and there were 150 outdoor boards. In sizing up the strategy, Gibbons states, "You need to have tactical promotions that have a real compelling call to action, and the best way is to offer added value for customers."

The campaign ran in the spring of 2002 and produced double-digit growth in customer counts. Gibbons decided to repeat the promotion, with a few new wrinkles, in the fall of 2003, a period when other chains would not be running their promotions. The prize package was similar to the initial contest but advertising, in the form of print ads in *Famous Players* magazine and television spots, was added to the mix. The results again were spectacular.

Since the company had been floundering before these promotions, it is difficult to compare recent success to past marketing efforts. Gibbons does say, however, that since they fixed the company and started to market and advertise with some consistency, there has been a positive change in attitude among franchisees and double-digit increases in customer traffic.

From the outside looking in, a person might accuse Country Style of copying Tim Hortons's famous "RRRoll up the Rim" promotion, hardly a unique approach to marketing. But, points out Gibbons, "'Turn Up a Winner' has been an annual event for 20 years. People just didn't know about it."

Over the long term, more changes will be implemented. The chain has opened its first drive-through-only location in Toronto and there are more to come. Other changes will include faster service, a drive-through focus by revamping existing locations, and better menu boards. Gibbons is striving for a disciplined approach to operations and marketing, citing consistency as a good strategy for attracting and retaining customers.

Adapted from Sarah Dobson, "Turning Up a Winner," *Marketing*, December 2, 2002, pp. 12–13.

Country Style Food Services
www.countrystyle.com

CONSUMER PROMOTION EXECUTION

As indicated earlier, an organization will combine various consumer promotion activities with trade promotion activities so that there is balance between the pull and push strategies. It is that combination of pull and push that creates a synergistic effect in the marketplace. This section will discuss the various forms of consumer promotions that are often included in sales promotion plans.

The major types of consumer promotions include coupons, free samples, contests, cash rebates and related incentives, premiums, and loyalty programs. The popularity of the various alternatives varies from one industry to another. In the packaged goods industry, all alternatives are used but coupons seem to be the most popular. A survey conducted by NCH Promotional Services ranked coupons as the most important form of promotion for companies in the food, household, and personal care products industries. Following in order of importance were samples, contests, cash refunds, and premiums.[2]

In the computer software industry, samples of software can be downloaded directly to a person's computer. Timing mechanisms are built into the software program so the consumer can only use it for a short period of time. Based on the satisfaction gained from trial usage the consumer may be motivated to buy the software. The automotive industry is now bound by a variety of financial incentives that include cash-back rebates and extremely low financing terms. Does anyone actually buy a car that doesn't have some kind of incentive offer? Let's analyze the various consumer promotions and determine the conditions for which each type of promotion is best suited.

Coupons

Coupon
A price-saving incentive offered to consumers to stimulate quick purchase of a specified product.

Coupons are price-saving incentives offered to consumers to stimulate quick purchase of a designated product. The motivation for distributing the coupons is the same across all industries, although the value of the coupons varies considerably. Grocery coupons, for example, may only be valued at $0.75, while a trial coupon for a restaurant may be valued at 50 percent of the cost of the meal. A common offer is "Buy one meal at regular price and save 50 percent off the price of the second meal."

In packaged goods markets, coupons are the dominant form of sales promotion activity. The latest data available from NCH Promotional Services, which keeps records on coupon distribution and redemption in Canada, reveal that more than 2.32 billion coupons are distributed annually. A total of 110 million are returned, for a total savings on goods of about $120 million. The average value of a redeemed coupon is $1.07.[3]

Coupons are an excellent medium for achieving several marketing objectives at various stages of the product life cycle. First, coupons can encourage *trial purchase* among new users (and encourage competitive brand users to switch brands) and they can encourage *repeat purchases* by current users. In the latter situation, the coupon is a means of building brand loyalty. The method by which the coupons are distributed to consumers is based on the objectives of the coupon offer. When a product is new or relatively new, trial purchase is the marketer's primary objective, so **media-delivered coupons** are popular. Options for delivery include **freestanding inserts (FSI)** in newspapers, magazines, direct mail, in-store distribution, and the internet. Using the internet to deliver coupons is a fairly new practice. Websites such as save.ca distribute coupons on behalf of manufacturers. Many companies distribute coupons to consumers who request them while visiting their website. NCH Promotional Services reports that online coupons are growing fast, but from a small base. At present, they account for only 0.1 percent of coupons distributed and 0.1 percent of coupons redeemed.[4]

Once a product moves into the late growth and early mature stages of its life cycle, a marketer's attention shifts from trial purchase to *repeat purchase*. By now there are many competing brands, all of which have a certain degree of consumer loyalty. As a defensive measure, it is important to reward current customers in one form or another. The package itself becomes an important medium for distributing coupons. The insertion of a coupon in or on a package, for example, is an incentive for a customer to keep buying the product.

Coupons contained inside a package are called **in-pack self-coupons**, because they are redeemable on the next purchase. Usually the face panel of the package makes mention of the coupon contained inside. A coupon that appears on the side panel or back panel is called an **on-pack self-coupon**. Another option is the **instantly redeemable coupon**, which is on the face panel of the package and can be removed immediately and used on the purchase of the product. Sometimes two different products collaborate on a coupon offer. Too illustrate, Tetley Tea includes an in-pack coupon for Christie cookies and Christie cookies places a Tetley tea coupon in its package. The relationship between the

Media-delivered Coupon
A coupon distributed by traditional media alternatives such as newspapers, magazines, and direct mail.

Freestanding Insert (FSI)
A booklet featuring coupons, refunds, contests, or other promotional advertising distributed by direct mail or with newspapers, magazines, or other delivery vehicles.

In-pack Self-coupon
A coupon for the next purchase of a product, packed inside the package or under a label.

On-pack Self-coupon
A coupon that is printed on the outside of a package redeemable on the next purchase of the product.

Instantly Redeemable Coupon
A removable coupon often located on the package or a store shelf that is redeemable on the current purchase of the product.

Cross-ruff or Cross-coupon

A coupon redeemable for one product that is packed in or with another product

Redemption Rate

The number of coupons returned expressed as a percentage of the number of coupons that were distributed.

two brands is obvious. Each brand capitalizes on the other's consumer franchise in its effort to attract new users. This type of coupon is called a **cross-ruff or cross-coupon**.

The success or failure of a coupon offer is often determined by the redemption rate that is achieved. The **redemption rate** for coupons refers to the number of coupons returned to the manufacturer and is expressed as a percentage of the total coupons in distribution. If, for example, 1 million coupons were distributed and 45 000 were returned, the redemption rate would be 4.5 percent (45 000 divided by 1 000 000).

For budgeting purposes, it is important to know the average redemption rates of the various methods of delivering coupons. For example, NCH research shows the average redemption rate for direct mail coupons to be 6.5 percent, while the range can be anywhere from 1.9 percent to 22.6 percent. Why is there so much variation? Several factors influence the rate of return. Based on the average figures that appear in Figure 8.8, the primary influence is the method of delivery. The direct mail rate seems very high when compared to the average redemption rate for newspapers and magazines, and package-delivered coupons are high because they appeal to current users of the brand (thus encouraging brand loyalty). Another factor is the consumer's perception of the value of the discount offered by the coupon in relation to the regular price of the product. If it's not a worthwhile incentive, it won't be acted upon.

FIGURE **8.8**

Average Redemption Rates by Distribution Media

Media	Range	Average
FSI	0.1 – 1.8%	0.6%
In-store	1.2 – 32.7%	9.8%
In/On Pack	0.3 – 51.4%	6.1%
Direct mail addressed	1.9 – 22.6%	6.5%
Direct mail unaddressed	0.1 – 3.3%	1.2%
Magazine	0.1 – 7.0%	0.8%
Charity	0.5 – 28.5%	16.9%
Other	0.3 – 30.6%	2.7%
Internet	0.3 – 14.9%	3.9%

Ranges exclude top and bottom 10% of cases.

Sample Interpretation: The average redemption rate for a coupon distributed by magazine is 0.8% (a low rate). The average redemption rate for an in-store delivered coupon is 9.8% (a high rate).

COUPON DISTRIBUTION AND REDEMPTION BY METHOD OF DELIVERY

Delivery Method	% Distributed 2000	% Redeemed 2000	% Distributed 2002	% Redeemed 2002
FSI	55	10	64	10
In-store	17	48	13	46
In/On Pack	13	29	8	23
Direct mail	5	6	6	8
Magazine	5	2	6	6
Other	5	5	3	7

Sample Interpretation: Freestanding inserts (FSI) account for 64% of all coupons distributed but only 10% of coupons actually redeemed. Packages deliver 8% of all coupons and account for 23% of all redemptions. The redemption rate is higher for packages, because current users are redeeming the coupons.

Source: Reprinted by permission of NCH Promotional Services Ltd.

Free Samples

Free Sample

Free distribution of a product to potential users.

Product sampling is a powerful, yet expensive way to promote a product. It is an effective strategy for encouraging trial purchase, but due to the costs involved, many manufacturers do not select this option. Traditionally, **free sample** programs involved the distribution of trial-size packages (small replicas of the real package) or actual-size packages (see Figure 8.9). The latter option is obviously an expensive proposition. In order to implement a sampling program, the marketer must appreciate the true benefit of such an offer. In a nutshell, it is unlike any other form of promotion in that it is the only alternative that will convert a trial user to a regular user solely on the basis of product satisfaction. Essentially, the marketing organization has eliminated any perceived risk the consumer may have about buying the product. That's a compelling reason for using samples. Gillette followed this strategy when it launched the Mach3Turbo, a razor that was targeted to males 16 to 29 years

FIGURE **8.9**   **Trial-Size Samples Delivered Directly to Households Encourage Trial Usage and Initial Purchase**

Source: Dick Hemingway.

of age. The company provided samples directly to players and coaches of 326 Junior A teams across Canada and handed out 100 000 razors to fans at junior hockey games.[5]

There are less expensive ways to implement sample programs, but they lack the impact of household distribution of free goods. A tried and true approach, particularly for food products, is in-store sampling. Costco uses this approach extensively by setting up sample stations at the ends of food aisles. A smart shopper can practically have a free lunch while shopping at Costco on a Saturday. When packaged good grocery manufacturers do sample tasting in local supermarkets, they usually outsource the promotion to an independent company that specializes in this activity. Booths are strategically set up in stores to intercept customers as they shop.

Companies are discovering new ways of delivering samples while at the same time generating positive publicity for the brand involved in the promotion. Some refer to it as **on-site sampling**; others call it **experiential marketing**. To illustrate, consider a recent campaign for Lady Speed Stick Clean Glide antiperspirant. Picture this: two female rollerbladers wheel through a downtown crowd. They strip down to their T-shirts and they are perspiring. On the front of the T-shirts is the phrase "Tired of white residue?" Arrows point to the corners of their shirts. Tied around their wastes are fanny-packs containing deodorant samples. Curious pedestrians are shown how the product does not leave a mark on clothing, and receive small samples.

Larry Burns, co-chair of U.S.-based Promotion Marketing Association (PMA), says "Targeted, well thought-out programs like the one for Lady Speed Stick are the way to go in today's market." He cites research findings to back up his claim. From a survey conducted by the PMA, 94 percent of respondents view sampling as a way of increasing their comfort level when buying a product. A further 68 percent said they were "excited" about receiving the sample.[6]

Strategically, there was a connection between the product and the target market in the Lady Speed Stick sample program. According to Carolyn Thompson, product manager at Colgate-Palmolive Canada, which produces Lady Speed Stick, "The sampling program is innovative, there is positive interaction with consumers, and the action—rollerblading and gliding—induces perspiration and ties nicely to the sub-brand name."[7] Lady Speed Stick also uses print advertising in women's magazines and web-based communications to round out its marketing communications strategy (see Figure 8.10).

When deciding whether to use a free sample program a review of the benefits and drawbacks is essential. Samples are an expensive proposition due to product, package, and handling costs. In spite of these costs, samples rank second to coupons among marketers, so clearly the long-term benefit outweighs the short-term costs. The fact that it eliminates the risk usually associated with new product purchases is a benefit. On the downside, a sample is the fastest and surest way to kill an inferior product.[8] In terms of timing, sample programs are best suited to the early stage of the product life cycle when the primary objective is to achieve trial purchase. For certain, the delivery of samples adds excitement to any new product launch.

Contests

Contests are designed and implemented to create temporary excitement about a brand. For example, offering a grand prize such as an automobile, vacation, or dream home can capture the consumer's imagination, even though the odds of winning are very low. Contests can be classified into two categories: sweepstakes and games. A **sweepstakes** is a chance promotion involving the giveaway of products and services such as cars, vacations, and sometimes cash. It's like a lottery: winners are randomly selected from the entries received. Typically, consumers enter a contest by filling in an entry form that is available at point-of-purchase, through print advertising, or at a website.

When companies are searching for the right sweepstakes idea, their objective is clear. It must light a fire under sales. Experience reveals that successful contests have longevity.

On-Site Sampling or Experiential Marketing

A promotion in which potential customers interact directly with a product.

Promotion Marketing Association
www.pmalink.org

Contest

A promotion that involves awarding cash or merchandise prizes to consumers when they purchase a specified product.

Sweepstakes

A chance promotion involving the giveaway of products or services of value to randomly selected participants.

FIGURE **8.10** **Lady Speed Stick Provides Additional Product Information through Web-based Communications**

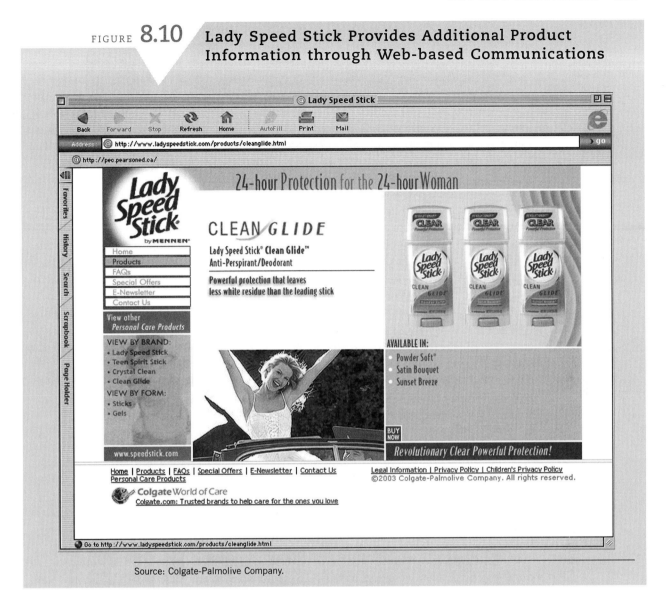

Source: Colgate-Palmolive Company.

They are not just one-time offers but are a concept that can be integrated into the annual marketing plan. To illustrate, consider that Gillette has used the "Cavalcade of Sports" contest for more than 30 years. This contest embraces a variety of Gillette's premium brands, appeals to consumers and trade customers, and runs across North America. The grand prize is always dramatic and sports-related, like a trip to the NCAA Final Four Basketball Tournament, the Super Bowl, or the Stanley Cup finals. Secondary prizes include automobiles, vacations, and sporting goods equipment. Consumers are drawn to the promotion by the marketing efforts of numerous promotional partners including General Motors, TSN, and Shoppers Drug Mart. The retail trade is also very active in promoting the brands and providing in-store displays. In Canada alone, Gillette spends $2 million a year on this contest.[9]

Games are also based on chance but can be more involving because they often require repeat visits for game pieces. This makes them a good device for encouraging continuity of purchase by consumers. McDonald's is somewhat of an expert in this area. Its "Monopoly" game is a regular feature in annual marketing plans. As the saying goes, "You have to play to win," and the only way to play is to go to a McDonald's.

(Instant-Win) Game

A promotional contest that includes a number of pre-seeded winning tickets; instant-win tickets can be redeemed immediately.

An offshoot of the game contest is the **instant-win** promotion, which involves pre-determined, pre-seeded winning tickets, in the overall fixed universe of tickets. For example, if the promotion is implemented nationally, prize tickets should be regionally dispersed based on population patterns. Variations of instant wins include *collect-and-wins* and small instant-wins combined with a grand prize contest. Tim Hortons's annual "RRRoll Up the Rim" is an example of a contest combining instant-wins with a series of grand prizes. Most of the instant-win prizes involve food products available at the organization's restaurants, but it is the roster of bigger prizes that draws the consumer in. As mentioned earlier, "RRRoll Up the Rim" is another example of a longstanding successful promotion. It delivers a consistent theme and has a catchy and memorable slogan. According to Tim Hortons, the promotion is now less of a promotion and more like a brand unto itself: "RRRoll Up the Rim" has become recognized as its own entity, much as a product would. Franchisees indicate that sales increase 10 to 15 percent during the promotion period.[10] This promotion is an integral part of the company's annual marketing plan.

Planning any kind of contest is a challenge. Most manufacturers rely on external suppliers to develop and implement a contest. In this regard, there is much upfront discussion with suppliers to ensure proper briefing on objectives and expectations. The success of a contest depends on the consumer's perception of the value and number of prizes being awarded and on the odds of winning. As well, the prizes must match the image of the product and the lifestyle of the target market. Successful contests tend to have a grand prize that captures the imagination of the target market, or have prizes of less value but awarded in large numbers to compensate for the disappointment factor associated with most contests (see Figure 8.11).

A cost–benefit analysis should be done prior to getting involved with a contest. In terms of benefit, a contest is a good device for achieving repeat purchase objectives. A well-designed contest encourages customers to come back or buy more frequently. By returning or buying more goods, consumers exhibit a certain degree of loyalty. As such, contests are ideal promotions for products in the mature stage of the product life cycle. They can boost brand sales in a time of need. According to Tony Chapman, president of Capital C Communications, "Contests have the ability to excite consumers, excite a sales force, sell incredible volume, and build brand equity, and that's a sweet spot every marketer dreams about."[11]

On the cost side of things, a contest requires a significant investment in media advertising to create awareness and interest. Contests such as the "Cavalcade of Sports" and "RRRoll Up the Rim" are supported by multimedia advertising campaigns. A combination of media advertising and in-store promotional materials tends to be effective. When the cost of prizes and the cost of having an external organization implement the contest are factored in, the amount required for a contest promotion can be a sizeable portion of a marketing budget.

Thinking long range, however, Maxwell House Coffee once ran a contest called "The Dream House Sweepstakes." The grand prize was $1 million to be put toward the winner's dream home. More than 250 000 entries were submitted, making it the largest contest ever run by Kraft Canada. The immediate impact of the contest was a 10 percent increase in brand sales. The long-term benefit was the addition of 250 000 names to Kraft's database.[12] For some tips on planning an effective contest, see Figure 8.12.

Legal issues are another concern of marketers when they get involved in contests. The manager must be familiar with some of the basic laws that govern contests in Canada. Section 189 of the *Criminal Code* and sections 52 and 59 of the *Competition Act* regulate most contests in Canada, and there are certain fairly standardized rules and regulations for what information must be communicated to participants. The following information must be clearly conveyed:

• the number of prizes and the value of each;
• the odds of winning, if known;

FIGURE **8.11**   **An Example of a Contest Promotion Communicated by In-store Shelf Pads and Point-of-Purchase Displays**

Source: Courtesy of Gillette.

- whether a skill-testing question will be administered;
- whether facsimiles are acceptable in the case of a sweepstakes;
- how to enter, and what proof of purchase is required; and
- the contest's closing date.

To say the least, the fine print that appears on the back of contest entry forms or in promotional literature is exhaustive, and is meant to ensure that the organization

FIGURE **8.12**

Tips for Planning an Effective Contest

Effective contests do not happen by chance. They are carefully planned to spark interest and action and achieve specific marketing objectives. Here are some pointers from those in the business.

- Choose prizes that spark wish-fulfillment fantasies.
- Give consumers a decent chance of winning (low odds of winning create ill will).
- Plan an engaging media component to drive consumer awareness and generate publicity.
- Keep the company name in the contest moniker (again for positive press).
- Use strategic partnerships; co-brand the contest to leverage each other's equity.
- Make sure contest rules are clear and unambiguous.
- Ensure that fulfillment (awarding of prizes) occurs quickly.
- If it ain't broke, don't fix it! Stay with a successful contest if it's producing desired results.

Source: Adapted from "Tips for Creating Killer Contests," Special Report on Premiums and Incentives, *Strategy*, August 26, 2002, p. 24.

promoting the contest is abiding by all appropriate laws and regulations. Figure 8.11 shows the back panel of a shelf pad sheet that communicates the legal information for a typical contest promotion.

Rebates

Rebate

A predetermined amount of money returned directly to customers by the manufacturer after the purchase has been made.

A **rebate** is a predetermined amount of money returned directly to the customer by the manufacturer after the purchase has been made. It is an incentive to get consumers to buy in greater volume during the promotion period. Initially, rebates were the promotion of choice among packaged goods marketers, but they are now an integral element of marketing programs for durable goods such as automobiles and major appliances.

The most common type of rebate is the *single-purchase refund*, in which the consumer receives a portion of money back for the purchase of a specified product. Such an offer is one method of achieving trial purchases. Other variations of rebates include making an offer according to an escalating schedule. For example, an offer could be structured as follows: buy one and get $1.00 back, buy two and get $2.00 back, and buy three and get $5.00 back. The nature of the offer encourages consumers to buy three items at one time. This type of offer helps achieve multiple purchase objectives and can help boost sales over a short period.

Slippage

The situation of a consumer collecting labels in a promotion offer but failing to follow through and request the refund.

Though many people buy a product because of the possibility of a rebate, many rebates go uncollected due to the hassle of filling out a form and mailing it in with proofs of purchase and receipts. This phenomenon is referred to as **slippage**, when the consumer collects labels but fails to follow through and request the refund. In a survey among grocery shoppers, it was found that one half of all refund participants neglect to submit a request for a refund even though they were enticed to buy the product on the basis of the refund and intended to follow through with the offer.[13]

In recent years, incentives and rebates have become commonplace among automobile manufacturers. Offers such as zero percent (or an incredibly low percentage) financing and cash-back deals of between $1000 and $2500 try to entice consumers to buy now. These types of incentives were first instituted to help car companies reduce inventories, while making way for the introduction of new models each year. But, in an uncertain economy, they have become more of an ongoing practice. In fact, so common are they now that many consumers have adopted an attitude that they won't buy a new car unless there is some kind of incentive provided.

Automobile incentives can boost sales in the short term, but in the long term they have made the cost of an automobile higher and have affected the profitability of domestic manufacturers. In 2001, the Ford Motor Company offered incentives on many of its models but market share dropped a full percentage point to 16.0 percent by the end of the year. At the same time, the Japanese automakers, which rely far less on expensive incentive packages to lure buyers, reported solid gains in volume.[14] Perhaps there is a lesson to be learned here about rebates and their relationship to other marketing variables—particularly product quality.

Rebate offers are best suited to products in the mature stage of the product life cycle. As indicated above, they are a good incentive for encouraging multiple purchases of inexpensive packaged goods products. Encouraging multiple purchases or building frequency of purchases is a common objective of mature products. At this stage in the life cycle, maintaining customer loyalty is critical. Apart from the rebates offered by automobile companies, which tend to be very high, a rebate promotion is not that expensive to implement. Since it is current users who tend to take advantage of rebate offers, advertising support can be confined to the package and various in-store opportunities, such as shelf cards and product displays. Ad pads located at the point-of-purchase help draw attention to the offer and provide the necessary details about how consumers can take advantage of the offer.

PREMIUM OFFERS

Premium

An additional item given free, or greatly discounted, to induce purchase of the primary brand.

A **premium** is an additional item given free, or greatly discounted, to induce purchase of the primary brand. The goal of a premium is to provide added value in order to tempt consumers to buy. McDonald's frequently uses premiums because they are effective with its primary target market of families with young children. A "Happy Meal" becomes a "Nintendo Happy Meal" when Mario Brothers toys become part of the product mix. Recently, fast food restaurants have focused their premium efforts on characters from popular movies. KFC linked up with Spiderman, and McDonald's has a 10-year agreement with Disney to distribute its toy characters.

Premiums are offered to consumers several ways: either as a mail-in, by sending in proofs of purchase so the item can be delivered by mail; as an in-pack or on-pack promotion, where the item is placed inside or attached to a package; and by an order form that is usually available at point-of-purchase. Packaged goods companies frequently use their packages to distribute free premiums. One of General Mills's most successful promotions involved inserting Hasbro CD-ROM games ("Clue," "Monopoly," "Junior Yahtzee," and "Boggle") inside boxes of Cheerios cereal (see Figure 8.12). These games are instantly recognizable by kids and the parents who buy the cereal. Another example was Cheerio's offering of CDs containing video footage of Canada's gold medal winning games (men and women) from the 2002 Salt Lake City Winter Olympics. An offer like this certainly delivers added value for consumers.

General Mills
www.generalmills.com

Many marketers firmly believe that there is something to be said for offering a tangible quality gift, which can surprise the consumer and build long-term equity through association. Beauty product marketers and department stores regularly count on such giveaways to spur sales and traffic. Sears, for example, recently offered a free watch with the purchase of any Givenchy fragrance worth $55 or more. The Bay offered a free bag of cosmetics with any Lancôme purchase of $27 or more. According to Melanie Stewart, owner of the Toronto-based promotional company Two Crazy Ladies, "People still like instant gratification. The best way to build a long-term relationship is to give a quality product—the quality boosts your name."[15]

FIGURE **8.13**   **Cheerios Cereal Offers High-Value Premiums Inside Packages to Attract New and Current Users**

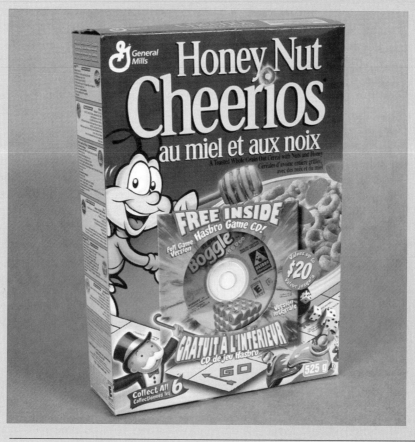

Source: Dick Hemingway.

Coca-Cola Canada introduced a unique twist to premium promotions when it went live with a web auction among customers in its database. Coca-Cola collected 20 000 names from a summer promotion and contacted all of them by e-mail. As soon as the e-mail went out, people started bidding online. According to Arlene Lebovic, national brands promotion manager at Coca-Cola, "The Internet promotions provide an ideal means for building loyalty. It's where our consumers are. It's more active and involves more people than a simple giveaway."[16]

Bonus Pack

The temporary offering of a larger package size for the same price as the regular size.

An offshoot of a premium offer is the **bonus pack**. The traditional bonus pack offers the consumer more for less. For example, a brand offers a package size that gives the consumer 20 percent more product for the regular price. Another option is to bundle a product in pairs and offer a deal like "Buy One Get One Free." Offers like these, if implemented properly, will attract new users and reward current users. If done wrong, they can cheapen the image or value perception of the brand.

Marketing managers tend to rank premiums lower in terms of popularity, but they do offer some tangible benefits. They achieve several marketing objectives: they can increase the quantity of brand purchases made by consumers during the promotion period; they help to retain current customers, therefore building brand loyalty; and they provide a merchandising tool to encourage display activity in stores.

A good premium offer will help differentiate one brand from another at a crucial point in time, the time when consumers decide which brand to buy. Some premiums produce a huge spike in sales, as was the case with Labatt Blue's "NHL Crazy Coldie Program." Throughout the 2002 NHL playoffs, Labatt's Double Blue 24 cases included one of 30 NHL insulated bottle holders shaped like the jersey of each hockey team. Blue tapped into the number one sport among young Canadian men, and the coldies' ability to keep the beer cold made the promotion a sure thing. Market share grew 300 percent during the promotion period and sales were double the original forecast.[17] The promotion was supported with television advertising, an online contest, and on-site advertising in bars and pubs across Canada. Labatt even dressed guys in life-sized versions of the coldies and sent them to popular hockey events. It was an integrated effort!

Loyalty Programs

Loyalty programs take the short-term premium offer a step further—they encourage long-term brand loyalty. How many loyalty cards do you have in your wallet? It seems that consumers are collecting points to obtain something for free years from now. In the meantime, we keep going back to the loyalty sponsor to earn more points. By definition, a **loyalty program (frequent buyer program)** offers consumers a small bonus, such as points or play money, when each time they make a purchase. The bonus accumulates and can be redeemed for merchandise or some other benefit at a later date.

Shoppers Drug Mart has a frequent buyer program that is updated electronically. Member customers swipe their Optimum card each time they make a purchase. Shoppers can cross-reference transaction data electronically and tailor offers and services to specific customers in-store or by e-mail. One such offer included a free Gillette Mach3 razor along with coupons for replacement blades and Gillette shaving foam or gel, an attractive combination offer that promotes a family of branded products (see Figure 8.14). These samples were distributed by mail to a select group of Shoppers' customers. As discussed elsewhere in this book, the true benefit of a loyalty program is the information it collects for database marketing.

Perhaps the longest running and most successful loyalty program in Canada is Canadian Tire money. It rewards regular shoppers who pay by cash or Canadian Tire credit card, with Canadian Tire "money" worth up to 5 percent of the value of the purchase. Now at an advanced stage, customers can collect virtual money at Canadian Tire's website. Canadian Tire money represents the true essence of a loyalty program: customers can actually receive something for free. In contrast, a program like Air Miles takes considerable time before the consumer can get even the smallest of rewards.

Given our wallets bulging with loyalty cards, it is safe to say that loyalty programs are popular with consumers. In fact, a study conducted by Kubas Consultants reveals that more Canadians participate in loyalty programs (76 percent participate in at least one program) than voted in the last federal election (61 percent of the eligible population).[18] What consumers fail to realize is that while they are chasing a dream vacation or a state-of-the-art, theatre-style television, the cost of merchandise they are buying is going up. Loyalty programs add to the costs of a business in the form of additional employees, call centres, catalogues, and computers. As well, investment in media advertising is needed to draw attention to the loyalty program.

More recently, customer fatigue is setting in and some marketing organizations are questioning the value of a loyalty program. Several retailers, including Second Cup, Pizza Pizza, and HMV, have cancelled their frequent buyer programs. Second Cup cited the degree of clutter in the loyalty club market and decided to focus on other marketing issues such as customer service, product quality, café design, and new products.

Wal-Mart, the world's largest retailer, doesn't offer any loyalty promotions and it may have the most loyal customers. Wal-Mart's takes a straightforward view. It is not interested in activities that increase the cost of merchandise. Costs get passed onto consumers in the form of higher prices and that's contrary to Wal-Mart's marketing strategy.

Loyalty Program (Frequent Buyer Program)

A program that offers consumers a small bonus, such as points or play money, each time they make a purchase; bonus accumulates and can be redeemed for merchandise or some other benefit.

Second Cup
www.secondcup.com

FIGURE **8.14** **Selected Shoppers Drug Mart Customers Receive a Free Sample of the Gillette Mach3 Razor**

Source: Courtesy of Shoppers Drug Mart.

Given these views, marketing organizations must carefully consider the decision to use loyalty programs. In some cases, consumers perceive the "free" reward as a real incentive, but they don't realize they are paying for the privilege. Since loyalty programs add costs, customers may eventually tire of paying more for the goods they buy. The true benefit for the organization is the information it is collecting about customer purchase behaviour. The electronic capture of transaction data that will be mined at a later date is extremely useful as organizations move toward individualized marketing programs. There is no good time to implement a loyalty program—once an organization starts a loyalty program, it is an ongoing program.

Canadian Tire has integrated several promotional offers into an integrated marketing communications campaign. For insight into its campaign, read the IMC Highlight **Canadian Tire Scores Big**.

TRADE PROMOTION EXECUTION

Trade customers are the link between manufacturers and consumers, and in Canada they have incredible control in many markets. In the grocery industry, for example, the combination of two large wholesale/retail operations, Loblaws and Sobeys, controls more than half of all food store sales. In the hardware market, the combination of Canadian Tire and Home Hardware controls a significant portion of volume. Distributors make money by selling your products, but they are also in business to sell anyone's products. Consequently, their loyalty to any supplier can waver if they do not receive the trade promotion offers they feel they deserve.

IMC Highlight

CANADIAN TIRE SCORES BIG

Canadian Tire money... a simple concept. Yet it is the cornerstone of Canadian Tire's marketing mix. According to Eymbert Vaandering, vice-president of marketing at Canadian Tire, "Canadian Tire money is the most successful and popular customer reward program and has a 90 percent redemption and participation level. It is the very heart of what Canadian Tire stands for in today's competitive marketplace."

Canadian Tire recently launched a fully integrated marketing communications campaign called the "Big Spender Giveaway." The campaign was born out of an ad campaign called "Big Spender," which marked the first time that Canadian Tire money was the central focus of advertising. The campaign featured the customers' love of the money and the relationships they have with the company.

Using Canadian tire money as the focal point, the integrated campaign included media advertising, an in-store contest supported by flyers, credit card statement stuffers, point-of-purchase display materials in stores and gas bars, and an online contest.

Canadian Tire money was originally introduced in 1958 to attract customers to the company's new gasoline business and to get more traffic into stores. Today, there is a fully integrated customer rewards program in place that allows the company to leverage a multi-channel approach to increase traffic and loyalty that Canadian Tire money always delivered. By taking an integrated approach to promote the contest, the aim was to use a privileged asset—Canadian Tire money—to leverage the creative equity of the Big Spender TV campaign and to extend the excitement and fun to customers in stores, online, and at gas bars.

The Big Spender contest prize pool featured $250 000 in Canadian Tire money and merchandise prizes. Entry forms were collected at stores or submitted online. There were three grand prizes of $50 000 in Canadian Tire money. The online component featured daily prizes of $1000 in Canadian Tire money and hundreds of draws for prizes.

According to Vaandering, "The focus on Canadian Tire money held tremendous appeal for customers as it is an important aspect of the shopping experience. People love the money because it is simple to use. It can be redeemed anytime, anywhere, on any item." From a marketing perspective, the program allows the company to further differentiate itself and provides immense competitive advantage. It drives traffic to the stores and Canadian Tire's website is one of the top three e-commerce sites in Canada.

For the record, Canadian Tire is the most-shopped retailer in Canada: 90 percent of Canadians shop there, 40 percent shop there weekly. There is a very loyal customer base equally split between males and females. The Canadian Tire brand is one of the top five most-recognized brands in the country.

Adapted from Eymbert Vaandering, "Hey, Big Spender," *Marketing*, January 14, 2002, p. 8.

Simply stated, the trade looks for the best offers and makes buying decisions accordingly. A marketing organization needs them, and they need the marketing organization. As with consumer promotions, trade promotions must be designed to deliver the highest possible value to the trade while costing as little as possible for the manufacturer. A quick example demonstrates how trade promotions work. Someone might question Tide detergent's affiliation with NASCAR events (stock car racing in the United States). American women are not influenced to buy Tide because of such a relationship. However, trade executives at southern U.S. grocery chains found free trips to NASCAR events an incentive to buy more Tide and place it in prominent positions in their stores. That gives the brand a real "push" through the channel.

Manufacturers choose between many trade promotion options when developing trade promotion plans. Typically, the options work together to generate a high degree of impact during the promotion period. This section explores the various trade promotion options.

Trade Allowances

Trade Allowance
A temporary price reduction that encourages larger purchases by distributors.

A **trade allowance** is a temporary price reduction that encourages larger purchases by distributors. It can be offered several ways: a percentage reduction from the list price, a predetermined amount off the list price, or free goods. A free goods offer may be something like "Buy 10 cases and get one free."

In addition to encouraging larger volume purchases, the manufacturer would like to see a portion of the allowance devoted to lowering the price of the product at retail for a short period. In the grocery industry, products are commonly offered on sale for one week. The manufacturer absorbs the discount offered to consumers. Trade allowances can be deducted from the invoice immediately, and in such cases are called *off-invoice allowances*. Or they can be offered on the basis of a *bill-back*, in which case the manufacturer keeps a record of all purchases shipped to the distributor and, when the deal period expires, reimburses the distributor for the allowances it earned.

Performance Allowance

Performance Allowance
A discount offered by a manufacturer that encourages a distributor to perform a merchandising function on behalf of a manufacturer.

A **performance allowance** is a discount that encourages the distributor to perform a merchandising function on behalf of the manufacturer. As indicated above, a trade allowance helps lower prices but additional incentives are required in order to make the promotion a real success. It is common for the manufacturer to request automatic distribution of goods to retail stores, displays in stores, and a mention of the sale price in the retailer's weekly advertising flyer. The additional funds provided in the performance allowance help cover the distributor's costs of implementing these activities. The distributor may or may not comply with all of the requests of the manufacturer, but some kind of deal is negotiated and agreed to. Before paying the allowance, the manufacturer requires proof of performance by the distributor.

Given this information, you can now appreciate that many of the advertising flyers and in-store promotional activities that are undertaken by large retail chain stores are actually subsidized by the manufacturers' brands involved in the promotions. The costs of trade promotions are significant and take a considerable portion of a brand's marketing budget each year.

Cooperative Advertising Allowance

Cooperative Advertising Allowance, or Co-Op
The sharing of advertising costs by suppliers and retailers or by several retailers.

A **cooperative advertising allowance,** or **co-op** as it is commonly referred to as, is a fund allocated to pay for a portion of a distributor's advertising. Marketing organizations often pay a percentage (often 50 percent or more) of the distributor's ad cost, provided the marketer's brand is featured prominently. An example of a co-op campaign that you see frequently is "Intel Inside." By featuring those two words and the logo, the computer manufacturer receives partial funding for its advertising from Intel.

To maximize the effectiveness of allowances offered to the trade, the above allowances are frequently combined in order to develop an integrated promotion plan. If a bigger plan is in place, the trade promotion plan will be integrated with consumer promotions and brand advertising. Combining the allowances is attractive to the retailers. The financial rewards will be much greater and the funds available are sufficient to support their own advertising and merchandising activities. Financial incentives are a great motivator among distributors.

Dealer Premiums

Dealer Premium
An incentive offered to a distributor to encourage the special purchase of a product or to secure additional merchandising support from the distributor.

A **dealer premium** is an incentive offered to a distributor by a manufacturer to encourage the special purchase of a product or to secure additional merchandising support from a retailer. Premiums are usually offered in the form of merchandise and distributed by sales representatives of the company offering the premium. Some common premiums include golfing equipment, cameras, audio equipment, and leisure clothing. The offering of premiums is a controversial issue. Some distributors absolutely forbid their buyers to accept them. They argue that the buyer is the only beneficiary and the buying organization might be purchasing more goods than they really need. Many believe the practice of offering premiums, often referred to as "payola," to buyers is unethical. However, dealings between sellers and buyers sometimes occur under the table.

Spiff
An incentive offered to retail salespeople to encourage them to promote a specified brand of goods to customers.

An offshoot of a premium offer is a **spiff**. Next time you're in a store, ask yourself why did that retail sales representative recommend the Canon camera (or any other popular brand name) to me? It could be that the manufacturer encouraged the sales representative to promote its brand by providing some kind of incentive. The retail sales representative stands to gain if more Canon products are sold. Such a practice is common in product categories where consumers have a tendency to ask for recommendations. In the camera illustration above, the buyer wants a certain type of camera but choosing the brand to buy always presents risk—there are many good brands to choose from. The seller's job is to help eliminate such risk but that may not always happen if spiffs are in play.

Clearly, the use of premiums and spiffs achieves certain marketing objectives. Many companies employ them when they are facing unusual circumstances, such as when trying to meet year-end sales objectives, and it's a touch-and-go situation. Compared to other forms of sales promotion, though, they are not the kinds of activity that will be used with regularity.

Collateral Material

Collateral Material
Visual aids used by sales representatives in sales presentations.

The role of the sales representative cannot be underestimated, particularly in business-to-business selling situations. Companies invest significant sums in programs that tell consumers about their goods and services, but, as indicated above, it is important also to invest in programs that help push the product through the channel. Sales representatives need selling resources, and that's where **collateral material** comes into play. A variety of visual aids that are specific to special promotions or simply ongoing for the variety of products being sold must be available. Collateral materials include price lists, catalogues, sales brochures, pamphlets, specification sheets, product manuals, and audiovisual sales aids.

In the age of electronics, it is now common for much of this material to be available in CD-ROM format or on a company's website. Either medium is capable of communicating lengthy and complex information. Form a buyer's point of view, sales information on a CD can be reviewed at a more leisurely pace and perhaps a more convenient time than during a sales call. Sometimes when a sales representative is selling the goods, the pace can be rapid and there isn't time to really digest the information. Therefore, the use of hard-copy and soft-copy collateral materials is a good combination.

Dealer Display Material

Dealer Display or Point-of-Purchase Material

Advertising or display materials located in a retail environment to build traffic, advertise a product, and encourage impulse purchasing.

As indicated earlier, one of the objectives of trade promotion is to encourage merchandising support from retail distributors. The manufacturer can assist in this area by providing **dealer display material**, or **point-of-purchase material**, as it is often called. Dealer display material includes posters, shelf talkers (mini posters that hang or dangle from store shelves), channel strips (narrow bands that fit into the side of a store shelf), and advertising pads (tear-off sheets that hang from pads attached to shelves). Figure 8.15 illustrates a shelf talker.

Material of a more permanent nature includes display shippers (shipping cases that convert to display stands when opened and erected properly) and permanent display racks. Certain categories of goods often require special shelving to accommodate regular displays of products. For examples, spice bottles are very small, so shelves with wire dividers lock the bottles in place. The spice manufacturer may agree to provide the retailer with special shelves to merchandise its products only.

One of the problems with display material is it frequently goes to waste. In many retail outlets, permission to erect displays must be granted by the store manager and sometimes by the head office of the retailer. Some retailers do not allow manufacturer-supplied

FIGURE **8.15** **A Shelf Talker Creates Awareness for a New Flavour of Oreo Cookies**

Source: Kraft Canada.

display material at all. To be effective, displays must be erected in a visible location. The retailer makes the location decision and it may not be to the liking of the manufacturer. A poor location will diminish the intended impact of the display.

TRADE SHOWS

Trade Show
An event that allows a company to showcase its products to a captive audience and generate leads.

Trade shows are an effective way for a company to introduce new products to the marketplace. There is no better opportunity to showcase something special than at a trade show. Where else will a manufacturer find as many customers, all in one place, actively and willingly seeking product information? All industries seem to have trade shows and in many cases they move around the country to make it more convenient for prospective customers to visit. Depending on the nature of the show, it may attract consumers, trade distributors, or both.

The automobile industry and the recreation and leisure products industry are among the largest users of trade shows. Here, all manufacturers gather to show their latest models (see Figure 8.16). Auto shows are magnets for the media, so they generate all kinds of positive press for the participating companies. From a manufacturer's perspective, a trade show provides an opportunity to develop a prospect list that the sales force can follow up on. When visiting a trade show, customers leave a trail of valuable information about themselves, which can be added quickly to a database for analysis and use later. The very nature of a trade show, however, requires considerable planning by participants along with a considerable financial investment. There is a simple rule of thumb about participating in trade shows: "If you are going to do it, do it right." It's a great opportunity to outshine the competition.

Additional Considerations for Sales Promotion Planning

Sales promotions are not usually the focal point of a brand's marketing communications strategies but, as mentioned above, play a complementary role in achieving certain objectives. Therefore, sales promotions must be carefully planned so they effectively integrate with advertising, public relations, and any other marketing communications plans. Decisions must be made regarding how frequently promotions are offered, what types of promotions will have a positive effect on brand image, and how they will build brand value in the long term. Let's look at each situation briefly.

FREQUENCY OF PROMOTIONS

How frequently should a brand offer sales promotions? All kinds of influencing factors contribute to this decision: the type of product, the activities of the competition, the stage of the brand in the product life cycle, and the receptiveness of customers toward promotions. A theme running throughout this chapter is that promotions are complementary in nature. So they should never disrupt the flow of regular and more dominant communications activities. There is a risk that too many promotions could cheapen the image of a brand. Short-term gain for long-term pain! In general, coupon activity can be implemented more frequently than cash refunds, premium offers, and contests. It is less disruptive to the regular message expressed through media advertising.

BRAND IMAGE AND PROMOTIONS

Much of the discussion about promotion strategies in this chapter mentioned lowering prices so that consumers get a better deal. In the short run, such a strategy brings positive results. However, if this practice becomes frequent, consumers will perceive the sale price to be more of a regular price. In the long term, such a practice will hurt the brand's image and lower profit margins. Domestic automobile manufacturers are facing this dilemma

FIGURE **8.16** Trade Shows Bring the Customer to the Marketer

Source: Canadian National Sportsmen's Shows.

right now. Advertising is so focused on rebates and low financing packages that much less time is devoted to building an image, the former priority of these companies.

The fast food industry is in the midst of a price war that focuses on value-priced menus. Discount fever is sweeping the business and chains are struggling to boost stagnant sales. McDonald's, Burger King, Harvey's, and others are all going head to head to see who can offer the best deal. The discounting has done more harm than good by cutting into profit margins and restraining sales growth. These restaurants have conditioned consumers to expect a deal, when they should have been introducing higher-margin innovative items to boost the amount of the average sale.[19]

Consumers who are continually exposed to low prices may begin to believe a brand is in trouble. They could desert it for another brand. When you consider the psychology of buying, brands are often a personal statement, and people like winning brands.

BUILDING BRAND EQUITY

The cumulative force of all marketing communications is a key factor in building brand equity. Marketers must be aware that sales promotions are a rather chaotic sequence of deals and events that create noise in the marketplace. They are not a sustaining message.

It is preferable to adopt a view about promotions that will pay attention to long-term brand values and a consistent approach that will build good relationships with the trade and consumers. A few of the promotions mentioned in this chapter do just that. Among them are Tim Hortons's "RRRoll Up the Rim," Gillette's "Cavalcade of Sports," and Canadian Tire's reward money. Another famous and successful promotion is Budweiser's "Bud Bowl," a staple promotion that is part of each year's Super Bowl football telecast. Promotions like these become a positive part of the brand's heritage and reinforce relationships with the trade and the consumer.

Summary

Sales promotions are incentives offered to consumers and the trade customers to encourage more immediate and larger purchases. Strategically, consumer promotions are designed to help pull a product through the channel of distribution, while trade promotions help push a product through the channel of distribution. A good sales promotion plan usually balances between pull and push.

Sales promotion planning involves a series of steps or decisions. After an assessment of the situation is made, specific objectives and strategies are established and the appropriate offers or incentives are determined. The plan must also consider fulfillment obligations at the back end, and a means of assessing the effectiveness of the plan must be in place.

A key to a successful sales promotion plan lies in how it is integrated with other marketing communications strategies. For certain, sales promotion strategies must be integrated with advertising strategies. Because sales promotions are short term in nature, they often become the focus of the advertising message while the promotion is in place. When the overall plan is implemented, advertising creates awareness for the promotion while in-store displays and websites provide additional details.

Some specific objectives of consumer promotions are to achieve trial purchase by new users and to achieve repeat and multiple purchases by current users. The types of activities commonly used to achieve these objectives include coupons, free samples, contests, rebates, premium offers, and loyalty programs.

Specific marketing objectives of trade promotions are to secure new listings and distribution, build volume on a preplanned cyclical basis, and encourage merchandising support at point-of-purchase. Trade promotion activities that help achieve these objectives include trade allowances, performance allowances, cooperative advertising funds, dealer premiums, point-of-purchase display materials, collateral materials, and trade shows.

The impact of sales promotions are short term in nature and therefore complement other integrated marketing communications strategies. As such, sales promotions should not disrupt regular brand advertising. They must be integrated into advertising strategies to enhance the overall impact on consumers and trade customers. When planning promotions, a manger should guard against running them too frequently so as to not harm the image of the brand. A good sales promotion concept will fit with the brand's image and help build brand equity.

Key Terms

bonus pack   234

collateral material   239

consumer promotion   213

contest   228

co-op   238

cooperative advertising allowance   238

coupon   225

cross-coupon   226

cross-ruff   226

dealer display material   240

dealer premium   239

experiential marketing   228

free sample   227

freestanding insert (FSI)   225

frequent buyer program   235

game   229–230

Review Questions

1. What is the difference between a pull strategy and a push strategy, and how do sales promotions complement both strategies?

2. What are the primary objectives of a consumer promotion plan?

3. What are the primary objectives of a trade promotion plan?

4. Briefly explain how sales promotion strategies are integrated with advertising strategies. Why is such integration essential?

5. In sales promotion planning, what is meant by logistics and fulfillment?

6. Briefly describe the following consumer promotion terms:
   a) redemption rate
   b) in-pack self-coupon
   c) cross-ruff
   d) on-site sampling
   e) instant-win promotion
   f) slippage
   g) bonus pack

7. What types of coupon distribution are appropriate for the early stages of the product life cycle? What distribution is appropriate for the later stages? Why?

8. What are the benefits and drawbacks of a free sample offer?

9. What elements contribute to the success of a contest offer?

10. What is the objective of a consumer premium offer and when is the best time to implement such an offer?

11. What are the benefits and drawbacks of loyalty promotions?

12. How do trade allowances, performance allowances, and cooperative advertising funds complement each other when implementing a trade promotion plan?

13. Briefly describe the following trade promotion terms:
    a) spiff
    b) dealer premium
    c) collateral material
    d) point-of-purchase material

Discussion and Application Questions

1. Assume you are a brand manager launching a new snack food or confectionary product. What balance would you recommend among consumer promotion, trade promotion, and media advertising? What specific sales promotion activities would you recommend? Justify your choices.

2. Conduct some secondary research on consumer and trade promotion budgets and spending patterns in various industries. Is there undue pressure placed on

marketing organizations to spend more on trade promotions and less on other activities? Does the situation vary from one industry to another?

3. A common criticism of consumer premium offers is that they only encourage temporary brand switching. Once the offer is over, consumers switch back to their regular brand. Therefore, in the long run, the promotion will not contribute to sales objectives. Conduct some secondary research on

this issue and determine if such a criticism is valid.

4. This chapter suggests that consumers could be suffering from "loyalty promotion fatigue." Conduct some secondary research on loyalty promotions to find out how organizations view loyalty promotions. Do loyalty promotions provide real benefits to consumers and the sponsor? What are the elements that make a loyalty promotion a success?

5. What forms of sales promotion are best suited for the following brands? (Hint: you may want to consider the life cycle stage the brand is in). Justify your position.
   a) Secret deodorant
   b) Quaker Chewy Granola Bars
   c) Goodyear tires (replacement tires)
   d) Valvoline motor oil
   e) Hewlett Packard laser printer
   f) New Balance running shoes

6. Evaluate the sales promotion strategies employed by Canadian Tire. What marketing and marketing communications objectives do they meet? How effective are the programs? How does Canadian Tire integrate sales promotions with other components of its marketing communications plan?

7. Evaluate the sales promotion strategies used by Tim Hortons. What marketing and marketing communications objectives do they meet? How does Tim Hortons integrate sales promotions with other components of the marketing communications mix?

8. It was stated in the chapter that Lady Speed Stick Clean Glide antiperspirant had success with on-site sampling. Conduct some secondary research to determine the effectiveness of on-site sampling or experiential marketing. Do you think this form of sales promotion will become more popular in the future? Justify your position.

9. Automobile manufacturers have used rebate programs for years to provide consumers with an incentive to buy (and buy now!). Is this an effective sales promotion strategy? Conduct some secondary research on rebate incentives and develop some kind of cost benefit analysis for using this form of promotion.

End Notes

1. "Promotional Offers Can Do More to Bolster Image," *Marketing*, February 24, 1986, p. 10.
2. Wayne Mouland, "General Information on the Coupon Industry in Canada," *NCH Promotional Services*, May 2001.
3. Wayne Mouland, "General Information on the Coupon Industry 1997–2002," *NCH Promotional Services*, March 2003.
4. Leslie Young, "Save.ca Looks for High Redemption," *Marketing*, October 30, 2000, p. 3.
5. News Line, Gillette Canada, *Marketing*, October 21, 2002, p. 3.
6. Geoff Dennis, "Sampling Growth Spurs Creativity," *Strategy*, May 20, 2002, pp. 1, 10.
7. Ibid.
8. "A Special Presentation on Coupon Promotion Fundamentals," *NCH Promotional Services*, 1998.
9. Wendy Cuthbert, "Gillette Scores with Cavalcade of Sports," *Strategy*, May 22, 2000, pp. 21, 23.
10. Laura Pratt, "Roll Up the Rim Major Player for Tim Hortons," *Strategy*, May 22, 2000, p. 22.
11. Terry Poulton, "A Winner Every Time," *Strategy*, August 26, 2002, p. 19.
12. Sandy Brown, "Maxwell House Sweeps Beats 30-year Entry Level," *Strategy*, March 12, 2001, pp. 8, 9.
13. "A Marketer's Guide to Promotion," *NCH Promotional Services*, 1996, p. 4.
14. Paul Brent, "Car Sales Keep Soaring on Incentives," *Financial Post*, August 2, 2002, p. FP5.
15. Lucy Saddleton, "Extending the High," *Strategy*, May 20, 2002, p. B11.
16. Ibid., p. B12.
17. Michelle Halpern, "Labatt's Big Promo! Score," *Marketing*, October 6/13, 2003, p. 28.
18. John Heinzl, "You May Be Loyal, But It's Costing You," *Globe and Mail*, January 31, 2003, p. B8.
19. John Heinzl, "Fast-Food Discounting Hard to Swallow," *Globe and Mail*, February 27, 2003, pp. B1, B4.

9

PUBLIC RELATIONS

After studying this chapter you will be able to:

identify and assess the various roles of public relations communications in achieving marketing and business objectives,

describe the various steps in public relations planning,

identify and evaluate various public relations execution techniques for potential application in public relations plans, and

identify and assess the various evaluation and measurement techniques that determine the effectiveness of public relations strategies.

Public relations are an often misunderstood form of marketing communications. The term often conjures up negative images of a company trying to cover something up or trying to put its own spin on a situation. Certainly, with all the news coverage that companies receive when they are in trouble, there is some truth to such perceptions, but public relations can have a very positive impact on a brand or company's performance, and are responsible for communicating all kinds of positive information.

The theme of this book deals with how messages from various disciplines in communications are integrated and how, whatever the discipline, all must work together to give the consumer a unified message. In that regard, public relations play a key role today. For example, many companies are questioning the value of so much spending on television advertising. Technology such as TiVo and Replay (video equipment that automatically eliminates commercials) is forcing marketers to rely more on product placements within TV shows to get across brand awareness. If this trend continues, other traditional forms of public relations will be left to explain what the product is all about. The future is bright for integrating public relations strategies into the marketing communications mix.

In the age of hyper-competition and advancing electronic technology, marketers are looking for multiple solutions to brand building. This position further suggests the need for the integration of various forms of marketing communications. To rely too much on any one medium or channel of marketing communications could be harmful. This chapter will show how public relations play a role in creating brand awareness and building relationships with customers.

Defining Public Relations

Public Relations

A form of communications designed to gain public understanding and acceptance.

Public relations are a form of communication that is primarily directed toward gaining public understanding and acceptance. Unlike advertising, which is a form of communication paid for by the company, public relations use publicity that does not necessarily involve payment. Public relations communications appear in the news media and, as such, offer a legitimacy that advertising does not have. Recently, public relations have been used to extol the merits of a company's products by assisting in new product launches or reporting eventful occurrences of the product.

Internal Publics

The publics with which an organization communicates regularly; can include employees, distributors, suppliers, shareholders, and customers.

External Publics

Those publics that are distant from an organization and are communicated with less frequently.

The practice of public relations is used to build rapport with the various publics a company, individual, or organization may have. These publics are either internal or external. **Internal publics** involve those with whom the organization communicates regularly and include employers, distributors, suppliers, shareholders, and regular customers. **External publics** are more distant and are communicated with less frequently. They include the media, governments, prospective shareholders, the financial community, and community organizations. The goal of public relations is to conduct communications in such a way that an organization builds an open, honest, and constructive relationship with its various publics. In comparison to advertising once again, public relations communications are not controlled by the organization. Instead, the media determine what is said about the company regardless of what information the company provides. In other words, the media act as a "filter" for the information an organization releases.

The Role of Public Relations

The role of public relations is varied but generally falls into six key categories: corporate communications, reputation management, publicity generation, product placement and seeding, community relations and public affairs, and fundraising. The diversity of this list indicates how public relations can be company-oriented or product-oriented. Let's examine each category in more detail.

CORPORATE COMMUNICATIONS

Corporate Advertising
Advertising designed to convey a favourable image of a company among its various publics.

Advocacy Advertising
A form of advertising paid for by a sponsor that promotes a particular view on a recognized, controversial issue.

An organization that believes in the benefits of public relations communications will take positive and constructive action to disseminate useful information about itself. Such communications may be in the form of **corporate advertising**: advertising designed to convey a favourable image of a company among its various publics. It can do so by showing how the resources of the organization resolve customers' problems, by promoting goodwill, or by demonstrating a sense of social responsibility. For example, Shell Canada shows how it integrates economic progress with environmental issues, often a delicate challenge for a company in the oil exploration business (see Figure 9.1). This advertisement is an example of social responsibility marketing and reflects an attitude of corporate conscience that anticipates and responds to social problems.

A company can also be active in the area of issue management. In such cases, the company delivers messages to the public to show where it stands on a particular issue, usually an issue that is important to its various publics. The Shell example shows a proactive stance on protecting the environment. An alternative is **advocacy advertising**, a

FIGURE **9.1** An Illustration of Corporate Responsibility: Shell Canada Promotes Economic Progress and Concern for the Environment

NOT ALL THE EXPERTS WE LISTEN TO ARE EXPERTS, YET.

Last year, university student Meherzad Romer had the summer job of his dreams. As one of the inaugural Shell Conservation Interns, he participated in the stewardship of some of Canada's most fragile and endangered landscapes.

Meherzad and 15 other interns worked to maintain and safeguard some of the properties protected by the Nature Conservancy of Canada (NCC). Working on-site, the Shell Conservation Interns increased the ecological value of these important natural habitats by enhancing and preserving biodiversity. At the same time, they gained relevant experience in their chosen fields.

At the end of the summer, the interns had the opportunity to meet with top management at Shell to share the results of their work. Together, they discussed priorities for nature conservation in Canada and the importance of continued efforts.

The NCC and Shell Canada partnership spans more than two decades. Jointly, they have completed land conservation projects across Canada, spanning thousands of hectares. Since the inception of this partnership, Shell has donated more than $3.5 million in financial resources, volunteer support and land and mineral rights. NCC, Shell Canada and tomorrow's ecological experts: a natural partnership.

For more information, visit Shell Canada's web site at shell.ca.

Profits. Principles. Or both?

Source: J. W. Thompson, Toronto. Reprinted by permission of Shell Canada Limited.

form of communication paid for by the sponsor that presents information or a point of view on a publicly recognized, controversial issue. The organization's objective is to influence public opinion, encourage others to support the cause or issue, and possibly take action to correct the problem, if that is the case. An illustration of advocacy advertising appears in Figure 9.2.

FIGURE **9.2** **An Illustration of Advocacy Advertising: Shell Canada Works toward Finding Environmental Solutions**

HELPING CANADIANS
Turn Good Ideas into Action

Shell Canada congratulates all of the Canadian Environment Awards 2003 nominees. We salute your dedication and hard work towards the preservation or renewal of the environment.

Shell is pleased to participate as a sponsor of the awards for a second year. This awards program is a celebration of Canadian groups and individuals that are passionate about taking care of our environment.

We believe that individuals, communities and businesses have the power to bring about change. Finding solutions to today's environmental challenges takes the commitment and ideas of all Canadians.

For our part, we at Shell will continue to incorporate the principles of sustainable development into how we think and what we do. We must integrate economic, environmental and social priorities in our business decisions. We must listen, not only to our shareholders, but also to our customers, neighbours, employees and all those influenced by our business.

Together we can turn good ideas into action.

Tim Faithfull
President and CEO
Shell Canada Limited

Thirteen years ago, Shell created the Shell Environmental Fund to help individuals and groups make a positive contribution to our environment. For more information about the Shell Environmental Fund visit www.shell.ca/sef

Source: Céline Parisien/*Canadian Geographic*. Reprinted by permission of Shell Canada Limited.

REPUTATION MANAGEMENT

Chances are that a company in the headlines is there for all the wrong reasons. Something went wrong and key executives are being called upon to defend the company's position. Public relations play a vital role when a company finds itself in a crisis situation, because the final outcome often depends on how effectively an organization manages its communications during the crisis.

In April 2003, the City of Toronto found itself in a crisis situation, because the out-break of SARS (sudden acute respiratory syndrome) led to the World Health Organization advising travellers to avoid Toronto. Public officials representing the city, the province, and the country felt the blacklisting was unfair, even though people were dying at an alarming rate (23 deaths in Ontario by the end of April). As communications challenges go, how do officials persuade tourists and business people it's safe to visit Toronto at a time when medical and other health officials were struggling to contain the SARS virus?

With the high tourist season fast approaching, quick action had to be taken by Toronto. In such cases, rapid and positive action is vital. A group known as the Toronto Tourism Industry Community Coalition was established to develop a marketing campaign to rebuild Toronto's image locally, nationally, and internationally. The coalition was composed of stakeholders in the travel and tourism business along with elected city officials.[1] The coali-tion called upon all levels of government to contribute to the campaign. The first step was to lobby the World Health Organization aggressively in order to lift the travel ban, and there was compelling statistical evidence to suggest the SARS outbreak was under control. Once the ban was lifted a week after it was announced, an advertising campaign was launched to assure people the city was safe and open for business. A massive print campaign supported by a coalition of Toronto hotels, restaurants, sports and entertainment venues was implemented immediately. As well, pertinent information was released to the media to generate positive news stories, which also played a key role in rebuilding Toronto's image.

In such a situation, it is important for organizations to be prepared. Having a plan in place to meet disaster head on makes more sense than simply reacting to an unforeseen circumstance. To illustrate, consider the highly publicized case involving Bridgestone/Firestone tires. Bridgestone did not handle the situation effectively. It mis-handled concerns about tire safety by not addressing the public's questions and concerns soon enough. The tires were linked to more than 200 deaths, and as many as 6.5 million tires were eventually recalled. Bridgestone/Firestone acted only after being warned by the U.S. government. The public questions the moral values of such a company and demon-strates its anger by not buying its products.

Being prepared, thus, is clearly essential. Senior executives must be ready to act instant-ly and demonstrate they are in control of the situation. All messages sent to the public must be credible and based on fact from the outset. Company executives must be ready to meet the demand of a more sophisticated and more demanding consumer audience, or suffer the consequences of its wrath.

PRODUCT PUBLICITY

Publicity

News about an organiz-ation, product, service, or person that appears in the media.

Publicity is news about an organization, product, service, or person that appears in the media. There is often a tendency for people to confuse publicity and public relations, thinking they are one and the same. Publicity is but one aspect of many public relations activities. Essentially, publicity is something that a company, and the media, deem to be newsworthy. Most of the time, the media don't see things the same way as a company does. Big news for a company is not necessarily big news for the media. One of the major opportunities for a product or company to generate positive publicity is during a new product launch. To illustrate, consider that Botox achieved US$300 million in sales in its first year without any advertising. The brand relied solely on public relations and publicity to get the message out. In its second year, a US$50 million advertising campaign was launched in order to create primary demand for the product and explain the product's benefits in more detail. The same communications strategies were employed when Viagra was introduced.[2] The rush to Viagra was fuelled by massive media coverage. A previously taboo subject (erectile dysfunction) was now being discussed openly on prime-time television. A subsequent advertising campaign encouraged men to ask their doctor for more information. One such campaign included famous hockey player Guy Lafleur speaking about erectile difficulties.[3]

These examples seem to indicate that public relations in the past have been undervalued. Public relations and advertising have been traditionally treated as separate disciplines running along similar tracks. Only recently have the two been integrated so that their full potential can be exploited. Perhaps the current reality of advertising clutter enhances the opportunity for public relations to break through the clutter by placing effective messages in newspapers, on news broadcasts or shows, and on websites. Jeanne Milne, owner of the Calgary-based store The Art of Hardware, believes fully in the power of publicity. Her store was featured in such media as HGTV's program *House and Home* and in full-colour spreads in the *Calgary Herald*. Says Milne, "The sales impact was immediate and noticeable. As soon as the stories hit the press, we were all hands on deck in the store. The media coverage is far more effective than any ad you could place anywhere."[4]

PRODUCT PLACEMENT AND PRODUCT SEEDING

Product Placement or Branded Content

The visible placement of brand name products in television shows, movies, radio, video game, and other programming.

Product Placement
www.productplacement.biz

Product placement, or **branded content**, is the insertion of a branded product into a show, movie, video game, or other programming. Changing technology is one reason why product placement is growing in popularity. Since the introduction of the remote control device, television viewers have been compelled to watch numerous shows simultaneously; essentially, the viewer does whatever possible to avoid commercials. More recently, the TiVo recording device allows for commercials to be removed entirely. Marketers are fighting back!

Ironically, product placement was a popular strategy in the early days of television, as several cigarette companies would have their brands included in shows. The theory behind placement is simple: a product featured in a TV show or movie, as opposed to a 30-second spot, will have more credibility with viewers and have a better chance of being noticed and remembered. To illustrate, consider that *The Best Damn Sports Show Period*, a Fox Network program, shows the cast enjoying meals provided by KFC and Outback Steakhouse, relaxing on a deck finished by Home Depot, and sitting in a bar advertising Labatt USA's brands. Movies have become saturated with product pitches. The James Bond film *Die Another Day*, starring Pierce Brosnan, showcases brands such as Aston Martin, Ford, Sony, and Heineken, and *Minority Report*, starring Tom Cruise, plugged the Gap, Burger King, and American Express.[5] Even popular reality-based TV shows such as *Survivor* are in on the action. *Survivor* features brands such as Reebok, Mountain Dew, Budweiser, and Doritos. So much for roughing it in the wilderness.

Product placement has expanded opportunities for integration with other forms of marketing communications, particularly advertising campaigns and sales promotions. For more insight into the phenomenon of product placement, refer to the IMC Highlight **Marketers on the Bond Wagon**.

Product Seeding or Buzz Marketing

Giving a product free to a group of trendsetters who promote the product to others by word of mouth.

Product seeding is different from product placement in that the product is given free to a group of trendsetters who, in turn, influence others to become aware of the product and, one hopes, purchase the product. While the product is in the hands of the trendsetters, they are creating "buzz" for the product, by chatting it up whenever and wherever they can. For this reason, product seeding is often referred to as **buzz marketing**.

To illustrate, consider what Reebok did when it launched the new U-Shuffle DMX shoe for women. The shoe is a laceless black and red sneaker, a trendy style. The company gave

MARKETERS ON THE BOND WAGON

Is product placement a good strategy or a bad strategy? If consumers are tired of excessive advertising on television, will they soon object to the blatant placement of branded products in television shows and movies? Will marketers take product placement a step too far? Thus far, the answer is no!

In the product placement business, nobody does it better than James Bond movies, and the popularity of these movies attracts an upscale list of advertisers. Take, for example, the most recent Bond film, *Die Another Day*. There was a Samsonite suitcase, an Omega wristwatch, a Philips heart rate monitor, Bollinger champagne, a Norelco shaver, Heineken beer, a Sony security camera, an Ericsson cellphone, a British Airways jet, and several Bombardier Ski-Doos. And of course there were cars: a $228 000 Aston Martin Vanquish driven by Bond and the Ford Thunderbird driven by co-star and arch enemy Halle Barry.

This and other Bond films have taken product placement to new limits. In total there were 24 promotional partners worldwide that spent $120 million on marketing campaigns tied to the film. Not all companies pay directly for product exposure. Some agree to promote the film in their own advertising campaigns in exchange for seeing their product in the movie. Philips, for example, whose razor makes only a brief appearance in the movie, launched a global Bond-themed ad campaign for the new Norelco XL Spectra James Bond shaver.

With so many companies wanting a piece of the action, will product placement become a victim of its own success? Because so much of it is out there, the technique may become uninteresting, if not annoying. According to Gary Ruskin, executive director of Commercial Alert, "This is the way movie producers are going. People don't pay $10 to see a movie and then get hammered with ads. It's disrespectful to moviegoers." Producers use the money to defray rising production costs, but one has to wonder how many additional scenes were produced and included in *Die Another Day* simply to plug a product.

In television, reality-based shows such as *Survivor* and *American Idol* also employ product placement. In *Survivor*, CBS struck a deal with Pontiac Aztek as part of an exclusive agreement for the automaker. The price tag for Pontiac was $12 million. Product placement pacts can take many shapes. Some are rewards for extensive media buys (such as the CBS case), while others have a separate price tag with the television production company of up to $1 million for a reality series. Others cost as much as $50 000 per episode, with the producer guaranteeing between one and three visuals per episode. Coca-Cola and Ford have product placement deals with *American Idol*. Beverage cups with the Coke logo sit in front of the judges, the green room was renamed the Coca-Cola Red Room, and taped segments are called "Coca-Cola Moments."

Placing products in TV shows and movies is a direct response to technology that makes life more comfortable for the couch potato and less so for the advertisers. The remote control device spawned zipping, zapping, and muting of commercials. With personal video recorders, the viewer can skip the commercials all together. Product placement is one way around these problems.

Despite the increased usage of product placement, there is little consensus among marketing executives on whether the technique has any measurable effect on sales. By measuring how long a product is on the air, and its context within the program, a rough estimate of impact can be determined, but it's very difficult to get an exact rating.

Adapted from Kate Fitzgerald, "Growing Pains for Placements," *Advertising Age*, February 3, 2003, p. S2; John Heinzl, "The Spy Who Endorsed Me," *Globe and Mail*, November 22, 2002, p. B7; Wayne Friedman, "Product Integrators Tackle Learning Curve," *Advertising Age*, October 21, 2002, p. 18; and Katherine Macklem, "Ready for Your Close-Up, Pepsi," *Maclean's*, August 12, 2002, p. 34.

90 young women from across Canada a free pair ($150 value) and asked them to wear them around town. These trendsetters would influence others to buy the shoe. And it worked. The trendsetters were asked all kinds of questions, including where could they be purchased.[6]

Product seeding offers several advantages. First, it is a low-cost strategy that is nowhere near the cost of an advertising campaign. Second, it can reach a narrowly defined target. In the case of Reebok, it was targeting young adult women and screened 1000 women to select the right 90 people for the seeding. If seeding works, it will attract the attention of the media, and the next thing you know, there is a complete story about it in the newspaper or on a news broadcast. Now that's good public relations!

COMMUNITY RELATIONS AND PUBLIC AFFAIRS

Companies today are operating in an environment where social responsibility is very important. Consequently, they place much higher value on programs that foster a good public image in the communities where they operate. Sponsoring community events, local groups, and sports teams is part of being a good corporate citizen. The effect of such an investment on sales is indirect and long term in nature. Very often, being part of the fabric of a community takes precedence over sales. Leaders of companies that place a high value on public relations will tell you that the public has to "like you before they will buy you." Tim Hortons is a good example of a community-minded company. It supplies sports jerseys to local hockey and soccer teams through its Timbits program, offers free ice skating in local communities during the Christmas break, and sends thousands of needy children to camps each summer through the Tim Hortons's Children's Foundation (see Figure 9.3).[7]

Lobbying

Activities and practices designed to influence policy decisions that will affect an organization or all organizations in a particular industry.

Public affairs involve strategies to deal with governments and to communicate with governments. **Lobbying** involves activities and practices designed to influence policy decisions that will affect an organization or all organizations within a particular industry. It is very common for a national association to represent the interests of industry members. Naturally, a company or association wants government policy to conform to what's best for business. For example, the Packaging Association of Canada (PAC) has advocated successfully in all areas of government packaging policy and regulation—from the *Consumer Packaging and Labelling Act*, to the National Packaging Protocol and the North American Free Trade Agreement. The PAC is the focal point for action on environmental packaging initiatives and competitive measures for Canadian packagers.[8]

Greenpeace
www.greenpeace.org

Independently funded organizations such as Greenpeace actively lobby governments to ensure industry maintains environmental standards. Recently, Greenpeace has been active trying to ensure that Fortune 500 companies support the Kyoto Protocol (an issue dealing with the long-term effects of climate change largely caused by industry practices). Many leading companies, including oil exploration companies and automobile manufacturers, do not support the Protocol and lobby the government from a different angle. The lobbying and counter-lobbying help shape national government policy on such issues. When making policy decisions, governments must balance economic well-being with social and environmental well-being, and therein lies the conflict for government, business, and special interest groups.

FUNDRAISING

In the not-for-profit sector, public relations play a key role in fundraising. National organizations such as the Canadian Cancer Society, the Canadian Heart and Stroke Foundation, and the United Way face huge financial challenges each year. For these and similar organizations, public relations help educate the public about how funds are used. The message is designed to predispose people to give, to solicit commitment, and to make people feel good about giving. The overall goal of such campaigns is to create a positive image and secure support by sending a message that clearly states what the organization is all about. Such campaigns use a variety of techniques to deliver the message. Media strategies include direct mail, telemarketing, print advertising (outdoor, newspaper, and magazines), and websites (see Figure 9.4).

Public Relations Planning

As a component of the integrated marketing communications mix, public relations plans are designed to fit directly with the needs of the organization's marketing objectives. They can be active (help support a brand or company positively) or reactive (help out in a crisis situation). Regardless of the situation, as already stated, a plan must be in place.

FIGURE **9.3** Public Relations Is Key to Building Community Relationships and Enhancing a Company's Image in the Community

Source: Courtesy of Morgan MacLean.

As with advertising, a good public relations plan can help build an image and assist in developing relationships with customers. Furthermore, a well-timed public relations plan can play a key role in the launch of a new product, especially in times when budget resources are scarce. Advertising is a very expensive endeavour; public relations is much more economical. In companies searching for greater effectiveness at lower cost, public relations look like a better option than advertising, or, at the very least, the two disciplines must work effectively together to achieve objectives efficiently.

FIGURE **9.4** Public Relations Communications Play a Key Role in Fundraising Campaigns

"The Salvation Army gave me back my life. And my dignity."
—Bonnie G., Former Prostitute and Heroin Addict

Behind Bonnie's middle class upbringing, was a childhood damaged by sexual abuse. In her teens, she slid into prostitution and the numbing effects of heroin. Then a Salvation Army Community worker found her. Gradually, she was weaned off the drugs and the street scene. For the first time, she began to think that her life might actually be worth something. Looking back at that time, Bonnie says, "I was a broken, broken soul". Today Bonnie has not only pulled her own life together, she is helping others do the same, as a Salvation Army Community Worker. And while not every story ends this happily, The Salvation Army is saving lives in communities across Canada every single day. But we need your help. Please give what you can afford. And Get Behind The Shield.

Please give from your heart to The Salvation Army Red Shield Appeal.

To donate call: 1 888 321 3433 SalvationArmy.ca

GET BEHIND THE SHIELD

Source: ACLC Advertising Actor/model: Ana V. Flanders, The Byron Agency.

Based on the discussion presented so far in this chapter, it is very apparent that the planning of public relations communications is best left to specialists. It is not an area of expertise in most organizations, though many have a senior ranking officer assigned the responsibility. Typically, the in-house public relations specialist is a liaison with outside agencies that prepare and implement public relations plans. If there is an in-house public relations department, its responsibilities might focus on public affairs and community relations. For the preparation and implementation of corporate and product public relations plans, there is a tendency to hire an organization that specializes in these areas. Hill and Knowlton and National Public Relations are examples of leading public relations agencies in Canada. The specialist is briefed by the organization on its needs and expectations. Then, the specialist assesses the information and prepares a strategic plan that will meet the client's objectives. Figure 9.5 illustrates the public relations planning process. Let's discuss each stage of the planning process.

GOALS AND OBJECTIVES

Public relations objectives typically involve creating awareness, shaping attitudes, and altering behaviour. As marketing campaigns become more integrated and seamless, the ability both to quantify and to measure objectives becomes more difficult. On the surface,

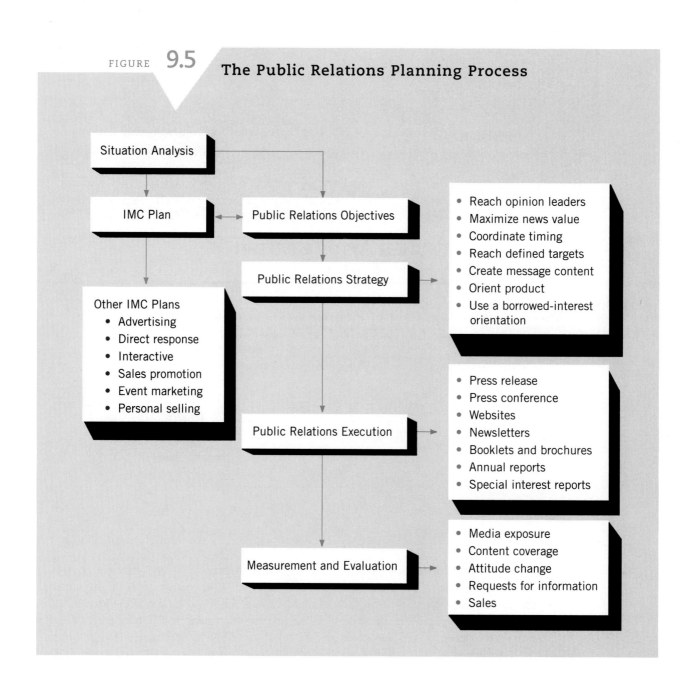

FIGURE 9.5 **The Public Relations Planning Process**

Situation Analysis

IMC Plan ⟷ Public Relations Objectives

Public Relations Strategy
- Reach opinion leaders
- Maximize news value
- Coordinate timing
- Reach defined targets
- Create message content
- Orient product
- Use a borrowed-interest orientation

Other IMC Plans
- Advertising
- Direct response
- Interactive
- Sales promotion
- Event marketing
- Personal selling

Public Relations Execution
- Press release
- Press conference
- Websites
- Newsletters
- Booklets and brochures
- Annual reports
- Special interest reports

Measurement and Evaluation
- Media exposure
- Content coverage
- Attitude change
- Requests for information
- Sales

public relations objectives are very similar to advertising objectives. Therefore, to try to distinguish between the two is difficult. Increased awareness and predisposition to buy are influenced by numerous factors well beyond the scope of public relations, so trying to evaluate public relations in terms of sales and increased market share is next to impossible.

What can be measured, however, is the level of publicity generated by a public relations plan. Typically, the goal of public relations is to achieve media exposure, so quantifiable objectives can be established in this area. Publicity objectives should consider the media through which the message will be communicated and consider the target audience reached by the media. Surprisingly, even very targeted public relations plans can catch the attention of the national media, because good stories, no matter where they come from, are good stories on national news broadcasts, in national newspapers, and in general interest magazines.

Media exposure can be measured in terms of **_gross impressions_**, the number of times an item was potentially seen. If a news story appears in a large-circulation newspaper, what is the circulation or readership (circulation multiplied by the readers per copy) of that newspaper? An objective could be stated in terms of impressions. For example, the objective is to achieve 10 million gross impressions nationally in Canadian daily newspapers.

Another objective could entail matching the message with the appropriate medium. To illustrate, assume you are doing a campaign for TaylorMade golf clubs and the nature of the message deals with how your clubs add distance to the average swing. The objective would be to reach golfers in a medium they refer to frequently. Some options include the Golf Channel and _Golf Digest_ as well as a host of other golf-related publications. Reaching your audience in highly targeted media offers several benefits: the message will be read or seen by influencers who will create a word-of-mouth network, and the message could influence the editorial agenda of the publication or station. The media are constantly looking for new and innovative ideas to promote. If they don't find you, you have to find them. Figure 9.6 is an example of a press release announcing improvements in TaylorMade's R360 XD driver. Even subtle improvements such as these can be big news to golfers. Golf magazines and a variety of golf show on the Golf Channel report on stories like this.

PUBLIC RELATIONS STRATEGY

Every form of marketing communications has its strengths and weaknesses. With public relations, the company cannot control the media or dictate the manner in which the message is communicated. Getting past the media gatekeepers is the first challenge; the second challenge is ensuring the message is communicated with reasonable accuracy. On the positive side, public relations messages provide enhanced credibility. When the consumer reads a story in a newspaper or hears and sees something positive on a news broadcast about a product or company, it is much more authentic than an advertisement.

The role of public relations is determined in advance and is outlined in the marketing communications plan. Typically, that role is to reach influential individuals such as industry analysts, key media representatives, and early adopters of products (refer back to discussion about product seeding).

The strategic role of public relations should be examined based on how best to

- reach the opinion leaders, including professionals, industry analysts, trade audiences, and media, well in advance of the public.
- maximize the news value of new product introductions, new advertising campaigns, and event sponsorships. Messages must be written creatively and visuals must grab attention.
- time public relations events to reinforce advertising and promotion campaigns and to maintain visibility between campaigns.
- reach markets that are defined by demographics, psychographics, or geographic location that might not be targeted by advertising.[9]

FIGURE **9.6** **A Press Release That Presents a Brand Favourably to the Media**

THE BEST PERFORMANCE GOLF BRAND IN THE WORLD.

To download high-resolution visuals of the R360 XD driver,
please go to http://www.tmag.com/media
(please use the password provided to you by the TMaG PR department.)

TaylorMade Introduces R360 XD Titanium Driver

CARLSBAD, Calif. (May 27, 2003) – TaylorMade Golf has introduced the R360 XD titanium driver, a new and improved version of TaylorMade's popular 360 Ti driver. Designed with distance in mind, the R360 XD driver features:

- TaylorMade's Pull-Face, titanium construction, which allows for a strong-walled clubhead and thin-yet-strong clubface.
- An expansive, 360cc clubhead that boasts a high MOI for greater stability and less twisting on off-center hits.
- A clubface engineered thicker and thinner in strategic areas, resulting in a larger COR zone (the part of the clubface that delivers high coefficient of restitution), meaning that even off-center hits can go far.
- Precision-placed center of gravity (CG) that fuels a high, long-carrying trajectory.
- XD-60 Extra Distance graphite shaft that weighs just 60 grams and which features a soft tip that helps launch the ball into the air.

"Fans of the TaylorMade 360 driver will flip over the new R360 XD," says Sean Toulon, vice president, global product and brand creation. "The XD stands for extra distance, and is a nod to the improved launch conditions that the R360 XD was designed to deliver, which can result in added yardage."

The R360 XD comes equipped with a TM Crossline non-cord grip and is available in S, R and M flexes; and in right-handed lofts of 8.5°, 9.5° and 10.5°, and left-handed lofts of 9.5° and 10.5°. Manufacturer's suggested retail price is $299.

About TaylorMade Golf Company, Inc. dba TaylorMade-adidas Golf Company
TaylorMade Golf has led the golf industry's technological evolution since being founded in 1979. In 1998 the company joined with adidas Golf, becoming a wholly owned subsidiary of adidas-Salomon AG. Dedicated to being the best performance golf company in the world, consumers can find more information on TaylorMade-adidas Golf at (800) 888-CLUB or www.tmag.com , www.taylormadegolf.com , www.adidasgolf.com , www.maxfli.com or www.rossaputters.com.

For more information contact:
TaylorMade-adidas Golf
John Steinbach
Tel: 760.918.6330
eMail: john.steinbach@tmag.com

| 5545 fermi court   carlsbad   california   92008 | phone   760.918.6000   fax   760.918.6014 | |
| www.taylormadegolf.com | www.adidasgolf.com | |

© 2003 Taylor Made Golf Co., Inc. All Rights Reserved
Legal | Privacy

Source: Taylor Made.

A public relations strategy allows an organization to tell a longer story about itself and its products. Strategy deals more with informing and educating, rather than motivating someone to buy something. Therefore, when claims are made about a product, proper substantiation should be provided. Unlike advertising, where time and space are often restricted, public relations communications can spend additional time expanding on something of importance. News editors might edit the length of the story, but they will strive to maintain the credibility of the message. Should an organization not have anything newsworthy to say directly about a product, another opportunity is to develop a **borrowed-interest strategy**. A borrowed-interest strategy will typically promote a marketing activity that is related to the product. Perhaps a new sales promotion offer is about to be announced or the product (or company) is about to become involved sponsoring a major event. An Olympic sponsorship involving significant sums of money is certainly a newsworthy item for companies such as Coca-Cola, McDonald's, and Visa. Refer to Figure 9.7 for an illustration.

Krispy Kreme is a company that relies heavily on public relations to spread the word. For insight into how it uses public relations communications, read the IMC Highlight **Krispy Kreme Plants the Seeds**.

PUBLIC RELATIONS EXECUTION

The tools available to execute public relations programs are diverse. Some are used routinely to communicate newsworthy information and some are brought out periodically or only on special occasions. This section examines some of the more routinely used media tools.

Press Release

A **press release** is a document containing all the essential elements of the story (who, what, when, where, and why). Editors make very quick decisions on what to use and what to discard, so the release must grab their attention quickly. Copies of the release are delivered to a list of preferred editors, for example those with whom an organization has a good relationship. Alternatively, the release could be distributed to a national wire service as well as posted on the company's website. Figure 9.8 is an illustration of a press release. Note that contact information is provided should the media require any additional information. This press release deals with the recall of a coffee thermos that was sold through Tim Hortons restaurants. Signs posted in each Tim Hortons outlet also advised consumers that the recall was underway. Tim Hortons took positive and constructive action in this case.

Press Conference

A **press conference** is a meeting of news reporters invited to witness the release of important information about a company or product. Because a conference is time consuming for the media representatives, it is usually reserved for only the most important announcements. A crisis, for example, is usually handled by an initial press conference. When a professional sports team is about to announce a new star player entering the fold, a press conference is very common. A conference allows the media to interact by asking questions, which results in the transfer of additional and perhaps more meaningful information for the story they will publish or broadcast.

A media kit is usually distributed at a press conference. A **media kit** usually includes a schedule of conference events, a list of company participants, including biographical information, a press release, historical fact sheets if applicable to the situation, a backgrounder that tells something about the character of the organization and the nature of what it does, a page of standalone facts about the company, photographs, copies of speeches, videos, and any other relevant information. Depending on need, any combination of these materials can be included. The key to developing a good media kit is to evaluate who is will use it and what that person is likely to need. For example, a media kit for a special event or new sales promotion activity would be very different in tone, style, and content from one needed for a crisis situation.

Borrowed-Interest Strategy
A plan to promote a marketing activity that is related to a product.

Press Release
A document prepared by an organization containing public relations information that is sent to the media for publication or broadcast.

Press Conference
A meeting called by an organization to present information to representatives of the media.

Media Kit
A package of relevant information associated with a product or organization, distributed at a press conference.

FIGURE **9.7** A Press Release Using a Borrowed-Interest Strategy to Promote a Company

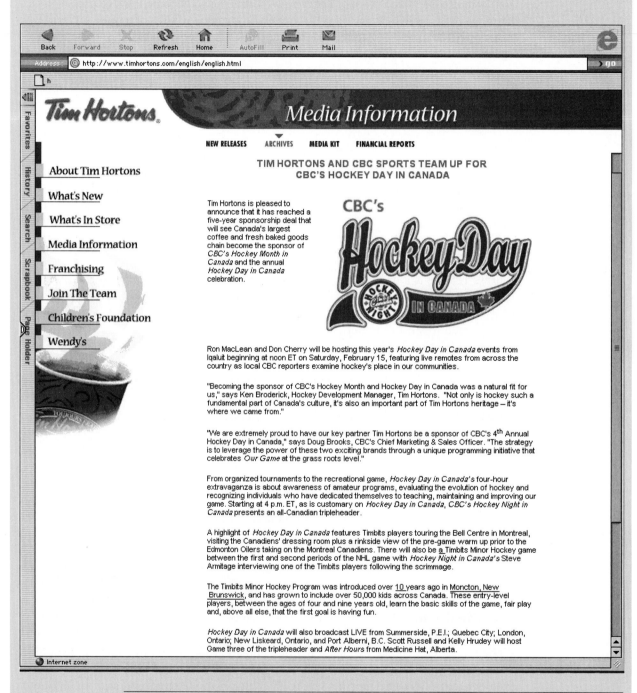

Source: The TDL Group Corp.

IMC Highlight

KRISPY KREME PLANTS THE SEEDS

What is it about Krispy Kreme that makes its donuts so popular with Americans—and now with Canadians, too? Is it a massive advertising campaign that creates so much buzz, or is it simply nothing more than a great product? Well, in the view of public relations specialists, Krispy Kreme is somewhat of a legend for its effective public relations communications that have spread the word. It is unique, but public relations is the tail that wags the Krispy Kreme marketing communications dog.

Krispy Kreme is one of those rare brands to have achieved cult status. A cult brand seizes the imagination of a small group, who spread the word, make converts, and help turn a fringe product into a mainstream name. Another key to Krispy Kreme's success is the simplicity of its marketing concept: the brand character is fun for people of all ages, and outlets sell only donuts and coffee. There never has been and never will be an expanded menu.

The only way to experience a Krispy Kreme donut is to visit a store, and that's where public relations enters the picture. The passion people portray for the product is just plain difficult to explain and show in ordinary advertising. When Krispy Kreme opened its first Canadian store in Mississauga, Ontario, public relations dominated the marketing plan. In fact, the media buzz about Krispy Kreme entering Canada started 13 months prior to the store opening. According to Mat Wilcox of the Wilcox Group (Krispy Kreme's public relations agency in Canada), the company fielded media inquiries that resulted in more than 500 stories. Part of the strategy was to ensure that management was very responsive to any request for information, but never pushing for coverage if there wasn't anything to announce.

The key element of the public relations launch plan was the "donut drop." Initially, 2500 dozen donuts were strategically dropped in key traffic areas of Mississauga and Toronto. There was also a steady stream of hot, fresh donuts delivered to media outlets, as well as toques bearing the Krispy Kreme logo—a distinctly Canadian premium.

The night before the store opened there were 200 people waiting in line. On opening day, it took about one hour waiting in line to get into the store. The opening had enthusiastic coverage by the Toronto media and there was national coverage by the *National Post*. Opening week sales set a company record by raking in $465 000, a true testament to the public relations strategies.

Wilcox suggests that media hype and free donuts are just the beginning of the public relations campaign. The next step is to connect Krispy Kreme with the local communities in which its stores are located. The company ensures that employees reflect the area they operate in, and they are known to be actively involved in community-based fundraising campaigns.

Adapted from Angela Kryhul, "The Krispy Cult," *Marketing*, January 28, 2002, p. 11.

Krispy Kreme
www.krispykreme.com

Websites

Since the primary purpose of a website is to communicate information about a company or brand, it can be a very useful public relations tool. Visitors to a website quickly form an impression about the company based on the experience they have at the site. Therefore, the site must download quickly and be easy to navigate. Providing some kind of entertainment or interactive activity also enhances the visit. Unlike other media, the web can be updated easily and quickly, so the very latest news about a company and its products can be made available for public consumption. It is now very common to post all press releases about a company on the corporate website.

Newsletters

Newsletter
A document sent to a predetermined audience that contains news about an organization.

The **newsletter** is a very common public relations tool. By nature it is a concise reporting of the news related to the organization, and is very clear and to the point. A successful newsletter conveys information in a unique way so that the people who receive it pay attention to it. Newsletters are distributed regularly to their intended audience, so they are an efficient method of conveying information.

FIGURE **9.8** The Essential Elements of a Good Press Release: Who, What, When, Where, and Why

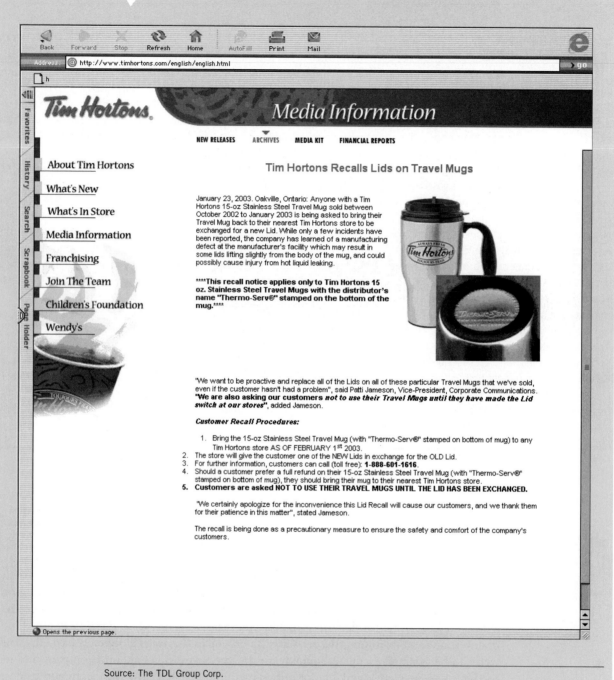

Source: The TDL Group Corp.

There are various types of newsletters, but most are published by companies that want to communicate regularly with employees, by recreation and sports clubs that wish to keep in touch with their members, and by professional associations that regularly publish information to members who are geographically dispersed. Typically, a newsletter is distributed by internal or external mail or email, and relies on an accurate database of names and addresses. The frequency of publication is based on budget, timelines, and serialization. Small budgets may dictate quarterly distribution as opposed to monthly; if timeliness is an issue, then more frequent distribution is required.

For companies wishing to keep in touch with employees, a newsletter is a useful tool for communicating company policies, for announcing social and recreational events, and for acknowledging individual and team success within the organization. As well, they are useful for informing employees of news (good or bad) about the company before it is announced to the general public. The newsletter often assumes this role. *Special interest newsletters* are distributed by a wide variety of lifestyle clubs and organizations, and by professional associations (refer to Figure 9.9). Investors in the stock market, for instance, often receive newsletters from a bank or other financial institutions. In another example, members of the Canadian Public Relations Society receive a monthly newsletter from the Society. Such a newsletter keeps the public relations practitioner abreast of new developments, new techniques in public relations, and even career opportunities.

Booklets and Brochures

A **booklet or brochure** is a brand-sponsored, multiple-page document that is distributed to consumers and other interested stakeholders. The information in a booklet is usually related to a product or service. For example, it may promote usage of a product in a variety of ways or it may appeal to the lifestyle of the target audience it is intended for. Campbell's Soup is well known for distributing recipe booklets in food stores, through direct mail, and through its website. These booklets encourage consumers to use Campbell's products more frequently in cooking recipes as well as in other non-traditional ways. Greater usage equals greater sales. Figure 9.10 shows a similar application.

Streamlined versions of brochures or single-page documents are referred to as flyers or leaflets. A **flyer** is usually a single sheet, and a **leaflet** typically has a fold or several folds, even if the leaflet is a small size.

Annual Reports and Special Interest Reports

The primary purpose of an **annual report** is to provide current and prospective investors and stakeholders with financial data and a description of an organization's operations. But it can do much more to promote the company. In terms of public relations, it is a good opportunity for the organization to tell the public how it stands on social and environmental issues, for example. In fact, the annual report is often seen by audiences beyond the primary target—such as the media, community leaders, and employees. Word can spread fast about what a company stands for.

Special interest reports can be integrated into an annual report or can be standalone documents. For companies that want to portray to the public that there is more to business than a healthy bottom line, a special interest report is an ideal vehicle to get a different message out. Special interest reports are designed to appeal to a very selective audience—usually opinion leaders—and focus on issues that affect the organization and the target audience. To illustrate, General Motors issues the "Corporate Responsibility and Sustainability Report," which documents the social accountability practices of the company and goes a long way in building trust with customers, suppliers, and distributors. The report shows that GM is a good corporate citizen. The 2002 report focused on several environmental issues, including GM's research leadership, emission technology research, research into alternate fuels, waste reduction and recycling, and the partnerships it has formed with other companies and organizations.[10] In a similar fashion, RBC Financial Group publishes an annual "Corporate Responsibility Report" (see Figure 9.11). It shows the financial contributions the

Canadian Public Relations Society
www.cprs.ca

Booklet or Brochure
A multiple-page document distributed to consumers and other interested stakeholders.

Flyer
A single-sheet document that contains information about a product or service.

Leaflet
A one-page flyer that offers relevant information about a direct mail offer.

Annual Report
A document published annually by an organization primarily to provide current and prospective investors and stakeholders with financial data and a description of its operations.

FIGURE **9.9** An Illustration of a Special Interest Newsletter

Business Alumni Association of Ryerson

BAAR

Message from BAAR's President

A new year is well under way and like a professional sports club that's being rebuilt, we've assembled a diverse and dynamic new management team. Our plan is to continue to build the Business Alumni Association of Ryerson (BAAR) into an organization that meets the growing needs of its membership - Ryerson Business Alumni like yourself.

As you may know, BAAR started just over 4 years ago. Our mission is to be a solid and dependable force for our existing alumni, as well as a support vehicle for new alumni as they begin their respective careers; thereby bridging past accomplishments with future endeavours.

We believe your Alumni Association should play a key role in your professional and personal development. We have made it a mandate to become more involved in the School of Business Management student's lives as they make their way through their studies at Ryerson. We shall strive to build a solid network among SBM students, faculty, alumni and the community at large, thereby enabling life long learning and friendships.

We remain firmly committed to our core vision of assisting the Ryerson School of Business Management in becoming the Most Respected Undergraduate Business School in Canada. While 2002 proved to be a successful year for BAAR, it also highlighted the need to continue our efforts towards carrying out our vision. The realization of this vision depends on the ideas, values and capabilities of the Executive Committee and all of our alumni. Your support, goodwill and enthusiasm will help us in this journey. We hope that you will keep in touch and remain vocal about how you envision your Alumni Association and what we can do to help one another to grow.

In closing, I would like to take this opportunity to thank Gregg Lee and his board. They have contributed a great deal of time and energy in initiating BAAR. They have laid

Executive Board (Left to Right): Lynden Henriques, Lilia Salva, Michael Chersey and Andreas Konnafis

a solid foundation for all of us to build on. I would also like to thank and formally introduce you to your new Executive Board: Lynden Henriques (Vice-President), Andreas Konnafis (Treasurer), Lilia Salva (Director of Event Management) and David Lee (Communications Officer).

In closing, I would like to extend my personal invitation to you to join SBM alumni, students, faculty and friends at our 5th Annual BAAR Golf Tournament on Monday, June 23 at Granite Ridge Golf Club in Milton. Also, read through the newsletter for details of other planned events - I'm confident you'll find something that captures your interest. Finally, please share with us your ideas or suggestions of what you'd like your Alumni Association to do for you, either through our new website (www.ryerson.ca/baar) or call us at 416-979-5000, extension 7720.

Thank you for your continued support and we look forward to seeing all of you at an upcoming BAAR event.

Sincerely,
Michael Chersey
President

Source: Business Alumni Association of Ryerson.

company makes in the areas of youth and education, community economic development, health, civic causes, and the environment. RBC's annual donations are considerable. The latest report shows total donations to be $37.1 million worldwide with $27.4 million allocated to Canadian organizations and communities.[11]

Figure 9.12 offers some insight into additional and unique public relations tactics appropriate for special occasions.

FIGURE **9.10** ▼ **Recipe Books Encourage Consumers to Use Company Brands More Frequently**

Source: Photography by Doug Bradshaw, as seen in *Bakefest 2002*.

TIMELINE AND BUDGET

As with other communications plans, a timeline is essential so that all activities are carefully coordinated with other marketing communications activities. In the case of a new product launch, for example, public relations programs can be put in place well before the product is actually available. One strategy is to start the public relations communications in a small way, slowly building credibility, and proceed with a slow rollout. This strategy creates demand in such a manner that the public is eager to buy the product once it is launched. The Viagra and Botox examples cited above followed this strategic approach. They also show how important it is to coordinate timing and activities across the two disciplines of integrated marketing communications, public relations and advertising.

Public relations programs cost much less than advertising programs, but they are nonetheless costs that must be accounted for. If a company employs corporate advertising, the costs are similar to brand advertising programs. There are costs associated with producing print and broadcast materials and with buying time in the broadcast media and space in the print media. A company might also employ newsletters, brochures, annual reports, and media kits, and the costs of producing these materials must also be included in the public relations budget.

FIGURE **9.11** **RBC Financial Publishes a Corporate Responsibility Report That Documents Its Contribution to Communities across Canada**

Good Business:

THERE IS NO SINGLE DEFINITION OF "CORPORATE CITIZENSHIP" OR "CORPORATE RESPONSIBILITY." BUT ONE THING IS CLEAR: A COMPANY CAN'T SIMPLY WRITE CHEQUES FOR CHARITIES AND CONSIDER THE JOB DONE. RESPONSIBILITY MEANS MUCH MORE – COMPANIES MUST BE RESPONSIBLE TO THEIR EMPLOYEES, CUSTOMERS AND SHAREHOLDERS, AS WELL AS TO THEIR COMMUNITIES.

As a financial services institution, RBC pays particular attention to ensuring we are a leader in developing sustainable and ethical business policies and practices. "Good Business" includes highlights from these areas:

- Governance and ethical conduct
- Community investment
- Human resource policies and practices
- Consumer protection measures
- Access to personal and business banking services
- Care for the environment
- Risk management

GOVERNANCE AND ETHICAL CONDUCT

The year 2002 was one of increased scrutiny of corporate governance, practices and policies. RBC's proactive corporate governance culture ensures industry-leading standards; as an economically and socially responsible corporation, we believe it is important for our conduct to be ethical and transparent.

Board of Directors
RBC believes it is critical for our Board of Directors to be well informed about our business and the competitive, economic and regulatory environments in which we operate. The board must be well balanced in terms of experience and skills, independent while retaining a good relationship with management, focused on continuous improvement and flexible to adapt to changing circumstances.

To ensure board independence from management, RBC split the role of Chairman and Chief Executive Officer in 2001, and an outside director acts as Chairman of the Board. In 2002, of RBC's 19 directors, 16 were independent, as defined by the Toronto Stock Exchange bylaws and regulations of the Bank Act.

All board committees are composed exclusively of non-management directors.

Financial Reporting
RBC uses the services of two auditing firms. The Audit Committee of the Board of Directors approves RBC's quarterly financial statements and has the authority to hire and fire external auditors. RBC's unaudited quarterly and annual financial statements are reviewed by the full board.

2002
Canada's Most
Respected
Corporation

"A lot of things go hand in hand with integrity: professionalism, trust, confidentiality and accountability," says RBC's Meghan Meger.

28 GOOD BUSINESS

Source: Courtesy of RBC Insurance.

MEASUREMENT AND EVALUATION

To justify a financial investment in any form of marketing communications, certain expectations and results must be delivered. There must be some kind of financial return, increase in awareness, or change in behaviour. Walter K. Lindenmann, senior vice-president and director of research at Ketchum Public Relations, has identified levels for measuring public relations effectiveness: outputs, outgrowths, and outcomes.

- *Outputs* measure the transmission, that is, the amount of exposure in the media, the number of placements and audience impressions, and the likelihood of reaching the target audience.

- *Outgrowths* measure message reception by the target audience. Did the target pay attention to, understand, and retain the message?

- *Outcomes* measure attitude and behavioural change. Was there a change in attitude and did the recipient do something as a result of the message?[12]

FIGURE **9.12**

Some Unique and Innovative Public Relations Techniques

With so much advertising out there, it is increasingly difficult to get a product message through the clutter. Companies are turning to public relations techniques that simply approach customers a different way in order to catch their attention. Sometimes, the customers don't even realize they're being sold something!

THE CELEBRITY PITCH

Drug companies are hiring Hollywood stars to discuss illnesses and treatments on the talk show circuit. Lauren Bacall speaks openly about Visudyne (a drug that treats macular degeneration, an eye disease). Bacall is financially rewarded by Novartis, the drug's manufacturer. Kathleen Turner plugs Enbral, an anti-arthritis drug marketed by Wyeth, and Rob Lowe promotes Neulesta, a drug that treats febrile neutropenia (a kind of fever condition often related to cancer). It all sounds technical, but these stars speak to the issues when interviewed on talk shows.

THE LOCAL ACTOR PITCH

Marketers hire local actors to pose as tourists in a bid to generate buzz about a new product. Sony Ericsson's undercover operatives ask strangers at tourist destinations across the United States to snap their picture with the new camera/cellphone device. The purpose is to create the illusion of a spontaneous encounter with someone who bought the gadget. The actors talk up the gadget once they are asked questions about it.

CEOS

A company's top executive could be the company's most effective spokesperson. His or her presence in the media can have a significant impact on a company's financial performance. Some great ones past and present include Lee Iacocca at Chrysler, Bill Gates at Microsoft, and Dave Thomas at Wendy's. Dave Thomas's personality reflected the personality of the entire organization. Since his death in 2002, his sense of humour and warm demeanour are no longer part of Wendy's television advertising.

ROAD SHOWS

A brand hits the road with a decorated vehicle as a means of attracting attention. Product samples can be given away at each stop. Red Rose Tea reshaped a Volkswagen Beetle to look like a teapot (handle on the back hood and spout on the front hood). Other popular brands that use this technique include Microsoft Xbox, Sony Music, and Pepsi-Cola. In the case of Microsoft, the vehicle was a travelling gaming arcade that encouraged experiential contact. In the sky, there's the Goodyear blimp, the Met Life Blimp with Snoopy, and the Fuji blimp.

Toronto Star
www.thestar.ca

Output measures are the most common means of evaluating public relations effectiveness. There are companies that specialize in tracking everything that is written and broadcast about a company and its brands. For example, if an article appears in the front section of the *Toronto Star*, a newspaper with a weekday circulation of more than 400 000, how many impressions will be made? If there are 2.5 readers for every newspaper, the potential number of impressions is 1 million (400 000 × 2.5). If a similar story appears in other newspapers, the number of total impressions accumulate.

It is also possible to attach an equivalent advertising value to such an article. The tracking firm examines the size of the article, the location in the publication, the number of brand mentions, and so on, and, through the magic of mathematical calculations, determines the value in terms of advertising. While this may not be exact science, it does appease senior executives who are looking for some kind of return for their investment. While there is no real agreement on such matters, public relations experts believe that a good article about a product is worth anywhere from three times as much to ten times as much as an equivalent size ad in the same publication.

Measuring for outgrowths involves determining if the target audience received and understood the message. Collecting this information involves a combination of qualitative and quantitative research methodologies, so it is much more costly. Since creating awareness is the primary objective of most public relations campaigns, many firms do not proceed with research in this area. Among those that do, many prefer to use focus groups and telephone surveys.

Marketing research is required to measure for outcomes such as a shift in behaviour. As with research conducted for any other marketing activity, this form of evaluation involves pre-campaign and post-campaign research. The initial research firmly establishes a benchmark. For example, the research identifies how consumers perceive and use a product or company before being exposed to the public relations message. The initial research group is then divided into a test group and a control group. The test group receives the public relations messages and the control group does not. Post-campaign research determines the differences between the two groups in terms of what they know and if their attitudes have changed.

More detailed information about specific procedures for measuring and evaluating public relations activities is included in Chapter 12, "Evaluating Marketing Communications Programs."

Public Relations as a Communications Medium

Senior executives today are starting to have a better understanding of the role played by public relations in achieving their organization's marketing objectives. As a communications discipline, the status of public relations has been considerably elevated. The examples in this chapter show how public relations can play a key role in specific situations, and it will certainly continue to grow in terms of its contribution to marketing communications strategies and the achievement of an organization's objectives. Those responsible for corporate and brand communications should be aware of the basic benefits and drawbacks of public relations communications.

ADVANTAGES OF PUBLIC RELATIONS

If public relations is done properly, it can be a **credible source** of information. Unlike advertising, public relations messages are delivered by third parties who have no particular interest in the company or product. They are communicating information that they deem useful to their readers, listeners, viewers, and so on. Consumers reading or viewing such messages perceive those messages to be more objective than they do advertisements. If a company can win favourable press coverage, its message is more likely to be absorbed and believed.[13]

Third-party endorsements by trusted media personalities can have a **positive impact on sales**. To illustrate, consider what happened when the CBS news program *60 Minutes* announced that drinking a moderate amount of wine each day could prevent heart attacks by lowering cholesterol. The effect was so astonishing that red wine sales in the United States jumped 50 percent after the broadcast. Figure 9.13 also illustrates how good public relations can increase sales.

FIGURE 9.13

Successful Public Relations Campaigns Have a Positive Impact on Sales

This public relations plan for Dunlop Tires demonstrates how a carefully planned public relations campaign can increase brand sales.

CLIENT

Goodyear Canada and its Dunlop Tire brand

AGENCY

Environics Communications, Toronto

PUBLIC RELATIONS OBJECTIVE

To increase consumer awareness for the Dunlop Tire brand and drive sales.

PUBLIC RELATIONS CAMPAIGN

The campaign theme revolved around the Dunlop name. Dunlop challenged people whose last name was Dunlop to change their name to Dunlop-Tire for a cash reward. It was promoted as the "Tired of Your Name Challenge."

The story received prominent coverage across Canada and the United States, including front- page stories, television features, and radio interviews.

MEASUREMENT AND EVALUATION

- 100% of media stories mentioned the name Dunlop Tire.
- Many stories were front-page or top stories reported on television news.
- The tone of all news coverage was positive and/or humourous.
- Forty-nine people named Dunlop inquired about changing their name.
- Four people legally changed their name to Dunlop-Tire.
- Sales increased 59 percent over two years in a market only growing by 3 percent.
- Canadian Tire (the largest distributor of tires) agreed to sell Dunlop tires, a decision attributed to the public relations support received by the brand.

Adapted from Sara Minogue, "Proving Value," *Strategy*, November 18, 2002, p. 18.

Indirectly, public relations also play a role in developing sound *customer relationships*. Public relations campaigns offer a means to build rapport through ongoing dialogue with consumers and other stakeholders. Such a benefit is important, considering the rising costs of media advertising, the fragmentation of the media, and the clutter of commercial messages. A good public relations campaign can cut through the clutter faster and may encourage the desired attitude or behaviour change to occur more immediately.

DISADVANTAGES OF PUBLIC RELATIONS

One of the biggest drawbacks of public relations is the *absence of control* experienced by the sponsoring organization. Through press releases and press conferences, the company does its best to ensure that factual information is available and presented accurately to the public. In the process of communicating the information, however, the media might add their own opinions, which detract from the intent of the original message. Companies facing crisis situations often see stories in the media that misrepresent the company or mislead the public.

A second disadvantage deals with the sheer *waste* of time, energy, and materials that go into a public relations campaign. This is not to say that the effort isn't worthwhile, but the challenge of catching the attention of editors (the media gatekeepers) is an onerous one. Enormous amounts of material flow into media newsrooms daily, so standing out in the crowd is part of the public relations challenge. Senior management must recognize the waste factor and be prepared to absorb the costs that go along with it. Finally, what is important to management may not be perceived as important by the media. End of story!

Summary

Public relations are a form of communications directed at gaining public understanding and acceptance. They are used by organizations to change or influence attitudes and behaviour. Unlike advertising, which is a very costly means of communications, public relations go largely unpaid for. The organization presents information to the media in the hopes they will publish or broadcast it in a news story.

The primary roles of public relations are diverse. They constitute a useful channel for communicating corporate-oriented messages designed to build the organization's image. Public relations are also the most important form of communications when an organization finds itself in a crisis situation. In such times, an organization must be honest and forthright with the public. Public relations specialists help prepare organizations to handle crisis situations. At the product level, public relations help generate positive publicity by distributing news releases and by holding press conferences when there is newsworthy information to announce. As well, relatively new communications alternatives, such as product placement and product seeding, fall under the umbrella of public relations. Product placement is proving to be an effective alternative to regular television advertising, and product seeding offers a means of getting the product in the hands of trendsetters who influence the public's attitudes and behaviour.

Public relations planning begins with a situation analysis. Usually the client organization provides a brief containing all relevant background information to a public relations agency. Public relations is a form of communications that does require external expertise. The public relations firm establishes the goals and objectives, develops the communications strategy, selects the best execution techniques, and, after receiving the client's approval, implements the plan.

The primary objectives of public relations programs tend to dwell on creating awareness, altering attitudes, and motivating a change in behaviour. The public relations strategy focuses on reaching opinion leaders, maximizing the news value of the story, and reinforcing other communications campaigns such as advertising, sales promotions, and event marketing activities. There are several techniques for getting a story into distribution. The most commonly used options include the press release, press conferences, websites, newsletters, booklets and brochures, and videos.

Once the public relations plan is implemented, research is necessary to determine the effectiveness of the campaign. Output measurements are the most common evaluation technique. They measure message transmission, that is, the amount of exposure in the media, the number of placements and audience impressions, and the likelihood of the message reaching the intended target audience. If pre-campaign and post-campaign research is conducted (budget permitting), an organization can measure the impact of public relations messages in terms of influencing attitudes and altering behaviour.

Key Terms

advocacy advertising	248	buzz marketing	251
annual report	263	corporate advertising	248
booklet or brochure	263	external publics	247
borrowed-interest strategy	259	flyer	263

Review Questions

1. What are the essential differences between media advertising and public relations communications?

2. Identify and briefly explain the role of public relations in the following areas:
   a) corporate communications
   b) reputation management
   c) product publicity
   d) product seeding
   e) community relations

3. What is the difference between product placement and product seeding?

4. What is lobbying and why is it necessary for an organization to conduct such a practice?

5. What are the key elements of a public relations strategy?

6. What is a borrowed-interest public relations strategy? Provide a new example of this strategy.

7. What is a media kit and what role does it serve?

8. What are the roles of special interest newsletters and special interest reports that are distributed by companies, organizations, and associations?

9. Public relations effectiveness is measured based on output, outgrowth, and outcome. Briefly explain each form of measurement.

10. What are the advantages and disadvantages of using public relations as a marketing communications medium? Briefly explain.

Discussion and Application Questions

1. Considering the nature of the business environment today, do you think that public relations will play a more significant role or less significant role in future marketing communications strategies? State your position and justify it based on your vision of the future business environment.

2. What is your opinion of product placement? Is it a fad or will it continue to grow in importance? Is it really more effective than regular forms of brand advertising? Review the IMC Highlight **Marketers on the Bond Wagon** for essential insights about product placement.

3. Review the IMC Highlight **Krispy Kreme Plants the Seeds**. Public relations are the primary form of marketing communications in the United States and the company has adopted the same strategy in Canada. Considering the nature of the Canadian quick-serve food market and the degree of competition in this particular market segment, will Krispy Kreme have to rethink its marketing communications strategies as it pursues expansion? Analyze the situation and prepare a response.

4. Conduct some secondary research that involves an organization facing a crisis situation. How did it handle the situation from a public relations perspective? Were its strategies effective or ineffective?

5. Conduct some secondary research that involves an organization using public relations strategies to launch a new product. How important was public relations in the marketing communications mix? What were the objectives of the public relations effort? Was the plan effective in achieving its goals?

6. Find some examples of organizations that are involved in advocacy advertising. Can you determine why that organization is involved in communicating that specific message?

7. Identify two different companies that compete with each other in the same industry or markets. Analyze the information they provide on their websites in terms of public relations value. Are these companies maximizing the potential of the web for communicating vital information to customers? Sample sites to visit include Procter & Gamble and Colgate-Palmolive, Coca-Cola and Pepsi-Cola, Bell and Telus, Hudson's Bay Company and Sears, etc.

8. Visit some company websites of your choosing. Usually, there is a link to the press release section of the site. Review that company's latest five press releases. What subject matter did they deal with? Try to determine how that company uses public relations to its advantage.

End Notes

1. John Heinzl, "How Toronto Can Counteract Its Blacklisting," *Globe and Mail*, April 25, 2003, p. B11.

2. Justin Smallbridge, "Is Advertising a Dead Language?" *Financial Post*, July 29, 2002, p. FP6.

3. Judy Lewis, "Building Buzz," *Marketing*, January 28, 2002, p. 17.

4. Kristen Vinakmens, "Publicity Helps The Art of Hardware Carve Its Niche," *Strategy*, March 10, 2003, p. 5.

5. John Heinzl, "Product Placement Reaches New Highs—Or Is That Lows?" *Globe and Mail*, January 10, 2003, p. B9.

6. John Heinzl, "If the Shoe Fits, Sell It," *Globe and Mail*, September 7, 2001, p. M1.

7. Tim Hortons, <**www.timhortons.com/english/english.html** (November 2003).

8. Packaging Association of Canada, "Lobbying," <**www.pac.ca/Services/lobbying.html**> (November 2003).

9. Thomas L. Harris, *Value-Added Public Relations* (Chicago, NTP Publications, 1998), p. 243.

10. General Motors, "Corporate Responsibility and Sustainability Report," <**www.gm.com/company/gmability/sustainability/reports/02/index.html**> (November 2003).

11. RBC Financial Group, "Community Centre," <**www.rbc.com/community**> (November 2003).

12. Walter K. Lindenmann, Ketchum Public Relations, "It's the Hottest Thing These Days in PR," a presentation at PRSA Counselors Academy, Key West, Florida, April 25, 1995.

13. Kevin Goldman, "Winemakers Look for More Publicity," *Wall Street Journal*, September 29, 1994, p. 53.

EVENT MARKETING AND SPONSORSHIPS

After studying this chapter you will be able to:

explain the importance of event marketing and sponsorships in contemporary marketing,

differentiate among the various forms of event sponsorships,

evaluate the role of event marketing and sponsorships in the marketing communications mix,

assess the criteria that a marketing executive considers before participating in event marketing and sponsorships,

describe the steps in event marketing planning,

evaluate various marketing strategies for making an event successful,

identify and explain the key elements of event marketing execution, and

identify and assess the various evaluation techniques that determine the effectiveness of event marketing and sponsorship activities.

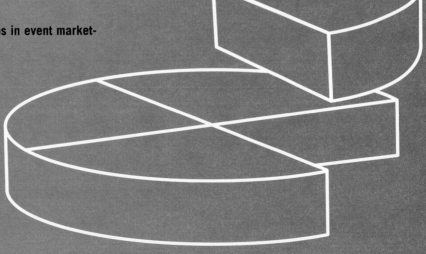

Event marketing and sponsorships are fast becoming important elements of the marketing communications mix, and for very good reasons. According to David Lackie, public relations manager for Harry Rosen Inc., "Events can build loyalty that's steadfast and unshakeable. They take time, are an investment, and quite often do not show immediate results. But if you are consistent and commit to it for a number of years, the payoff in customer loyalty can be tremendous."[1] This chapter explores the exciting world of event marketing and shows how a variety of companies reap the benefits of event and sponsorship participation.

An Introduction to Event Marketing

Event Marketing

The process, planned by a sponsoring organization, of integrating a variety of communications elements with a single event theme.

There is a distinct difference between event marketing and event sponsorship. **Event marketing** is the process, planned by a sponsoring organization, of integrating a variety of communication elements with a single event theme (e.g., Molson's coordination of advertising, public relations, and sales promotion activities for the Molson Indy car race). In other words, the costs of developing or participating in an event are only part of the costs. To maximize the true benefit of event marketing, a significant investment must be made in other forms of marketing communications. Such investments are necessary to generate awareness of the event, sell tickets to it, and to generate publicity for it.

Event Sponsorship

The financial support of an event in exchange for advertising privileges associated with that event.

Event sponsorship is the financial support of an event, say, an auto race, theatre production, or a marathon, by a sponsor, in return for advertising privileges associated with the event. Visa, for example, is the lead sponsor of the Visa Triple Crown, thoroughbred horseracing's most prestigious series of races in the United States—the Kentucky Derby, the Preakness Stakes, and the Belmont Stakes. As in other sports sponsorships Visa is involved with, television advertising supports the event to reinforce Visa's designation as "The Official Card of the Visa Triple Crown." The brand is linked to one of America's premier sporting events. At the centre of Visa's sponsorship lies a $5 million bonus—one of the largest single payouts in the history of professional sports—awarded to the winner who captures all three races.[2] (It happens rarely that one horse wins all three races.)

Usually, an event marketer offers sponsorships on a tiered basis. For instance, a lead sponsor or sponsors would pay a maximum amount and receive maximum privileges. Other sponsors would pay less and receive fewer privileges. In the case of the Visa Triple Crown sponsorship, Visa receives significant on-track and on-air visibility through point-of-sale signage, out-rider jackets, and on-track Visa Triple Crown signage. In addition, the president and CEO delivers a "Chairman's Message" that is broadcast on NBC before each race.

Event marketing is big business! According to IEG Consulting, a Chicago-based sponsorship measurement firm, the North American sponsorship market is valued at $9.57 billion. IEG projects a reshuffling of where sponsorship dollars will be going over the next few years based on corporate belt tightening and a lingering concern over consumers' willingness to travel to big-ticket events. Even though sports sponsorships attract the lion's share of sponsor dollars, IEG is forecasting a decline in spending on sports and modest increases in other sponsorship areas.[3] Given that Canada is 10 percent of the size of the U.S. in almost everything (our population is 10 percent of that of the U.S.), the Canadian market size is traditionally estimated at 10 percent of the U.S. for everything from toothpaste to beer. So why not also apply the 10 percent rule to investment in sponsorship? Sponsorships here could be worth as much as $950 million annually.

Investment in event marketing and sponsorships is mainly divided between five areas: sports; entertainment tours and attractions; festivals, fairs, and annual events; causes; and the arts. Refer to Figure 10.1 for a summary of how event sponsorship investments are allocated. Visa, for example, is an established, diversified sponsor—in addition to the Triple Crown, it sponsors the Olympic Games, a host of film festivals in Canada, the United States, and Europe, and the Dubai Shopping Festival, among many other sponsorships.

FIGURE **10.1** **Allocation of Event Marketing and Sponsorship Investments in North America**

Type	Dollars Invested	Growth
Sports	$6.43 billion	+0.4%
Entertainment, tours, and attractions	$865 million	+3.1%
Festivals, fairs, and annual events	$834 million	+12.7%
Causes	$828 million	+13.0%
Arts	$610 million	+3.6%

Sports receive the lion's share of the sponsorship investment, but other areas of investment are now growing at a faster pace. All figures are for 2002.

All figures compiled by IEG, Inc., "Where the Dollars Go," <**www.sponsorship.com/Learn/wheredollarsgo.asp**> (November 2003).

SPORTS MARKETING SPONSORSHIP

Sports sponsorship occurs at amateur and professional levels and can be subdivided into classifications from local events to global events (see Figure 10.2). The sports share of the sponsorship pie in North America accounts for $6.43 billion, about 67 percent of all sponsorship spending. Sports sponsorships tend to be dominated by certain industries and manufacturers. In Canada, for example, the automobile industry is well represented by General Motors and Ford, the brewing industry by Molson and Labatt, and the financial industry by RBC Financial Group, BMO Financial Group, and Visa and MasterCard. The BMO Financial Group has been actively supporting professional women's golf and the LPGA by making a multimillion-dollar commitment to the Canadian Women's Open and several smaller women's golf events. BMO also sponsors junior golf development across Canada in a program called Future Links. According to Maurice Hudon, president of the personal banking division at the Bank of Montreal, "The involvement with golf has proven to have big benefits for the bank's profile. It's an important business vehicle for us."[4] See Figure 10.3 for an illustration.

As noted in Figure 10.2, an organization's involvement in sports sponsorship does not have to be extravagant. The extent of involvement and the financial commitment depends upon the organization's marketing objectives and its overall strategy. To illustrate, Visa associates with national and international events, a reflection of the card's status around the world. In contrast, Tim Hortons prefers to sponsor local sports programs all across Canada. The initiative stems from the local franchisees and their desire to be involved with local market events. Through the Timbits program, Tim Hortons sponsors minor hockey and soccer programs, which fit neatly with the target audience the company strives to reach. Sunlight detergent is another brand actively involved with children's soccer leagues across Canada. Muddy soccer uniforms fit like a glove with Sunlight's positioning strategy of "Go ahead. Get dirty." Local participation at much lower cost can produce attractive results.[5]

FIGURE **10.2** **The Various Levels of Sports Event Marketing**

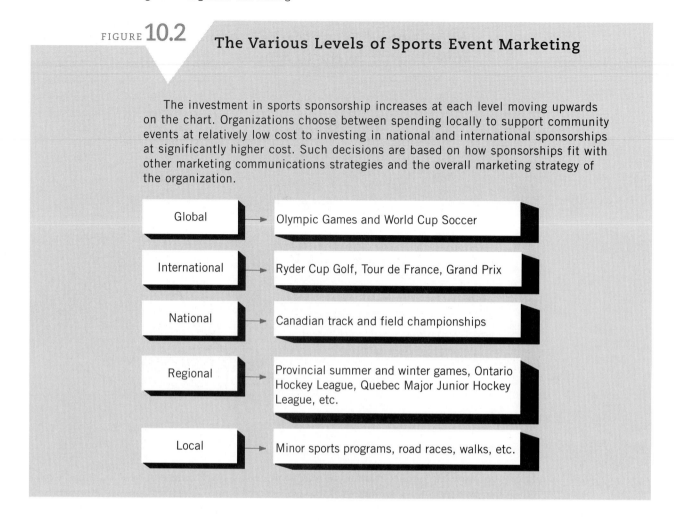

The investment in sports sponsorship increases at each level moving upwards on the chart. Organizations choose between spending locally to support community events at relatively low cost to investing in national and international sponsorships at significantly higher cost. Such decisions are based on how sponsorships fit with other marketing communications strategies and the overall marketing strategy of the organization.

Global	→	Olympic Games and World Cup Soccer
International	→	Ryder Cup Golf, Tour de France, Grand Prix
National	→	Canadian track and field championships
Regional	→	Provincial summer and winter games, Ontario Hockey League, Quebec Major Junior Hockey League, etc.
Local	→	Minor sports programs, road races, walks, etc.

Ambush Marketing

A strategy used by non-sponsors of an event to capitalize on the prestige and popularity of the event by giving the false impression they are sponsors.

A recent phenomenon associated with event sponsorship is the practice of ambush marketing. **Ambush marketing** is a strategy used by non-sponsors to capitalize on the prestige and popularity of an event by giving the false impression they are sponsors. Such a strategy works especially if people are confused about who the real sponsors are. To illustrate, consider what happened in the 2002 Winter Olympic Games in Salt Lake City. Labatt's was a major advertising sponsor on the CBC network (which held the broadcast rights in Canada). During the Olympic period, Molson placed Olympic-themed television ads (showing Canada's Olympic hockey opponents as being afraid to face our national team) on competing networks—a classic case of ambush marketing.[6]

Venue Marketing or Venue Sponsorship

Linking a brand name or company name to a physical site such as stadium, arena, or theatre.

Venue marketing or **venue sponsorship** is another form of event sponsorship. It was one of the hottest trends in the 1990s. Here, a company or brand is linked to a physical site such as a stadium, arena, or theatre. In Canada, there is the Corel Centre in Ottawa (home of the Ottawa Senators), the Air Canada Centre (home of the Maple Leafs and Raptors), and GM Place (home of the Vancouver Canucks). Inside the Air Canada Centre, there's the Sears Theatre and inside GM Place there's the Air Canada Club. Pre-eminent title positions like these break through the clutter of other forms of advertising, but venue marketing does come at a cost. Air Canada spent $20 million for a 20-year agreement for the naming rights to the Leaf's home rink. Hummingbird, a software development company, paid a flat fee of $5 million to have its name on a performing arts theatre in Toronto.[7]

Houston Astros
houston.astros.mlb.com

There are certain perils associated with venue marketing, many of which cause embarrassment for sports teams performing in the stadiums and arenas adorned with corporate names. The Houston Astros played at Enron Field, a corporate name now strongly

FIGURE **10.3** **BMO Financial Actively Sponsors Junior Golf and Women's Golf in Canada**

®/TM Trademarks of Bank of Montreal.

$$38 + 36 = 74$$

$$38 + 36 = 2 \text{ Over par}$$

We're helping young golfers recognize their potential.

Since 1996, the Future Links junior golf development program has introduced nearly 200,000 kids to the game of golf. As well, we've also given them the chance to witness the true artistry of the game by sponsoring the BMO Financial Group Canadian Women's Open. At BMO Financial Group, we're proud to bring the spirit of the game to all Canadians.

BMO ⛰ Financial Group

For the world you live in.™

Source: Courtesy of BMO.

associated with corporate malfeasance. It has since been renamed Minute Maid Park. Minute Maid is a Coca-Cola brand name. Other stadiums that will probably be renamed include the United Centre in Chicago (United Airlines has filed for bankruptcy) and the Adelphia Coliseum in Nashville (the company founders are accused of using company money as a personal piggy bank).[8] For a more detailed list of corporations involved in venue marketing, see Figure 10.4.

FIGURE **10.4**

Venue Marketing Is Popular among North American Corporations

AIR CANADA CENTRE ($20 MILLION, 20-YEAR DEAL)

Sponsor: Air Canada
Toronto Maple Leafs (hockey), Toronto Raptors (basketball), Toronto Rock (lacrosse)

PEPSI CENTRE ($68 MILLION, 20-YEAR DEAL)

Sponsor: PepsiCo.
Colorado Avalanche (hockey), Denver Nuggets (basketball)

CONTINENTAL AIRLINES ARENA ($29 MILLION, 12-YEAR DEAL)

Sponsor: Continental Airlines
New Jersey Devils (hockey), New Jersey Nets (basketball)

COORS FIELD ($15 MILLION OVER INDEFINITE PERIOD)

Sponsor: Adolph Coors Co.
Colorado Rockies (baseball)

DELTA CENTRE ($25 MILLION, 20-YEAR DEAL)

Sponsor: Delta Air Lines
Utah Jazz (basketball)

FIRST UNION CENTRE ($40 MILLION, 30-YEAR DEAL)

Sponsor: First Union Corp.
Philadelphia Flyers (hockey), Philadelphia 76ers (basketball)

HEINZ FIELD ($57 MILLION, 20-YEAR DEAL)

H.J. Heinz Company
Pittsburgh Steelers (football)

STAPLES CENTRE ($116 MILLION, 20-YEAR DEAL)

Sponsor: Staples
Los Angeles Clippers (basketball), Los Angeles Lakers (basketball), Los Angeles Kings (hockey)

Reprinted with permission from the October 28, 2002 issue of *Advertising Age*, Special Report on Sports Marketing, "Naming Rites," p. S7. Copyright, Crain Communications Inc., 2002.

What's thriving in sports marketing is the concept of **value-added sponsorships**, where hefty doses of public relations and media exposure accompany a marketer's sponsorship agreement. The key in this strategy is a lucrative player endorsement. The Ford Motor Company has inked its first player endorsement in golf, signing Phil Mickelson as its spokesperson. On the professional golf tour, Mickelson now displays the Ford logo on his shirt. He makes public appearances on behalf of the company, attends company business-building functions, and appears in branded advertising campaigns. Showing its commitment to golf, Ford extended its role with the PGA Tour by taking title sponsorship at the Doral tournament in Miami.[9] Sears Canada recently struck a deal with Mike Weir, Canada's best professional golfer and now a Masters Champion, a position of distinction among all professional golfers. Ironically, the deal with Sears happened just before Weir won the Masters Championship. Sears will be marketing a line of golf accessories bearing the Mike Weir label.

Why do corporations invest in sports marketing and how effective is the investment? The true benefits of event marketing are discussed later in the chapter. For now, simply consider that key indicators of success are awareness and association with the event. For example, which beer company is closely associated with *Hockey Night in Canada*? If you cannot answer this question, the sponsor has a problem. Until recently, Labatt was the exclusive beer sponsor, but that has changed. Labatt did not renew its exclusive rights deal with the CBC. As of the 2003–04 season, Molson beer advertising is also part of *Hockey Night in Canada*—a showdown between Canadian and Blue is brewing! Labatt had paid the CBC $80 million for its current exclusive arrangement. Such an investment is now deemed too expensive.[10]

Hockey Night in Canada
www.cbc.ca/sports/
hockey

Our economy and heightened sensitivity about responsible spending in an era of corporate scandals are having a negative influence on sports marketing decisions. For more insight into the present state of affairs with sports sponsorships, read the IMC Highlight **Scrambling for Sponsors**.

IMC Highlight

SCRAMBLING FOR SPONSORS

Despite the potential benefits of a corporation sponsoring a major event, the cost of events is scaring sponsors away. Major sports such as professional golf and tennis are starting to feel the pinch as corporations assess their overall marketing communications strategies and where event marketing and sponsorships fit in. In Canada, for example, Air Canada (a financially troubled company) decided not to continue its sponsorship of the Vancouver Professional Golfers Association (PGA) tour event. Event organizers were not successful in finding a replacement willing to meet the US$5 million requirement and the event was eventually cancelled. Air Canada also announced it would not continue its sponsorship of the Formula 1 Grand Prix in Montreal beyond 2003, a $15 million investment.

According to Keith McIntyre, a leading sports marketing consultant, "Companies are taking a second to look at everything they are doing. The sponsorship market is in transition, there's no question." The reality of the situation is simple: companies are more concerned with plunging stock prices and earnings statements than finding funds for sporting events.

The pool of sponsorship money has shrunk for several reasons. As the global economy slows, companies are under pressure to re-evaluate budget items such as sports sponsorship, whose effectiveness is hard to measure. In Canada, the 1997 *Tobacco Act* placed restrictions on where and when tobacco companies could promote sponsorships. Being one of the largest groups of companies to provide sponsorship money, they simply pulled out of sports, entertainment, and art events. Technology companies that were flush with cash during the dot-com boom have vanished. Nortel Networks Corp., for example, which sponsored all kinds of events, was one of the biggest dot-com bombs. "Sponsorships are not a key strategic element in our efforts to move forward," says Tina Warren, a Nortel spokesperson.

Given these examples, there is no question that sponsors are becoming more prudent about where their marketing dollars go. Companies have less money to spend right now so they must make sure they are putting it in the right place to target their audience. They want return on their investments and perhaps sport marketing is not the best alternative.

Before committing to a sponsorship deal a company should establish specific criteria that must be met. The event must be a solid strategic fit with its brand and target market and it wants proof that the sponsorship will create awareness and generate solid business results. Even then, the benefits of sports sponsorship have to be evaluated against investments in other marketing strategies.

Adapted from John Heinzl, "Sports Events Do the Sponsor Scramble," *Globe and Mail*, August 10, 2002, p. B9.

ENTERTAINMENT, TOURS, AND ATTRACTIONS

Canadian corporations invest huge amounts of money to sponsor concerts and secure endorsements from high-profile entertainment personalities in the hope that the celebrity-company relationship will pay off in the long run. Companies such as Molson, Coca-Cola, and Pepsi-Cola, which are interested in targeting youth and young adult segments, use entertainment sponsorship as a vehicle for developing pop-music and youth-lifestyle marketing strategies. According to Dave Perkins, vice-president of marketing at Molson, "Sponsorships are part of Molson's commitment to provide our consumers with the best in sports and entertainment." By plastering the Molson banner on tickets and publicity, the company hopes to attract the young drinker on the verge of forming lifelong brand loyalties.[11]

Teens and young adults are a difficult target to reach, but MuchMusic gets through. An entertainment event called SnowJob (an annual event that ran from 1993 to 2002) encouraged anyone with a ski pass to travel up a mountain to watch the music and other activities during the six days the event took place. Around 200 000 skiers and snowboarders and 25 contest winners checked out the event each year; the resulting footage filled hours of time on MuchMusic in the month of March. Over half the audience was 12- to 17-year-olds. The event attracted sponsors like Nike, Pantene, and Sprite.[12]

Film Festivals

Film festivals are enticing because they reach a cross-section of adult target audiences. At a top film festival, a corporate sponsor hitches a ride on the most glamorous coattails of all—movie stars! For two prominent film festivals, the Toronto International Film Festival and the Festival des Films du Monde in Montreal, there are waiting lists for platinum sponsorships. These events showcase branded products not only to filmgoers, but also to the thousands of deep-pocketed domestic and international wheeler-dealers who do business at festivals. Key clients get to hobnob with the movie stars.

Sponsorship revenue for the Toronto International Film Festival averages $4 million annually, with top sponsor spots occupied by AGF, Bell Canada, *National Post*, Visa, and Volkswagen. Visa leverages its sponsorships of film festivals in Toronto, Montreal, and Vancouver in several ways. There are exclusive ticket packages that include advance purchase opportunities to Visa cardholders, and there are "Visa Screening Rooms": posh, branded lounges where purchasers of special passes can avoid long lines and enjoy a relaxing environment with refreshments for up to one hour before a screening. Pass holders enter the theatre before other patrons and have first choice of seats. As for corporate hosting, Visa entertains its best clients at film festival events.[13]

The *National Post* is the Toronto International Film Festival's official daily newspaper and the association "has conferred huge cachet on the paper," according to vice-president of promotion Lynn Munro.[14] The *National Post* sells more newspapers by making all of its readers feel as if they are a part of the festival, whether or not they have tickets to a film. The *Post* and its strategic partners at Global Television and CHFI radio pull out all the stops with coverage throughout the festival. The *Post* publishes an official supplement listing all films and events, offers special prize packages, and sponsors related events.

National Post
www.nationalpost.com

Television

Canadian Tire signed a television sponsorship deal with *Open Mike* with Mike Bullard. On the show, Canadian Tire sponsors the "Canadian Quiz," a live segment in which Bullard quizzes celebrity guests on their knowledge of Canada. According to Eymbert Vaandering, vice-president of marketing for Canadian Tire retail, "We wanted to find different ways, outside the selling environment, to allow customers to interact with our brand, without feeling they're being sold to." The audience does not experience product benefits directly. They are associating with the entertainment value and star power surrounding it. The association is a good fit because Canadian Tire's customers are the same psychographic group as *Open Mike*'s audience: hard working, middle class, and 100 percent Canadian. It's an interesting approach that hits the target audience in a creative way. The Canadian Quiz is a small extension of a much larger multimedia campaign to revitalize the brand. Canadian Tire's brand repositioning was launched in 2002 under the "Let's Get Started" slogan.[15]

CULTURE AND THE ARTS SPONSORSHIPS

Arts and cultural event opportunities embrace such areas as dance, film, literature, music, painting, sculpture, and theatre. What separates cultural events from sports and entertainment events is the audience size. Depending on the sponsor, this is an advantage or a disadvantage. A company such as Molson might prefer the mass audience reach of a sports event, whereas Mercedes-Benz and BMW might prefer to reach a more selective and upscale audience through an arts event. Perhaps only 2500 people attend the cultural event, but those people can be powerful. Typically, their education level would be above average, as would their income. Such an audience profile would be a good match for promoting a new luxury car. A financial services company such as the RBC Financial Group (Royal Bank) or MasterCard may sponsor both large audience and small audience events given the diversity of age and income of its customers.

The primary benefit these companies gain by sponsoring the arts is goodwill from the public. Most firms view this type of investment as part of their corporate citizenship objectives; that is, they are perceived as a good, contributing member of society. Bell Canada has always invested in the communities it serves and has a varied sponsorship portfolio that includes major cultural and sporting events that enable it to be present in the community throughout the year. Some of the cultural events sponsored by Bell include the Stratford Festival, the Shaw Festival, and the *Just for Laughs* Festival in Montreal. The RBC Financial Group is another civic-minded organization. In Hamilton, for example, there is the RBC Aquafest, a week-long summer music festival, set in a downtown waterfront park. Family activities include dragon boat races, midway rides, a children's play area, and crafters.[16]

CAUSE MARKETING SPONSORSHIPS

Cause-related marketing is relevant in the minds of consumers, corporations, and not-for-profit organizations that mean something to consumers. This feeling, when associated with a brand or company, can have a positive effect on the consumer's perception of the brand. Such is the benefit that the CIBC derives from its ongoing title sponsorship of the Canadian Breast Cancer Foundation CIBC "Run for the Cure," where the overall goal is to raise funds to help find a cure for breast cancer (see Figure 10.5). Other large corporations involved with this event include Air Canada and the Ford Motor Company of Canada.

In today's competitive business world, brands drive marketing, but as brand loyalty diminishes, marketing executives are searching for new ways to connect with consumers emotionally. Not-for-profit organizations are proving to be good business partners to achieve this goal. The right combination produces a win-win situation for both parties. Coca-Cola, for example, has a successful association with Harry Potter. Coca-Cola committed to the development of reading skills for youth and Warner Bros. provided access to material and support. Coca-Cola was sensitive to the need for a low-key grassroots-type program and made donations to the communities where the children lived.[17]

Other organizations develop and foster their own causes. McDonald's has the Ronald McDonald Children's Charities and Tim Hortons has the Tim Hortons Children's Foundation. Both organizations long ago recognized the benefits of touching their audience on an emotional level. The Tim Hortons Children's Foundation is a non-profit charitable organization committed to providing a fun-filled camping experience for children

FIGURE 10.5 CIBC Is the Proud Title Sponsor of the Canadian Breast Cancer Foundation CIBC "Run for the Cure"

CIBC Run for the Cure

- **CIBC Run for the Cure**
- Thank You
- About the Run
- Who are you running for?
- 2003 Run Highlights
- Français

Who are YOU running for?

Thank you

Thank you for your support for the 2003 CIBC Run for the Cure!
On Sunday, October 5, 2003, 39 communities and thousands of women, men and children rallied together for the largest ever CIBC Run for the Cure. This year, over 160,000 participants raised over $17 million for the Canadian Breast Cancer Foundation. Join us next year and become part of the cure. Read More

About the Run

Exhilarating. Inspiring. Encouraging. These are just some of the ways participants describe the CIBC Run for the Cure. Each year, thousands join together in the fight against breast cancer. Join us and be part of the energy on Sunday, October 3, 2004. With your help, we can beat this disease and create a future without breast cancer.
Read More

Who are you running for?

Angie Fera, Dorey Fox and Margaret Grobisen are not only connected because they work at CIBC — they're connected because each one of them has had a very personal experience with breast cancer. Angie and Dorey are breast cancer survivors and Margaret lost her mother-in-law to the disease. Read More

2003 Run Highlights

This year's run was our largest and most successful yet! Over 160,000 people in 39 communities across the country participated and raised over $17 million to help the Canadian Breast Cancer Foundation find a cure for breast cancer. Here are the run results for each site as well as some pictures and stories from Sault Ste. Marie, Toronto, Montreal, Red Deer and Saint John. Read More

About The Canadian Breast Cancer Foundation

The Canadian Breast Cancer Foundation (CBCF) is the largest charitable organization in Canada dedicated exclusively to supporting the advancement of breast cancer research, education, diagnosis and treatment. Its fundraising efforts — through the annual CIBC Run for the Cure, special events and corporate sponsorship and donations — has enabled the Foundation to fund innovative and leading edge breast cancer projects and services since 1986. The Foundation has chapters in BC/Yukon, Alberta/NWT, Ontario and the Atlantic Region, with several community-based branch offices across the country. The CBCF National Office is located in Toronto, Ontario. Read More

Return to CIBC.com

Trademarks and Disclaimers

Source: Canadian Breast Cancer Foundation.

from economically disadvantaged homes. The foundation is dedicated to fostering within children the quest for a bright future.[18] It raises funds from donation containers at point-of-purchase, donations from other organizations, and an annual fundraiser where franchisees donate all monies raised from the sale of coffee one day each year. The program is fully supported by media advertising that encourages consumers to visit Tim Hortons on the fundraising day.

PRODUCT PROMOTIONAL TOURS AND TOUR SPONSORSHIPS

Experiential Marketing
A promotion in which potential customers interact directly with a product.

Growing in popularity is a concept called experiential marketing. **Experiential marketing** is about finding ways for a target audience to interact directly with a product. Tour events play a key role in experiential marketing. Oscar Mayer has been doing it for years with its Weinermobile, and the Hershey's Kissmobile still attracts a crowd wherever it stops. This brand-on-wheels concept is now moving to another level.

Marketers from film studios, music labels, and video games recently jumped on the bandwagon. Independent event management companies plan and implement such tours, arriving at targeted locations, using on-board staff and promotional techniques that include sampling and built-in billboard advertising. Columbia TriStar used the tour technique when it launched the Vin Diesel film *XXX* in the summer of 2002. The tour team hit summer fun spots in Ontario such as Wasaga Beach and the Molson Indy, handing out *XXX* T-shirts and *XXX* tattoos.[19]

These types of events work especially well with the 15- to 29-year-old age group. One product that has recognized the value of tours is Pepsi-Cola's Mountain Dew brand. For years, Mountain Dew has capitalized on the popularity of skateboarding, developing many television spots and print ads. The skateboarding theme is integrated into the much larger "Do the Dew" advertising campaign. It's an edgy style of advertising that appeals to younger audiences. Mountain Dew has conducted numerous skateboard tours, including the Mountain Dew Free Flow Tour, visiting 12 cities with skateboarding demonstrations and contests. Prizes and giveaways at each stop included free Mountain Dew, Mountain Dew branded merchandise, and skateboard paraphernalia branded with the Mountain Dew name. From Mountain Dew's perspective, the tour encourages audience participation, and kids get a chance to interact with the best skateboarders in the country.[20] Mountain Dew closely associates with BMX racing, inline skating, and snowboarding as well.

Considerations for Participating in Event Marketing

Companies enter into events and sponsorships in an effort to create a favourable impression with their customers and target groups. For this to be accomplished, the fit between the event and the sponsor must be a good one. For instance, Nike sponsors national and international track and field events as well as community-based events, such as fun runs. Much of the company's success has been based on event sponsorship and the distribution of merchandise that bears Nike's trademark logo—the swoosh. Generally, event sponsorship is a vehicle for enhancing the reputation of a company and the customer's awareness of a brand. The most effective sponsors generally adhere to the following principles when considering participation in event marketing.

- *Select Events Offering Exclusivity:* If a company need to be differentiated from its competition within the events it sponsors, it calls for exclusivity so direct competitors are blocked from sponsorship. Also, sponsors are often concerned about the clutter of lower-level sponsors in non-competing categories that reduce the overall impact of the primary sponsor.

- *Use Sponsorships to Complement Other Promotional Activity:* The role that advertising and promotion will play in the sponsorship must be determined first.

Sponsoring the appropriate event will complement the company's other promotional activities. For example, FedEx sponsors drivers' baseball caps and tiny logos on the Championship Auto Racing Teams (CART) circuit. It has corporate banners at the site, its trucks do pace laps, and uniformed employees present trophies.[21] Is there a better angle for a speedy delivery company than race cars? FedEx's message in traditional media advertising emphasizes speed of delivery, so the sponsorship integrates well with other forms of marketing communication.

- *Choose the Target Carefully:* Events reach specific targets. For example, while rock concerts attract youth, symphonies tend to reach audiences that are older, urban, and upscale. As suggested earlier, it is the fit—or matching—of targets, that is crucial, not the size of the audience.

Mercedes-Benz
www.mercedes-benz.ca

- *Select an Event with an Image That Sells:* The sponsor must capitalize on the image of the event and perhaps the prestige or status associated with it. For example, a luxury car, such as the Mercedes-Benz, may be a suitable sponsor for a significant art or cultural event, or a major national golf championship. Mercedes-Benz sponsors the Mercedes Hawaii Open Golf Championship each year. The prestigious image and status of such events have an impact on the sale of products that project a comparable image—the image and status that come with ownership of a Mercedes-Benz automobile.

- *Establish Selection Criteria:* In addition to using the criteria cited here, companies should consider the long-term benefit that sponsorship offers compared with the costs in the short term. For example, being associated with an event that is ongoing, popular, and successful is wise, because there is less risk for the sponsor. Before committing financial resources to an event, a company should also consider whether it is likely to receive communications exposure through unpaid media sources and whether the event organizers will be able to administer the event efficiently. The company must establish objectives in terms of awareness and association scores, image improvement, and sales so it can properly evaluate its participation in the activity.

Event Marketing Planning

Should an organization decide to develop its own event, it must be comfortable with an exhaustive planning process. Putting the plan into place is one thing, executing it is quite another! As in the case of many other forms of marketing communications, a more prudent approach may be to outsource the activity, allowing experts in this field to do the job.

An organization's marketing team carefully considers the role of an event or sponsorship to ensure it is an appropriate opportunity for achieving its business objectives. The organization's primary role is to identify the overall goal and marketing objectives, identify the target audience and timing, consider the financial implications (revenues, costs, and profit), and evaluate the results. Working with the client organization, the event planner develops the event theme, identifies the best venue, and establishes the marketing strategy and implementation plan. The event planner's role is tactical in nature at the implementation stage, as all kinds of concerns need to be addressed. Among these concerns are staging the event, having adequate and trained staff, operations and logistics planning, and safety and security. Successful events run smoothly, moving like clockwork from one activity to another. To do so requires careful planning down to the minutest of details (see Figure 10.6).

EVENT CONCEPT DEVELOPMENT

The initial stage of planning is developing the concept. In determining the nature of the event, the planner considers the event's purpose, the audience it will reach, available resources, potential venues, and timing. In terms of *purpose*, an event that is designed to

FIGURE **10.6** **The Event Marketing Planning Process**

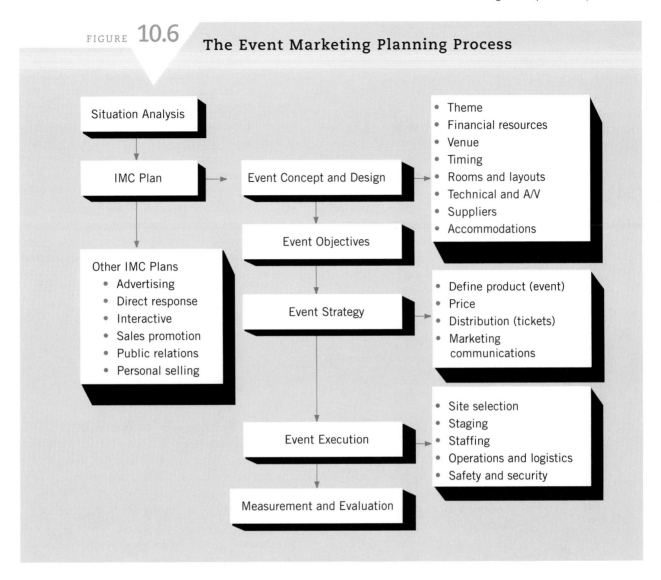

transfer information to prospective clients would be much different from one intended to entertain an audience. The former might have a business tone and style while the latter would be much more upbeat and participative. To illustrate, an event with a trade show orientation (e.g., some kind of business fair where new products are introduced to the market) is much different from the annual Calgary Stampede. The Calgary Stampede is a community event that is presented with all the enthusiasm and passion that the people of Calgary and all of Alberta can muster. The Stampede represents the historical and cultural fabric of the West.

The **theme** of the event should be linked to the purpose and consider the needs of the audience. Events tend to adopt a colour scheme and a tagline that tie various components of the event together. For example, tickets, programs, promotional literature, and signs are usually designed to look like they are all part of a package. Key influences on theme development are one's imagination and money. The latter always brings a sense of reality to one's imagination! Potential themes could involve history (the organization's history), geography and culture (the location of the organization or the event), sports (being part of a sports event that fits with the product), music and entertainment (offers significant appeal to younger audiences), and so on.

Once the theme is determined, the next decision is *venue*. Will the venue be a traditional setting such as a hotel, convention centre, arena, or stadium? Or will it be something unusual such as a parking lot or a site at a company facility, or will it move from location to location, as in the case of product promotional tours, mentioned earlier? Regardless of the venue, the planner must carefully consider factors such as sound, lighting, and other technical issues, along with parking and public transportation issues. And of course, there's always the unpredictability of the weather. Should the event be inside or outside?

The *financial resources* must be considered immediately. Much like an advertising budget, where a relatively small budget precludes the use of television advertising, an event's budget quickly determines the degree of extravagance. What an event planner would like to do and what the planner can actually do are usually quite different—a good idea is only a good idea if it is financially viable. Therefore, the event planner must carefully balance creative instincts with the financial resources of the organization.

The *timing* of an event is often linked to the season or weather. For example, the Canadian Home Show, an annual show held at Exhibition Place in Toronto, is held in early April each year. The show is timed to coincide with the public's interest in home improvements and renovations, which tends to peak in the early spring. Essentially, there are four time-related factors to consider: season, day of the week, time of day, and duration of the event. Business trade shows, for example are usually scheduled on weekdays. In contrast, home and leisure shows cover weekends as well as weekdays, with traffic at the show peaking on the weekends.

DESIGNING THE EVENT

Once the concept decisions have been made, the next stage is *design*. For the purpose of illustration, let's assume we are planning a two-day business conference at which several prominent business speakers will make presentations about various aspects of marketing communications. Attendees will include advertising agency personnel, marketing executives, as well as managers employed in sales promotion and public relations. The theme of the conference is "How to Communicate Effectively with Youth," a hot topic among marketing communications practitioners.

In designing this conference, key decision areas include venue, room layout, technical requirements, food and beverage requirements, material suppliers, and hotel room availability. Regarding venue, a downtown hotel location in a major city would likely be a logical choice because the target audience works in that environment. The hotel's banquet room facilities will be considered, because a room for 250 to 300 attendees is required, and an additional banquet room will be needed for some of the meals. For example, it is common for keynote speakers to make their presentations after a meal in the main banquet room. Meals without keynote speakers are often in an adjacent room where the atmosphere is less formal.

The layout of the banquet room has a bearing on how well the audience and speakers interact with each other. A common layout at this type of conference includes carefully spaced, round tables with eight people seated at each. Attendees usually like this arrangement because a table can be reserved for a large group from one company. Such an arrangement encourages collegiality at the table even if the people did not know each other initially. The speakers usually address the audience from an elevated podium at the front of the room.

In the age of technology, the use of proper and effective technology is crucial. Most speakers today use slides or video presentations as their primary visual aid to illustrate the key points. Therefore, an event planner must consider all possible audiovisual needs in advance. Typically, the audiovisual aspect of the conference is outsourced to an expert company in this field. That company brings in all the equipment and does its own set-up and tear-down, and is responsible for coordinating the visual aspect of the presentation with the speaker. For extremely large conferences where attendees are distant from the speaker, it is common to have additional screens that display the speaker making the presentation.

Attending a marketing communications conference involves a considerable investment in time and money. Therefore, the attendee expects good-quality food and efficient service by hotel staff. A poor experience in this area can negate any other positive experiences the attendee has at the conference. Buffet-style meals, for example, seem efficient, but only if there are enough serving stations so the lineups aren't too long. If the meal is served directly to tables, adequate staff must be on duty so that the meal is served within the time allocated. Conferences must stick to their schedule. Light snacks and beverages must be readily available in convenient locations during the break periods.

Dealing with **suppliers** behind the scenes is another key decision area. At our example of the marketing communications conference, print materials were prepared and copied by a printing company to be distributed at registration. It is quite common to have a booklet containing an event schedule, profiles of the various speakers, information about the host sponsor, and copies of the various presentations. As indicated earlier, audiovisual supply requirements must also be confirmed in advance. Food and beverage supplies are the responsibility of the hotel, but all meal requirements must be confirmed in advance between the event planner and catering manager.

The final decision area involves having adequate **hotel rooms** available for the anticipated number of attendees. Hotels usually block off rooms until a specified date before the conference. If there aren't enough rooms at the host hotel, additional rooms should be reserved nearby. All promotional materials should include hotel information and indicate the key dates and reservation procedures.

SETTING OBJECTIVES

As indicated earlier in the chapter, an organization must establish concrete objectives in order to justify any financial investment in event marketing. Therefore, as with other aspects of marketing communications planning, quantitative objectives are identified. The event planner identifies objectives that are realistic, achievable, and measurable. They must be within the realm of what event marketing is capable of achieving. A direct link to sales is not possible, but it may be possible to measure changes in awareness about a company's product as a result of event participation.

Some of the more common aspects of events and sponsorships related to objectives include size of audience reached, the ability to reach a specific target audience (e.g., the quality of reach), sponsor recognition levels, sales of sponsor products, the economic impact of the event, and profit. In the example of the marketing communications conference, the event's objective may have been to attract 300 participants (perhaps any number above 200 participants would produce a profit for the event). Since the event will attract a quality target audience of marketing communications practitioners, it could attract additional sponsors who will help defray the costs of planning and executing the conference.

To draw a comparison, consider the logistical implications for planning the 2003 "SARS-Stock" benefit concert in Toronto, with the Rolling Stones as headliners. The objective of this undertaking was to alter the city's image, specifically to help remove the stain of SARS. It was promoted as "the largest global event ever," and was attended by almost 500 000 people and watched by 1 billion around the world. The initial target of one of the main sponsors, Molson, was to raise $300 000, but when all the receipts were counted it had in fact raised $500 000. The event also brought in people from around the world, which benefited the city's economy, particularly in the hospitality and restaurant industries.[22]

To demonstrate the economic impact an event can have, another Toronto event suffered due to the SARS outbreak. Sponsorship interest in Toronto's gay and lesbian Pride

Pride Toronto
www.pridetoronto.com

Week celebrations was low leading up to the June 2003 event, even though it is immensely popular each year. The event typically draws about 1 million participants and injects an estimated $76 million into the city's economy.[23]

PLANNING TOOLS

The initial stage of planning is the preparation of an event proposal. The *proposal* should include the objectives of the event, as well as details about organization, layout, venue, technical requirements, and any other key considerations such as those discussed above (see Figure 10.7). Certain planning tools are essential in the planning stages. Most important is a *timeline chart* that indicates when various planning activities start and finish. As well, a schedule of daily events, often called a *run sheet*, is essential to list the various dates, times, and location of activities (see Figure 10.8). The importance of the timeline chart will become clear in the discussion of execution issues later in this chapter. With so many logistical things to consider, it is important to identify a critical path for those elements of the plan that are essential for a successful outcome.

Event Marketing Strategy

With event marketing strategy, the key decisions involve carefully defining the product and then positioning it in the minds of the target audience in a favourable way. Motivating people to attend the event depends on the quality and quantity of marketing communications activities. This section examines some of the essential strategic planning elements.

PRODUCT STRATEGY: DEFINING THE EVENT

In defining the event, the planner must identify the essential features and benefits of the event that can ultimately be used in messages directed at the target audience. For example, is the purpose to entertain, to provide a learning experience, or to simply have fun with friends? The marketing communications conference cited earlier in the chapter offers a learning experience for participants, who gain from the success and expertise of others. In contrast, attending the Molson Indy race in Toronto or Vancouver brings auto race enthusiasts together to cheer and celebrate racing excellence. Clearly, the nature of communications to motivate attendance for these two events would be very different. Promotional information for the Molson Indy stresses words such as speed, thrill, and emotion. In contrast, promotional information for a series of conferences conducted by Brunico Communications use the theme "Great insight. Great inspiration. Great contacts." For one conference titled "Maximizing Media," the following pitch was used to attract attendees:

> To reach increasingly fragmented audiences, you must understand today's changing media landscape. Through dynamic group interaction and case studies, this conference offers marketers vital insights into the current media planning and buying environment. It explores the different mediums available and shows how to make cost-effective, high-impact decisions.[24]

In defining the product (event) and understanding the motivation of the target audience, the event planner discovers what buttons to press to motivate participation.

PRICING STRATEGY

Price also plays a role in motivating attendance. Literature promoting professional seminars and conferences is easily discarded if the price-value relationship is incongruent. Charge too much for a conference and the value is questioned. Charge too little and people may think they won't learn anything important by attending. All things considered, the pricing decision is a delicate one. To put things in perspective, the registration fee for

FIGURE **10.7** Key Elements of an Event Proposal

An event proposal is drafted in the preliminary stages of planning to highlight key elements. As planning progresses, the proposal becomes more detailed and execution oriented.

EVENT DESCRIPTION

- Type of event and event name
- Location
- Timing
- Event concept (including goals and objectives)

EVENT MANAGEMENT

- Management responsibilities
- External supplier requirements
- Facility requirements (venue, rooms, layout, etc.)
- Identification of target audience

MARKETING

- Assessment of audience needs
- Competitor analysis (similar events, timing, etc.)
- Product (event definition)
- Price strategy (price ranges, ticket availability, etc.)
- Marketing communications strategy (media advertising, web, public relations)
- Distribution strategy (registration procedures, methods, etc.)

FINANCIAL

- Budget (consideration of all associated costs)
- Profit and loss statement

STAGING

- Theme
- Decor
- Layout

- Sound and lighting
- Catering
- Services (parking, transportation, vehicle requirements, electricity, etc.)

STAFFING

- Recruitment of staff
- Staff training (roles and responsibilities)
- Recruitment of volunteers
- Volunteer training

SAFETY AND SECURITY

- Risk identification and management
- Safety strategy (audience, presenters, entertainers, etc.)
- Security strategy (premises, equipment, cash, etc.)
- Reporting procedures and communications
- First aid

OPERATIONS AND LOGISTICS

- Bump-in (setup)
- Room layout
- Technical execution (sound, lighting, computers, projectors, etc.)
- Attendee traffic flow (venue layout, room locations, meeting rooms, etc.)
- Contingencies (weather, technology failure, accidents, etc.)
- Bump-out (teardown)

EVALUATION

- Actual versus plan (based on objectives)
- Profitability

the two-day "Maximizing Media" conference mentioned above was $1300, not including hotel and travel costs. Such an event might attract 150 people and could prove to be profitable for the sponsoring organization. However, if the price were lowered to less than $1000, would it attract a larger audience? Pricing an event is much like pricing a product—a lot of psychology is involved.

FIGURE **10.8** **A Sample Run Sheet**

A run sheet is an indispensable planning tool that is updated as needed during planning. It is particularly useful for hotels and conference centres at the execution stage of an event. The schedule below was used at the Ambassador Hotel and Conference Centre, Kingston, Ontario, when it hosted the Ontario Colleges' Marketing Competition in 2002.

THURSDAY NOVEMBER 14, 2002

2:00–4:00 p.m.	Registration and Team Photographs (Atrium)
5:30–7:00 p.m.	Complimentary Buffet Dinner (Ballroom)
7:00–7:15 p.m.	Opening Ceremonies (Ballroom)
7:15–9:30 p.m.	Marketing Quiz Bowl (Ball Room)
10:00–11:30 p.m.	Faculty Social (Prime Minister's Suite)

FRIDAY NOVEMBER 15

7:00–8:00 a.m.	Judges' Breakfast (East Ballroom)
7:00–8:00 a.m.	Continental Breakfast, Students and Faculty (West Central Ballroom)
8:00 a.m.	First Participants Enter Prep Rooms (refer to event schedules)
8:00 a.m.–12:00 p.m.	Judging Begins for Cases, Job Interview, and Sales Presentation
12:00–1:00 p.m.	Judges' Lunch and Faculty Lunch (East Ballroom)
1:00–4:00 p.m.	Competition Continues
6:30–7:30 p.m.	Reception (Ballroom)
7:30–10:00 p.m.	Awards Banquet (Ballroom)

All activities take place at the Ambassador Resort Hotel and Conference Centre.

In contrast, ticket prices for the Toronto Molson Indy are based on location at the track. A three-day Gold Grandstand seat (near Pit Row and the start and end of the race) goes for $233.50. The cheapest three-day seats are in Thunder Alley (the back straightaway) and sell for $78 each. In this case, the degree of thrill that consumers are looking for determines how much they will pay. Over three days, attendance at this event exceeds 100 000 people.

A second pricing consideration involves a plan for purchasing tickets. The sale and distribution of tickets for an event or the registration process for a business conference must be convenient for the participant. As well, the planning organization must decide if it will sell the tickets directly or outsource this task to a specialist in this area such as Ticketmaster. Consumers now find online ticket buying and event registration very convenient. Therefore, registration could be handled by an organization's website, or handled by the website of a ticket intermediary.

MARKETING COMMUNICATIONS STRATEGY

The success of any event is often dictated by the effectiveness of the marketing communications strategy. What message will be delivered to the target audience to motivate participation and what media will be used to efficiently reach that audience? A separate budget must be drawn up for marketing communications, because it may take a considerable portion of the event's overall budget.

The initial marketing communications decisions are basically *branding* decisions. Typically, an event will adopt a distinctive name, logo, colour scheme, and image. Every component of the communications mix, including tickets, will bear the same logo and colour scheme. Such consistency of presentation gives the event a branded look. At an event such as the Molson Indy, branded merchandise such as T-shirts and caps will have the same look (see Figure 10.9).

Among the various elements of the marketing communications mix, advertising, public relations, and internet communications frequently play key roles in promoting an event. The *advertising strategies* for the event are based on the target market profile and how best to reach the target given the financial resources available. The content of the message and the style of delivery must combine effectively in order to meet the

FIGURE **10.9**   **An Event Is a Brand with a Branded Look**

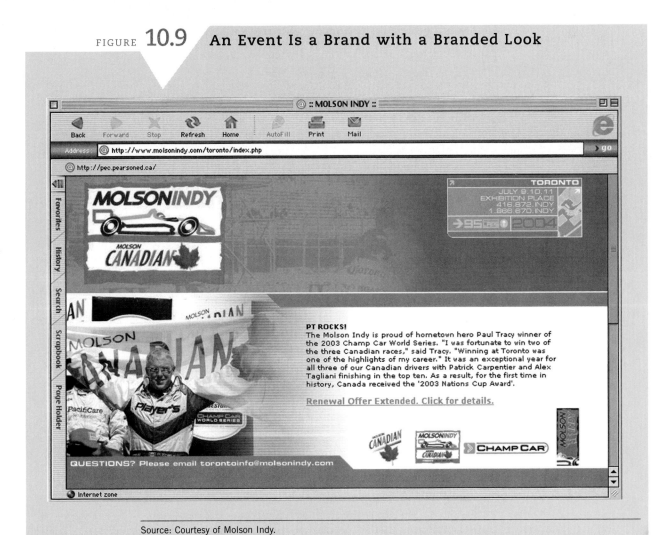

Source: Courtesy of Molson Indy.

motivational needs of the audience. Media alternatives include television and radio advertising, magazine and newspaper advertising, direct mail (letters, brochures, and pamphlets), and the internet. The size of the media budget obviously dictates media decisions. An event like the Molson Indy that attracts a broad cross-section of ages will adopt a multimedia strategy to create awareness and rely heavily on the internet for actual ticket sales. All media advertising now includes a website address so people can get more complete details of the event and find out how to buy tickets. In contrast, an event like the "Maximizing Media" conference will use targeted media such as direct mail and business-oriented print media in order to effectively reach business executives.

An event like the Molson Indy also has sponsorship partners. Partners such as FedEx, Dodge (Chrysler), and Canon also sponsor the three-race Canadian circuit. In order to take full advantage of their participation and achieve their business objectives, such partners often provide advertising assistance. For example, Canon might run a contest in the months leading up to the actual races. Any advertising it does for the contest will refer to the Molson Indy.

Public relations are also essential in generating positive publicity for an event. Organizers of large events frequently hold press conferences, timed appropriately, in order to build some pre-event publicity. It is the organizer's opportunity to introduce celebrities involved with the event (e.g., race car drivers and their cars), issue press releases, and interact with the media. Smaller and more local events send a press release to all local media and then hope for the best—and take care to invite the press to the actual event. Molson constantly issues press releases to promote its activities. Refer to Figure 10.10 for details.

Event Marketing Execution

Execution involves dealing with specific details about an event. A planner usually works from a checklist to ensure that all details are taken care of in the planning stage and the execution stage of an event. For the purpose of illustrating event execution, this section assumes that a planner is planning a marketing conference. Discussion will focus on several key areas, including site selection and staging, staffing, leadership and delegation, logistics, and safety and security. Event execution is complex and a full discussion of such a topic is beyond the scope of this textbook.

SITE SELECTION AND STAGING

In the theatre, the *stage* is the scene of action. The same is essentially true in event marketing. The scene of action for an event involves a site selected according to considerations such as theme development, sound and lighting, and availability of essential services. The choice of venue should be consistent with the event's purpose and theme and it should provide all of the essential services that are required. Some of the key factors influencing site selection include:

• the size of the event (e.g., number of participants),
• the suitability of the site for planned activities (e.g., formal and informal activities),
• the primary field of play (e.g., the theatre or conference room where the main event will be held),
• the availability of, or proximity to, accommodation, food, and attractions, and
• the availability of on-site technical support and venue management experience.

Theme development was discussed earlier in the chapter. At the event, the theme should be supported in every aspect, including sound and lighting, decor, and special effects. For example, the theme at a marketing conference could be very subtle and communicated only by signage and colour schemes. At much larger events of a longer

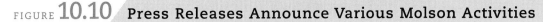

FIGURE **10.10** Press Releases Announce Various Molson Activities

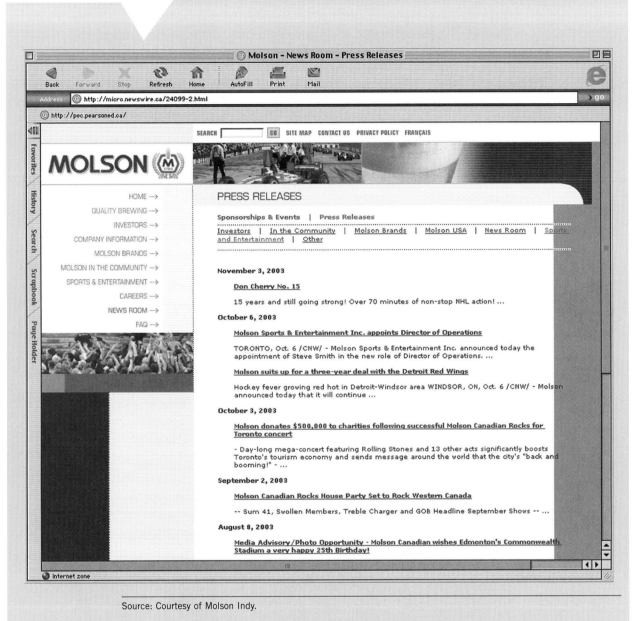

Source: Courtesy of Molson Indy.

duration, music and entertainment (e.g., specific acts revolving around the theme) could be included, along with special props appropriately placed around the venue. If the latter is the choice, an event planner is wise to seek advice from staging and rental companies that offer specialized services in this area.

For the purpose of illustration, let's assume for our one-day marketing conference we need a hall that can accommodate 150 people. The conference theme will be billed as "Marketing in the Future. What Lies Ahead?" The purpose of the conference is to educate and inform concerned marketing managers about what trends and external environments will influence marketing strategies over the next decade. Influential guest speakers from the ranks of industry, government, and the services sectors will present their views on what the future holds and provide insights into how they are already responding.

At this type of a conference, most of the speaker's presentations involve computer-generated shows, so a planner must be concerned about room layout, the stage where the speakers are positioned, sound, lighting, and vision. Let's start with *room layout*. Since a standard, rectangular-shaped banquet room is the theatre, the speakers will be placed at one long side of the room, reducing the distance between the front and back of the room. The seating will be laid out in a way conducive to making notes. For this type of a presentation, there are four basic seating layouts: cabaret, banquet, classroom, and theatre (see Figure 10.11). Of the options available, the cabaret layout seems most appropriate, because it allows for good eye contact for all participants and encourages communication among participants at each table.

The guest speakers will be on an elevated platform at one side of the room. The height of the platform considers the sight lines of the audience. The audience must be able to see the speaker and the screen clearly. Appropriate backdrops should be on stage to isolate the presentation area and create a more intimate feeling. At such a conference, the speaker rarely controls the slide presentation—technical coordination is usually the responsibility of an audiovisual expert who is located at the side of the room.

Proper *sound* and *lighting* are essential to create mood and ambience. Professional advice from a sound and lighting expert is recommended. Such advice is usually readily available at conference centres. If audience communication is going to be important, microphones should be strategically situated throughout the conference room.

With all details addressed, the final aspect of staging is *rehearsal*. The rehearsal is an opportunity for everyone to integrate their efforts and to ensure that all technical glitches are remedied. Contingency plans should be established in case the unexpected occurs, and it often does occur! For example, there should be a plan in place in case a speaker falls sick at the last minute or the projector breaks down.

FIGURE **10.11**

An Event Planner Can Choose from a Variety of Room Layouts

An event planner chooses the room layout based on such factors as ease of serving meals, note taking by participants, audience participation, sub-group activities, and entertainment.

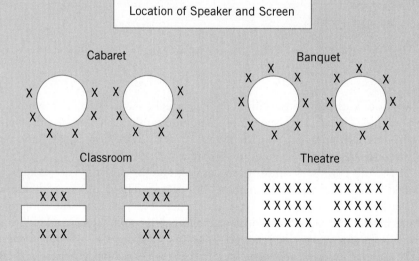

Additional staging considerations include making arrangements for **catering** and **accommodations**. Since the marketing conference is being held at a conference centre, food and beverages are readily available. Decisions involve the style of service (e.g., buffet or set menu with table service), the timing and availability of snacks and beverages (e.g., during planned breaks), and choosing the menu for each meal. Hotels and conference centres usually offer food and beverage packages that are available in a range of prices (see Figure 10.12). Of course, the planner must negotiate room rates with the host hotel or conference centre. Typically a group rate is negotiated based on number of rooms that will be booked.

FIGURE **10.12** **A Sample of Various Meal Packages Offered by a Conference Centre**

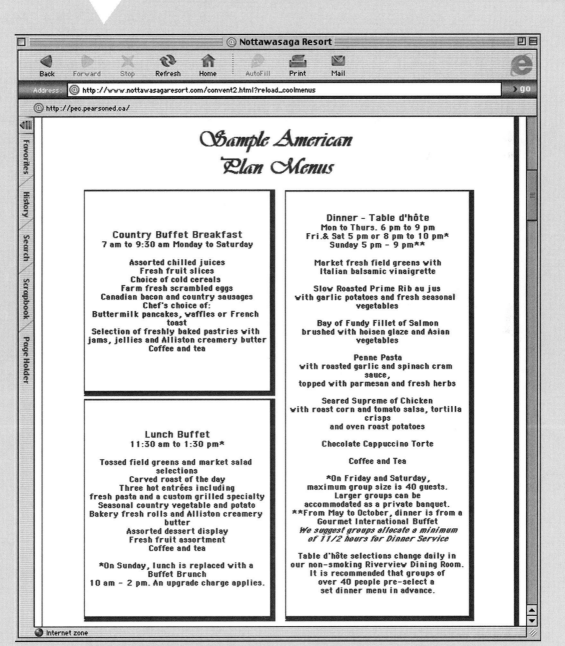

Sample American Plan Menus

Country Buffet Breakfast
7 am to 9:30 am Monday to Saturday

Assorted chilled juices
Fresh fruit slices
Choice of cold cereals
Farm fresh scrambled eggs
Canadian bacon and country sausages
Chef's choice of:
Buttermilk pancakes, waffles or French toast
Selection of freshly baked pastries with jams, jellies and Alliston creamery butter
Coffee and tea

Lunch Buffet
11:30 am to 1:30 pm*

Tossed field greens and market salad selections
Carved roast of the day
Three hot entrées including fresh pasta and a custom grilled specialty
Seasonal country vegetable and potato
Bakery fresh rolls and Alliston creamery butter
Assorted dessert display
Fresh fruit assortment
Coffee and tea

*On Sunday, lunch is replaced with a Buffet Brunch
10 am – 2 pm. An upgrade charge applies.

Dinner - Table d'hôte
Mon to Thurs. 6 pm to 9 pm
Fri.& Sat 5 pm or 8 pm to 10 pm*
Sunday 5 pm – 9 pm**

Market fresh field greens with Italian balsamic vinaigrette

Slow Roasted Prime Rib au jus with garlic potatoes and fresh seasonal vegetables

Bay of Fundy Fillet of Salmon brushed with hoisen glaze and Asian vegetables

Penne Pasta with roasted garlic and spinach cram sauce, topped with parmesan and fresh herbs

Seared Supreme of Chicken with roast corn and tomato salsa, tortilla crisps and oven roast potatoes

Chocolate Cappuccino Torte

Coffee and Tea

*On Friday and Saturday, maximum group size is 40 guests.
Larger groups can be accommodated as a private banquet.
**From May to October, dinner is from a Gourmet International Buffet
We suggest groups allocate a minimum of 1 1/2 hours for Dinner Service

Table d'hôte selections change daily in our non-smoking Riverview Dining Room. It is recommended that groups of over 40 people pre-select a set dinner menu in advance.

Source: Nottawasaga Resort, **http://www.nottawasagaresort.com**

STAFFING

Planning and executing an event are complex undertakings and, depending upon the size and scope of the event, the human resources required can vary considerably. Can you imagine the number of people that would be required (paid and volunteers) when a city hosts the Olympic Games or a national sports championship? For large-scale events the roles and responsibilities of all individuals must be spelled out in detail. Therefore, organization charts are needed for various stages of event planning: pre-event, event, and post-event. In the pre-event stage, the focus is on planning, so anyone connected with marketing, financial, and human resource planning is involved. During the event itself, human resources capacity expands to its fullest, so it is essential that reporting relationships for all operations are delineated. After the event, only those people involved with evaluation and financial planning play a key role.

OPERATIONS AND LOGISTICS

To illustrate the importance of operations and logistics, consider the planning required to get a major golf championship such as the Bell Canadian Open Golf Championship up and running. For the participants alone, a plan is needed to ensure that

- all golfers, their entourage, and their equipment arrive on time;
- golfers are settled in the correct accommodation and that all equipment is safe and secure;
- the golf course is in immaculate condition (a process that starts months before the competition) and that spectator stands, scoreboards, and crowd barriers are in place; and
- golfers arrive in time for their tee-off each day.

Bump-In or Setup

The setting up of structures and other equipment at an event.

This set-up process is referred to as the bump-in. **Bump-in,** or **setup**, involves setting up structures and facilities required for an event.[25] For an event such as our marketing conference example, tasks such as installing sound and lighting equipment, computers, projectors, and screens involve the services of a specialist. Regardless of how the bump-in occurs, it is essential that all facilities and equipment are in place and in working condition prior to the official start of the event. Simply stated, logistics is about getting equipment and people into the right place at the right time so that things run smoothly, and then, once the event is complete, taking everything down. The process of dismantling is referred to as **bump-out,** or **teardown**.

Bump-Out or Teardown

The process of dismantling everything after an event.

SAFETY AND SECURITY

Imagine the potential safety and security concerns the City of Toronto faced when close to 500 000 people congregated in one location for the Rolling Stones SARS concert. For this and similar events that involve large crowds in arenas and stadiums, safety and security issues must be given priority. There must be a plan in place that considers potential crowd behaviour and methods proposed for controlling crowds should the need arise.

At an event everyone must feel safe, including the audience, the staff, and the subcontractors (e.g., technical crews). At large events, accidents can occur, people might fall ill unexpectedly, or something completely unexpected could occur that forces evacuation of the facility. Potential risks include fires, bomb threats, gas leaks, overzealous fans (even riots), and so on. Crowd management—the orderly flow of spectators in and out of the venue—is very important. Signage indicating direction and staff barking out commands where necessary play a key role in moving audience pedestrian traffic smoothly.

To demonstrate the importance of safety and security, consider some of the disasters that have occurred at championship soccer matches over the years. In Johannesburg, South Africa, 2001, 42 people were crushed to death and 150 people injured when excited fans tried to get into a capacity stadium. People were literally crushed to death against barricades at the side of the field. An inquiry into the disaster concluded, "There was an appalling lack of event pre-planning, preparation, risk assessment, and an arrogant indifference to public safety by crucial organizations involved in a highly anticipated championship match."[26] Gross underestimation of the possible crowd attendance at the match was cited as the fundamental cause of the tragedy.

Proper security measures for property, equipment, and cash must also be planned for. As well, the planner must ensure that only certain people have access to specific areas and must act responsibly in case of emergency. Typically, people in positions of authority or special responsibility wear badges identifying their role at the event. Vehicles may be necessary to transport security personnel to areas where emergencies occur. Event planners have a choice of hiring private security firms or members of the local police force.

Measuring the Benefits of Event Marketing and Sponsorship

One reason many companies are reluctant to enter into sponsorship programs is that results are difficult to measure. Large sums of money are spent at one time for a benefit that may be short lived. The basic appeal of event marketing is that it provides an opportunity to communicate with consumers in an environment in which they are already emotionally involved. Beyond this, companies conduct marketing research in order to determine the impact of the sponsorship association. The following indicators, many of which are obtained from research, are used to measure the benefits of sponsorship.

- *Awareness:* How much awareness of the event is there within each target group? How well do people recall the brand or product name that sponsored the event?
- *Image:* What change in image and what increase in the consumer perception of leadership or credibility result from the sponsorship? For additional details regarding image enhancement refer to the IMC Highlight **The Big One!**
- *New Clients:* How many new clients were generated as a result of the company's sponsoring an event? Entertaining prospective clients in a luxury box at an event goes a considerable way in building a relationship.
- *Sales:* Do increases in sales or market share occur in the period following the event? Be aware that the real sales benefit may take years. It takes time for a sponsor to become closely associated with an event.
- *Specific Target Reach:* Do the events deliver constituency? Carefully selected events reach specific targets that are difficult to reach by conventional communications. For example, pre-teens and teens are difficult to reach through conventional media but can be reached effectively through sponsorship of concerts and music tours. As discussed earlier, events need not be big in terms of attendance to attract constituency.
- *Media Coverage:* What value was derived from editorial coverage? Did the sponsorship result in free publicity for the sponsor? The industry benchmark for sports sponsorship is currently four to one, meaning $4 in exposure (e.g., free air time) for every $1 spent on sponsorship and its marketing support.

For sponsorships to be successful, they must be seamlessly integrated into corporate marketing and marketing communications plans. All forms of communications must be complementary. The organization must leverage the use of its website and incorporate the sponsorship into public relations campaigns as well as run thematic promotions to get all customer groups (trade and consumers) involved. Above all, it has to make a financial commitment above and beyond the rights fees. A general ratio for spending should be three to one: for every dollar spent on securing the rights, $3 should be spent to promote the relationship to the event.[27]

THE BIG ONE!

Is sponsoring the Olympics a wise investment? For certain, a select group of international companies, including McDonald's, Coca-Cola, and Visa, and Canadian companies, such as Roots, make a point of associating themselves closely with the Games. Others, such as Air Canada and IBM, have had enough. After 40 years as an Olympic sponsor, IBM did not participate in the Salt Lake City Winter Games in 2002.

When evaluating a sponsorship property, marketers consider quantifiable audience data along with such intangibles as what an audience thinks of the property. Despite bribery allegations against officials, drug scandals among athletes, and tainted judging, people continue to watch the Olympics in droves. The size of the viewing audience brings the advertisers back for more. The Olympics are also popular with companies because the Games appeal to all age groups. Entire families watch the events for two solid weeks, a rarity in television advertising.

The Canadian Olympic Association signs its own slate of sponsors. General Mills, a packaged goods manufacturer, jumped on board for the Salt Lake City Games. To maximize the association, General Mills launched a national, on-pack promotion featuring six Canadian Olympic hopefuls: long-track speed skater Catriona Le May Doan, women's hockey player Cassie Campbell, men's hockey players Steve Yzerman and Martin Brodeur, and figure skaters Jamie Salé and David Pelletier—great selections as they all won gold! Leading up to the Games, pictures and biographies of the athletes appeared on the boxes of Cheerios, Golden Grahams, and Honey Nut Chex cereals.

Eric Lucas, General Mill's vice-president of marketing, explains the Olympic association this way: "It is very important for Canadians to see the company as part of the support system for Canadian Olympic athletes. Just as friends and families play a role, so do corporations.

General Mills is associating itself with the Olympic values of partnership and excellence." The payoff occurs when consumers begin to associate the brand with the event, as is the case with Roots and the Olympics.

Roots participation in the Olympics has been a financial bonanza. Outfitting Canadian teams with trendy styles is always the talk of the Games. Roots also clothed the American team at Salt Lake City. People flocked to their Olympic village store to buy Canadian and American hats, berets, and other items. Says Michael Budman, co-founder of Roots, "Demand for our product is unprecedented. On some items we had to limit the number people could buy."

The scope of the Olympics equates to huge costs for sponsors. Worldwide rights for global sponsors such as Coca-Cola, Samsung, and Xerox were in the range of $50 million for the 2002 Winter Olympics. Air Canada, a long-time sponsor of the Canadian Olympic Association, bowed out of the Winter Olympics, because of "prohibitive" costs. IBM also bowed out, citing a need for more return on investment. IBM re-evaluated its entire sponsorship portfolio and determined that sports will be less important in its future. According to Rick Singer, director of worldwide sponsorship marketing, "Our business strategies are shifting, and we need to pick the right properties to reflect that. Each event we sponsor must generate real stories of how problems are solved for IBM customers."

So you be the judge. The costs are high but the potential payoff could be even higher. Is it a wise investment or a waste of money?

Adapted from Jim Byers, "Toronto-Based Clothier Reaps Gold at Winter Olympics," *Toronto Star*, February 20, 2002, pp. E1, E12; Patrick Allossery, "Will Sponsors Start Keeping a Distance from the Olympics?," *Financial Post*, February 18, 2002, p. FP7; Chris Zelkovich, "Corporations Love Games," *Toronto Star*, January 23, 2002, p. C6; and Patrick Allossery, "The Biggest Game Going," *Financial Post*, January 14, 2002, p. FP6.

Olympic Movement
www.olympic.org

For smaller events such as the marketing conference discussed in this chapter, success or failure is determined by the financial outcome of the event. Key indicators of success would be the profit the event generated. The event planner and perhaps a financial executive would scrutinize all the revenues and costs associated with planning and operating the event to determine if a profit or loss was ultimately generated. For this reason, it is imperative that proper marketing communications strategies are implemented to create awareness and interest in the conference and that operational costs are kept within the financial resources allocated for the event. In the pre-planning stage, the budget statement and profit and loss statement were based on anticipated revenues and cost estimates, and after the event it is time to compare plan figures to actual figures.

Summary

Event marketing and sponsorships are now an important element of a firm's marketing communications mix. Sponsorships tend to be concentrated in four areas: sports; entertainment, tours, and attractions; causes; and the arts. Events and sponsorships can be local in nature or they can be expanded to become regional, national, and international in scope. Sports sponsorships and events attract a majority of the sponsorship pie but interest is now growing faster in the other areas. Organizations that are involved in sports marketing are now pursuing opportunities such as venue marketing and value-added sponsorships.

Prior to getting involved with sponsorships an organization should establish specific criteria for participation. Factors to consider include product category exclusivity, relationships with other marketing communications programs, the event's ability to reach the desired target market effectively, and the image-building potential offered by the event.

Should an organization decide to plan its own event, it must be comfortable with a rather exhaustive planning process. The first decision is to evaluate the role of the event or sponsorship to ensure it offers a good opportunity for achieving business objectives. An organization often works with an event planner (a specialist in this area). The organization is responsible for establishing goals and objectives, identifying the target audience, determining the best time for the event, providing adequate financial resources, and evaluating the event for effectiveness. The event planner develops strategies for staging the event, making available properly trained staff to execute the event, planning operations and logistics to make sure everything runs smoothly, and preparing for safety and security issues that could arise during an event.

The first stage in developing an event is to determine the event's concept and design. This involves decisions about the type of event, the name, and theme of the event. Once these decisions are made, attention focuses on issues such as venue alternatives, financial resources required, timing, room layouts, and technical requirements. To secure proper technical advice and support, a planner usually works with a specialist. Technical support is commonly outsourced.

As with other forms of marketing communications planning, qualitative and quantitative objectives are established. Typically, event marketing objectives focus on quality and quantity of target audience reach, potential new business and product sales, the economic impact of the event, and profit. Event marketing strategies involve carefully defining the product (the event) and then positioning it in the minds of the target audience. A good event title and theme become the foundation for building an effective communications strategy for motivating attendance at the event. An effective price strategy is also crucial, because potential participants evaluate the potential benefits against the cost of attending. To promote the event, a combination of media advertising, web-based communications, and public relations is an effective mix. All communications must have a branded look and present a similar message to the target audience.

At the execution stage, concerns focus on specific details in the following areas: site selection and staging, staffing, operations and logistics, safety and security. All details must be checked and re-checked to ensure smooth flow of activities and people.

Once the event is over, attention turns to evaluation. In relation to objectives that were established for the event, measures are determined for criteria such as awareness, image enhancement, new business clients, product sales, target market reach, and media coverage. There will be an assessment of all revenues and costs to determine profitability, and to make recommendations for improvements should the event be planned for another occasion.

Key Terms

ambush marketing   276
bump-in   296
bump-out   296
event marketing   274
event sponsorship   274

experiential marketing   283
setup   296
teardown   296
venue marketing   276
venue sponsorship   276

Review Questions

1. What is the difference between event marketing and event sponsorship?

2. What is ambush marketing and what benefits does it offer?

3. Identify and briefly explain the main classifications of event marketing.

4. What is experiential marketing and what benefits does it offer?

5. Briefly explain the criteria an executive considers before pursuing an event marketing opportunity.

6. Identify the basic steps in the event marketing planning process.

7. Developing the event concept is the initial stage of planning an event. What are the key decision areas in this stage? Briefly explain.

8. Designing the event is the second stage of event planning. What are some of the key decision areas in this stage? Briefly explain.

9. Briefly explain the purpose of the following planning tools:
   a) proposal
   b) timeline chart
   c) run sheet

10. A key element of event marketing strategy is defining the event. What decisions are associated with defining the event?

11. Briefly explain the following stages of event marketing execution:
   a) site selection and staging
   b) staffing
   c) operations and logistics
   d) safety and security

12. What are the measures commonly used to evaluate the effectiveness of event marketing participation?

Discussion and Application Questions

1. Marketers seem to be growing wary of sports event marketing, particularly at the professional level. Can you suggest any reasons why this is so?

2. Why are companies becoming more actively involved in cause-related event sponsorships? Conduct some secondary research on this issue and formulate a position on the matter.

3. Do value-added sponsorships such as the one between the Ford Motor Company and Phil Mickleson or between Sears and Mike Weir offer significant benefit to the sponsoring organization? If so, what are the benefits? Discuss.

4. Tobacco companies are traditionally among Canada's largest sponsors of prominent sports, entertainment, and cultural events. Since October 1, 2003, these companies are no longer allowed to advertise at such events, which has led to event cancellations. Conduct some research on the ethical issues associated with tobacco advertising and event sponsorships. Should advertising and sponsorships be allowed or not? Justify your position.

5. What classification of event sponsorship is appropriate for the following companies or brands? (More than one can apply.) Justify your decision.
   a) Becel margarine
   b) Michelin tires
   c) Perrier water
   d) BMW automobiles
   e) McDonald's

6. Assess the effectiveness of product promotional tours. Does this form of grassroots marketing really work? Provide some real examples to justify your position.

7. Assume you are responsible for planning and event such as a marathon/half-marathon race to raise funds for the Alzheimer Association of Canada or some similar not-for-profit organization. What are your objectives? Consider both qualitative and quantitative objectives. Provide examples of a few objective statements. What marketing strategies will you employ to create awareness and interest in the event? Provide details of the activities you recommend.

8. Provide some examples of companies and brands that are involved with "experiential marketing." Based on your observations of their activities, identify the strengths and weaknesses of this form of event marketing.

Endnotes

1 Justin Smallbridge, "The Main (Retail) Event," *Financial Post*, November 25, 2002, p. FP7.

2 Visa, "Visa USA 'Lists' the Best Things about the Visa Triple Crown," <usa.visa.com/personal/newsroom/press_releases/nr158.html> (November 2003).

3 IEG Inc., "Where the Dollars Go," <www.sponsorship.com/Learn/wheredollarsgo.asp> (November 2003).

4 Robert Thompson, "BMO Likes Links to Women's Golf," *Financial Post*, August 9, 2002, p. FP6.

5 Carrie Toane, "Soccer's New Game," *Marketing*, August 21, 2001, p. 12.

6 Chris Zelkovich, "Corporations Love Games," *Toronto Star*, January 23, 2002, p. C6.

7 "Your Name Here," *Report on Business Magazine*, May 2002, p. 31.

8 "Cursed," *Advertising Age*, September 16, 2002, p. 19.

9 Kate Fitzgerald, "Masters, Baseball Flaps Zap Magic," *Advertising Age*, October 28, 2002, p. S10.

10 John Heinzl, "Labatt Scales Back Sponsorship," *Globe and Mail*, February 15, 2001, pp. B1, B6.

11 Mark Evans, "Brewers Cheer Concert Boom," *Financial Post*, July 6, 1992, p. S25.

12 Michael Gillings, "Edgy SnowJob Helps Sponsors Reach Youth," *Strategy*, March 12, 2001, p. B8.

13 Terry Poulton, "Basking in the Starlight," *Strategy*, September 9, 2002, p. 21–24.

14 Ibid., p. 24.

15 Sharon Younger, "Grabbing the Spotlight," *Marketing*, December 2, 2002, p. 18.

16 RBC Financial Group, 2002–2003 *Corporate Responsibility Report*, Ontario, p. 5.

17 Mike Lang, "Getting It Right," *Strategy*, September 9, 2002, p. 24.

18 Tim Hortons, "Children's Foundation," <www.timhortons.com/english/english.html> (November 2003).

19 Kristen Vinakmens, "Brands on Wheels," *Strategy*, March 24, 2003, p. 19.

20 Kate Fitzgerald, "Summer Tour Lure," *Advertising Age*, June 17, 2002, p. 36.

21 Bob Weeks, "New Name Coming to Brier," *Globe and Mail*, March 9, 2001, p. S1.

22 Molson Canada, "Molson Donates $500 000 to Charities Following Successful Molson Canadian Rocks for Toronto Concert," press release, October 3, 2003.

23 Jennifer Lewington, "Pride Week's Fate Uncertain Due to SARS, Organizers Say," *Globe and Mail*, May 29, 2003.

24 2002/2003 Conference Calendar, *Strategy*, <www.strategymag.com/conferences> (November 2003).

25 Lynn Van Der Wagen, *Event Management* (Elsternwick, Australia: Hospitality Press, 2001), p. 196.

26 John Van Stan, *The Ellis Park Stadium Soccer Disaster Interim Report*, 2001 <www.crowdsafe.com> (November 2003).

27 Wendy Cuthbert, "Sponsors Pump ROI with Experimental Approach," *Strategy*, March 12, 2001, p. B7.

CHAPTER 11

PERSONAL SELLING

After studying this chapter you will be able to:

LEARNING OBJECTIVES

understand the role of personal selling in retail, business-to-business, and direct selling environments and its relationship to integrated marketing communications;

describe the evolution of personal selling strategies and evaluate the role that relationship selling plays in integrated marketing communications programs;

identify the human variables that contribute to the successful application of personal selling strategies;

learn how to apply this knowledge to a variety of personal selling situations;

identify the fundamental roles and responsibilities of a sales representative;

identify the essential steps in the selling process and the key elements required for preparing a successful sales presentation; and

assess how selling strategies need to adapt to a changing business environment.

Among the various components of the integrated marketing communications mix, personal selling differentiates itself due to its personal nature. Advertising and promotions rely on the media to spread the word, public relations uses various tools to seek the media's support in spreading the word, and direct response communications rely on the mail, telemarketing, and the internet. All these forms of communications are impersonal. In spite of all of the changes that have occurred in the marketplace, and in spite of the fact that industry has come to rely on technology as a means of communication, personal selling nonetheless remains a vital component. Organizations continue to sell— they just sell differently than they used to.

To demonstrate, customer relationship management practices affect all forms of communication, but none more than personal selling. The human contact and the ability to negotiate form the foundation of customer relationship management (CRM) practices. Furthermore, all of the technical wizardry in the world can only go so far. Once the show is over, someone has to ask for the order. And that's the responsibility of personal selling. This chapter examines the role of personal selling in the context of integrated marketing communications.

Personal Selling and Integrated Marketing Communications

Personal Selling
Face-to-face communication involving the presentation of features and benefits of a product or service to a buyer.

Personal selling is a personalized form of communications that involves sellers presenting the features and benefits of a product or service to a buyer for the purpose of making a sale. It is an integral component of marketing communications, because it is the activity that in many cases clinches the deal. Advertising and promotions create awareness and interest for a product. Personal selling creates desire and action. In creating desire and action, the interaction between the seller and buyer is crucial.

Personal selling can be divided into three main areas: retail selling, business-to-business (B2B) selling, and direct selling, either to consumers or other businesses (see Figure 11.1). In all these areas, personal selling is connected to other aspects of integrated marketing communications planning. For example, a sales representative for Kraft Foods who calls on the head office of a grocery chain such as Safeway or Sobeys does more than just communicate the benefits of various product lines. If the salesperson's presentation involved a new product launch, the objective would be to get the product listed by the chain's head office so that retail stores in the chain could order it. Buyers want to know what kind of marketing support will be provided by Kraft. Therefore, at the very least, the salesperson must include information about advertising plans and sales promotion plans (both consumer and trade promotions) that will help create demand for the new product. Details about when advertising is scheduled, what markets it will run in, and what incentives will be offered to the consumer and the trade are all critical factors that influence the buying decision. Similar situations exist in other industries. Personal selling is directly linked to other communications strategies.

Kraft Foods
www.kraft.com

RETAIL SELLING

Transactions occur on the sales floor of a department store, in a checkout line of a grocery store, at an insurance agent's office, and at the service desk of an automobile maintenance shop, to name just a few examples of retail selling. In these situations, the nature of the sale is defined as a single transaction or a repeat transaction. The quality of service offered at the point of sale and the degree of satisfaction the customer receives usually influence repeat transactions. A **single transaction** occurs when a salesperson spends time with a customer and eventually closes the sale on the spot. In many organizations, **order taking** is becoming popular. Stores such as Canadian Tire, Wal-Mart, Home Depot,

Single Transaction
A retail sales situation where a salesperson spends time with a customer and closes the sale on the spot.

Order Taking
In retail sales, a floor clerk provides product information and shows goods to the customer, who then goes to the checkout counter to pay for purchases.

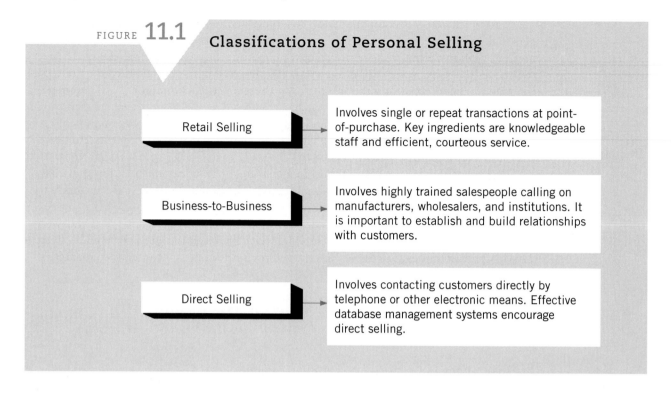

FIGURE **11.1** **Classifications of Personal Selling**

Retail Selling → Involves single or repeat transactions at point-of-purchase. Key ingredients are knowledgeable staff and efficient, courteous service.

Business-to-Business → Involves highly trained salespeople calling on manufacturers, wholesalers, and institutions. It is important to establish and build relationships with customers.

Direct Selling → Involves contacting customers directly by telephone or other electronic means. Effective database management systems encourage direct selling.

Ikea, and other large retailers have popularized the concept of self-serve. In these stores, floor personnel assist customers in locating the goods they need and provide useful information, but the customer simply passes through the checkout when purchasing the goods.

In situations where **repeat transactions** occur, there is an ongoing relationship between the buyer and seller. For example, a customer will return to the same automobile repair shop after getting to know the people who are working on his or her car. The customer wants to avoid potential risk in dealing with different repair shops. The relationship between the buyer and seller is usually based on factors such as trust, respect, and satisfaction with the goods or services provided. These factors must be present if the retailer is to profit in the long run.

Successful retailers continuously stress the importance of customer contact at point-of-purchase. How a retail salesperson interacts with the customer has a significant impact on how the customer perceives the retailer and helps determine if that individual will make a purchase. It is the seller's responsibility to clarify what the customer actually needs, usually by politely asking a few questions. The seller must then offer some product suggestions and demonstrate knowledge by presenting the essential benefits of the products to the customer. When the purchase decision is made, the seller should look for opportunities for add-on sales, or suggest service warranties to protect the customer's long-term interests. In retail stores where single transactions are the goal, high-pressure sales tactics are often applied. Although these kinds of tactics may work in the short term, many customers react negatively to them, and simply leave the store feeling frustrated. Generally speaking, a low-key approach involving positive customer contact, in a pleasant and courteous manner, is the main ingredient for retail selling success. In retail, the salespeople are the most essential point of contact in the purchasing process—integral to a well-planned integrated marketing communications program.

Repeat Transaction

A retail sales situation that involves a relationship between the buyer and the seller; the customer returns to the same store for similar goods and services.

BUSINESS-TO-BUSINESS SELLING

Business-to-business salespeople either sell products for use in the production and sale of other products, or sell products to channel members who in turn resell them. For example, a Xerox sales representative sells photocopiers to another business for use in its daily operations; a representative from Nike sells a line of running shoes to the head office of a specialty retailer such as the Forzani Group, which in turn, distributes the running shoes through its retail locations (Sport Chek).

Thoroughly trained and adequately prepared sales representatives are crucial in all these examples. Investment in other forms of marketing communications could be all for naught if the personal selling execution is weak. B2B organizations usually have different types of sales personnel. A **field sales force** is composed of sales representatives who call on customers regularly. They make presentations to existing and new customers, and provide ongoing customer contact in order to establish a good business relationship. The roles and responsibilities of the field sales force are discussed later in the chapter. An **inside sales force**, often referred to as order takers, also seek out new customers and provide useful information to them. Working from the organization's premises, an order taker handles orders that are received by telephone, fax, or online.

DIRECT SELLING

Direct selling to customers either by telephone or the internet can be accommodated in the retail selling and B2B selling situations described above. **Telemarketing** involves using the telephone as an interactive medium for a marketing response. It uses highly trained people and database marketing techniques to seek and serve new customers. Figure 11.2 summarizes the role that telemarketing can play in the selling process. Telemarketing improves productivity by reducing direct-selling costs, specifically the costs associated with keeping sales representatives on the road (automobile, accommodations, and related travel expenses). It is also useful in screening and qualifying incoming leads, generating leads from various database directories and mailing lists, and for calling on current customers to secure additional orders, offer additional services, and determine the level of customer satisfaction. Telemarketing techniques prosper in business today because they capitalize on the database management systems employed by sophisticated marketing organizations.

Online selling refers to the use of websites in order to conduct sales transactions. Consumers who are looking for convenience now include the web as part of their shopping experience. Figure 11.3 shows how Grocery Gateway, an online supermarket, provides its consumers convenience. Websites such as Grocery Gateway's are capable of

Field Sales Force
An organization's external sales representatives who regularly call on customers to pursue orders.

Inside Sales Force
An internal group of sellers, often referred to as order takers, who accept orders from customers by telephone or other means.

Telemarketing
The use of telecommunications to promote the products and services of a business.

Online Selling
Using the internet to conduct sales transactions.

FIGURE **11.2** **Some of the Roles Played by Telemarketing in Personal Selling**

Sales Support
- Generate leads
- Qualify leads
- Schedule appointments
- Collect market intelligence

Selling
- Open new accounts
- Call marginal accounts
- Sell to existing customers

Customer Service
- Operate customer help lines
- Handle inquiries and complains
- Offer after-sales service
- Conduct satisfaction surveys

accepting and processing orders, receiving payment, and arranging for the delivery of goods and services directly to consumers and businesses. Since all transactions are electronically recorded, companies accumulate huge databases of information that can be used for marketing purposes in the longer term.

FIGURE **11.3** **Online Selling Offers Convenience to Consumers**

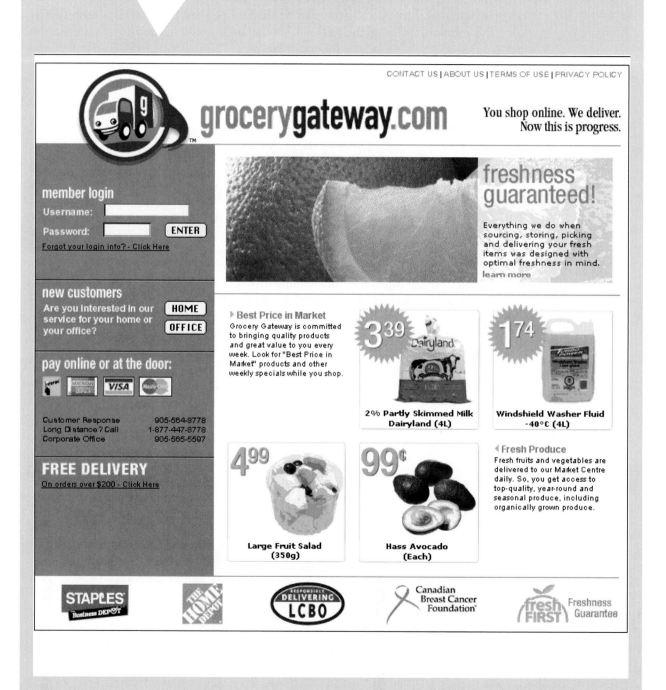

Source: Grocery Gateway Inc., Mississauga, Ontario.

The Evolution of Selling

Over the years, the nature of selling has changed. Since the 1970s, personal selling has passed through three distinct stages: consultative selling, strategic selling, and relationship selling.[1] Relationship selling has been extended a step further as companies adopt electronic data interchange practices. For these companies, partnership selling is now the name of the game. Let's start with an examination of consultative selling. **Consultative selling** stresses open two-way communication between sellers and buyers. The initial task of the seller is to discover a need or set of needs by asking questions and listening carefully. The seller then uses that information to formulate appropriate product recommendations—acting as a consultant. Once the sale is complete, the seller gets involved with after-sales service and customer care programs. A satisfied customer remains a customer!

The marketplace has changed and so the nature of personal selling has had to change. Several trends have fuelled that change: products and services are now more sophisticated and complex, competition is more intense and occurs on a broader (global) scale, and customer expectations of quality, price, service, and individualized solutions have increased considerably. These trends paved the way for strategic selling. Much like strategies that are developed for advertising, sales promotions, public relations, and event marketing programs, strategic selling strategies are influenced by an organization's strategic marketing plan. Remember, the strategic marketing plan establishes objectives, plots overall strategic direction for the company or its individual divisions or products, and allocates resources to put the strategic plan into action. The marketing plan acts as a guide for the strategic selling plan. Refer to Figure 11.4 for an illustration of the planning model.

Strategic selling takes consultative selling to the next level. It considers the most recent yet continuously changing conditions in the marketplace, adds in technology to enhance the methods of presenting products to buyers, and focuses on serving customers one customer at a time. The goal is to remain flexible while providing solutions unique to each customer. There are three key factors to be considered when formulating a strategic sales strategy. First, the seller must do what is necessary to form a good relationship with the customer. Second, the seller must effectively match products and position them so that they meet customer needs. And third, the seller must develop a compelling presentation that will clearly portray the usefulness of a product in resolving a customer's problem.

In **relationship selling**, the goal is to develop a plan of action to establish, build, and maintain customers. In involves taking a long-term perspective on selling and considers the fact that good relationships don't necessarily form very quickly. Instead, a seller must take the necessary steps to form a relationship, such as establishing rapport and building trust and respect, over a long period of time. Having a positive attitude, projecting a good image, and being able to get along with all kinds of different people and personalities are key factors that contribute to a sales representative's ability to build a solid relationship with customers.

Establishing a good relationship depends on how well the seller positions products in the minds of customers, how effectively (persuasively) the product's benefits are presented, and how well the seller guards the relationship in the long run. The latter requires ongoing customer contact and the implementation of customer care programs. Figure 11.5 reviews the key aspects of relationship selling.

Typically, a seller has several products that will satisfy the customer's needs. And, of course, competitors will offer similar alternatives. Therefore, it is the seller's responsibility to match the right product to the customer and then develop the communications strategy that will position it appropriately in the customer's mind. As a good ad for toothpaste would effectively position Crest as the best solution for preventing cavities in a consumer's mind, a good sales presentation for Apple computers to an educational facility will effectively portray the computers as being unique, innovative, and reliable, promoting Apple as the right computer for students pursuing careers in the creative aspects

Consultative Selling
A form of selling that stresses open two-way communication between a buyer and seller.

Strategic Selling
A form of consultative selling that involves dealing with each customer as an individual, stressing that in the transfer of product information.

Relationship Selling
A form of selling with the goal of developing a plan of action that establishes, builds, and maintains a long-term relationship with customers.

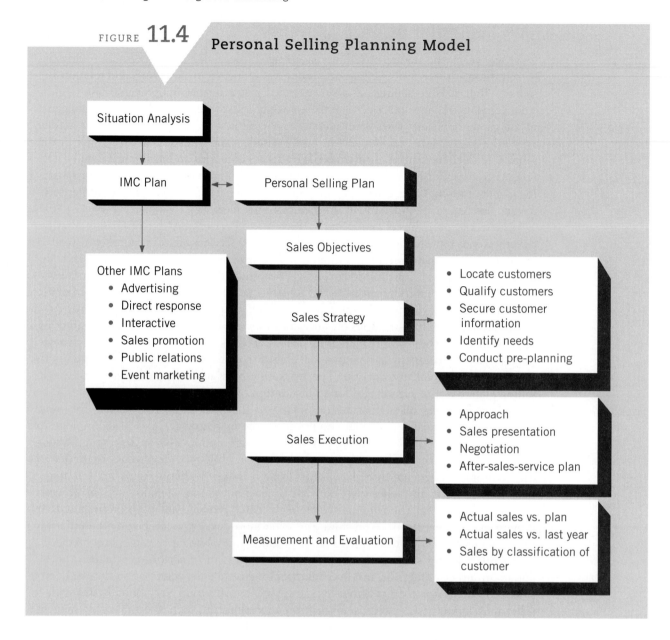

FIGURE **11.4** Personal Selling Planning Model

Apple Computers
www.apple.com

Presentation Strategy

A plan of what to say to a customer in a sales presentation to identify customer needs, summarize benefits, and prepare for potential objections.

of business, and so on. In this example, the sales representative adapts Apple's overall positioning strategy, as it appears in all forms of its marketing communications, to the sales situation at hand. Apple representatives will differentiate their product offerings from the rest of the pack by identifying market segments its products are ideally suited for.

The formation of the right positioning strategy depends largely on the seller's knowledge of the customer. The more knowledge the seller has going into the presentation, the easier it is to structure the presentation. A good salesperson continuously updates his or her files with customer information. In the age of technology, such a practice is easy to do and vital to success. People in organizations move around, so it is very important to be constantly on top of who is responsible for what.

A good salesperson formulates a **presentation strategy** that focuses on what to say to customers when presenting the product. A good plan is based on the seller's knowledge of the customer and his or her immediate needs; it summarizes potential benefits that will be stressed (often prioritized from most important to less important) and considers

FIGURE **11.5** The Key Elements of Relationship Selling

Overall Goal	To establish, build, and maintain customers.
Personal Strategy	The seller must initiate steps that will build rapport with customers. The seller must earn the trust and respect of the customer. The salesperson must have a strong and positive self-image and be flexible when dealing with many different people and personalities.
Selling Strategy	The salesperson must effectively position the product (a solution) in the customer's mind by relating the right benefits to a unique problem or situation that the customer presents. The benefits should be related to the rational needs of the buying organization and the emotional needs of the buyer. A salesperson must make a convincing presentation and be flexible enough to adapt to the unexpected while the presentation is in progress. A persuasive presentation should lead the buyer to the right decision.
Building Relationships	Customers not only want good products, but also want good relationships. Selling today is not about selling products—it's about selling solutions!

potential objections that the buyer might raise. As with most marketing communications strategies, a sales strategy must remain flexible. The seller, for example, must be able to adapt the presentation based on new information that surfaces during a presentation, or to rephrase relevant benefits if the buyer introduces the benefits of a competitor's product. The importance of knowledge in a variety of areas and the key elements of a presentation are discussed in more detail later in this chapter.

PARTNERSHIP SELLING

Increased competition, the need to deliver greater customer satisfaction, and internal demands to reduce costs are driving companies to transform their selling procedures and methods.[2] The concept of relationship selling took hold in the 1990s. Relationship selling was based on the premise that longer term relationships between buyers and sellers would bear greater fruit for both parties. It was a concept based on personalization. Sellers customized their approach for each customer.

Today, customers not only want good products—they want good relationships, too. Buying organizations want to deal with selling organizations that are willing to invest significant time and resources into finding good solutions. It's not just about selling products any more. It's about selling solutions! IBM, for example, has transformed itself from a seller of computer hardware to a company that provides complete business and e-business solutions. IBM is now more of a services and solutions company than a product company. The company has evolved its marketing and marketing communications practices with the changing conditions in the marketplace. In similar fashion, UPS has moved from a courier service to a supply chain management and distribution company, with the goal of assisting customers with their long-range growth needs (see Figure 11.6).

United Parcel Service
www.ups.com

FIGURE **11.6** **Sophisticated Marketing Organizations such as UPS Offer Business Solutions to Current and Prospective Customers**

Source: Courtesy of UPS and The Martin Agency.

Partnership Selling

A strategically developed long-term relationship that involves selling products and providing comprehensive after-sales service and effective two-way communications to ensure complete customer satisfaction.

The concept of customer relationship management plays a role in selling today. As discussed elsewhere in this textbook, the cost of keeping a current customer satisfied is significantly less than attracting a new customer. **Partnership selling** is part of CRM. It is a strategically developed, long-term relationship that involves selling products, providing comprehensive after-sales service, and effective two-way communications to ensure complete customer satisfaction.

British Telecom
www.bt.com

Changing conditions in the marketplace have fostered the concept of partnership selling. With so many companies offering so many good and similar products, sellers look to the relationship as a means of differentiation from the competition. As well, technology has changed the very essence of selling. Computers and other telecommunications devices allow for quicker and better communications with customers and more efficient reporting procedures with managers and technical and service support personnel at the head office. For additional insight into how personal selling is changing, read the IMC Highlight **Change Essential for Survival**.

> ### IMC Highlight
>
> # CHANGE ESSENTIAL FOR SURVIVAL
>
> According to Danny McLaughlin, managing director for British Telecom, the old way of selling will not work in the future. He cites increased competition, the need to deliver greater customer satisfaction, and internal demands to reduce costs as driving forces for transforming sales forces. In the case of British Telecom, it was a process akin to recreating the company.
>
> Selling the old way involved squads of salespeople calling on customers to drum up business. "We had to make a fundamental shift to a multi-channel sales organization," says McLaughlin. "We could see that the one-channel way of doing business just wouldn't work in the future." The very nature of British Telecom's business was also being transformed. Formerly it faced competition from a host of network providers, but by the late 1990s, most of its competitors simply dealt with British Telecom as a wholesaler. The company's future, it appeared, would come from the services it offered. The goal was to find ways of delivering the services, matching the right delivery channel to the right customer, and at the right cost.
>
> According to McLaughlin, the key to changing the face of the company—the face it presented to customers—was to change it inside first. And that involved a change in sales mentality. There were three main challenges. As in most organizations, there is an initial resistance to change. The company was experiencing double-digit growth, so why change? The second challenge was to create new skill sets among existing staff while introducing new recruits with different skills. The third challenge was changing the behaviour of more than 5000 existing sales staff.
>
> The key to success was a trio of programs. First, British Telecom created an online learning course designed to challenge sales staff from selling products to selling solutions. Everyone had to pass the course! The second program involved a web portal offering all the information necessary to make sales. And the third program involved a targeted approach to selling that provided a sales strategy using a single glossary of terms and way of dealing with customers. As well, new customer relationship management software was employed across the entire organization.
>
> In less than two years, British Telecom has switched from a single way of selling to major customers to a multi-faceted approach that includes 300 telemarketing people, indirect selling through resellers, and an internet marketing channel. McLaughlin advises that the process of change is ongoing.
>
> Adapted from Terrence Belford, "Re-arm Your Sales Force," *National Post*, May 5, 2003, p. BE1.

Personal Selling: The Human Communications Element

If establishing and building effective relationships are the keys to modern-day success, what strategies must the salesperson use to form a good working relationship? To be successful, a salesperson must focus on three primary areas: personal characteristics, verbal communications, and non-verbal communications. A well-prepared and energetic salesperson knows how to communicate effectively both verbally and non-verbally, and, as a result, will be successful. Let's examine each area briefly.

PERSONAL CHARACTERISTICS

To survive in selling, certain personal characteristics are required. Typically, successful salespeople are self-confident, motivated, flexible, and optimistic, and project a good image when confronted with social and business situations. Fortunately, these characteristics are things that can be learned and practised, and, given time and proper training, poorly performing salespeople can be transformed into prosperous salespeople. All that is required are dedication and a desire to confront the challenges of selling.

Self-Image
One's own idea about oneself and one's relationship with others.

Self-image is a psychological term referring to one's attitude and feelings about oneself and one's roles in relation to others. It certainly plays a key role in selling. Perhaps the most important aspect of self-image is one's confidence. For example, an individual who approaches a challenge with enthusiasm, or possesses that "I'm going to win" attitude, is likely to succeed. In contrast, an individual who tends to forecast failure, or has a "doom and gloom" attitude, will almost certainly get disappointing results. To succeed, therefore, you have to think you can succeed.

Developing the proper mindset is the responsibility of an organization's sales managers and the training programs it provides its salespeople. Among all the theories about building self-confidence that exist, three essential strategies stand out. First, a positive self-image will exist if a person does not dwell on past mistakes. Instead, people must learn from those mistakes, and move forward. Second, a salesperson should develop some expertise in a certain area, because there is special status in being an expert. Others will call upon you for advice. Third, a salesperson should develop a positive outlook. For example, taking courses that reinforce the principles of success and simply associating with other positive and successful people are both good practices to follow.

Non-Verbal Communication or Body Language
The expression of thoughts, opinions, or information using non-verbal cues such as body movement, facial expressions, and eye contact.

Non-verbal communication or **body language** is another essential aspect of self-confidence. Non-verbal communication refers to the imparting of thoughts, opinions, or information without using spoken words. An observer (in this case the buyer) will notice non-verbal cues such as body movement, facial expressions, and eye contact.[3] A buyer's perceptions of a salesperson are often determined by body language. For example, does the seller squirm in the chair while conversing or does the seller fidget with a small object while speaking? Such body language could be perceived as a lack of confidence. Alternatively, does the seller make direct eye contact? Was that handshake firm and friendly? Such body language suggests positive self-confidence. For a summary of the essential characteristics and traits for successful selling, refer to Figure 11.7.

There are numerous theories, well beyond the scope of this book, that discuss the relationships between verbal communication and non-verbal communication. Rather than dwell on which aspect is most important, let's simply suggest that successful salespeople effectively blend together verbal and non-verbal communications. They communicate the message in a positive and enthusiastic manner and reinforce it with body language that is consistent with what they say. Such a combination builds confidence in the buyer and gives the buyer the impression you can be trusted. Such perceptions certainly go a long way in building and maintaining a business relationship.

Other non-verbal characteristics that influence buyers' perceptions include facial expressions, personal appearance, and manners. The old expression that "the lips say one thing, but the eyes say another" applies to selling situations. Facial gestures can communicate confidence, as does a smile; boredom, as does a grin; or evaluation or judgment, as in a frown or perplexed expression. Given that the goal in selling is to express confidence, successful salespeople always wear a sincere and winning smile when they approach customers and when they present information to them.

Dress codes have changed drastically in recent years. The business world moved away from formal attire (business suits) and toward informal attire (business casual) for a period of time. The "Casual Friday" concept spread to the entire week. Recently, however, there has been a return to a more formal dress. Wardrobe experts believe clothing makes a significant difference in building one's credibility and likeability with customers. Experts also offer lots of differing opinions on how to dress. If there is one common theme in all the advice they provide, it is that the situation (or appropriateness) dictates the style of dress. For example, if you are meeting your customer in a business office or boardroom setting, formal dress is appropriate. If the meeting is in a factory or at a construction site, less

FIGURE **11.7** **Personal Characteristics and Planning Lead to Selling Success**

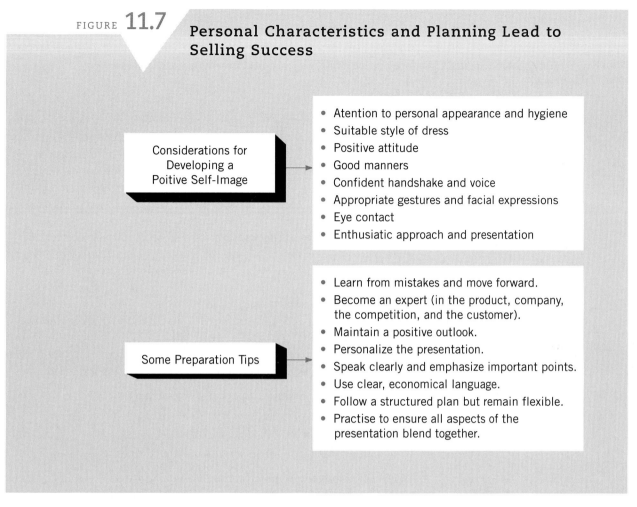

Considerations for Developing a Poitive Self-Image

- Atention to personal appearance and hygiene
- Suitable style of dress
- Positive attitude
- Good manners
- Confident handshake and voice
- Appropriate gestures and facial expressions
- Eye contact
- Enthusiatic approach and presentation

Some Preparation Tips

- Learn from mistakes and move forward.
- Become an expert (in the product, company, the competition, and the customer).
- Maintain a positive outlook.
- Personalize the presentation.
- Speak clearly and emphasize important points.
- Use clear, economical language.
- Follow a structured plan but remain flexible.
- Practise to ensure all aspects of the presentation blend together.

formal attire is suitable. Other traditional guidelines for wardrobe focus on simplicity, quality, and the selective use of accessories.

In terms of simplicity of clothing, it is wise to consider the combination of colour and design. Going on the golf course with a customer allows the seller to express a little flamboyance. If the meeting is in an office, dressing more conservatively is wise, if the salesperson is to be taken seriously. Quality also projects a certain image. No one suggests or expects that salespeople should spend a fortune on clothing, but they must view their clothes as an investment. Therefore, buying quality designs that will remain in style for an extended period is a good strategy to follow. Finally, what role do accessories play? The seller's role is to command attention to what he or she is saying. Accessories such as earrings, necklaces, and facial jewellery can be a distraction for the buyer. Anything that will cause a distraction should be avoided. A conservative approach is wise.

PREPARATION AND THE IMPORTANCE OF KNOWLEDGE

In a nutshell, the primary task of a salesperson is to provide a customer with a solution to a problem by matching the right product or service at a price that is agreeable to the customer. It sounds so simple! But it requires much advance preparation, and that preparation is divided into three primary areas: product knowledge, company knowledge, and competitor knowledge. With regard to product knowledge, the salesperson must become an expert and know exactly what benefits to stress with any particular customer. For example, two different customers might require the same product but one customer is motivated by quality, the other by service. The salesperson would have to adapt the presentation to offer different perspectives based on each buyer's unique needs and priorities. In complex situations, such as when various products must be combined to form a solution, the salesperson must be capable of bringing the right products and services together. This process is called **product configuration**.

Product Configuration

The bringing together of various products and services to form a solution for the customer.

Product Knowledge

Essentially, product knowledge can be classified into four key areas: product development and quality improvement processes, performance data and specifications, maintenance and service, and price and delivery. The various combinations of this information make up the essential elements of a planned sales presentation. To grow, companies develop new products to solve new needs. It is important for a salesperson to know how a product was developed, how much it cost to develop, and why it was developed. This sort of information strongly suggests to a customer that the company takes research and development seriously and strives to build better products for its customers. In terms of performance and quality, a salesperson should be familiar with quality control standards so that information regarding product claims can be substantiated and compared with claims made by competitors. Knowing that a product meets or exceeds certain standards often provides competitive advantage in a sales presentation.

A buyer usually poses all kinds of questions (referred to as objections) about performance data and specifications in the middle of a sales presentation. To illustrate, assume you were considering various conference centres for a business conference you are planning. What kinds of questions would you ask the sales managers? Here are a few examples:

- Does the conference centre offer technical support if we need it?
- Is there an internet connection available to delegates and at what cost?
- Is there sufficient accommodation for 200 delegates?
- How efficient is the catering department in serving a buffet dinner to 200 people?

Certainly the list could be longer and much more diverse. And that is the key point. A good salesperson must be ready to respond to the expected and unexpected.

If the competing products are similar, it could be that information about maintenance and service provide product differentiation. If service is provided as part of a package deal, all specifications regarding additional services must be part of the sales presentation. Specifications must be agreed upon about who is responsible for what service, when it will happen, how often it will happen, and so on. It is very common for selling companies to draw up official service contracts based on specific requirements provided by the buying organization. Such contracts play a vital role in the relationship building process.

Other knowledge that helps differentiate one product from another is knowledge about price and delivery. The easiest and most common objection that buyers raise is price: "Your price is too high!" Knowing how to respond appropriately is crucial to closing the sale. If your price is higher than the competition, that fact must be acknowledged, and additional and tangible product benefits must be presented to justify the higher price. In such situations, the buyer simply wants more information; the salesperson must show good product knowledge.

Company Knowledge

Since the salesperson is the customer's primary source of contact, the salesperson is the company. The perceptions formed by a customer or prospective customer about a company depend largely on the attitude, style, behaviour, and communications ability of the salesperson. Simply stated, good feelings about a company are key to an eventual sale and the development of a long-term business relationship. A salesperson, therefore, should integrate essential information about the company into a sales presentation. In situations where competing products are judged to be similar, the buyer could make a decision based on which company he or she prefers to do business with. To demonstrate, consider that Canada has five very large banks: RBC Financial Group, BMO Financial Group, CIBC, TD Canada Trust, and the Bank of Nova Scotia. All banks offer similar products and services, so customers very often choose where to do business based on their overall perceptions of each institution. These perceptions are influenced by contact the customer has with the bank, by the attitudes projected by employees, and by marketing communications in other forms.

Business organizations exist in order to serve their customers, and all employees must recognize that they contribute to this effort. This attitude, often referred to as **corporate culture**, is defined as the values, norms, and practices shared by all employees of an organization. A good corporate culture always puts the customer first. A successful and diversified organization such as 3M thinks "customer" all of the time. All employees are part of a marketing team and consider themselves to be in the customer care business. In fact, 3M uses the phrase "From need to…3M Innovation" as its advertising slogan. At the 3M website there are other phrases such as "From Imagination to Innovation" and "Leading through Innovation." 3M identifies customer needs and develops innovative products to satisfy those needs. Such information should be passed on to prospective customers by sales representatives, because it sends out a clear signal about the type of company 3M is: a company willing to develop new products and to respond to new challenges in an ever-changing marketplace. Figure 11.8 provides some insight into the innovations of 3M in the consumer marketplace and the B2B marketplace.

What services a company provides after the sale is also crucial information to provide to customers. As many experts say, "the relationship begins once the sale is made." Therefore, after-sales service, which is a function that is usually implemented by other departments of a company, must be integrated into a sales presentation. It is important for a company to track the level of satisfaction that customers are experiencing, so it is quite common for organizations to contact customers directly by telephone or mail. The results of surveys, for example, can be passed on to sales representatives for follow-up.

Competitor Knowledge

A good salesperson knows the competitor's products almost as well as his or her own. In a sales presentation, comparisons inevitably crop up, making it essential to know the benefits and weaknesses of competing products and adapt the selling strategy accordingly. If a seller cannot respond to the challenges posed by a buyer, the chances of making a sale are lost.

Talking about competing products is usually awkward. Obviously, a salesperson does not want to acknowledge a competitor's strengths but at the same time a seller cannot be too critical of what is being offered. The customer may already be doing business with the competition. Here are a few basic guidelines for dealing with competing products.[4]

- Do not deliberately include reference to competitors in your presentation as it shifts the focus off your own product. Do, however, respond to questions about the competition.

- Do not make statements about the competitor if you are uncertain of the facts. Your credibility will suffer if you make inaccurate statements.

- Do not criticize the competition. State the facts as you know them and avoid emotional comments if you have to make a comparison.

Remember, prospective customers are forming perceptions of you and your company when you are making the sales presentation. How you handle competing products goes a long way in creating a favourable or unfavourable impression.

Roles and Responsibilities of Salespeople

The primary tasks of a salesperson, particularly in a business-to-business environment, are to gather market intelligence, solve customers' problems, locate and maintain customers, and provide follow-up service. This section examines each key responsibility.

Corporate Culture
The values, beliefs, norms, and practices shared by all employees of an organization.

3M
www.3m.com

FIGURE **11.8**   **3M Responds to the Challenge of Developing New and Innovative Products for a Changing Marketplace**

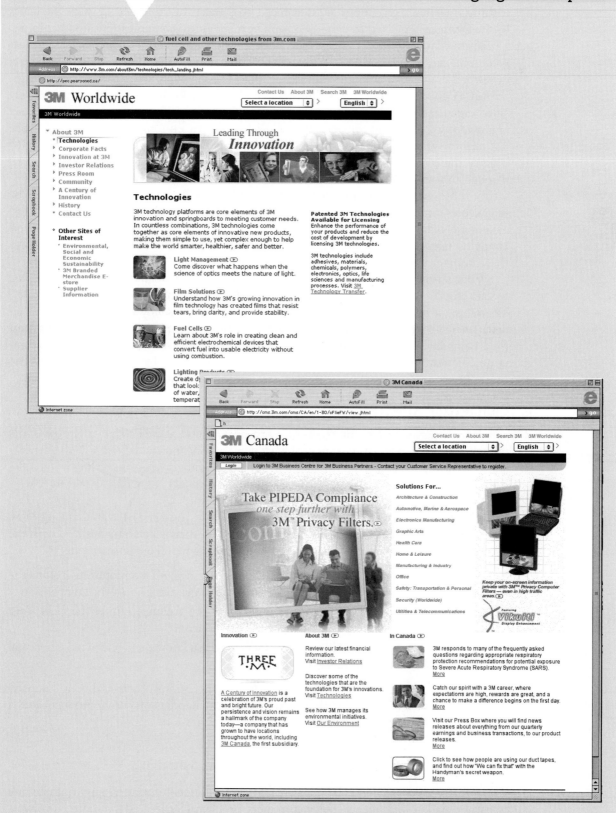

Source: © 3M 2003.

GATHERING MARKET INTELLIGENCE

In a competitive marketplace, salespeople must be attuned to the trends in their industry. They must be alert to what the competitor is doing, to its new product projects, and to its advertising and promotion plans, and they must listen to feedback from customers regarding their own products' performances. As indicated earlier, competitive knowledge is important when the salesperson faces questions involving product comparisons. Data collected by a salesperson can be reported electronically to the company's head office. Managers can retrieve the information and use it appropriately at a later date.

PROBLEM SOLVING

The only way a salesperson can make a sale is to listen to what a customer wants and ask questions to determine his or her real needs. Asking, listening, and providing information and advice that is in the best interests of the customer are what consultative selling is all about. The seller must demonstrate a sincere concern for the customer's needs.

LOCATING AND MAINTAINING CUSTOMERS

Salespeople who locate new customers play a key role in a company's growth. A company cannot be satisfied with its current list of customers because aggressive competitors are always attempting to lure them away. To prevent shrinkage and to increase sales, salespeople actively pursue new accounts. Their time is divided between finding new accounts and selling and servicing current accounts.

FOLLOW-UP SERVICE

The salesperson is the first point of contact should anything go wrong or should more information be required. Maintenance of customers is crucial and, very often, it is the quality of the follow-up service that determines if a customer will remain a customer. Since the salespeople are the company's direct link to the customer, it cannot be stressed enough how important it is that they handle customer service well. The sale is never over! Once the deal has closed, numerous tasks arise: arranging for delivery, providing technical assistance, offering customer training, and being readily available to handle any problems that might emerge during and after delivery. The personalized role of the sales representative is instrumental in building relationships.

Personal Selling Strategies

Before discussing the various steps involved in successful personal selling, let's first explore the difference between features and benefits. A product feature is anything that can be felt, seen, or measured. **Features** include such things as durability, design, and economy of operation. They provide a customer with information but do not motivate a customer to buy. A **benefit** provides the customer with advantage or gain, and shows how a product will help resolve a specific problem. Benefits provide motivation! To demonstrate, consider all of the technical features usually associated with a laptop or desktop computer. The list seems endless and includes much technical jargon. Assuming the customer wants quick access to information when using the computer (information the seller would seek out by asking a few questions), the seller can quickly zoom in on the appropriate features, and translate them into benefits that are appropriate for and meaningful to the customer.

Some of the key concepts involved in B2B buying behaviour were discussed in Chapter 1. A successful salesperson uses such knowledge of the buying situation when developing a sales strategy for approaching new and existing customers. Regardless of the

Feature
Tangible aspects of a product, such as durability, design, and economy of operation.

Benefit
The value a customer attaches to a brand attribute.

FIGURE **11.9**

The Seven Essential Steps in the Personal Selling Process

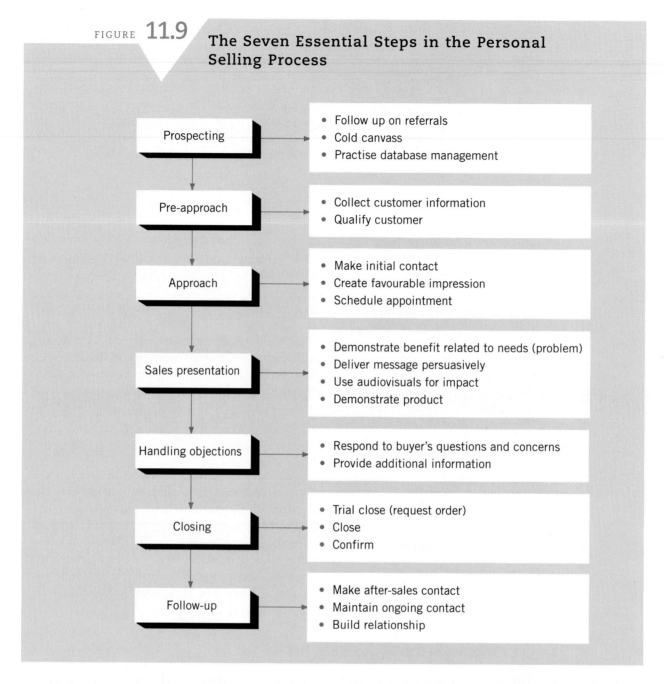

Prospecting
- Follow up on referrals
- Cold canvass
- Practise database management

Pre-approach
- Collect customer information
- Qualify customer

Approach
- Make initial contact
- Create favourable impression
- Schedule appointment

Sales presentation
- Demonstrate benefit related to needs (problem)
- Deliver message persuasively
- Use audiovisuals for impact
- Demonstrate product

Handling objections
- Respond to buyer's questions and concerns
- Provide additional information

Closing
- Trial close (request order)
- Close
- Confirm

Follow-up
- Make after-sales contact
- Maintain ongoing contact
- Build relationship

sales situation—whether retail selling, business-to-business selling, or direct selling—the stages in the selling process are similar. They are simply adapted to each situation. This section covers the seven essential stages of the selling process (see Figure 11.9).

PROSPECTING

Prospecting

A procedure for systematically developing sales leads.

The first step is **prospecting,** which is a procedure for systematically developing sales leads. If salespeople do not allocate enough time to finding new customers, they risk causing a decline in sales for their company. If their income is geared to the value of the business they produce, they risk the loss of personal compensation as well. Prospecting is also important because of attrition. Attrition refers to the loss of customers over a period of time. Even with extensive CRM programs in place as a means of retaining customers, buyers switch suppliers when better products and services become available.

Potential customers, or prospects, are identified by means of published lists and directories, such as Scott's industrial directories, the *Frasers Trade Index*, and the *Canadian Key Business Directory*. Another strategy for seeking new customers is the referral. A **referral** is a prospect that is recommended by a current customer. The salesperson also seeks new customers by **cold canvass**, the process of calling on people or organizations without appointments or advance knowledge of them. Other sources of leads include names obtained from trade shows, advertising, direct response communications, telemarketing and online communications, sales promotion entry forms, and channel members.

PRE-APPROACH

The **pre-approach** involves gathering information about potential customers before actually making sales contact. During the pre-approach stage, customers are **qualified**, which is the procedure for determining if a prospect needs the product, has the authority to buy it, and has the ability to pay for it. There is little sense in pursuing customers who lack the financial resources or have no need to make the business relationship successful. In the process of qualifying customers, the seller also gains insights that can be used in the sales presentation: information such as the buyer's likes and dislikes, personal interests and hobbies, buying procedures, and special needs and problems.

APPROACH

The **approach** is the initial contact with the prospect, often in a face-to-face selling situation. Since buyers are usually busy, little time should be wasted in the approach. In the first few minutes of a sales interview, the salesperson must capture the attention and interest of the buyer and create a favourable first impression so that there is an effective environment for the presentation of the product's benefits.

SALES PRESENTATION

As discussed in Chapter 1, it is common for a salesperson to make presentations to individuals (one-on-one selling) or to buying teams (one-on-group selling). Buying teams were classified as buying centres (an informal grouping of people in the buying group) or buying committees (a formal group with a structured buying procedure in place). In dealing with buying committees, the salesperson must listen attentively and observe body language, in order to determine which members of the group are the real influencers and decision makers.

The actual **sales presentation** consists of a persuasive delivery and demonstration of a product's benefits. An effective sales presentation shows the buyer how the benefits of the product satisfy his or her needs or help resolve a particular problem. In doing so, the seller focuses on the benefits that are most important to the buyer. Critical elements usually focus on lower price, the durability of the product, the dependability of supply, the performance of the product, and the availability of follow-up service.

At this stage, asking proper questions and listening attentively are particularly important. A salesperson listens to and analyzes what buyers are saying, then uses what has been discovered when presenting the appropriate benefits. Being flexible and adapting a presentation in mid-stream could be the difference between making a sale and not making a sale.

Demonstrations play a key role in a sales presentation. A **demonstration** is an opportunity to show the product in action and substantiates the claims being made about the product. A good demonstration (something the buyer can see) adds to the convincing nature of the presentation. It helps hold the buyer's attention and create interest and desire. It is wise to rehearse the demonstration so that what the salesperson says and what the salesperson demonstrates are in harmony with each other.

Referral

A recommendation by a current customer of a potential new customer to a sales representative.

Cold Canvass

The process of calling on people or organizations without appointments or advance knowledge of them.

Pre-approach

The gathering of information about customers before actually making sales contact.

Qualifying

Assessing if a prospect needs a product, has the authority to buy it, and has the ability to pay for it.

Approach

The initial contact with a customer.

Sales Presentation

A persuasive delivery and demonstration of a product's benefits.

Demonstration

A sales technique that involves showing the product in action to portray its benefits to a buyer.

FIGURE **11.10** Useful Reminders for Planning a Sales Presentation

- Ask the buyer questions and listen attentively to the responses.
- Include useful information about the company.
- Watch for cues by observing body language.
- Include a product demonstration (rehearse to make sure it works).
- Involve the buyer in the presentation.
- Remain flexible throughout the presentation and adapt it based on feedback.
- Add technology where appropriate to enhance the presentation.
- Respond to objections pleasantly (be prepared for the expected and unexpected).
- Ask for the order (always be closing).

Laptop computers and changing technology now allow for multimedia presentations and very effective demonstrations. Sellers often rely on PowerPoint or other software presentations; video can also be integrated into the presentation. While technology certainly helps put the spotlight on the product, it is important not to get carried away with it—the content of the presentation is always what is most important. A useful tactic in the presentation is to involve the prospect by letting him or her handle the product and the materials relevant to it. This action results in a feeling of ownership and helps in the decision-making process.

As a supplement to a presentation, catalogues on CD-ROM that show photos of products along with prices and specifications can be left with the customer. Lengthy and complex information should also be available on a website for the customer to refer to at any time. In situations where technology is part of the presentation, the salesperson must be certain all equipment is in good working condition. A failure with the technology is embarrassing for the salesperson and costly in terms of potential time lost for the presentation. Figure 11.10 lists useful reminders for planning a sales presentation.

HANDLING OBJECTIONS

Objection

An obstacle that a salesperson must confront during a sales presentation.

An **objection** is an obstacle that the salesperson must confront during a presentation and resolve if the sales transaction is to be completed. Prospects almost always express resistance when contemplating the purchase of a product. An objection is a cue for more information. The buyer is suggesting that the presentation of a product has not revealed how the product will satisfy a particular need. The objection, therefore, is feedback to be analyzed and used. It may enable the salesperson to discover another benefit in the product, a benefit that can then be presented to the buyer.

Typical objections involve issues related to the following: product quality or product-related issues such as its popularity or lack of popularity; the price or the level of discounts suggested, for example the price may be too high, discount too low, or credit terms unacceptable; the level of service and technical assistance; and sourcing issues such as how the buyer feels about the company in comparison to other potential suppliers. The salesperson must remain calm and not take these objections personally, recognizing that they are the normal reactions of a buyer. Instead, the salesperson should ask questions of the buyer to confirm his or her understanding of the situation, then answer the objection, and then move on to the next benefit or attempt to close the sale. A good salesperson develops effective strategies for handling buyer concerns. Being prepared for the expected and unexpected is essential. When responding to objections, the salesperson can call upon the product itself, photos and illustrations, testimonials and case histories of success, test results shown in a variety of formats (e.g., graphs and charts), electronic spreadsheets, and other forms of audiovisual support.

CLOSING

Closing
Asking for the order at the appropriate time in a sales presentation.

Trial Close
A failed attempt at closing a sale.

Closing Cue
An indication that the buyer is ready to buy; can be expressed verbally or nonverbally.

Does the buyer voluntarily say "Yes, I'll buy it"? The answer is "rarely"! Getting the buyer to say "yes" is the entire purpose of the sales interview, but this task is only accomplished if the salesperson asks for the order. **Closing** consists of asking for the order, and it is the most difficult step in the process of selling. Salespeople are reluctant to ask the big question, even though it is the logical sequel to a good presentation and demonstration. In fact, a good salesperson attempts a close whenever a point of agreement is made with the buyer. If the buyer says "no," the close is referred to as a **trial close**, or an attempt to close that failed. The salesperson simply moves on to the next point in the presentation.

The close can occur at any point in a sales presentation. Knowing when to close is essential. Therefore, as the sales presentation progresses, the salesperson must be alert to closing clues. A **closing cue** is an indication that the buyer is ready to buy. The cue may be verbal or non-verbal. If a cue is detected, a close should be attempted. Verbal clues include statements such as "What type of warranty do you provide?" Such a statement shows that the buyer is thinking ahead. Another clue is "The delivery and installation schedule fits well with our factory conversion schedule." Such a statement suggests confirmation of a key benefit. Or another: "We need the product in one week." In other words, if you can supply it, we'll buy it! Statements such as these are closing cues that must be acted upon.

Positive non-verbal communications include changing facial expressions, a change in buyer's mood (e.g., buyer becomes more jovial), or the buyer nods in agreement or reads the sales information intently. Good salespeople do not miss such opportunities, even if they are not finished their presentation. The buyer is telling you it is time to close. Do it!

Timing a close is a matter of judgment. Good salespeople know when to close—it is often referred to as the "sixth sense" of selling. The salesperson assesses the buyer's verbal and non-verbal responses in an effort to judge when that person has become receptive, and at the right moment, asks the big question with a high degree of self-confidence. When the time to close arrives, the seller can use one of the following commonly used techniques.

- *Assumptive Close:* The salesperson assumes the prospect has already decided to buy and makes a statement such as "I will have this model delivered by Friday," or asks a question such as "What is the best day for delivery?" An agreement or answer confirms the assumption that the customer has chosen to buy.
- *Alternative-Choice Close:* The seller assumes that the sale has been made and simply inquires which option is preferable. For example, the representative asks, "Would you prefer the metallic blue or cherry red colour?"
- *Summary-of-Benefits Close:* The salesperson summarizes the key benefits that the buyer acknowledged during the presentation, such as the favourable credit terms, the dependability of the product, the availability of frequent service, and the prompt delivery. When the summary is complete, the seller then poses a direct closing question, such as "Do we have a deal?" or "When would you like delivery?"
- *T-Account Close:* The buyer evaluates the pros and cons of the purchase. The salesperson lists the positive and negative points in a manner suggesting that the positive points outweigh the negative, and in doing so, leads the prospect to the decision that now is the time to buy.
- *Direct Close:* The seller asks a direct question such as "Can I deliver the order on Friday?" Once the question is asked the seller stops talking to let the buyer ponder the

question and waits for the response. Nothing is more clear than this strategy, and for that reason many sellers (and buyers) find it attractive. It is used when the buyer has definitely expressed interest. It is not a strategy to be used early in a presentation.

Once the sale has been closed, it is time to reassure the customer that a good decision has been taken and to confirm that you will provide all the essential services that were promised in the presentation. Parting on a positive note is crucial, because buyers very often experience cognitive dissonance. **Cognitive dissonance** refers to a feeling of doubt or regret once the buying decision has been made. The buyer wants to be reassured that the best choice has been made. This is the start of the relationship building process.

Cognitive Dissonance
A feeling of doubt or regret in a consumer's mind once a buying decision has been made.

FOLLOW-UP

There is an old saying: "The sale never ends." There is truth to this statement, because a new sale is nothing more than the start of a new relationship. Keeping current customers satisfied is the key to success. Effective salespeople make a point of providing **follow-up**; that is, they keep in touch with customers to ensure that the delivery and installation of the goods are satisfactory, that promises are kept, and that, generally, the expectations of the buyer are met. When problems do occur, the salesperson is ready to take action to resolve the situation.

Follow-Up
Maintaining contact with customers to ensure that service has been satisfactory.

In the current competitive business environment, good follow-up strategies help reduce customer attrition. Companies realize that a satisfied customer is a long-term customer. Furthermore, research shows that it is four or five times more costly to attract a new customer than it is to retain a current customer.[5] Moreover, poor customer service plays a key role in customer attrition. Larry Rosen, president of upscale clothier Harry Rosen, firmly understands this concept. Harry Rosen has implemented programs that ensure the utmost in customer service and care. "We don't look at a person in terms of an immediate sale. We look at him in terms of potential lifetime value."[6]

Harry Rosen
www.harryrosen.com

Success in selling requires dedication, determination, and discipline. What separates the successful salesperson from the unsuccessful one usually boils down to how well an individual follows an established set of principles. While the wording of these principles might vary from one source to another, the intent behind them is consistent. See Figure 11.11 for some pointers on what separates the professionals from the average salespeople.

For additional insight into how a good salesperson makes someone buy, read the IMC Highlight **Let's Make a Deal**.

Selling in a Changing Business Environment

The nature of selling is changing rapidly. To be successful in the future, a salesperson and his or her company must consider the importance of teamwork in communicating with customers (another aspect of integration), the importance of building long-term relationships, and the importance of adapting to technologies that directly influence the selling process.

SELLING IS A TEAM EFFORT

Traditionally, selling has been thought of as an individual effort (e.g., the salesperson calling on the customer and presenting a product to an individual or to a committee of buyers). Today, selling is a team effort involving everyone in an organization, spearheaded by the salesperson. For example, selling sophisticated technical equipment in a B2B environment requires a team of experts, including research and design specialists, engineers, accountants, and other marketing personnel, in addition to the salesperson. They all bring different expertise to the presentation and make the customer feel more at ease with the decision-making process.

FIGURE **11.11** **Tips for Successful Selling**

1. SELLING SKILLS ARE LEARNED SKILLS

Successful salespeople take the time to develop their skills. They ask meaningful questions, listen attentively, and observe buyer behaviour. Through learning, they can relate appropriate product benefits to the customer's needs. Knowledge of the product, company, customer, and competition is essential.

2. THE SALESPERSON IS THE MOST IMPORTANT PRODUCT

Successful salespeople sell themselves. They project a positive image about themselves and their company. If the customer isn't sold on you, he or she won't buy your product.

3. EMOTIONS, FEELINGS, AND RELATIONSHIPS ARE IMPORTANT

Successful salespeople present more than just facts. They create positive emotions about themselves, their products and services, and their company. Through effective communications, they bring the buyer into the relationship, showing how their problems will be resolved.

4. PREPARATION IS CRUCIAL

Be prepared! A sales presentation is like a stage performance. You may not get a second chance. Command the buyer's attention immediately and encourage participation throughout the presentation. Through participation, the buyer will discover the product's benefits. Ensure that all components of the presentation are coordinated and all electronic aids are in working condition.

5. NEGOTIATION SKILLS ARE IMPORTANT

A successful salesperson can deal with any and all concerns raised by the buyer. Be prepared to meet challenges by offering additional information and package together all points of agreement in order to close the sale.

6. ALWAYS BE CLOSING

Closing begins at the start of a presentation. The challenge is to build agreement and help the prospect decide how to buy, not whether to buy. When the prospect agrees, ask for the order. If the buyer refuses, continue with the presentation and ask for the order again when the prospect agrees. Persistence pays off!

Buyers also form teams to better evaluate the product offerings of sellers. From a buying perspective, the team approach helps eliminate financial risks and other risks that are associated with large and complex buying decisions. As well, the personalities of people on both sides of the relationship are put to a test. If the chemistry is good, it is a good sign that the business relationship will grow and prosper.

COMPANIES SELL RELATIONSHIPS, NOT PRODUCTS

Organizations abiding by contemporary corporate culture—that is, those that believe in relationship marketing—actively pursue relationships in the selling process. Making a sale, or getting the order, is simply one step in the sales continuum. It symbolizes the start of a new relationship or the solidification of an existing one.

LET'S MAKE A DEAL

Here are some insights from some very successful salespeople from across Canada. Working in a variety of companies, these individuals earn a good living doing what they do best...selling! Here's why they are successful.

John Monster is a home theatre sales associate at a Future Shop in Kelowna, British Columbia. His annual income is $50 000. John cites product knowledge as a means of differentiating himself from other sellers. He also prides himself on figuring out the dynamics of who is making the decision in a "couples-doing-the-buying situation." It's matter of paying attention to the customers. He says you can recognize when people are ready to buy. They'll start talking about the warranty or delivery. They are thinking about the future rather than the moment. That's when you close! John closes about four or five of every ten customers he talks to.

Ken Nolin is a senior financial consultant with Investors Group in Winnipeg, Manitoba. His annual income is $150 000. He works with a client base of couples in their fifties or sixties with $200 000 in investable assets. He tries to be their advisor, not to just be there with the sales hat on. "My goal is to find out their needs and fill them," he says. Ken likes to meet clients in his office, where the technology is readily available. His strategy is to sit beside the couple so he can analyze their body language at the same time. If they ask questions and lean forward,

he knows they are interested. If they're backing off, crossing their arms and legs, that shows a barrier. He relates their current incomes to the lifestyle they want to have later on in life. Once the picture is painted, there is enough motivation to invest. He realizes investing is a step-by-step process for most individuals and that the level of investment can change once the relationship is established. Ken doesn't press for too much too soon!

Kelly Gray is a managing director for RBC Dominion Securities Inc. in Toronto. Her annual income is mid six figures. In the securities business, which is fast paced, knowledge is power. Kelly differentiates herself from the competition by offering her own value-added input. She keeps her messages short and calls back with more specifics. In this business, the telephone is the lifeline! When recommending companies to invest in, she tries to understand what's going to drive the company both conceptually and fundamentally, and then she packages the information. Since her clients, who are portfolio managers, have limited time to listen, the packaging is very important. Once the dialogue gets going, you have to circle continuously to answer questions and deal with concerns. Then you ask for the order. Says Kelly, "It's all about relationship building and that takes a long time to develop."

Adapted from Rod McQueen, "Closing Arguments," *National Post*, May 2001, pp. 59–60.

The key for the seller is to determine how the company's resources can give the customer an edge. It is a consultative process in which the seller proves to the buyer that there is an advantage in doing business together. The search for a good fit between sellers (suppliers) and buyers stems from customers' relentless search for value in everything they purchase.

THE IMPACT OF TECHNOLOGY

The nature of selling is changing in many industries due to the advances in communications technology. Members of a channel of distribution that includes raw material suppliers, manufacturers, wholesalers and retailers, and end users are working cooperatively on supply chain management programs. By electronically transferring information among the participants in the supply chain—a cornerstone of true CRM programs—basic buying decisions are automated. Therefore, the challenge facing creative sellers is how to get their products into such a system. The practice of online marketing is a threat to the traditional ways of selling. Companies that do not pursue relationship and partnership selling strategies risk losing sales.

As mentioned earlier, firms are increasing their investment in direct response and online marketing techniques because of the cost savings associated with these practices. As a consequence, the role of personal sellers is changing. For starters, technology makes it possible to use fewer people in personal selling. But those sellers find themselves spending less time with personal contact and more time with electronic contact. They are also scouring databases for the best possible prospects and spending much more time providing customer service in order to retain present customers. Companies using technology to help market goods and services are finding that geographical boundaries are being eliminated, as buyers search for the best value in what they require. Because customers contact companies in a variety of ways, such as by telephone, in person, by email, or through websites, it is important to send out a consistent and integrated marketing communications message.

Summary

Personal selling refers to personal communications between sellers and buyers. Typically, personal selling is divided into three main areas: retail selling, business-to-business selling, and direct selling. In all forms, the immediate goal is to complete a sales transaction, and then adopt appropriate strategies to encourage repeat transactions, thus building a relationship with the customer that will last for an extended period.

The nature of selling has evolved with the changing marketplace. Since the 1970s, selling has moved from consultative selling to strategic selling to relationship selling. Relationship selling involves strategies to establish, build, and maintain customers. It approaches selling from the perspective of the lifetime value of a customer and the concept that retaining satisfied customers is much more profitable than constantly finding new customers. In many cases, relationship selling has extended into partnerships between sellers and buyers. Partnership selling is but one aspect of customer relationship management programs, and is strategically developed to encourage a profitable long-term relationship.

There are several essential attributes for successful selling today. A good salesperson possesses the right combination of personal characteristics (characteristics that can be learned and practised) and communications skills (both speaking and listening). A good self-image and positive approach to selling are essential. A successful outlook breeds success! The ability to read a customer is also necessary. Observing and interpreting verbal and non-verbal cues from the customer allow the salesperson to adapt a presentation while in progress, and to close the sale at the appropriate time.

Adequate advance preparation is another key to successful selling. A good salesperson possesses sound knowledge in four key areas: product, company, competition, and customer. The task of the salesperson is to match the right product or combination of products and services with the customer's needs. In doing so, the salesperson plans a presentation strategy that shows how the products meet customer needs better than the competition's products. Other essential roles of the salesperson include gathering market intelligence, solving problems, locating and maintaining customers, and providing follow-up service.

The selling process involves seven distinct stages: prospecting, pre-approach, approach, presentation and demonstration, handling objections, closing, and follow-up. Contemporary selling strategies involve the presentation of appropriate product benefits to meet customer needs. A benefit provides the customer with a gain or advantage and shows how the product will resolve a specific problem. Product benefits that are identified as important for a particular buyer are built into a pre-planned presentation designed to resolve a unique problem. During the presentation, a seller's negotiation skills are called upon in order to respond to the buyer's objections and concerns. Once those are answered, the seller closes the sale by asking for the order. Assuming a satisfactory response, the sale is confirmed and follow-up strategies are implemented. This is the start of the CRM process that, if nurtured carefully, will be profitable for both parties.

Advancing technology is changing the nature of personal selling. Less time is now spent on personal contact, while more time is devoted to electronic contact and activities designed to service and retain customers. As in other forms of marketing communications, the challenge is to develop effective strategies to solidify relationships.

Key Terms

approach   319

benefit   317

body language   312

closing   321

closing cue   321

cognitive dissonance   322

cold canvass   319

consultative selling   307

corporate culture   315

demonstration   319

feature   317

field sales force   305

follow-up   322

inside sales force   305

non-verbal communication   312

objection   320

online selling   305

order taking   303

partnership selling   310

personal selling   303

pre-approach   319

presentation strategy   307

product configuration   314

prospecting   318

qualifying (customers)   319

referral   319

relationship selling   307

repeat transaction   304

sales presentation   319

self-image   312

single transaction   303

strategic selling   307

telemarketing   305

trial close   321

Review Questions

1. What are the distinctions between single transactions and repeat transactions?
2. What are the fundamental differences among consultative selling, strategic selling, and relationship selling?
3. In relationship selling what is meant by the phrase "positioning the product in the customer's mind"?
4. Briefly define partnership selling and explain its importance.
5. What personal and non-personal characteristics are essential for successful selling?
6. Advance preparation is crucial to successful selling. Briefly describe the importance of knowledge in the following areas: product, company, and competition.
7. Briefly explain the roles and responsibilities of a salesperson.
8. List and briefly describe the seven steps in the selling strategy process.

Discussion and Application Questions

1. "Advances in communications technology will dramatically change the role and nature of selling in the future." Discuss and provide examples of changes that are already influencing selling strategies or will have an influence on them in the future.
2. Conduct some secondary research on the concept of partnership selling. How prevalent is partnership selling in business today? Provide some new examples of organizations that have adopted this strategy.
3. Conduct an interview with a salesperson involved in business-to-business selling. Ask if he or she has a relationship strategy for working with customers. How are the relationship strategies adapted to the changing conditions in the marketplace? Present a brief outline of what those strategies are and if they are effective.

4. Assess the role of follow-up in the context of customer relationship management practices. How important is it and how much emphasis do sales representatives place on this aspect of selling?

5. Evaluate the personal selling strategies of the following retail businesses: Future Shop, The Brick, and Canadian Tire. Do the style and nature of personal selling vary from one business to the other? Which approach is more effective at selling goods at retail? Justify your opinion.

6. Conduct a brief interview with a business-to-business sales representative for a company in your area. Inquire about his or her role in the context of integrated marketing communications. Are there links to other aspects of marketing communications that offer assistance in selling goods and services? Explain the various links as best you can.

7. Conduct some secondary research on telemarketing practices in Canada. Is telemarketing an effective form of personal selling? What are the strengths and weaknesses of this type of selling? Why is it becoming more popular in the communications mix?

8. Pre-planning is an essential step in making a sales presentation. Assume you are working for IBM and plan to make a sales presentation to your school. The school is going to purchase or lease desktop computers for a new 50-station lab and is in the process of securing information from various computer suppliers. What questions would you ask in order to determine your prospect's specific needs? What benefits would you stress when planning the sales presentation and why? What objections do you foresee the buyer will raise? You may wish to discuss this question with the individual responsible for information technology at your school.

Endnotes

1 Gerald Manning, Barry Reece, and H. F. MacKenzie, *Selling Today* (Toronto: Prentice Hall, 2001), pp. 9–16.

2 Terrence Belford, "Re-arm Your Sales Force," *National Post*, May 5, 2003, p. BE1.

3 Dictionary of Marketing Terms, Barron's Educational Series Inc., 1994, p. 367.

4 Gerald Manning, Barry Reece, and H.F. MacKenzie, *Selling Today* (Toronto: Prentice Hall, 2001), p. 110.

5 Geoffrey Brewer, "The Customer Stops Here," *Sales and Marketing Management*, March 1998, pp. 31–32.

6 "Relationship Marketing," *Venture* (Canadian Broadcasting Corporation), broadcast on April 7, 1998.

PART IV

Measuring Plan Performance

Part 4 takes a look at the role of marketing research in evaluating the effectiveness of marketing communications programs. Because so much of the evaluation process relies on the collection of qualitative and quantitative data, it is essential to develop an appreciation of the various research techniques and procedures available.

Chapter 12 introduces some fundamental methodologies for collecting primary research data and distinguishes between qualitative and quantitative data. It discusses the relationships between data analysis and interpretation and their impact on the development and evaluation of marketing communications strategies and executions.

EVALUATING MARKETING COMMUNICATIONS PROGRAMS

After studying this chapter you will be able to:

LEARNING OBJECTIVES

define the role and scope of marketing research in contemporary marketing organizations,

describe the methodologies for collecting primary research data,

distinguish between qualitative data and quantitative data,

determine the influence of primary data and information on the development of marketing communications plans,

assess a variety of marketing research procedures and methodologies that measure and evaluate behavioural responses to communications messages, and

identify the unique methods that measure the effectiveness of individual components of marketing communications.

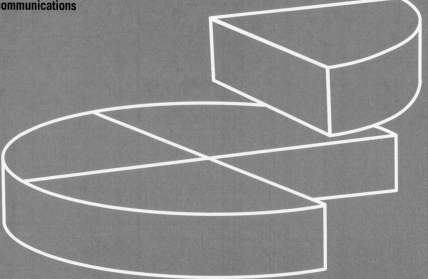

Because a considerable amount of money is invested in marketing communications activities, a marketing organization is very concerned about protecting its investment. In addition, its desire to remain competitive and be knowledgeable about consumers' changing needs makes it necessary to collect appropriate information before and after critical decisions are made. Certainly, a firm understanding of relevant and contemporary consumer behaviour will play a major role in the development of a marketing communications campaign (refer to Chapter 1 for details). Carefully planned and well timed marketing research is the tool that provides organizations with the insight necessary to take advantage of new opportunities. This chapter will discuss some fundamental concepts about the marketing research process and present various specific research techniques that are used to measure and evaluate the effectiveness of marketing communications programs.

The Role and Scope of Marketing Research

Research provides an organization with data. The data do not guarantee that proper decisions and actions by the firm will be taken, because data is always open to interpretation. The old saying that "some information is better than no information" puts the role of marketing research into perspective. A vital marketing tool, it is used to help reduce or eliminate the uncertainty and risk associated with making business decisions. Of course, this principle applies to marketing communications decisions as well.

In many ways, marketing research is a form of insurance. It ensures that the action a company might take is the right action. For a multi-million dollar advertising decision, a manger would want to have good information (a foundation, so to speak) available to make sure the right decision is made. To demonstrate, consider a marketing communications problem once faced by Molson Canadian, a popular brand of beer. When Brett Marchand, vice-president of marketing first showed senior executives a commercial called "Rant," it wasn't greeted with overwhelming applause. The ad showed a young guy working himself into a feverish pitch over what it means to be a Canadian. In fact, the ad zeroed in on things that separate Canadians from Americans. From marketing research, however, Molson had discovered a pent-up sense of patriotism among young Canadians. "Rant" ended up touching a nerve with Canadians who related to "this proud Canadian message," says Marchand.[1] The ad generated much publicity, even in the United States, and helped Canadian recover some lost market share. The moral of the story is simple: research provided useful information to develop an effective advertising strategy.

Marketing Research
A marketing function that links the consumer to the marketer through information.

Marketing research links the consumer/customer/public to the marketer through information—information used to define marketing opportunities and problems, to generate, refine, and evaluate marketing actions, to monitor marketing performance, and to improve the understanding of marketing as a process. Marketing research specifies the information required to address these issues. It designs the method for collecting information, manages and implements the information collection process, analyzes the results, and communicates the findings and their implications.[2]

The scope of marketing research seems endless. In a marketing communications setting, research is useful for testing advertising for impact and effectiveness, conducting surveys to measure customer satisfaction, tracking brand awareness compared to the competition, pre-testing advertising strategies, and measuring changes in behaviour based on the effects of marketing communications activities. Regardless of the nature of the research study, the information obtained will assist managers in their decision-making.

The very nature of marketing research, however, requires significant investment by a marketing organization. Due to the diversity of marketing communications and the complementary ways in which the various components blend together, it is difficult to isolate one communications component and state definitively that it determined success or failure. Wise marketing managers rely on their own experience and intuitiveness as well as whatever information is available when making decisions. When the situation so dictates, marketing research should be undertaken.

How do managers go about collecting information? Prudent marketing decision makers combine their intuition and judgment with all other information sources available. They use the scientific method, which implies that the data generated are reliable and valid. **Reliability** refers to degree of similar results being achieved if another study were undertaken under similar conditions. **Validity** refers to the research procedure's ability to measure what it was intended to.

Research Techniques for Marketing Communications

When an organization attempts to measure the potential impact of its advertising messages on consumers, it implements a variety of primary research techniques. Students should be aware of the basic steps involved in planning various research procedures in order to appreciate the value of the data. Essentially, the evaluation of advertising messages or any other form of marketing communications involves the collection of primary data.

PRIMARY RESEARCH

Once the organization decides it requires input from customers and potential customers before making a decision, the research process moves to the stage of collecting primary data. **Primary research** refers to the process of collecting and recording new data, called **primary data**, in order to resolve a specific problem, usually at a high cost to the sponsoring organization. Primary research is custom designed and focuses on resolving a particular question or obtaining specified information. A procedure is developed and a research instrument designed to perform the specific task. Figure 12.1 summarizes the steps involved in collecting primary data.

In directing the primary research, the marketing organization identifies the precise nature of the problem, the objectives of the study, and the hypotheses associated with it. **Research objectives** are statements that outline what the research is to accomplish, while **hypotheses**, which are statements of predicted outcomes, are confirmed or refuted by the data collected. The outcome of the research often leads to certain actions to be taken by the marketing organization. Refer to Figure 12.2 for an illustration of research objectives, hypotheses and action standards.

Conducting a marketing research study is beyond the scope and expertise of most marketing organizations in Canada. Consequently, independent market research firms such as Millward Brown are hired to perform the task. For example, Millward Brown conducts a considerable amount of research on advertising campaigns under consideration by General Motors of Canada. Usually, a marketing research manager from the sponsoring organization is responsible for supervising the research study and works directly with the marketing research firm in designing the project.

Sample Design

Prior to implementing a research study, the researchers identify the characteristics of the people they would like to participate in the study. This process is referred to as sample design. A **sample** is defined as a portion of an entire population used to obtain information about that population and must form an accurate representation of the population if the information gathered is to be considered reliable. Some basic steps must be taken to develop a representative sample:

- *Define the Population (Universe):* A **population (universe)** is a group of people with certain specific age, gender, or other demographic characteristics. Defining a population involves identifying its basic characteristics. For the purposes of primary research, a description of a population might be "single or married females between the ages of 21 and 34 years living in cities with more than 500 000 residents." A proper research procedure will screen potential respondents for these characteristics.

Reliability

Degree of similarity of results achieved if another research study were undertaken under similar circumstances.

Validity

A research procedure's ability to measure what it is intended to.

Primary Research

The collection and recording of primary data.

Primary Data

Data collected to resolve a problem and recorded for the first time.

Research Objective

A statement that outlines what the marketing research is to accomplish.

Hypothesis

A statement of outcomes predicted in a marketing research investigation.

Sample

A representative portion of an entire population that is used to obtain information about that population.

Population or Universe

In marketing research, a group of people with a certain specific age, gender, or other demographic characteristics.

FIGURE **12.1**   **The Steps Involved in Primary Research**

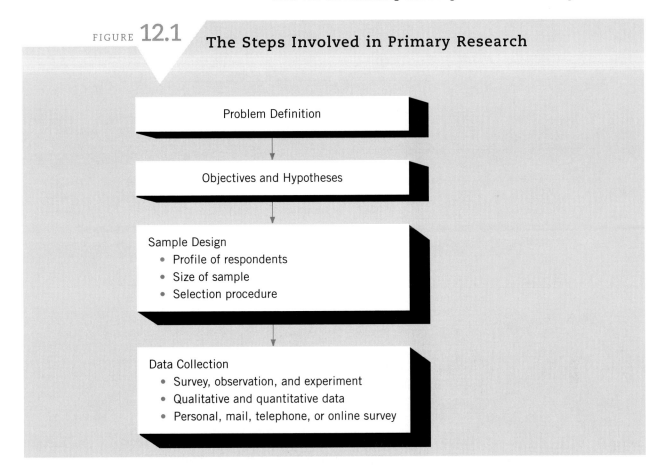

Sampling Frame

A list used to access a representative sample of a population.

Probability Sample

A sample of respondents who are known to have an equal chance of selection and are randomly selected from the sampling frame.

Non-Probability Sample

A sample of respondents who have an unknown chance of selection and are chosen because of factors such as convenience or the judgment of the researcher.

- *Identifying the Sampling Frame:* The **sampling frame** refers to a list that can be used for reaching a population. The telephone directory could be used as a sampling frame for the population described above. If Sears wanted to conduct research among its current customers about the style of advertising it uses, it could use its credit card account holder list as a means of access.

- *Determining the Type of Sample:* The researcher has the option of using a probability sample or a non-probability sample. If a **probability sample** is used, the respondents have a known or equal chance of selection and are randomly selected from across the population. For example, the researcher may use a pre-determined and systematic procedure for picking respondents through a telephone directory. The known chance of selection enables statistical procedures to be used in the results to estimate sampling errors and determine the reliability of the data collected. In a **non-probability sample**, the respondents have an unknown chance of selection, and their selection is based on factors, such as convenience for the researcher or the researcher's judgment. The researcher relies on experience to determine who would be most appropriate. For example, Sears could randomly stop shoppers inside its stores to seek their input on a variety of marketing concerns. Factors such as cost and timing are other reasons for using non-probability samples.

- *Determining the Sample Size:* Generally, the larger the sample, the greater the accuracy of the data collected and the higher the cost. The nature of the research study is a determining factor in the number of participants required. Some researchers use a one percent rule (one percent of the defined population or universe), while others state absolute minimums of 200 respondents. The accuracy of the sample is usually calculated statistically and stated in the research report. Therefore, a researcher considers the margin of error that is acceptable and the degree of certainty required.

FIGURE **12.2**

A Sample of Research Objectives, Hypotheses, and Sample Design for a Marketing Communications Study

PRODUCT

Labatt Blue

PROBLEM

Labatt Blue has been using a humorous appeal technique in its "Cheers to Friends" advertising campaign. The brand manager is less than satisfied with the impact of this campaign on current customers and would like to evaluate alternative appeal techniques.

OBJECTIVES

1. To determine the potential impact of a lifestyle appeal technique on current Labatt Blue drinkers.
2. To determine the potential impact of a sexual appeal technique on current Labatt Blue drinkers.

HYPOTHESES

1. The communication of lifestyle appeals may have impact initially but over the long term will not be viewed as unique and distinctive because so many competing brands use lifestyle imagery.
2. The communication of sexual appeal will break through the clutter of competitive beer advertising and separate Blue from other leading brands.

ACTION STANDARD

Given the assumption that research results indicate a preference for either the lifestyle appeal technique or the sexual appeal technique, and preference can be sustained for an extended period, then a new creative campaign will be devised for Labatt Blue. The implementation date for a new campaign will be May 2005.

SAMPLE DESIGN

Population

Input will be sought from Blue's primary target market, described as males, 19 to 29 years old, living in urban markets.

Sampling Frame

Current Blue drinkers will be recruited by telephone and by using telephone directories in three cities: Toronto, Edmonton, and Vancouver. A series of qualifying questions will be asked of potential respondents to determine their degree of brand loyalty.

Type of Sample

A probability sample is essential to ensure accurate and reliable data. A systematic procedure will be devised to recruit respondents in each city.

Sample Size

It is anticipated that a mixture of qualitative research and quantitative research will be employed. A focus group will be conducted in each city to derive qualitative information. Survey research will require a minimum of 200 respondents in each city to secure accurate quantitative data.

The above is a hypothetical example and is intended for illustration purposes only.

Figure 12.2 contains a sample design. It should be noted that errors in the design and implementation of a research sample could distort the validity and reliability of the data collected.

Data Collection Methods

There are three primary methods a researcher can use to collect data: surveys, observation, and experiments (see Figure 12.3), and the data collected can be qualitative or quantitative in nature.

Survey Research

The systematic collection of data by communicating with a representative sample by means of a questionnaire.

Fixed-Response (Closed-Ended) Questioning

Questions that include pre-determined questions and set answers for the respondents to choose from.

For **survey research**, data are collected systematically through some form of communication with a representative sample by means of a questionnaire that records responses. Most surveys include pre-determined questions and a selection of responses that are easily filled in by the respondent or the interviewer. This technique is referred to as **fixed-response (closed-ended) questioning**. Survey research can be conducted by personal interview, telephone, mail, or online.

Most surveys are designed with a high degree of structure. The questionnaire follows a planned format: screening questions at the beginning, central issue questions (dealing with the nature of the research) in the middle, and classification (demographic) questions at the end. Closed-ended or fixed-response questions—those that include a list of possible answers (e.g., tick-off or multiple-choice questions)—are the most popular. They permit the data to be easily transferred to a computer for tabulation and subsequent analysis.

Observation Research

A form of research in which the behaviour of the respondent is observed and recorded; may be by personal or electronic means.

In **observation research**, the behaviour of the respondent is observed and recorded. In this form of research, participants do not have to be recruited; they can participate in a study without knowing it. In other situations, respondents are usually aware of being observed, perhaps through a two-way mirror, by a hidden camera while being interviewed, or by electronic measurement of impulses. All of these techniques can be used when consumers are asked to evaluate advertising messages.

FIGURE **12.3** Data Collection Methods

SURVEY

- Data are collected systematically by communicating with a representative sample, usually using a questionnaire.
- Questionnaires can be disguised (purpose hidden) or undisguised (purpose known), and structured (fixed responses provided) or unstructured (open-ended question format).

OBSERVATION

- The behaviour of respondent is observed by personal, mechanical, or electronic means.

EXPERIMENTS

- Variables are manipulated under controlled conditions to observe respondents' reactions.
- Experiments are used to test marketing influences such as product changes, package changes, and advertising copy tests.

Cookie

An electronic identification tag sent from a web server to a user's browser to track the user's browsing patterns.

Electronic observation on the internet tracks the surfing behaviour and purchase behaviour of people. Electronic observation is achieved through cookies. A **cookie** is a file that websites store on a user's computer (browsers contain features that allow users to control whether cookies are stored). The contents of those files can contain information about a user's preferences—and that information is a valuable resource to marketers. The code tracks the computer, not the individual user (as several people in a household may use the same computer). The evaluation of internet communications is discussed in more detail later in this chapter.

Experimental Research

Research in which one or more factors are manipulated under controlled conditions, while other elements remain constant, so that the respondent's actions can be evaluated.

Test Marketing

Placing a commercial or ad campaign in one or more limited markets to observe impact.

In **experimental research**, one or more factors are manipulated under controlled conditions, while other elements remain constant so that respondents' reactions can be evaluated. Test marketing is a form of experimental research. In a marketing communications context, **test marketing** involves placing a commercial or set of commercials in a campaign (could be print ads as well) in one or more limited markets, representative of the whole, in order to observe the potential impact of the ads on consumers. Do the ads generate the desired level of awareness and preference? Do they provide sufficient motivation so that consumers take the desired action? Good test marketing provides valuable experience prior to an expensive regional or national launch of the campaign. If the test market proves the campaign to be less than effective, a pending disaster can be avoided.

Qualitative Data versus Quantitative Data

According to the nature of the information sought, research data are classified as qualitative or quantitative. There are significant differences between these classifications.

Qualitative Data

Data collected from small samples in a controlled environment; describe feelings and opinions on issues.

Focus Group

A small group of people brought together to discuss issues related to the marketing of a product or service.

Qualitative data are usually collected from small samples in a controlled environment. They result from questions concerned with "why" and from in-depth probing of the participants. Typically, such data are gathered from focus group interviews. A **focus group** is a small group of people (usually eight to ten) with common characteristics (e.g., a target market profile), brought together to discuss issues related to the marketing of a product or service. A typical qualitative project consists of four to six groups representing various regions or urban areas of Canada.

The word "focus" implies that the discussion concentrates on one topic or concept. A trained moderator usually conducts the interview over a period of a few hours. The role of the moderator is to get the participants to interact fairly freely in order to uncover the reasons and motivations underlying their remarks. Probing uncovers the hidden interplay of psychological factors that drive a consumer to buy one brand rather than another. With regard to advertising evaluations, it provides a multitude of favourable and opposing views on how effective a message might be. Consumers' reactions to the message, the characters that present the message, the campaign theme and slogan, and their general likes and dislikes of the ad can be discussed at length.

The major drawback of using focus groups concerns the reliability of the data. The sample size is too small to be representative of the entire population, and most people in a focus group do not like to show disagreement with a prevailing opinion. For that reason, interviews are usually held in several locations.

Pop Culture—The Coke-Pepsi Market Wars
www.css.edu/users/
dswenson/web/
525ARTIC/
popwars.html

Marketing decisions involving considerable sums of money are very risky if based on such limited research. One of the most spectacular focus group failures, the launch of new Coke in the 1980s, came about because the soft drink maker was not asking the right questions. Worried that archrival PepsiCo had a better-tasting product, Coca-Cola asked consumers if they liked its new formulation without ever asking if they wanted its tried-and-true beverage changed.[3] The new version of Coke failed miserably when it was launched, and the public backlash was so significant that Coca-Cola had to re-introduce the original Coke as Coca-Cola Classic.

The Coca-Cola example shows the potential weakness of focus groups—they are exploratory in nature. A follow-up quantitative survey is often required to establish numbers, which costs organizations additional money and time. On the positive side, attitudes that are revealed in a focus group can be used as a foundation for forming questions and questionnaires if and when quantitative research is required. The attitudes uncovered can be expressed as answers for closed-ended questions in a questionnaire.

Quantitative Data

Measurable data collected from large samples and a structured research procedure.

Quantitative data provide answers to questions concerned with "what," "when," "who," "how many," and "how often." This research attempts to put feelings, attitudes, and opinions into numbers and percentages. The data are gathered from structured questionnaires and a large sample to ensure accuracy and reliability. The interpretation of the results is based on the numbers compiled, not on the judgment of the researcher. For this reason, qualitative data are a tool for measuring and evaluating rather than for investigating and exploring. Figure 12.4 briefly compares qualitative and quantitative research.

With so much risk involved in major decisions about marketing communications, the wise organization should use both forms of data collection. Molson, for example, has a vice-president accountable for marketing research. Molson does focus groups and qualitative research, but it also does quantitative research on all television ads before production of the ad takes place. Each ad must hit a specific persuasion level. "We do not shoot ads until we know they will persuade beer drinkers to drink that brand," says Michael Downey, Molson's senior vice-president of global marketing.[4]

Survey Methodology

Personal Interview

The collection of information in a face-to-face interview.

Telephone Interview

The collection of information from a respondent by telephone.

There are four primary means of contacting consumers when conducting surveys to collect quantitative data: telephone, personal interview, mail, and the internet. **Personal interviews** involve face-to-face communication with groups (e.g., focus groups) or with individuals, and are usually done through quantitative questionnaires. Popular locations for interviews are busy street corners, shopping malls, and the homes of respondents. **Telephone interviews** involve communication with individuals by the telephone. Usually, the interviews are conducted from central locations (i.e., one location that can reach all Canadian markets), and, consequently, there is supervised control over the interview process. Telephone technology is now so advanced that research data can be transferred from the telephone directly to a computer.

FIGURE **12.4**   **A Comparison of Qualitative and Quantitative Data**

QUALITATIVE DATA

- Collected from a small sample, usually in a focus-group environment.
- Unstructured questions.
- Questions seek attitudes, feelings and opinions.
- Data not always reliable because of small sample.

QUANTITATIVE DATA

- Collected from a large, representative sample of target market.
- Structured questions with predetermined responses.
- Deals with who, what, when, how many, and how often.
- Statistically reliable, with calculated degree of error.

Mail interviews are a silent process of collecting information. Using the mail to distribute a survey means that a highly dispersed sample is reached in a cost-efficient manner. The main drawbacks are the lack of control and the amount of time required to implement and retrieve the surveys.

Online surveys allow an organization to be much less invasive in collecting information. Some companies have found that consumers seem more willing to divulge information over the internet, compared with the more traditional means of surveying. As well, it takes less time to get results. Procter & Gamble is experimenting with online research for new product concept testing. In a paper environment, P&G would spend $25 000 and get results in two months. Online the same test costs $2500 and results are available in two weeks.[5] On the downside, recruiting participation can be a lot like fishing—participation is left up to the fish. Therefore, the validity of the information is questionable.[6]

The decision about which technique to use is based on three primary factors:

- *Nature of Information Sought:* The amount of information to be collected and the time it will take to complete the survey are considerations. For example, if discussion is necessary to get the answers, personal interviews in a focus group may be best. If large amounts of information are required, the best option may be the mail.

- *Cost and Time:* When time is critical, certain options are eliminated. The telephone and the internet are the best means of obtaining quick, cost-efficient information. Costs must also be weighed against benefits. The net financial gains expected to result from the research may determine which method is to be used.

- *Respondents:* The selection of a survey method can be influenced by the location of the respondents and how easily they can be reached. For example, if the participant is to be reached at home, any method—personal interview, telephone, mail, or online—can be used. Responding online is very convenient for people. In contrast, if the participant is to be reached in a central location, such as a shopping mall, a personal interview is the only choice.

Figure 12.5 summarizes the advantages and disadvantages of each survey method.

Data Transfer and Processing

Once the data have been collected, then editing, data transfer, and tabulation take place. In the **editing** stage, completed questionnaires are reviewed for consistency and completeness. Whether to include questionnaires with incomplete or seemingly contradictory answers is left to the researcher to decide. In the **data transfer** stage, answers from questions are transferred to a computer. Answers are pre-coded to facilitate the transfer. In the case of telephone surveys, it is now common to enter the responses directly into the computer as the questions are being asked.

Once the survey results have been entered into a computer, the results are tabulated. **Tabulation** is the process of counting the various responses for each question and arriving at a frequency distribution. A **frequency distribution** shows the number of times each answer was chosen for a question. Numerous cross-tabulations are also made. **Cross-tabulation** is the comparison and contrasting of the answers of various subgroups or of particular subgroups and the total response group. For example, a question dealing with brand awareness could be analyzed by the age, gender, or income of respondents.

Data Analysis and Interpretation

Data analysis refers to the evaluation of responses question by question, a process that gives meaning to the data. At this point, the statistical data for each question are reviewed, and the researcher makes observations. Typically, a researcher makes comparisons between responses of subgroups on a percentage or ratio basis.

FIGURE **12.5**

The Advantages and Disadvantages of Various Survey Methods

	ADVANTAGES	DISADVANTAGES
Personal Interview		
	• High rate of participation	• Higher cost due to time needed
	• Visual observations possible	• Respondents reluctant to respond to certain questions
	• Flexible (can include visuals)	• Interviewer bias possible
Telephone Interview		
	• Convenient and allows control	• Observation not possible
	• Costs less	• Short questions and questionnaires
	• Timely responses	• Privacy concerns (bad time of day)
Mail Surveys		
	• Cost efficient	• Lack of control
	• Large sample obtainable	• Potential for misinterpretation by respondent
	• Relaxed environment	• Time lag between distribution and return
	• Impersonal nature produces accurate responses	• Low response rates
Online Surveys		
	• Efficient and inexpensive	• Immature medium compared to alternatives
	• Less intrusive (respondent driven)	• Limited sample frame (internet users only)
	• Convenient for respondent	• Image concerns associated with spam
	• Fast response time (days)	• Reliability of information suspect

Data Interpretation
The relating of accumulated data to the problem under review and to the objectives and hypotheses of the research study.

Data interpretation, on the other hand, involves relating the accumulated data to the problem under review and to the objectives and hypotheses of the research study. The process of interpretation uncovers solutions to the problem. The researcher draws conclusions that state the implications of the data for managers.

For additional insight into the role of research, analysis, and interpretation, read the IMC Highlight **Positive Perceptions Lead to Saturn Campaign**.

Recommendations and Implementation

The recommendations outline suggested courses of action that the sponsoring organization should take in view of the data collected. Once a research project is complete, the research company will present its findings in a written report. Frequently, an oral presentation of the key findings is also made to the client. Very often, the senior management is informed of the information when it becomes known, so that the managers are better prepared for possible actions or changes in strategic direction.

POSITIVE PERCEPTIONS LEAD TO SATURN CAMPAIGN

If you know anything about the Saturn automobile, it's likely that it is a "different kind of car and a different kind of company." Past advertising campaigns have effectively instilled that message into our minds. Saturn Canada wanted to develop a new way of expressing the Saturn difference. Marketing research would play a key role.

The research started with a series of workshops with Saturn owners. There, the buyers' "superior ownership experience" surpassed all other observations. The workshops were followed by focus groups. Many participants could easily recall past commercials, so there was a high level of awareness of what Saturn was about. In the focus groups, brand attributes were expressed as rational or emotional statements and tested by the "Benefits Explosion" methodology, a system for consumers to rank specific benefit statements about a product. The "relationships that customers had with the car, and the dealer," topped the list.

The research provided input for a new ad campaign that demonstrates the personal nature of the Saturn buying and ownership experience, while reinforcing Saturn's offerings and its commitment to "do things differently." One new commercial explains the benefits of the 30-day or 2500-kilometre money-back guarantee. A young woman loses her job shortly after buying a Saturn. Regrettably, she returns the car but the Saturn dealer is there to help when she gets a new job. Another new commercial gives car buyers the option of buying a Saturn online from anywhere. Featuring a woman named Susan, the ad shows her face lighting up when her Saturn dealer meets her at the airport with the keys to her new car. These ads were based on Saturn customers' actual experiences.

Viewers were touched emotionally by the ads in the campaign, and an unprecedented number of positive comments were received from consumers. Saturn used research effectively—the data provided a lead on how to get to the heart of Saturn customers and potential customers.

Saturn used qualitative and quantitative research to test the relevance of the commercials. Once they were on air, they were measured for appreciation, wearout (whether the target is tiring of the message), brand measures (how the target views the brand character), brand linkage, message comprehension, reach, and likeability.

By doing research at various stages of the advertising development process, Saturn is enjoying the benefits of an effective advertising campaign.

Adapted from Eric Leblanc and Kate Tutlys, "The Heart of the Matter," *Marketing*, July 16, 2001, p. 10.

These days, thanks to changing technology and fast turnaround times, market research is more streamlined, with clients expecting solid decision-making results—yesterday. It is quite common for research companies to present their findings in personal presentations, using PowerPoint or the like to display succinct objectives, results, and recommendations.

For a more complete look at how marketing research influences the direction of marketing strategy refer to Figure 12.6. It identifies a problem faced by Kraft Dinner, outlines the research procedures used to obtain information, and shows how Kraft used the information to develop a new advertising campaign.

Measuring and Evaluating Advertising Messages

One of the first steps in measuring advertising messages is an evaluation of agency creative ideas by the client. It seems that a creative idea is just that—an idea—until it is sold to the client for approval. Very often, these kinds of evaluations are subjective in nature, because they rely on opinions put forth by brand managers, marketing directors, and presidents of companies. The chain of command for approving advertising creative and media expenditures can go very high in an organization.

FIGURE **12.6**

Psychological Profiling Leads to New Advertising for Kraft Dinner

BACKGROUND

Kraft Dinner is the country's number-one selling grocery item with a 75 percent share of its category and Kraft Canada's biggest volume business. Despite such a lofty status, sales were flat and had been for some time.

PROBLEM

To discover just what was ailing this powerhouse brand. It was hypothesized that erosion in brand confidence among consumers was due to the fact there was no communication with people about what they love about Kraft Dinner.

MARKETING RESEARCH PROCEDURE

A methodology was employed that would create a personality profile for the brand. There would be an exclusive focus on the emotional aura around the brand. The notion of a brand carrying human traits is nearly as old as advertising itself, but it is only lately that psychiatric profiling has been gaining momentum.

To determine Kraft dinner's personality profile, *two specific exercises* were undertaken by research participants:

1. "Kraft Dinner has died. You have to write the obituary that goes in your local newspaper."
2. "You're a psychiatrist and Kraft Dinner has come to see you. Analyze the problem and tell him a solution."

THE RESEARCH FINDINGS

From the obituary pages

- "Tragically yesterday the hero of many a Canadian meal died accidentally."
- "He was affectionately known as KD by his many friends."
- "There was an easy way about him that was both knowing and comforting."
- "KD valued his time with friends."

From the psychiatrist's couch

- "Kraft has low self-esteem and insecurity."
- "Kraft Dinner is feeling guilt and anxiety about his image."
- "Kraft has low self-esteem, is old, lethargic, and withdrawn."

ANALYSIS AND INTERPRETATION

Kraft Dinner is

- dependable
- comfortable
- a friend
- nonjudgmental
- easy-going
- unpretentious
- trustworthy
- loved by all

RECOMMENDED THERAPY

- Build self-confidence
- Remember and promote the immortal place he holds in our hearts
- Raise self-esteem
- Get across the point that you are worth more

ACTIONS TAKEN

Kraft raised the price of Kraft Dinner, redesigned the packaging, launched a new KD website, and created a series of television commercials targeting young people who grew up eating the product. The ads touched on a person's relationships with Kraft Dinner.

RESULTS

Testing of the commercials revealed that the spots outperformed all others in the category in North America. Although the product was already the biggest seller on the grocery shelves, base brand sales experienced a significant increase.

Adapted from Peter Vamos, "Psychological Profiling Gets Inside a Brand's Head," *Strategy*, August 27, 2000, p. 2.

CLIENT EVALUATION

Creative can be tested at several stages of the development process. The first step is usually a qualitative assessment by the client to determine if the message conforms to the strategic direction that was provided the agency. This evaluation is conducted by means of a managerial approach. In this evaluation, a client needs to resist the impulse to assess the creative on personal, subjective bases. However, if a "to proceed or not to proceed" decision must be made, the client reserves the right to conduct consumer research prior to making the decision.

Clients using the *managerial approach* for evaluating creative may apply some or all of the criteria listed here:

1. ***In terms of content, does the advertisement communicate the creative objectives and reflect the positioning strategy of the brand (company)?*** The client reviews the creative for its ability to communicate the key benefit and support claims that substantiate the benefit. All creative objectives would have been outlined in the creative brief. As well, the client would determine if the message strategy and execution conform to the overall positioning strategy of the brand. If it is off strategy, the ad will be rejected.

2. ***In terms of how the ad is presented (strategy and execution), does it mislead or misrepresent the intent of the message?*** *Is it presented in good taste?* The client must be concerned about the actual message and any implied message since it is responsible for the truthfulness of the message. Legal counsel often has the final say regarding message content. Consumers frequently lodge complaints about ads they find offensive or that encourage risky behaviour. Consumer complaints forced Labatt Breweries to pull a Blue commercial called Cart Chase. In the commercial several young people were shown racing through busy downtown streets in shopping carts. Consumers felt it was a reckless and dangerous representation that younger people might be tempted to try.

3. ***Is the ad memorable?*** Breaking through the clutter of competitive advertising is always a challenge, and a lot of advertising that is approved doesn't quite cut it. Is there something that stands out that customers will remember—what will they take away from the ad? For instance, Dave Thomas, the founder of Wendy's was once closely associated with advertising for Wendy's. His character and charm were such that consumers would automatically know they were watching a Wendy's commercial. Since Dave's death, Wendy's has altered its message strategy and execution to focus more on the menu items.

4. ***Is the brand recognition effective?*** There must be sufficient brand registration in the ad. Some companies go as far as to stipulate how many times the package should be shown in a television commercial or how many times the brand name should be mentioned. The creativity of the commercial or print ad should not outweigh the product. It should complement the product. For example, people often recall funny ads and they can talk openly about the humorous situations that were presented until they are asked for the name of the product that appeared in the ad. So much for the laughs!

5. ***Should the advertisement be researched?*** When it comes to assessing the impact and effectiveness of the advertisement, subjective judgments by the client have the disadvantage of not being quantifiable. Prior to spending money on production, the client may decide to conduct consumer research to seek quantifiable data that will help the decision-making process. Better safe than sorry.

The evaluation process can occur at any stage of the creative development process. A television commercial, for example, could be evaluated by consumers at the storyboard, rough-cut, or finished commercial stage. Although it is not practical to test commercials at all stages, if the quality or effectiveness of the commercial is ever in question, the client should conduct research to avoid costly and embarrassing errors in judgment.

It is difficult to isolate any particular form of marketing communications and state categorically that it had an impact on sales. There are simply too many factors that influence buying decisions by consumers and business customers. The source of motivation to take action could be any combination of product quality, services offered, price, availability, advertising, public relations, sales promotions, and so on. Some forms of marketing communications have a short-term impact while others have a longer term impact, so the time to generate impact could be a factor. Furthermore, as this book reiterates time and time again, it is the integrated effort of all forms of marketing communications that ultimately influences the customer's buying decision. For these reasons, it is very difficult to measure the direct effect on sales.

When evaluating the impact of advertising messages, the objectives of the advertising plan must be considered. What did the brand set out to achieve? As discussed in Chapter 2 on strategic planning and Chapter 4 on creative planning, common objectives of advertising are to create and increase awareness, attract new target markets, encourage trial purchase by including incentives with advertising, create brand preference in the consumer's mind, and alter consumers' perceptions about the brand. Various primary research techniques can be used to evaluate whether or not advertising achieved these kinds of objectives.

EXTERNAL RESEARCH TECHNIQUES AND PROCEDURES

Creative evaluation involves a variety of research techniques. The objective of most creative research is to measure the impact of a message on a target audience. Creative research is conducted based on the stage of creative development. It is either a pretest or a post-test situation. **Pre-testing** is the evaluation of an advertisement, commercial, or campaign before it goes into final production or media placement, in order to determine the strengths and weaknesses of a strategy and execution. By getting input from the target market at an early stage, a company will have more confidence in the creative once it is placed in the media. **Post-testing** is the process of evaluating and measuring the effectiveness of an advertisement, commercial, or campaign during or after it has run. Post-testing provides information that can be used in future advertising planning.

Common techniques used to measure the effectiveness of creative are ***recognition*** and ***recall testing***, ***opinion-measure testing***, and ***physiological response testing***. Procedures such as inquiry tests and controlled experiments used in post-testing also measure the effectiveness of the message.

Recognition and Recall Testing

In **recognition tests**, respondents are tested for awareness. They are asked if they can recall an advertisement for a specific brand or any of the points made in the advertisement. For example, consumers who have read a publication in which an ad has appeared are asked if they remember the editorial content of an advertisement, or the advertisement itself. Are they aware of the brand name that was advertised? Typically, an individual is asked a series of questions to determine what they know of an ad.

Several factors affect the level of recognition of an ad. For example, a large print ad occupying a full page usually has a higher level of recognition than an ad occupying only a portion of a page. The inclusion of a celebrity might draw more attention to an ad simply because consumers like the celebrity. The amount of text in the ad may also be a factor. Ads with lots of copy might get lower recognition simply because readers don't read all of the copy.

In **recall** tests, respondents are tested for comprehension to measure the impact of advertising. The test can be an ***aided*** situation (some information is provided the respondent to stimulate thinking) or an ***unaided*** situation (no information provided). In either

Pre-Testing
The evaluation of commercial messages prior to final production to determine the strength and weaknesses of the communications.

Post-Testing
The evaluation and measurement of a message's effectiveness during or after the message has run.

Recognition Test
A test that measures a target audience's awareness of a brand, copy, or of the advertisement itself, after the audience has been exposed to the message.

Recall Test
A test that measures an ad's impact by asking respondents to recall specific elements.

situation, respondents are asked to name or recall ads, and asked to recall specific elements of an advertisement or commercial, such as its primary selling points, the characters in it as presenters, and its slogan. Test scores are usually higher when some form of aid is provided. For that reason, researchers tend to prefer the unaided recall technique, citing it as a truer test of an ad's impact on people.

Recognition and recall both help develop a brand's image with consumers over a period of time. Therefore, once an advertiser finds an ad or advertising campaign that is performing well, it must resist the temptation to make changes. In the long run, effective advertising plays a role in building sales and market share. A summary of some specific recall and recognition test procedures offered by Gallup & Robinson, a marketing research company, is included in Figure 12.7.

Two of the most common methods for collecting recognition and recall information are Starch readership tests and day-after-recall tests. A **Starch readership test** is a post-test recognition procedure applied to both newspaper and magazine advertisements. The objectives of the test are to measure how many readers have seen the ad and to measure the percentage of those who saw it who atually read it.

In a Starch readership test, a consumer is given a magazine to read, after which an interviewer goes through it ad by ad with the respondent. For each advertisement in the magazine (the entire magazine is "starched"), responses are divided into three categories:

- *Noted:* the percentage of readers who remember seeing the ad in this issue.
- *Associated:* the percentage of readers who saw any part of the ad that clearly indicated the brand or advertiser.
- *Read Most:* the percentage of readers who read half or more of the written material.

The Starch readership test offers several benefits: the client can measure the extent to which an ad is seen and read; the extent of clutter breakthrough can be determined by reviewing the results of other ads that were tested; and various layout and design options can be evaluated for effectiveness by reviewing scores obtained by other products in previous tests.

In the broadcast media, particularly television, the use of **day-after-recall (DAR) testing** is common. As the name implies, research is conducted the day after an audience has been exposed to a commercial message for the first time. By means of a telephone-survey technique, a sampling of the client's target market is recruited and asked a series of questions to determine exposure to, and recall of, particular commercials. Respondents who saw the commercial are asked what the ad actually communicated. The test seeks specific information about the primary selling message, what the respondent likes and dislikes about the ad, areas of disbelief or confusion, and purchase motivation.

The actual quantified measures obtained in a DAR test are described as total related recall levels. Total related recall measures two dimensions of the test commercial: intrusiveness and impact. Related recall refers to the percentage of the test-commercial audience who claim to remember the test execution, and who are also able to substantiate their claim by providing some description of the commercial.[7] The higher the percentage is, the more intrusive the message with respect to the audience. For measuring the impact of a commercial on an audience, the total related recall score is broken down into categories: unaided (by brand name mention) versus aided, specific versus non-specific, communication-objective or selling-message playback, and central-situation playback.

Opinion-Measure Testing

Measuring attitudinal components is another means of evaluating advertising effectiveness. Attitudes and opinions can be gathered from surveys or focus groups. The intent of attitude surveys is to delve a bit deeper with consumers in order to determine their true feelings about an ad and the product. Marketing research organizations use a combination of closed-ended and open-ended questions to uncover attitudes and opinions.

Starch Readership Test
A post-test recognition procedure that measures readers' recall of an advertisement, ability to identify the sponsor, and whether they read more than half of the written material.

Day-After-Recall (DAR) Testing
Research conducted the day following the respondent's exposure to a message to determine the degree of recognition and recall of the advertisement, the brand, and the selling message.

FIGURE **12.7**

A Selection of Research Services Offered by Gallup & Robinson

COPY TESTING

Tests for the performance of individual advertising executions and campaigns, their strengths and weaknesses in the context of other alternatives, past experience, and category norms. Among the services are:

- *InTeleTest*—Commercials are exposed using an at-home, in-program context via VCR cassettes among widely dispersed samples.
- *InView*—Respondents are invited to view a show in which the commercial is aired for testing. Recall and persuasion scores are obtained from the test.
- *Magazine Impact Research Service (MIRS)*—Ads are tested using an in-home, in-magazine context. The system offers standardized measures. Test ads may naturally appear or are inserted for testing.
- *FasTrac*—A pre-testing service yielding qualitative and quantitative analysis in a mall-intercept environment. FasTrac provides a full range of measures for clients operating on a tight time frame.

TRACKING STUDIES

Assesses the aggregate effect of a company's advertising in terms of creating awareness, building knowledge, enhancing attitudes, and generating purchase intent.

CONCEPT TESTING

Gauges the potential of the concept or idea behind new advertising before time and material are invested in it.

CLAIMS SUBSTANTIATION

Determines reaction to advertising messages claims, usually to support or challenge possible actions by media review bodies, regulatory agencies, or courts.

SPOKESPERSON OR ICON TESTING

Assesses how the use of spokespersons, celebrities, and icons in advertising influences attitudes toward the brand.

MEDIA INFLUENCES RESEARCH

Explores how people think about and use media content and how the medium itself influences the value of the advertising to help determine which media choices are more effective than others for communicating the message.

Adapted from Gallup & Robinson, "Services," <**www.gallup-robinson.com**> (November 2003).

Opinion-Measure Testing
A form of research yielding information about the effect of a commercial message on respondents' brand name recall, interest in the brand, and purchase intentions.

With television commercials, **opinion-measure testing** exposes an audience to test-commercial messages in the context of special television programs. In a research setting, respondents view commercials on a large screen (theatre) or on television monitors. Once all of the ads are viewed, participants respond to a series of questions.

The test commercial is usually presented twice during the program, in cluster situations. Also included in the cluster is a set of control commercials, against which the test commercial or commercials (sometimes more than one commercial is being tested) can be compared. The position of the test commercial is different in each cluster. The test measures three key attributes: the audience's awareness of the commercial based on brand name recall, the extent to which the main idea of the ad is communicated, and the effect the commercial could have on purchase motivation—that is, the likelihood of the respondent buying the brand. This final measure is based on a comparison of pre-exposure brand purchase information and post-exposure brand preference data.

This procedure is often referred to as a ***forced exposure test***, a name that suggests its potential weakness: the artificial environment in which it occurs. However, the results for commercials are compared to results from previous tests, and since the procedure remains constant, the data should provide reasonable direction to advertisers. Millward Brown, a marketing research company, uses a procedure it calls TVLink™ to predict how well an ad will perform (see Figure 12.8).

Millward Brown
www.millwardbrown.com

FIGURE **12.8**

A Television Advertising Research Service Offered by Millward Brown

Predicting how an ad will perform in real life is difficult but a research technique known as TVLink™ provides advertisers with relevant information to make an informed decision about an ad's potential.

TVLink™, conducted in-mall or online, tells an advertiser

- whether an ad communicates the intended strategy. It determines how clearly the creative idea is understood and how well the proposition is communicated.
- how consumers will react to the ad emotionally and rationally.
- how many consumers will remember the ad in real life.
- whether consumers will register that the ad they have seen is actually for the advertised brand.
- how well the ad will affect sales of the brand

The results of this testing technique are interpreted against a database of norms, the client's objectives, and an understanding of how to project copy test findings to what happens in real life.

TVLink™ works alongside the rest of the Link™ family:

- CinemaLink™
- PrintLink™
- RadioLink™
- OutdoorLink™
- Link4Kids™
- TotalLink™

This research procedure can evaluate the potential impact of multimedia campaigns.

Adapted from Millward Brown, Inc., "Solutions: Link" <**www.millwardbrown.com**> (November 2003). Courtesy of Millward Brown, Inc.

Physiological Testing

Advertisers also have access to a variety of physiological testing methods that measure involuntary responses to a specific element of an advertisement. In an *eye movement–camera test*, consumers read an advertisement while a hidden camera tracks their eye movements. Such a test gauges the point of immediate contact, how a reader scans the various components of an ad, and the amount of time spent reading it. The *pupilometer test* measures the dilation of a person's pupil to see how it changes based on emotional arousal. For example, a person's pupils widen when frightened or excited and are smaller when the response is negative. In a *voice-pitch analysis test*, a person's voice response is recorded. It measures changes in voice pitch caused by emotional responses. The change in pitch indicates how strongly a person is affected.

These types of tests are popular with researchers, because emotions trigger physiological responses that can be measured. Physiological responses to something a person sees or hears are difficult to mask. In two of the tests mentioned above, reactions are monitored with no words being spoken. Sometimes respondents try to hide their true feelings by saying something that contradicts their physiological reaction. For example, a person might respond in the desired way physiologically to a print ad with sexual imagery but might state that the ad should not be shown in a magazine. In such a case, physiological reactions speak louder than words.

Taxi Advertising
www.taxi.ca

Testing procedures and the need for them are controversial issues in the industry, particularly among advertising agencies, whose work is being tested. Many creative directors argue that too much testing defeats the creative process (because it stifles creativity) and that what people say in research and do in the real world can be completely different. In recent years, clients have relied heavily on focus groups to try to gain insight into how people feel about their advertising. Paul Lavoie, CEO of Taxi Advertising, offers strong and negative feelings about focus groups, citing their tendency to inhibit innovation. Prior to founding Taxi, Lavoie was a creative director at Cossette Communication Marketing, Quebec's largest advertising agency. "Focus groups are good for research and development," he says. "Beyond that, they reduce, homogenize and compromise fresh ideas."[8] Nevertheless, clients like to know how customers will react to their messages, preferably before the clients spend money on them.

For additional insight into how research influences the development of advertising messages, refer to the IMC Highlight **Branding Oregon**.

Measuring and Evaluating Sales Promotions

The overall goal of sales promotions is to produce an increase in sales in the short term. As discussed in Chapter 8, promotions are classified as consumer promotions and trade promotions. Consumer promotions embrace activities such as coupons, contests, free samples, cash rebates, and premium offers. These activities are designed to encourage trial purchase by new customers, repeat purchases by existing customers, and, generally, brand loyalty. Therefore, consumer promotions are measured against these objectives.

Trade promotions include activities such as trade allowances, performance allowances, cooperative advertising allowances, dealer premiums, and dealer display materials. These activities are designed to secure listings of new products with distributors, build sales volume in the promotion period, and secure merchandising support from distributors. Trade promotions are measured against these objectives.

Specific sales promotion measures include response rates to coupon offers, the number of entries received for a contest, and the number of cash rebate forms returned to the company. A marketing manager typically compares response rates for current promotions to response rates received for past and similar promotions. For example, some brands may run a major contest each year in the peak season. Brands like Pepsi-Cola and Coca-Cola

BRANDING OREGON

How consumers perceive a brand and how an organization would like consumers to perceive a brand can be two different things. The latter is the ideal situation, because it suggests that the marketing and marketing communications strategies actually had an effect on people. A primary role of marketing communications is to influence perceptions or alter perceptions. The state of Oregon and the Pacific Northwest are well known as an outdoors region. The area has the beautiful Pacific coastline, majestic mountains, great camping, and scenic vistas. People instantly think of its natural beauty, but they generally know little else about the region.

Ten years ago, the Oregon Tourism Commission implemented a branding campaign to portray the state as having a special quality of life where nature and the built environment co-exist, where 'fresh' and 'clean' permeate everything, where culture is alive and the heritage showcased. The slogan for the campaign was "Oregon. Things Look Different Here." Wieden and Kennedy, an ad agency renowned for its Nike advertising, created the campaign.

To determine how well the campaign was working, a three-tiered research program was devised and implemented by Longwoods International, a U.S. marketing research company. The research involved an overnight visitor profile, an advertising effectiveness study, and an image study. The primary goal was to determine how well Oregon compared to other regional and national norms for tourism communications.

The commission found that the campaign did encourage new visitors to the region but that Oregon's image did not compare well to Washington, British Columbia, and California in terms of excitement, unique opportunities, and entertainment. Looking critically at its advertising, it determined that there was too much focus on the pristine environment. There was little emphasis on things to do.

The commission also discovered that visitors rated their experiences very highly, and that Oregon's actual tourism product is rated much higher than its image. In other words, Oregon's image did not live up to the product! Oregon recognized that a good communications solution would correct this problem. New advertising was developed to build Oregon's image in specific areas such as being exciting, showing cultural amenities, and being a real adventure. The new campaign focused on "capturing the moment" and "people having fun."

To supplement media advertising, the commission also formed partnerships with cultural organizations and destinations to launch a cultural tourism campaign, with public relations and other marketing communications elements. High-end resorts, world-class golf courses, regional cuisine, and historic trails serve as backdrops for advertising. It's culture packed with beauty!

The commission's investment in research demonstrates the importance of crafting a message that communicates what life in Oregon is really like. The research helped to identify information that really helped develop an effective marketing communications campaign.

Adapted from Julie Curtis, "How Research Shapes a Message," Longwoods International, <www.longwoods-intl.com/case-study-Oregon.htm> (November 2003).

Travel Oregon Online
www.traveloregon.com

usually run a summer contest. If a particular contest generates significantly more entries than usual, the manager will attempt to isolate the elements of the promotion that lead to the higher degree of interest.

Coupon offers are usually evaluated based on the redemption rate, that is, the number of coupons returned, expressed as a percentage of the number of coupons distributed. The higher the redemption rate, the more successful the coupon promotion. For example, if a magazine coupon draws a 2 percent return rate and the norm for magazine coupons is only 1 percent, the offer is an overwhelming success.

Historical redemption rates for coupon offers are used to develop budgets for new coupon offers. Again, should response to a particular coupon offer be significantly higher than past offers, the manager would try to identify the elements of the offer that contributed to the increase in redemptions. Was it the face value of the offer? Was it the timing of the offer? Are consumers generally more price sensitive than previous? Marketing managers have the necessary information available to forecast coupon redemptions. Actual redemptions received are compared to forecasted redemptions to determine the success or failure of the coupon promotion. For an illustration of such a calculation, refer to Figure 12.9.

The absolute number of entry forms received from contests and rebate offers are a means of measuring the effectiveness of these types of offers. The names collected provide an additional marketing benefit; they can be added to the company's database. Smart marketers seek additional information about consumers on the contest or rebate entry form, such as demographic and psychographic information that can be used to plan direct response communications programs.

The use of dealer display material affects the success of sales promotions. Point-of-purchase advertising helps create awareness for promotion offers and reminds consumers about a product at precisely the right time—the purchase decision time. This medium provides a good finishing touch to a well-integrated advertising and promotion program.

FIGURE **12.9**

Measuring the Effectiveness of a Coupon Promotion

ASSUMPTION

A manufacturer offers a $1.00 coupon on a branded box of cereal that has a regular retail price of $4.09. The coupon is distributed through a cooperative direct mail package. For the purposes of budgeting, an average coupon redemption rate for cooperative direct mail will be used. A misredemption rate of 20% is considered, because on average only 80% of coupons redeemed are on valid purchases. The manufacturer receives about 65% of the retail price when wholesale and retail profit margins are considered.

COUPON INFORMATION

Face value:	$1.00
Handling charge (retailer)	$0.10
Handling charge (clearing house)	$0.03
Distribution cost	$15.00/M
Printing cost	$10.00/M
Total coupons in distribution	2.5 million
Redemption rate	5.0%

COSTS

Distribution	2 500 000 x $15.00/M	$37 500
Printing	2 500 000 x $10.00/M	$25 000
Redemption	2 500 000 x 0.05 x $1.13	$141 250
Total cost		**$203 750**

REVENUES

Revenue from each purchase	$4.59 x.65	$2.98
Total revenue	2 500 000 x 0.05 x 0.80 x $2.66	**$266 000**

PAYOUT

Total revenue minus total cost	$266 000–$203 750	**$62 250**

From the total revenue line, it can be determined that the coupon offer generated 100 000 purchases (2 500 000 x 0.05 x 0.80).

FIGURE 12.10

Measuring the Effectiveness of Point-of-Purchase Communications

FORM OF COMMUNICATION	INCREMENTAL RESPONSE RATE
Brand signage	+2%
Sign plus base wrap	+12%
Display stand and sign	+27%
Display stand, sign, and mobile	+40%
Display stand plus sign about sports tie-in	+65%

On average, point-of-purchase communication generates incremental sales ranging from +2% to +65%, independent of any price reductions. The above figures were based on research in 250 stores in 22 cities, and 94 brands in eight different product categories (beer, salty snacks, cold and allergy products, dog food, soft drinks, laundry detergent, shampoo, and conditioner).

Adapted from "Initial Results from Supermarket Phase of POPAI/ARF Study Reveal Insights into POP Advertising," *Point-of-Purchase Advertising International*, March 27, 2000.

Studies conducted by the Point-of-Purchase Advertising Institute in the United States found that when imagery of a television commercial is graphically repeated in an in-store display, sales increase significantly.[9] Figure 12.10 shows that a significantly higher purchase response is achieved if various combinations of in-store merchandising activities are implemented. The importance of these activities is highlighted by the fact that 70 percent of brand purchase decisions are made in-store.[10]

Measuring and Evaluating Direct Response and Internet Communications

One method of measuring direct mail and direct response television messages is to include a toll-free telephone number or website address. The number of inquiries received or the actual sales that result from a particular offer can be compared to those of offers in the past, and an observation can be made about the effectiveness of a new offer. As well, a great deal of information can be collected about consumers responding to phone calls. Sales data can be recorded and demographic information gathered. Sales data can be tied to demographic information to determine who is actually buying the product. Knowing who is responding to each offer helps a firm better understand its customers and provides insight into how to develop better marketing communications strategies to reach particular targets.

Response cards are another means of assessing impact and collecting information about customers. Typically, these cards are filled in at the time of purchase. Any information that is collected can be added to the organization's database and be combined with other information that may be available on a particular customer.

The use of cookies was discussed in Chapter 7 and briefly mentioned earlier in this chapter. Cookies enable an organization to track online responses. The web is a unique communications medium that has built-in technology unlike any other medium. That technology allows for all communications to be measured for effectiveness. In fact, internet communications is much easier to measure in terms of hard numbers than any other form of media advertising.

Response Card

A card filled in, usually at the time of purchase, that collects information about customers that can be added to the organization's database.

Ad Clicks

The number of times users click on a banner (clicking transfers the user to another website).

Ad Views

The number of times a banner is downloaded to a user's screen.

Hit

Each time a server sends a file to a browser.

Visitor

A unique user of a website.

Visit

A sequence of page requests made by a visitor to a website; also called a session or a browsing period.

Stickiness

A website's ability to keep people at the site for an extended period or to have them return to the site frequently.

Online observation is a common form of recording and analyzing usage patterns. Banner advertising, for example, is measured in terms of **ad clicks** (the number of times users click on a banner) and **ad views** (the number of times a banner ad is downloaded). Every time a server sends a file to a browser, it is recorded in that organization's server log. This statistical information, frequently referred to as **hits**, is readily available for analysis and interpretation. The higher the number of hits, the more effective the message in generating the hits.

The number of visitors to a website and the number of visit that each visitor makes over a period of time are factors that measure a website's ability to communicate. A **visitor** is a unique user who comes to a website. A **visit** is a sequence of page requests made by a visitor at a website. Websites are evaluated on their **stickiness**—how long visitors stayed at the site. Sticky sites are ones that people are interested in, as shown by their tendency to revisit favourite sites frequently. A plethora of factors influence visits: site design, navigation speed and ability to move from page to page conveniently, site content, and more.

Many organizations are now experimenting with online surveys and are finding that online consumers are more responsive and generous with the information they provide. Surveys are structured in a manner similar to personal interviews or telephone surveys as predetermined responses to select from are provided. Online surveys offer several advantages: they are fast and inexpensive compared to traditional methods, and there are no fees for personal contact or mailings and no data entry errors. Some researchers have discovered that online respondents answers questions more openly and honestly when an interviewer is not present. The primary disadvantage of online surveys is their inability to draw a probability sample. Researchers do not have access to the multitude of predetermined lists commonly used in other forms of quantitative research. As database lists grow, and as organizations fine tune their online information gathering processes, this problem will gradually be eliminated.

Measuring and Evaluating Public Relations Communications

There are several ways to evaluate public relations communications: counting clippings, calculating the number of impressions based on the numbers of clippings, and employing a mathematical model that equates public relations to an advertising value. The latter is referred to as an *advertising equivalency*.

Clipping Service

An organization that scans the print and broadcast media in search of a company's or brand's name.

Many organizations that are active in public relations subscribe to a **clipping service**, which scans the print and broadcast media in search of a company's name. Each time the name is found, it is recorded and compared to the numbers of press releases that were issued. For example, if 500 press releases were issued and there were 50 clippings, the return rate would be 10 percent. The success of the campaign would be based on historical comparisons of return rates.

The number of *impressions* generated is based on the circulation of the medium in which the organization's name is mentioned. For example, if an article appears in *The Toronto Star* on a Tuesday and the circulation that day is 450 000, the total number of impressions is 450 000. A company may also "gross up" the number of impressions by considering the actual readership of the paper. If the average number of readers is 2.5 per copy, the gross impressions would be 1 125 000 (450 000 x 2.5).

There is a problem associated with counting clippings and impressions. Such a procedure ignores the nature of the article written or broadcast about the organization. Was it positive or negative? There is a presumption that an article that is critical of a company is of equal value to one that praises a company. It could be argued that positive articles and negative articles should be separated. For certain, companies receive a lot of negative publicity when they face a crisis situation, and such publicity negates much of the positive publicity that is generated by planned public relations communications. There are also those that believe that any publicity is good publicity.

Trying to equate public relations to a corresponding advertising value is an attempt to eliminate the problems associated with clippings and impressions. A technique called **advertising equivalency** involves an evaluation of the space occupied by a public relations message and relating it to a similar amount of advertising space. To demonstrate, consider that a one-page article about a company appeared in *Canadian Business* magazine. If a one-page ad costs $25,000, then that is the value of the public relations to the organization. Similar calculations can be made for the broadcast media. Based on this type of calculation, the sum total of a public relations campaign can be considerable. Specialist companies exist to provide this service.

Ideally, some form of evaluation in relation to specific public relations objectives would be preferable, but rarely does a company have sufficient funds to perform precampaign and post-campaign research—the techniques required for such an evaluation. For instance, if the objective of public relations were to increase awareness of a company's name, the pre-campaign research would establish a benchmark figure. Once the campaign is over, a second research study would determine how the level of awareness increased. Justifying such an investment for so many different types of communications programs is often difficult. Again, it is the combination of marketing communications activities that determines true success or failure.

> **Advertising Equivalency**
> A mathematical model that equates public relations to an advertising value by evaluating the space occupied by a public relations message in relation to advertising space.

Measuring and Evaluating Event Marketing and Sponsorships

Among all of the integrated marketing communications components, event marketing and sponsorships are the most difficult to evaluate, particularly on a quantitative basis. At their best, sponsorships are a pointed, high-profile way to increase sales and improve brand recognition. At their worst, they're a haphazard form of promotion. It is difficult to tell which is which.[11]

Event marketing is absorbing a bigger piece of the marketing communications pie each year, but it doesn't get the respect it deserves because there aren't any widely accepted, standardized methods of measuring its results. Examples of proposed event measurement systems include adopting accepted methods of measuring attendance, total number of consumer contacts, and the level of consumer immersion in an event. Despite measurement flaws, event marketing and sponsorship programs continue to be a valued element in a good many marketing plans.

The most common measure of an event's success is *how well the event reaches the target audience*. If some form of return on investment can be added to the evaluation mix, so much the better. But, unless you are establishing leads or selling something at the event, the true impact of the sponsorship won't be felt immediately. Nowhere are sponsorships more visible than in the world of sports. In professional football, basketball, and hockey leagues, there is no shortage of sponsors willing to jump in. The MBNA credit card company has been a sponsor of the National Hockey League for the past few years. At rinks around the league, fans can sign up for a credit card bearing the symbol of their favourite professional team. MBNA can track the success of its sponsorship based on the number of people who sign up.

Most managers rely on less concrete evidence to justify investing in event marketing and sponsorships. Having Tiger Woods walking around a golf course wearing a Nike hat, for example, has a positive impact for all kinds of Nike products, and it extends well beyond golf products. Seeing Tiger Woods driving a Buick Rendezvous adds an element of prestige to the automobile; it also has a halo effect on the image of General Motors.

MBNA Canada
www.mbna.com/canada

But to measure the direct impact of such an association on the sales of that automobile is next to impossible, because of the influence of other forms of communication.

Greg Cyr, manager of sponsorship marketing at General Mills Canada, offers a perspective on the benefits of sponsorship. His company's association with the likes of Elvis Stojko and Catriona Le May Doan creates a credibility that trickles down to the customer level. "People look at them as gold medal champions. They're the best, and they think we're the best. People feel pretty good about buying Cheerios because it exhibits the same qualities as Jamie Salé and David Pelletier, Martin Brodeur, and Cassie Campbell."[12] Such an association is a guaranteed bonus for the brands involved. Refer to Figure 12.11 for an illustration.

FIGURE **12.11** **Association with Celebrities Enhances a Brand's Image with Consumers**

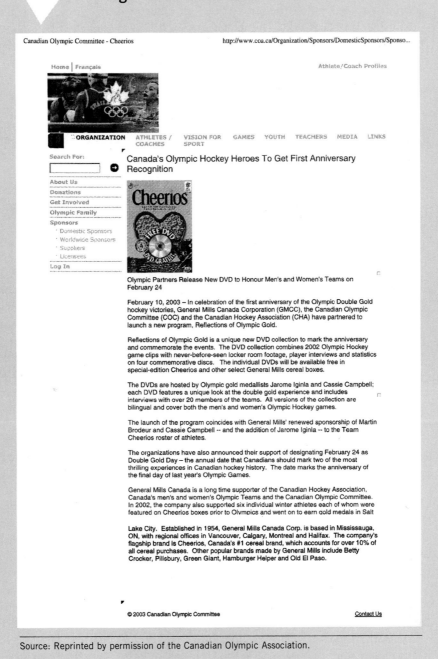

Source: Reprinted by permission of the Canadian Olympic Association.

As discussed in Chapter 10, certain indicators are commonly used to measure the benefits of sponsorship. For example, an organization might look at *awareness* and association measures as well as changes in *image perceptions* among its customers. However, to measure for changes in awareness and image, pre-event and post-event marketing research is necessary. Is the organization willing to invest further in order to get some measure of how well an event is contributing to achieving certain marketing objectives? Many managers presume that if an event effectively reaches the desired target audience, then measures for awareness, event association, and image will be positively affected and no investment in research is necessary.

Another common measure is the impact on *brand sales*. Is it immediate, during the event period, or will it happen after the event? Consider Molson's sponsorship of the NHL playoffs in 2003. Molson launched the Molson Canadian Don Cherry Bubba pack specifically for the playoffs and supported it with an extensive television advertising campaign (remember the young beer-drinking males marching down the street wearing Cherry-style suits?). The campaign garnered all kinds of media publicity, both positive and negative. For certain, the Bubba pack was a strong seller during the playoffs.

Sharp Dressed Beer
www.iam.ca/
doncherryedition/
sharp.php

Measuring the Integrated Marketing Communications Effort

Because integrated marketing communications is a coordinated and collaborative effort among many different individuals and organizations, and many different communications disciplines, perhaps the best form of measurement and evaluation is to look at the big picture. In other words, how healthy is a particular brand or the company as a whole, based on all of the marketing and marketing communications strategies that have been implemented over the past year (a typical planning cycle)?

Some typical indicators of success or failure include market share, productivity, sales and profitability, customer satisfaction levels, and social responsibility. As in most evaluation systems already discussed in this chapter, the organization should look back at the corporate objectives it established in these areas to see how well it performed.

An increase in *market share* would indicate greater acceptance by more customers, a higher degree of brand loyalty among current customers, and a strong competitive position. A well-planned IMC program would have contributed to such an outcome. *Productivity* measures are more difficult to come by, but where tangible results can be attributed to a specific communications activity, it should be noted. Did the IMC program generate new customers? Was brand awareness higher than previous? Was the company's or brand's image altered in a positive way? These kinds of measures indicate whether or not a plan is working.

Marketing managers are responsible for producing sales while keeping marketing and marketing communications investments at reasonable levels. *Sales* must generate an adequate level of *profit* in order for the company to thrive and survive in the long term. Most brands in an organization have their own profit and loss statement, which is reviewed continually to ensure that sales, costs, and profit targets are always within sight. Alterations and adjustments to a marketing plan or marketing communications plan will occur during the year when necessary.

As discussed elsewhere in the text, every employee of an organization plays a role in providing *customer satisfaction;* all employees must adopt a marketing attitude. Therefore, it is very important for all employees to be aware of the marketing and marketing communications strategies. Informed employees play a key role in implementing the strategies: they thus directly influence how customers perceive the organization.

With regard to *social responsibility* objectives, planned public relations programs play a key role. An organization must promote its positive contributions while eliminating, as best it can, the negative outcomes. Brand equity and company image are directly influenced by the quality of social programs and ethical behaviour that a company and its employees demonstrate to the public.

In summary, the real challenge for an organization is to develop an integrated marketing communications strategy that will communicate clearly and effectively with its various publics. The company that does so stands a very good chance of achieving success in the short run and long run.

Summary

Marketing research must be viewed as a tool that assists the manager in the decision-making process. It is a systematic procedure that, if used properly, will produce reliable and valid data.

The research process begins with a firm's becoming aware of a problem situation. Problems associated with evaluating marketing communications typically involve primary research. Primary research is the gathering of new data from a representative sample. Primary data are collected from surveys, observation, and experiments. Survey data are qualitative or quantitative in nature. Qualitative data are collected by focus group interviews or by one-on-one interviews and answer the question "why." Quantitative data are obtained by questionnaires through personal interview, telephone, mail, or online and involve translating thoughts and feelings into measurable numbers. Once the data are secured, they are processed for analysis and interpreted by the researcher.

Experimental research involves testing a marketing mix activity within a controlled situation in order to measure the effectiveness of the activity. Test marketing is an example of experimental research. In a test market involving marketing communications, an advertisement, a commercial, or set of ads in a campaign is placed in designated geographic markets to evaluate the potential impact on consumers. Knowledge gained from such tests allows an organization to make changes to a campaign before it is launched in additional markets.

In order to measure the effectiveness of marketing communications program, various research procedures are implemented. In advertising, several pre-test and post-test techniques are available. If recognition and recall are a concern, a Starch readership test, a day-after-recall test, and opinion measure tests can be applied. These tests generate data on brand identification and message comprehension. If there is a desire to measure emotional responses, various physiological tests that evaluate eye movement, pupil dilation, and voice-pitch analysis are available.

Sales promotions measures include response rates to coupon offers and the number of entries received for contest and cash rebate offers. Response rates for current promotions are compared to response rates of previous promotions. The manager will evaluate the various elements of the promotion in order to determine what elements contributed to success or failure.

Direct response communications and internet-based communications are easier to evaluate quantitatively. Direct response communications usually include a toll-free telephone number, a website address, or response cards. Inquiries can be tracked and any sales that occur can be attributed to specific customers. With internet communications, the use of cookies allows an organization to track responses. Other forms of internet measures include ad clicks, impressions, hits, numbers of visitors to a website, and time spent visiting a website. Online surveys are becoming popular. Companies find they can access information from customers quickly and for a fraction of the cost of traditional survey methodologies.

The most common ways of measuring public relations communications include counting actual clippings that appear in the print and broadcast media, calculating the number of impressions that the press clippings generate, and converting the press coverage (the size of space or amount of time it occupies) to some kind of advertising equivalency. The latter places a monetary value on public relations, and is a popular means of justifying investment in public relations.

Event marketing and sponsorships remain difficult to measure. Nonetheless, events and sponsorships are popular among marketing executives because they are perceived as a high-profile way to increase sales and improve brand recognition. The most common measure of an event's success is determined by how well the event reaches the target audience. Other commonly used measures include changes in brand awareness levels and image, both of which are based on how well a brand associates with an event. Measures of this nature involve pre-event and post-event research.

When measuring the success of an integrated marketing communications campaign, an organization looks at the bigger picture. Typical indicators of success or failure include shifts in market share, productivity, sales and profitability, employee performance and attitude, and the public's perceptions of an organization's social responsibility. A carefully planned marketing communications program contributes to achieving objectives in all of these areas.

Key Terms

Review Questions

1. In the context of marketing research, what is the relationship between the following sets of terms?
   a) secondary data and primary data
   b) research objectives and hypotheses
   c) observational and experimental techniques
   d) population and sampling frame
   e) qualitative data and quantitative data
   f) probability sample and non-probability sample
   g) frequency distribution and cross-tabulation
   h) tabulation and cross-tabulation
   i) data analysis and data interpretation

2. What is the problem-awareness stage of the marketing research process?

3. Briefly explain the four steps in the sample design process.

4. What purpose does a test market serve?

5. What is a focus group? What are the benefits of focus group research?

6. Under what circumstances would you use the telephone for collecting survey data? When would you use the personal interview?

7. In terms of measuring the effectiveness of advertising, what is the difference between pre-testing and post-testing? What benefits does each form provide?

8. What is the difference between a recognition test and a recall test?

9. What are the three categories of measurement in a Starch readership test? Briefly explain each category.

10. What does opinion-measure testing refer to?

11. What are the three primary ways of measuring the effectiveness of public relations campaigns? Briefly discuss each form of measurement.

Discussion and Application Questions

1. Compare and contrast the nature of qualitative data and quantitative data. Is it essential to have both types of information prior to investing in a new advertising campaign? Refer to the IMC Highlight **Positive Perceptions Lead to Saturn Campaign** for some initial insight into this issue. Prepare a position and provide appropriate justification for it.

2. You are about to devise a new advertising strategy (a message strategy) for the Porsche Boxster. You do not know how to present the automobile to potential customers and would like to find out more about them. What information would you like to obtain, and what procedure would you recommend to obtain it?

3. "Too much information obtained from marketing research ultimately stifles creative thinking and the production of innovative creative." Many creative

directors have expressed this opinion. Conduct some secondary research on this issue and present an opinion on the issue. Justify your position with appropriate examples.

4. Companies are now using online surveys to learn more about their customers and how they feel about products they market. What are the benefits and drawbacks of using online research? Is it as useful and effective as traditional survey methodologies? Briefly discuss the key issues.

5. If event marketing and sponsorships are so difficult to measure for tangible business results, why do so many large and prosperous companies pursue such associations? What are the advantages and disadvantages of being involved in this form of marketing communications? Is it a worthwhile investment? Present an opinion supported with appropriate justification.

Endnotes

1 Chris Daniels, "Canuck vs. Yanks," *Marketing*, May 22, 2000, p. 26.

2 "New Definition for Marketing Research Approved," *Marketing News*, January 22, 1987, p. 1.

3 "Managers Should Rethink the Power and Limitations of Focus Groups," *Financial Post*, December 14, 1999, p. C4.

4 Wendy Cuthbert, "Hold the Numbers," *Strategy*, June 4, 2001, pp. B6, B7.

5 Jack Neff, "P&G Weds Data, Sales," *Advertising Age*, October 23, 2000, pp. 76, 80.

6 Perry Vanier, "Polling Online," *Marketing*, June 25, 1999, p. 22.

7 Cherie Hill, "In Defense of DAR Testing," *Marketing*, June 1984, p. 28.

8 Matthew McKinnon, "Focus Pocus," *National Post*, August 1, 2002, pp. 56–63.

9 "In-store Merchandising, The Power of P.O.P.," insert in *Marketing*, n.d., p. 1.

10 Ibid.

11 Patrick Maloney, "Do Sponsorships Measure Up?" *Marketing*, July 8, 2002, p. 13.

12 Ibid., p. 13.

Media Buying Principles and Media Information Resources

This appendix presents the essential aspects of media buying and acquaints the student with a variety of media rate cards and how to read them. The rate cards used in this section have been gathered from online sources and *Canadian Advertising Rates and Data* (CARD). Rate cards are usually posted on a media company's website under a title like "Advertise with Us" or "Products and Rates." Students can refer to *CARD*, a publication usually available in the reference section of college and university libraries. *CARD* contains summary rate cards for all media in Canada except television.

In addition, this section exposes the student to a variety of media information sources often referred to by marketing organizations and communications agencies when planning campaigns. In most cases, specialized software available by subscription is required to access specific data. However, students are encouraged to visit the various websites listed under Media Information Resources to gain exposure to basic information that is available for free.

Media Buying Principles

NEWSPAPER ADVERTISING

Agate Line
A non-standardized unit of space measurement, equal to one column wide and 1/14" deep, used in newspaper advertising.

Broadsheet
A large newspaper with a fold in its middle.

Tabloid
A smaller newspaper that is sold flat.

Modular Agate Line (MAL)
A standardized unit of measurement equal to one column wide and 1/14" deep, used in newspaper advertising.

Newspaper space is sold on the basis of agate lines or modular agate lines. An **agate line** is a non-standardized unit of space measurement, equal to one column wide and 1/14" deep. For **broadsheets**, a standard page is 11 1/2" wide with column widths of 1 1/16". The number of columns ranges from 7 to 10, so full-page lineage ranges from 1800 to 3150 agate lines. In **tabloids**, the number of columns ranges from 6 to 10 and full-page lineage ranges from 1134 to 2000 agate lines. Most broadsheets and tabloids use agate lines to determine the size of an advertisement.

A **modular agate line (MAL)** is a standardized unit of measurement equal to one column wide and 1/14" deep. Standard column widths are 2 1/16" in broadsheets. An MAL is wider than an agate line. For a broadsheet, the full-page lineage ranges from 1800 to 1848 MALs. For a tabloid, the full-page lineage ranges from 890 to 1050 MALs.

Note that in this context "lines" and "columns" are not physical lines and columns. They are invisible lines and columns that the newspaper industry uses to measure the size of an ad.

The basic procedure for buying newspaper space is to determine the size of the ad either in agate lines or modular agate lines. In either case, the cost is calculated by multiplying the width of the ad (number of columns) by the depth of the ad (inches of depth). One column inch of depth equals 14 agate lines. Other factors that influence costs include the number of insertions, creative considerations such as the use of colour, and position charges, if applicable.

Some newspapers offer standard-size ads that are easier to understand in terms of size. With reference to *The Globe and Mail* (see Figure A1.1), some of the standard-size options include full page (1800 agate lines), 1/2 page (900 agate lines), magazine page (616 agate lines), and 1/4 page (453 agate lines).

FIGURE **A1.1** **Some Standard-Size Ad Page Options in Newspapers**

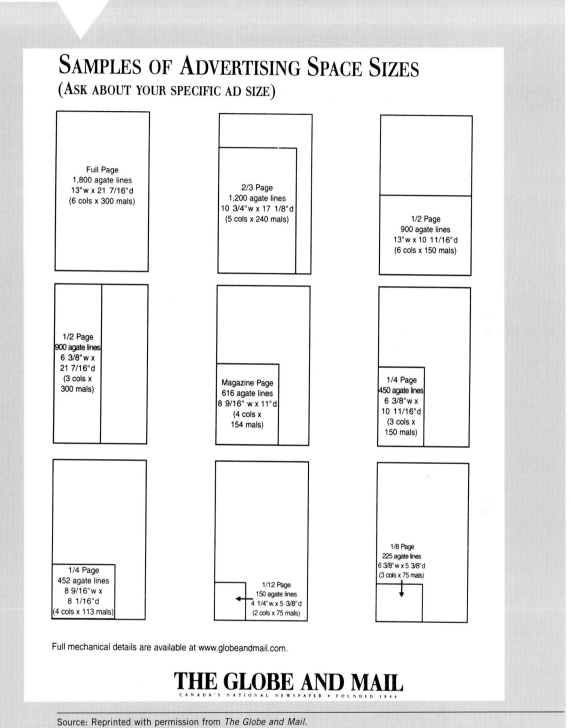

SAMPLES OF ADVERTISING SPACE SIZES
(ASK ABOUT YOUR SPECIFIC AD SIZE)

Full Page
1,800 agate lines
13"w x 21 7/16"d
(6 cols x 300 mals)

2/3 Page
1,200 agate lines
10 3/4"w x 17 1/8"d
(5 cols x 240 mals)

1/2 Page
900 agate lines
13"w x 10 11/16"d
(6 cols x 150 mals)

1/2 Page
900 agate lines
6 3/8"w x
21 7/16"d
(3 cols x
300 mals)

Magazine Page
616 agate lines
8 9/16" w x 11"d
(4 cols x
154 mals)

1/4 Page
450 agate lines
6 3/8"w x
10 11/16"d
(3 cols x
150 mals)

1/4 Page
452 agate lines
8 9/16"w x
8 1/16"d
(4 cols x 113 mals)

1/12 Page
150 agate lines
4 1/4"w x 5 3/8"d
(2 cols x 75 mals)

1/8 Page
225 agate lines
6 3/8"w x 5 3/8"d
(3 cols x 75 mals)

Full mechanical details are available at www.globeandmail.com.

THE GLOBE AND MAIL
CANADA'S NATIONAL NEWSPAPER • FOUNDED 1844

Source: Reprinted with permission from *The Globe and Mail*.

Determining Space Size

To illustrate the concept of agate lines, let's assume the size of the ad is 4 columns wide by 10 column inches deep. Considering that each column inch of depth equals 14 agate lines, the size of the ad would be calculated by the following formula:

$$\text{Number of columns wide} \times \text{inches of depth} \times 14$$

$$4 \times 10 \times 14 = 560 \text{ agate lines}$$

If the size of the advertisement is 5 columns wide by 8 inches deep, the size of the ad in agate lines will be:

$$5 \times 8 \times 14 = 560 \text{ lines}$$

These two examples illustrate that different configurations of ads (combinations of width and depth) can produce the same size of ad in terms of space occupied and rates charged.

The calculations above would be the same for modular agate lines. The only difference is that the modular agate line is slightly wider than the agate line. Before calculating the costs of an ad the planner must be aware of what system the newspaper is using: agate lines or modular agate lines.

Modular Agate Unit

A standardized unit of measurement in which a newspaper page is divided into equal-sized units each 30 modular agate lines deep.

Newspaper space can be sold on the basis of **modular agate units**, though only a few daily newspapers use this system. In this system, the size of the ad is expressed in terms of units of width and units of depth (e.g., 4 units wide by 6 units deep). In effect, the page is sectioned off into equal size units with each unit being 30 modular agate lines deep. Therefore, to calculate the actual size of an ad that is 4 units wide by 6 units deep, the calculation would be as follows:

$$\text{Number of columns wide} \times \text{units deep} \times 30 = \text{Modular agate lines}$$

$$4 \times 6 \times 30 = 720 \text{ MAL}$$

Rate Schedules

Line Rate

The rate charged by newspapers for one agate line or one modular agate line.

Line rate is defined as the rate charged by newspapers for one agate line or one modular agate line. With regard to rate schedules, several factors must be noted. First, rates charged by line go down as the volume of the lineage increases over a specified period. Second, costs for the addition of colour or preferred positions are quoted separately. Third, the line rates may vary from one section of the paper to another. For example, the transient rate (the highest rate paid by an advertiser) for advertisers in *The Globe and Mail's* News and Report on Business sections is higher than in the Review, Technology, Travel, and Special Interest sections. *The Globe and Mail* rate card in Figure A1.2 (pages 361–362) contains more details about line rates.

Transient Rate

A one-time rate, or base rate, that applies to casual advertisers.

In the chart in Figure A1.2, the rates quoted start with a **transient rate**, which is defined as a one-time rate, or base rate, that applies to casual advertisers. Discounts are offered to advertisers purchasing volume linage over a more extended period of time, usually one year.

To illustrate how costs are calculated in newspapers, let's develop a hypothetical plan and consider the use of modular agate lines and agate lines. For the sake of accuracy, however, it should be noted that *The Globe and Mail* quotes rates in terms of space occupied measured by MALs.

Newspaper: *The Globe and Mail*—National Edition, News Section

Size of ad: 4 columns wide × 10 column inches deep

Rate: Transient Rate—General

Frequency: Once

The first calculation determines, as follows, the total number of modular agate lines:

$$4 \text{ columns wide} \times (10 \text{ column inches deep} \times 14) \times 1 = 560 \text{ MAL}$$

The next step is to multiply the number of modular agate lines by the line rate by the frequency to determine the cost of the insertion. In this case, the **transient rate** applies because there is not enough linage to earn a discount.

$$560 \times \$30.37 = \$17\,007.20$$

FIGURE **A1.2**   **The Globe and Mail Rate Card**

2003 THE GLOBE AND MAIL
ON-LINE MEDIA KIT AT ADRATES.GLOBEANDMAIL.COM

GENERAL RATES

Advertising Rates effective January 1, 2003

Canada's largest and leading national newspaper is, without a doubt, the No. 1 choice for reaching affluent and educated Canadians from coast to coast*.

Industry studies repeatedly confirm that The Globe and Mail dominates the national newspaper market in Canada – and by a widening margin.

The Globe and Mail is a unique medium with the most influential, affluent and loyal readers in Canada – an audience you can't find anywhere else.

No matter what you need to advertise, The Globe and Mail delivers more of your best prospects in numbers too significant to ignore.

When quality customers with money to spend and intent to purchase matter to your media buy, buy The Globe and Mail.

NEWS, REPORT ON BUSINESS, SPECIAL REPORTS
Report on Business appears Monday through Saturday – National Edition only.

Monday to Friday

MALS**	National	Ontario	Metro
Transient	$30.37	$26.22	$24.14
900	29.46	25.45	23.42
1,800	28.71	24.68	22.73
3,600	27.95	23.99	22.06
5,400	27.03	23.20	21.36
7,200	26.57	22.85	21.04
10,000	25.67	22.07	20.33
13,000	25.21	21.69	19.96
16,000	24.76	21.31	19.62
20,000	24.43	21.05	19.39
25,000	24.00	20.66	19.03
32,000	23.54	20.26	18.66
43,000	23.23	19.98	18.43
58,000	22.63	19.46	17.93
75,000	22.02	18.92	17.43
100,000	21.26	18.25	16.81
135,000	20.50	17.61	16.22
175,000	19.59	16.82	15.50

Saturday

MALS**	National	Ontario	Metro
Transient	$31.88	$27.53	$25.35
900	30.93	26.71	24.60
1,800	30.15	25.92	23.87
3,600	29.35	25.20	23.17
5,400	28.38	24.36	22.42
7,200	27.91	23.99	22.09
10,000	26.95	23.18	21.35
13,000	26.47	22.78	20.96
16,000	25.99	22.37	20.60
20,000	25.66	22.10	20.36
25,000	25.21	21.69	19.98
32,000	24.73	21.27	19.60
43,000	24.39	20.98	19.35
58,000	23.76	20.44	18.82
75,000	23.11	19.87	18.30
100,000	22.33	19.17	17.65
135,000	21.52	18.49	17.03
175,000	20.56	17.66	16.28

Advertising rates shown are per line per day.

* SOURCE: NADbank 2002, 41 National Markets.

** Volume rates based on modular agate lines. All rates are gross. Prices in Canadian dollars.

GLOBE REVIEW, TRAVEL AND SPECIAL INTEREST REPORTS
Globe Review appears Monday through Saturday. Travel appears Wednesday and Saturday.

Monday to Friday

MALS**	National	Ontario	Metro
Transient	$18.94	$16.42	$15.07
900	18.25	15.81	14.49
1,800	17.71	15.34	14.04
3,600	17.09	14.89	13.46
5,400	16.64	14.39	13.06
7,200	16.44	14.20	12.95
10,000	15.92	13.75	12.55
13,000	15.62	13.51	12.32
16,000	15.39	13.30	12.15
20,000	15.19	13.14	11.98
25,000	14.95	12.91	11.78
32,000	14.68	12.66	11.56
43,000	14.49	12.51	11.41
58,000	14.18	12.23	11.15
75,000	13.87	11.96	10.91
100,000	13.46	11.63	10.59
135,000	13.05	11.28	10.26
175,000	12.48	10.76	9.80

Saturday

MALS**	National	Ontario	Metro
Transient	$19.89	$17.23	$15.82
900	19.17	16.61	15.21
1,800	18.59	16.10	14.74
3,600	17.95	15.63	14.14
5,400	17.47	15.11	13.72
7,200	17.25	14.91	13.60
10,000	16.72	14.44	13.17
13,000	16.40	14.19	12.93
16,000	16.17	13.96	12.76
20,000	15.95	13.79	12.58
25,000	15.71	13.56	12.37
32,000	15.42	13.30	12.14
43,000	15.21	13.14	11.98
58,000	14.89	12.85	11.71
75,000	14.57	12.57	11.46
100,000	14.14	12.21	11.12
135,000	13.71	11.84	10.77
175,000	13.10	11.30	10.30

CONTACT INFORMATION:
Toronto
tel 416.585.5600
toll-free 1.800.387.9012
fax 416.585.5682

Montreal
tel 514.982.3050
toll-free 1.800.363.7526
(from NFLD, NS, PEI, NB, PQ)
fax 514.845.8766

Western Canada
tel 604.685.0308
toll-free 1.800.663.1311
(from BC, AB, SK, NT)
fax 604.685.7549

United States and international advertising representatives
Publicitas, New York, NY
tel 212.599.5057
fax 212.599.8298

YOU ALSO NEED TO KNOW:
Any advertising published by The Globe and Mail in the newspaper or any of its other publications may, at our discretion, be published, displayed, retained and archived by us and anyone authorized (including any form of licence) by us, as many times as we and those authorized by us wish, in or on any product, media and archive (including print, electronic and otherwise).

All advertising must meet Globe and Mail terms and conditions – ask for a printed copy from your Globe and Mail advertising representative.

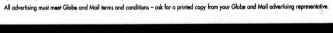

continued

GENERAL RATES

SPORTS, STYLE, AND CLASSIFIED

Style appears Saturday.

Monday to Friday

MALS**	National	Ontario	Metro
Transient	$14.42	$12.52	$11.47
900	13.90	12.05	11.04
1,800	13.32	11.69	10.56
3,600	12.85	11.32	10.09
5,400	12.50	10.95	9.79
7,200	12.48	10.81	9.71
10,000	12.15	10.48	9.47
13,000	11.91	10.30	9.30
16,000	11.73	10.13	9.21
20,000	11.60	10.01	9.11
25,000	11.38	9.84	8.95
32,000	11.19	9.66	8.82
43,000	11.04	9.52	8.70
58,000	10.80	9.32	8.50
75,000	10.56	9.12	8.29
100,000	10.23	8.85	8.07
135,000	9.94	8.58	7.80
175,000	9.55	8.25	7.45

Saturday

MALS**	National	Ontario	Metro
Transient	$15.14	$13.15	$12.04
900	14.60	12.65	11.59
1,800	13.99	12.27	11.08
3,600	13.49	11.89	10.60
5,400	13.13	11.50	10.29
7,200	13.10	11.35	10.19
10,000	12.76	11.01	9.94
13,000	12.50	10.81	9.76
16,000	12.32	10.63	9.68
20,000	12.18	10.51	9.56
25,000	11.95	10.33	9.41
32,000	11.75	10.15	9.26
43,000	11.59	10.00	9.13
58,000	11.34	9.78	8.93
75,000	11.08	9.57	8.71
100,000	10.75	9.29	8.48
135,000	10.44	9.01	8.19
175,000	10.02	8.65	7.83

COLOUR CHARGES

	National	Ontario	Metro
Spot	$3,936	$3,582	$3,294
Full	7,813	7,105	6,536

REPORT ON BUSINESS

Appointment Notices	$49.89
Financial Notices/Tombstones	38.22

GLOBE CAREERS

Includes 3 insertions – Wednesday, Friday and Saturday or Monday	$37.50

REGIONAL EDITIONS

Eastern Edition

Monday to Friday	$6.90 transient
Saturday	7.25 transient

Includes Ottawa, Quebec and Atlantic Canada.

Western Edition

Monday to Friday	$8.51 transient
Saturday	8.94 transient

Includes British Columbia, Alberta, Manitoba and Saskatchewan.

Eastern and Western editions published daily in front news.

Colour subject to availability. Colour rates available upon request.

RESERVATIONS AND CLOSINGS

Issue Day	Space Booking		Pub-set Material	
Mon.	Thurs.	4.30pm	Wed.	4.30pm
Tues.	Fri.	4.30pm	Thurs.	4.30pm
Wed.	Mon.	4.30pm	Fri.	4.30pm
Thurs.	Tues.	4.30pm	Mon.	4.30pm
Fri.	Wed.	4.30pm	Tues.	4.30pm
Sat.	Thurs.	4.30pm	Wed.	4.30pm
Mon. Careers	Thurs.	2:00pm	Wed.	2:00pm
Wed. Careers	Mon.	2:00pm	Fri.	2:00pm
Fri. Careers	Wed.	2:00pm	Tues.	2:00pm
Sat. Careers	Thurs.	2:00pm	Wed.	2:00pm
Wed. Travel	Fri.	4:30pm	Fri.	4:30pm
Sat. Travel	Tues.	4:30pm	Tues.	4:30pm
Sat. Style	Tues.	4:30pm	Mon.	4:30pm
Weekend Review	Thurs.	4:00pm	Wed.	4:30pm

All deadlines are based on Eastern Standard Time.

Complete deadlines listed on our Web site: adrates.globeandmail.com

Colour advertising

4 days in advance for space booking and material.

Double truck

4 days in advance for space booking and material.

COPY CHANGES

News, Report on Business, Sports, Globe Review (excluding Weekend Review)

2:00pm day prior to publication date.

Wednesday Travel

Monday 4:30pm.

Style

Thursday 12:00pm.

Saturday Travel

Thursday 4:30pm.

Weekend Review

Friday 12:00pm.

Saturday Books

Thursday 12:00pm.

ADDITIONAL INFORMATION

- Deadlines and specifications available separately.
- There is a $64.50 production charge for ads under 50 MAL that are not camera-ready.
- Minimum display space in News, Style, and Report on Business is 30 MAL; unless specified, it is 15 MAL in other sections.
- Advertising columns 251 MAL or more in depth are charged full column depth.
- Double Trucks: Gutter is charged as full column.
- Regional copy changes: $419 per plant.
- Position charge: +25 per cent.
- Front News Banner: +50 per cent.
- Page 3, News: +40 per cent.
- Pages 2 & 3, ROB: +40 per cent.
- Charge for Globe and Mail box number: $64.50.

- Charge for affidavits: $64.50.
- Cancellation charge: 50 per cent for ads cancelled after deadline. No cancellations for colour advertising two days prior to publication. No cancellations accepted the day prior to publication.
- The Publisher shall not be liable for errors in advertisements beyond the actual space paid. No liability for non-insertions of any advertisement.
- Not responsible for return of advertising material.

NEWSPAPER SPECIFICATIONS

Complete mechanical and digital specifications available separately.

Number of columns: 6.

Column width: 50mm
11.9 picas
1.96" (approx. 1 15/16")

Column depth: 300 modular agate lines for full page ads (1,800 lines per 6 column page).

THE GLOBE AND MAIL

CANADA'S NATIONAL NEWSPAPER • FOUNDED 1844 • GLOBEANDMAIL.COM

Source: Reprinted with permission from *The Globe and Mail*.

FIGURE **A1.3**

Newspaper Cost Calculations Including Colour and Position Charges

The following illustrations consider two important aspects of newspaper advertising: adding colour and requesting specific locations. The size of the budget often dictates whether colour and position charges can be accommodated. Refer to Figure A1.2 for rates for each illustration.

ILLUSTRATION 1: THE ADDITION OF COLOUR

Newspaper:	*The Globe and Mail*, National Edition, ROB section
Size of ad:	6 columns wide by 15 column inches deep
Colour:	Black & white plus one colour (spot colour)
Timing:	Two insertions per week (Tuesday and Thursday)
Continuity:	6 weeks

The cost calculation would be as follows:

Total Number of Lines

$(6 \times 15 \times 14) \times 2 \times 6 = 15\ 120$ lines

Cost of Ad in Black & White

$15\ 120 \times \$25.21 = \$381\ 175.20$

Additional Colour Cost

$\$3936 \times 12 = \$47\ 232.00$

Total Cost

$\$381\ 175.20 + \$47\ 232.00 = \$428\ 407.20$

ILLUSTRATION 2: POSITION REQUEST

Newspaper:	*The Globe and Mail*, National Edition
Size of ad:	6 columns wide by 11 inches deep
Colour:	Black & white
Frequency:	10
Location request:	page A5 (News Section)

The cost calculation would be as follows:

Total Number of Lines

$(6 \times 11 \times 14) \times 10 = 9240$ lines

Cost of Ad

$(9240 \times \$26.57) \times 1.25 = \$306\ 883.50$ (there is a 25 percent premium for the page request)

As indicated in the rate schedule in Figure A1.2, the cost of each advertisement is less if the ***volume of lines purchased*** meets or exceeds the line requirements on the volume scales. To illustrate, let's assume the same information as in the preceding example, with one change. This time, the ad will run eight times (twice a week, Monday and Wednesday for four weeks). In this case, the total lines purchased would be as follows:

4 columns wide × (10 column inches deep × 14) × 8 insertions = 4480 MAL

Based on the rate schedule (Figure A1.2), the rate per line in the National edition is $27.95. Therefore, the total costs of the campaign would be calculated as follows:

Total lines purchased × Line rate = Total cost

4480 × $27.95 = $125 216.00

Where the cost of the advertisement in the original example was $17 007.20, the cost of each advertisement in this campaign would be $16 497.60 ($131 980.80 divided by eight insertions). For additional illustrations of how to calculate costs, refer to Figure A1.3.

Position Charges

Position Charge
The cost of requesting a preferred position in a newspaper.

Since one disadvantage of newspaper advertising is clutter, advertisers and agencies normally request positions in the newspaper that are deemed to be favourable. The request may be for a particular section, or it could be for the first few pages of the newspaper. With reference to Figure A1.2, *The Globe and Mail* charges more for preferred locations. A request for any position in the paper will increase rates by 25 percent, while a request for an ad to appear on page 3 of the News section or page 2 or 3 of the ROB section will increase rates by 40 percent. The privilege of having a preferred position in a newspaper at a higher cost incurs a **position charge**. An advertiser usually justifies the additional expense of a position request by referring to the improved recognition and recall that will result from the better position.

Colour Charges

Although newspapers are often referred to as the black-and-white medium, colour is available to advertisers willing to pay for it. With reference to *The Globe and Mail's* rate schedule in Figure A1.2, the addition of spot colour (one colour) adds $3936 to the cost of an ad. Full colour would add $7813. There are minimum size requirements for ads that include colour. Generally speaking, there is higher recognition and recall of ads that appear in colour, but given the constraints of most budgets, the use of colour in newspaper advertising is reserved for very large advertisers. Figure A1.3 offers cost examples that include colour and position charges.

Pre-Printed Inserts

Pre-printed inserts, such as advertising supplements for supermarkets, drug stores, and mass merchandisers, are inserted into most newspapers and distributed by them. Costs are usually quoted on a cost per thousand (CPM) basis, with rates increasing with the size of the insert. For example, a 24-page catalogue insert would cost more than a four-page folded insert. Insert rates are quoted separately on newspaper rate cards. In many cases, there is only a reference to the rates on the rate card. Advertisers must contact the newspaper for details.

Comparing Newspapers for Efficiency

In large metropolitan markets, where several newspapers compete for advertising revenue, advertisers must decide which papers to place advertising with. If using a shotgun strategy, the advertiser may use all newspapers. Conversely, if the budget is limited and the target market is more precisely defined, the advertiser might be more selective.

Cost Per Thousand (CPM)
The cost of delivering an advertising message to 1000 people.

Since the circulation and the cost of advertising (line rates) vary among newspapers, the advertiser must have a way of comparing the alternatives. To make this comparison, the advertiser may use a standard figure called the **cost per thousand (CPM)**. CPM is the actual cost of reaching 1000 readers in a market. The formula for calculating CPM is as follows:

$$\frac{\text{Cost}}{\text{Circulation (in thousands)}} = \text{CPM}$$

To illustrate the concept of CPM, an advertiser that wants to reach adults in the Toronto market can choose among three daily newspapers. Refer to Figure A1.4 for specific details of how the newspapers are compared.

As shown by Figure A1.4, the newspaper CPM is strictly a quantitative figure and the results vary considerably. If the advertiser bases the decision of which newspaper to use solely on this principle, the decision is an easy one—*The Toronto Star* and the *Toronto Sun* have a lower CPM. Not shown in a CPM calculation, however, is the demographic profile of the readers of the various newspapers. *The Toronto Star* and the *Toronto Sun* offer mass appeal to a broad cross-section of the Toronto population at very reasonable costs compared to those of *The Globe and Mail*. So if the target market is more upscale in terms of income, occupation, and educational background, *The Globe and Mail* might be selected, despite the higher CPM.

MAGAZINE ADVERTISING

The procedure for buying magazine space begins with deciding on the size of the ad, which involves choosing from among the variety of page options sold by the magazines under consideration. The rates quoted are based on the size of page requested. Other factors that influence the cost of advertising in magazines include the frequency of insertions and appropriate discounts, the use of colour, guaranteed-position charges, and the use of regional editions.

Size of an Advertisement and Rate Schedules

Magazines offer a variety of page options or page combinations. For example, *Canadian Geographic* sells space in the following formats: double-page spread, double 1/2 page spread, one page, 2/3 page, 1/2-page digest, 1/2-page horizontal, and 1/3 page. See Figure A1.5 for illustrations of various magazine ad sizes. The size selected for the advertisement determines the rate to be charged. Magazine rates are typically quoted for all page combinations.

FIGURE **A1.4**   **Comparing Newspapers for Efficiency**

The CPM or cost per thousand is used to compare newspaper alternatives. It is calculated by dividing the cost of the advertisement by the circulation (in thousands) of the newspaper.

Specifications	The *Toronto Star*	*Toronto Sun*	The *Globe and Mail*
Ad size	1000 lines	1000 lines	1000 lines
Cost per line	$15.90	$6.89	$27.43
Ad Cost (rate x lines)	$15 900	$6890	$27 430
Circulation	454 831	230 644	354 574
CPM	$34.96	$29.87	$77.36

The Globe and Mail reaches an audience characterized by higher education and higher income. An advertiser will have to pay more to reach such a selective audience.

Adapted from *Canadian Advertising Rates and Data*, September 2002.

FIGURE **A1.5** **Various Sizes of Magazine Ads**

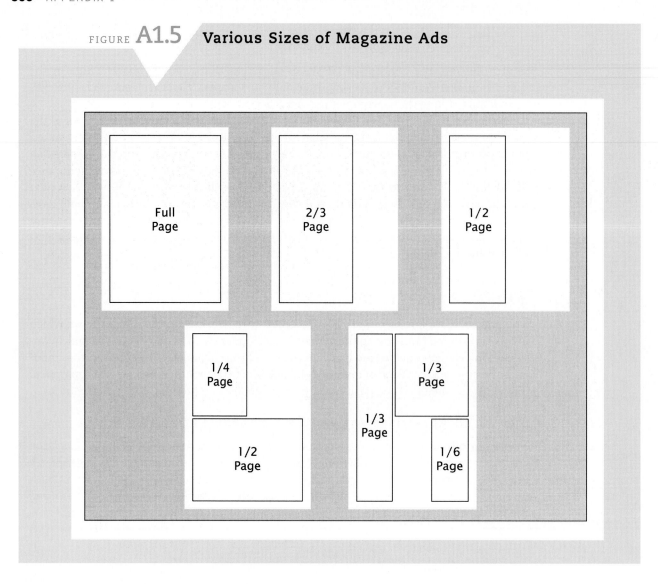

To illustrate how costs are calculated, let's consider a simple example. Assume an advertiser would like to purchase a one-page, four-colour ad in *Canadian Geographic* for January/February and March/April (see Figure A1.6 on pages 367–368). *Canadian Geographic* is a bi-monthly publication. Because the frequency of the advertising does not reach the first discount level (three insertions), the advertiser would pay the one-time rate. The cost calculation would be as follows:

$$\text{One-page rate} \times \text{Number of insertions} = \text{Total cost}$$

$$\$14\,590 \times 2 = \$29\,180$$

Discounts

Advertisers that purchase space in specific magazines with greater frequency will qualify for a variety of discounts. The nature of these discounts varies from one publication to another. Some of the more common discounts include frequency, continuity, and corporate discounts. In magazines, a **frequency discount** refers to a discounted page rate, with the discount based on the number of times an advertisement is run. The more often the ad is run, the lower the unit cost for each ad. In the *Canadian Geographic* rate card, the unit rate is reduced when the ad is run three times, six times, nine times, and twelve times.

Frequency Discount

A discounted page rate based on the number of times an advertisement runs.

FIGURE A1.6 **Canadian Geographic Magazine Rate Card**

RATES AND DATA 2003

MAGAZINE OF THE YEAR

Winning Awards

In 2002, *Canadian Geographic* received two significant national honours. For the third time in four years, it was recognized as "Best Magazine" by the Canadian Society of Magazine Editors. In May, *Canadian Geographic* was named "Magazine of the Year" by the National Magazine Awards (NMA) Foundation.

In nominating *Canadian Geographic* for the award, John Macfarlane, president of the NMA, said:

Canadian Geographic is:

- unapologetic about celebrating Canada in all its glory
- excellent cover to cover, and an example of editorial commitment
- rigorously edited
- well-written
- published to consistently high standards of research, design, writing, photography and graphics
- handsome
- entertaining

Publishing Schedule

Issue	Features and Supplements	Closing Date (Insertion orders & materials)	On Newsstand
Jan/Feb 2003	**Special Issue on Canadian Housing & Shelter**	November 20, 2002	December 23, 2002
Mar/Apr 2003	**TBA**	January 29, 2003	March 3, 2003
	Travel and Adventure Spring/Summer	January 15, 2003*	March 3, 2003
May/June 2003	**Report on the Environment**	March 26, 2003	April 28, 2003
July/August 2003	**TBA**	May 28, 2003	June 30, 2003
Sept/Oct 2003	**TBA**	July 30, 2003	September 1, 2003
Nov/Dec 2003	**TBA**	October 1, 2003	November 3, 2003
	Travel and Adventure Fall/Winter	September 17, 2003*	November 3, 2003
Jan/Feb 2004	**TBA**	November 26, 2003	December 29, 2003

* Closing date for supplements only.

2003 Advertising Rates

National	1x	3x	6x	9x	12x
IFC Spread	29,805	28,905	28,040	27,195	26,375
IBC	16,655	16,145	15,660	15,190	14,730

Rates for 2003					
OBC	17,370	16,845	16,345	15,850	15,380
DPS	25,915	25,135	24,380	23,650	22,940
Full Page	14,590	14,150	13,725	13,305	12,910
1/2 Spread	17,050	16,535	16,035	15,550	15,090
2/3 Page	11,570	11,225	10,885	10,560	10,245
1/2 Page Digest	10,575	10,255	9,945	9,645	9,355
1/2 Horizontal	10,340	8,995	8,725	8,460	8,195
1/3 Page	6,945	6,735	6,530	6,330	6,135

Ontario/Western CAN	1x	3x	6x	9x	12x
DPS	19,435	18,860	18,290	17,745	17,210
Full Page	10,940	10,615	10,295	9,985	9,690

Travel & Adventure Digest	
Full Page	7,500
1/2 Page	3,900

All rates in gross Canadian dollars.

Your **country** — your **magazine**.

continued

MECHANICAL SPECIFICATIONS

Generic Book Specifications

Trim Size	8" x 10 7/8"
Bleed	Minimum 1/8" bleed
Colour	CMYK throughout
Printing	Web Offset, coated stock, 150 lpi.
Binding	Perfect bound

Standard Unit Sizes

	Non-Bleed	Bleed
Full Page	7" x 10"	8" x 10 7/8"
Double Page Spread	15" x 10"	16" x 10 7/8"
Double 1/2 Page Spread	15" x 4 7/8"	16" x 5 1/4"
1/2 Page Horizontal	7" x 4 7/8"	8" x 5 1/4"
1/2 Page Digest	4 1/2" x 7 3/8"	5 1/6" x 7 7/8"
2/3 Page (2 Column)	4 1/2" x 10"	5" x 10 7/8"
1/3 Page Vertical	2 3/16" x 9 7/8"	2 11/16" x 10 7/8"
1/3 Page Square	4 1/2" x 4 7/8"	5 1/16" x 5 1/4"

NON-BLEED ADS

Ads that are not intended to bleed must be sized to fit within the non-bleed sizes listed above.

BLEED ADS

• Ads that are intended to bleed must be sized to be trimmed to the bleed sizes listed above.
• All live matter (text, images not to be trimmed) must be kept within the non-bleed measurements. Any matter that extends past the non-bleed safe area may be trimmed due to folding and bindery variations.
• Any image or background colour intended to bleed must extend a minimum of 1/8" past the trim dimensions on all four sides of the ad. Right or left hand positioning is not guaranteed.
• Be aware of common crossover limitations in "double-page-spread" configurations (adjoining pages can shift up to 1/8" in the binding process on certain copies).

AUTHOR'S ALTERATIONS AND LATE FEE

Changes to supplied material will be made only when accompanied by written instructions from the client. Changes will be made only if received before the ad submission date, and clients may be charged an AA fee of $60 depending on the production stage. *Canadian Geographic* endeavours to comply with all advertisers' changes, but assumes no responsibility for errors or omissions resulting from requested changes. Requested changes are assumed to be final. A courtesy proof will be sent to the client upon request.

Any material supplied after the published submission date will be subject to a charge of $60.

PRODUCTION REQUIREMENTS

Canadian Geographic does not accept film. Electronic files must be supplied. Any charges incurred to convert film to electronic format will be charged to the client.
• Upon confirmation of an ad booking, each ad will be assigned a reference number. This number must be included in the file name and marked clearly on the supplied proof.

• Electronic files must be supplied as Mac QuarkXpress 4.1 (or earlier) with all support files and fonts included, or PDF (Press Optimized). Extra charges may be applied to convert PC files.
• Acceptable removable media include 100 mb Zip, 1 or 2 Gb Jaz, or CD.
• Compressed files must be saved as self-extracting archives (.sea).
• Type should be converted to outline when possible (Adobe Illustrator, Macromedia Freehand, Corel Draw).
• Press-ready proof must be supplied to guarantee accurate colour reproduction.
• *Canadian Geographic* will not assume responsibility for type reflow or accurate colour reproduction if all necessary fonts, support files, and press-ready proofs are not included.

GENERAL INFORMATION

Acceptability: The content and design of all advertisements are subject to the publishers' approval.
Commissions: 15% of charges for space, position and colour allowed to recognized agencies.
Cash Discount: 1% on net if paid within 15 days of date of invoice.
Terms: Net 30 days; 2% interest charged per month on overdue accounts; 24% per annum.
GST: Rates do not include Goods and Services Tax. Where applicable, a 7% GST will be added to the price of all advertising and services in *Canadian Geographic*.

SHIPPING:

1) All insertion orders and contracts are to be sent to:

Canadian Geographic Enterprises
ADVERTISING SALES OFFICE
70 The Esplanade, Suite 400
Toronto, ON M5E 1R2
Tel: (416) 360-4151
Fax: (416) 360-1526
E-mail: adsales@canadiangeographic.ca

2) All creative should be shipped to:

Canadian Geographic Enterprises
PRODUCTION MANAGER
39 McArthur Avenue
Ottawa, ON K1L 8L7
Tel: (613) 745-4629
Fax: (613) 744-0947
E-mail: elston@canadiangeographic.ca

or contact your sales representative for FTP information.

Your **country** — your **magazine**.

Source: Courtesy of *Canadian Geographic*.

Continuity Discount

A discount offered to advertisers that purchase space in consecutive issues of a publication.

A **continuity discount** is an additional discount offered to advertisers that agree to purchase space in consecutive issues of a magazine (such as buying space in 12 issues of a monthly magazine). When continuity discounts are combined with frequency discounts, lower unit costs per page of advertising result.

Large advertisers that use the same magazine to advertise a variety of products (note that such an advertiser would likely be a multi-product firm with products that share similar target markets) may qualify for corporate discounts. A **corporate discount** involves consideration of the total number of pages purchased by the company (all product lines combined), and a lower page rate for each product. Companies such as Procter & Gamble or Unilever that advertise extensively in women's magazines such as *Chatelaine* and *Canadian Living* would earn preferred rates for the advertising pages they buy in those magazines.

Corporate Discount

A discount based on the total number of pages purchased by a single company (all product lines combined).

Colour and Position Charges

Most magazines publish in colour. Therefore, rates for black and white ads or ads that only include spot colour ads are usually quoted separately. Additional costs for requesting a guaranteed position are also quoted separately on the rate card. For a guaranteed position, such as the outside back cover (OBC) or the inside front cover (IFC) and inside back cover (IBC), the additional costs are usually in the +20 percent range. With reference to the *Canadian Geographic* rate card, the rate for the outside back cover is $17 370, compared to a full-page ad inside the magazine at $14 590. The difference is about 20 percent.

To illustrate the cost calculations of buying magazine space, let's develop a few examples based on the *Canadian Geographic* rate card (see Figure A1.6) and the following information:

Example 1:

Magazine:	*Canadian Geographic*
Size of ad:	one-page, 4-colour ad
Number of insertions:	one-page ad to run in 4 consecutive issues

The calulation for this buying plan will be as follows:

Costs for one page, 4 colour:

Base rate	= 3–5 times rate
$14 150 × 4	= $56 600

Example 2:

Magazine:	*Canadian Geographic*
Size of ad:	double-page spread, 4-colour ad
Number of insertions:	6 issues

The calulation for this buying plan will be as follows:

Costs for DPS, four colour:

Base rate	= 6–8 times rate
$24 380 × 6	= $146 280

Comparing Magazines for Efficiency

Let's assume the advertiser has decided to use magazines because they usually have a well-defined target audience based on demographic variables. The advertiser still must choose particular magazines in which to advertise. Because costs and circulation figures vary, the advertiser needs a way to compare alternatives. As with newspapers, CPM is an effective quantitative means of comparing competing magazines.

In most magazine classifications, there is usually a group of publications competing for the same market. For example, *Chatelaine*, *Homemaker's*, and *Canadian Living*, among others, compete against each other in the women's classification. Although the editorial content varies from one magazine to another, each reaches a similar target, so advertisers must look at the efficiencies of each.

Figure A1.7 contains the comparative calculations for two of the magazines in the women's classification. In terms of a purely quantitative measure, both magazines are almost equal and that is why they attract the same types of advertisers. Advertisers wanting to reach the demographic profile of readers of these magazines have little choice but to allocate dollars to both. They reach different readers but readers with the same profile. Therefore, to advertise in both increases the reach of the magazine campaign. The question is, How much weight does each magazine receive?

TELEVISION ADVERTISING

As indicated earlier, stations and networks tend not to publish a rate card. There are a variety of factors that influence the costs of television advertising: the supply of advertising time available and the demand for that time, the type of program, the time of day the ad will appear, and the length of the commercial.

Supply and Demand

For major networks such as CTV, CBC, and Global, fundamental economic principles rule the cost of advertising. Advertising space is restricted to 12 minutes per hour, so the network has to maximize advertising revenues on shows that are popular. Top-rated shows such as *Survivor* (Global), *CSI* (CTV), and the *NHL Playoffs* (CBC) attract advertisers willing to pay a premium price for being on a popular (highly watched) show. The low supply and high demand for the space drives the rates upward. National ads on *Survivor* in 2003 were expected to be $80 000 for each 30-second spot, followed by *CSI* and *ER* at $65 000 apiece. By comparison, *Hockey Night in Canada* sells for about $25 000.[1]

The rates paid by advertisers for these and other shows depend largely on their advertising agency's ability to negotiate with the networks. To illustrate, the quoted 30-second spot on *CSI Miami* in 2002 was $22 600. For 2003, the price more than doubled to $49 500, indicating the show's popularity. The negotiated rate, typically given to larger year-round advertisers after negotiations, packaging strategies, and agency agreements, was $34 000. The negotiated rate in 2002 was $18 100.[2] Again, negotiation skills play a key role in the rates an advertiser actually pays.

FIGURE **A1.7**

Comparing Magazines for Efficiency

Similar to newspapers, CPM (cost per thousand) comparisons are made between magazines that reach similar target markets. In this case, *Chatelaine* and *Canadian Living* compete head-to-head for advertisers.

Specifications	Chatelaine	Canadian Living
One-time, four-colour rate	$39 765	$30 035
Circulation	735 059	547 793
CPM	$54.10	$54.83

Both magazines charge different rates and have different circulations, but their CPM is almost identical. Both magazines are good alternatives for reaching career women and homemakers.

Adapted from *Canadian Advertising Rates and Data*, September 2002.

Types of Programs

Special programming such as drama specials, sports events, and miniseries is usually distinguished from regular programming. They are designated as special buys and are sold separately from regular programs. In the case of sports programs, for example, hockey and baseball broadcasts tend to appeal to a particular demographic: males between 18 and 49. They are attractive shows for certain types of advertisers. For these shows networks need sponsors that are willing to make a long-term commitment, and there are separate rates and discount schedules for those that make such a commitment. Canadian Tire, for example, is a committed advertiser for *Hockey Night in Canada* and the *NHL Playoffs*.

Time of Day

Television is divided into three time categories: ***prime time***, ***fringe time***, and ***day time***. Prime time is usually between 7 p.m. and 11 p.m., fringe time between 4 p.m. and 7 p.m., and day time from sign-on to 4 p.m. Because television viewing is highest in prime time, the advertising rates are higher in that time period. Rates vary from show to show and are based solely on the size of viewing audience each show reaches. As indicated above, shows like *CSI* and *ER* reach a very large audience, so their rates are among the highest. Other shows in prime time with a smaller audience have rates that are adjusted downward proportionately. To illustrate, a spot on *Everybody Loves Raymond* might fetch $30 000 but the show that precedes it, *Still Standing*, only brings in about $18 000. The difference is based on the popularity of the show and the size of the audience.

Television viewing in fringe time and day time is much lower, so the advertising rates are adjusted downward. Program content is of a different nature: talk shows, children's shows, reruns of popular programs, and so on. CKCO-TV does publish a rate card, which illustrates how rates fluctuate based on time of day and the popularity of the show (see Figure A1.8).

Length of Commercial

Most advertisers run 30-second commercials, so rates are normally quoted based on that length. Due to the rising costs of television advertising, advertisers frequently use 15-second commercials. There is a slight premium for using 15-second commercials; rates are normally about 65 percent of the cost of a 30-second commercial on the same network or station. A 60-second commercial is normally twice the cost of a 30-second commercial. If an advertiser can accomplish creatively what it desires by using 15-second commercials, it will cost less to advertise in absolute dollars. This is an important budget consideration.

Gross Rating Points

Gross Rating Points (GRPs)
An expression of the weight of advertising in a media schedule.

The weight of advertising in a market is determined by a rating system referred to as gross rating points. **Gross rating points (GRPs)** are an aggregate of total ratings in a schedule, usually in a weekly period, against a predetermined target audience. GRPs are based on the formula:

$$\text{GRPs} = \text{Reach} \times \text{Frequency}$$

Rating
Television and radio audience estimates expressed as a percentage of a population in a defined geographic area.

To illustrate how GRPs work, assume a message reaches 40 percent of target households three times in one week. The GRP level would be 120 (40×3). If the message reaches 35 percent of households with an average frequency of 3.6 per week, the GRP level would be 126 (35×3.6). The reach of a television show is referred to as a **rating**. For example, if *Friends* reaches 40 percent of households during its weekly time slot, the show has a 40 rating. Therefore, another way to calculate GRPs is to multiply a show's rating by the frequency of messages on that show. See Figure A1.9 (p. 373) for an illustration of this calculation.

Decisions about reach and frequency are difficult. Traditional wisdom suggests frequency is the more important variable, because it is necessary to drive the message home before people take action. Traditional models are based on achieving awareness, attitude,

FIGURE **A1.8** **CKCO-TV Rate Card**

CKCO KITCHENER
2000-2001 RATE CARD

REVISED EFFECTIVE: Mar 23/01
30 SECOND – PUBLISHED RATE (GROSS)
FOR INTERNAL USE ONLY
RATES ARE PROTECTED FOR 5 WORKING DAYS

PRIME

DAY	TIME	PROGRAM	GROUP #	SPRING FEB 19/01– JUN 10/01	SUMMER JUN 11/01– SEP 16/01	52WK SEP 18/00– SEP 16/01
M–FR	5:57–7P	EARLY NEWS	015	$1,240	$700	$1,080
SA–SU	5:58–7P	WEEKEND NEWS	162	$830	$540	$740
M–SA	7–7:28P	WHEEL OF FORTUNE (S)	160	$1,410	$720	$1,240
M–F	7:28–8P	JEOPARDY (S)	001	$1,410	$530	$1,240
MO	8–9P	MYSTERIOUS WAYS	089	$1,360	$820	$1,090
TU	8–9P	MILLIONAIRE (S)	206	$2,170	$1,090	$1,850
TU	9–930P	DREW CAREY (PRE)	146	$1,330	$760	$1,120
TU	930–10P	WHAT ABOUT JOAN? (S)	057	$880	$530	$790
WE	8–830P	MY WIFE AND KIDS	034	$990	$490	$810
WE	830–9P	WHOSE LINE IS IT ANYWAY (S)	054	$2,460	$1,550	$2,060
WE	10–11P	LAW & ORDER (S)	076	$2,410	$1,210	$2,120
TH	9–10P	CSI (S)	068	$710	$320	$600
FR	8–9P	THE FUGITIVE (Pre)	008	$490	$330	$430
FR	9–10P	MILLIONAIRE (S)	291	$2,460	$1,410	$2,270
SA	7–730P	COMMITTED	047	$170	$130	$160
SA	730–8P	ENOW	048	$190	$130	$160
SA	9–10P	COLDSQUAD	020	$340	$130	$290
SA	10–11P	COMEDY NOW	282	$390	$130	$320
SU	7–8P	SEVENTH HEAVEN	327	$1,310	$860	$1,110
SU	9–10P	MILLIONAIRE (S)	242	$2,350	$1,270	$2,090

Source: Courtesy of CKCO Kitchener.

and action. But there is a threshold at which an advertiser starts to turn the consumer off.[3] Consequently, many advertisers buy into a relatively new concept called recency. **Recency** is a model that suggests advertising works best by reminding consumers about a product when they are ready to buy.[4] The debate goes on!

Recency
A model that suggests advertising works best by reminding consumers about a product when they are ready to buy.

Since reach, frequency, and GRPs are discussed in the negotiation process, along with a host of other factors, it is next to impossible to illustrate its application in this book. However, to illustrate the basic use of a television rate card, let's look at a few examples. The rate card included in Figure A1.8 will be used as reference for these illustrations.

Example 1:

Wheel of Fortune:	2 spots per week
Drew Carey:	1 spot per week
Whose Line Is It Anyway:	1 spot per week
Early News:	3 spots per week

All spots run 52 weeks per year.

Cost Calculations:

A discounted rate applies (refer to the cost columns in Figure A1.8).

Wheel of Fortune:	$1240 \times 2 \times 52 = \$128\,960$
Drew Carey:	$1120 \times 1 \times 52 = \$58\,240$
Whose Line Is It Anyway:	$2060 \times 1 \times 52 = \$107\,120$
Early News:	$1080 \times 3 \times 52 = \$168\,480$
Total cost:	**$462 800**

Example 2:

Law & Order:	2 spots per week (13 weeks from February 19 to May 14)
Mysterious Ways:	1 spot per week (13 weeks from February 19 to May 14)

FIGURE **A1.9** **Calculating GRPs for Television**

The weight of advertising in a market or on a particular show is determined by a rating system. Media weight is expressed in terms of gross rating points (GRPs). **GRPs** consider two key variables: the size of the audience reached and frequency with which the ad is run against that audience. The chart shows some sample calculations to arrive at total GRPs.

Audience Demographic	Rating	Number of Spots	GRPs
18–49	30	2	60
18–49	25	2	50
18–49	20	2	40
18–49	23	2	46
Total		**8**	**196**

If the eight spots were scheduled in a one-week period, the weight level for the advertising would be expressed as 196 GRPs for the week.

Cost Calculations: The continuity discount does not apply because the spots only run during a portion of the year.

Law & Order:	$2410 × 2 × 13 = $62 660
Mysterious Ways:	$1360 × 1 × 13 = $17 680
Total cost:	**$80 340**

A variety of discounts are usually available to television advertisers. A **frequency discount** is usually earned by purchasing a minimum number of spots over a specified period. A **volume discount** is linked to the dollar volume purchased over an extended period, usually 52 weeks. The greater the volume purchased, the greater the discount. A **continuity discount** is earned when advertisers purchase a minimum number of spots over an extended period (also usually 52 weeks). The value of the continuity discount increases with the number of spots purchased. Discounts are not usually published. Instead, they are part of the discussion when buyers and sellers are negotiating with each other.

Volume Discount

A discount linked to the dollar volume purchased over an extended period; the more volume purchased, the higher the discount.

RADIO ADVERTISING

The rates paid by radio advertisers are affected by several factors: the season or time of year in which commercials are placed, the time of day at which the commercials are scheduled, the use of reach plans, and the availability of discounts offered by individual stations.

Seasonal Rate Structures

Radio stations use grid-rate schedules that reflect seasonal listening patterns and reach potential. Refer to Figure A1.10 for an illustration of specific grid-level rates. Generally, radio rates fluctuate with the seasons, as follows:

Time Period	Rate
May–August (summer) and December	Higher
September–October	Mid-range
March–April	Mid-range
January–February	Lower

Dayparts

Daypart

A broadcast time period or segment on radio or television.

Since the size and nature of the audience vary according to the **daypart** (a broadcast time period or segment), different rates are charged for each. Generally, the dayparts are classified as follows:

Classification	Time
Breakfast	6 to 10 a.m.
Midday	10 a.m. to 4 p.m.
Drive	4 to 7 p.m.
Evening	7 p.m. to midnight
Nighttime	Midnight to 6 a.m.

Dayparts vary from one station to another, with some stations having more or fewer classifications than those listed above. In addition, weekend classifications are often different from weekday ones, as the listening patterns of the audience change on weekends.

Reach Plans

Radio advertisers can either purchase specific time slots and schedule a particular rotation plan during the length of the media buy, or they can purchase a reach plan. For the

FIGURE A1.10 **CJAZ-FM Rate Card**

CJAZ-FM Radio
101.7 JAZ-FM
Jazz that Rocks!

30-sec spot rates

Daypart/Grid	1	2	3	4	5
Breakfast 6:00 to 10:00 am	300	275	250	225	200
Daytime 10:00 am to 3:00 pm	245	225	205	185	165
Drive 3:00 to 7:00 pm	250	230	210	190	170
Evening and Sunday	220	200	180	160	140

Reach Plan - 30 sec spots

	1	2	3	4	5
Breakfast 25% Daytime 25% Drive 25% Evening and Sunday 25%	250	225	200	175	150

Discount Schedule

Contract Buy (Continuity)		*Volume (Spots)*	
14 to 26 weeks	Grid 3	250	Grid 3
27 to 39 weeks	Grid 4	450	Grid 4
40 to 52 weeks	Grid 5	700	Grid 5

Rotation Plan

The placement of commercials in time slots purchased on radio; can be vertical according to the time of day or horizontal according to the day of the week.

Reach Plan

Rotation of commercials in various dayparts on radio according to a predetermined frequency.

first option, a **rotation plan**, the advertiser specifies the time slots and pays the rate associated with it. Two types of rotation plans are available:

- **Vertical Rotation:** the placement of commercials based on the time of day (within various dayparts)
- **Horizontal Rotation:** the placement of commercials based on the day of the week (same daypart on different days)

Radio stations sell reach plans so that advertisers can maximize reach. In a **reach plan**, commercials are rotated through the various dayparts according to a predetermined frequency, in order to reach different people with the same message. As shown in Figure A1.10, the reach plan divides spots equally between breakfast, daytime, drive time, and evening/Sunday dayparts. For the advertiser, the benefit of the reach plan is twofold. First, the reach potential is extended, and second, the rates charged for the reach plan collectively are lower (because of the discounts) than those that would result from the individual purchase of similar time slots. Reach plans do require a minimum spot purchase on a weekly basis.

Discounts Offered by Radio

Advertisers that purchase frequently from specific stations qualify for a variety of discounts.

A **frequency discount** is a discounted rate earned through the purchase of a minimum number of spots over a specified period of time, usually a week. Having earned such a discount, advertisers are referred to a lower-rate grid schedule, or could be quoted a percentage discount, such as 5 percent for 15 to 20 spots per week, 8 percent for 21 to 30 per week, 10 percent for over 31 spots, and so forth. With a **volume discount**, the advertiser is charged a lower rate for buying a large number of spots; the discount might be 5 percent for 260 spots, for example, or 10 percent for 520 spots. A **continuity discount** applies when an advertiser agrees to place ads over an extended period such as intervals of 26, 39, and 52 weeks.

Advertisers can increase reach by buying a **reach plan**. The reach plan offers a minimum number of weekly spots across all dayparts in return for a packaged discount rate. Refer to Figure A1.10 for examples of discounts.

Buying Radio Time

A strategic plan guides the purchase of radio commercial time. In order to get the best possible rate from a station or network of stations, all details of the plan must be known by the radio station. Factors such as volume and frequency (the total number of spots in the buy), the timing of the schedule in terms of time of day or season in which the plan is scheduled, and continuity (the lengths of the plan) collectively affect the spot rate that is charged the advertiser. It places an advertiser on a particular grid with the station. Refer to Figure A1.10 for a listing of grid rates and how an advertiser arrives at a certain grid. For advertisers that purchase large amounts of time, the discounts described above usually apply.

To illustrate some basic cost calculations used in buying radio time, let's develop some examples based on the CJAZ-FM rate card in Figure A1.10.

Example 1:

30-second spots

10 breakfast spots per week

15 drive spots per week

12-week schedule

Cost Calculations:

The advertiser does not qualify for a continuity discount. Therefore, the first calculation is to determine the total number of spots in the buy to see if a volume discount applies.

Total number of spots	= spots per week × number of weeks
Breakfast	= 10 per week × 12 weeks = 120
Drive	= 15 per week × 12 weeks = 180
Total spots	= 300

Based on the total number of spots (300), the rate charged will be from Grid 3. In this case, the 30-second rate is $250 for breakfast and $210 for drive time. The cost calculations are as follows:

Total cost = number of spots × earned rate	
Breakfast	= 120 spots × $250 = $30 000
Drive	= 180 spots × $210 = $37 800
Total cost	= $67 800

Example 2:

The advertiser would like to evaluate a reach plan (involving 16 commercials per week) against a specific buying plan. Details of each plan are as follows:

Plan A: Reach Plan (30-second spots)

Involves 16 spots per week

Rotated between breakfast, drive, day, and evening/Sunday

Runs for 16 weeks, June through September

Plan B: Specific Plan (30-second spots)

8 breakfast spots per week

8 drive spots per week

16-week schedule

Cost Calculations for Plan A:

The advertiser qualifies for a continuity discount because of the 16-week schedule. The rate would be in Grid 3 in the reach plan. The earned rate is $200 per spot.

Total Cost = total number of spots × earned rate

= (16 spots per week × 16 weeks) × $200

= $51 200

Cost Calculations for Plan B:

The total number of spots is:

Breakfast   = 8 spots per week × 16 weeks = 128 spots

Drive   = 8 spots per week × 16 weeks = 128 spots

Total spots   = 256

Based on this calculation, the advertiser does not qualify for a volume discount, but since the contract runs for 16 weeks, a continuity discount does apply. The advertiser is charged the rate from Grid 3.

Breakfast   = 128 spots × $250 = $32 000

Drive   = 128 spots × $210 = $26 880

Total cost   = $58 880

In conducting a comparative evaluation of Plan A and Plan B, the advertiser must weigh the more selective reach potential of Plan B against the savings of Plan A. Perhaps the advertiser wants to reach business commuters in drive time to and from work. With Plan A, the advertiser can reach a somewhat different audience by means of a daypart rotation of spots. The net result is a cost difference of $7680 in favour of Plan A. Should the advertiser decide to go with the cost savings of Plan A, or with the more selective reach of Plan B at greater cost?

OUT-OF-HOME ADVERTISING

Out-of-home advertising offers a variety of outdoor poster options, street-level advertising, transit shelters, and transit vehicle and station advertising. Regardless of the alternative, the media buying procedure is similar. Out-of-home rates are based on GRPs, so factors such as reach and frequency are built into the rate cards.

Referring to Figure A1.11 on page 378, let's assume an advertiser wants to buy 50 GRPs in Toronto. That means the advertiser will reach the equivalent of 50 percent of Toronto's population. The word "equivalent" is important because vehicle and pedestrian traffic in a

FIGURE **A1.11** **Outdoor Rate Card for Transit Shelters**

⌐MEDIACOM⌐

Member
OAAC

PMB
ASSOCIATE

Audited by
COMB

The Poster Network

Data confirmed for Aug./00 CARD

TRANSIT SHELTERS:

Market	Estimated 1999 5+ Population	25 DAILY GRPs approx panels	4-week rate	50 DAILY GRPs approx panels	4-week rate	75 DAILY GRPs approx panels	4-week rate
ATLANTIC							
St. John's(CMA) Nfld. ...	174,700	6	$2,928	11	$4,796	17	$7,412
Halifax(CMA) N.S.........	329,600	10	4,331	19	8,250	28	12,375
Sydney(C)	32,300	1	740	2	1,410	3	2,115
Annapolis Valley...........	58,000	2	1,080	5	2,700	7	3,780
Moncton(C)..................	95,300	3	848	6	1,615	9	2,423
Saint John(C)...............	95,600	3	1,079	5	2,055	7	3,083
Total Atlantic	785,500	25	11,006	48	20,826	71	31,188
QUEBEC							
Quebec City District	503,100	13	9,214	26	17,551	39	26,327
Chicoutimi/Jonquiere.....	111,900	3	1,652	6	3,148	9	4,721
Trois Rivieres District	101,900	4	1,487	7	2,833	10	4,249
Sherbrooke(CMA)	145,800	3	1,796	6	3,421	9	5,132
Montreal District	3,085,100	51	32,853	101	62,578	151	93,866
Hull C & District............	212,200	7	1,916	13	3,650	19	5,475
Total Quebec	4,160,000	81	48,918	159	93,181	237	139,770
ONTARIO							
Pembroke(CA)..............	22,500	1	625	2	1,200	2	1,200
Toronto(CMA)/ Hamilton(CMA)/ Oshawa(CMA)..........	5,367,900	92	61,747	183	117,614	274	176,421
Toronto(CMA)...............	4,464,300	75	57,873	149	110,234	224	165,351
Oshawa(CMA)...............	292,400	12	5,465	12	5,465*	12	5,465*
Hamilton(CMA).............	611,200	15	9,235	29	17,590	44	26,385
Stratford(CA)	28,000	3	2,067	3	2,067*	3	2,067*
Kitchener(C)	178,500	5	2,894	10	5,513	15	8,269
London(CMA)	396,400	8	4,961	16	9,450	24	14,175
Windsor(CMA) & District	329,900	8	4,134	16	7,875	23	11,813
Sarnia(CA)...................	80,800	3	21,63	6	4,120	8	6,180
Owen Sound(CA)	29,500	3	772	3	772*	3	772*
Barrie(CA)	138.600	5	1,588	10	3,025	15	4,538
Barrie(CA)/Orillia(CA)....	177,400	7	1,800	14	3,429	20	5,143
Sault Ste. Marie(CA)	77,700	2	775	4	1,550	5	1,938
Thunder Bay(CMA)	117,900	4	1,045	7	1,991	10	2,987
Timmins(C).................	44,500	2	1,000	4	1,680	6	2,400
Sudbury(CMA)..............	154,300	3	2,007	6	3,750	9	5,391
Total Ontario..............	7,744,200	149	91,750	290	172,531	426	256,036
PRAIRIES/B.C.							
Winnipeg(CMA)	631,100	8	6,169	16	11,750	24	17,625
Regina(CMA)................	181,400	4	2,025	8	3,856	12	5,784
Calgary(CMA)...............	826,600	18	11,551	35	22,003	53	33,004
Grande Prairie(C).........	152,500	—	—	—	—	—	—
Red Deer(CA) & District	229,200	7	3,280	14	7,000	21	10,290
Edmonton (CMA)	831,500	14	11,197	14	11,197*	14	11,197*
Okanagan Valley..........	199,200	8	5,678	15	10,815	22	16,223
Vancouver Metro..........	711,200	12	11,000	24	20,900	36	31,350
Total Prairies/B.C.	3.762.700	71	50.900	126	87,521	182	125,473
Canada	15,666,900	326	202,574	623	374,059	916	552,467

Source: Courtesy of Canadian Advertising Rates and Data.

FIGURE A1.12   **Outdoor Rate Card for Posters**

MEDIACOM

Member
OAAC

PMB ASSOCIATE
The Poster Network

Audited by
COMB

Data confirmed for Aug./00 CARD

Markets	Pop'n	25 DAILY GRPs app. pan.	25 DAILY GRPs 4-week rate	50 DAILY GRPs app. pan.	50 DAILY GRPs 4-week rate	75 DAILY GRPs app. pan.	75 DAILY GRPs 4-week rate
ATLANTIC:							
St. John's(CMA) NFLD ...	174.700	5	$3.960	9	$7.128	12	$9.000
Charlottetown(CA) PEI ...	71.700	3	2.451	5	3.855	7	5.397
Amherst(C) & District N.S.	30.000	6	4.488	6	4.488*	6	4.488*
Truro(CA) N.S.	42.900	1	825	1	825*	1	825*
Halifax(CMA) N.S.	329.600	7	5.738	13	10.929	19	16.393
Acadian Peninsula	52.900	4	2.200	6	3.000	6	3.000
Sydney(C) N.S.	32.300	2	1.422	3	2.709*	4	4.063
Bathurst (CA)	43.600	2	1.390	4	2.600	4	2.600
Miramichi & District	35.600	2	1.390	4	2.600	4	2.600
Fredericton(C) N.B.	44.300	2	1.456	4	2.773	6	4.159
Moncton(C) N.B.	95.300	3	1.517	6	2.889	8	4.333
Saint John(C) N.B.	95.600	3	1.712	5	3.260	7	4.890*
Total Atlantic:	1,048.500	40	28.549	66	47.056	84	61.748
QUEBEC:							
St. Lawrence Basin/Matapedia	150.300	11	6.143	21	11.700	32	17.550
Charlevoix North Shore...	71.600	5	3.276	10	6.240	15	9.360
Beauce District	61.700	7	5.733	14	10.920*	21	16.380*
Thetford Mines (CA)/Victoriaville (CA) & Dist.	78.500	6	4.505	12	8.580	17	12.870
Québec City (CMA)	666.700	13	17.206	25	32.774	37	49.161
Chicoutimi/Jonquiere & Dist.	165.600	5	3.377	10	6.433	15	9.649
Northwestern Quebec	60.200	4	2.796	8	5.325	12	7.988
Trois-Rivieres (CMA) & Dist.	193.800	5	4.067	10	7.746	15	11.619
Granby (CA)/Drummondville (CA)	124.400	4	4.389	4	4.389*	4	4.389*
Sherbrooke CMA	145.800	4	4.117	8	7.841	11	11.762
Montreal Dist.	3.085.100	28	53.051	55	101.050	82	151.575
Montreal ESA	3.196.100	30	54.582	59	103.966	88	155.949
Hull(C) & District	212.200	5	4.218	9	8.035	13	12.053
Total Quebec:	5,126.900	99	114.409	190	213.949	280	318.730
ONTARIO							
Pembroke(CA) & Dist	64.700	4	3.160	8	6.080	11	8.085
Kingston (CA)/Belleville (CA)/Brockville (CA) & Dist..	294.000	9	7.781	17	14.820	25	22.230
Kingston (CA)	144.500	4	4.787	8	9.119	11	13.678
Ottawa(ESA)	763.200	19	23.859	38	45.446	57	68.169
Peterborough (CA)	99.100	6	3.249	6	3.249*	6	3.249*
Peterborough (CA)/Lindsay (CA) & Dist.	143.400	8	4.138	8	4.138*	8	4.138*
Toronto (CMA)/Hamilton (CMA)/Oshawa (CMA).	5.367.900	75	85.223	149	162.329	223	243.493
Toronto (CMA)	4.464.300	60	80.534	120	153.399	180	230.098
Oshawa (CMA)	292.400	7	6.864	14	13.075	14	13.075
Hamilton (CMA)	611.200	13	13.194	25	25.131	37	37.697
Kitchener(CMA)/Brantford (CA)	488.400	12	11.576	12	11.576*	12	11.576*
St. Catharines/Niagara (CMA)	358.800	12	9.211	23	17.545	23	17.545*
Brantford (CA)	97.300	4	3.638	4	3.638*	4	3.638*
Woodstock (CA)	32.500	—	—	—	—	—	—
London (CMA)	396.400	8	8.680	16	16.533	16	16.533
Strathroy (CA)	12.500	2	1.217	2	1.217	2	1.217
Windsor (ESA)	373.000	9	8.289	17	15.789	26	23.684
Sarnia	80.800	3	2.130	5	4.056	5	4.506*
Owen Sound (CA)/Collingwood (CA) & Dist.	176.100	12	10.369	24	19.750	35	29.625
Barrie (CA)/Orillia (CA)/Central Ont.	282.100	11	15.602	22	29.718	32	44.576
Barrie (CA)	138.600	6	8.831	11	16.821	17	25.232
Beaverton & Dist.	19.700	—	—	—	—	—	—
Sault-Ste-Marie (CA)	77.700	2	1.500	4	2.940	6	4.320
Sault-Ste-Marie (CA)	77.700	2	1.470	4	2.940	6	4.410
Sudbury (CMA)/North Bay (CA)/North Shore & Dist.	229.800	8	6.600	15	11.550	23	17.480
Thunder Bay (CMA)	117.900	3	2.171	6	4.135	8	6.203
Timmins (C) & Dist	121.600	7	4.515	14	8.190	21	11.760
Timmins (C)	44.500	2	1.430	4	2.540	6	3.720
Total Ontario:	9,382.600	204	205.991	380	375.812	533	534.780
PRAIRIES/B.C.							
Winnipeg (CMA)	631.100	6	9.126	12	17.383	18	26.074
Brandon (CA) & Dist.	37.700	2	919	4	1.751	6	2.627
Regina (CMA)	181.400	3	3.300	6	6.285	9	9.428
Yorkton (CA)	16.000	3	2.433	5	4.635	5	4.635*
North Battleford (CA)	16.300	1	770	2	1.468	3	2.201
Rural Saskatchewan	437.000	—	—	—	—	—	—
Moose Jaw (CA)	31.300	2	1.121	3	2.135	4	3.203
Saskatoon (CMA)	209.000	4	3.771	8	7.183	12	10.774
Calgary (CMA)	826.600	17	16.675	33	31.763	33	31.763*
Edmonton (CMA)	831.500	14	16.456	27	31.345	40	47.018
Vancouver District	673.600	14	20.396	14	20.396*	14	20.396*
Total Prairies/B.C.:	3,891.500	66	74.967	114	124.344	144	158.119
Total Canada:	19,449.500	409	423.916	750	761.161	1,041	1,073.377

Source: Courtesy of Canadian Advertising Rates and Data.

city is habitual, that is, people tend to travel the same routes each day. Therefore, in the Toronto example, the advertiser might reach 25 percent of the population twice a day for a total of 50 daily GRPs.

All out-of-home advertising rates are quoted on a four-week basis and are sold on a market-by-market basis. Posters and transit shelters are sold on the basis of a four-week minimum purchase. The other options (backlits, mall posters, and superboards) have a 12-week minimum purchase requirement. To illustrate outdoor cost calculations, let's consider a few media buying examples. Rates and data from Figure A1.11 (transit shelter rates) and Figure A1.12 (outdoor poster rates) are used to calculate costs.

Example 1: Outdoor Buying Plan

Medium:	Transit shelters (Mediacom)
Markets:	Toronto (CMA), Montreal District, Calgary (CMA), and Edmonton (CMA)
Weight:	25 GRPs weekly in Toronto and Montreal and 50 GRPs weekly in Calgary and Edmonton
Contract length:	16 weeks in all markets

Cost Calculation:

The costs for a four-week period for each market would be as follows:

Toronto	$57 873
Montreal	$32 853
Calgary	$22 003
Edmonton	$11 197
Total	**$123 926**

Because the contract is for 16 weeks, the costs are multiplied by four (16 weeks divided by four-week rates). The gross cost would be:

$123 926 × 4 = $495 704

Although not shown in this particular illustration and rate card, outdoor media usually offer advertisers volume discounts (e.g., a reduced rate based on dollar volume purchased) and continuity discounts (e.g., a reduced rate for extended buys such as 12 weeks, 16 weeks, etc.).

Example 2: Outdoor Buying Plan

Medium:	Horizontal outdoor posters (Mediacom)
Markets:	Toronto (CMA), Montreal (ESA), and Ottawa (ESA)
Weight:	Toronto and Montreal at 50 GRPs and Ottawa at 25 GRPs
Contract length:	16 weeks in Toronto; 12 weeks in Montreal and Ottawa

Cost Calculation:

Using the data from Figure A1.12, the appropriate costs for each market over a four-week period would be:

Toronto	$153 399 × 4	= $613 596
Montreal	$103 966 × 3	= $311 898
Ottawa	$23 859 × 3	= $71 577
Gross cost		**= $997 071**

Because the length of the contract in Toronto is 16 weeks, the costs are multiplied by four (16 weeks divided by four-week rate). In Montreal and Ottawa, the contract is

12 weeks. Therefore, the costs are multiplied by a factor of three (12 weeks divided by the four-week rate). Should volume and continuity discounts apply, they would be deducted from the gross amount shown in this illustration.

DIRECT MAIL ADVERTISING

Three basic steps are involved in buying direct mail: obtaining a proper prospect list, conceiving and producing the mailing piece, and distributing the final version.

Obtaining Direct Mail Lists

The direct mail list is the backbone of the entire campaign. Both the accuracy and definition of the list can have a significant bearing on the success or failure of a campaign. Companies recognize that it costs about six times as much to acquire a new customer as it does to keep an existing one.[5] As a result, companies compile databases to keep track of existing customers and form relationships with customers through the mail and electronic means. Internal lists compiled from a database management system are referred to as **house lists**.

House List
An internal customer list.

Prospective names are also gathered from external sources. People with a history of responding to mail offers tend to be attractive prospects for new offers. Buying by mail is part of their behaviour. Therefore, the challenge is to find prospects that have a demographic profile and, perhaps, a psychographic profile that mirror the profile of current customers. A **list broker** can assist in finding these prospects. The buyer provides the broker with the profile of the target customer, and the broker supplies a list of possible prospects on a cost-per-name basis. Generally, a high-quality list is developed through a **merge/purge** process on a computer, whereby numerous lists are purchased, combined, and stripped of duplicate names.

List Broker
A company specializing in finding or developing lists for direct response purposes.

Merge/Purge
The process of purchasing lists, combining them, and then stripping them of duplicate names.

For example, TargetSource, a database management company, compiles lists on the basis of demographics (e.g., income, home ownership, marital status, and type of dwelling). The base rate for names is $90/M ($90 per thousand). As the quality of the list requested becomes more sophisticated or specialized, the rate per thousand increases.[6]

Canada Post also supplies information vital to the accurate targeting of messages. For example, a postal code can isolate a small geographic area—say, a city block—and can then be combined with census data to provide relevant statistics regarding the ages and incomes of homeowners in the area, and whether children are present in the households.

A few types of lists are available: *response lists, circulation lists,* and *compiled lists.* A **response list** is a list of proven mail-order buyers. Such lists include book-of-the-month-club buyers, CD music buyers, or people who order from cooperative direct mailing firms. Because these lists include proven mail-order buyers, they tend to cost more. For example, customers of Time Life Products (an established direct mail marketing company) rent for $365/M ($365 for each one thousand names). The list includes buyers of books, videos, and children's products. A minimum purchase of 5000 names is required.[7]

Response List
A list of direct mail buyers who have previously bought based on direct response offers.

Circulation lists are magazine subscription lists that target potential customers according to an interest or activity. A publishing company, for example, might sell its list of subscribers to another business interested in a similar target. Rogers Media offers a consumer database (English) composed of unduplicated active subscribers to *Maclean's, Chatelaine,* and *Flare.* A total of about 1 million names are available at a base cost of $125/M.[8]

Circulation List
The circulation of a newspaper or magazine that is generated by subscription sales and newsstand sales.

Compiled lists are prepared from government, census, telephone, warranty, and other publication information. These are the least expensive of the lists and are not always personalized. Provincial and national associations, such as the Canadian Medical Association, commonly provide mailing lists of their members. A list broker, for example, could compile a list of a cross-section of professionals from various occupations, if required by a client.

Compiled List
A direct mail list prepared frpm government, census, telephone, warranty, or other publication information.

Production

Direct mail packages are usually designed by a specialist agency. Once the mailing package is designed, it is ready for printing. Various factors that influence cost include size, shape, number of pieces, use of colour, and so on. Costs are usually quoted CPM, with larger runs incurring lower unit costs. Once printed, the mailing pieces are turned over to a letter shop that specializes in stuffing and sealing envelopes, affixing labels, sorting, binding, and stacking the mailers. Once this task is complete, the mailing units are sent to the post office for distribution.

Distribution

Distribution costs of direct mail replace placement costs in traditional forms of media advertising. The most common means of delivery is Canada Post. Several options are available through the postal system: first-class mail, third-class mail, and business-reply mail. Obviously, the quicker the means of delivery the higher the costs will be. Most direct mail pieces—whether single pieces, bulk items, catalogues, or cooperative mailings—are delivered third class. The advantage over first class is the cost savings.

Direct Mail Buying Illustration

The procedures for estimating the cost of solo direct mail and cooperative direct mail are similar. However, with a solo direct mail campaign, the advertiser absorbs all the costs rather than sharing them with other advertisers. Taken into consideration are factors such as distribution costs, printing costs, mailing costs, and costs associated with fulfillment. For this example, we will assume a cooperative direct mail program will be undertaken in the *Open & Save* Cooperative Mailing package (see Figure A1.13).

Buying Information:

Open & Save Cooperative Mailings (Transcontinental Publications)

The offer:	one-page folded ad that includes a $1.50 coupon
Redemption rate:	3 percent
Distribution:	3 000 000 households

Cost Calculations:

Distribution costs (cost to insert an offer into an envelope)	3 000 000 × $12/M	= $36 000
Printing costs (estimated at 3/4 cost of mailing)	3 000 000 × $9.00/M	= $27 000
Redemption costs (estimated at 3 percent of total coupons distributed)	3 000 000 × 0.03 × $1.50	= $135 000
Total cost		**= $198 000**

Depending on how the coupon offer is returned, there could be additional costs for the advertiser. For example, there is a handling fee provided to the retailer for conducting the coupon transaction. As well, coupons are usually sent from the retailer to a clearing house for processing. The clearing house pays the retailer and provides periodic reports to the advertiser about how many coupons are being redeemed. The advertiser pays a fee for this service.

INTERNET ADVERTISING

The most common model for quoting advertising rates on the internet is CPM. Other pricing models include pay for performance and flat fees.

FIGURE A1.13   Open & Save Cooperative Mail Rate Card

CPM Model

CPM is the price charged for displaying an ad one thousand times. The calculation for CPM is cost divided by impressions (number of impressions divided by 1000). For online advertising, an organization pays a rate for every 1000 impressions made. Therefore, if the total number of impressions is 500 000 and the CPM was $30, the total cost of the advertising campaign will be $15 000 (500 000 impressions/1000) × $30.

CPM rates vary according to the level of targeting desired by the advertiser and they range anywhere from $10 to $100. Typical options include *run of site, run of category*, and *keyword targeting*. With reference to the rate card for Canada.com shown in Figure A1.14, if **run of site** or **run of network** is selected, the rates charged are those quoted for the various sizes and styles of advertising for ads that will appear anywhere on the website. For example, a banner ad rate is $13/M, a skyscraper is $20/M, and a pop-up ad is $30/M. If **targeting requests** are applied a 10 percent premium is charged for each targeted request. Volume discounts might be offered based on the total dollar value of the advertising space that is purchased.

CPM rate cards vary from one site to another, but the high-traffic sites of course charge a higher CPM. Popular sites such as Canoe, Sympatico.ca, Yahoo!, and various sports and media sites (TSN, The Score, *The Globe and Mail*, etc.) attract significant traffic and price their CPMs accordingly.

To demonstrate how costs are calculated on the Canada.com website, refer to Figure A1.14 for rate information for the following buying examples.

Run of Site or Run of Network

Ad rate for placements anywhere on a website.

Targeting Request

An ad placed to reach a specific target audience of a website, for which a premium is usually paid.

Example 1:

Type of ad:	Banner
Impressions desired:	1 000 000
CPM:	$13

Cost Calculation:

(1 000 000/1000) × $13 = $13 000

Example 2:

Type of ad:	Pop-up
Impressions desired:	1 500 000
CPM:	$35
One target request	+ 10%

Cost Calculation:

(1 500 000/1000) × $35 × 1.10 = $57 750.00

The advertiser earns a 12 percent volume discount (refer to the dollar volume discount scale in Figure A1.14). Therefore, the additional calculation would be:

$57 750 – ($57 750 × 0.12) = $57 750 – $6930 = $50 820

Although these rates are those quoted, the reality of the situation is similar to offline advertising. CPM rates are negotiable, and depend on factors such as length of the campaign, season, and relationship between client and vendor. Effective negotiation skills in the media buying process could result in lower CPM rates.

Pay for Performance Model

Advertisers must remember that the purpose of online advertising is to create interest so that the viewer clicks the ad for more information. Once clicked, the viewer sees the ad in its entirety, usually via a link to a page at the advertiser's website. Since clicking is the desired action, many advertisers feel they should pay on the basis of cost-per-click instead

FIGURE **A1.14**

Online Advertising Rate Card for Canada.com

AD TYPE

Banners: $13 CPM

- 468 × 60 pixels/GIF format and rich media
- Placement: Headers on all pages of Canada.com

Buttons: $10 CPM

- 120 × 90/GIF format
- Placement: near right hand top of most Second Level Pages

Skyscraper Ads: $20 CPM

- 120 × 240, 120 × 600, or 160 × 600 pixels
- GIF format and Rich Media
- Placement: fourth column

Pop-up and Pop-under Windows: $35 CPM

- File size limits: GIF format – 15K/Rich Media formats – 15K Initial download/25K in total
- Placement available on most Canada.com pages

Bid Box Ads (In Story): $30 CPM

- 250 × 250 pixels
- GIF format and Rich Media
- Placement: within editorial content

CONTESTS

Regional: Starting at $10 000
National: Starting at $20 000

OTHER ADVERTISING OPTIONS

Interstitials and Superstitials: $60 CPM
All pricing is based on Run of Network rotation.
A 10% premium is charged for each applied target specification.

DOLLAR VOLUME DISCOUNTS

$15 000–25 000	5%
$25 000–50 000	10%
$50 000–75 000	12%
$75 000–100 000	15%
$100 000+	20%

Adapted from CanWest Media Sales, a division of CanWest Interactive Inc.,
<canada.com/aboutus/advertising/rate_card.html> (June 2003). By permission of CanWest Interactive.

of CPM. The benefit of such a system is clear: the advertiser knows from the start what the internet campaign will cost per click.

If the success of an ad is based on the clickthrough rate, then many current campaigns are not doing very well. In fact, latest industry surveys peg the average click rate at about 0.5 percent. The quality of the creative (e.g., its cleverness, its animation, and so on) along with a certain degree of targeting can improve the clickthrough rate.

From a publisher's perspective, the clickthrough system has several drawbacks. First, the publisher has to rely on the quality of the advertiser's message (the banner) for advertising revenue. If it does not stimulate clicks, it will not generate revenues for the website. The job of the media is to offer access to an audience, not to share in the responsibility for the quality of the advertising itself. Second, such a model completely discounts what a banner can do to build brand image. There has to be an advertising cost associated with this benefit. To date, advertising rates based on clickthroughs are the exception rather than the rule.

Flat-Fee Model

Some websites charge a flat fee for advertising—typically, it is a set amount for the length of time the ad appears on the site. Sponsorships, for example, are usually sold on a flat-rate basis rather than on the number of impressions. The *Maclean's* website, for example, charges $1000 net per week (net means the agency commission has been deducted) for one banner ad at the top of the home page with two rotations. Rates on other pages on the site are lower. Contract advertisers that commit to periods longer than 13 weeks earn significant discounts.[9] Fee structures vary considerably from site to site. Lower traffic sites are more likely to use the flat fee system.

Media Information Resources

Media planners rely on secondary research data provided by specialist media organizations. Secondary research refers to data compiled and published by others for purposes other than resolving a specific problem. In advertising, secondary sources are frequently used to gain access to media information that benefits media analysis and planning. This information is available through various media associations, specialized media research companies, and individual media outlets (e.g., a daily newspaper, national magazine, or a local television station).

Most organizations that provide media data also provide appropriate software for users to sift through the data (e.g., data can be cross-tabulated with product and service consumption data to determine the best way of reaching a specific target audience). Much of the information is made available through the media research companies and organizations mentioned above, or through specialist companies that develop software for use with database information provided by these organizations.

TELEVISION RESOURCES

The organizations that compile television media data on a continuous (year to year) basis include BBM Bureau of Measurement, Nielsen Media Research, and the Television Bureau.

BBM Bureau of Measurement

The BBM Bureau of Measurement is divided into two divisions for recording and analyzing data: BBM TV and BBM Radio. BBM TV collects audience data through a combination of electronic observation and diaries that are returned by mail. In the case of electronic observation, the BBM has metering devices installed in approximately 2100 households across Canada. The meter registers what is being watched every minute of every day in every metered household.[10] Because the households are a representative sample, extrapolations are made about how people view programs on local, regional, and national bases.

When the diary system is used, participants complete a seven-day log by recording the television viewing for all television sets in the household, for each quarter hour of the day from 6 a.m. to 2 a.m. Information from returned diaries is keyed into computers for processing and verification.

BBM data focus on local markets. The BBM conducts its surveys three times a year—fall, winter, and spring—in 40 television markets. Their reports contain current audience ratings and share data, as well as full coverage data for local market stations. The data are presented in four sections: time block, program, time period, and trend. The BBM also conducts a "sweep" survey in the fall and spring that covers the national market (television viewers two years of age and older). The data collected during the ratings period are used to estimate the audiences of programs on individual stations and networks. **Ratings** are audience estimates expressed as a percentage of a population in a defined geographic area. For example, if a show has a rating of 20, it reaches 20 percent of that market's population. For some examples of basic trend data available from the BBM, visit **<www.bbm.com>**.

Nielsen Media Research

The data available from Nielsen refer to channels watched and audience composition. The Nielsen Television Index (NTI) network reports cover audiences for all programs, 52 weeks a year, for national and regional networks. Network reports provide viewing information 24 hours a day for the entire year. Data are organized according to age, education, income, and occupation of audience members. Nielsen electronically collects information from a sample panel of 2500 households across Canada. Respondents indicate their viewing responses using a remote-control device. Among the data recorded are program rankings, audience composition, and average weekly cable television and VCR penetration.

The Nielsen Broadcast Index (NBI) is a local market service that provides continuous audience estimates for regional networks within a localized geographical area. For both indexes, the information is available to ad agencies through Nielsen software called Media Advisor. For organizations wanting up-to-the-minute information, Nielsen also provides the Overnight Report. This report gives preliminary audience reports due 24 hours from the broadcast date.[11]

Nielsen Media Research also offers a variety of competitive tracking services that provide the quantitative information necessary for strategic determination and tactical execution of communications plans. Nielsen provides estimates of media expenditures by measuring advertising activity in the traditional mass media: television, daily newspapers, magazines, and out-of-home advertising. The information observed is translated into advertising dollars using published rates in *Canadian Advertising Rates and Data (CARD)*. Nielsen also receives information from billing statements from the broadcast representative companies and information from the broadcasters themselves. For additional information about Nielsen Media Research, visit **<www.nielsenmedia.ca>**.

Television Bureau of Canada

The Television Bureau of Canada (TVB) is a sales and marketing resource centre for the commercial television industry. Its mandate is to promote television as an effective advertising medium. Each year, this organization publishes a booklet, "TV Basics," that contains the latest data on television trends. It covers viewing trends by demographic and geographic variables, programming preferences by demographic variables, and television-station circulation by gender and age for all station markets. The TVB provides such data as viewing by time of day, day of week, and by time of year. For additional information about the data provided by the TVB, visit **<www.tvb.ca>**.

RADIO

The organizations that compile radio consumption data on a continuous basis are the BBM Bureau of Measurement and the Radio Marketing Bureau.

BBM Bureau of Measurement

BBM Radio conducts three surveys per year in more than 115 radio markets across Canada using a seven-day diary. In addition to collecting tuning data, the diary contains questions collecting product usage and lifestyle data. Market reports are published three times a year in the nine largest markets. Regional Reports (Atlantic, Quebec, Ontario, Manitoba/Saskatchewan, Alberta, and British Columbia) are published twice a year to supplement the Market Reports. Tuning data are reported in the market and regional reports on up to 22 demographics for more than 30 dayparts.

The data compiled by the BBM include hours tuned per week, listening by daypart, and listening by location (e.g., home, automobile, and other locations). Other standard data include market share and audience profiles, and listening locations tuning. For some samples of basic trend data published by the BBM, visit **<www.bbm.ca>**.

Radio Marketing Bureau

The Radio Marketing Bureau is the marketing, sales development, and resource centre for radio advertising in Canada. It provides statistical data to advertisers and agencies, which can then make objective assessments regarding how best to use radio as an advertising medium. In conjunction with the BBM, the Bureau conducts a Radio Product Measurement (RPM) study in selected major markets. This study is designed to generate information about product usage and media consumption of radio, television, magazines, and newspapers.[12] For more information about the Radio Marketing Bureau, visit **<www.rmb.ca>**.

MAGAZINES

The companies and organizations involved in magazine research and data collection include the Audit Bureau of Circulations, Canadian Circulations Audit Board, and Print Measurement Bureau. The audit boards also audit daily and community newspapers.

Audit Bureau of Circulations

The Audit Bureau of Circulations (ABC) issues standardized statements verifying circulation statistics for paid-circulation magazines (consumer and business publications) and most daily newspapers in Canada. All publications that are members of ABC receive an audited publisher's statement. This statement is the authority on which advertising rates are based (verified circulation is used to establish the advertising rate base as shown in the publication's rate card). The statement is issued twice each year. A publisher's statement includes the following information: average paid circulation for the past six months, paid circulation for each issue in the last six months, an analysis of new and renewal subscriptions, paid circulation by county size, and geographic analysis of total paid circulation. For a selection of sample data published by ABC, refer to **<www.accessabc.com>**.

Canadian Circulations Audit Board

The Canadian Circulations Audit Board (CCAB) audits the circulation data of member publications and issues standardized statements twice a year for use by advertisers and advertising agencies. More than 425 business, trade, professional, and farm publications, consumer magazines, and community and daily newspapers subscribe to auditing by the CCAB. Statements include type of circulation (e.g., paid or controlled circulation), recipient qualification (e.g., distribution to a pre-determined target based on demographic data), circulation for the past six months, average paid circulation per issue, and a geographical breakdown of the circulation. Additional information about CCAB is available at **<www.bpai.com>** or **<www.ccab.ca>**.

Audited circulation data provided by the ABC or CCAB provide several benefits to the advertiser and the advertising agency. First, circulation figures, current versus past, can be analyzed to determine whether the publication is growing or declining in popularity. Second, the circulation audience of the publication can be compared with the target market of the advertiser, and, third, efficiency comparisons (i.e., comparisons of the amounts being spent on reaching the target audience) can be made with competing publications reaching similar target audiences to determine which publications are the most cost-effective.

Print Measurement Bureau

The Print Measurement Bureau (PMB) provides standardized readership information for members, a group that includes advertisers, agencies, publishers, and other related companies in the Canadian media industry. The PMB publishes Canada's leading single-source multimedia study.

The major data component of the annual PMB study is the detailed readership data for more than 90 magazines and newspapers and the linking of those data with information on readers' product usage patterns, their usage of brands, their retail shopping habits, and their lifestyles.

The product usage section of the PMB study provides usage data on more than 2600 products, 3000 brands, and 37 retail shopping habits. PMB provides extensive information on demographic data as well as information on consumer lifestyles, leisure habits, and psychographics. Data provided by the PMB's product-profile studies benefit advertisers and agencies in the media planning process. Based on cross-tabulations of data concerning media, product, brand, and lifestyle, the information can be used to identify target markets more precisely, to assist in budget allocation, and to make better decisions regarding media selection and placement. PMB information is available to clients electronically and requires special software to access it. For additional information about the PMB, visit **<www.pmb.ca>**.

NEWSPAPERS

Data about newspaper circulation and readership are available from the Audit Bureau of Circulation and the Canadian Circulations Audit Board. These organizations were discussed in the previous section. Readership information is compiled by an industry-sponsored measurement organization known as NADbank Inc.

NADbank Inc.—Newspaper Audience Databank

NADbank provides advertisers, advertising agencies, and daily newspapers with accurate and credible information on newspaper readership, retail data, and consumer behaviour. NADbank is an annual survey among 31 000 adults 18 years and older, representing 86 percent of Canada's urban population. It provides readership data for 66 daily newspapers in 46 urban markets. The nature of information produced by NADbank includes weekday and weekend readership, demographic profiles of readers, product ownership and purchase intentions, media habits (e.g., other media referred to), and shopping habits (e.g., malls visited and frequency of visits). Additional information and some sample data published by NADbank is available at **<www.nadbank.com>**.

OUT-OF-HOME MEDIA

Canadian Outdoor Measurement Bureau

The Canadian Outdoor Measurement Bureau (COMB) audits the circulations of outdoor posters, superboards, mall posters, backlit posters, and street-level advertising (e.g., transit-shelter ads). Circulation data concerning all outdoor media except mall posters are based on municipal and provincial traffic counts, and converted to circulations according to an established traffic-variation factor. COMB currently uses an average occupancy factor of 1.75, which represents the average number of people in an automobile.[13] Mall counts are based on observation (head counts) in each location by an independent research firm.

COMB maintains a national database of all products for all member suppliers. The data are used to produce a quarterly publication, the *Market Data Report*. The report calculates new daily or weekly audience averages for each supplier, each product, in each market. Verification reports are also provided. These reports verify that suppliers are delivering what they are contracted to deliver and compare the percentage of audience delivered to what was contracted.

INTERNET DATA SOURCES

Measuring the numbers of people who notice web-based advertising has been a difficult and controversial task, but two organizations have emerged to provide useful information on internet traffic and related activities: Media Metris Canada and Nielsen//NetRatings. The Internet Advertising Bureau (IAB) represents the interests of members of the Internet advertising industry.

Interactive Advertising Bureau

The Interactive Advertising Bureau (IAB) is a national organization of internet publishers, advertisers, and agencies, acting as the collective voice to represent companies engaged in selling advertising on internet-based media. IAB promotes the value of internet advertising to advertisers and agencies and serves as an educational resource through which advertisers can increase their knowledge and gain a competitive edge in the marketplace. For more information about the IAB, visit **<www.iab.com>**.

Media Metrix Canada

Media Metrix Canada provides independent, meter-based internet and digital audience measurements in Canada and other countries. The metering methodology captures actual usage data from a randomly recruited population base of 6000 households. The meter is a software application that monitors all user activity in real time, click by click, page by page, and minute by minute.

Media Metrix publishes a monthly syndicated report called *The Web Report*. It includes a variety of reports dealing with internet usage and consumption. Of particular interest to advertisers is a document called *The Key Measures Report*. The key measures include unique visitors, reach, average usage days per user, average unique pages per user per day and month, average minutes spent per person per page, per day, and month, gender consumption, and demographic trends.[14] Refer to **<www.MyMetrix.com>** for additional information.

Research Data by Individual Media

The specific media vehicles often conduct their own marketing research, or use research data provided by independent sources such as those just described. These data provide advertisers and agencies with objective, reliable information showing the relative strengths of the given medium as an advertising vehicle. In local market situations, a daily newspaper or a local radio station provide advertisers and agencies with data to assist them in the decision-making process. Here, local media compete with each other for advertising revenue, so comparisons on criteria such as reach, readership, number of people listening and watching, and so on are inevitable. When assessing this type of data, the advertiser should ensure that it is audited data and that it has been verified by an independent organization.

Key Terms

Endnotes

1. Rick Westhead, "Networks Wooing Ad Dollars," *Toronto Star*, June 10, 2003, pp. D1, D13.

2. Chris Powell, "Rate Hikes Confound Media Buyers," *Marketing*, June 30/July 7, 2003, p. 4.

3. Andrea Zoe Aster, "How Much Is Way Too Much?" *Marketing*, August 16, 1999, p. 14.

4. Chris Daniels, "Media Buying Gets Scientific," *Marketing*, July 31, 2000, pp. 11, 12.

5. Franzi Weinstein, "Short, Sweet, and Smarter Creative," *Marketing*, April 29, 1996, p. 17.

6. "Canada's Best Sources of New Consumer Responders," brochure, *Target Source*, 1998.

7. Based on costs obtained from Accountable List Brokers, <www.listbroker.com>, direct responders *Time Life*.

8. Direct Mail Services, List Rental Data Card, Maclean Hunter Publishing Limited, 1998.

9. *Maclean's* Online Media Kit, <www.macleansmediakit.com/home.htm> (November 2003).

10. Patti Summerfield, "BBM Plans for National Meter Rollout," *Strategy*, April 12, 1999, p. 8.

11. Nielsen Media Research, "Services" <www.nielsenmedia.ca> (November 2003).

12. Canadian Media Directors' Council, *Media Digest*, pp. 59, 60.

13. *Market Data Report*, Canadian Outdoor Measurement Bureau, 1986, p. 4.

14. Ibid., pp. 60–61.

Mobicox: An Integrated Marketing Communications Plan

A Unique Approach to Launching a Pharmaceutical Product—In Positioning and Creative Treatment

This marketing communications plan describes the essential elements of a launch plan, written in June 2000, for a new arthritic pain relief product in Canada. A unique and controversial message strategy is delivered to the intended targets by print advertising (magazines), direct mail, and a website. A public relations strategy is also employed in the pre-launch phase of the new product introduction.

The marketing of prescription pharmaceutical products in Canada is governed by a more rigid set of laws and regulations. These laws make it difficult to communicate a complete message about the brand name to the public. Essentially, there are limits to what branded advertising can say about the product.

Company:	Boehringer Ingelheim Canada
Advertising Agency:	Euro RSCG Life
Product:	Mobicox
Product Category:	Arthritis pain relief medication (prescription)

Introduction

Prescription drugs have a scientific or generic name and a brand name. The generic name for this drug is meloxicam. The brand name is Mobicox. Mobicox is in a class of drugs called NSAIDs (Non Steroidal Anti-Inflammatories). It is taken orally to ease pain and inflammation mainly by older people with osteoarthritis or rheumatoid arthritis.

Aspirin is an NSAID and is a remedy that has been used for decades to treat arthritis. While aspirin is effective in relieving pain and inflammation, it can cause gastro-intestinal bleeding in some patients. Medically, this is potentially a serious problem.

The discovery of a new class of NSAIDs called Cox-2 selective inhibitors was a major step forward. The Cox-2s act on pain and inflammation but have few gastro-intestinal side effects. Not surprisingly, these new drugs did well. Pfizer launched Celebrex in April 1999 and Merck launched Vioxx in November 1999 and very quickly became the leading brands in the Canadian market.

Initially, there was some debate as to whether Mobicox was a legitimate Cox-2. Some opinion leaders in the medical community said the chemical compound was different from Celebrex and Vioxx. Given the different medical properties, these leaders dubbed Mobicox as a "Cox-One-and-a-Half." Eventually, Health Canada, the regulator of prescription drugs in Canada, decided that Mobicox was a full Cox-2 product—helped by the efforts of Boehringer Ingelheim that form part of this plan.

Marketing Communications Plan

MARKET AND COMPETITOR ANALYSIS

- Primary competitors are Pfizer Canada and Merck Frosst Canada. Both companies are established leaders in prescription pharmaceuticals.
- Pfizer and Merck dominate the arthritis pain relief market (prescription category) in Canada. They were the first to launch Cox-2 entries into the NSAID category: Pfizer with Celebrex and Merck Frosst with Vioxx. Pfizer and Merck are extremely large and resourceful companies, and they invest heavily to develop and market new prescription medicines.
- Pfizer Canada is closely associated with the Arthritis Society in Canada. Pfizer sponsors the Society's website and other initiatives that the Society undertakes.
- Other leading brands marketed by Pfizer include Viagra (erectile dysfunction) and Lipitor (cholesterol reduction). Other leading brands marketed by Merck include Zocor (cholesterol reduction) and Singulair (asthma medication).
- At present, 4 million Canadians suffer from arthritis, with the market projected to reach 7 million by 2031. Growth in this segment is attributed to the aging population.
- Pricing in the category is a concern. Patients with arthritis take medication daily and costs can run as high as $55 per month. Drug costs are typically covered by the patient, a private health plan, or by the provincial government, depending on the situation. The rising cost of medical coverage plans is always a controversial issue.
- Given the high cost of medication today, the medical community and insurers seem keen to hear about lower priced alternatives. This represents opportunity for Boehringer Ingelheim and its Mobicox brand.

COMPANY INFORMATION

- Boehringer Ingelheim is a successful medium-sized pharmaceutical company that also spends considerable sums developing new medical products. In comparison to Pfizer and Merck, however, Boehringer Ingelheim is competitively disadvantaged, especially in the area of funds available for marketing support.
- Boehringer Ingelheim is an international pharmaceutical company with corporate headquarters in Germany. The company pursues innovative solutions to evolving healthcare issues. Successful products in its prescription pharmaceutical division include Spiriva and Atrovent (for chronic obstructive pulmonary disease), Micardis (for hypertension), and Viramune (HIV/AIDS).

PRODUCT INFORMATION

- Mobicox is a powerful oral pain reliever used mainly to treat older people with serious and chronic arthritic conditions. It is in a class of prescription drugs called nonsteroidal anti-inflammatories (NSAIDs).
- Existing prescription medication for chronic arthritis patients is costly depending on the dose they need to take. Mobiocox is a less expensive alternative to Celebrex and Vioxx.

THE MARKETING OPPORTUNITY

The higher price levels established by the two Cox-2s, combined with a need for less expensive prescription medications, represent a significant market opportunity for Boehringer Ingelheim. Opportunities to advance are based on the following considerations:

- There must be full coverage of Mobicox on all or most provincial formularies as soon as possible after launch. Each province operates its own healthcare coverage of the provincial formulary, and so the same product can get different coverage by province, or in some cases not be covered at all. Thus far, only three provinces have granted Celebrex and Vioxx full coverage. This does not include Ontario.
- Ontario will be given priority for Mobicox, because it represents 40 percent of dollar market share.
- To ensure preferential coverage in Ontario and other provinces, Mobicox will be priced 40 percent less than Celebrex and Vioxx. It is assumed Mobicox will be granted full listing status in Ontario. [In fact, this was granted in March 2001, following the launch in November 2000.]

THE MARKETING CHALLENGE

Boehringer Ingelheim indicates that time is extremely important and summarizes the key marketing challenges as follows:

- *Immediate Time Pressure:* It is June 2000 and Mobicox will be launched in November. This is super-fast compared to the 24 months that are usually available for launching a new drug.
- *Life Cycle Time Pressure:* Mobicox was developed several years earlier, but never launched. Its patent has actually expired (June 1998), so there is only a two-year window of opportunity before intense generic competition is expected. Mobicox must get off to a fast start.
- *Powerful Competitors:* Pfizer and Merck are renowned for their business and marketing prowess. They will counterattack with all guns blazing.
- *Spending Levels:* Mobicox will not have the same level of marketing support as Merck and Pfizer brands.
- *The "Cox and a Half" Issue:* This issue must be rebutted, especially in the pre-launch period, before Mobicox receives full Cox-2 status from the regulators.
- *Pricing:* Boehringer Ingelheim has managed to cover Mobicox's development costs in the past, and (as noted) will be able to price Mobicox significantly below Celebrex and Vioxx—at a 40 percent saving. The low cost will be beneficial to securing formulary coverage. However, with pharmaceutical products, there can be a sting in the tail with lower pricing. Doctors can perceive the drug as providing lower efficacy, and quite a number of lower priced drugs have failed. Mobicox cannot be seen as a "cheap" drug.

OVERALL GOAL

Doctors have to know the drug will work. They won't prescribe a drug that is cheaper if they believe it doesn't work as well. Therefore, the overall goal for the launch campaign is as follows:

> *To demonstrate to the medical community that Mobicox, a drug that doesn't cost as much as the leading Cox-2 brands, provides the same medical benefits for patients suffering from arthritis.*

POSITIONING STRATEGY

Mobicox is positioned as a quality arthritis pain relief medication that provides doctors with a less expensive alternative to prescribe to patients. The positioning strategy is summarized in the following statement:

> *To convince doctors that Mobicox is a full-blooded Cox-2, every bit as effective and tolerable as Celebrex and Vioxx, and at a considerably more attractive price.*

Mobicox cannot be perceived as a cheap me-too product. Strategically, it must be emphasized that the product represents equivalent performance to the market leaders.

BRANDING STRATEGY

The name "Mobicox" can be divided into two parts. "Mobi" echoes the improved mobility that comes from using the brand and "cox" echoes Cox-2. In approving this name, the regulators agreed that Mobicox is a full Cox-2—an important step in establishing the Mobicox credentials.

Given the competitive situation, Boehringer Ingelheim and the advertising agency identify two distinct directions for Mobicox's brand strategy.

1. Even though Mobicox is a long way from being a brand leader, it will act as though it is already a leader. The analogy is similar to what Apple did to IBM back in the 1980s and what Pepsi-Cola did to Coca-Cola with its Pepsi Generation campaign. As a result of sound marketing communications strategies, both Apple and Pepsi-Cola were perceived as innovator brands.
2. The brand message will shake up the competition in a very public way. In traditional pharmaceutical marketing, this just isn't done. If Boehringer Ingelheim can get the competition to respond, it will legitimize Mobicox. In fact, Boehringer Ingelheim representatives will be able to say to doctors, "Why are Pfizer and Merck over-reacting? It's because Mobicox is a fully legitimate alternative."

Both Boehringer Ingelheim and its advertising agency decided that a swaggering brand character is needed. The brand character statement will be:

"Confidence Bordering on Arrogance."

All creative materials will be evaluated for acceptance based on the brand character statement.

The advertising agency will then go on to develop a brand logo, brand colour scheme, and positioning line (tagline for the campaign) that suit the brand character. The design is clean and simple and includes an unusual colour combination. The "cox" part of the name is emphasized through colour. The tagline for the branding effort is *"Even the Price is a Relief."*

TARGET MARKET

Several unique target markets will be addressed:

- **General Practitioners:** Medical practitioners all across Canada will be made aware of Mobicox.
- **Insurance Companies and Governments:** Senior managers and government officials, responsible for drug coverage plans in the private sector and the public sector, will be interested in the cost savings offered by Mobicox.
- **Company Sales Force:** A contract sales force, hired for the launch, needs to be trained on product knowledge to the highest level.

CREATIVE OBJECTIVES

1. To create a high level of awareness for the Mobicox brand name and its primary benefits: a product for arthritic pain relief with all the benefits of the leading Cox-2s, but at a much lower price.

2. To show actual cost comparisons with the leading Cox-2s, in order to stimulate interest and desire among the medical community to prescribe Mobicox.

Key Benefit Statement

"Mobicox delivers all the benefits of the leading Cox-2s, but at a considerably more attractive price."

Creative Strategy (Tone, Style, and Theme)

Considering the marketing challenges and the desired brand character, communications have to offer immediate impact. The ads will:

* be provocative in nature
* be consistent in look and feel
* project a David versus Goliath tone
* be designed to create a stir (be controversial)
* communicate the positioning strategy by using the tagline *"Even the Price is a Relief."*

CREATIVE EXECUTION

* All ads include provocative headlines to capture the attention of readers.
* A consistent brand image is projected for Mobicox by using the same typography and photo style in all ads.
* A comparative tactic will be employed to dramatize the cost savings for patients and insurance program managers.
* Budget restrictions and message considerations dictate the use of print media, direct mail, and a website.
* A branding block that includes the brand logo, colour scheme, and tagline will appear in the lower right corner of all print ads.
* Ads will vary in length from one page to multiple page spreads. The spread format will effectively grab the reader's attention, as will the provocative headlines.

PRE-LAUNCH AD: "THE PARTY'S OVER."

This double-page spread will appear in medical magazines and magazines directed at health benefits managers. The ad takes direct aim at the competition and states that the high price being paid by patients, insurers, and governments will soon be over. The execution represents the classic "teaser" approach (see Figure A2.1 on page 400).

Ad 2—Launch Ad: "We Imagine" and "Low Blow"

This multiple-page spread is designed to establish the price advantage very dramatically. By quoting actual prices, it provides factual proof to the message in the teaser ad while taking dead aim at Celebrex and Vioxx. This ad maintains the David versus Goliath tonality to a degree not seen in pharmaceutical marketing. It also breaks tradition by placing the competitors' names front and centre. The visual shows the actual amount of money an average patient can save over a period of time. This ad will spark controversy in doctors' offices and the Pfizer and Merck boardrooms. See the advertisement in Figure A2.2 (on pages 401 and 402).

An alternative rough for this ad shows a picture of arthritic hands taking bills out of a wallet and the heading "Now more of your Cox-2 patients can avoid this painful exercise." (This double-page spread was seen as being too aggressive by the client, even though it does reflect the brand's character and personality.) See the advertisement in Figure A2.3 (on page 403).

Ad 3—Direct Mail: "There's a Time Bomb Ready to Go Off"

The direct mail piece focuses on price savings to the insurance industry. It communicates how prevalent arthritis is and how much it costs employers. Consequently, a drug such as Mobicox—fully effective but at a lower price—can reduce costs by thousands of dollars. The mailer includes a CD-ROM that contains an electronic spreadsheet that allows users to compare their current costs of Celebrex and Vioxx to Mobicox. The technology in the mailer helps sell the less expensive positioning strategy. See the advertisement in Figure A2.4 (on page 404).

Media Plan

MEDIA OBJECTIVES

- *Who?* Medical practitioners and health benefits managers in the private and public sectors.
- *What?* All media will deliver a similar message. Mobicox is of a quality equal to leading competitor brands but at a substantial cost savings to patients, insurers, and publicly funded medical plans.
- *When?* The launch media plan will commence November 2000 and extend until the end of 2002.
- *Where?* The plan will focus on high-potential provinces where Mobicox can expect preferential coverage on the provincial formulary.
- *How?* A priority is given to reach, and the plan will be front-loaded at a level that will create an equal share of voice to Celebrex and Vioxx.

MEDIA BUDGET

A budget of $1.8 million has been allocated for the launch period November 2000 to the end of October 2001.

MEDIA STRATEGY

- Given the nature of pharmaceutical marketing and the amount of information that must be communicated, print media are the preferred choice. Print media offer the space necessary to explain the Mobicox promise carefully. There is an excellent list of specialized medical publications and health benefit publications (rifle media strategy) available that reach the intended targets (medical practitioners and health benefits officers) both directly and efficiently.
- Direct mail is added to the mix because additional space is needed to explain the product benefits and cost-savings proposition fully to managers of insurance benefit programs. Direct mail messages avoid the problem of advertising clutter associated with other forms of print advertising. Furthermore, specific lists to reach the intended target audience are available at reasonable cost.
- All information regarding the nature and benefits of Mobicox will be posted on the company's website. The print ads will help draw the reader's attention to the website.

MEDIA EXECUTION

The print ad campaign includes the following publications:

- *Medical Post*
- *Canadian Family Physician*
- *Canadian Medical Association Journal*
- *Patient Care*
- *Canadian Journal of Continuing Medical Education*
- *Doctor's Review*
- *Stitches*
- *Pain and Research Management*
- *Journal of Rheumatology*
- *New England Journal of Medicine*
- *Pharmacy Post*

The various ads will be rotated through each publication. The timing of each ad is a key consideration. For example, the "We Imagine" ad is to be used in the pre-launch and early launch phase. Once the launch is underway, the emphasis will shift to the other ads. Refer to the timing considerations on the blocking chart in Figure A2.5.

The average number of insertions per month in the 12-month period November 2000 to October 2001 will be 8. The average time that each ad will run in the 12-month period will be 20. The pre-launch ad will run a total of 23 times while the "There are Now/But Only" will dominate the launch period, running 37 times.

Public Relations Plan

With many new product launches, it is customary for advertising to "sell the sizzle." There isn't a need for too much information transfer. In contrast, prescription medications such as Mobicox require large amounts of technical information to be communicated. Hence there is a need for alternative marketing communications strategies. In this case, public relations will play a key role in delivering the Mobicox message. The primary role will be to quell the anticipated "Cox-One-and-a-Half" challenge that will be raised by Pfizer and Merck before Mobicox will be launched.

PUBLIC RELATIONS OBJECTIVES

- To quash the anticipated response from Pfizer and Merck regarding the perceived "Cox-One-and-a-Half" issue that is associated with Mobicox.
- To provide opinion leaders, industry analysts, and medical practitioners with a thorough understanding of Mobicox, its primary benefits, and cost-savings compared to other Cox-2s.
- To time public relations activities so they will reinforce pre-launch advertising programs for Mobicox.

PUBLIC RELATIONS STRATEGIES

- Press releases containing relevant details about Mobicox will be delivered to appropriate stakeholders.
- A speaking tour featuring a third-party endorser will reach stakeholders in major cities across Canada.

PUBLIC RELATIONS EXECUTION

Boehringer Ingelheim secured the services of Sir John Vane from the United Kingdom. Sir John is an extremely credible individual, being a Nobel Prize winner for discovering the mechanism of how Aspirin works. He is also a strong supporter of the Mobicox molecule. Since he believes in the product and its Cox-2 status, he was willing to present data on it. His presence will help secure the desired credibility Boehringer Ingelheim needs in the marketplace. Word about Mobicox will spread as he tours major cities.

To deliver the Cox-2 message, Sir John will engage in a cross-Canada health education tour that is designed to influence key opinion leaders in major cities. Special invitations will be delivered to target members in each city. The press will also be invited.

FIGURE **A2.5**   **Media Blocking Chart: Print Media**

Ad and Month	"We Imagine"	"Party Over"	"There are now/ But only"	"Do You Think"	"Until Recently/ Older Lady"
November	8	2			
December	13				
January	2			15	
February				12	
March			23		
April			14		
May					2
June					8
July					
August					
September					
October					

Note: The figures represent the number of insertions in the various publications each month.

FIGURE **A2.1** "The Party's Over."

Source: Courtesy of Remtulla Euro RSCG and Boehringer Ingelheim.

FIGURE A2.2   **Launch Ads: "We Imagine" and "Low Blow"**

We imagine Vioxx™ and Celebrex™ would prefer that you skipped over the next 2 pages.

continued

FIGURE **A2.3** Alternative Mobicox Ad

Source: Courtesy of Remtulla Euro RSCG and Boehringer Ingelheim.

There's a 17.8 billion dollar time bomb ready to explode in Canadian companies.*

It's called Arthritis.

* Arthritis costs Canadians $17.8 billion annually.
Arthritis in Canada: Facts and Figures, Canadian Rheumatology Association & The Arthritis Society.

continued

And if you think arthritis is painful for employees, wait until you see these numbers:

PRIVATE PAYOR SPEND ON NONSTEROIDAL ANTI-INFLAMMATORY DRUGS (NSAIDS):

154% overall increase in spending 1998–2000
since the arrival of the first two COX-2 selective NSAIDs – Vioxx™ and Celebrex.™

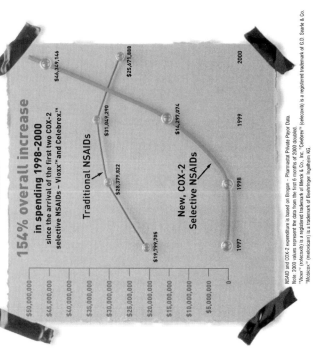

Traditional NSAIDs

New, COX-2 Selective NSAIDs

$46,349,146
$25,671,888
$31,049,290
$14,297,074
$28,379,822
$19,299,705

1997   1998   1999   2000

NSAID and COX-2 expenditure is based on Brogan – Pharmastat Private Payor Data.
Note: 2000 values represent the data from the first 6 months of 2000 doubled.
'Vioxx'™ (rofecoxib) is a registered trademark of Merck & Co., Inc. 'Celebrex'™ (celecoxib) is a registered trademark of G.D. Searle & Co.
'Mobicox'™ (meloxicam) is a trademark of Boehringer Ingelheim KG.

What is Arthritis?

There are over 100 types of arthritis, but 2 of the most common are osteo and rheumatoid arthritis.

Osteoarthritis (OA)
• Affects 1 in 10 Canadians.
• Affects hips, knees, hands and spine.
• Affects women and men equally.
• Develops usually after age 45.

Rheumatoid Arthritis (RA)
• Affects 1 in 100 Canadians.
• Affects primarily hands and feet.
• Affects twice as many women as men.
• Develops between age 25 and 50.

Adapted from The Arthritis Society website.

How does it affect employees?

• Arthritis is the leading cause of disability.
• It accounts for more than 25% of all long-term disability in Canada.
• 21% of the working population between 45 and 64 have some form of arthritis.
• OA is second to ischemic heart disease as a cause of work-related disability in men over 50.

How is it treated?

• Exercise/physiotherapy
• Heat/cold
• Assistive Devices
• Relaxation
• Over-the-counter pain medication, e.g. acetaminophen
• Over-the-counter NSAIDs, e.g. ASA, ibuprofen
• Prescription – traditional NSAIDs, e.g. naproxen, diclofenac, piroxicam
• Prescription – COX-2 selective NSAIDs, e.g. Mobicox,™ Vioxx,™ Celebrex™
• Surgery

Why are your arthritis drug costs rising?

The new COX-2 selective NSAIDs are replacing traditional NSAIDs – and they're more expensive.

Why are the new COX-2 selective NSAIDs so popular?

They represent an advance in anti-inflammatory therapy because the incidence of gastrointestinal side effects is lower.

How can this cost escalation be managed?

There's now a new COX-2 selective NSAID in Canada that's affordably priced – new Mobicox.™

Introducing new Mobicox.™ Canada's most affordable COX-2 selective NSAID.

Although new in Canada, Mobicox™ has been prescribed over 44 million times worldwide.¹ With favourable coverage of Mobicox™ on your drug plan, employees will finally have a much more affordable option to higher-priced Vioxx™ or Celebrex.™

How you can find out more about how Mobicox™ can help reduce your arthritis drug spending:

Send away for our complimentary CD-ROM containing an easy-to-use budget impact model. Simply fill out the attached business reply card to find out more about how Canada's most affordable COX-2 selective NSAID could reduce your drug plan expenditure.

¹IMS Health MIDAS 2000, January 1996 and January–June 2000.

Source: Courtesy of Remtulla Euro RSCG and Boehringer Ingelheim.

Acquisition strategy – A plan of action for acquiring companies that represent attractive financial opportunities.

Ad click rate (clickthrough rate)– The percentage of ad views that resulted in an ad click; determines the success of an ad in attracting visitors to click on it.

Ad clicks – The number of times users click on a banner (clicking transfers the user to another website).

Ad views (impressions)– The number of times a banner is downloaded to a user's screen.

Advertising – A form of marketing communications designed to stimulate a positive response from a defined target market.

Advertising equivalency – A mathematical model that equates public relations to an advertising value by evaluating the space occupied by a public relations message in relation to advertising space.

Advocacy advertising – A form of advertising paid for by a sponsor that promotes a particular view on a recognized, controversial issue.

Agate line– A non-standardized unit of space measurement, equal to one column wide and 1/14" deep, used in newspaper advertising.

Ambush marketing – A strategy used by non-sponsors of an event to capitalize on the prestige and popularity of the event by giving the false impression they are sponsors.

Animated ad – A online ad that has a spinning motion or other form of action.

Annual report – A document published annually by an organization primarily to provide current and prospective investors and stakeholders with financial data and a description of its operations.

Approach – The initial contact with a customer.

Attitude – A individual's feelings, favourable or unfavourable, toward an idea or object.

Attribute – A descriptive feature of a product.

Backlit poster – A luminous outdoor sign printed on polyvinyl material.

Banner – In outdoor advertising, a large-size printed ad that is framed and mounted on the exterior of a building. Online, an ad that stretches across a webpage; the user can click on the ad for more information.

Benefit – The value a customer attaches to a brand attribute.

"Big idea" – See **Central theme**.

Billboard– see **Poster**.

Blitz schedule – The scheduling of media advertising so most spending is front-loaded in the schedule; usually involves a lot of money spent in a short period.

Blocking chart – See **Media calendar**.

Bonus pack – The temporary offering of a larger package size (e.g., 20 percent more) for the same price as the regular size.

Booklet (brochure) – A multiple-page document distributed to consumers and other interested stakeholders.

Borrowed-interest strategy– A plan to promote a marketing activity that is related to a product.

Bounce back– See **Statement stuffer**.

Brand – An identifying mark, symbol, word or words, or combination of mark and words that separates one product from another product; can also be defined as the sum of all tangible and intangible characteristics that make a unique offer to customers.

Brand development index (BDI) – The percentage of a brand's sales in an area in relation to the population in that area; determines if the brand is underdeveloped or over-developed in each area.

Brand equity – The value (monetary or otherwise) of a brand to its owners; determined by the success of marketing activities; influenced by brand name awareness, degree of customer loyalty, perceived quality, etc.

Brand insistence – A situation where the consumer searches the market for the specific brand.

Brand loyalty – The degree of attachment to a particular brand expressed by a consumer. There are three stages of brand loyalty: brand recognition, brand preference, and brand insistence.

Brand manager – An individual assigned responsibility for the development and implementation of marketing programs for a specific product or group of products.

Brand name – That part of a brand that can be spoken.

Brand preference – The situation where a brand is perceived as an acceptable alternative by a customer and will be purchased if it is available.

Brand recognition – Customer awareness of the brand name and package.

Branded content – See **Product placement**.

Brandmark or logo – A unique design, symbol, or other special representation of a brand name or company name.

Broadsheet – A large newspaper with a fold in its middle.

Brochure – See **Booklet**.

Build-up schedule – The scheduling of media advertising so that the weight of advertising starts out light and gradually builds over a period of time; also called a teaser campaign.

Bump-in (setup) – The setting up of structures and other equipment at an event.

Bump-out (teardown) – The process of dismantling everything after an event.

Business-to-business (B2B) market – A market of goods and services needed to produce a product or service, promote an idea, or operate a business.

Button – A small online ad; can be any shape.

Buying centre – An informal purchasing process in which individuals in an organization perform particular roles but may not have direct responsibility for the actual decision.

Buying committee – A formal buying structure in an organization that brings together expertise from the various functional areas to share in the buying decision process.

Buzz marketing– See **Product seeding**.

Call centre – A central operation from which a company operates its inbound and outbound telemarketing programs.

Catalogue – A reference publication, usually annual or seasonal, distributed by large retail chains and direct marketing companies.

Category development index (CDI) or market development index – The percentage of category sales in a geographic area in relation to the total population of that area; determines if a category is underdeveloped or overdeveloped in a particular region.

Central theme ("big idea") – The glue that binds various creative elements of a campaign together; transferable from one medium to another.

Channel positioning – A marketing strategy based on an organization's position in its distribution channel and its market coverage.

Cinema advertising – Print advertising inside film theatres and broadcast advertising on screens; options include television-style ads on screen, slides, posters, and ads printed on tickets.

Circulation – The average number of copies per issue of a publication sold by subscription, distributed free to predetermined recipients, carried with other publications, or made available through retail distributors.

Circulation list – A publication's subscription list that targets potential customers based on specified demographic characteristics, interests, or activities.

Classified advertising – Print advertising in which similar goods and services are grouped together in categories under appropriate headings.

Clickthrough rate – See **Ad click rate**.

Clipping service – An organization that scans the print and broadcast media in search of a company's or brand's name.

Closing – Asking for the order at the appropriate time in a sales presentation.

Closing cue – An indication that the buyer is ready to buy; can be expressed verbally or nonverbally.

Cluster – Ads grouped in a block of time during a break in a program or between programs, or in a section of a publication.

Cluster profiling – See **Geodemographic segmentation**.

Clutter – The amount of advertising in a particular medium.

Cognitive dissonance – A feeling of doubt or regret in a consumer's mind once a buying decision has been made.

Cold canvass – The process of calling on people or organizations without appointments or advance knowledge of them.

Collateral material – Visual aids used by sales representatives in sales presentations, such as price lists, product manuals, sales brochures, and audiovisual material.

Communication – The transmission, receipt, and processing of information between a sender and a receiver.

Compiled list – A direct mail list prepared from government, census, telephone, warranty, or other publication information.

Consultative selling – A form of selling that stresses open two-way communication between a buyer and seller.

Consumer behaviour – The combined acts carried out by individuals choosing and using goods and services, including the decision-making processes that determine these acts.

Consumer promotion – Incentive(s) offered to consumers to stimulate purchases or encourage loyalty.

Contest – A promotion that involves awarding cash or merchandise prizes to consumers when they purchase a specified product.

Contingency plan – The identification of alternative courses of action that can be used to modify an original plan if and when new circumstances arise.

Continuity – The length of time required in an advertising medium to generate the desired impact on the target audience.

Continuity discount – A discount offered to advertisers that purchase space in consecutive issues of a publication.

Controlled circulation – The circulation of a publication that is distributed free to individuals in a specific demographic segment or geographic area; this segment receives the publication for free.

Cookie – An electronic identification tag sent from a web server to a user's browser to track the user's browsing patterns.

Cooperative advertising allowance (co-op) – The sharing of advertising costs by suppliers and retailers or by several retailers.

Cooperative direct mail – A mailing containing specific offers from non-competing products.

Core values – The primary attributes and benefits a brand delivers to the customer.

Corporate advertising – Advertising designed to convey a favourable image of a company among its various publics.

Corporate culture – The values, beliefs, norms, and practices shared by all employees of an organization.

Corporate discount – A discount based on the total number of pages purchased by a single company (all product lines combined).

Corporate objective – A statement of a company's overall goal, used to evaluate the effectiveness or ineffectiveness of a company's strategic plan.

Corporate plan – A strategic plan formulated at the executive level of an organization to guide the development of functional plans in the organization.

Corporate strategy – see **Strategic planning**.

Cost per thousand (CPM) – The cost of delivering an advertising message to 1000 people; calculated by dividing the cost of the ad by the circulation in thousands.

Coupon – A price-saving incentive offered to consumers to stimulate quick purchase of a specified product.

Creative brief – A document developed by a client organization that contains vital information about the advertising task at hand; is a useful tool for discussions between the client and its advertising agency.

Creative objective – A statement that clearly indicates the information to be communicated to the target audience; usually involves a key benefit statement and a support claims statement.

Creative plan – A plan that outlines the nature of the message to be communicated to the target audience; involves the development of creative objectives, creative strategies, and creative execution.

Creative strategy – A plan of action for how the message will be communicated to the target audience, covering the tone and style of message, the central theme, and the appeal techniques.

Cross-ruff (cross-coupon) – A coupon redeemable for one product that is packed in or with another product. The other product is the means of distributing the coupon.

Cross-tabulation – The comparison of answers to questions by various subgroups with the total number of responses.

Customer relationship management (CRM) – A process that enables an organization to develop an ongoing relationship with valued customers; the organization captures and uses information about its customers to its advantage in developing the relationship.

Data analysis – The evaluation of responses question by question; gives meaning to the data.

Data interpretation – The relating of accumulated data to the problem under review and to the objectives and hypotheses of the research study.

Data mining – The analysis of information to determine relationships among the data and enable more effective marketing strategies to be identified and implemented.

Data transfer – In marketing research, the transfer of answers from the questionnaire to the computer.

Database management system – A system that collects information about customers for analysis by managers in order to facilitate sound business decisions.

Database marketing – The use and analysis of accumulated information on customer buying behaviour in order to develop more effective marketing strategies.

Day-after-recall (DAR) test – Research conducted the day following the respondent's exposure to a message to determine the degree of recognition and recall of the advertisement, the brand, and the selling message.

Daypart – A broadcast time period or segment on radio or television.

Dealer display material (point-of-purchase material) – Advertising or display materials located in a retail environment to build traffic, advertise a product, and encourage impulse purchasing.

Dealer premium – An incentive offered to a distributor to encourage the special purchase of a product or to secure additional merchandising support from the distributor.

Demographic segmentation – The identification of target markets based on characteristics such as age, income, education, occupation, marital status, and household formation.

Demonstration – A sales technique that involves showing the product in action to portray its benefits to a buyer.

Direct competition – Competition from alternative products and services that satisfy the needs of a common market.

Direct (customized) segmentation – The identification of a target audience at the level of the individual; marketing programs designed for and communicated to individual customers.

Direct home shopping – A shopping service provided by cable television stations that offers products or services for sale by broadcast message (e.g., The Shopping Channel).

Direct mail – A printed form of direct response advertising distributed by Canada Post or independent delivery agents.

Direct marketing – A marketing system for developing products, sending messages directly to customers, and accepting orders through a variety of media, and then distributing the purchase directly to customers.

Direct response advertising – Advertising placed in a medium that generates an immediate and measurable response from the intended target.

Direct response communications – The delivery of a message to a target audience of one; message can be distributed by direct mail, direct response television, and telemarketing.

Direct response print – An ad in print media that issues a direct call to action via a toll-free number, return mail address, or online.

Direct response television (DRTV) – Advertising that appears on television and encourages viewers to respond by telephoning a toll-free number, by mail or online; often referred to as infomercials.

Directory database – A commercial database that provides information about a company (e.g., size, sales, location, number of employees).

Editing – In marketing research, the review of questionnaires for consistency and completeness.

Elevator advertising – Advertising in display frames on elevator walls and on televisions mounted in the corner or above the door.

Encoding – The transformation of a message into a meaningful format such as an advertisement, a mailing piece, or an article in a newspaper.

Endorsement – A situation where a celebrity speaks highly of an advertised product.

Eprocurement – An online, business-to-business marketplace through which participants can purchase goods and services from one another.

Even schedule – The uniform schedule of media advertising over an extended period; also referred to as a continuous schedule.

Event marketing – The process, planned by a sponsoring organization, of integrating a variety of communications elements with a single event theme.

Event sponsorship – The financial support of an event in exchange for advertising privileges associated with that event.

Experiential marketing (on-site sampling) – A promotion in which potential customers interact directly with a product (e.g., sample give-aways).

Experimental research – Research in which one or more factors are manipulated under controlled conditions, while other elements remain constant, so that the respondent's actions can be evaluated.

External publics – Those publics that are distant from an organization and are communicated with less frequently.

Eye movement–camera test – A test that uses a hidden camera to track eye movement to gauge the point of immediate contact in an advertisement, how the reader scans the ad, and the amount of time spent reading.

Feature – Tangible aspects of a product, such as durability, design, and economy of operation.

Field sales force – An organization's external sales representatives who regularly call on customers to pursue orders.

Fixed-response (close-ended) questioning – Questions that include pre-determined questions and set answers for the respondents to choose from.

Flight – A period of time in which advertising is scheduled.

Flyer – A single-sheet document that contains information about a product or service.

Focus group – A small group of people with common characteristics brought together to discuss issues related to the marketing of a product or service.

Folder – A direct response sales message printed on heavy stock that can be mailed with or without an envelope; may be several pages in length.

Follow-up – Maintaining contact with customers to ensure that service has been satisfactory.

Format – The type and nature of the programming offered by a radio station.

Free sample – Free distribution of a product to potential users.

Freestanding insert (FSI) – A booklet featuring coupons, refunds, contests, or other promotional advertising distributed by direct mail or with newspapers, magazines, or other delivery vehicles.

Frequency – The average number of times a message has been exposed to an audience over a period of time, usually a week.

Frequency discount– A discounted page rate based on the number of times an advertisement runs.

Frequency distribution – The number of times each answer in a survey was chosen for a question.

Frequent buyer program– See **Loyalty program**.

Game (including instant-win) – A promotional contest that includes a number of pre-seeded winning tickets; instant-win tickets can be redeemed immediately.

Geodemographic segmentation (cluster profiling) – The identification of target markets according to dwelling areas defined by geographic and demographic variables, based on the assumption that like people seek out residential neighbourhoods in which to cluster with their lifestyle peers.

Geographic segmentation – The identification of a target markets based on the regional, urban, or rural location of the customers.

Gross rating points (GRPs)– An expression of the weight of advertising in a media schedule; calculated by multiplying reach by frequency.

Head-on positioning – A marketing strategy in which one product is presented as an equal or better alternative than a competing product.

Hit– Each time a server sends a file to a browser.

House list – An internal customer list.

Hypothesis – A statement of outcomes predicted in a marketing research investigation.

Image positioning – See **Lifestyle positioning**.

Impressions – See **Ad views**.

Incentive– A free gift or offer included in a direct mail package.

Indirect competition – Competition from substitute products that offer the same benefit as another type of product.

Infomercial– A long commercial (e.g., 10 to 30 minutes) that presents in detail the benefits of a product or service; usually includes a call to action (e.g., a 1-800 number).

Innovation positioning – A marketing strategy that stresses newness (based on a commitment to research and development) as a means of differentiating a company or a brand from competing companies and brands.

In-pack self-coupon– A coupon for the next purchase of a product, packed inside the package or under a label.

Insert – A preprinted, free-standing advertisement (e.g., a leaflet, brochure, or flyer) specifically placed in a newspaper or magazine.

Inside sales force – An internal group of sellers, often referred to as order takers, who accept orders from customers by telephone or other means.

Instantly redeemable coupon – A removable coupon often located on the package or a store shelf that is redeemable on the current purchase of the product.

Instant-win – See **Game**.

Integrated marketing communications – The coordination of all marketing communications in a unified program that maximizes the impact on the intended target audience.

Interior card – A transit ad in the rack above the window or near the door of a bus or subway car.

Internal publics – The publics with which an organization communicates regularly; can include employees, distributors, suppliers, shareholders, and customers.

Internet – A world-wide network of computer networks linked together to act as one in the communication of information; like a global mail system in which independent entities collaborate in moving and delivering information.

Interstitial (pop-up or pop-under) – An online ad that appears in a separate browser window while another Web page is loading; a pop-up appears in a window in front of the active window, and a pop-under appears in a window behind the active window.

Key benefit statement – A statement of the basic selling idea, service, or benefit promised the consumer by the advertiser; appears in the creative plan section of an advertising plan.

King poster – An oversized poster attached to the sides of buses.

Leadership positioning – A marketing strategy in which a product presents itself as a preferred choice among customers.

Leaflet– A one-page flyer that offers relevant information about a direct mail offer.

Line rate– The rate charged by newspapers for one agate line or one modular agate line.

Lifestyle (image) positioning – A marketing strategy based on intangible characteristics associated with a lifestyle instead of tangible characteristics.

List broker – A company specializing in finding or developing lists for direct response purposes; finds prospect lists based on target market criteria established by marketing organizations.

Listing– An agreement made by a wholesaler to distribute a manufacturer's product to the retailer it supplies.

Lobbying– Activities and practices designed to influence policy decisions that will affect an organization or all organizations in a particular industry.

Local spot – Advertising bought from a local station by a local advertiser.

Logo– See **Brandmark**.

Loyalty program (frequent buyer program) – A program that offers consumers a small bonus, such as points or play money, each time they make a purchase; bonus accumulates and can be redeemed for merchandise or some other benefit.

Mail interview – In marketing research, the collection of information from a respondent by mail.

Mall poster – A form of advertising located inside shopping malls; relies only on pedestrian traffic.

Market segmentation – The division of a large market into smaller homogeneous markets based on common needs and characteristics.

Market share – The sales volume of one product or company expressed as a percentage of total sales volume in the market the company or brand is competing in.

Marketing communications plan – A plan that identifies how the various elements of marketing communications will be integrated into a cohesive and coordinated plan.

Marketing control – The process of measuring and evaluating the results of marketing strategies and plans and of taking corrective action to ensure marketing objectives are achieved.

Marketing objective – A statement that identifies what a product will accomplish in a one-year period, usually expressed in terms of sales, market share, and profit.

Marketing plan – A short-term, specific plan of action that combines strategy and tactics.

Marketing planning – The analysis, planning, implementing, and controlling of marketing initiatives to satisfy target market needs and achieve organizational objectives.

Marketing research – A marketing function that links the consumer/customer/public to the marketer through information; information used to define marketing opportunities and problems, generate marketing strategies, evaluate marketing actions, and monitor performance.

Marketing strategy – A plan of action that shows how the various elements of the marketing mix will be used to satisfy a target market's needs.

Mass customization – The development, manufacture, and marketing of unique products to unique customers.

Media brief – A document that contains essential information for developing a media plan; used to stimulate discussion between a client and agency.

Media calendar (blocking chart) – A document that shows allocation of a brand's media budget according to time of year and type of medium; shows coordination of various media recommendations.

Media execution – The translation of media strategies into specific media action plans; involves recommending specific media to be used in the plan and negotiating the media buys.

Media kit – A package of relevant information associated with a product or organization, distributed at a press conference.

Media objective – A statement that outlines what a media plan is to accomplish (who, what, when, where, or how).

Media plan – A strategy that outlines the relevant details about how a client's budget will be spent; involves decisions about what media to use and how much money to invest in the media chosen in order to reach the target audience effectively and efficiently.

Media strategy – A plan for achieving the media objectives stated in the media plan; typically justifies the use of certain media.

Media-delivered coupon – A coupon distributed by traditional media alternatives such as newspapers, magazines, and direct mail.

Merge/purge – A process in which numerous mailing lists are combined and then stripped of duplicate names.

Micro-segmentation (micro-marketing) – The identification of very small yet profitable market segments.

Mission statement – A statement of an organization's purpose and operating philosophy; provides guidance and direction for the operations of the company.

Modular agate line– A standardized unit of measurement equal to one column wide and 1/14" deep, used in newspaper advertising.

Modular agate unit – A standardized unit of measurement in which a newspaper page is divided into equal-sized units each 30 modular agate lines deep.

Monopolistic competition – A market in which there are many competitors, each offering a unique marketing mix; consumers can assess these choices prior to making a buying decision.

Motive – A condition that prompts an individual to take action to satisfy a need.

Mural advertisement – A hand-painted outdoor ad painted on the side of a building.

National advertisement – Advertising of a branded product or service wherever that product or service is available across the country.

Need – The perception of the absence of something useful.

Network advertising – Advertising from one central source broadcast across an entire network of stations.

New product development strategy – A marketing strategy that calls for significant investment in research and development to develop innovative products.

Newsletter – A document sent to a predetermined audience that contains news about an organization (e.g., a newsletter is sent to alumni of a school or to all employees of an organization).

Noise – Any potential form of disruption in the transmission of a message that could distort the impact of the message; competitive advertising or the clutter of advertising messages in a medium are forms of noise.

Non-probability sample – A sample of respondents who have an unknown chance of selection and are chosen because of factors such as convenience or the judgment of the researcher.

Non-verbal communication (body language) – The expression of thoughts, opinions, or information using nonverbal cues such as body movement, facial expressions, and eye contact.

Objection– An obstacle that a salesperson must confront during a sales presentation.

Observation research – A form of research in which the behaviour of the respondent is observed and recorded; may be by personal or electronic means.

Oligopoly – A market situation in which only a few brands control the market.

Online advertising– Advertising on a website in the form of a banner, pop-up ad, text ad, or animated ad, or delivered electronically through e-mail, cell phones or personal digital assistants.

Online database – An information database accessible online to anyone with proper communications facilities.

Online selling– Using the internet to conduct sales transactions.

Online survey – In marketing research, using an online questionnaire to collect data from people.

On-pack self-coupon – A coupon that is printed on the outside of a package redeemable on the next purchase of the product.

On-site sampling – See **Experiential marketing**.

Opinion-measure testing – A form of research yielding information about the effect of a commercial message on respondents' brand name recall, interest in the brand, and purchase intentions.

Opt-in list – A list of people who have agreed to receive messages via email.

Order taking – In retail sales, a floor clerk provides product information and shows goods to the customer, who then goes to the checkout counter to pay for purchases.

Overall goal – The objective of an advertising campaign.

Page views – The number of times an ad was potentially seen online or in print; also referred to as "gross impressions." In online marketing, the number of times a user requests a page that may contain a particular ad.

Paid circulation – The circulation of a newspaper or magazine that is generated by subscription sales and newsstand sales.

Partnership selling – A strategically developed long-term relationship that involves selling products and providing comprehensive after-sales service and effective two-way communications to ensure complete customer satisfaction.

Peer group– see **Reference group**.

Penetration strategy – A plan of action for aggressive marketing of a company's existing products.

Perception – The manner in which individuals receive and interpret messages.

Performance allowance – A discount offered by a manufacturer that encourages a distributor to perform a merchandising function on behalf of a manufacturer.

Permission-based email – Email sent to recipients who have agreed to accept email advertising messages.

Personal interview – In marketing research, the collection of information in a face-to-face interview.

Personal selling – Face-to-face communication involving the presentation of features and benefits of a product or service to a buyer; the objective is to make a sale.

Personality – A person's distinguishing psychological characteristics that lead to relatively consistent and enduring responses to the environment in which that person lives.

Point-of-purchase material– See **Dealer display material**.

Pop-up and pop-under – See **Interstitial**.

Population (universe) – In marketing research, a group of people with a certain specific age, gender, or other demographic characteristics.

Portal – A website that serves as a gateway to a variety of services such as searching, news, directories, email, online shopping, and links to other sites.

Position charge – The cost of requesting a preferred position in a newspaper.

Positioning – The selling concept that motivates purchase, or the image that marketers desire a brand to have in the minds of consumers.

Positioning strategy statement – A summary of the character and personality of a brand and the benefits it offers customers.

Post-buy analysis – An evaluation of actual audience deliveries calculated after a specific spot or schedule of advertising has run.

Poster (billboard) – A common form of outdoor advertising; usually a picture-dominant advertisement with a minimum of copy.

Post-testing – The evaluation and measurement of a message's effectiveness during or after the message has run.

Pre-approach – The gathering of information about customers before actually making sales contact.

Premium– An additional item given free, or greatly discounted, to induce purchase of the primary brand.

Presentation strategy – A plan of what to say to a customer in a sales presentation to identify customer needs, summarize benefits, and prepare for potential objections.

Press conference – A meeting called by an organization to present information to representatives of the media.

Press release – A document prepared by an organization containing public relations information that is sent to the media for publication or broadcast.

Pre-testing – The evaluation of commercial messages prior to final production to determine the strength and weaknesses of the communications.

Price positioning – A marketing strategy based on the premise that consumers search for the best possible value given their economic circumstances.

Primary data – Data collected to resolve a problem and recorded for the first time.

Primary medium – A medium that receives the largest allocation of an advertiser's budget; the dominant medium in a media plan.

Primary research – The collection and recording of primary data.

Probability sample – A sample of respondents who are known to have an equal chance of selection and are randomly selected from the sampling frame.

Problem statement – A brief statement that summarizes a particular problem to resolve or an opportunity to pursue and serves as the focus of a marketing strategy.

Product advertising – Advertising that provides information about a branded product to help build its image in the minds of customers.

Product as hero – A creative execution technique in which the advertised product is shown coming to the rescue (e.g., of a consumer in a difficult situation).

Product configuration – The bringing together of various products and services to form a solution for the customer.

Product differentiation strategy – A plan of action for communicating meaningful attributes and benefits of a product to a target market.

Product placement (branded content) – The visible placement of brand name products in television shows, movies, radio, video game, and other programming.

Product seeding (buzz marketing) – Giving a product free to a group of trendsetters who promote the product to others by word of mouth.

Profile-matching strategy – A media tactic that involves matching the demographic profile of a product's target market with a specific medium that has a similar target profile.

Promotional advertising – Advertising that communicates a specific offer to encourage an immediate response from the target audience.

Prospecting– A procedure for systematically developing sales leads.

Psychographic segmentation – The identification of a target market according to lifestyle characteristics such as activities, interests, and opinions.

Public relations – A form of communications designed to gain public understanding and acceptance.

Publicity – News about an organization, product, service, or person that appears in the media.

Pull – Demand created by directing promotional activities at consumers or final users, who in turn pressure retailers to supply the product or service.

Pulse schedule – A scheduling of media advertising in flights of different weight and duration.

Pupilometer test – A device that measure pupil dilation (enlargement) of a person's eye when reading; measures emotional response to an advertisement.

Push– Demand created by directing promotional activities at intermediaries, who in turn promote the product or service among consumers.

Qualifying (a customer) – Assessing if a prospect needs a product, has the authority to buy it, and has the ability to pay for it.

Qualitative data – Data collected from small samples in a controlled environment; describe feelings and opinions on issues.

Quantitative data – Measurable data collected from large samples using a structured research procedure.

Ratings– Television and radio audience estimates expressed as a percentage of a population in a defined geographic area.

Reach– The total unduplicated audience exposed one or more times to a commercial message during a specific period (usually a week).

Reach plan– Rotation of commercials in various dayparts on radio according to a predetermined frequency.

Rebate– A predetermined amount of money returned directly to customers by the manufacturer after the purchase has been made.

Recall test – Test that measures an ad's impact by asking respondents to recall specific elements (e.g., the selling message) of the advertisement; can be aided (some information provided) or unaided.

Recency – A model that suggests advertising works best by reminding consumers about a product when they are ready to buy.

Recognition test – A test that measures a target audience's awareness of a brand, copy, or of the advertisement itself, after the audience has been exposed to the message.

Rectangular ad– A large ad, slightly wider than it is tall, on a web page.

Redemption rate – The number of coupons returned expressed as a percentage of the number of coupons that were distributed.

Reference group (or peer group) – A group of people who share common interests that influence the attitudes and behaviour of its members.

Referral– A recommendation by a current customer of a potential new customer to a sales representative.

Related recall – The percentage of a test commercial audience who claim to remember the test commercial and can provide, as verification, some description of the commercial.

Relationship selling – A form of selling with the goal of developing a plan of action that establishes, builds, and maintains a long-term relationship with customers.

Reliability (of data) – Degree of similarity of results achieved if another research study were undertaken under similar circumstances.

Repeat transaction – A retail sales situation that involves a relationship between the buyer and the seller; the customer returns to the same store for similar goods and services.

Research objective – A statement that outlines what the marketing research is to accomplish.

Response card – A card filled in, usually at the time of purchase, that collects information about customers that can be added to the organization's database.

Response list – A list of direct mail buyers who have previously bought based on direct response offers.

Retail advertising – Advertising by a retail store; involves advertising the store name, image, location, and the re-advertising of branded merchandise carried by the store.

Rich media – Streaming video, audio, and special effects similar to television and used online.

Rifle strategy – A strategy that involves using a specific medium that effectively reaches a target market defined by a common characteristic.

Rotation plan– The placement of commercials in time slots on radio purchased; can be vertical according to the time of day or horizontal according to the day of the week.

Run of site (run of network)– Ad rate for placements anywhere on a website.

Run sheet – A schedule of daily events that shows the various dates, times, and locations of activities at an event.

Sales presentation – A persuasive delivery and demonstration of a product's benefits; shows buyers how the product's benefits will satisfy their needs.

Sales promotion – An activity that provides incentives to bring about immediate response from customers, distributors, and an organization's sales force.

Sales promotion plan– An action plan for communicating incentives to appropriate target markets at the right time.

Sample– A representative portion of an entire population that is used to obtain information about that population.

Sampling frame – A list used to access a representative sample of a population; it is a means of accessing people for a research study.

Seasonal schedule – Scheduling media advertising according to seasonal sales trends; usually concentrated in the pre-season or the period just prior to when the bulk of the buying occurs.

Secondary media – Media alternatives used to complement the primary medium in an advertising campaign; typically less money is allocated to these media.

Selective direct mail – See **Solo direct mail**.

Selective spot – Commercial time during a network show that is allocated back to regional and local stations to sell; advertisers buy spots on a station-by-station basis.

Self-image – One's own idea about oneself and one's relationship with others.

Setup – See **Bump-in**.

Seventy poster – A small poster usually affixed to the back of a bus.

Shotgun strategy – A tactic involving the use of mass media to reach a loosely defined target audience.

Single transaction – A retail sales situation where a salesperson spends time with a customer and closes the sale on the spot.

Skip schedule – The scheduling of media advertising on an alternating basis, such as every other week or every other month.

Skyscraper – A vertical box-shaped ad that appears on a web page.

Slippage– The situation of a consumer collecting labels in a promotion offer but failing to follow through and request the refund.

Slogan– A short phrase that captures the essence of an entire advertising campaign; reflects the positioning strategy of the brand and is shown in all ads in all media.

Solo direct mail (selective direct mail) – A unique advertising offer mailed directly to a target audience by a marketing organization.

Spam– Unsolicited e-mail.

Spectacular– see **Superboard**.

Spiff– An incentive offered to retail salespeople to encourage them to promote a specified brand of goods to customers.

Sponsored email – Email that includes a short message from a sponsor along with a link to the sponsor's website.

Sponsorship – The act of financially supporting an event in return for certain advertising rights and privileges. Online sponsorship is when a company or brand commits to advertise for an extended period or sponsors a web page.

Starch readership test – A post-test recognition procedure that measures readers' recall of an advertisement (noted), their ability to identify the sponsor (associated), and whether they read more than half of the written material (read most).

Statement stuffer (bounce back) – An ad or offer distributed in monthly statements or with the delivery of goods purchased by some form of direct response advertising.

Station poster – An advertisement located on the platform or at the entrance or exit of subways and light rail transit systems.

Stickiness (sticky) – A website's ability to keep people at the site for an extended period or to have them return to the site frequently.

Strategic alliance – The combination of separate companies' resources for the purpose of satisfying their shared customers; the companies have strengths in different areas.

Strategic planning– The process of determining objectives (setting goals) and identifying strategies (ways to achieve the goals) and tactics (specific action plans) to help achieve objectives.

Strategic selling – A form of consultative selling that involves dealing with each customer as an individual, stressing that in the transfer of product information.

Streaming media – Audio or video delivered online in small, compressed packets of data that are interpreted by a software player as they are received.

Superboard (spectacular) – Outdoor advertising that is larger than a normal poster and much more expensive to produce; can include extensions beyond borders and electronic messaging.

Superbus advertising – An advertisement painted on the exterior of a bus; advertiser also has exclusive use of interior cards.

Support claims statement – A substantiation of the promise made in the key benefit statement; appears in the creative plan.

Survey research – The systematic collection of data by communicating with a representative sample by means of a questionnaire.

Sweepstakes– A chance promotion involving the giveaway of products or services of value to randomly selected participants.

SWOT analysis – An analysis procedure that involves an assessment of an organization's strengths, weaknesses, opportunities, and threats; strengths and weaknesses are internal variables, whereas opportunities and threats are external variables.

Tabloid – A smaller newspaper that is sold flat (not folded).

Tabulation – The process of counting various responses for each question in a survey.

Tactics (execution) – Action-oriented details that outline how a strategic plan will be implemented.

Tagline – A short phrase that captures the essence of an advertised message.

Target profile – A description of a customer group based on demographic, psychographic, and geographic variables.

Targeting request – An ad placed to reach a specific target audience of a website, for which a premium is usually paid.

Teardown – See **Bump-out**.

Telemarketing – The use of telecommunications to promote the products and services of a business; involves outbound calls (company to customer) and inbound calls (customer to company).

Telephone interview – In marketing research, the collection of information from a respondent by telephone.

Test marketing – Placing a commercial, set of commercials, or print ad campaign in one or more limited markets, representative of the whole, in order to observe the impact of the ads on consumers.

Text messaging – The transmission of short text-only messages using wireless devices such as cell phones and personal digital assistants.

Theme – See **Central theme**.

Tip-in – An insert that is glued to a page in the publication using a removable adhesive.

Torture test – A creative execution technique in which the product is subjected to extreme conditions to demonstrate its durability.

Trade allowance – A temporary price reduction that encourages larger purchases by distributors.

Trade promotion – An incentive offered to channel members to encourage them to provide marketing and merchandising support for a particular product.

Trade show – An event that allows a company to showcase its products to a captive audience and generate leads.

Trademark – A brandmark or other brand element that is granted legal protection so that only the owner can use it.

Transient rate – A one-time rate, or base rate, that applies to casual advertisers.

Transit shelter advertising – Street-level advertisements incorporated into the design of the glass and steel shelters located at a bus stop.

Transmission – The sending of a message through a medium such as television, radio, newspapers, magazines, outdoor advertising, internet, and so on, or through personal selling.

Trial close – A failed attempt at closing a sale; the buyer said no.

Unique selling point (USP) – The primary benefit of a product or service that distinguishes it from its competitors.

Universe– See **Population**.

Validity (of data) – A research procedure's ability to measure what it is intended to.

Venue marketing (venue sponsorship) – Linking a brand name or company name to a physical site such as a stadium, arena, or theatre.

Viral marketing – Online marketing that encourages the receiver of a message to pass it along to others in order to generate additional exposure.

Visitor– A unique user of a website.

Visit– A sequence of page requests made by a visitor to a website; also called a session or a browsing period.

Voice-pitch analysis test – A test that uses a recording of a person's voice response to measure change in voice pitched caused by emotional responses to the communications.

Volume discount– A discount linked to the dollar volume purchased over an extended period; the more volume purchased, the higher the discount.

Washroom advertising – A mini-poster ad located in a public or institutional washroom; usually placed above the urinal and on the back of the stall door.

Wordmark – The stylized treatment of the brand name; serves the same function as a symbol.

World Wide Web – A system of internet servers that publish websites, which are specially formatted documents that contain graphics, audio, and video files and links to other websites.

Index